THE IRISH STAGE IN THE COUNTY TOWNS

1720 TO 1800

The Adelphi Club, Belfast, 1783

(1) Cherry; (2) Atkins; (3) Griffith; (4) Rowe; (5) Bernard

THE IRISH STAGE IN THE COUNTY TOWNS

1720 TO 1800

BY

WILLIAM SMITH CLARK

OXFORD

AT THE CLARENDON PRESS

1965

Oxford University Press, Amen House, London E.C.4

GLASGOW NEW YORK TORONTO MELBOURNE WELLINGTON
BOMBAY CALCUTTA MADRAS KARACHI LAHORE DACCA
CAPE TOWN SALISBURY NAIROBI IBADAN
KUALA LUMPUR HONG KONG

PRINTED IN GREAT BRITAIN

PREFACE

THIS volume continues the account of theatricals in Ireland that commenced with *The Early Irish Stage: The Beginnings to 1720*. Professional dramatic entertainment before 1720 had been confined almost wholly to Dublin; by 1800 it had become a distinctive feature of town life throughout Ireland. The establishment of a country-wide stage tradition, accompanied as it was by persistent, though tentative, manifestations of literary patriotism, provided a requisite step towards the full flowering of the Irish genius for dramatic art. This interesting and significant expansion of theatrical enterprise outside Dublin between 1720 and 1800 is described in the form of a tour of nine leading county seats, circling counterclockwise from the west to the north. Each town is introduced with an historical vignette in order to establish a setting for the local dramatic activities thereafter recorded. Notable physical and social changes that had a bearing upon these activities up to the year 1800 are reported along with other events relevant to the stage history of each town.

The interspersed vignettes, anecdotes, and observations are not supposed, however, to be a comprehensive summary of the conditions and developments in eighteenth-century Ireland. For the first two-thirds of the century the entire island suffered, at the hands of the English Ascendancy, humiliating impoverishment and subjugation and, for the last third, endured an unfinished struggle for economic, political, and religious emancipation. Yet the grave distress and unrest that existed before and during the fifteen years of partial independency (1783–98) caused little fluctuation in the spread of theatrical production among the county towns and in the resulting island-wide growth of interest in the drama. The stage managers and their companies looked for support primarily to the gentry and the merchants. These two classes generally enjoyed increasing wealth and security between 1720 and 1800, since the gradual removal of limitations upon domestic industry and foreign exports brought prosperity to the larger estates and to the centres of trade. Therefore, the narrative of this volume, whenever it moves beyond strictly theatrical matters, stresses for the most part the progressive opulence and social elegance of the county seats, though it also includes occasional evidences of their unhappy aspects.

The Irish Stage in the County Towns: 1720 to 1800 covers a subject that has been investigated only in a fragmentary manner by either local historians or theatre scholars. Dr. W. J. Lawrence, that eminent Irish writer upon the affairs of the English-speaking stage from Elizabethan times onwards, more than sixty years ago prepared for publication a history of the Belfast Theatre before 1820, but never succeeded in getting it printed. Between 1890 and 1940 he published a large number of newspaper articles dealing with the drama in eighteenth-century Ireland outside Dublin. Over fifty of his more important contributions have been listed in the bibliographical appendix. These must be honoured as pioneer accounts, even when careful scrutiny discloses extensive repetition of substance and incomplete research. Dr. Lawrence, however, never pretended to have exhausted the available documentary sources relating to the theatres of the towns, and, towards the end of his life, generously urged the present author to pursue the topic and undertake an integrated study. Early in the twentieth century Dr. Lawrence had redirected his efforts to the gathering of data in regard to Dublin theatricals. Consequently, the valuable collection of his Irish stage notebooks purchased by the Charles Phelps Taft Memorial Fund of the University of Cincinnati contains few references to activities outside the capital. Drawing upon the Lawrence newspaper articles, Miss La Tourette Stockwell in *Dublin Theatres and Theatre Customs: 1637–1820* included brief notes on the chronology of some early playhouses erected elsewhere in Ireland. A few histories of the larger towns contain scraps of fact regarding their playhouses, but never an adequate paragraph.

This volume, therefore, devotes considerable space to locating and depicting the various eighteenth-century theatres of the selected county seats. A large amount of new information about these buildings, their inhabitants, and their facilities was discovered in the course of examining all the known Irish provincial newspapers for the period and such invaluable contemporary manuscripts as the letters of the Drennan family and the stage account books of Sir Vere Hunt. The repertoire and personnel named in the recorded professional performances outside Dublin between 1720 and 1800 have been assembled in Appendixes A and B. The list of plays reveals many hitherto unknown dramatic works of Irish origin. The roster of actors brings to light not only a multitude of forgotten stage figures, but also numerous fresh details of the Irish careers of performers prominent on the London and provincial English circuits. Elizabeth Farren, Sarah Siddons, John Philip Kemble, Charles Macklin, and many others during the seventeen-seventies, eighties, and nineties, were tempted beyond Dublin by the flattering rewards of applause as well as coin that town audiences bestowed upon them.

The host of writers who contributed to the making of this history is gratefully enumerated in the bibliography. Mr. Michael Breen of the National Library, Dublin, Mr. Brian Trainor of the Public Record Office of Northern Ireland, Belfast, and Mr. John T. Collins of Cork assisted me as skilful investigators and copyists. My fellow theatre historians—Dr. James G. MacManaway of the Folger Shakespeare Library; Dr. C. Beecher Hogan of Yale University; and the late Dr. William B. Van Lennep, Curator of the Harvard Theatre Collection—offered expert advice and called to my notice important items of evidence. For access to unique documentary sources I am indebted to Mr. Robert Cussen, Newcastle West, Co. Limerick; Ald. T. Lynch, T.D., Waterford; John Gillan, City Manager and Town Clerk of Waterford, and his assistant, Mr. T. F. Ryan; Mr. P. J. Neylon, Ennis; Mr. Christopher Townley, University College Library, Galway; Mr. Dermot Foley, Cork Public Library; Mr. R. Naughton of the former *Limerick Chronicle* staff; the late Mr. Robert Herbert, Limerick Public Library, and his successor, Miss Maíre Lanigan; Miss Kathleen Magone, Newry Free Public Library; Miss Agnes M. McAulay, Magee University College Library; Mr. William Kenealy, Kilkenny Journal Ltd. Mr. James Delehanty, Kilkenny, provided unforgettable hospitality as well as much informative counsel. The following institutions and their staffs extended indispensable help during my research: in Dublin, the National Library of Ireland, the Royal Irish Academy, the Pearse Street Library, the Trinity College Library, Marsh's Library, the National Gallery, the Record Office, Dublin Castle; in London, the British Museum and its Colindale branch, and the Victoria and Albert Museum; the Houghton Library at Harvard University; the Folger Shakespeare Library in Washington, D.C.; and the University of Cincinnati Library.

Other innumerable benefactors came to my aid as I wandered around Irish towns, up and down the streets, in and out of shops and public houses, seeking traces of players and play-houses long gone. Their delighted interest in my inquiries gave powerful encouragement to this recital of a fascinating era in Ireland's theatrical past.

W. S. C.

CONTENTS

LIST OF PLATES

LIST OF PLATES

I · A STROLLING PRELUDE

PROFESSIONAL stage entertainment had become deeply rooted in the life of Dublin by 1720. Between that year and the Act of Union in 1800 community interest in and support of dramatic performances spread from the capital to all sections of the country. Indeed, it was during the eighteenth century that the theatrical inclinations of the townspeople of Ireland were aroused and shaped into a permanent, nation-wide tradition which was affected by but never dependent upon any of the movements for Irish political autonomy that flared and faded.

A sociable, beneficent attitude in a majority of the upper classes, and a remarkable sense of humour in the lower orders, made the eighteenth-century Irish towns an alluring 'Ultima Thule' for English as well as native performers.[1] The seventeenth-century concept of players as vagabonds or inferior persons disappeared from the minds of both the profession and the public perhaps more quickly in Ireland than in Britain. For instance, in 1743, a Dublin clergyman's son, John Carteret Pilkington, in a fit of adolescent depression over his musical career, had given up 'hopes of being a gentleman'. During the summer, on a visit to Cork, he suddenly decided to join the troupe at the Theatre Royal because he found the members, by dress, manners, and education, assuming the character of 'gentlemen' and being accepted as such in the city.[2] Thus the gratifying status that actors and actresses generally enjoyed long before 1800 throughout the Emerald Isle proved a decisive factor in giving it fame abroad as '*the* Hot-Bed for Actors'.[3]

In the course of the eighteenth century the more important Irish towns came to be divided into three groupings of theatrical *foci*. Cork, Limerick, and, later, Waterford and Newry became satellites of Dublin. Ultimately Belfast emerged as an indepen-

[1] John Bernard, *Retrospections of the Stage* (Boston, 1832), i. 200.

[2] J. C. Pilkington, *The Real Story of John Carteret Pilkington* (London, 1760), p. 74.

[3] *An Answer to the Memoirs of Mrs. Billington* (London, 1792), p. 33.

dent centre and attached Derry as a satellite. To the end of the century the other large towns continued as vantage points for strolling organizations. At first such companies originated for the most part at Dublin and embarked in the summers on sporadic tours. The Smock Alley Theatre corps, after a pioneer visit to Cork in 1713 to initiate a new playhouse, was not again recorded on a similar travelling venture for fifteen years. Then on 13 June 1728 it assisted Drogheda in celebrating 'the riding of the franchises' by a performance of *The Beggar's Opera* and evidently stayed on there for a few more days of acting.[1] Years later, on 4 July 1735, the Aungier Street company was reported to be setting out for Carlow 'to divert the Ladies and Gentlemen who may resort to the Races'.[2] Two eminent London entertainers, Dennis Delane and Henry Giffard, 'favoured that company with their Presence, thereby to render the Diversions more agreeably pleasant to the Ladies'.[2] The same Dublin group went in 1736 to Cork to open a summer Theatre Royal and presumably travelled thither every year henceforth.[3] In the summer of 1736 also, the Smock Alley players undertook a trip as far north as Belfast and Derry,[4] and journeyed over the identical route at least once more in 1741.[5] On the other hand, in 1738 and again in 1740, the Smock Alley troupe directed their touring to Carlow and Drogheda from August to late October.[6] On Saturday evening, 11 October 1740, in festive observance of the anniversary of George II's coronation, the Mayor requested Manager Lewis Duval to 'give a Play to the [Drogheda] Corporation'.[7] It was acted on a temporary stage in the yard of the Crown and Thistle Inn, where the Smock Alley company also performed for Duval's benefit on 31 October, their last night before returning to Dublin.[8]

[1] DDI, 15 June 1728. The abbreviations used throughout this volume in references to Irish newspapers are listed after each title in the newspaper section of the Bibliography. [2] DEP, 5 July 1735.

[3] In 1737 the Aungier Street company performed during July and August, first at Clonmel, then Cork, and finally Carlow. See FDJ, 28 June, 16 and 27 Aug. 1737.

[4] Robert Hitchcock, *An Historical View of the Irish Stage* (Dublin, 1788–94), i. 97.

[5] Ibid., i. 114; FDJ, 11 July and 12 Sept. 1741.

[6] *Reilly's Dublin News Letter*, 8 Aug. and 9 Sept. 1738; FDJ, 23 Aug., 16, 20, and 27 Sept. 1740. DEP, 27 Sept. 1740; *Reilly's Dublin News Letter*, 26 Aug. 1740.

[7] DEP and FDJ, 14 Oct. 1740.

[8] *Reilly's Dublin News Letter*, 25 Oct. 1740.

From 1740 onwards towns all over Ireland advertised their summer Race Week with notices like the following:

Plays and Assemblies each Night by Turns, for the Entertainment of the Ladies. (Tralee.)[1]

Balls and Plays for the Amusement of the Ladies every Evening. Good Fox hunting and Hare hunting every Morning for the Gentlemen. (Ballinasloe, County Galway.)[2]

The week of the county assizes, spring, summer, or autumn, also called for unusual diversion in town. As early as 1739 the Aungier Street company departed for Cork at the beginning of April 'to play at the Assizes'.[3] The racing and the court sessions at first offered the most lucrative periods for itinerant entertainers, but the taste for dramatic amusement grew so swiftly that before 1750 a few bands of strollers were criss-crossing Ireland at all seasons.

These travelling players fascinated the populace wherever they put up. And, in turn, the spectators at the inns along the road always delighted one of the century's outstanding itinerant comedians, John O'Keeffe.[4] A 'great variety of personages' were sure to assemble at every stopping-place to welcome the troupers and to speed them on their way. Their modes of transport provided the bystanders with a subject for voluble and whimsical repartee: 'The post chaise, the gig, the whiskey, the noddy, the single horse, the double horse, the car', and, above all else, those most humble Irish beasts of burden, 'St. Francis's mules'. As the moment of departure approached, the manager of a strolling band used to round up his fellows like a mother hen overseeing her chicks. On one occasion, O'Keeffe recalled,[5] the manager stood 'at the inn-door, his hands in his fobs, looking anxiously around', and an Irish countryman, pointing at him, loudly addressed another onlooker: 'Hush! look! that's the ringleader of them all!'

The manager was the 'ringleader' of a troupe organized in most cases on a 'commonwealth' or shareholding basis. Under such an arrangement each performer shared equally in the profits of each performance after the expenses had been deducted, but the manager customarily enjoyed, in addition to

[1] FDJ, 15 July 1740. [2] Ibid., 6 Oct. 1744. [3] Ibid., 31 Mar. 1739.

[4] John O'Keeffe, *Recollections of the Life of John O'Keeffe, Written by Himself* (London, 1826), i. 225. [5] Ibid. i. 226.

his individual portion, an allotment of four 'dead' shares, two for costumes and two for scenery.[1] On this account a disgruntled or jealous player might refer to his manager as 'the Leviathan for a Great Swallow'.[2]

Every sharer supplemented his income by the profit arising from one or more benefit performances. Each benefit was allocated usually to only one beneficiary or to a married couple, though, sometimes, in the case of a minor or novice actor, to two beneficiaries. Professional seniority normally determined the order of the benefits, the manager and the leading performers taking the earlier ones.[3] Those of about the same rating arrived at precedence by mutual agreement or by lot, or, occasionally, by managerial decision. 'A pretty female might have a Secret Interest with the Manager.'[3] All ranks looked upon the benefit as the ultimate harvest. Failure to reap an appreciable profit wounded not only the player's purse but also 'his feeling in the tenderest point'.[4] Then, as now, 'the Theatre was a Temple of Vanity',[5] in which the acting profession constantly worshipped.

The benefit system, though it added considerably to the gains of the majority of the acting profession, also disturbed the self-respect of many. The system forced both men and women into the dependent position of begging patronage, particularly from the merchants and the gentry. Each performer was expected to go around the town, knocking 'humbly' at doors with or without rappers, as well as 'supinely' calling at shops and stalls, to leave a playbill and request the favour of Mr. and Mrs. ——'s company at his benefit.[6] Occasionally a popular actor might be aided by a local friend or official. At Drogheda in 1791 'the Mayor politely waited upon the most respectable in the town to induce them to take a number of Tickets' for William Palmer's benefit.[7] Illness or pregnancy, both sometimes feigned, provided a sufficient excuse for the beneficiary to avoid the tedious round of personal solicitation. When Mr. and Mrs. William Dawson at Tralee in 1756 gave notice by bills of their benefit on 7 May, they took pains to announce that 'as Mrs.

[1] Anthony Pasquin, *The Eccentricities of John Edwin, Comedian* (Dublin, 1791), ii. 141; Thomas Snagg(e), *Recollections of Occurrences* (London, 1951), p. 106.

[2] Snagg(e), p. 106.

[3] Ibid., p. 107.

[4] EC, 1 Apr. 1790.

[5] Tate Wilkinson, *Memoirs of his Own Life* (Dublin, 1791), ii. 274.

[6] Ibid. ii. 248.

[7] *The Diary*, 7 Sept. 1791.

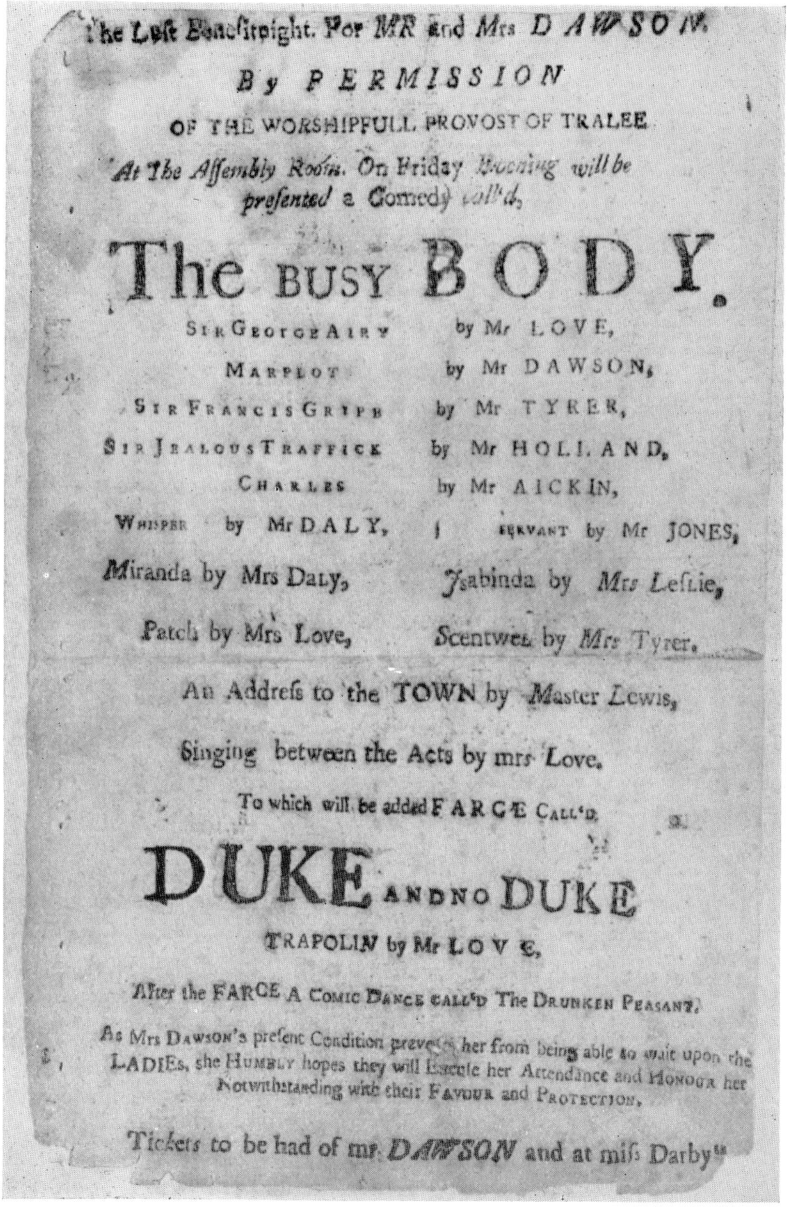

The Last Benefitnight. For MR and Mrs DAWSON.

By PERMISSION

OF THE WORSHIPFULL PROVOST OF TRALEE

At The Assembly Room. On Friday Evening will be presented a Comedy call'd,

The BUSY BODY.

SIR GEORGE AIRY by Mr LOVE,

MARPLOT by Mr DAWSON,

SIR FRANCIS GRIPE by Mr TYRER,

SIR JEALOUS TRAFFICK by Mr HOLLAND,

CHARLES by Mr AICKIN,

WHISPER by Mr DALY, SERVANT by Mr JONES,

Miranda by Mrs DALY, *Isabinda* by *Mrs Leslie*,

Patch by Mrs Love, *Scentwel* by *Mrs Tyrer*.

An Address to the TOWN by *Master Lewis*,

Singing between the Acts by mrs Love.

To which will be added FARCE CALL'D

DUKE AND NO DUKE

TRAPOLIN by Mr LOVE,

After the FARCE A COMIC DANCE CALL'D The DRUNKEN PEASANT.

As Mrs DAWSON's present Condition prevents her from being able to wait upon the LADIES, she HUMBLY hopes they will Excuse her Attendance and HONOUR her Notwithstanding with their FAVOUR and PROTECTION.

Tickets to be had of mr. *DAWSON* and at miss Darby's

Tralee Playbill, Friday, 7 May 1756

Dawson's present condition prevents her from being able to wait upon the Ladies, she humbly hopes they will excuse her Attendance and Honour her notwithstanding with their Favour and Protection.'[1]

The Dawsons at this time belonged to a band of strollers under the management of James Love [Dance], an actor with a dozen years of experience in England, Scotland, and Ireland, and the son of George Dance, London's city architect. In addition to Mr. and Mrs. Dawson, and Mr. and Mrs. Love, the troupe included two other couples, the Dalys and the Samuel Tyrers; a single woman, Mrs. Leslie; and six unmarried men, three sharers and three novices on salary without benefits. One of the three unmarried sharers was ten-year-old William Thomas Lewis, son of Mrs. Dawson by her first husband, William Lewis. 'Master' Lewis played at Tralee a variety of youthful roles—Prince John in *Henry IV*, Duke of York in *Richard III*, Peter in *Romeo and Juliet*, Fleance in *Macbeth*, Dickey in *The Constant Couple*, the Boy in *The Committee*—and, on the season's last night, he gave the farewell address to the town. Already 'Master' Lewis, later known as 'Gentleman' Lewis, was well launched on the stage career that brought him eminence in both Dublin and London.

The complete record of this company's stay at Tralee during the spring of 1756 has survived in handbills to afford a unique vignette of Irish strolling practices.[2] As the very first handbill indicated in its heading, Manager Love, observing ancient precedent, got permission of Tralee's highest official, the Provost, to act in town and to use the best public hall, the Assembly Room, as a theatre.[3] Since the Assembly Room possessed neither boxes nor gallery, its accommodation corresponded to pit seats. Admission therefore was set at 2*s*.,[4] the usual pit price outside Dublin, with the not uncommon provision of half-price for children. The undivided and close seating demanded that, in order to prevent what numerous persons of the period considered unpleasant social contact, no

[1] Playbill, Folger Shakespeare Library, Washington, D.C.

[2] A complete list of the thirty Tralee bills, now in the possession of the Folger Shakespeare Library, may be found under Tralee in the playbill section of the Bibliography.

[3] See the bill for Saturday, 6 Mar.

[4] All monetary references throughout this volume are in English currency. 1*s*. English = 1*s*. 1*d*. Irish.

'servants' be admitted. Ordinarily, at town theatres, the servants of 'persons of quality' were permitted to enter at the opening of the doors and hold seats in the boxes or pits for their employers. Then, on the arrival of the latter, the servants retired to the gallery 'to answer the commands of their respective masters and mistresses'.[1]

The season at the Tralee Assembly Room began on Saturday, 6 March, and ended on Monday, 10 May. Performances took place on the customary town schedule of three days a week: chiefly Tuesday, Thursday, Saturday in the first half of the season, and Monday, Wednesday, Friday in the second half. The curtain rose at the conventional hour of six o'clock except on the final evening when a curtain-time of seven permitted the large and rather more heterogeneous charity audience to be seated without disorderly pressure at the doors. During a little over nine weeks, embracing thirty performances, James Love's group of only fifteen players presented, as after-pieces, twenty-two different farces and, as principal entertainment, thirteen tragedies and fourteen comedies. Of those twenty-seven dramas, eight, or almost one-third, were written by Shakespeare: *Hamlet*, *Macbeth*, *Othello*, *Richard III*, *Romeo and Juliet*, *Henry IV*, *Merchant of Venice*, *Merry Wives of Windsor*. The popularity of this Shakespearian octet continued in the Irish towns throughout the century. Five plays contained humorous Irish characterizations—Howard's *The Committee*, Thomas Sheridan's *The Brave Irishman*, and *The Constant Couple*, *The Recruiting Officer*, *The Stage Coach*, all by Farquhar—but only two of them roused enough popular demand to warrant repetition as much as once. Though the large and ambitious repertoire exhibited by Love's small company would have done credit to a much stronger city organization, such a varied store of entertainment was inevitably required if an itinerant troupe hoped to attract profitable audiences in a sojourn of any considerable duration.

The last two weeks of the Tralee season in 1756 were given over to benefit nights. Manager and Mrs. Love took the privilege of holding theirs first. Mr. and Mrs. Dawson, the least important of the four married couples, had to wait until the close of the second week. In accordance with the general custom in Irish town theatricals, the actors, after completing

[1] BNL, 2 Mar. 1784.

their benefits, performed once more on behalf of local impoverished citizens. Tralee showed a rare unsectarian spirit by advertising this charitable affair as for the relief of both 'the Protestant and Roman Poor'.[1]

On neither the charity night nor earlier in the season did Manager Love evidently face the annoyance of persons wishing to go behind the scenes or on to the stage. At Belfast, however, where in 1751 he originally appeared as an Irish manager, he encountered a more inquisitive public and, in consequence, had to issue a polite but firm admonition: 'It is hoped, No Gentleman will attempt to come behind the Curtain, or into the Dressing Room this Night, on any Account whatever; the Play being so extremely full of Business, that but the presence of a Single Person behind the scenes must greatly disconcert the Representation.'[2] Love's notice is the earliest known of the innumerable similar pronouncements by managers outside Dublin, because the wayward inclinations of the curious and vain theatregoers plagued management everywhere in Ireland up to 1800. As late as May 1799 Mr. Smithson at Kilkenny found prohibition to be necessary and announced with unequivocal brevity: 'No admittance behind the Scenes.'[3]

The persistence of the backstage problem may be attributed in some measure to the long-standing tradition of allowing persons on the stage at special performances, such as the nights for the Masons or the Friendly Brothers of St. Patrick. On these occasions rising tiers of boards were erected in the form of an amphitheatre at the rear of the stage to accommodate the guests of honour. The fraternal orders always wore their 'proper Cloathing and Jewels',[4] and sat all evening 'in their formalities'.[5] The chief official of the local group was often provided with a seat of distinction at the centre of the amphitheatre. At Cashel, on 25 February 1771, when the Masons in a body attended a performance at the town theatre and took their places in front of 'a brilliant and respectable audience', the Master occupied 'a throne covered with a canopy of purple velvet edged with ermine'.[6] However, Manager Tate Wilkinson, himself a Mason,

[1] Playbill for Monday, 10 May.

[2] Playbill, Shaw Collection, Harvard University Library. See under Belfast in the playbill section of the Bibliography.

[3] LJ, 25 May 1799.

[4] HC, 14 Sept. 1775.

[5] LJ, 13 Feb. 1768.

[6] WC, 5 Mar. 1771.

viewed an assemblage of this sort as without glamour: 'Their heads reached the theatrical cloudings [i.e. cloudlike flats suspended in mid-air upstage]; their seats were closed in with dirty, worn-out scenery, to enclose the painted round [i.e. amphitheatre] from the first wing [flat]; the main entrance to the amphitheatre being up steps from the middle of the back scene.'[1] Yet neither uncomfortable seats nor unpicturesque surroundings dimmed the appeal of onstage location for eighteenth-century Irish townsmen.

Admission behind the footlights was only one of numerous details in manners and management not recorded by the Tralee handbills. These bills do evidence, however, the simple, basic organization and procedure of the early theatrical companies that travelled around Ireland, performing at the smaller towns in mostly improvised playhouses. By the 1760's the Dublin Theatre Royal had established seasonal touring calendars and destinations; regular playhouses had begun to be constructed in the larger centres of population; and, as a result, strolling troupes had grown larger, more stable, and more talented. Such fundamental developments greatly increased the complexity of theatrical production and administration. In a tour of leading Irish towns, circling counterclockwise from the west to the north, the succeeding chapters will describe the evolving pattern of stage enterprise in each town up to the year 1800, together with multifarious events and influences that accompanied the evolution.

[1] Wilkinson, iii. 164.

II · GALWAY

GALWAY, the famed 'City of the Anglo-Norman Tribes', had been in the sixteenth century the commercial hub of the west of Ireland, but by the mid-eighteenth century the ravages of war, land confiscation, and anti-Catholic persecution had greatly reduced the importance of Connacht's ancient port. The once flourishing wine and provision trade had declined a great deal and had been replaced only in part by fishing and smuggling.[1] The old walls still pretty well contained the slowly growing city of five to six thousand inhabitants.[2] Many of the fine houses built of grey hewn stone by wealthy sixteenth-century merchants continued to line the narrow paved streets.[3] Galway's business and social activity centred in the Tholsel or Exchange, a large stone two-storied edifice, situated at the junction of High and Shop Streets.[4] On the front, the second floor extended out over a long spacious piazza faced with six archways and provided with seats on the inner wall. Here both ladies and gentlemen gathered for conversing and promenade. In the Tholsel's commodious upper hall they held assemblies, balls, and civic celebrations. There are no indications, however, that the Tholsel ever served for a playhouse as did similar public structures elsewhere in Ireland.

The first known reference to theatricals at Galway occurred in 1739 when a Dublin newspaper reported a colourful episode. On Thursday, 6 December, Mr. Lewes, the town 'stock officer', and Mr. Lynch, a merchant, 'exchanged some words in the Playhouse. When the Play was done, they both drew at the door and Mr. Lewes was killed on the spot'.[5] This brief but vivid recital discloses that Galway then possessed a building

[1] Richard Pococke, *A Tour in Ireland in 1752* (ed. Rev. G. T. Stokes, Dublin, 1891), p. 105; James Hardiman, *The History of the Town and County of Galway* (Galway, 1820: reprinted Galway, 1926), pp. 180–9.

[2] Edward MacLysaght, *Irish Life in the Seventeenth Century: After Cromwell* (London, 1939), p. 195.

[3] Hardiman, p. 291.

[4] Ibid., p. 309.

[5] DDP, 15 Dec. 1739.

associated with dramatic performances, perhaps a warehouse converted into a theatre, as at Cork in 1713.[1]

In the 1740's, and subsequently, reports of strolling companies in the City of the Tribes occasionally appeared. Sometime during the autumn of 1742 Mrs. Cassandra Parker, an attractive widow with two children, visited there with a troupe which she had newly organized.[2] Impressed with the acting of James Augustus Whiteley, aged eighteen, assistant Smock Alley prompter, whom she had observed at Waterford in the previous summer, she had persuaded him to join her forces. Because of a good singing voice he made his Galway début as the lead in the ballad opera *A Cure for a Scold*, adapted from *The Taming of the Shrew*. Before long, 'Jemmy' had been lured into marriage with the manageress, his senior by eight years. This strangely matched pair soon broke with their fellow players and went off to England.

As early as 1744 the celebrated Galway races were being run. The Race Week announcements advertised plays for six evenings, starting on Monday, 1 October, along with 'other diversions for the entertainment of the ladies'.[3] The local belles gradually won country-wide renown for their gaiety and elegance. One tourist later in the century commented that 'if playing at Cards, even upon a Sunday, is an evidence of politeness, the ladies of Galway are extremely polite'.[4] Their love of fashionable amusements could not overcome, however, the city's geographical isolation and uncertain prosperity. Though a stroller at his benefit in the summer of 1774 termed Galway 'the actor's patron' and proclaimed 'the bounty of its fost'ring hand',[5] the truth was that the town did not even then promise enough business to draw the established companies which toured out of Dublin or Belfast.

At the beginning of the 1780's the Volunteer Movement, the removal of many Roman Catholic disabilities, and the general increase of Irish trade abroad, much invigorated the City of the Tribes.[6] Simultaneously a sponsor for local theatricals

[1] William Smith Clark, *The Early Irish Stage* (Oxford, 1955), p. 138.

[2] Charles Lee Lewes, *Memoirs* (London, 1805), i. 36–40.

[3] FDJ, 11 Sept. 1744.

[4] Chief Justice (Baron) Edward Willes, Letters, B.M. Additional MS. 29252, p. 97.

[5] FJ, 15 Oct. 1774.

[6] Hardiman, p. 196.

appeared from one of the oldest and wealthiest families, the Martins. Richard Martin, a short, thick-set, energetic man, familiarly called 'Hair-Trigger Dick' by reason of his notorious skill with the duelling pistol, had sailed off at the age of twenty-one to see New England just as the American Revolution broke out.[1] Very soon returning to Ireland, he got elected to the Irish Parliament in 1776, married Elizabeth Vesey of Lucan, County Dublin, in 1777, became head and colonel of the Galway Volunteers at their birth in 1779, was called to the Irish bar in 1781, and was appointed High Sheriff of Galway in 1782. Early in the autumn of this latter year the well-known actor Robert Owenson turned up at Galway with a troupe whom he had been leading on a tour through Castlebar, Sligo, and other towns of the north and north-west. He evidently met with so encouraging a reception that on 9 October he was reported to be preparing to erect 'a new and elegant theatre' at Galway.[2] Prime support for this venture came from Colonel Richard Martin, who was 'passionately fond of acting' and regularly attended the Dublin performances when he was sojourning in the capital.[3]

Martin not only put up money for the building but also presumably furnished its site in Kirwan's Lane, a section of which earlier had been called Martin's Mill Lane. This very narrow and short thoroughfare runs in the form of a tilted L between Cross and Quay Streets to the rear of the old Martin family residence, which still stands at the junction of these two streets.[4] The new playhouse was apparently located at the elbow of Kirwan's Lane so that the entrance would be equally accessible from two directions.[5] An extremely small structure, it contained an auditorium without boxes or gallery, but with a sloping pit so well designed that, according to a contemporary visitor, 'each person sat perfectly at ease, without incommoding those behind, or being themselves inconvenienced by those who sat before them'.[6] The pit, which accommodated 'about one hundred

[1] Wellesley Pain, *Richard Martin* (London, 1925), pp. 10–34. [2] HJ, 9 Oct. 1782.

[3] Theobald Wolfe Tone, *The Autobiography* (ed. Sean O'Faolain, London, 1937), p. 10. [4] Hardiman, pp. 179, 326.

[5] Christopher Townley, 'Galway's Early Association with the Theatre', *The Galway Reader*, iv. (1953), 65. Mr. Townley has kindly supplied further evidence, based upon local lore and personal survey, in letters to the author, 1956–8.

[6] FJ, 11 May 1786.

persons', looked upon a stage decorated with an elaborate proscenium. Along the top of the latter a gaudy fillet of roses and ribbons joined two medallions bearing figures of the Tragic and Comic Muse respectively. Below, on either side, the lively motto of 'Vive la Bagatelle' embellished the frame.[1]

By the summer of 1783 the theatre in Kirwan's Lane had been completed and put into use. Colonel and Mrs. Martin had assembled from the county gentry and the Volunteers an amateur company to act under the management of Robert Owenson. A unique Kirwan's Lane playbill for Friday, 8 August, records an occasion of great historical interest.[2] On this August evening two widely popular dramas, the tragedy of *Douglas* and the farce of *All the World's a Stage*, were presented before a most select audience. Special raised prices prevailed for admission to the gala programme, which was to begin 'precisely at seven o'clock'. Places in the pit cost 4*s.*; seats on the stage, which must have been exceedingly few in number, sold at the princely sum of £1 1*s.* In order to seat the maximum number of persons in the limited accommodations, the performing ladies and gentlemen issued the unusual warning to all female playgoers that 'no Hoops may be worn at the theatre'.

Colonel and Mrs. Martin took the leading roles in both the tragedy and the farce, but the Mr. Tone who acted Lord Randolph in *Douglas* and Diggory in *All the World's a Stage* emerges today as the pre-eminently important member of the two casts. This young man was none other than Theobald Wolfe Tone, the gay, high-minded patriot who suffered martyrdom in the Rebellion of 1798.[3] While a student at Trinity College, Dublin, the twenty-year-old Tone met Mrs. Martin about the beginning of 1783, fell in love, and not long thereafter followed her to the west of Ireland to become a house guest and an actor in the

[1] FJ, 11 May 1786.

[2] The author examined this playbill in June 1939, when it was in the possession of the late Philip O'Gorman of the O'Gorman Printing House, Ltd., Galway. A descendant of a county family represented in the cast had given the bill to Mr. O'Gorman about 1900. He permitted it to be reproduced in the *Journal of the Galway Archaeological and Historical Society*, iii. (1903–4), 144. The bill is now preserved in the Library of the University College, Galway.

[3] The author privately arrived at this identification upon being shown the playbill by Mr. O'Gorman. Professor Liam O'Briain of University College, Galway, later made the same identification and wisely published his discovery in *The Irish Sword*, ii. (1955), 228–9, 'Theobald Wolfe Tone in Galway'.

At the THEATRE, KIRWAN's-LANE.

ON Friday Evening, the 8th of Auguſt, 1783, will be preſented the celebrated Tragedy of

DOUGLAS.

Douglas,	Captain NUGENT.
Old Norval,	Major TRENCH.
Lord Randolph,	Mr. TONE.
Officer,	Lieutenant MOOR.
And, Glenalvon,	Colonel MARTIN.
Anna,	Mrs. SOPHIA CHEVERS.
AND. LADY RANDOLPH,	Mrs. R. MARTIN.

To which will be added a Farce call'd

ALL THE WORLD's A STAGE.

Sir Gilbert Pumpkin,	Colonel MARTIN.
Captain Stanly,	Captain NUGENT.
Harry Stukely,	Lieutenant MOOR.
Simon,	Lieutenant COSTELLO.
Watt,	Lieutenant DALY.
And, Diggory,	Mr. TONE.
Miſs Kitty Sprightly,	Mrs. SOPHIA CHEVERS.
And, Miſs Bridget Pumkin,	Mrs. R. MARTIN.

By particular Deſire of the Ladies and Gentlemen,

STAGE 1l. 2s. 9d. PIT 4s. 4d.

Tickets to be had of Mrs. R. MARTIN; and of Mr. Owenſon at the Theatre.

The Ladies and Gentlemen requeſt that no Hoops may be worn at the Theatre on the above Occaſion.

To begin preciſely at Seven o'clock.

GALWAY: Printed by B. CONWAY, at the Volunteer Print-

Galway Playbill, Friday, 8 August 1783

Martins' amateur troupe.[1] Tone's Galway romance as well as his theatrical endeavours in that town aroused little, if any, notice and faded from history until the publication of Tone's unexpurgated *Autobiography* a century and a half later revealed a dramatic tale that even now is generally unknown to his countrymen.

According to Tone's frank account, Mrs. Martin, 'independent of a thousand other attractions', fascinated him as one of the first actresses he had ever watched.[2] Not only did he 'live in the house with her' but 'as somewhat of an actor, [he] was daily thrown into particular situations with her, both in rehearsals and on the stage'.[2] Since he possessed an 'imagination easily warmed, without one grain of discretion to regulate it', he very soon became in love 'to a degree almost inconceivable'. Because Colonel Martin neglected his wife a good deal and Tone was 'continually on the spot', the latter by degrees engaged Mrs. Martin's affections so that at length she reciprocated his intense feeling.[3] During the two years of their infatuation Tone made to the Martin house in Galway three visits of four or five months each, 'without, however, in a single instance overstepping the bounds of virtue, such was the purity of [his] extravagant affection'.[3] In the course of these visits he no doubt performed on the Kirwan's Lane boards in other plays besides the *Douglas* of August 1783, his sole recorded stage appearance. Little did the Galway audiences imagine that this spirited Dublin collegian would become in the next decade a revolutionary leader and one of Ireland's outstanding heroes.

Tone broke off his friendship with the Richard Martins sometime in 1785,[4] but his action did not diminish their enthusiasm for theatricals. On 11 May 1786 the *Freeman's Journal* of Dublin reported exciting entertainment at 'Richard Martin's private theatre' during the week of the Galway assizes. A 'very splendid' audience, including numerous black-garbed judges and lawyers, enjoyed a production of that perennial favourite, *The Fair Penitent*, by local amateurs under the leadership of Colonel and Mrs. Martin. The *Freeman*'s correspondent indulged in flowery comments about several performers. Miss Westrop's Lavinia exhibited 'all that youth, innocence and

[1] Tone, pp. 9–10. [2] Ibid., p. 10.
[3] Ibid., pp. 10–11. [4] Ibid., pp. 11–12.

beauty, elegance and grace could give to the wife of Horatio'. Mr. Burke's animation made his Lothario 'hot with Tuscan grape and high in blood'. In regard to Colonel Martin as Sciolto, the correspondent remarked: 'I had known him to be the best mimic of public men, but it remained for me to know that he is also one of the best actors.' Mrs. Martin in her acting of Calista received, however, the most audacious compliment: 'She excelled Mrs. Siddons, and every other woman in the world.' Intoxicated by Mrs. Martin, or by the 'supper' which followed the dramatics, or by both, the *Freeman*'s correspondent at the evening's close 'regretted that such a stupid thing as sleep was necessary for beings of so exalted a kind as I felt'.

No further account of theatrical activity on the part of the Martins was ever published, but the Kirwan's Lane Theatre by no means fell into disuse. In 1790 the veteran actor-manager William Joseph Smithson, who had experienced a rewarding year at his newly erected theatre in Ennis, brought his company, starring the talented singer Mrs. Castelli, to Galway in late August for at least a month of performances.[1] The city, now grown to a population of 8,000 or more, was beginning a notable expansion of social and cultural enterprises.[2] In 1791 the Amicable Literary Society was formed by Protestants and Roman Catholics to encourage discussion of the arts and sciences, and to support a reference library. In the following year the Mercantile Coffee Room started as a meeting-place for the more thoughtful and public-minded business men. Assemblies, drums and promenades multiplied. A French traveller found 'the greatest gaiety and ease' reigning in the west-of-Ireland metropolis at this period.[3]

Meanwhile, in 1791, Colonel Richard Martin lost to a more appealing Englishman his very attractive wife and, thereby, his chief incentive for theatrical sponsorship.[4] By the spring of 1792 Martin evidently had sold out his interest in the Kirwan's Lane playhouse to a new proprietor, Alexander Macartney, who antedated Smithson as an actor-manager in various Irish towns. Macartney, incited by Galway's fresh prosperity, ventured

[1] EC, 19 Aug. and 13 Sept. 1790.

[2] MacLysaght, p. 195; Hardiman, pp. 196–8.

[3] DeLatocnaye, *A Frenchman's Walk through Ireland, 1796–7* (trans. John Stevenson, Dublin and Belfast [1917]), p. 150.

[4] Tone, p. 12.

an ambitious enlargement of Martin's bandbox theatre.[1] He unroofed the structure, raised the walls seven feet, and added an elegant circular set of boxes with a regular gallery above. The pit was also redesigned, and the level of the stage lifted somewhat. A reconstruction of the passageways improved the access to every part of the house.

To open the 'New Theatre, Galway', in the summer of 1792, Macartney secured Smithson and his strolling company. Their leading actress, Mrs. Garvey, offered for her benefit on Thursday, 16 August, two widely popular works—*The Country Girl*, Garrick's purification of Wycherley's *The Country Wife*, followed by *The Romp*.[2] The benefit met with such generous patronage that she was moved to publish in the local paper a statement of thanks, especially to the ladies for their 'flattering' response.[3] During the first week of September, the Galway assizes took place, and in consequence Smithson put on plays every night with an outstanding Dublin vocalist, Miss W. Brett, as the special feature.[4] Fresh from triumphal appearances in Kilkenny and Waterford, she delighted 'a brilliant and crowded audience' on her benefit night, Friday, the fourteenth, not only by her singing of 'Whither My Love?' and 'Sweet Birds' in the comic opera of *The Haunted Tower*, but also by her impersonation of debonair Jack Rover in *Wild Oats*.[5] Proprietor Macartney for his benefit two weeks later arranged a festive programme intended to elicit the support of his fellow Masons: a parade to the theatre by the lodge members 'in the Insignia of their different Orders'; the seating of the marchers on the stage; a prologue and epilogue addressed to the brethren; Masonic songs, choruses, and gun salutes between the acts.[6] The proprietor went to the expense of advertising his hope that 'the brethren around the Country will be so good as to attend'.

By the end of the season Mrs. Garvey had established herself in strong favour with the gentlemen of the garrison and the neighbourhood. A number of them, at her second benefit on Monday evening, 22 October, carried minor roles in *Percy, Earl of Northumberland*, and in *The Waterman*, the musical afterpiece.[7]

[1] CJ, 23 Apr. 1792.
[2] Ibid., 13 Aug. 1792.
[3] Ibid., 20 Aug. 1792.
[4] Ibid., 27 and 30 Aug. 1792.
[5] Ibid., 10 and 17 Sept. 1792.
[6] Ibid., 24 and 27 Sept. 1792.
[7] Ibid., 11 and 15 Oct. 1792.

The politic actress took grateful leave of Galway with a printed acknowledgement that 'to the Commanding Officers of both Regiments she feels herself most particularly indebted, but it is impossible for her to express her high sense of the Obligations she is under to Mr. Blair of the 22nd Regiment for his kind exertions'.[1]

In July of 1793 Smithson returned to Kirwan's Lane as actor-manager and entertained the city with almost four months of plays. He staged performances three times a week—usually Monday, Wednesday, and Friday—with the doors opening at six o'clock and the curtain rising at seven-thirty.[2] In accordance with tradition, the week of the summer assizes saw plays daily.[3] In turn, tradition prohibited during the next week any productions by reason of the death of Mayor Daly on 11 August.[4] Only tickets for the boxes were sold before the evening of the performance. These could be obtained at the theatre from Mr. Dunn, the housekeeper, between the hours of eleven and three.[5] Though the Galway purchasers well knew that a box ticket guaranteed no specific seat in the boxes, late arrivals none the less proceeded to complain to the management over the disagreeable locations forced upon them. Smithson, rightly tiring of such unfair complaints after three weeks, published a polite request that 'Ladies and Gentlemen will send Servants to Keep Places in the Boxes, as there is no other mode of securing them'.[6] Somewhat more speedily he became annoyed by the disturbing circulation of fashionable theatregoers backstage and announced that 'the Manager, having a wish to conduct the Business with that degree of Regularity justly due to a Galway audience, hopes no Person will be offended at being refused Admittance behind the Scenes'.[7]

Smithson kept up public interest during the 1793 season by a succession of guest stars all advertised as from the Theatre Royal, Dublin. He led off with Mrs. Coates on the season's opening night, Monday, 1 July. She excelled in comic parts such as Lady Townley in *Journey to London* and Lady Amarinth in *Wild Oats*, but she also attempted Juliet for her benefit and Ophelia for her last appearance on 19 July.[8] Smithson next put

[1] CJ, 5 Nov. 1792. [2] Ibid., 1 July 1793. [3] Ibid., 5 Aug. 1793.
[4] Ibid., 12 Aug. 1793. [5] Ibid., 1 July 1793. [6] Ibid., 18 July 1793.
[7] Ibid., 8 July 1793. [8] Ibid., 3, 8, 15 and 18 July 1793.

forward with a fanfare the veteran Thomas Betterton and his daughter Julia, 'a Child of eleven years old whose astonishing Abilities are the admiration of the first Critics'.[1] This pair, who had been playing with much success at Wexford in April and at Kilkenny in the subsequent two months, remained at Galway till the season's close on 25 October. Miss Betterton concentrated on prologues, epilogues, entr'acte dances, recitations, and such light, boyish parts in afterpieces as Captain Flash in *Miss in Her Teens*.[2] For her final benefit her father thought to introduce a bit of novelty by his own designing and painting of 'a View of the Sea and a Shipwreck', the opening set in *No Song, No Supper* which concluded the evening's programme.[3] Smithson's third attraction, the sparkling Miss Maria Campion, started playing on Monday, 22 July, in an engagement supposedly limited to six nights,[4] but the town discovered 'her extraordinary abilities, added to her angelic person', so powerful a drawing-card that the manager twice extended her contract.[5] She acted a variety of serious as well as comic roles, and chose Portia in *The Merchant of Venice* for her final performance on 4 September.[6] Mrs. William Dawson, wife of the one-time Dublin manager, concluded the featured list of players at Kirwan's Lane. Her forte consisted of mature or elderly woman characters like Polly Peachum in *The Beggar's Opera* and the Nurse in *Romeo and Juliet*.[7]

Smithson's repertory displayed throughout the season a freshness well above the average of the smaller Irish theatres. It included, for example, Mrs. Inchbald's comedy *Every One Has His Fault* and the farce *The Irishman in London*, which were still enjoying their first run of popularity in London.[8] His most distinctive venture, however, was the production on Friday, 30 August, of a highly political tragedy concerning the French Revolution, entitled *Democratic Rage: or, Louis the Unfortunate*, and written by William Preston of Dublin—a work which had been staged first at Crow Street two months before and then at Cork. Smithson, announcing this Irish-born drama as 'the Tragedy that has so much attracted the Notice of Europe',

[1] CJ, 11 July 1793.
[2] Ibid., 15 July 1793.
[3] Ibid., 3 Oct. 1793.
[4] Ibid., 22 July 1793.
[5] Ibid., 19 Aug. 1793.
[6] Ibid., 2 Sept. 1793.
[7] Ibid., 25 July and 3 Oct. 1793.
[8] Ibid., 7 and 10 Oct. 1793.

doubtless believed it to be in tune with the predominantly anti-proletarian sentiment of his Galway clientele.[1] His publicity called special attention to one of the stage sets because it depicted 'a View of the Guillotine that put a period to an illustrious Monarch'. Marie Antoinette in the person of Maria Campion must have been portrayed as a most glamorous and pathetic victim of mob violence.

After two apparently prosperous seasons, Smithson seems to have turned his back on Galway. Indeed, the scanty city annals available reveal little further activity at Kirwan's Lane before the Union. Macartney, still proprietor of the theatre in 1795, issued a notice on 31 August that 'with a view to Alleviate the heavy loss he would of course sustain by the Theatre lying idle this year', he had permitted 'several Gentlemen of Rank' to use it.[2] These amateur performances, as in the days of the Richard Martins, were intended to be fashionable events for the county society. Therefore the playhouse interior was splendidly illuminated with wax rather than tallow candles, and seats in the boxes, pit, and gallery 'were thrown into one', that is, were all sold at the one price of 3*s*.[3] During September the company of ladies and gentlemen gave at least two evenings of plays, a serious and a comic piece on each programme. For the second occasion, Tuesday, 22 September, they selected *The Fair Penitent*, a tragedy done by the Martins and their friends at Kirwan's Lane a decade before. A local critic, damning the female impersonations with faint praise as 'very respectful', singled out Lothario for approbation since 'he was presented with all the spirit and fire of this *ne plus ultra* of tragic rakes'.[4]

After the mild outburst of theatricals by Galway's high society in 1795, the curtain stayed down on the Kirwan's Lane stage for the remaining years of the eighteenth century. The City of the Tribes was still a community too ill-balanced in wealth and too heavily divided by class politics and religion to support professional dramatic amusement with that largesse which 'Hair-Trigger Dick' Martin and his wife had once provided.

[1] CJ, 29 Aug. 1793.
[2] Ibid., 31 Aug. 1795.
[3] Ibid., 31 Aug. and 14 Sept. 1795.
[4] Ibid., 24 Sept. 1795.

III · ENNIS

ENNIS, the county seat of Clare, forty miles south of Galway on the post road to Limerick, twenty miles beyond, was in the later eighteenth century an unpretentious and unwalled market town of considerably less population and wealth than either of these neighbouring centres. Trade in cattle and sheep formed the principal basis of its moderate prosperity. Without commanding families of large means and property, its social life was characterized by the conventional yearly round of drums and assemblies, which reached its peak in Race Week during the autumn. Plays became a source of amusement only at very rare intervals when some strolling company happened to pay a brief visit and set up a temporary stage in the market house or town hall.

Towards the close of 1789 the theatrical situation at Ennis underwent a marked and significant change with the appearance of the enterprising William Joseph Smithson, who had greatly invigorated dramatic activity at Wexford in the previous winter and spring.[1] On the very last day of the year the *Ennis Chronicle* congratulated the town on the fact that Smithson had arrived with 'his excellent Company of Players', and was fitting up a 'regular' theatre. A week later the paper published the encouraging news that 'from the rapidity with which the workmen proceed, our Theatre will be completely finished in the course of this week. . . . It will be as neat and comfortable, for the size, as any in the Kingdom, an Agreeable Surprise to those who were accustomed to the temporary theatres hitherto made use of in this Town'.[2] Smithson, however, encountered the usual difficulties in readying a new building and had to announce:

Notwithstanding that every exertion has been made use of to complete our theatre, we find that it will not be fit for the reception of Company for a few days—and, in order that it may be thoroughly

[1] See WH, 18 Dec. 1788 to 23 Mar. 1789.
[2] EC, 7 Jan. 1790.

aired and properly fitted up, the Manager has determined not to open till Monday, January 18, when our Theatrical Campaign will positively commence.[1]

A few days afterward the manager confirmed this date of commencement with a burst of grandiloquence:

The mode in which the Business will be arranged, together with a watchful endeavour to please, will, he presumes, recommend him to the countenance of a people whose unlimited generosity on former occasions he holds a grateful remembrance of.[2]

The Ennis playhouse contained a pit and gallery but no boxes. Of the approximate size of the Galway theatre, probably, it must have held about two hundred persons. Contrary to the usual eighteenth-century design the Ennis structure originally did not have separate entrances to the pit and the gallery.[3] A single door at the front served as a common means of access to ground floor and upstairs—an awkward retrogression introduced to save on the cost of construction. The new building was erected in a central but very unprepossessing location on Cooke's Lane, earlier called Bridewell Lane.[4] This thoroughfare formerly led to the old 'bridewell' or jail, which long occupied the spot where the orphanage of the Sisters of Mercy now stands. Cooke's Lane, almost as narrow and constricted as Kirwan's Lane in Galway, goes eastward from the town's main artery, O'Connell Street, a little north of its junction with Market Street. Since 'no less than eleven dwelling houses' stood in the near vicinity of the theatre,[5] its site appears to have been well along Cooke's Lane towards the present Convent of Mercy gate, presumably along the lane's south side on one of the two corners adjoining the alley that runs at present between an amusement hall and a venerable warehouse. Though the latter appears of the right vintage, height, and ground dimensions—50 feet by 30 feet—to be the shell of Smithson's playhouse, its interior fails to disclose evidence of the transformations which that playhouse certainly experienced when it was made, first, a schoolhouse in 1814 and then, in 1817, a fever hospital.[6]

[1] EC, 11 Jan. 1790. [2] Ibid., 14 Jan. 1790. [3] Ibid., 19 Aug. 1790.
[4] 'Around the Town of Ennis with Father Clancy', *Molua* (Dublin, 1945), pp. 23–24.
[5] Ibid., pp. 26–27. [6] Ibid., p. 25; *Clare Journal*, 25 and 28 Nov. 1817.

The *première* of Ennis's first permanent theatre occurred on Monday, 18 January 1790, with Cumberland's comedy, *The West Indian*, and a musical farce, *The Farmer*, as the main entertainment.[1] The doors opened at six o'clock and the performance began at seven. Pit seats were priced at 2*s*., those in the gallery at half of that figure. Perhaps because of the inexperience of his Ennis public Smithson put into effect at once a set of strict rules in regard to admission. Patrons of a casual or thrifty turn of mind could not expect to attend part of an evening's performance at a cut rate: 'Nothing will be taken under *full price* during the whole of the Entertainment.' Furthermore, the manager warned: 'Children or Servants will not be admitted without Payment, nor any Person allowed to go behind the Scenes, or attend Rehearsals; as such practices render the Performance very defective, impede the Satisfaction of the Audience, and prove a dreadful inconvenience to the Actors.'[1]

On the night of Wednesday, 27 January, the 'New Theatre, Ennis' presented, in addition to Otway's masterpiece of *Venice Preserved*, *Peeping Tom of Coventry*, a farce. According to a local critic, Smithson as Peeping Tom 'displayed great comic powers and kept the House in peals of laughter'. The same observer, describing the theatre as filled with 'the genteelest audience we have witnessed for a long time', ventured the hope that the manager's 'taste and liberality' would continue to be rewarded with 'the applauding smiles of such crowds of our lovely country women as graced the house last night'.[2]

Monday, Wednesday, and Friday comprised the days of performance except when other local amusement promised to reduce attendance too severely. For instance, Smithson shifted the programme for Friday, 29 January, to Saturday 'in consequence of a Drum interfering'.[2] During that same week-end he encountered interference of a more violent sort. Marauders tried to break into the playhouse. Their action provoked him to publish in Monday's newspaper an amusingly gentle protest: 'Those evil minded persons who attempted to make a burglarous entry on the East end of the theatre are desired to desist.'[3]

This bit of unpleasantness was soon overshadowed by the festive plans for Smithson's benefit night. Since he counted

[1] EC, 14 Jan. 1790. [2] Ibid., 28 Jan. 1790.
[3] Ibid., 1 Feb. 1790.

heavily on the fraternal patronage of Ennis Freemasons, he solicited their co-operation with an elaborate verbal flourish:

By Desire of the Masters, Wardens, and Brethren of the Ennis Lodge No. 60, who will walk to the theatre in their proper Regalia, for the Benefit of Brother Smithson. On Monday evening, February 22, will be presented Shakespeare's comedy *As You Like It.* This Play is allowed by the most judicious Critics to be the Flower of the Author's Writings. In the Course of the Entertainment several Mason Songs will be sung.[1]

The evening's bill opened with a prologue delivered by Mrs. Brennan in the character of a Mason's wife, and closed with O'Keeffe's latest comic opera, *The Highland Reel.* The whole affair so delighted the manager that he could not find language sufficiently fulsome to describe his appreciation:

Smithson, Bound by every Tie of Gratitude, thus offers his public acknowledgement to the Master and Brethren of Lodge No. 60 for their generous attention at his Benefit. . . . Nor is he less indebted to those Ladies and Gentlemen who formed an audience so crowded and splendid. For this, and former favours equally liberal, he uses this occasion for presenting all that in his power lies—all, indeed, worthy their acceptance, which are simply—*Thanks.*[2]

Though the town generously responded to Smithson on this occasion, it apparently did not display equal liberality toward the other players whose benefits followed during February and March.[3] The resulting sense of discouragement and insecurity among the members of the local company moved the *Ennis Chronicle* to a very perspicuous editorial on the critical importance of supporting the benefit system for the sake of both the profession and the community:

The support of the stage depends in a great measure on the excellence of its professors; and what actors, or actresses, of merit will remain in any place where the public patronage does not reward their merits and exertions? The harvest of an actor is his *Benefit*—if that fails him it renders him liable to numerous inconveniences and distresses, as the failure of the entire crop does the farmer, and at the same time wounds his feeling in the tenderest point. If he is a

[1] EC, 15 Feb. 1790.

[2] Ibid., 1 Mar. 1790.

[3] See ibid., 25 Feb., 4, 11, 22 and 29 Mar. 1790.

favourite with the public he very naturally expects they will evince their regard on the single annual night on which alone they can do it to his advantage. . . . The writer is led into these reflections from the disappointment he has witnessed in the attempt of our Performers for their Benefits, and as the only means to ensure us the return of persons of merit he wishes to see their future endeavours better attended; and that while we have candour enough to applaud, we shall not be found deficient in generosity to reward those talents by which we are improved and entertained.[1]

This is perhaps the most pointed summary of the problem of actors' benefits to appear in Irish theatrical commentary of the eighteenth century.

Two of the Ennis actors, Cunningham and Hall, encouraged by this editorial, decided to stage on Friday, 9 April, another benefit for themselves by reason of 'a failure in their former attempts'.[1] They offered an abundant and thrilling programme: a tragedy, Otway's *The Orphan;* a comic opera, Dibdin's *The Deserter;* a 'Pantomimical Ballad Dance' called 'Vauxhall Champêtre, or Easter Gambols'; and a 'Pantomimical Epilogue', *Harlequin.* In this finale Mr. Cunningham made his escape 'through a grand display of FIREWORKS and through a brilliant Sun of variegated FIRE, each SIX FEET HIGH'.

On the closing night of Monday, 3 May, Smithson took the second benefit customary for an actor-manager. His bill consisted of the ballad opera, *Flora; or Hob in the Well*, 'at the instance of several Ladies and Gentlemen of distinction'; and the comedy, *A School for Wives*, by Hugh Kelly, who was patriotically advertised as 'the famous Poet of this Country'.[2] On departing from Ennis the manager published the company's thanks to the town for the season's success: 'a Circumstance they will always remember and gratefully acknowledge.'[3]

Smithson directed his troupe back to Ennis at the beginning of August for three weeks of plays. Before the performances started, however, the Cooke's Lane playhouse underwent a notable improvement by the addition of a gallery entrance 'on the outside of the Building'. What had formerly been the only public door to the theatre now admitted solely to the pit. This rearrangement enabled the pit to be appreciably enlarged and

[1] Ibid., 1 Apr. 1790. [2] Ibid., 29 Apr. 1790.
[3] Ibid., 17 May 1790.

'totally prevented any possibility of confusion in admitting persons to the House'.[1]

As a novel attraction for the opening on Monday night, 2 August, the shrewd manager selected his new Ennis-bred actress, Mrs. Hall.[2] The *Ennis Chronicle* gave the occasion much attention since 'our Country woman will make her début' as Stella, the principal female role in the opera of *Robin Hood, or Sherwood Forest.* That fact, the newspaper said, 'cannot but excite the inhabitants of this her native town'.[3] The *Chronicle* also did its best to build up the audience for the benefit night of Mrs. Castelli, the chief singer and most experienced actress in the company. She was to sing five current 'hits'—'The Lass of Richmond Hill', 'The Rising Aurora', 'Tantivy', 'The Dreadful Din of War', and 'Tally Ho'—as well as to perform in Bickerstaffe's comic opera, *The Padlock.*[4] The newspaper urged the public to attend with this telling exhortation: 'It seldom occurs that an Actress of Mrs. Castelli's merit deigns to visit a small town like this; and to ensure us the return of that excellent Actress we have now an opportunity to shew appreciation of those talents and abilities which we so much admire and applaud.' Mrs. Castelli's popularity aroused malicious gossip to the effect that she was going to leave the Smithson troupe. Therefore she thought it 'necessary to inform the Public that such report is totally groundless and only fabricated for sinister views'.[5] She further disproved the likelihood of any parting by her generous contributions to the manager's benefit, namely, the feminine lead in the operatic farce *The Flitch of Bacon,* plus a variety of songs before and after.[6] The newspaper appeal for support of this finale on Tuesday, 24 August, stressed that the 'judicious and well-conceived' alterations in the playhouse 'must be attended with great expense to the Manager, who is indefatigable in his endeavours to please', and that therefore the proceeds of the evening would be 'for the purpose of discharging the debts incurred by the late improvements'.[7]

Following his benefit, Smithson took his company off to Galway for an engagement at the Kirwan's Lane Theatre, but

[1] EC, 19 Aug. 1790. [2] Ibid., 29 July 1790. [3] Ibid., 26 July 1790.
[4] Ibid., 16 Aug. 1790. [5] Ibid., 13 Sept. 1790. [6] Ibid., 23 Aug. 1790.
[7] Ibid., 19 Aug. 1790.

he expected to be performing again in Ennis during Race Week a month later.[1] His intention, however, was completely thwarted by the visit of a rival organization under the leadership of Sir Vere Hunt, a wealthy baronet and devotee of the stage who had set himself up as a professional manager. After opening a new theatre at Limerick in January of the current year, Sir Vere had also assumed charge of the Waterford theatre and conducted a summer season there. Then he had brought his company back to Limerick for August and early September. Now, in the absence of Smithson, he invaded Ennis 'at the request of the Nobility and Gentry of the County of Clare'.[2] His players, extravagantly designated 'the Company of the United Theatres of the South', numbered fourteen actors, eight actresses, a treasurer, a carpenter, a hairdresser, a musician, two scene painters, and two permanent stage hands.[3] Of the acting group, Mrs. Achmet, Miss Harriet Westropp Atkins, Mr. Brown, Mr. Hurst, and Mr. Wells represented the top talent. The first three had special contracts, terms unknown. The stipends of Messrs. Brown, Hurst, and Wells apparently included the stage services of their wives—the same arrangement as that which held for their Limerick engagements. Mr. Hurst received a weekly salary of £2. 3*s*. 6*d*.; Mr. Wells, £2. 2*s*. at the start, but £3. 13*s*. 4*d*. after the first week.[3] The remuneration of the lesser actors ranged from £1. 12*s*. per week down to 7*s*. 6*d*. for Miss Webb, a young and inexperienced performer.[3] Mr. Whitmore, an able scene painter well known throughout Ireland, was paid £2. 2*s*. a week.[3] No one else on the staff earned over half of this latter sum, and for the majority the range lay between nine and sixteen shillings.[3] The bill-posters, charwomen, guards, porters, and extra stage-hands got compensation of one shilling for each day of service.[3]

Sir Vere Hunt's company began its Ennis performances on Monday, 6 September, with the comic opera of *Inkle and Yarico*, in which Wells and Mrs. Achmet impersonated the two characters named in the title.[4] Since the races were being run

[1] Ibid., 19 Aug. 1790. Actually he led his players from Galway to Kilkenny, and opened a playhouse there in November. See LJ, 6 Oct., 3 and 7 Nov. 1790.

[2] EC, 6 Sept. 1790.

[3] Sir Vere Hunt, MSS.: Account Books, 1790–1.

[4] EC, 6 Sept. 1790.

during the second week of the company's visit, plays were given daily from Monday to Saturday inclusive, 13–18 September. Mrs. Achmet enjoyed a benefit on Thursday, 23 September, with the celebrated operetta *Lionel and Clarissa* and the farce *The Citizen.*[1] Miss Atkins took hers on Friday night when she acted the heroine, Charlotte Rusport, in *The West Indian* and afterwards entertained the audience with 'a Dissertation on Jealousy, describing its various effects on the Italian, Frenchman, Spaniard, Dutchman, and Englishman'.[2] Mr. McCrea in the 'Animation and Dying Scenes of Harlequin' furnished a vivid culmination to the evening by 'leaping through a Hogshead of Fire'.

The most spectacular piece in his repertory Sir Vere Hunt saved, however, for the fourth and last week. On Monday, 27 September, he presented 'to the general satisfaction of a brilliant and crowded audience' *The Death of Captain Cook*, 'that grand serious Pantomime, or sublime *Ballet d'Action*, in three acts, as now appearing in London, Dublin and Paris, with universal applause'.[3] Its final scene reached the *ne plus ultra* of spectacle in showing, amidst the uproar of cannon and thunder, molten lava running down the mountains in the background. All the pantomime's elaborate scenery and machinery were brought by cart to Ennis from Limerick where it originally had been produced.[4] The manager did not have transported, however, one impressive stage property needed towards the end, the coffin for Captain Cook; instead, he rented a casket in Ennis for two shillings.[5] Since so extraordinary a specimen of theatrical exhibitionism appealed to an audience far larger than the ordinary theatregoing public of Ennis and vicinity, the pantomime was repeated on Friday and Saturday nights.[6] Mr. Wells's benefit, featuring Mrs. Achmet in Garrick's *The Irish Widow* and intended for Wednesday, had to be postponed until Saturday, 'on account of the melancholy event of a much respected young gentleman's death'.[6]

The advertisement for this closing performance on Saturday, 2 October, bore the arresting headline: 'The Last Night of

[1] EC, 20 Sept. 1790. [2] Ibid., 23 Sept. 1790. [3] Ibid., 30 Sept. 1790.
[4] Ibid., 23 Sept. 1790; Hunt MSS.: Account Books, 1790–1.
[5] Hunt MSS.: Account Books, 1790–1.
[6] EC, 30 Sept. 1790.

Performing until the New Theatre Royal opens'.[1] The reference to 'the New Theatre Royal' was simply a neat bit of publicity connected with the theatrical empire-building which had prompted Sir Vere Hunt to lead his forces to Ennis. Perhaps even before he had arrived there in September, he had initiated among his County Clare acquaintances a movement to replace the unimpressive playhouse in Cooke's Lane with a more handsome structure on a more attractive site. Certainly his campaign was well advanced when the *Ennis Chronicle* on 23 September gave its hearty endorsement to the project:

> Our intended new Theatre Royal, modelled on the beautiful one at Limerick [the one opened by Sir Vere Hunt in January 1790], will not only afford us an unexhausted fund of the most rational entertainment, but have such an effect on our intellects, morals, and manners; and, in a word, on all that is interesting to humanity, as to render it the first object of the attention of the Nobility and Gentry in the county of Clare and town of Ennis.[2]

The same issue of the *Chronicle* printed the announcement of a meeting of the subscribers to the New Theatre Royal at two o'clock on Friday, 24 September, at the Grand Jury Room, in order to approve a plan and appoint a Treasurer. Such gentlemen as could not attend were requested to supply a proxy. The current subscribers, a dozen in number—Edward Armstrong, C. P. Bolton, F. N. Burton, Edmond Carroll, George Crowe, Cunningham, Francis Macnamara, Charles Mahon, O'Callaghan, Anthony Sheehan, John and William Stacpoole (by proxy)—met again on Sunday, 3 October, with Armstrong in the chair, and approved the following three resolutions:

1. That the Subscribers approve of Mr. Armstrong's ground for building the theatre on.
2. That we pay our Subscriptions into the Hands of C. P. Bolton, Treasurer, in the proportion of £20 per cent. at each payment when applied to by the Treasurer.
3. That the Treasurer be empowered to pay the different Artificers employed in the Building of said Theatre Royal, and to make all the payments relative and necessary to same.[3]

[1] Ibid., 30 Sept. 1790. [2] Ibid., 23 Sept. 1790. [3] Ibid., 4 Oct. 1790.

The last item of business decided upon, namely, that proposals for building the theatre be sent sealed to Sir Vere Hunt at Curragh, near Limerick, revealed this baronet's directing hand in the whole enterprise. His campaign, however, came to nothing in the end despite the careful and determined intentions evinced in these Ennis proceedings of September and October 1790. In all probability, the constructional costs, when at last ascertained, exceeded by far the subscriptions of the local group, and the original Limerick promoter was not of a mind to guarantee the further amount necessary. Therefore the little playhouse in Cooke's Lane continued without a competitor.

Smithson, undaunted by Sir Vere Hunt's temporary invasion, returned to Ennis in the autumn of 1791 for a season of six weeks beginning on 30 September.[1] During Race Week, Monday to Saturday, 17–22 October, performances were given every night. Knowing that many strangers would be in town, the manager took pains to reiterate in the press his rule that no person would be admitted 'under full price'.[2] John Macnamara, Treasurer of the Ennis Races, stood patron on the first night, when Smithson augmented a thin dramatic programme by his starless company with titillating acts by members of a touring troupe from Astley's Circus of London. These circus strollers put on two hilarious dances—'the celebrated Fricasee Dance after the manner of the Boulevard Ladies from Paris' and 'the Jockey's Hornpipe, or a Trip to Newmarket'—as well as exhibitions of 'Slack Rope, Vaulting, Ground and Lofty Tumbling consisting of fore springs, back springs, flipflaps, somersets, etc.'. The acrobatics culminated with 'The Egg Hornpipe (blindfolded)', and 'Balancing with the Force of Hercules in which a Number of Men were supported on the Hands and Feet'.[2]

The last night of performance, 14 November, Smithson chose as his benefit and therefore proceeded to solicit a large Masonic turn-out.[3] Ennis Lodge No. 60 were to 'walk to the theatre in their proper clothing, where an Amphitheatre will be erected for their reception on the stage'. 'Such of the Brethren as [were] not Sitting Members' (that is, such Masons as could not or

[1] EC, 29 Sept. 1791.
[2] Ibid., 17 Oct. 1791.
[3] Ibid., 10 Nov. 1791. At Dunn's benefit on 14 Oct. the local lodge had held a procession to the theatre, but had not sat on the stage. See EC, 13 Oct. 1791.

would not march and sit on the stage in their regalia) were urged to attend anyway and take seats in the usual locations. The manager, promising the appearance of three new but unidentified performers, arranged a very colourful bill. It started with *The Sheep Shearing* (an adaptation of Shakespeare's *The Winter's Tale*) in which Smithson played Autolycus, 'the Ballad Singing Pedlar', and rendered a comic song describing 'the pretty, ugly, black-haired, red-haired, six-feet, three-feet, pale-faced, plump-faced, dainty, dowdy, etc., Ladies that were smitten with his Person'. Then there came a humorous piece, *Irish Simplicity*, not recorded in any other Irish town and possibly Smithson's invention. Next was acted O'Keeffe's 'last new after-piece', *Modern Antiques; or, The Merry Mourners*, which the publicity rightly claimed 'not yet in Print'. Since this was the first production of O'Keeffe's farce in Ireland outside Dublin, the manager advertised with understandable pride that he had given 'a considerable Sum' for the manuscript—a pirated copy, of course. Two more or less original skits followed: 'The Magic Ring, or a Peep into a Lodge of Free and Accepted Masons', and 'A Swadling Sermon'. In keeping with the excitement still felt toward the French Revolution, the entertainment concluded with a 'Grand Transparency of that terrifick Mansion, the Bastille, on Fire' and, to offset any slightest subversive implication in the foregoing spectacle, a curtain chorus of 'God Save the King'.

When, at the end of this gala evening, the Cooke's Lane playhouse shut its doors, no one could have foreseen that they would remain closed for almost five years. Smithson evidently discovered the pastures greener elsewhere than in Ennis;[1] perhaps he also grew to believe the playhouse accommodations there unattractive. Since no other strolling manager meanwhile sought to explore Ennis's possibilities, it remained for Smithson to raise once again the curtain on the Cooke's Lane stage in the spring of 1796. After a month of fitting up 'the old theatre in the best style of convenience and elegance at great expense',[2] he commenced on Wednesday, 27 April, with a rather apologetic announcement: 'The Manager has suited the Entertainment to the present strength of the Company: He hopes for the

[1] He and his troupe appeared at Galway in the summers of 1792 and 1793.

[2] EC, 21 Mar. 1796.

accustomed Protection and liberal Patronage of his Ennis friends.'[1] His current aggregation of actors presumably did not measure up to past standards. The days of playing continued to be Monday, Wednesday, Friday, with admittance from 6.00 and the curtain up at 7.30 p.m.

The actors' benefits in May fared so meagrely that the *Ennis Chronicle* embarked on a series of puffs to swell the audiences. Of Mrs. Williams it remarked that she was an actress 'certainly entitled to a share of Public Patronage' with her abilities 'far above mediocrity' and her exertions to please 'always conspicuous'.[2] It then exhorted the ladies and gentlemen of the town to be 'as ambitious to reward merit as they are discerning to discover and applaud it'. A week later the *Chronicle* appealed on behalf of Miss Stewart, saying that she depended for her emolument entirely upon her benefit night, 'having covenanted with the Manager to that effect'.[3] The next week the newspaper put forward as its candidate for public favour 'our little Miss Grant' who, along with 'a child of this town', was on 13 June to play in the interlude of *The Children in the Wood*. Miss Grant's characterization was reputed 'as natural a piece of acting as any that has been seen'.[4] On Friday, 24 June, Dawson, daring a second benefit because 'his last one met with ill success', billed himself to dance an Irish jig as the novelty of the day.[5]

Manager Smithson appropriately commenced the entertainment on the last night, Monday, 27 June, with Colman's prelude *The Manager in Distress*.[6] At the moment the Ennis manager was feeling distressed about the playhouse in Cooke's Lane. In fact, he had gone so far as to take a lease on a fresh site, so the *Chronicle* reported in mid-June, because he had resolved to establish a 'regular' theatre.[7] The news article, commending Smithson's 'honest character, which he has preserved in spite of calumny', called for the utmost encouragement of his 'spirited undertaking'. Subsequently, in connexion with his benefit on 27 June, the manager announced that he would 'thankfully receive a few Subscribers to assist in the Establishment of a regular Theatre worthy such a spirited and liberal Public'.[8] As late as 18 July advertisements asking for subscriptions to a 'new'

[1] EC, 25 Apr. 1796. [2] Ibid., 2 June 1796. [3] Ibid., 6 June 1796.
[4] Ibid., 13 June 1796. [5] Ibid., 20 and 23 June 1796.
[6] Ibid., 23 June 1796. [7] Ibid., 13 June 1796. [8] Ibid., 23 June 1796.

theatre appeared. Mr. Foster Parsons, the printer of the *Ennis Chronicle*, would furnish all inquirers with the 'conditions' of subscription as well as receive their pledges.[1] This venture of Smithson, however, like the similar effort of Sir Vere Hunt in 1790, soon dwindled into silence.

Undismayed by the lack of response to his dreams of a fine new building, Smithson turned up in Ennis for the spring assizes of 1797, 20–25 March. The nightly performances at 7.30 were promised to finish before 11.00 in order to permit those living at a distance from town to ride home at a decent hour.[2] The manager, in the hope of stimulating attendance, made it known that the company's stay would be 'but short',[2] and then, a few days thereafter, that the theatre would close on 8 April.[3] Perhaps the flattering comment of the *Ennis Chronicle* helped to prolong the theatricals. The newspaper adjudged the performance of 7 April 'the most compleat we have ever witnessed in Ennis',[4] and on 24 April redoubled its praise: 'In our recollection we have not seen a Company of Itinerant Players—take them all in all—to equal them; and candour prompts us to say we never saw them excelled.'[5] Nevertheless, the next issue spoke of the theatre as 'thinly attended hitherto'.[6] On at least one occasion Smithson, striving to increase receipts, abrogated his firm rule of 'no admittance under full price during the whole performance' and made an exception in the case of children.[7] For his first benefit on Monday, 1 May, 'the manager, ever anxious to entertain his Ennis friends, prepared at a most enormous expense the unparalleled pantomime, *Don Juan; or, The Libertine Destroyed*, composed of such Scenery, Machinery, etc., as he presumes will further recommend him to the notice of a Public he so much reveres'.[8] At the last moment this gala event was put off two days because of 'the indispensable necessity' to avoid conflict with an unanticipated ball.[9] Spectacular pantomimes and other eye-filling devices now drew the Ennis theatregoers above all else. For his second benefit, therefore, Smithson, 'yielding to the general wish of the Town', chose 'that inimitable pantomime of *Robinson Crusoe*, with all the Scenery,

[1] Ibid., 18 July 1796.
[2] Ibid., 23 Mar. 1797.
[3] Ibid., 30 Mar. 1797.
[4] Ibid., 10 Apr. 1797.
[5] Ibid., 24 Apr. 1797.
[6] Ibid., 27 Apr. 1797.
[7] Ibid., 13 Apr. 1797.
[8] Ibid., 20 Apr. 1797.
[9] Ibid., 1 May 1797.

Music, Dresses, Grand Savage Dance, etc.'.[1] He gave assurance that the well-known story of Robinson Crusoe was founded on facts and had excited 'the Admiration of All Europe'. The *Ennis Chronicle*, loyal as ever, came out with an eloquent appeal for an overflow audience as proof of the town's capacity 'to estimate proper principles' in a theatre manager. The appeal described his conduct over the nine years since his first coming as 'uniformly upright, just, and honest', and finished its eulogy with the assertion that 'as an Actor he has been much caressed, as a Brother much beloved, and as a Fair Dealer, greatly admired'.[2] These words of praise well described the esteem that was amply demonstrated at the season's final performance on 30 May by 'the crowded and brilliant' gathering of Smithson's admirers, who included 'the Brethren of the South Cork Militia'.[3]

The Cooke's Lane playhouse saw no further performances for two and a half years. Then at the beginning of 1800 Smithson returned with a troupe that boasted four men from the Dublin Theatre Royal and, as leading actress, Mrs. Courtney, formerly at Covent Garden.[4] Prices of tickets (2*s.* for the pit and 1*s.* for the gallery) and the days of playing (Monday, Wednesday, Friday) continued as they had ever since 1790. The rise of the curtain, however, was changed from 7.30 to 7.00 p.m., the original local starting-hour. Now, for the first time, the Ennis management offered admission tokens good for the entire season, but, regarding their sale, it published a single laconic notice, 'a few Silver Tickets to be disposed of', which appeared in connexion with the announcement of the opening performance on Monday, 13 January.[4] For the first time also, the management issued an admonition about behaviour. The Ennis audience had begun to contain a bolder male set. Its too insistent attentions to the ladies led to the public request that 'a certain description of men' allow 'the Fair Sex . . . to enjoy the Entertainments with that tranquil happiness which is the lawful right of any individual that pays for admission'.[5]

The highlight of the first half of the season proved to be 'Monk' Lewis's noted melodrama *The Castle Spectre*, which, after its original showing on 31 January, the *Ennis Chronicle*

[1] EC, 22 May 1797. [2] Ibid., 29 May 1797. [3] Ibid., 1 June 1797.

[4] Ibid., 10 Jan. 1800. All five of the players named had performed with Smithson's company at Kilkenny in the summer of 1799. [5] Ibid., 7 Feb. 1800.

pronounced 'a production of considerable merit'.[1] The alternating simplicity and magnificence of the scenes occasioned 'unceasing applause . . . from a very numerous and respectable audience'. Subsequently the newspaper pointed to *The Castle Spectre* as the most delightful of the new entertainments, with the business-minded observation that its preparation must have been attended with very great expense.[2] Then on Friday, 14 February, the *Chronicle* asserted that 'the public are all anxious for another Representation of *The Castle Spectre*' and that if the manager would have it performed on the succeeding Monday, he would 'find his account in it', that is, he would gain profit from it. Nevertheless Smithson did not select the Lewis work for his first benefit but preferred to stress new comic songs—especially 'More Grist to the Mill; or, All the World Turned Grinders'.[3] On that occasion, according to the manager, 'never was an House so crowded in this town'.[4] More people were turned away than gained entrance.

The next benefit, on Monday, 10 March, honoured Mrs. Smithson, the sole record of this lady's existence in Irish theatrical history. Because of her physical condition at the time it is very doubtful whether she participated in the night's programme, consisting of two principal attractions: (1) *The Irishman in Naples*, a new musical play never before given outside Dublin; (2) *Romeo and Juliet*, 'with a solemn Dirge and Funeral Procession'.[5] Juliet could scarcely have been acted by Mrs. Smithson since she was in a very advanced state of pregnancy. Indeed, the selection of Shakespeare's tragedy with its mournful finale of death seems hardly appropriate to the situation of a beneficiary who was facing both the joy and travail of imminent motherhood. Yet no ill fortune came out of the affair, and a week later, on Tuesday, 18 March, Harriet Constance Smithson was born. Nursed on the stage from her Ennis infancy, she developed during the 1820's into a gifted actress of international reputation, who put the final touch to her celebrity by marriage to the famous French composer Hector Berlioz in 1833.

Not long after the birth of this future star the theatrical season began to approach its end. One of the company's young

[1] Ibid., 4 Feb. 1800. [2] Ibid., 7 Feb. 1800. [3] Ibid., 21 Feb. 1800.
[4] Ibid., 28 Feb. 1800. [5] Ibid., 7 Mar. 1800.

women, Miss Nicolle, tried a second benefit, which the *Ennis Chronicle* publicized with a heart-rending plea to 'the Ladies of Ennis': 'We know of none who has a stronger claim than Miss Nicolle—an unprotected female—unsuccessful in a former attempt, which involves her in pecuniary embarrassment—and now presuming on the kindness of her sex. There remains no doubt, if the Ladies smile assent but that the House will overflow—so will the grateful heart.'[1] The last benefit, that of the manager, took place on the closing night, Saturday, 5 April, under the patronage of his brother Masons. With a canny eye to receipts he had postponed the performance from Thursday on account of 'the cold and disagreeable rain which rendered that day unpleasant'.[2] When the curtain fell that April evening of 1800 on Thomas Dibdin's new comedy of *Five Thousand a Year*, Smithson had rounded out a decade of conscientious association with theatricals at Ennis—a decade which he had opened auspiciously by his founding of the town's first and only playhouse in the eighteenth century. As he now said farewell on the brink of a new era, he quite justly hoped to enjoy in the future 'the patronage of an audience who have so frequently testified their approbation of his endeavour to please'.[3]

[1] EC, 25 Mar. 1800. [2] Ibid., 28 Mar. and 4 Apr. 1800.
[3] Ibid., 4 Apr. 1800.

IV · LIMERICK

LIMERICK, the historic capital of Munster, had more than recovered from the sieges and confiscations of the Williamite wars by the middle of the eighteenth century. Indeed, by then 'the City of the Violated Treaty' was well on its way to becoming the third city of Ireland.[1] Yet it still retained its medieval walls, narrow crooked streets, and segregated districts for English and Irish residents.[2] The ancient fortifications, which surrounded both the 'English Town' on King's Island and also the 'Irish Town' to the south across the Abbey River, unhappily confined a fast-growing population of twenty-five to thirty thousand.[3] Travellers, viewing the city's thriving commerce, were surprised at its shabby precincts, especially the dirty and crowded quarters of the Irish Town.[4] In truth, Limerick's citizens had been so much absorbed in business enterprises that civic as well as cultural and recreational facilities had by no means kept pace with the increasing stature of the community.

Up to 1760 no tholsel, exchange, custom house, assembly rooms, or promenades existed worthy of a visitor's attention. The theatre of that day was also an undistinguished building with a history that may have extended back to the beginnings of local stage entertainment. From 1736 onwards Dublin troupes, while on their summer tours to the south of Ireland, often stopped to perform at Limerick.[5] Thither in 1754 a veteran stroller, James Love, migrated from Edinburgh to manage a summer company.[6] Though unpleasing in person and voice, he attained a considerable reputation by reason of

[1] Rev. P. Fitzgerald and J. J. M'Gregor, *The History, Topography, and Antiquities of the County and City of Limerick* (Dublin, 1827), ii. 465.

[2] John Ferrar, *An History of the City of Limerick* (Limerick, 1767), p. 67.

[3] Ibid., p. 148.

[4] Pococke, p. 113; Willes, p. 50.

[5] Robert Hitchcock, *An Historical View of the Irish Stage* (Dublin, 1788–94), i. 97, 114.

[6] James Love, *Poems on Several Occasions* (Edinburgh, 1754), p. xi; Benjamin Victor, *Original Letters* (Dublin, 1776), i. 222.

two quite diverse accomplishments:[1] (1) his writing of the recitational prologue 'Bucks Have at Ye All', a steady favourite throughout Ireland during the latter half of the eighteenth century; (2) his acting of Falstaff, which one informed colleague praised as 'the best of his time'.[2]

In 1760, when Spranger Barry, manager of the Dublin Crow Street Theatre, opened the fine new theatre at Cork, he instituted regular summer seasons at Limerick as a supplementary undertaking. For the next decade the Dublin Theatre Royal company played almost every year at the small inconvenient structure called 'the Theatre in Peter's Cell'. The district known as Peter's Cell, comprising the ruined properties of an Augustinian nunnery dedicated to St. Peter, lay along the walls in the north-eastern section of the English Town.[3] About 1760 a number of professional men and others of some means, such as Anne O'Dell with her fine house and garden, resided there.[4] The lane which led from Bishop Street as the principal entry into the area still survives, bearing the quaint name of 'Peter's Cell'. Today, however, it exhibits no vestiges of the eighteenth century; it is flanked on the north by the modern St. Mary's Convent and School and, on the south, by a large public playground. Some ingenious theatrical entrepreneur transformed the refectory of the one-time nunnery into a playhouse containing boxes, pit, one gallery, stage, and a few dressing rooms.[5] Seats in the 1760's sold at 3*s.* in the boxes, 2*s.* in the pit, and 1*s.* in the gallery.[6] The refreshments served at the Peter's Cell performances constituted the theatre's one distinction: they were not oranges, as in London and Dublin, but peaches.[7] The fruit sellers circulated with baskets of luscious four-inch specimens at a halfpenny each.

In September and October of 1767 the Crow Street actors were performing at Limerick under the leadership of William Dawson, Barry's deputy.[8] During their stay the company's famous tumbler, Sully, married one of the *ingénues*, Miss Shepherd, daughter of an Irish strolling manager, Charles

[1] *Theatrical Biography* (London, 1772), i. 135–9.
[2] Snagg(e), p. 105.
[3] John Ferrar, *The History of Limerick to the Year 1787* (Limerick, 1787), pp. 187–8; O'Keeffe, i. 176.
[4] Maurice Lenihan, *Limerick; Its History and Antiquities* (Dublin, 1866), p. 363.
[5] O'Keeffe, i. 177, 287.
[6] LC, 13 Oct. 1768.
[7] O'Keeffe, i. 287–8.
[8] Ibid. i. 176.

PLATE IV

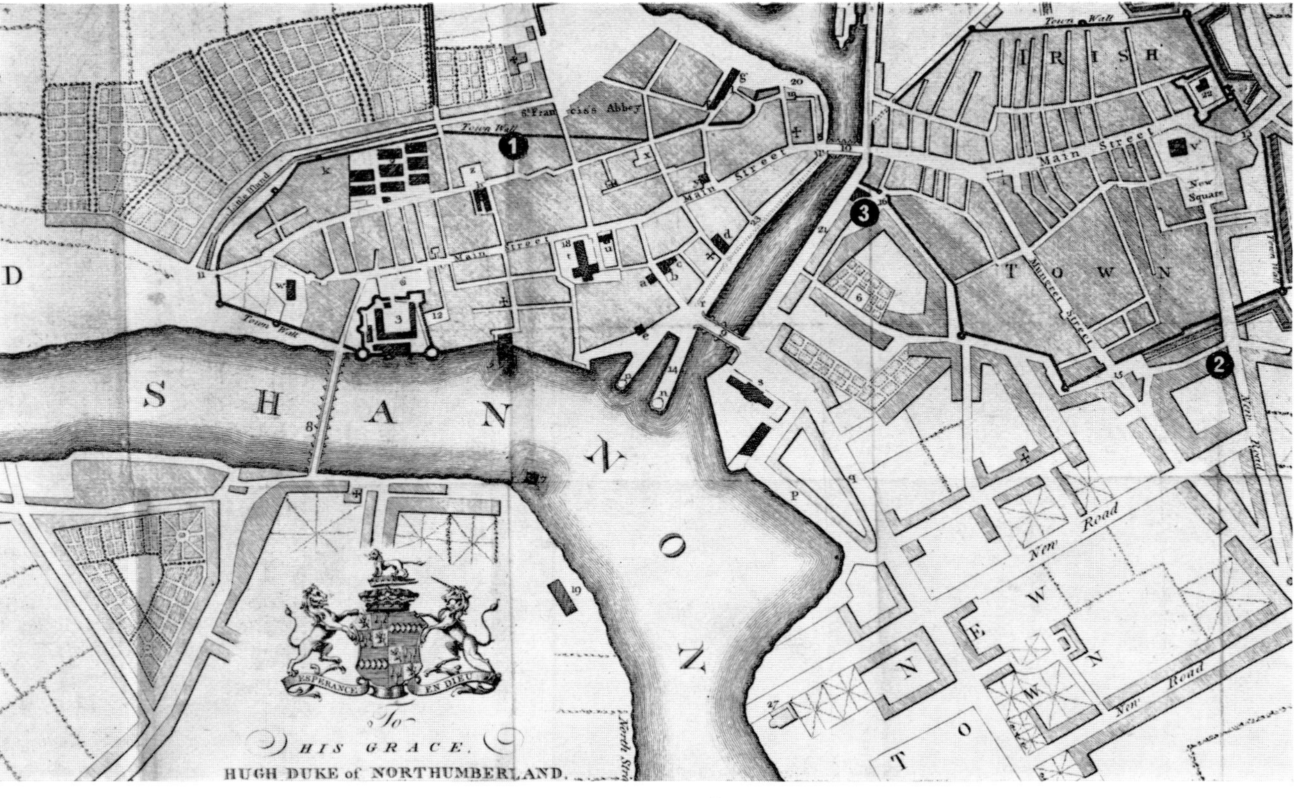

Limerick in 1786

Theatre Sites: (1) Peter's Cell; (2) Cornwallis Street; (3) The New Assembly House

Shepherd.[1] This romance must have caused little stir among the players, however, in the midst of the almost daily excitement surrounding the Peter's Cell performances. The mean and cramped interior of the playhouse made for very informal and prankish behaviour. On one occasion the Badgers Club, composed of the county's first gentlemen, sponsored *Romeo and Juliet*.[2] The club members as privileged spectators sat on the stage and imbibed freely from the contents of a near-by sideboard. Towards the close of the play, at the moment of Juliet's death, the Grand Badger, an old man dressed in a high cap of badger's skin, could not contain himself. Crying out, 'Oh, my poor pretty little soul! don't be lying there', he stepped forward, lifted Juliet up in spite of her remonstrance, and took her to the sideboard for refreshment. On that day Shakespeare's tragedy ended in laughter!

At another performance a Limerick buck, familiarly called 'the Grand Bugle', mounted to the stage in order to show himself off after the prevailing fashion, discovered too many of his kind ahead of him between the scene wings at the sides, and therefore walked behind the scene at the back.[3] Then in the nicely painted and valuable flat he cut with his penknife a hole large enough to show his face. There he stood at his ease, boldly looking out at the audience. The Grand Bugle had a worthy rival for public attention in a personage known as 'the Child' because 'Frolic was his whole affair in this world'. One evening at Peter's Cell 'the Child' was sitting in the gallery with a crowd of fellow roisterers, bottles in hand, leading the crowd in shouting toasts.[4] 'A clap for Mahon the player on the stage' was followed by hearty clapping from the gallery bucks. 'A groan for my aunt in the side-boxes' brought a loud response. The whole house got into an uproar. The sheriff, 'Hero' Jackson, left his box, climbed to the gallery, grasped 'the Child' by the scruff of the neck and shoved him down the gallery stairs into the street. After the sheriff had reached his seat again, he looked across the stage and there he saw 'the Child' sober and quiet beside his aunt in the side-box opposite.

The boisterous interruptions from the Peter's Cell audiences infected the manners of the actors. In a performance of *The*

[1] FDJ, 13 Oct. 1767.
[2] O'Keeffe, i. 176–7.
[3] Ibid. i. 184.
[4] Ibid. i. 180–2.

Beggar's Opera West Digges as Captain Macheath had just put on his fetters at Newgate prison.[1] He found himself unpleasantly bound with chains that were not the customary set. Turning in irritation to 'the Grand Bugle' who was seated near by, he complained in a loud voice about the property-man: 'Look here, sir, what a pair of fetters he has brought me—they've cut through my ankles! Instead of giving me proper light tin ones, he has got them out of the gaol, and they have been on some murderer!' Such persistent goings-on caused the playhouse in Peter's Cell to be remembered with unusual vividness by John O'Keeffe, the far-strolling Dublin comedian.

In 1768 Henry Mossop, the new manager of the combined Dublin theatres, transferred his touring company from Cork to Limerick on the last week-end of September and played at Peter's Cell until 29 October.[2] This, his first, experience at the antiquated playhouse prompted him to think of improving Limerick's stage facilities in accord with the spirit of progress now pervading the city. Recent demolition of the old walls had made way for the extension of main thoroughfares and for the construction of new quays along the Abbey River: George's Quay (1763); the South Mall, later known as Charlotte's Quay (1766); Sir Harry's Mall (1767).[3] The introduction of handsome buildings commenced with the erection of the City Court House in 1764 and the Custom House in 1769.[3] A year later the elegant Assembly House, containing shops on the ground floor and vaults underneath, was completed at a cost of £4,000.[4] It stood towards the eastern end of Charlotte's Quay near the old West Water Gate of the Irish Town.[5] All these large edifices rose on the edge of Newtown-Pery, a splendid tract of land owned by the Right Honourable Edmond Sexton Pery, son of a wealthy Limerick merchant and Speaker of the Irish House of Commons in 1768. Pery, showing the vision of a modern city planner, laid out his ground in a design of broad straight streets cutting across one another to form spacious blocks.[6] Newspaper

[1] O'Keeffe, i. 187.
[2] LC, 24 Oct. 1768.
[3] Fitzgerald and M'Gregor, ii. 466–8.
[4] LC, 26 July 1770; Constantia Maxwell, *Country and Town in Ireland under the Georges* (Dundalk, 1949), p. 244.
[5] See 'A Plan of the City of Limerick' (1786) in Ferrar, *The History of Limerick to the Year 1787*.
[6] Fitzgerald and M'Gregor, ii. 486–7, 505.

advertising of 1769 described the Newtown-Pery sites in the picturesque style of eighteenth-century landscape painting that Irish stage settings of the time often copied:

> An extensive view up and down the river, commanding a full prospect of many agreeable objects, particularly the romantic grandeur of the county Clare mountains.—A large Cascade and spacious Basin alternately as the tide ebbs and flows.—All the shipping, etc., passing and repassing, and at the several Quays and the Pool.—The Ruins of Carrig O'Gunnell, etc. . . . In short, the most elegant Town Residence in the Kingdom, or perhaps in the World, cannot boast such rural Beauty or so fine a Landscape, and the Variety is daily encreasing.[1]

The rapid development of Newtown-Pery into a district of handsome brick residences and shops for well-to-do mercantile families as well as for the gentry from the surrounding country beautified the face of Limerick to an extent which no Irish town other than Dublin enjoyed in the eighteenth century.

The prevailing atmosphere of expansion and opulence soon crystallized Mossop's thinking in regard to the betterment of Limerick's theatrical situation. His future designs he set forth in the *Limerick Chronicle* of 24 October 1768, together with an appeal for funds towards a suitable new playhouse:

> With the approbation and patronage of some of the principal Gentlemen of the City of Limerick and of the Counties of Limerick, Clare and Tipperary, [Mr. Mossop] has undertaken the Establishment of a regular theatre in this City. As Mr. Mossop is under the necessity of immediately setting out for Dublin in order to open the Theatre Royal, he thinks it proper to take this opportunity of assuring the publick, that it is his Intention to exhibit Dramatic Entertainments in the most perfect and extensive Manner in the City of Limerick. He proposes to bring down every Summer the best and most approved of those Performers whom he shall have employed in Dublin on each preceding Winter; he also proposes to perform here himself each Summer, and designs to commence the opening of the New Theatre some time before the next Summer Assizes. He further begs leave to assure the Publick . . . to exert his warmest Endeavours . . . in order that the Theatre of Limerick may be allowed to be, in every particular, as well regulated, as elegant, and as compleat, as any other Theatre in the Kingdom.

[1] LC, 13 Mar. 1769.

The Proposals at large, with the Plan of the Theatre drawn by a proper Architect, are in the hands of Alderman Sexton Baylee, the Reverend Jaques Ingram, Alexander Franklin and Nicholas Smith, Esquires, who are so obliging as to undertake the trouble of receiving Subscriptions. . . . All those who are desirous to patronize their Undertaking will be pleased to send their Names to the above Gentlemen or to Mr. Mossop in the City of Dublin.

On the following day the *Leinster Journal* at Kilkenny interpreted the vague opening sentence of Mossop's announcement as a specific declaration that 'the mayor of Limerick and most of the principal gentlemen of the city of Limerick and of the counties of Limerick, Clare, and Tipperary have become subscribers'. No matter what local subscriptions may have been forthcoming in the autumn and winter of 1768, the grave difficulties which Mossop soon encountered in the management of his Dublin theatres made it impossible for him to carry on with the Limerick project.

Within the next year and a half the Dublin manager sold his theatrical rights in Limerick to a native of that city, Tottenham Heaphy, who had been connected with the Irish stage for over twenty years. In the spring of 1770 Heaphy proceeded to erect a theatre, since he had secured £600 towards the venture from twenty-four subscribers, each of whom paid £25 for a silver transferable admission ticket valid indefinitely.[1] The new building, located at the south-west corner of Cornwallis (now Gerald Griffin) Street and Playhouse Lane (now Little Gerald Griffin Street),[2] presented in its inelegant appearance and arrangements a great contrast to the Assembly House finished a little earlier in the same year. Heaphy's structure lacked a conventional theatre façade with centre doors, because the forward section, abutting on Cornwallis Street, was designed for dwelling and business purposes. Edward Gubbins, noted carriage and coach builder, for years occupied these front premises.[3] Access to the playhouse boxes could be gained only by a long and inconvenient passage that ran from Cornwallis Street through Gubbins's kitchen to the theatre in the rear.[3] Often so many persons crowded together in this narrow corridor that it was 'very difficult, especially for Ladies, to get

[1] Ferrar, *The History of Limerick*, p. 206.

[2] See 'A Plan of the City of Limerick'.

[3] Lenihan, p. 364.

out without being hurt'.[1] The entry leading to the pit door opened off Playhouse Lane;[2] perhaps it survives in the small old passage on the west side of Little Gerald Griffin Street a short distance north of the corner. The theatre itself measured 80 feet long by 40 feet wide,[3] less than two-thirds the size of the Theatre Royal in Aungier Street, Dublin, built forty years before. It had a small stage in comparison with the area of the house and no green-room for the actors;[4] but it did possess, adjoining the one gallery, a second tier of side-boxes termed 'lattices' as in Dublin.[5] The prices for seats Heaphy established at the prevailing Dublin scale: 4*s.* in the boxes and lattices, 2*s.* 6*d.* in the pit, and 1*s.* in the gallery.[6]

As late as April of 1770 the old playhouse in Peter's Cell was still being used. The *Limerick Chronicle* carried advertisements of a performance to be given there on 14 April by an unnamed group of players, presumably local amateurs.[7] Heaphy opened the new theatre in Cornwallis Street during the summer of 1770[8] either before or after his company's visit to Cork, 24 August to 6 September. The personnel, drawn mostly from Dublin, included, besides Manager Heaphy and his wife, Mr. and Mrs. William Dawson, the youthful light comedian William Thomas Lewis, and Mrs. Spranger Barry as the principal figures. Of their bills, none is on record; of their playing, a Limerick resident said 'tolerably decent'.[9]

The following year Heaphy and many of 'His Majesty's Servants' from the Crow Street Theatre, Dublin, played Limerick before Cork. On the opening night, Thursday, 15 August, 'a numerous and polite audience' gave the players 'repeated Plaudits' during the performance of *The Provok'd Husband.*[10] The presence of the famous Dublin comedian Isaac Sparks and his son Richard, of John O'Keeffe the expert in farce, and of Robert Mahon the character actor considerably improved the company's playing of comedy during this season. Late in

[1] LC, 25 Aug. 1792. [2] Lenihan, p. 364.
[3] Ibid., p. 425. [4] Charles Mathews, *Memoirs* (London, 1839), i. 110.
[5] LC, 17 Oct. 1771. [6] Ibid., 23 Sept. and 17 Oct. 1771.
[7] LC, 12 and 29 Mar. 1770, advertised 'at the Theatre in Peter's Cell . . . a Comedy, never perform'd in this Kingdom, called, The Brothers. With new Scenery paint'd for the Occasion. And the Musical Entertainment of Thomas and Sally.' [8] Ferrar, *The History of Limerick*, p. 206.
[9] HJ, 13 July 1772. [10] LC, 19 Aug. 1771.

August the Heaphy troupe went to Cork for the court assizes and then returned to Limerick to perform until the end of October. The manager, having set Monday, 23 September, as his benefit, expected, in accordance with custom, to solicit in person the sale of tickets. His 'dangerous state of health', however, prevented him from 'waiting on those Ladies and Gentlemen to whom he has the honour of being particularly known'.[1] Instead, tickets could be procured from Mr. Heaphy 'at his house near the Theatre'.

On the following Friday, Lewis the comedian, who throughout the season had been exhibiting a perverse ambition for the important roles of Shakespearian tragedy, chose to do Hamlet for his benefit.[2] This attempt and his earlier efforts in the tragic vein provoked one indignant spectator to protest against 'the disrespect offered by the farcical, ridiculous gesture of Lewis, who certainly had not weight enough for the character of Richard, Hamlet, Lear, etc.'.[3] At Mrs. Heaphy's benefit, on 22 October 1771, Lewis reinstated himself in local esteem by his acting of Belcour, the genteel hero of *The West Indian*, the part which in the previous winter had elevated him to the elect of the Dublin stage and bestowed upon him the sobriquet of 'Gentleman'.[4]

The new theatre did not wholly cure the Limerick audience of the unruly conduct in which it had so freely indulged at Peter's Cell. On Thursday, 10 October, the *Limerick Chronicle* took prominent space to express the public's appreciation 'to the gentlemen who corrected a most clamorous, indecent, troublesome young man in the Gallery of the playhouse last Tuesday night'. By now the local playgoers had invented a more subtle form of misbehaviour; they forged the special printed tickets which were issued in advance for the benefit nights of both individual actors and local charities. In connexion with the end-of-the-season performance on behalf of the Limerick Poor a stern warning had to be published a day ahead that 'Mr. Mayor has marked all the Tickets, and any Person who attempts to pass a Counterfeit one, will be severely punished'.[5] Not only the customers but also the physical plant caused difficulties for Heaphy. The long, dark passages from the

[1] LC, 19 Sept. 1771. [2] Ibid., 23 Sept. 1771. [3] HJ, 13 July, 1772.
[4] LC, 17 Oct. 1771. [5] Ibid., 28 Oct. 1771.

streets to the various doors of the playhouse required constant attention if they were to be kept decent and safe. To encourage attendance at Mrs. Heaphy's benefit her husband published an emphatic assurance that 'the utmost care will be taken to have the Avenues leading to the Theatre sufficiently Clean'd and Lighted'.[1] As a final means to engender goodwill the manager took pains over a week before departure to urge 'persons who have any demands on the Theatre' to submit their bills at once.[2]

In 1772, Heaphy with most of the chief performers from Crow Street, Dublin, occupied 'the New Theatre Royal, Limerick', at the beginning of July.[3] Soon afterwards an anonymous Limerick troublemaker berated the manager: 'Do you imagine a city so considerable will tacitly suffer such actors to mock so rational an amusement with impunity? . . . What greater indignity could you offer than bringing here that animal, Keeffe, who dared to inscribe some indecent lines under a picture at a publican's in Monastereven, to the Ladies of Limerick!'[4] This attack only succeeded in arousing a greater public interest in the local season. Business proved so good that the company did not leave for Cork until mid-August and then returned again for Assize Week, 14–19 September. In fact, the habit of playgoing had grown to such a point among the common people that prices for gallery seats were raised during the season another sixpence to 1*s*. 6*d*.[5]

Even if irate letter writers did not prove disturbing, other matters did cause Heaphy concern. Numerous male patrons, as in Dublin and other towns, insistently desired to penetrate backstage. Therefore, in the first week of performances, the manager gave out a firm statement of policy: 'Since it is impossible to conduct the Performances with regularity if Gentlemen come behind the Scenes, it is humbly hoped that no Person will be Offended at being denied Admittance.'[6] Nevertheless the gentlemen did not abate their efforts. A month later the manager had to reaffirm his stand in more vehement language: 'Since it is impossible to carry on the Entertainments of the Stage with order or decency if the Performers are crowded

[1] Ibid., 17 Oct. 1771. [2] Ibid., 21 Oct. 1771.

[3] The earliest surviving advertisement for the season (LC, 6 July 1772) announced *The Fashionable Lover* and *The Mayor of Garrat* for 6 July, and added that 'the Company will perform but a few nights longer till the Assizes'.

[4] HJ, 13 July 1772. [5] LC, 30 July 1772. [6] Ibid., 6 July 1772.

or interrupted in their Business, therefore no Money will be taken at the Stage Door; nor will any Person be admitted behind the Scenes but those who belong to the Theatre.'[1] The weather too became troublesome. July turned out so hot that the playhouse threatened to be unbearable. On 13 July and again the next week Heaphy boldly stated that 'proper care will be taken to keep the House cool'.[2] The Limerick building, however, was certainly equipped with no more adequate means of ventilation than its Dublin counterparts, which, according to the newspapers, felt as hot as ovens sometimes in the summer seasons. Complaints about the dilatory commencement of the Cornwallis Street performances followed those in regard to the heat. At last the manager promised that 'for the future the Curtain will rise exactly at seven o'clock'.[3] In return, the Limerick ladies and gentlemen were requested to send servants to keep places at five o'clock instead of the former hour of six.[4]

These problems of management amounted to little in the face of a prosperous season. Its prosperity derived in large measure from the presence of Charles Macklin, the master of Irish comedians, and his twenty-year-old pupil, Henrietta Amelia Leeson, who had made a brilliant stage début at Dublin in the preceding winter. For their initial Limerick appearance (and Miss Leeson's first performance outside Dublin) on Friday, 10 July, they played together in *The Merchant of Venice* as Shylock and Portia.[5] Then they carried on their delightful collaboration as Sir Gilbert Wrangle and Charlotte in Cibber's comedy, *The Refusal*; as Iago and Desdemona in *Othello*; as Murrough O'Doherty and Mrs. Diggerty in Macklin's *The True-Born Irishman*; and as Sir Pertinax Macsycophant and Lady Rodolpha Lumbercourt in Macklin's *The True-Born Scotsman*, which concluded the main season on Wednesday, 12 August.[6]

Macklin and Miss Leeson did not return with the company to Limerick in September for the Assize Week performances. On Saturday the 19th the Crow Street troupers ended their 1772 tour, as they had commenced it, with the acting of *The Fashionable Lover*.[7] Manager Heaphy had staged this Cumber-

[1] LC, 3 Aug. 1772. [2] Ibid., 13 and 20 July 1772.
[3] Ibid., 30 July 1772. [4] Ibid., 27 July 1772. [5] Ibid., 9 July 1772.
[6] *The Refusal*, 13 July; *Othello*, 5 August; *The True-Born Irishman*, 21 July.
[7] LC, 17 Sept. 1772.

land comedy on the season's opening night with what he described as 'New Cloathes, Scenes, and Decorations'.[1] Thereafter he often called attention to the supposedly fresh costuming and scenery in the summer productions. For his benefit on Friday, 31 July, he got up *The Grecian Daughter* 'with New Dresses and Decorations'.[2] Again, 'New Dresses and Decorations' embellished *The True-Born Scotsman* at Vandermere's benefit on 12 August.[3] Thus the Limerick audiences in 1772 had little reason for raising against their present proprietor the common charge of excessive parsimony in regard to wardrobe and properties.

In the succeeding year the Crow Street company reversed the order of its touring and went to Cork first. Then it paid Limerick a visit of only three weeks, Monday, 2 August, to Friday, 20 August 1773, but gave at least a dozen performances to well-filled houses.[4] The enthusiastic audiences came principally to watch Heaphy's guest star, Thomas Sheridan of Covent Garden, in his famous tragic roles, such as Hamlet and the Roman Father.[5] On 6 August, when he impersonated Addison's Cato, the critic of the *Limerick Chronicle* described his portrayal as 'incomparably great' and went on to remark in a hyperbolic strain: 'Never were so many Eyes dissolved in tears as on that night.'[6] Yet Sheridan did not provide all the colour of the season. Heaphy and the Masons of the city planned an elaborate show for his benefit on 16 August: 'The Members of the Respective Lodges will walk in their Proper Cloathing, and usual order of Procession, to the Stage of the Theatre, which will be form'd into an Amphitheatre and properly decorated for the Reception of the Brethren.'[7] Heaphy in the dress of a Master Mason welcomed the Brethren with a prologue before the acting of *She Stoops to Conquer*. Three days later, at the benefit of 'Gentleman' Lewis, the manager found another opportunity for pageantry in presenting *Julius Caesar* with 'a grand procession of Lictors, Trophies, Fasces, etc.'.[7]

Thomas Wilks, a young light comedian over from England for the summer, acted his specialty, Sir Harry Wildair in Farquhar's *The Constant Couple*, as the closing attraction of this

[1] Ibid., 6 July 1772. [2] Ibid., 27 July 1772. [3] Ibid., 10 Aug. 1772.
[4] Snagg(e), pp. 93, 103. [5] LC, 9 and 12 Aug. 1773.
[6] Ibid., 6 Aug. 1773. [7] Ibid., 12 Aug. 1773.

short but profitable Limerick season.[1] The profits amounted to £502,[2] a high average of £42 per night if, as the advertising indicated, a dozen performances made up the season. Wilks for his playing during the three weeks netted £32,[2] a sum equal to a good Irish actor's usual salary for nine or ten weeks outside Dublin.

During the winter of 1773–4 a report began to circulate that a set of players other than Heaphy's would appear at the Limerick theatre in the spring or early summer. On 14 February Heaphy published in Dublin a denial of the report along with the declaration that as patentee of the Limerick playhouse he would not issue to anyone a licence to act there.[3] He had an ambitious intention of his own for enhancing the quality of Limerick theatricals, and he proceeded to reveal it in the *Limerick Chronicle* on 3 March. His notice began by stating that many ladies and gentlemen of Limerick had indicated a wish to remove the Theatre Royal from 'its present, inconvenient situation, to the ground next adjoining the New Assembly House'. The manager had been encouraged in 'the execution and expense of so great an undertaking' by the subscribers to the existing theatre, by several proprietors of the Assembly House, and by other persons who had desired 'to see those two edifices of entertainment mutually promote and assist each other'. Heaphy concluded his notice by promising to visit Limerick within a few days in order to report to interested ladies and gentlemen 'such measures as he had already conditionally entered into'. This was the first disclosure of a dream that in the ensuing fifteen years directed a recurrent civic movement. Heaphy, however, did not follow up the disclosure by going to Limerick for consultations.

The coming of summer found the Dublin players embarked once more on the Cork–Limerick circuit with yet another variation of schedule: six weeks in Cork, two weeks in Limerick, three weeks in Cork, and then two weeks at Limerick again before going back to Dublin. The opening of the 1774 season in the Munster capital was delayed until 11 August on account of the races held 4–6 August at Rathkeale, eighteen miles south-west.[4]

[1] LC, 16 Aug. 1773. [2] Snagg(e), p. 93.
[3] *The Public Advertiser; or, The Theatrical Chronicle*, 14 Feb. 1774.
[4] LC, 4 and 8 Aug. 1774.

In announcing the postponement on 4 August Heaphy once again promised that 'the much desir'd Scheme of erecting the Theatre adjoining the Assembly-House will be commenced on his Arrival in this City'.[1] Subsequently one of the city's leaders, Thomas Smyth, donated for the theatre site the piece of uncovered ground on Charlotte's Quay next to the Assembly House.[2] In spite of this donation and of the general recognition of the need for a more attractive and better located playhouse, Heaphy, like Smithson at Ennis, never succeeded in bringing about the fulfilment of his dream.

Except for the scheme to erect a new theatre the major interest in the summer's theatricals was furnished by the lively week of benefit performances beginning on Monday, 22 August. Heaphy's, the initial one as usual, consisted of *The Tempest* with Dryden's masque of Neptune and Amphitrite in Act V, Foote's interlude *Piety in Patterns*, and the comic opera of *The Deserter* with 'a Grand Garland Dance' in Act I.[3] So rich a dramatic feast required a special curtain time of 6.45 p.m. The rather less elaborate benefits of the leading tragedian, Lawrence Clinch, and the leading comedian, 'Gentleman' Lewis, followed on successive nights. Each of their bills, vying with the manager's selection of *The Tempest*, previously unseen, included at least one work 'never performed here'.[4] Both Clinch and Lewis tried to encourage the advance sale of their benefit tickets among the more wealthy patrons by a monetary arrangement that took advantage of the peculiar currency situation. In separate advertisements the two actors offered to accept in payment for tickets the sub-standard gold guineas which were then in common circulation. These 'light' guineas of 5 dwt. 3 gr. in weight they could use, presumably, in settling their local accounts. Limerick shopkeepers, for the time being, were permitted to send up to 5,000 'light' guineas to the Irish Treasury at Dublin and exchange them for the standard 'heavy' coins. Lewis would 'take gold . . . at Mr. Hayes's in Irish-town', where he was lodging; Clinch would 'take Guineas . . . at his residence opposite the Theatre', or through Mr. Evory at 'the Box Office'.[5]

[1] Ibid. [2] Ferrar, *The History of Limerick*, p. 206. [3] LC, 18 Aug. 1774.

[4] Ibid. Clinch offered Dibdin's comic opera, *The Wedding Ring*, on 23 Aug.; Lewis, Steele's comedy, *The Funeral*, on the 24th. [5] LC, 18 and 22 Aug. 1774.

Shortly after the end of the summer playing, two notable events occurred in the Limerick company. On Saturday, 1 October, John O'Keeffe, the popular low comedian, married in the Irish Town Mary Heaphy, the manager's daughter.[1] Ten days later the wife of a lesser-known comedian, Richard Sparks, 'was delivered . . . of Two Sons at Silvermines in the County of Tipperary', while *en route* to Dublin.[2] Mrs. Sparks, like numerous married actresses of the eighteenth century, evidently felt little discomfort or embarrassment in performance during the last month or two of pregnancy. She had been filling prominent roles as recently as 28 September, the day of her benefit. No ill effects seem to have resulted, for on 17 October the *Limerick Chronicle* reported that Mrs. Sparks and the two boys were 'in a fair way of doing well'.

The second summer after the birth of the twins Mrs. Sparks and her husband chose to play at Kilkenny rather than at Cork and Limerick. Heaphy experienced no loss by their secession, however, because the venerable tragedian Thomas Sheridan returned to Ireland for a farewell tour under Heaphy's management. Sheridan had found his south-of-Ireland visit in 1773 too rewarding in acclaim and money (he had 'picked up' £700, so his Dublin friend George Faulkner informed David Garrick[3]) to resist a second summer invitation. Heaphy's company with Sheridan as the star attraction performed in Limerick during the first three weeks of September 1776. Once more the citizenry turned out in large numbers to admire Sheridan's art, but the ageing actor had lost his zest for the limelight. Towards the close of his Limerick stay he wrote: 'I have been playing to crowded houses; but my time has not passed so agreeably as formerly.'[4]

The enthusiasm over Sheridan's farewell appearances was as nothing compared with the excitement over the Limerick Jubilee in August of the following year. Planned and directed by the enterprising mayor, Thomas Smyth, the Jubilee took the form of a week of varied entertainments. The magnificent celebration was intended to focus the attention of Britain and the Continent, as well as all Ireland, upon this vigorous city of

[1] O'Keeffe, i. 361–2.
[2] LC, 17 Oct. 1774.
[3] Letter of 9 Oct. 1773, Forster MS. 213.
[4] Lefanu Papers, microfilm 2975.

40,000 people,[1] and to demonstrate its coming-of-age as an enlightened European metropolis. The Jubilee opened on Tuesday, 12 August 1777, with the laying of the cornerstone of the impressive Exchange in Rutland Street.[2] At night the Fancy Ball took place at the Assembly House, where the ballroom was 'lighted in the Manner of the Rotunda in Dublin', and the supper room was 'illuminated with Lamps of various Colours, imitative of the Pantheon in London'.[3] Three hundred persons attended, all wearing costumes of Limerick material and manufacture to evidence the beauty of Irish textiles to the world at large.[4] Though no females dressed in native garb, a few patriotic males impersonated either Irish countrymen or hurlers. Most of the participants decked themselves out as fashionably exotic personages: Greek or Roman deities, harlequins, Indian princesses, Italian princes, and Turkish sultans. Because of the pleasant weather the populace crowded the streets near the quays to gape at these bizarrely attired figures of high society riding in carriages or sedan chairs and attended by footmen. Then a developing Irish democratic impulse seized the onlookers. 'The mob-ility, as usual on such occasions,' stated the contemporary reporter, 'forced the nobility and gentry out of their chaises and sedans, and made them walk from some distance to the Assembly-House, to the no small diversion of the numerous crowd.'[4] This ball, the most elaborate in Limerick's history before 1800, did not break up until four o'clock on Wednesday morning.

On Wednesday evening the theatrical programme commenced. Heaphy and his company interrupted their Cork summer season to travel to Limerick and perform for the Jubilee. One of the better comedians, Thomas Wilks, was thrown from his carriage near Mallow on his way from Cork and suffered a concussion.[5] The injury, though severe, did not result in death as the Dublin report asserted. With the exception of the rollicking O'Keeffe, Heaphy's troupe included no actor of repute. Nevertheless it played acceptably a series of old favourites in the four main types of current drama: (1) the

[1] *The Hibernian Magazine*, Jan. 1777, p. 22.
[2] Ibid., Aug. 1777, p. 574.
[3] LC, 4 Aug. 1777.
[4] *The Hibernian Magazine*, Aug. 1777, p. 574.
[5] Snagg(e), pp. 100–1.

comedy of *The Provok'd Husband* by Colley Cibber on the 13th; (2) the musical farce of *Lionel and Clarissa* by Isaac Bickerstaffe on the 14th; (3) the tragedy of *Jane Shore* by Nicholas Rowe on the 15th; (4) the comic opera of *The Duenna* by R. B. Sheridan on the 16th.[1]

The stage productions, however, could scarcely equal in glamour other of the later Jubilee festivities such as 'the Venetian Breakfast in the beautiful and romantic Garden' belonging to Mr. Robert Davis and located along the banks of the Shannon.[1] A river regatta, interspersed with band music on the water, followed this Thursday morning breakfast. The festivities extended over to Monday, 18 August, when the medieval ceremony of 'riding the franchises' of the city was carried out in gorgeous array.[1] The municipal procession, led by the 12th Regiment Band, started from King's Island at noon. 'Every one of the corporations took pains to provide fine cattle [i.e. horses], elegant cloaths, furniture, standards, ensigns, etc.'[1] The pageants of the fourteen trade guilds began with the Smiths' display of Venus and a child in a phaeton drawn by four beautiful pied horses with a mounted Vulcan alongside. The Tobacconists brought up the rear of the parade with a float showing the Black King of Morocco and Grimalkin the Snuff Grinder. Thus the Limerick Jubilee concluded in a truly grand finale which left one of the Week's participants recalling 'such a diversity of splendid objects, that the fancy, in a kind of controversy with itself, knew not which most to admire'.[1]

Two years after his direction of the very successful Jubilee Thomas Smyth headed the organization of the Limerick Volunteers, a militant defence corps which was forming throughout Ireland to secure her economic as well as her political liberties. As colonel of the local contingent Smyth ordered a command performance at the Limerick Theatre on Friday, 27 August 1779, the last night of the season as well as Mrs. O'Keeffe's benefit.[2] The evening's bill presented two melodramas appropriate to the insurgent mood of the times. Pilon's humorous *The Liverpool Prize* included a scene picturing a recent martial exploit on the high seas: 'The French Indiaman

1 *The Hibernian Magazine*, Aug. 1777, p. 574.
2 LC, 19 Aug. 1779.

brought in by the "Charming Sally" privateer.'[1] In the other piece, Home's *Douglas*, Mrs. O'Keeffe made her first appearance as Douglas, the young Scotsman, a free nature-loving soul. Spirited Mary Heaphy O'Keeffe was, however, far from the most notable of her father's players at Limerick in 1779. The well-known English actor John Henderson had joined Heaphy's summer tour as a fresh celebrity and, likewise, Richard Daly, a handsome dashing Irish novice.[2]

Daly, who played opposite the charming and talented Mrs. Lyster (*née* Barsanti) in genteel comedy, was to become in the next decade the most notorious personage on the Dublin stage. In December 1781, after assuming the managership at Smock Alley, Dublin, Daly brought Heaphy's reign as the proprietor of the Limerick Theatre to an end by leasing it 'for a term of years'[3] with the proviso that Heaphy might take possession for up to six months per year and might use any scenery found on the premises.[4] The new proprietor, in contrast to his predecessor, welcomed any chance for added income from rental of the theatre. Very shortly he leased the building to Alexander Macartney for six weeks in July and August of 1782 while the Daly company from Dublin was performing at Cork. Macartney, a strolling manager already well known to Kilkenny and Lisburn, presented a conventional repertory done by a group of obscure players. In accordance with the prevailing custom the manager exploited his Masonic connexions for his benefit evening on Friday, 26 July.[5] 'He issued a public request that 'every Brother of Town and Neighbourhood be so kind as to attend the Theatre that Night.' The members of Lodge No. 13 were instructed to 'walk in a Procession from their Lodge Room to the Theatre, dressed in the Insigns of their Order'. The rise of the curtain at 7.30 p.m. found them all accommodated upon an 'amphitheatre' erected on the stage. Macartney sought to make an impression not only upon the Masons but also upon the entire community. On 15 August he gave notice through

[1] Ibid.

[2] LC, 16 Aug. 1779, advertised Henderson's last performance for the 20th, and the first appearance of Daly and Mrs. Lyster for the 17th.

[3] FJ, 27 Dec. 1781.

[4] Letter of 8 Aug. 1797 from Richard Daly to Mr. Cooke in *Daly* v. *Jones*, Official Papers, 2nd series, 1790–1831, carton no. 511, 47/17, Record Tower, Dublin Castle.

[5] LC, 22 July 1782.

the local newspaper that he and his troupe would be leaving town in a few days, and he asked that all bills against them be submitted at once for prompt payment.[1]

No sooner had Daly's tenants departed in mid-August than he appeared with his company, featuring the Drury Lane débutante Anna Maria Phillips. For her benefit on Saturday evening, 31 August, she undertook a generous assortment of light musical roles: Laura in the prelude of *The Chaplet*, Polly in *The Beggar's Opera*, and Leonora in *The Padlock*.[2] On this special occasion the manager increased the size of the 'band' as well as engaged a pianoforte accompanist to heighten the 'airs'. The century's fad for musical interpolations was again exhibited in connexion with West Digges's benefit on the following Wednesday, 4 September, when he played Macbeth, and Mrs. Melmoth Lady Macbeth.[3] The bill for this last day of the Limerick season stressed the rendering of Purcell's *Macbeth* music and the fact that 'in this admired old Tragedy will be introduced the celebrated incantation of the Witches, assembled over their Caldron in the Pit of Acheron, and all their Magical Spells'.

During the summer of 1783 audiences held up so well in Dublin and then in Cork that Daly did not bring his actors to Limerick until the assizes at the beginning of October. During Assize Week the local regiment of Irish Volunteers under Colonels Burke and Smyth gained publicity and worked off patriotic energy by taking the guard of the theatre.[4] On Wednesday, 8 October, the two Masonic lodges observed a benefit night for 'Distressed Masons' with a procession starting for the playhouse at six o'clock.[4] Three days later a veteran cast in *Othello*—Clinch as Othello, Ryder as Iago, Mrs. Sparks as Desdemona—acted on behalf of Mrs. Heaphy. She made an urgent appeal for patronage, announcing 'with the most sincere Sentiments of Gratitude and the most tender Sensations of unalterable Respect and Esteem' that 'this will be the last Season of her performing in this City'.[4] As was often the case in pleas of this sort, the prophecy turned out quite wrong. The lady continued her appearances for five more years.

In the summer of 1784, as soon as it became known that Daly

[1] LC, 15 Aug. 1782.
[2] Ibid., 29 Aug. 1782.
[3] Ibid., 2 Sept. 1782.
[4] Ibid., 6 Oct. 1783.

and his Dublin troupe were not going to visit Limerick at all, William Henry Moss, an English actor of considerable experience in London and Dublin, attempted to turn Daly's by-passing of the Munster capital to his own profit. He drew up in Dublin a proposal 'to establish a theatre in Limerick upon a regular, respectable, and permanent footing for three months', commencing about November 1784. A sufficient number of advance subscriptions for transferable tickets to twelve nights of performance (about one month) would enable him 'to procure performers more suitable to the public taste than the customary and casual mode can possibly induce'. The needed amount of £54. 12*s.* would be raised by thirty subscriptions for box seats at £1. 10*s.* 6*d.* each, and by ten subscriptions for pit seats at 18*s.* each. These subscription figures represented a twenty-five per cent. reduction from the ordinary prices for single performances. The subscription money would be received and held by the High Sheriff of Limerick. A copy of this proposal, along with a request for support, Moss submitted on 12 August to the leading theatrical patron in the county, Sir Vere Hunt,[1] grandfather of the poet Aubrey de Vere, and owner of Curragh Chase, a rich and beautiful estate fifteen miles south-west of Limerick. Sir Vere apparently did not respond with the desired encouragement, and Moss pursued his scheme of a winter theatrical season no further.

The complete dearth of professional stage entertainment during 1784 provoked the formation of the Limerick Theatrical Society. On 17 January 1785 this organization of local gentlemen published its intention to perform for charitable purposes under the joint management of Sir Vere Hunt, Major Alcock of the 47th Regiment, and Captain Trevor Lloyd Ashe, a skilled instrumentalist, who later appeared at the Fishamble Street Theatre, Dublin, and elsewhere on the Irish stage circuit.[2] The Society leased from Daly the Theatre Royal, but sold no tickets at the door. They had to be purchased in advance from Mr. Watson the printer. Seats in the boxes and 'lattices' (the upper row of boxes on each side of the stage) cost 4*s.*; in the pit, 3*s.*; and in the gallery, 2*s.* The first performance on Tuesday, 25 January, consisted of two outstanding stage

[1] Hunt MSS.: Letter of 12 Aug. 1784 from Mr. Moss.
[2] LC, 17 Jan. 1785.

favourites: *The Poor Soldier* and *Venice Preserved*, to which Mr. Thomas Grady of Limerick wrote a new epilogue delivered by Captain Ashe.[1] On the second bill, a week later, Sir Vere Hunt took the leading part of Octavio in *The Duenna*.[2] For the fourth society production on Tuesday, 1 March, Mrs. Melmoth came down from Dublin to play the heroine in *Venice Preserved* and *Rosina*.[3] Anticipating a crowded house, the sponsors railed off the rear of the pit to be sold as box seats and thus swelled their proceeds. The curtain rose at six o'clock, an hour earlier than usual, in order that 'the Ladies might get in time to the Assembly' after the theatricals.[4] The Society had planned to end its season of charitable plays with *The Revenge* and *The Poor Soldier* on Saturday, 5 March,[5] but enthusiastic audiences and 'the principles of Humanity' induced it to act *The Beggar's Opera* and *The Poor Soldier* on Tuesday, 15 March, for 'the Relief of Fellow Creatures in Distress, many of whom are detained in a loathsome Prison for their Fees'.[6] On this lofty humanitarian note Limerick's exciting innovation of amateur public dramatics closed for the time being.

The successful activities of the Theatrical Society perhaps were responsible for Daly's paying the city greater consideration in the summer of 1785. At the end of the Smock Alley season he sent direct to Limerick the better portion of his company, including two star attractions: the noted impersonator of native Irish roles, Robert Owenson, and the young Covent Garden tragedian, Joseph Holman, who was visiting Ireland for the first time. He made his county début on Tuesday, 16 August, as a Romeo in love with a forty-five-year-old Juliet, Mrs. Egerton from Drury Lane.[7] His performance drew somewhat restrained approbation from the *Limerick Chronicle*, which termed his person 'elegant', his voice 'manly', and his action 'that of a finished Gentleman'.

For the next three years Limerick enjoyed more extended and unusual entertainment from Proprietor Daly, no doubt because the city's audiences were keeping pace with its rising population, now close to 50,000.[8] Each summer the Dublin players fitted

[1] LC, 20 Jan. and 3 Feb. 1785. [2] Ibid., 27 Jan. 1785.
[3] Ibid., 24 Feb. 1785. [4] Ibid., 28 Feb. 1785. [5] Ibid., 21 Feb. 1785.
[6] Ibid., 7 Mar. 1785. [7] Ibid., 15 Aug. 1785.
[8] DeLatocnaye in 1796 stated 50,000 inhabitants, but Arthur Young in 1779 estimated 60,000 (Maxwell, p. 228).

in two visits to the Munster capital between their sojourns at Cork and Waterford, and also introduced an increasing variety of guest actors. The 1786 performances, which occurred in the first two weeks of August and the last two weeks of September, presented Charles Bannister of Drury Lane and John Henry ('Jack') Johnstone of Covent Garden in their first Limerick appearance, plus Mr. and Mrs. Chalmers, and Richard Wilson, all three of whom were from Covent Garden and on their first Irish tour.[1] These five new faces constituted a superlative cast for *Love in a Village* on the opening night of 31 July. In 1787 the curtain was up at the Theatre Royal, Limerick, 16–28 July and 13–25 August, with the celebrated Michael Kelly, 'from Venice' via Drury Lane, and the charming Mrs. Crouch, also of Drury Lane, as the chief attractions. They chose to do *Lionel and Clarissa* for their *première* before an audience overflowing on account of the assizes.[2]

In 1788 Daly opened the theatre very early in order to profit from the crowds attending the Limerick races 7–12 July. For this year Sir Vere Hunt managed the race meeting, much to the displeasure of the Protestant Bishop of Limerick, who deplored the event as 'very injurious to the Community, promoting Idleness and Immorality amongst the Lower Class of People, and Gambling (that most destructive Vice) amongst the Higher Class'.[3] Despite the Bishop's opposition, Race Week had already begun to rival Assize Week as a local holiday period, especially for gathering in the county people of all classes. The Garter Inn 'at the back of the square opposite the Theatre' offered 'good stabling' at 8*d.* per night and served meals every day during the races at special prices: breakfasts 8*d.*, dinners 1*s.*, and suppers, even after the plays, 10*d.*[4] Limerick's picturesque racecourse, lying in a pretty valley, 'exhibited for the accommodation of spectators a long range of booths, in tent-like style, embellished with painted signs of various figures, as a boot, a pig, a gridiron, etc., reminding one of Tenier's celebrated Dutch Fair'.[5] The farmers' wives and daughters so adorned the surrounding slopes that their 'universal costume of blue and scarlet cloaks,

[1] LC, 27 July, 3 and 14 Aug., 14 Sept. 1786.
[2] Ibid., 12 July 1787.
[3] Hunt MSS.: Letter of 27 Mar. 1788 from the Bishop of Limerick.
[4] LC, 30 June 1788.
[5] W. T. Parke, *Musical Memoirs* (London, 1830), i. 229–30.

and white starched cocked-up caps, in the distance resembled a profusion of sweet comfits regularly disposed on a dessert cake'. To entice these racegoers at night Daly selected as his initial drawing-card seventeen-year-old Maria Hughes, a Tipperary beauty whose stage début three months previously had thrilled Dublin. She was soon joined by 'Jack' Johnstone and Wright Bowden of Covent Garden, and Mrs. Castelli of Norwich, the latter two on their first Irish tour.[1] Daly's troupe stayed on for most of July, and then came up again from Cork just to act during Assize Week in mid-August.

About this time a 'committee of Nobility and Gentry' revived Tottenham Heaphy's proposal of 1774 that a new playhouse be erected in conjunction with the Assembly House on Charlotte's Quay. The Smyth family, now represented by John Prendergast Smyth, M.P., renewed its offer of ground adjoining the Assembly House as a site. Witht his location in view, the promoters commissioned a London architect of some eminence, James Lewis, to draw up in 1788 appropriate building plans.[2] These, the only ones known for an eighteenth-century theatre in Ireland, called for a handsome three-storied structure of Palladian style to be connected with the Assembly House. It was conceived, however, as a structure that, like the existing Theatre Royal in Cornwallis Street, would combine under one roof residential apartments at the front and a theatre at the rear. The living quarters intended for Mr. Smyth's occupancy 'during his stay in the city' would look north upon the quay and river, and would possess an imposing ornamented façade, in brick and cut stone to match the Assembly House, with two large doors on the ground floor. The theatre area was to have entrances wholly unconnected with the house. Admittance to the boxes would be gained through the vestibule and hallway of the Assembly House, thence up the 'Great Stairs' to a landing, and finally through a broad door into the corridor encircling the first tier of boxes. The pit and the gallery were to be approached separately by doors from the back street at the south end of the building. The stage and dressing-rooms

[1] LC, 14–28 July 1788.

[2] James Lewis, *Original Designs in Architecture* (London, 1780–97), ii. 10–11. Lewis, born in South Wales about 1751, became a founding member of The Architects' Club, London, in 1791 and attained a considerable reputation before his death in 1820.

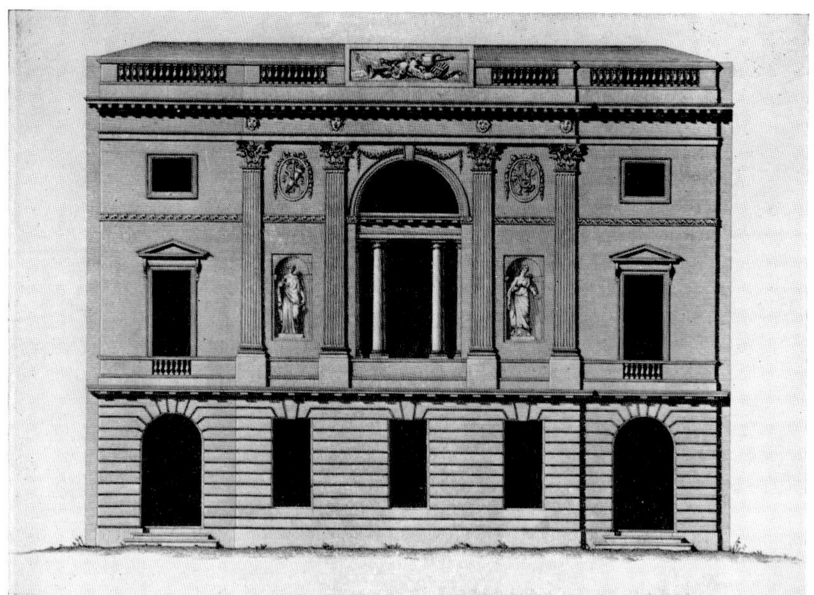

a

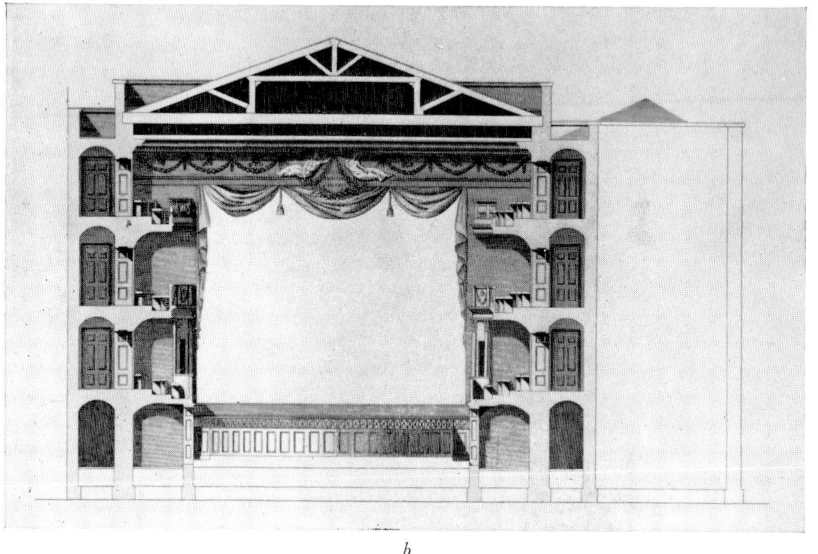

b

Designs of a Proposed Theatre for the City of Limerick
(*a*) Front Elevation (*b*) Cross-section of the Stage

would be situated at this end, but the actors' green-room, reached from backstage by a side passage, would be located in an adjacent card- or tea-room of the Assembly House.

The main stage was to be 32 feet at its greatest depth with a forestage or apron one-third as deep, in front of a proscenium 34 feet wide by 27 feet high. The auditorium, 50 feet by 50 feet, and therefore larger by a fifth than that in the Cornwallis Street playhouse, was designed unlike any other eighteenth-century public theatre in Ireland or Britain, namely, with a complete *upper* as well as lower horseshoe-shaped tier of boxes.[1] The upper tier, containing thirteen compartments, would include in the centre a larger box for Mr. Smyth with entry solely from the drawing-room of his house. The lower tier would have two fewer boxes to allow for the door on each side of the forestage under the upper box nearest the proscenium. Another unique feature of Lewis's plans in relation to the box arrangements was the apparent removal of the intrusive columns which traditionally supported the front of the tiers.

This projected Limerick theatre, though not equal in size or in impressiveness of entrance to the contemporary Theatre Royal at Cork, would have surpassed the latter in the elegance and novelty of its interior. Indeed, it would have been an edifice truly befitting the stature of Ireland's third city. A major obstacle to its construction, however, arose. The peculiar and limited 'form of the ground' donated by the Smyth family compelled the architect to design the backstage area in the shape of a right-angled triangle with the rear street as hypotenuse. The consequent space available for the requirements of production did not prove sufficient to meet professional acceptance.[2] This adverse judgement made clear the unfeasibleness of the site, and with that revelation the community interest in a new playhouse apparently evaporated. Once again the Munster capital, despite its prosperity, showed a lack of strong desire to establish a worthy home for its dramatic entertainment.

As a dismal aftermath to the failure of the theatre venture Daly sent 'the Dregs' of his Dublin company to Limerick in the

[1] Ibid., plates 21 and 22. The dimensions have been calculated according to the scale of measurement accompanying the plates.

[2] Ibid. ii. 10–11. Richard Southern in *The Georgian Playhouse* (London, 1948), pp. 28 and 33–34, mistakenly assumes that this Limerick theatre designed by Lewis was actually erected and put into use.

summer of 1789.[1] Under the assistant manager, William Dawson, they seem to have given bad performances during the August assizes. The audiences felt insulted and reacted with severity toward what one indignant observer called 'the remnant of a motley group of ragged strollers'.[2] This same critic wrote to Dublin a satiric description of the first evening when 'a discordant scraper and a blind fiddler attempted to grind opera tunes; and a gentleman of the bar, Mr. Lysaght, called out Deputy Dawson, alias Chief of the Monarch's eunuchs, on the stage, and he was obliged to make the *amende honorable*'. Saturday night, 22 August, saw the tension on both sides of the footlights at its height. Mrs. O'Reilly, one of the leading ladies, started to play Lucy in *The Beggar's Opera*, then 'changed her mind and quitted the house'. The irate audience shouted for her husband, and at O'Reilly's appearance on the stage, 'treated him so roughly that he set out for Cork that moment'.[2]

This unhappy summer produced strong repercussions among the playgoing enthusiasts of the city and vicinity. A group of young gentlemen, following in the steps of the former Limerick Theatrical Society, undertook a series of performances for charitable purposes during the autumn and early winter of 1789–90.[3] They leased the Theatre Royal; set up a price scale of 3*s*. for the boxes, 2*s*. for the pit, 1*s*. for the gallery; and sold admission tickets as well as box places in advance. The overwhelming response to their first effort led them to raise prices by one shilling for the box area, and by sixpence for the other parts of the house. The 'crowded and brilliant' audience at the opening on Friday, 9 October, brought in such a profit that 'it effected the liberty' of two men from the city jail where they had been confined a long time for debt in spite of their numerous dependants.[4] The second bill on Tuesday, 17 November, provided an ample evening of entertainment: *Venice Preserved*, *The Poor Soldier*, a recitation, and a duet.[5] The curtain rose at seven o'clock but did not go down until midnight by reason of the encores. Though 'the actresses were a little bashful, it being their first appearance', they received hearty applause from a full house that netted over twenty guineas for the Limerick poor.

[1] Hunt MSS.: Letter of 11 July from Mr. Crouch.

[2] DEP, 29 Aug. 1789.

[3] LC, 8 Oct. 1789.

[4] Ibid., 15 Oct. 1789.

[5] Ibid., 19 Nov. 1789.

Even greater profit was secured by railing in the rear of the pit with the boxes for the acting of *Cato* and *The Brave Irishman* on Monday, 21 December, when the proceeds went to 'the Relief of Confined Debtors, who now Labour under the greatest Distress for want of the common Necessaries of Life at this inclement Season'.[1] Two weeks later the Fever Hospital benefited from a repetition of the December programme, the final one of the charitable series.[2]

While these young gentlemen players were stirring up Limerick's interest in stage entertainment, Sir Vere Hunt felt the urge again, after five years, to engage in the theatrical business, but now as a bona-fide professional enterprise. Realizing the appeal of a fresh and more elegant milieu, he turned to the brick and cut-stone Assembly House and transformed its ballroom into a 'beautiful' theatre.[3] The magnificent ballroom—60 feet long, 40 feet wide, and 35 feet high—was coved and decorated in Ionic style, and equipped with handsome glass lustres.[4] Some of the adjoining small rooms the baronet doubtless fitted up as backstage quarters.

Sir Vere procured as his manager the veteran Dublin tragedian, Lawrence Clinch, a strong-minded actor who at the moment was enjoying one of his frequent disagreements with Richard Daly and therefore was not employed at Crow Street for the current winter. Clinch assembled a troupe of experienced strolling actors to open the 'New Theatre' with *As You Like It*, on Saturday, 30 January 1790.[5] Immediate success induced the aristocratic entrepreneur to expand his activities by taking over from Daly the proprietorship of the Waterford Theatre Royal. Thither he sent his players under Manager Clinch sometime in early summer for a stay that lasted till late July.[6]

When Sir Vere's company returned from Waterford to begin a summer season of five weeks at the Limerick Assembly House on Saturday, 31 July,[6] it had to compete against the Crow Street

[1] Ibid., 17 Dec. 1789.

[2] Ibid., 24 Dec. 1789.

[3] Charles T. Bowden, *A Tour through Ireland* (Dublin, 1791), p. 174; Lenihan, p. 359 n.

[4] Maxwell, p. 244.

[5] Lenihan, p. 359 n., places the opening on 31 Jan., a Sunday. No public theatrical performances occurred on Sunday in Ireland.

[6] Hunt MSS.: Account Books, 1790–1.

troupe under Daly till their departure on 13 August.[1] The Dublin players chose to appear just at this time so that they might share in the lucrative business provided by Assize Week, 2–7 August. At their Cornwallis Street theatre they performed for the most part comic operas with a strong quartet of vocalists in Bowden, J. Kelly, Mrs. Mountain, and Miss George. Thus, during this brief midsummer period, the Limerick playgoers could enjoy two competent companies with quite differing repertoires—a situation unparalleled in the city's stage history before 1800.

Many interesting details of Sir Vere Hunt's theatrical enterprise during the summer and the following winter season at Limerick can be gleaned from the surviving accounts of his treasurer, John Booker. Receipts ran large from the opening Saturday night, 31 July, through the ensuing Assize Week when daily performances were given. Income for these seven evenings totalled £130. 7*s*., with a maximum of £37. 19*s*. on Monday, 2 August, and a minimum of £4. 6*s*. on the next Saturday. During this period the door-keepers unwittingly accepted 13*s*. 6*d*. of 'bad silver', for which, according to custom, they had to be reimbursed by the proprietor.

In addition to the manager, a dozen men and a half-dozen women composed the regular acting personnel. Manager Clinch, of course, got the biggest compensation, £3. 13*s*. 6*d*. a week. The leading men—Richard Hurst, Ezra Wells, and J. Brown who had just come from Crow Street—received £2. 2*s*. for a normal week of three nights, but additional and variable amounts for extra performances; the ordinary actors—Adamson, Clare, Kelly, McCulloch, McCrea, Power—£1. 1*s*. to £1. 11*s*. 6*d*. per week; and the novices—Beaumont, Dempsey, Gotley—10*s*. 6*d*. weekly. The women's salaries were appreciably lower. The top figure of £1. 11*s*. 6*d*. was paid to Mrs. Achmet, a well-known Dublin actress recently back from Covent Garden. Young Harriet Westropp Atkins of Cork, *ingénue* and comedienne, played for £1. 1*s*. per week; the undistinguished Mrs. McCulloch and Mrs. Power, 10*s*. 6*d*. The irregular services of Mesdames Brown, Hurst, Kelly, and Wells appear to have been remunerated by extra payments to their respective husbands. The benefit nights added a good deal to the stated

[1] *Limerick Herald*, 12 Aug. 1790.

salaries, but the returns on these occasions always proved unpredictable. For instance, Miss Atkins at her August benefit took in £9. 4*s.*, while Wells with a comparable position in the company drew only £5. 11*s.* Miss Atkins's next benefit, in January 1791, yielded £19. 8*s.*, over twice the amount of her previous intake.

Sir Vere Hunt's backstage and house staff numbered between twenty and twenty-five. The scene designer, Samuel (?) Whitmore, an artist of repute, rated with the chief actors in salary at £2. 2*s.* per week. Byrne the assistant scene painter, Hoole the head carpenter, and the two regular musicians had a nightly wage of 10*s.* 6*d.* usually. Barney Murphy the head stage boy, Moore the tailor, and Ben Jones the hairdresser averaged 3*s.* a night. Bill posters, charwomen, doorkeepers, playhouse guards, stage boys, and other helpers got 1*s.* for each performance. The total wages of the New Theatre, Limerick, for the last week of its summer season, a typical week, amounted to approximately £36.

Sir Vere Hunt kept productional expenses at a minimum. Copy-books of individual parts in plays (for example, *King Lear* and *She Stoops to Conquer*) were procured at a charge of only 6*d.* Purchases of such petty materials as chains, cord, glass, ink, nails, painter's size, paper, pens, tar, and wine occurred often. A few unusual items were bought: green baize for the pit seats, 4*s.* 3*d.*; 'two Chamber Pots for the Dress Rooms', 2*s.*; an inkstand, 6*d.*; a pitcher and basin, 2*s.*; a prompter's whistle, 6*d.*; a dozen tin candlesticks, 2*s.* 3*d.* Hurst, wardrobe and property keeper as well as actor, made occasional outlays: 'stage properties', £2. 10*s.* on one date and £1. 1*s.* on another; 'dresses', £1. 1*s.* once, and, later, £1. 11*s.* A costume for Touchstone, done by Moore the tailor, cost 7*s.* The stage carpenter received 3*s.* for 'turning work' on Juliet's bier. Certainly these were very modest sums for outfitting.

Similar economy characterized the illumination of the theatre and the stage. During the summer season it must have been done entirely by oil lamps, because the sole lighting charge was for oil at 9*s.* a performance. The expense of oil lighting in the winter increased by 2*s.* Since the accounts mention 'toe for the lamps', that is, cord-like cloth or fibre for lamp wicks, it is apparent that Sir Vere Hunt had not installed the London 'patent' lamps, an improved type with cylindrical wick, which Daly had introduced to Ireland at the Crow Street Theatre in 1788. Wax tapers lighted the playhouse interior on rare occasions in the winter season. According to one entry, it cost 38*s.* 4*d.* to buy 'Candles for 4 nights'.

Pantomimes like *The Death of Captain Cook*, given several times in January 1791, required, according to one of the playbills,[1] 'a beautiful display of Scenes: the Wigwam of the Chiefs of O-Why-ee, a Kaiva or Festival, Grand Savage Dances, a Marriage Altar backed by a Dark Wood, a Nuptial Procession, the Arrival of Captain Cook, Nautical Manœuvres, the Assassination of Captain Cook, a Grand Tomb Scene, a Procession of Naval and Military Honours'. The hire of soldiers from the local barracks to act in the landing and processional scenes amounted to somewhat more than £1 per night. Four extra 'Black Men', impersonating South Sea islanders, had to be paid 3*s.* for each performance; 2*s.* an evening were spent on 'fagotts and toys' used by the 'natives'. Yet even these additional expenditures for a pantomime indicate simple and thrifty staging.

Sir Vere Hunt brought his summer season to an end on 4 September. Then, still of a mind to extend his theatrical reputation, he led his company to neighbouring Ennis for four weeks. Thereafter the troupe may have gone further afield or they may have taken a vacation; at any rate they did not start acting again in Limerick until Monday, 8 November.[2] The personnel remained much the same except for the absence of Clinch, who at the time of the Ennis tour had left for Dublin to join Daly's Crow Street organization once more. Performances until mid-December maintained the normal schedule of Monday, Wednesday, Friday, and business continued good. For the seven nights from Friday, 26 November, to Friday, 10 December, inclusive, the receipts amounted to £107. 14*s.*, compared with £130. 14*s.* for the first seven nights of the summer season. With the onset of more inclement weather, playing became more intermittent at the same time that attendance declined. From 10 December to the end of January the company acted only eleven nights and took in at the door £87. 7*s.* On Monday,

[1] Damaged playbill with date missing, City Library, Limerick.

[2] Hunt MSS.: Account Books, 1790–1.

7 February 1791, with the benefits completed, the thirteen weeks of winter performances at the Assembly House came to a close.

Sir Vere Hunt then prepared for another short season that would include the spring Assize Week, and to that end installed as manager, at a salary of £4. 4*s*. per week, the veteran William Moss of Dublin.[1] Back in 1784, Moss had vainly aspired to be a Limerick manager but had never appeared on the local stage until his arrival in December 1790, after a long sojourn in Edinburgh. The new manager persuaded Mrs. Castelli and Mr. Brennan, well-known singing strollers, to join the company, and thus he strengthened its musical repertoire. The new season at the Assembly House theatre commenced on 23 February 1791 and continued until 18 March. During these four weeks Moss raised the curtain on nine nights for total receipts of about £72, the same average per night as in midwinter.

After a month of inactivity following the cessation of the Limerick performances Sir Vere sent the company under Moss to play at Cork. In June a disagreement with Moss caused the Limerick baronet to withdraw from any further theatrical responsibilities.[1] *Faulkner's Dublin Journal* on 9 August reported that Sir Vere's playhouses at Limerick and Waterford were untenanted and his 'troops' were ranging the country. 'Having renounced the office of Field Marshal Manager, he has retired within the purlieus of the [Newtown-Pery] club house.'[2]

With Sir Vere's retirement Richard Daly once again exercised sole control of Limerick's professional stage entertainment. His Dublin players, however, no longer liked the venerable Theatre Royal on Cornwallis Street, and called it 'too small'[3] when in September 1791 they arrived with two guest stars from London, Charles Incledon and Mrs. James Billington, who were making their first Limerick appearance. The disgusted Mrs. Billington, who had been hailed 'divine, all-captivating, angelic', now 'mistook the respect due to an audience'.[4] Incensed by her disdain, the public returned the compliment by 'mistaking the night of her benefit'; they carefully refrained from buying any

[1] Ibid., Account Books, 1790–1; Journal, 1781–1807.

[2] FDJ, 9 Aug. 1791. The Newtown-Pery Club House was opened in Oct. 1788, with Sir Vere Hunt as president and John Prendergast Smith, another theatrical patron, as vice-president. *Limerick Herald*, 29 Sept. 1788.

[3] *The Diary*, 21 Sept. 1791.

[4] WH, 15 Sept. 1791.

box seats for that day. The celebrated actress in the face of this débâcle hurried from town without any reward.

The harsh reception accorded Mrs. Billington failed to deter one of her rivals, Madame Mara of Drury Lane, from performing at the Limerick Theatre Royal during the next summer. She appeared along with Daly's Crow Street troupe for Assize Week, 20–25 August 1792. This year the playhouse rather than the players aroused public condemnation: 'So large and so improving a City as this should be disgraced by such a Theatre. The Manager ought to pay some attention to the proper accommodation of the Inhabitants. The House is not only considerably out of repair, but many of the Seats in the Boxes are dirty beyond description.'[1] The same critic blamed the manager also for the 'disorderly and insolent behaviour in the gallery' where the spectators 'resemble Savages'. If the manager had shown the proper initiative and called on the 'magistrates', they would surely have assisted in preserving decent manners throughout the house.

Daly may not have heeded the urging of this angry patron to sweep out and repair his building, but at least he appeased the complaints of others by putting the theatre's subscription list in order for 1793.[2] Since the list had been 'mislaid' at the start of the previous season, 'some confusion' had attended the admission of season-ticket holders. No longer, however, would ladies and gentlemen be inconvenienced at the door, for the doorkeepers had in hand a new and correct list, so the proprietor announced before the first night. The Crow Street company came direct from Dublin in mid-July to present Limerick's playgoers with their first sight of two gifted actresses, Mrs. Frances Abington and Miss W. Brett. They paired off admirably as Lady Teazle and Maria in *The School for Scandal* for Mrs. Abington's benefit on Thursday, 25 July, when the curtain did not rise until 7.30 p.m., a half-hour later than usual because of the high society attending.[3] Miss Brett in connexion with her benefit on Monday the 29th adopted the unusual procedure of being present at the theatre on that Monday from ten until three o'clock to sell in person tickets as well as box places.[4] Her novelty on the evening's programme consisted in assuming for

[1] LC, 27 Aug. 1792.
[2] Ibid., 13 July 1793.
[3] Ibid., 24 July 1793.
[4] Ibid., 27 July 1793.

PLATE VI

(*a*) Isaac Sparks as the Right Comical Lord Chief Joker

(*b*) Elizabeth Farren

the first time the male role of Young Hob in the ever-popular ballad opera of *Hob in the Well.*

Another glamorous actress new to Limerick, Miss Elizabeth Farren from Drury Lane, furnished the main excitement of the 1794 season, which opened with Assize Week, 8–13 September.[1] Miss Farren 'was most rapturously received by a very elegant audience; for, besides numerous people of fashion residing near Limerick, the assizes brought together an immense number of people'.[2] Packed houses greeted her on all five nights of her week's engagement. To Proprietor Daly she proved a lucrative investment despite his publicity about the 'very great expense' connected with her visit.[3] Over the years the Theatre Royal had grown notorious because it contained no decent place of reception backstage. The prospect of Miss Farren's vexation at the absence of so important a facility moved Daly at last to remedy the situation. He built for her a fine dressing-room that in the future was to be used for the green-room.[4] In addition, he paid her the highest fee ever given to an actress in eighteenth-century Limerick, namely, £50 per night.[5] These outlays in conjunction with 'the smallness of the theatre' provided Daly with his excuse for raising the cost of seats to the current Dublin figures: 5*s.* for the boxes, 3*s.* for the pit, and 2*s.* for the gallery.[5] At these new prices a full house totalled about £130.[6] Therefore, with the theatre filled throughout Assize Week, the proprietor earned a large profit.

Miss Farren elected to entertain Limerick with the comic parts in which she excelled: Beatrice in *Much Ado About Nothing*, Estifania in *Rule A Wife*, Lady Bell in Arthur Murphy's *Know Your Own Mind*, and Violante in Mrs. Centlivre's *The Wonder: A Woman Keeps A Secret.* To play Lissardo opposite Miss Farren's Violante, Daly chose at short notice the youthful comedian Charles Mathews, who had made a promising début at Crow Street in June. This assignment led to a situation that developed as much comic melodrama as any scene in the troupe's repertory.[7]

Mathews, desirous of perfecting his role of Lissardo, decided to rehearse during the afternoon in the open air. He crossed the

[1] Ibid., 3 Sept. 1794.
[2] Mathews, i. 110.
[3] LC, 3 Sept. 1794.
[4] Mathews, i. 110.
[5] LC, 3 Sept. 1794.
[6] Mathews, i. 110.
[7] Ibid., i. 112–16.

bridge over the Shannon and was strolling along the river bank when he met a fellow actor, Seymour, also rehearsing. After reading lines to each other for a while, they parted. Soon Mathews, on account of the sultry weather, proceeded to strip for bathing, but 'never had a notion of swimming'. Suddenly he got in over his head and started to sink in panic. Like a man in a dream, he fell for a brief moment into conjecturing who could act Lissardo with Miss Farren that night if he were drowned. Then he rose, saw Seymour reading a little way off in the meadow, cried out feebly, and sank twice. Seymour providentially heard him, rushed up, and jumped into the river without undressing. Mathews, dragged to shore after a struggle, was hurriedly carried in the nude by Seymour and two by-standing soldiers to a public house, put on a table, and rubbed 'in all directions' with whisky. Curious onlookers gathered for joking comment on the reviving corpse:

'Sure, he went a swimming, and had never learnt?'

'He had one lesson only, I heard, and that was to teach him how to sink.'

'By my soul, then he was an apt scholar. What name's upon him?'

'Sure, I heard the Englisher red-coat say he was one of Daly's *divarters*.'

The whisky massage restored the nearly drowned Mathews with such surprising speed that by evening he went on stage and carried off his part to the complete satisfaction of both Miss Farren and the audience.

Another memorable episode enlivened Limerick's summer two years later. The Crow Street company came to the city direct from Dublin in order to take advantage of Assize Week. They opened on Monday, 18 July 1796, in the comic operas of *Robin Hood* and *The Farmer*, with the two principals, Joseph Munden and Miss Poole, making their first Limerick appearance.[1] Since Daly's players were staying for only ten days, he rashly promised that he would send at least a portion of his troupe up from Cork to perform during the Limerick races, 18–20 August.[2] When the time came, however, he dispatched five of his instrumentalists and singers to give evening concerts in the Cornwallis Street theatre with but pit and box seats available.[3] The substitution

[1] LC, 11 July 1796. [2] Parke, i. 230. [3] LC, 17 Aug. 1796.

of chamber music for plays irritated fashionable society at the same time that the closing off of the gallery vexed the general populace. In retaliation citizens and visitors alike boycotted the concert series. Four persons attended the *première*: one unidentified man in the pit, and Lord Barrymore with two guests, all three of whom entered a box late in the programme.[1] This fiasco concluded both the concerts and Daly's reign as proprietor of the Limerick Theatre Royal.

The Rebellion of 1798 caused the Crow Street organization to delay its annual visit to Munster's capital until the first of October, when the violence and tension had almost subsided in the south-west of Ireland. Then the Crow Street deputy manager, Thomas Bellamy, took on tour one of the strongest troupes that had ever set forth from Dublin. Its leading figure was not, as in recent summer tours, an actress, a comedian, or a singer, but a tragedian of repute, George Frederick Cooke from Covent Garden. He made his Limerick début in the role of Shylock on the season's opening night, Monday, 1 October.[2] A week later Manager Bellamy staged his own benefit with a calculated outburst of loyalty to the English Ascendancy.[3] For the evening's climax 'a Grand Emblematic Transparency', representing the Viceroy Marquess Cornwallis supported by Justice and Mercy, was gradually disclosed amid the singing of 'See the Conquering Hero', 'Rule, Britannia!', and 'God Save the King'. This display of allegiance typified the political bias that had dominated the entrepreneurs of the Irish theatre throughout the preceding two critical decades.

The final summer of the century found the Crow Street troupe at Limerick in time for the assizes, 22–26 July, with an even finer aggregation of talent, including Thomas Huddart of Covent Garden on his first Irish tour, young Miss Gough in her local début, Cooke, Fullam, and the popular comedian James B. Stewart.[4] For the troupe's last performance Huddart and Stewart employed the arrangement, rare among 'name' players, of 'blending their Nights', that is, combining their benefits.[5] Huddart proceeded to shine as Othello, and Stewart as a singer

[1] Parke, i. 231.

[2] William Dunlap, *The Life of George Frederick Cooke* (2nd ed., London, 1815), i. 125–7.

[3] LC, 6 Oct. 1798. [4] Ibid., 27 July 1799. [5] Ibid., 31 July 1799.

of comic lyrics, notably one entitled 'In Poaching All Mankind Delight'.

The truly superior groups of actors that now were yearly visiting Ireland's third city deserved there an attractive and commodious playhouse. Frederick Edward Jones, who in 1797 had taken over the Limerick as well as the Dublin and Cork Theatre Royal patents from Richard Daly, pronounced the thirty-year-old structure in Cornwallis Street to be in 'such a decayed and ruinous condition that it would be much more advantageous to build a new Theatre than repair the old'.[1] Therefore, to stir up agitation for an appropriate modern building, he advertised at intervals during the winter of 1799–1800 for 'Ground in a central situation . . . 50 feet in Front, by at least 130 feet in Depth', whereon to erect a new theatre.[2]

These advertisements, however, elicited neither offers of land nor any other material support. For the third time in the last quarter-century the undertaking to provide Limerick with a more suitable playhouse had been called to public attention; for the third time no effective response was forthcoming. Without any good excuse Limerick went forward into the era of the Union dependent upon a notoriously outdated theatre.

[1] FJ, 31 Dec. 1799.
[2] Ibid., 2 and 9 Jan. 1800.

V · CORK

THE eminence of Cork in the life of Ireland was recognized well before the middle of the eighteenth century by the title 'Capital of the South'. Situated a dozen miles up the River Lee estuary on an island intersected with canals like a Dutch city, this Irish metropolis exhibited more bustle than beauty. Its population, as well as its export trade in beef, butter, hides, and tallow, kept expanding rapidly.[1] In 1732 Cork contained less than 50,000 persons,[2] but in 1750 the number had risen to about 65,000,[3] considerably more than half the size of Dublin. Most of Cork's streets, however, remained very narrow, dirty, and badly lit.[4] Therefore coaches proved impracticable, while sedan chairs abounded. A chair to any point within the limits of the island cost 4*d.*; to a point outside, 6*d.*[5] The 'tolerably broad' Main Street, a half-mile in length, extended north and south across the island, and terminated at stone bridges over both channels of the river. Midway along this thoroughfare and jutting out into it stood the city's most prominent edifice, the Tholsel, or Exchange, built in 1709 of hewn stone with an arcaded front.[6] A quarter-mile to the west of the Exchange lay the district known as Hammond's Marsh, where both ladies and gentlemen enjoyed the 'very handsome large Bowling-Green, planted on its Margins with Trees, kept regularly cut, whose shade made it a pleasant walk'.[7] Here in fair weather a professional band played.[8] Adjacent to the Green was the Assembly House with a fine organ in the ballroom.[9] Weekly concerts were held at the House in addition to the dances and drums. One block due east of the Exchange, the Mall (now the Grand Parade) commenced, ran

[1] Willes, p. 43; *A Tour through Ireland in Several Entertaining Letters*, p. 93.

[2] 7,967 families, according to M. F. Cusack, *A History of the City and County of Cork* (Dublin and Cork, 1875), p. 394.

[3] 7,366 houses, according to Charles Smith, *The Ancient and Present State of the County and City of Cork* (2nd ed., Dublin, 1774), i. 395.

[4] Willes, pp. 40–41.

[5] *A Tour through Ireland*, p. 61.

[6] Ibid., p. 87.

[7] Smith, i. 395.

[8] *A Tour through Ireland*, p. 89.

[9] Smith, i. 399.

south beside a canal to the river, then turned eastwards along the Lee, bordering the district called Dunscomb's Marsh.[1] The Mall, though poorly surfaced with hard pebblestone paving, attracted the city's *beau monde* to promenade under its long row of elm trees.[2] During the summer assizes 'considerable numbers from the country' joined in the fashionable parading.[3]

Half-way down the Mall, George's (now Oliver Plunkett) Street led straight eastwards through Dunscomb's Marsh. On the south side of George's Street, less than a hundred yards off the Mall, Cork's second playhouse was erected.[4] The first theatre had been constructed from a malthouse in the old heart of the city.[5] Early in 1713 the directors of the Smock Alley Theatre, Dublin—Messrs. Joseph Ashbury, Thomas Elrington, John Evans, and Thomas Griffith—had leased property at Cork, and within a few months had converted 'a large room', 105 feet long by 21 feet wide, 'built over a yard just off the Great [i.e. Main] Street',[6] into a playhouse, the first in Ireland outside Dublin. There the Smock Alley company performed during the summer of 1713 and perhaps in occasional ensuing summers. Two decades elapsed, however, before any further theatricals were recorded at Cork. In mid-July of 1733 the Smock Alley players were again acting there with two Irishmen from the London stage, Lacy Ryan and Dennis Delane, as guest performers.[7] Two years afterwards the troupe of the Theatre Royal in Aungier Street, Dublin, accompanied by two London visitors, Delane and Henry Giffard, supplanted their Smock Alley rivals as summer entertainers on the southern circuit.[8]

In the summer of 1736 the Aungier Street company returned to the Capital of the South to open the new 'Theatre Royal on Dunscomb's Marsh'.[9] As far back as the winter of 1732–3 consultations had been held in Cork 'on the design of building a playhouse', and advice had been sought from Sir Edward Lovet Pearce, the architect of the Aungier Street Theatre, which was

[1] J. Rocque, 'A Survey of the City and Suburbs of Cork' (1759).

[2] *A Tour through Ireland*, p. 56; Smith, i. 399.

[3] Smith, i. 399.

[4] See Rocque's 1759 survey.

[5] See Clark, pp. 138–9.

[6] S. H. Lepper and P. Crossle, *A History of the Grand Lodge of Free and Accepted Masons of Ireland* (Dublin, 1925), i. 135.

[7] FDJ, 30 June and 10 July 1733; Robert Hitchcock, *An Historical View of the Irish Stage* (Dublin, 1788–94), i. 83.

[8] Hitchcock, i. 93.

[9] Ibid. ii. 40, 82.

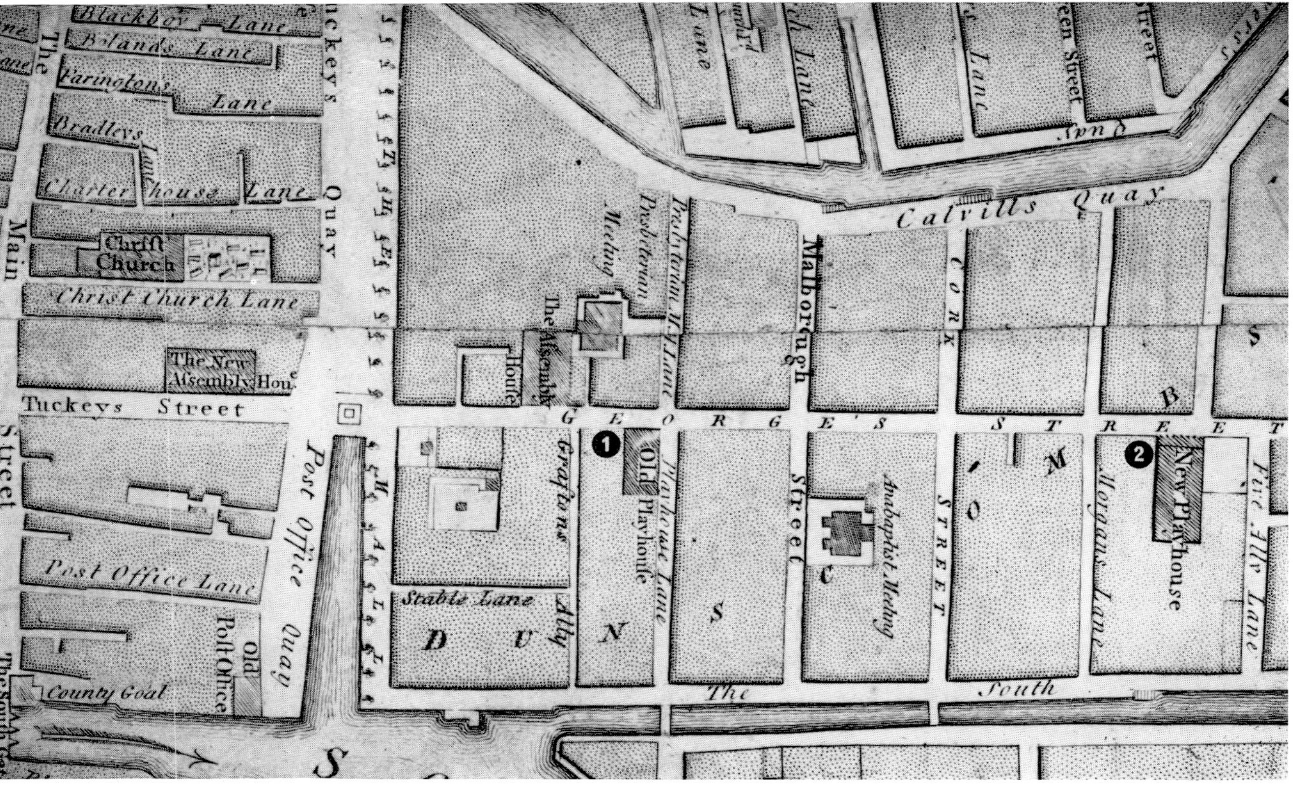

Cork in 1771
Theatre Sites: (1) Dunscomb's Marsh; (2) George's Street

then about to be constructed in Dublin. Pearce, in February 1732/3, recommended the plans he had drawn up for Dublin, but he also offered to make other proposals: 'If you really are upon such a design, and send me a plan of ye ground, with the streets that lead to it, and mention the money you expect to lay out, I will as soon as possible return you a plan fitted for y^r purpose, with our scheme at large, by which we raise the money and secure ourselves.'[1] No more is known of the planning that went on at Cork during the next three years. Presumably subscriptions from local citizens helped to underwrite the enterprise as in the Aungier Street project. A major portion of the needed funds, however, must have come from the estate of Thomas Elrington, who had died at Dublin in 1732, because it was his estate which held title to the new Cork playhouse.[2]

The design of Ireland's first actual theatre outside Dublin may well have been supplied by Sir Edward Pearce and have been based upon his Aungier Street plan. The Theatre Royal on Dunscomb's Marsh closely approached the size of its possible Dublin model; it measured approximately 88 feet in length by 44 feet in breadth, as compared to the Aungier Street dimensions of 94 feet by 46 feet.[3] The front with the box entrance faced north on George's Street. The gallery door was almost surely located on the theatre's east side around the corner in the alley-like thoroughfare which presently received the name of Playhouse Lane (now Prince's Street). The new Cork building possessed only one gallery[4] and did not follow the Aungier Street design of a lower and an upper gallery. The Dublin playhouse also contained a second or upper row of side-boxes, termed 'lattices', but no surviving advertisements mention box accommodations of this kind at the Theatre Royal on Dunscomb's Marsh. The Cork structure apparently could seat about 150 persons in the boxes, 100 in the pit, and 100 in the gallery.[5] Its rear yard exhibited a unique feature: eight six-pound cannon 'with a centinel for their guard and their mouths turned to the

[1] Linehan, p. 331.

[2] See note 7, p. 72.

[3] The dimensions of the Cork theatre have been calculated according to the scale of measurement accompanying Rocque's survey of 1759. The figures for the Aungier Street playhouse were reported in FDJ, 4 Feb. 1758.

[4] CEP and CJ, 1756–60, advertised only a single gallery.

[5] Hunt MSS.: Account Books, 1790–1.

South', that is, towards the river whence an enemy attack might be directed.[1]

Though the Cork military authorities never took over the interior of the Dunscomb's Marsh playhouse, the musicians often used it during the long off-seasons in order to conduct 'an Academy of Music weekly'.[1] Primarily, however, it served as the principal site of the city's dramatic entertainment for a quarter of a century. The greater portion of this period passed with only a few scattered notices of stage activities. In the summer of 1737 the mayor and sheriffs 'directed a Charity play to be acted for the Benefit and Relief of poor insolvent Debtors'.[2] Another kind of special performance, held at irregular intervals over the years, was a play given in honour of the Masons. On Thursday, 27 April 1738, 'the Free Masons . . . went in solemn manner from Mr. Keeling's house to the Theatre, where was acted by the desire of that Right Worshipful Society, *Harry the 8th*'.[3] This must have been the production of either local amateurs or a strolling troupe, because the two Dublin companies were both acting in the capital at that moment. In April of the next year a Dublin newspaper reported that the Aungier Street players were going to Cork for the spring assizes.[4] This company also acted there in 1741, probably about September, with a guest star from London, James Quin,[5] who as a novice with the Smock Alley organization had taken part in Cork's first professional theatricals twenty-eight years before.[6]

During the same summer the ownership of the Theatre Royal on Dunscomb's Marsh and of its sister theatre at Waterford changed hands. 'The cloaths, scenes, machines, decorations, &c., belonging thereto, as well as the estate, right, and title to the said theatres, and the leases of their sites' were sold on 11 August to the proprietors of the Aungier Street Theatre by the chief trustee of Thomas Elrington's estate, his widow Frances.[7] As payment she was guaranteed an annuity of £227. 10*s*. for life. Four months after this transaction the

1 *A Tour through Ireland*, p. 90.
2 FDJ, 6 Sept. 1737.
3 *The Medley*, 28 Apr. 1738. The next recorded Masons' Night at Cork took place on 5 Sept. 1753, when the audience must have overflowed the playhouse to bring in receipts of £90. *Dublin Gazette*, 8 Sept. 1753.
4 FDJ, 31 Mar. 1739.
5 Hitchcock, i. 114.
6 See Clark, p. 141.
7 Indenture of 11 Aug. 1741 between Frances Elrington and William Lord Mountjoy, Office of the Registry of Deeds, Dublin, old vol. 106, p. 420.

Aungier Street proprietors advertised the Cork and Waterford properties for sale,[1] and continued for some time to publicize the offer without finding a buyer. Again in 1748 they advertised the same properties for rent over a term of years.[2] Thomas Sheridan, the monopoly-minded Dublin manager, who took leases on the Aungier Street and Smock Alley playhouses from 19 March 1747/8, eventually leased the Cork facilities.

Meanwhile an independent group of players, calling themselves 'the Cork Company of Comedians', had opened a playhouse, smaller than the Theatre Royal, on Broad Lane, one of the chief connexions between Main Street and Hammond's Marsh.[3] This venture did not flourish long, because, as Cork's first historian wryly observed in 1750, 'one playhouse seems to be more than sufficient for this city'. By that date the Broad Lane building 'was not now made use of'.[4] It may have become the Broad Lane Chapel, an edifice about 60 feet long by 30 feet wide, located on the south side of Broad Lane between Cross Street and Hammond's Quay (now Grattan Street).[5]

Another 'company of comedians', headed by a well-known Dublin player, Michael Dyer, occupied the Theatre Royal for some time between the fall of 1741 and the summer of 1742. One of their offerings was locally printed: 'A Ballad Opera. A Wonder, or an Honest Yorkshireman, as it was acted in Cork at the Theatre Royal, Dunscomb's Marsh, by Mr. Dyer's Company of Comedians. Cork: 1741. Printed by George Harrison.' Dyer attracted notice for 'his prodigious flow of spirits and striking figure', but he demonstrated much similarity in his playing of various roles. The 'dancing and airy notes' of his voice and the 'pertness' of his manner fitted him only for lively comic characters such as Tattle the beau in Congreve's *Love for Love*.[6] On 15 May 1742 the *Dublin Mercury* published a startling Cork dispatch that 'Mr. Dyer, Master of the Company of Comedians at Cork', had been 'barbarously murdered'. This report, like the one of Robert Wilks's murder at Kilkenny a half-century earlier, turned out to be utter fiction.

[1] FDJ, 26 Dec. 1741.

[2] Ibid., 8 Mar. 1747/8.

[3] *A Tour through Ireland*, p. 89 n.

[4] Smith, i. 401.

[5] See Rocque's 1759 survey.

[6] *Theatrical Biography; or Memoirs of the Principal Performers of the Three Theatre Royals* (London, 1772), ii. 61–65; *The Theatrical Review: For the Year 1757 and the Beginning of 1758* (London, 1758), pp. 33–34.

An actual fatality did occur to an attendant of the Theatre Royal in the spring of 1749.[1] The future noted playwright Arthur Murphy, at that time eighteen years of age, was working in his uncle's counting-house on Cork (now Cook) Street and used to frequent the theatre only a block distant. One day his fellow apprentices became aggrieved at the theatre management over some supposed mistreatment, asked for an apology, and found none forthcoming. Murphy, quick to champion their cause, leaped upon the stage along with several other youths, all flourishing their swords. In the subsequent fracas a playhouse fruit-woman, Grace Lane, was hurt so seriously that she died within a few days. Her death occasioned an elegiac distich that lived on for years as neighbourhood folk jingle:

> Grace Lane, who graced our Play House Lane,
> By Graceless Murphy's band is slain.

'Graceless' Murphy, fearing prosecution for his part in the fatal affair, skipped to London. This Cork episode, hitherto unpublished, explains Murphy's sudden departure from the city in April 1749 to seek a career in English letters.

During the 1750's the full complement of the Smock Alley company under the management of Thomas Sheridan or his deputy, Benjamin Victor, performed every year at the Theatre Royal on Dunscomb's Marsh for at least two summer months and sometimes longer. The dates of the Cork sojourn varied according to the timing of the summer assizes at Cork and Limerick, because the company almost always visited Limerick for the Assize Week at least. The Cork season usually began in July and lasted until late September or early October, with a closed house, of course, during the Limerick visit. Three days a week—Monday, Wednesday, Friday—constituted the normal schedule of acting. Performances customarily began at seven o'clock, but the playhouse doors in general opened at five. A competing dance or party would often bring about an earlier rise of the curtain if the management decided to go on with the play. In 1756 Mr. Mynitt set his benefit for Monday, 13 September, and subsequently discovered an 'assembly' on that night.

[1] Thomas C. Croker, 'Recollections of Cork', Trinity College, Dublin, MS. 1206, ch. 9, pp. 14–16.

Then he put out a notice that 'the company are determined to be *Ready* to begin the *Play* at half an Hour after Six, on account of the Assembly'.[1]

The standard admission prices at the Theatre Royal on Dunscomb's Marsh did not follow the current Dublin scale, but were reduced in accordance with the Irish economy outside the capital. Boxes and pit cost 2*s*. 6*d*.; the gallery, 1*s*. 6*d*.[2] If a player thought he could nearly fill the theatre on his benefit night, he might 'lay his house at one price'. Beginning with Tom King on 16 August 1758, a number of the Smock Alley actors and actresses adopted this practice, and advertised all seats for their Cork benefits in 1758 or 1759 at the uniform figure of half a crown.[3] Benefits called for the advance sale of specially printed tickets, numbered, dated, and marked with the title of the main piece of entertainment. A change of day or bill therefore produced considerable annoyance. In 1756 Myrton Hamilton had announced *The Merchant of Venice* for his benefit on a certain September night and had distributed the usual printed tickets, marked 'The Merchant of Venice'. When the night arrived, however, 'by general advice the Play was dismiss'd'. A new night, 24 September, was set and *The Beggar's Opera* substituted as the main piece. Rightly concerned over this dislocation of time and programme, Hamilton approached his supporters with apology and reassurance curiously mixed: 'Mr. Hamilton humbly hopes that the dismission of *The Merchant of Venice* will not abate the interest of his friends. . . . Tickets for *The Merchant of Venice* will be taken on the above night [i.e. the 24th]. N.B. The Play will begin at the usual time, though there should not be ten persons in the Pit.'[4]

Charity plays often commanded raised prices but not always. On Tuesday, 26 September 1758, a very superior bill was presented on behalf of 'between fifty and sixty foundlings taken up in the Parish of Shandon, who must inevitably perish, if not relieved by the Charity of the Publick'. John Dexter and Mrs. Lawrence Kennedy, two of the chief Smock Alley performers in that season, acted Lord and Lady Townly in *The Provok'd Husband*. Tom King and Isaac Sparks, two other leading

[1] CJ, 9 Sept. 1756.
[2] Ibid., 1 Aug. 1757.
[3] CEP, 16 Aug., 4 and 7 Sept., 2 Oct. 1758; CJ, 23 Aug. 1759.
[4] CJ, 23 Sept. 1756.

actors, impersonated Dick the Apprentice and the Irish Actor, respectively, in the farce of *The Apprentice*. The sponsors of this charitable event had been urged to advance the prices of all sections of the playhouse to a uniform five shillings, but they were 'rather induced from the great confidence they have in the benevolence of the Ladies and Gentlemen of Cork to submit to their own Breasts what they will give above the usual Price'.[1] Yet the sponsors had the fortitude to refuse to establish for children a cut rate such as Irish theatre managements often permitted at regular performances: 'To prevent persons being disappointed by thinking that Children may be admitted gratis, or for a trifle, it is here published, that no Child whatever will be admitted under full Price, and as no Exception will be made to this Rule, it is hoped no Person will be offended.'[1]

Though the premier *comédienne* of the age, Peg Woffington, was acting at Smock Alley from 1751 to 1754, she did not see fit to go on the company's summer tours. Therefore the most colourful of its performers at Cork during the fifties was the Dublin-born low comedian, Isaac Sparks, a commanding figure with double chin, mischievous leer, and ingratiating brogue. Fond of clowning in public places as well as on stage, he repaired on off-nights to the Cork Arms Tavern on Castle Street near the Exchange and the County Court House. The proprietor, Richard Byrne, advertised the Tavern as 'a noted and well-established House, very convenient and pleasantly situated' and possessed of 'a curious sortment of enamel'd, stem and plain Drinking-glasses'.[2] At the Cork Arms during the theatrical season of 1753[3] and subsequent years Sparks amused the town by presiding as 'the Right Comical Lord Chief Joker' over a weekly mock trial. This 'Court of Nassau' took its name and procedure from the already celebrated Dublin judge-and-jury club which met Tuesday nights at a Nassau Street tavern under Sparks's presidency.[4] His buffoonery in the southern metropolis eventually achieved so much fame that a humorous summons, issued at Cork on Thursday, 7 August 1755, was reproduced by

[1] CEP, 25 Sept. 1758.

[2] CJ, 6 Sept. 1756.

[3] On 23 June 1753, at the Theatre Royal, before 'a crowded house . . . Chief Joker Sparks in the Character of Capt. O'Blunder [in *The Brave Irishman*] gave the Cork Ladies and Gentlemen such Satisfaction as they never met with before'. *Dublin Gazette*, 30 June 1753. See Sparks's portrait on p. 65.

[4] FDJ, 14 Nov. 1752.

Faulkner's Dublin Journal as an entertaining news item on the following Tuesday:

On Tuesday next, at the Corke Arms,
You are hereby required,
Your person desired,
To attend at the Court of Nassau;
If therein you fail,
You shall not give bail,
But be punished according to Law.
Signed by order, Lord Chief Joker Sparks.

Specialty dances and scenic display as well as the antics of 'Joker' Sparks provided novelty to the Cork theatrical seasons in the late 1750's. In 1757 a talented dancing-master, Mr. Harvey, appeared with the Smock Alley troupe. He offered to teach 'the Ladies and Gentlemen of Cork a Minuet, Country, and all Dances that is now taught at Paris and London, in the most polite and expeditious Manner'.[1] Interested pupils could apply 'at his Lodgings on Tuckey's Quay [i.e. the upper west side of the Mall] or at the Play-House'. The next year Signor Tioli succeeded Harvey and elaborated the *entr'actes* in the summer programmes. On 14 July, after *The Distrest Mother*, Tioli staged his 'new grand Pantomime Dance call'd the *Tartars*'.[2] On 11 August, in *Romeo and Juliet*, he introduced 'a grand Masquerade' during Act I and 'a grand Funeral Procession' at the end of Act IV.[3] A week later *May Day*, a comic ballet, exhibited Irish dances and tunes by Tioli.[4] His benefit on 21 August featured *The Merchant of Venice* with 'the Minuet and Louvre by Signor Tioli in Petticoats and Miss Baker in Man's Clothes' at the end of Act I, and, after the Shakespeare play, 'a Grand Pantomime Dance, The Inchanted Peasants'.[4] This dance required seven changes of costume and character, and presented 'Music, Scenery, Machinery, Dresses, and Decorations entirely new'. Tioli took unusual pains to preserve the beauty of the production by asking that 'no Gentleman will take it ill, that he cannot be admitted behind the Scenes, as it will be impossible to perform the Dance if it is in the least Incommoded'.

Other Shakespearian and classic plays displayed a variety of spectacle. The historical tragedy of *Douglas* opened with 'the

[1] CJ, 30 June 1757.
[2] CEP, 13 July 1758.
[3] Ibid., 7 Aug. 1758.
[4] Ibid., 14 Aug. 1758.

Curtain drawn up on the Ancient Scots ballad on which the play is based'.[1] The characters were 'dressed in the Habits of the Times', but the eccentric notions of Manager Sheridan about historicity in costuming must have resulted in some bizarre Highlanders. Increasingly spectacular performances had to be accompanied by more stringent regulations concerning stage and backstage spectators. Sheridan's version of *Coriolanus* on 11 September 1758 included in the first act 'a Grand Triumphal Procession in the shape of a Roman Ovation'.[2] 'As the Ovation, &c., will necessarily require the Scenes to be quite clear, it is humbly begg'd no Lady or Gentleman will take it amiss they can't be admitted on the Stage.' The presentation of *Macbeth* for Hurst's benefit on 27 August 1759 required him to announce that 'no Person can be admitted behind the Scenes on account of the Machinery and the Number of People employed in the Tragedy'.[3] He earnestly hoped 'no Gentlemen will take it ill that they can't be admitted on the Stage, as he has no other motive for refusing them, but his desire to render the representation as compleat as possible'. The Smock Alley company kept its stage environs at Dublin cleared of playgoers on all occasions; they did not operate so rigidly at Cork.

The unwillingness to enforce an absolute prohibition of spectators on the far side of the footlights may have resulted, at least in part, from the caustic attitude of many Cork theatregoers, an attitude calculated to put the actors constantly on the defensive. The unhappy close of the 1758 season illustrated the tensions on both sides. The company had intended to make their performance on Thursday, 5 October, their last, since 'no less than Seven of them were under a Necessity for setting out for Dublin the next morning'.[4] The remaining players, however, 'at the request of a worthy Gentleman, whom every one must be proud to oblige', undertook to put on *The Beggar's Opera* and *The Oracle* for a charity benefit that same day, Friday, 6 October, since these two pieces were the only ones that could be done on such short notice and with the few actors left. During *The Beggar's Opera* 'the great Croud on the Stage so much increased the Fatigue of a principal Performer (who had long struggled with a Nervous Complaint and still labours with it) that she

[1] CJ, 16 Aug. 1759.
[2] CEP, 7 Sept. 1758.
[3] CJ, 23 Aug. 1759.
[4] CEP, 9 Oct. 1758.

was rendered intirely incapable of finishing her Part'.[1] To make a bad situation worse, the prostrated actress was to have played the lead in *The Oracle*. The farce, however, could not be given, since the company in its depleted state had no substitute available. The actors 'were, therefore, very much against their own Inclinations, obliged to Apologize to the Audience for the Disappointment that they unavoidably met with'. In spite of the mitigating circumstances, the apology was not quietly accepted by a portion of the audience. These latter at once proceeded to 'some Insinuations, industriously spread to the Prejudice of Part of the Company of Comedians'.[1] The players then felt driven to re-explain and re-justify their action in print. This kind of agitation delighted a vocal cantankerous element in the city and foreshadowed more protracted altercations during the next decade.

In 1760 the theatrical situation at Cork underwent a very considerable alteration in keeping with the city's social and cultural advancement. Out of its 70,000 inhabitants most of the well-to-do gentlemen and many of their ladies were said to have visited France, Portugal, or Spain. As a result, Cork society had begun to display what tourists called 'a peculiar superiority' in dress, manners, and table fare.[2] The centre of local fashion had gravitated from Hammond's Marsh to the 'New City' on Dunscomb's Marsh and vicinity.[3] Here substantial brick houses with rather plain exteriors but expensively furnished 'interior apartments' were multiplying at a fast rate.[4] The Assembly House had been relocated just off the Mall on the north side of George's Street almost opposite the theatre erected in 1736. Once a fortnight 'a very Large and Brilliant Assembly of fine Girls' graced the ballroom, a hall as spacious as 'one of the Long Rooms at Bath' with 'white walls badly lighted and not unencumbered with ornament'.[5] The Mall, according to an English visitor, was still paved 'worse than the streets of London' but 'filled with very genteel company and a greater number of pretty women than I ever saw together in any other town'.[6]

To this Cork world of increasing wealth and elegance came

[1] Ibid.
[2] O'Keeffe, i. 236.
[3] Ibid. i. 237.
[4] Samuel Derrick, *Letters Written from Liverpoole, Chester, Corke, The Lake of Killarney, Tunbridge-Wells, and Bath* (Dublin, 1767), i. 34.
[5] Ibid. i. 37; Willes, p. 46.
[6] Derrick, i. 44.

the management of the Crow Street Theatre, Dublin, headed by Spranger Barry, with a proposal for a new playhouse more becoming to the second city of Ireland. In September 1759 Robert Wood, Master of the Revels, had transferred the Theatre Royal patent at Dublin from the Smock Alley Theatre to the Crow Street Theatre, and had appointed the latter's co-managers, Barry and Henry Woodward, as Deputy Masters of the Revels. This transfer of patent also gave control of the Theatre Royal at Cork to the Crow Street management in place of the Smock Alley organization. During the winter of 1759–60 Barry, securing 'in a few weeks' forty subscriptions from the Cork gentry, went ahead on the construction of the playhouse.[1] Each subscriber contributed £50; in return he received a silver transferable ticket bearing four per cent. interest and good for admission indefinitely.[2] The new building was situated three blocks east of the old Theatre Royal on the same side of George's Street between Morgan's Lane (now Morgan Street) and Five Alley Lane (now Pembroke Street).[3] Today the site is occupied by the Cork General Post Office.

The playhouse façade on George's Street possessed a ground-floor arcade or colonnade similar to that of the Crow Street Theatre.[3] Under this front portico, an ideal protection in bad weather, the sedan chairmen set down and picked up their passengers. All the chairs were numbered, and after the performance, the servants of the ladies and gentlemen who had chairs in waiting summoned them forward by calling out their numbers. At the same time the still unhired chairmen hovered around in pursuit of a fare. Eventually the traffic situation at the portico entrance necessitated more stringent regulations that proved difficult to enforce. On the eve of the theatrical season in 1787 the Mayor published orders that sedan chairmen were 'not to presume carrying their Chairs inside the Colonnade at the Play-House' and should 'not commit any disturbance whatsoever, by pressing improperly forward and fighting with each other for fares'.[4] Though very few playgoers probably ever

[1] Hitchcock, ii. 40.

[2] Memorandum enclosed in a letter of 6 Aug. 1797 from the Cork theatre manager, Richard Daly. See the case of *Daly* v. *F. E. Jones*, Official Papers, 2nd series, 1790–1831, carton no. 511, 47/17, Record Tower, Dublin Castle.

[3] J. Rocque, 'A Survey of the City and Suburbs of Cork . . . with all the new Improvements to 1771'.

[4] HC, 30 July 1787.

came by coach to George's Street, those who did drive thither could be discharged right at the east end of the portico in the theatre's early years when adjoining ground on the corner of Five Alley Lane remained uncovered.

The building completed in the early summer of 1760 measured approximately 136 feet long by 60 feet wide[1] to make it the biggest playhouse in eighteenth-century Ireland outside Dublin. Early observers described it as 'elegant', 'almost as large as Crow Street', and 'built upon the same plan' as that structure.[2] The interior, like Crow Street's, contained a second row of side-boxes, the 'lattices' or 'lettices', but had only one gallery as against two at Crow Street.[3] A full house brought in from £150 to £160 at the standard Dublin scale of prices which Manager Barry put into effect at Cork: 4*s*. for the boxes and lattices; 3*s*. for the pit; and 2*s*. for the gallery.[4] Though these figures represented considerable advances over the previous local charges, the public evidently had expected to pay more under the new régime and raised no protest.

The Theatre Royal in George's Street held its opening performance on Monday, 21 July 1760.[5] At the rise of the curtain, advertised for precisely seven o'clock, Barry delivered in honour of the occasion a dull and fulsome prologue that concluded with the customary appeal for generous support:

> Thanks to my friends—to all whose chearing ray
> Has dawn'd propitious on this first essay.
> But stop not here—still graciously go on
> To crown a work so gloriously begun!
> To infant weakness stretch a parent's hand!
> What force cou'd once, let reason now command![6]

'His Majesty's Company of Comedians' followed with Otway's tragedy of *The Orphan*, wherein Barry and Mrs. Ann Dancer played the leading roles. This was Cork's first view of the noted pair who later dazzled Drury Lane audiences. Barry at that period made a glamorous impression with his pale gold

[1] These dimensions have been calculated according to the scale of measurement accompanying Rocque's survey of 1771.

[2] Hitchcock, ii. 40, 83; Derrick, i. 36. CEP, 7 July 1760, boldly declared that 'the Elegance of this Theatre in Building, Painting, Machinery, and all other Decorations will excel those of London and Dublin'.

[3] CEP, 8 Sept. 1760.

[4] Ibid., 17 July 1760; Hitchcock, ii. 40.

[5] CEP, 17 July 1760.

[6] Ibid., 28 July 1760.

hair, bright blue eyes, mobile face, and almost six-foot height. Grace and dignity of movement gave him a kingly bearing. His sweet clear voice 'could wheedle a bird off the bush', so Arthur Murphy claimed. Yet with all these attributes he rarely communicated a natural passion; always he inclined to a studied manner of playing:

> Behold him for the solemn scene prepare.
> See how he frames his eye, poises each limb,
> Puts the whole body into proper trim—[1]

The ordinary Irish spectator, however, felt small concern for this defect in Barry's art and only saw in the handsome mellifluous fellow countryman a satisfyingly heroic figure. One Cork landlady, after watching him act Alexander the Great in Lee's *The Rival Queens* during that first season at George's Street, praised Barry as 'an Irish gentleman that beat all the actors England ever produced'.[2] Mrs. Dancer's soft femininity excelled at the pathetic; it offered an appealing contrast to the masculine force of her stage partner. An experienced theatregoer, Samuel Derrick of Bath, observed her at Cork in that same summer of 1760 and afterwards wrote down a short portrait—the first eyewitness description of a performer on the Irish stage outside Dublin: 'Her figure is well-proportioned, and very pleasing, of a middle size; her features regular and handsome: notwithstanding she is near-sighted, her eyes are piercing; and she marks the passions strongly: her voice is musical, but rather confined; her conceptions just; and she has great tenderness and feeling.'[3] Barry and Mrs. Dancer made tragedy their forte, impersonating Romeo and Juliet, Macbeth and Lady Macbeth, Othello and Desdemona, Antony and Cleopatra in Dryden's *All for Love*, Jaffeir and Belvidera in Otway's *Venice Preserved*, Horatio and Calista in Rowe's *The Fair Penitent*, and several others, during the current Cork season. For comedy the Theatre Royal troupe possessed equally qualified stars in Henry Woodward and Mrs. Frances Abington. Their lively postures and speech suited a broad range of parts from a Harlequin and a Columbine to the genteel Sir John Brute and Lady Fanciful in Vanbrugh's *The Provok'd Wife*. Indeed, this Dublin company

[1] Charles Churchill, 'The Rosciad', ll. 908–10, in *Poems* (ed. James Laver, London, 1933).
[2] Derrick, i. 27.
[3] Ibid. i. 36.

of at least twenty-four men and thirteen women who initiated the Theatre Royal in George's Street formed by far the best as well as the largest aggregation of players that had ever come to the city.

Nor had Cork ever before been presented in one season with so elevated and well balanced a repertory of drama: six Shakespearian pieces—*Hamlet*, *Henry V*, *Macbeth*, *Othello*, *Richard III*, *Romeo and Juliet;* nine current classics in tragedy—*All for Love*, *Barbarossa*, *Douglas*, *The Fair Penitent*, *Jane Shore*, *The Mourning Bride*, *The Orphan*, *The Rival Queens*, *Venice Preserved;* and six outstanding comedies of the century—*The Beggar's Opera*, *The Conscious Lovers*, *The Provok'd Husband*, *The Provok'd Wife*, *The Suspicious Husband*, *The Tender Husband*. A goodly number of farces and fewer musical plays accompanied the foregoing, but none of these lighter items was ever put forward as a primary attraction. One brand new tragedy, *The Royal Captive*, based on Aphra Behn's *Oroonoko* plot and written by 'a Gentleman of this Country', was reported on 25 September to be in rehearsal at the Theatre Royal.[1] Of this work the informant remarked that 'the Distresses are beautifully wrought up, . . . enhancing the Value of Conjugal Affection, and punishing Adultery and Injustice'. Despite the impressive moralism an actual performance seems never to have taken place.

The new Cork stage, nearly as capacious as that of Covent Garden Theatre, encouraged Barry's liking for 'grand tragic processions' and Woodward's for pantomimes.[2] They supported these spectacles, according to Samuel Derrick, with 'finely painted' scenes and an orchestra 'beyond anything we could expect'.[3] On 11 August the production of *Romeo and Juliet* showed 'an entire new Funeral Procession of Juliet to the Monument of the Capulets, accompanied with a Solemn Dirge'.[4] An original pantomime, *The Fairies*, written by Woodward and outfitted with fresh costumes, had its *première* at the author's benefit on 8 October.[5] It included some special dances arranged by Robert Aldridge, the finest Irish-born dancer of the day and a member of the Theatre Royal company.

Though Barry's initial season at Cork surely introduced the south of Ireland to a much higher level of theatrical entertainment

[1] CJ, 25 Sept. 1760. [2] Hitchcock, ii. 83. [3] Derrick, i. 36.
[4] CEP, 11 Aug. 1760. [5] CJ, 6 Oct. 1760.

than it had ever previously known or than it was often to know again, even so the season gave rise to irritations in one quarter or another. The more puritanical Protestant sects still frowned upon stage amusements. During August the famous Methodist leader, John Wesley, conducted a preaching mission in Cork and found the Theatre Royal a disturbing competitor. On Sunday the seventeenth he inserted in his *Journal* a sardonic comment about the local taste for playgoing: 'Our evening congregations this week were smaller than usual, as the gentry were engaged in a more important affair. A company of players were in town. However, many of [the gentry] came on Friday; for a watch night was newer to them than a comedy.'[1] In the second half of September, Barry, Mrs. Dancer, and Woodward succumbed to that mysterious stage ailment called 'indisposition'; by 1 October all three had recovered. Nevertheless the absences of these stars from the bills provoked uncomplimentary surmises. Barry ignored the gossip; Woodward at his benefit on 8 October poked fun at it by way of a prologue which he wrote and spoke in the character of Rumour—the entire recitation, so he announced, 'occasion'd by the many Rumours that have been spread relative to Himself'.[2] Mrs. Dancer, however, took the insinuations to heart and published a flowery rejoinder on 2 October:

> Whereas it has been maliciously reported that I have for some time past feigned Sickness, to avoid my Duty at the Theatre, I humbly beg leave to assure the Public that said Report is false and groundless. ... My real Indisposition (for the Truth of which I appeal to Doctor Frankland [a well-known Cork physician]) will, I flatter myself, remove any Impressions which have been conceived to my Disadvantage from misrepresentation, and excuse me for not waiting upon the Ladies who were so kind as to take Places for my Benefit [originally scheduled for 15 September], before I was under the Necessity of deferring it.[3]

This flurry of derogation, Mrs. Dancer little realized, was but renewed evidence that numerous Cork theatregoers quite enjoyed taking offence on the slightest excuse. In a more violent fashion they exhibited their quick resentment at the benefits for

[1] John Wesley, *Journal* (ed. Nehemiah Curnock, London, 1909–16), iv. 401.
[2] CJ, 6 Oct. 1760.
[3] CEP, 2 Oct. 1760.

the Charitable Infirmary on Monday, 6 October, when an all-star cast of Barry, Woodward, Mrs. Abington, and Mrs. Dancer appeared in *The Conscious Lovers*.[1] When too many persons pressed for admission on that evening, they had to be forcibly restrained. Then the disappointed crowd turned into an unruly mob, attacked a justice of the peace and the civic guard who were trying to keep order, and threw bricks as well as stones to the injury of many people.[2] Fortunately the riot commenced too late to prevent the evening's performance, so that the Charitable Fund netted an ample return of over £100. Barry and Woodward as co-managers remitted their usual expense charge of £17. 10*s.* apiece and also donated the music, the wax candles for the evening's illumination, and other items.[2] Their 'much Generosity', well publicized by the city's newspapers, perhaps soothed to some degree the aggrieved multitude who thought themselves unkindly shut out.

Barry and 'His Majesty's Company of Comedians at the Theatre Royal' ran into trouble again at the very beginning of their next Cork season. Though they had full right under their royal patent from Robert Wood, Master of the Revels, to act in any Irish town without permission of the mayor, they customarily asked the sanction of the local dignitary as a measure of goodwill. Out of seeming perversity they made no move on their arrival at Cork in the summer of 1761 to pay their respects to the city officials, and at once proceeded to advertise their opening performance for Monday, 6 July, with no reference to 'the Right Worshipful Mayor'.[3] Since the members of the Cork Council understandably viewed the actors' behaviour as an affront to municipal authority, they passed a stern resolution on Friday, 3 July: 'Whereas a set of players have lately come to this City, and have printed bills for acting on Monday night next, without asking the Mayor's permission, It is the opinion of this Council that Mr. Mayor ought to prevent their acting until they apply for his permission and publish same in their bills.'[4] The Mayor had no power, of course, to enforce such a prohibition, but apparently he did confront Manager

[1] Ibid.

[2] Ibid., 13 Oct. 1760.

[3] CJ, 2 July 1761.

[4] *The Council Book of the Corporation of the City of Cork* (ed. Richard Caulfield, Guildford, Surrey, 1876), 3 July 1761.

Barry with some kind of remonstrance, for the latter took pains to lay a copy of his patent from Wood before the Cork Council to vindicate his proceedings.[1] The manager continued to feel so incensed by what he considered officious interference that at the end of his company's stay he threatened legal retaliation against the mayor. In the face of this threat the Council resolved on 28 October to support their leader from the public purse: 'Whereas it is apprehended a suit is intended to be brought against Mr. Mayor for preventing the players from acting in this city, on account of their putting up bills without the Mayor's permission, ordered that in such case the Mayor's cost be paid out of the Corporation revenue.'[2] Though in the end Barry filed no suit, his tactless actions and talk stirred up an antagonism that lasted as long as his management.

The 1761 troupe at the Theatre Royal surpassed in size the large one of the previous season. Numbering thirty-one men and twenty-one women[3] it included not only most of the Crow Street actors, but also eight from the rival Smock Alley playhouse, of whom the most able was John Sowdon, a former manager and a sound versatile performer. In addition, the very popular comedian Ned Shuter arrived fresh from Covent Garden to provide the feature attraction of the season's opening night. For this, his first Cork appearance, he played his favourite role of Falstaff in *Henry IV, Part I*, while Sowdon acted Hotspur. In connexion with that occasion Barry announced a regulation which he had never before advertised at Cork, but one which earlier managements had imposed at times: 'No Person whatsoever admitted behind the Scenes.'[4] This laudable rule was often reiterated in subsequent years, but evidently had to be as often overlooked. It certainly was not observed when on Saturday, 26 September, Barry held the first 'Masons' Night' since he became Cork manager.[5] After a procession with a band from the Masonic Council Chamber to the George's Street stage, the brethren seated themselves on 'an Amphitheatre erected for their Reception'. On account of the enlarged seating arrangements places on the stage were openly advertised and at the same price, 3*s*., as seats in the pit and gallery. The brisk demand to see the Masonic display and Mrs. Dancer as 'a Mason's Wife'

[1] Hitchcock, ii. 41.
[2] *The Council Book*, 28 Oct. 1761.
[3] Hitchcock, ii. 84.
[4] CJ, 2 July 1761.
[5] Ibid., 24 Sept. 1761.

led to the theft of twenty-five pit tickets. These were specially printed slips or coupons, serially numbered so that the box office could keep a record of the tickets legitimately distributed. Two days before the gala affair the Theatre Royal cautioned the public against buying any of the stolen tickets, because the numbers, all known, would be 'stopped if offered to be brought into said theatre'.[1]

For two actors the 1761 sojourn would remain memorable. Henry Woodward, Barry's Crow Street partner, was paying his final visit to the south of Ireland and having a last fling at getting up a new pantomime of his own invention. On Wednesday, 29 July, he produced *Cupid's Frolick; or, Mid-Summer Mirth*, a piece never recorded in performance elsewhere.[2] Its original properties and 'machinery' included 'a travelling chaise without horses', and 'a beautiful and magnificent representation of an Ostrich'. These examples of costly *décor* explain why Barry complained of his partner's extravagance. Woodward thought Barry's 'processions', such as 'the entire new funeral procession and dirge' for *Romeo and Juliet* on Friday, 10 July, equally extravagant.[3] Therefore, after the ensuing Dublin season, he broke up the partnership to return permanently to England. At the same time that Woodward was saying his farewell to Cork on the closing night of the season—Friday, 2 October—Spranger Barry's eighteen-year-old son, Thomas, was making his stage début in the title role of *Douglas*. The father, to whet public curiosity, announced the event as 'a young gentleman's first stage appearance'.[4] After the occasion had come off to the manager's apparent satisfaction, he saw to it that a flattering review was dispatched to Dublin: '[Thomas Barry acted] with so much dignity, force and real judgement that every individual there was struck with uncommon admiration at his superior art in affecting so sensibly the tender passions and sufferings of the mind. Such vast merit and great talents in so young a gentleman . . . is beyond comprehension and fairly promises a genius of the first rank in theatrical performances.'[5] The ambitious parent handled the launching well, never dreaming how troubled and abbreviated the young man's career would turn out to be.

[1] Ibid. [2] Ibid., 27 July 1761. [3] Ibid., 9 July 1761.
[4] Ibid., 24 Sept. 1761. [5] FDJ, 10 Oct. 1761.

When Barry lost Woodward for good in the spring of 1762, he had already lured the distinguished Charles Macklin from England. During the summer the Irish comedian fascinated the Cork audiences with his male caricatures: Sir Archy MacSarcasm in *Love à la Mode*;[1] Sir Francis Wronghead in *The Provok'd Husband*, Macklin's first playing of the role in Ireland;[2] and, the most popular of all his impersonations, Murrough O'Dogherty in his newly finished comedy, *The True-Born Irishman*.[2] Capitalizing on his Irish 'character', the author advertised that tickets for his benefit night on 27 September might be procured in advance from 'the True-Born Irishman in George's Street near the Theatre'.[2]

With the exception of Macklin's accession for 1762 only, Barry maintained the Cork personnel and repertory without any notable changes for several years. Sometimes the Cork company interrupted its season to play at Limerick; sometimes it went directly from Dublin to Limerick in July and then came to Cork in August. The close of the Crow Street season and the dates of the summer assizes in Cork and Limerick determined the variations in the touring schedule. Relations between the Theatre Royal and the not inconsiderable group of fault-finding Cork playgoers continued in an uneasy truce. Some of them seem to have gone so far as to encourage the Smock Alley company under Henry Mossop in a projected descent upon the city. During the spring of 1763 a report circulated for a while that Mossop had engaged a playhouse at Cork for a season in opposition to Barry's troupe.[3] Yet the latter took no warning, but, on the contrary, allowed more and more obvious laxities to creep into its Cork performances. A serious lapse in the presentation of Farquhar's comedy, *The Recruiting Officer*, on Thursday, 18 August 1763, at last ignited the displeasure of the restive local critics. On the following Monday the *Cork Evening Post* gave prominence to this notice:

Whereas in the play of *The Recruiting Officer* . . . there was a *Scene* entirely left out, which led to the explanation of the under-plot, and the comedy necessarily concluded without giving proper information to the audience: The present Theatrical Company are desired to take

[1] CJ, 4 Oct. 1762. [2] Ibid., 23 Sept. 1762.

[3] *The Theatrical Review; or Annals of the Drama* (London, 1763), p. 170.

notice, that tho' a *Cork audience* have given repeated proofs of their good nature, they can when thus roused, give equal proofs of their resentment.

BOX, PIT, and GALLERY.[1]

After that sharp salvo the critical gentlemen took their time in organizing their campaign. They obtained the indispensable support of George Busteed when in 1764 he began to publish the *Cork Chronicle*, a newspaper which catered to the *élite* citizens. They did not, however, launch a persistent attack through the pages of the *Chronicle* until the next summer.

From the opening of the Theatre Royal on Monday, 12 August 1765, until the closing in October, the firing by the critics occurred frequently. The first-night performance of Spranger Barry in *Hamlet* elicited a sly ironic remark about 'this great Actor' commencing without all his company on hand and the stage in full order.[2] The Falstaff of Isaac Sparks on the next night was described as 'sometimes honest Isaac'; the Prince Hal of Robert Mahon, 'barely tolerable'.[2] Mahon, playing the Critic in *The Rehearsal* on 30 August, had to be 'constantly prompted' for both the lines and the business.[3] Two weeks later the same actor in *The Countess of Salisbury* exhibited 'such a familiarity or rather *vulgarity* of Manner, that we think him totally incapable of blank verse'.[4] William Glover, an implausible Apothecary in *Romeo and Juliet* on 2 September, was advised to act as Merry Andrew to 'Dr. Tuscano, who is at present in town, and stands in need of an Assistant'.[5] The production of *Othello* on 9 September not only had the minor parts 'as usual, very imperfectly done', but also the text badly abridged with the scene between Cassio and Bianca 'entirely left out'.[6] On the other hand, lavish praise greeted the performances of twenty-year-old Anne Cately as Rosetta in *Love in a Village;* she was thought 'a lovely Syren', 'indeed perfection', and so forth.[7] At her benefit on 16 September she displayed her 'elegant, fine figure' in boy's clothes as Captain Flash of *Miss in Her Teens*.[8] 'Every part of the house was filled two hours before the usual time of beginning.' The receipts were £160, the very maximum possible at normal prices. 'Many hundreds of people' had to be turned away.

[1] CEP, 22 Aug. 1763.
[2] CCh, 19 Aug. 1765, 'Theatrical Intelligence'.
[3] Ibid., 2 Sept. 1765.
[4] Ibid., 16 Sept. 1765.
[5] Ibid., 5 Sept. 1765.
[6] Ibid., 12 Sept. 1765.
[7] Ibid., 19 Aug. 1765.
[8] Ibid., 19 Sept. 1765.

Quite the opposite treatment was meted out to Mrs. Dancer when 'indisposition' prevented her from appearing in *Macbeth* on 27 September. Her absence at once drew blistering comment: 'The attack on this lady's constitution has been for some years past so Periodical that it generally seizes her after her own and Mr. Barry's benefit, and so continues till the beginning of the winter season in Dublin, where she perfectly recovers.'[1] Then on 3 October the *Chronicle* printed a sarcastic notice that Mrs. Dancer's health will '*permit* her to play' and that therefore she was 'to *oblige* the Town' in *Tancred and Sigismunda* on 9 October.

The most incendiary blast, however, took the form of a facetious 'Dramatic Scale' that rated members of the Theatre Royal company according to a point system applied to various phases of the art of acting. The sample ratings printed in the *Chronicle* for 30 September were designed in most cases to infuriate the persons named. For instance, Mr. Glover received 11 points (the maximum credit) for noise, 0 points for genius, and 0 points for 'capital' (i.e. leading) parts; Mr. Usher, 7 points for noise, 0 points for genius, and ? points for 'capital' parts. Myrton Hamilton and others among the players, believing themselves gravely insulted, tried to assault Busteed at the *Chronicle* office. Then in late October they brought suit against him. Therefore he was compelled to give bail 'in order to stand trial at the next assizes for publishing a false and scandalous paper relative to the performers of the Theatre Royal Cork'.[2] By spring the plaintiffs had lost their indignation and did not press the charge. The basis for further quarrels, however, had been unforgettably established.

Even before the summer season of 1766 had begun, the gibes of the critics in the *Chronicle* started up with greater intensity than ever. On 21 July 'Theatrical Intelligence Extraordinary', intending to satirize Manager Barry, printed a report about 'the noble acquisition of the Dutch Dogs and the Italian Monkeys by the High and mighty Field Marshal Othello' (that is, Spranger Barry, who upon his stage début at Dublin twenty years earlier had gained immediate fame in the role of Othello). Then the anonymous reporter went on to remark with irony that 'it is doubtful whether our tasteless Audience will sufficiently relish their sprightly and entertaining gambols in

[1] CCh, 30 Sept. 1765.

[2] *Sleater's Public Gazetteer*, 2 Nov. 1765.

preference to the dull, stupid scenes of Shakespeare, Gay, and Cibber'. A week later it was announced that 'the Quartermaster-general [Thomas Barry], his Lady, and family, arrived in Town; as did also a few inferiors of the Marshal's Troops'.[1] The Theatre Royal finally opened on Friday, 8 August,[2] without the presence of either Barry or Mrs. Dancer. According to the 31 July issue of the *Chronicle* 'the renowned Othello and his lovely Desdemona' had been at Mallow Spa for some time past. They crossed to London in August and never again played together at Cork.

The Theatre Royal audiences soon discovered the fact that Thomas Barry at the age of twenty-three could not fill his father's place as either actor or manager. Executive incapacity, combined with an unattractive personality, prevented him from exercising the needed leadership. 'An Enemy of Imposition' in a letter to the *Chronicle* accused him of 'intolerable insolence', of turning the gallery into 'a scene of obscenity', and of allowing the players on stage 'absolutely intoxicated'.[3] These charges did not irk the young deputy as much as the unfavourable criticisms of his acting. His several performances of the role of Hastings in *Jane Shore* resulted in the judgement that he would 'never shake off that Socratical Gravity so unsuitable to such a part'.[4] His playing in *The Fair Penitent* occasioned a similar stricture: 'We wish that the grave Lothario would be more gay and smile a little'.[5] At last, unable to endure any more adverse comment, he went to the *Chronicle* office to learn the identity of his critics that 'he might cane or horsewhip them on 'Change'. When Busteed the publisher refused to divulge the information, Barry denounced him and the commentators as 'Rascals and Scoundrels'.[5]

Then the enraged theatre manager set in motion a farcical series of contentions in court and out. He instituted an action of £1,000 damages against Busteed for the publication of derogatory remarks about the Theatre Royal performers, and he arranged for two of the latter, Philip Glenvil and Robert Mahon, to be appointed special deputy sheriffs to serve the writ.[6] At ten o'clock on Thursday evening, 4 September, the

[1] CCh, 28 July 1766.
[2] Ibid., 7 Aug. 1766.
[3] Ibid., 21 Aug. and 3 Nov. 1766.
[4] Ibid., 25 Aug. 1766.
[5] FDJ, 23 Sept. 1766.
[6] Ibid., 27 Sept. 1766; CCh, 8 Sept. 1766.

two actors called at Busteed's printing office on the pretence of wishing to insert an advertisement, but they could not gain admittance. They returned Friday morning to arrest Busteed, 'dragged him like a common felon through the streets', and clapped him into the city jail. After seven hours behind the bars he secured his freedom through the payment of £2,000 bail by several gentlemen friends. Immediately upon his release Busteed had Mahon arrested for drawing a pistol and threatening the publisher's life. This arrest in turn much delayed the benefit performance for the North Infirmary on the evening of 5 September.[1]

A group of local citizens, alarmed at Barry's suit against Busteed, now proclaimed themselves the 'Friends of Liberty' with the slogan: 'Liberty of the press, the privilege of a free born Irishman'.[2] At the same time they solicited, from Dublin as well as Cork, contributions towards the defendant's legal expenses.[3] On 2 October the City Recorder, affirming liberty of the press as an inviolable principle, declared Barry's affidavits of damage insufficient and discharged his bill of libel.[4] Five days later Busteed's *Chronicle* triumphantly carried a mock advertisement for subscriptions, at a half-crown each, to *Theatrical Intelligence; or, A Brief Criticism on the Merits and Demerits of the Theatrical Performers who have appeared on the Corke Stage, in the years 1764, 1765, 1766.*[5]

The defeated plaintiff, seeing a very meagre audience at his benefit play of *Cato* on 15 October, instructed his assistant Mr. Heaphy to announce at the rise of the curtain that 'Mr. Barry was suddenly and dangerously attacked with illness'. The *Chronicle* responded to this news with a mock elegiac couplet:

> The mighty Cato sick—Oh! fatal Stroke!
> Of empty Seats, and Boxes unbespoke.[6]

Not even a feigned illness, however, could stem a complete reverse of the manager's fortune. On Monday, 10 November, when he had thought his tempestuous sojourn in Cork at an end, he found himself committed to the city jail 'for having falsely and maliciously caused Busteed to be seized and

[1] CCh, 8 Sept. 1766. [2] Ibid., 25 Sept. 1766. [3] Ibid., 18 Sept. 1766.
[4] Ibid., 2 Oct. 1766. [5] Ibid., 7 Oct. 1766. [6] Ibid., 20 Oct. 1766.

imprisoned on an illegal action'.[1] The publisher apparently did not press his complaint after he had experienced the satisfaction of subjecting the proud Mr. Barry to the same indignity of imprisonment that he had suffered two months earlier.

Busteed also sought revenge upon another Theatre Royal opponent, William Frederick Glover, a low comedian. Like many actors of the period, Glover had a second occupation, that of surgery. Aware of this fact, the *Chronicle* critics in derision had called him 'Dr. Caius' after the grotesque French doctor in *The Merry Wives of Windsor*.[2] The actor had counter-attacked on stage by irritating impersonations of local citizens, including Busteed.[3] The latter finally brought suit against Glover. A constable came to the playhouse on Tuesday night, 28 October, to make the arrest, but the comedian escaped through a back door.[4] Busteed then advertised in the *Chronicle* a reward of two guineas for the apprehension of Glover, whom he labelled 'a strolling player'.[5] A week later the offer of reward was withdrawn, because the defendant had come out of hiding to give security for his appearance at the spring assizes.[6] In April 1767 'the Bills of Mr. Busteed against Mr. Glover . . . were unanimously thrown out by the Gentlemen of the Grand Jury'.[7]

More than a month before the start of Busteed's lawsuit Glover had attained notoriety by reason of his second occupation. On Wednesday, 10 September 1766, he strolled to Gallows Green to attend the execution of a tailor, Patrick Redmond.[8] Because a shower threatened, the city officials and the civil guard stayed only long enough to watch 'Jack Ketch', the executioner, supposedly complete Redmond's hanging. On their departure the tailor's friends hastened to cut his body down and carried it to a near-by cabin, named appropriately 'Resurrection House'. There Glover, out of the crowd, volunteered his skill as surgeon. He proceeded by massage and fumigation to restore Redmond's circulation. The latter soon regained consciousness, sat up, and helped himself to a proffered bottle of whisky to the 'no small admiration' of the onlookers. At this point Glover left for the Theatre Royal to take part in

[1] Ibid., 17 Nov. 1766.
[2] Ibid., 21 Aug. 1766.
[3] Ibid., 25 Aug. 1766.
[4] Ibid., 3 Nov. 1766.
[5] Ibid., 30 Oct. 1766.
[6] Ibid., 3 Nov. 1766.
[7] FDJ, 18 Apr. 1767.
[8] Croker, ch. 9, pp. 21–24; Anthony Edwards, *The Cork Remembrancer* (Cork, 1792), 10 Sept. 1766; O'Keeffe, i. 142–3.

his benefit night. He had just commenced his address to the audience with the words 'Patrons and Friends, to you how great my debt', when the resurrected tailor, drunk as a fool and waving a shillelagh, thrust himself through the orchestra and scrambled on to the stage. Then he shouted: 'Good Christians and Honest People, whativer debt Mr. Glover there is talkin' about, 'tis nothin' at all to what I owe him, for sure he saved my life.' Upon revelation of Redmond's identity a sheriff called out to seize him, but cool and friendly heads managed to hustle the man into concealment. Eventually he moved to Dublin to become tailor to the 'Corps Dramatique'.

A third member of the Theatre Royal troupe, its leading singer, Signor Guisto Ferdinando Tenducci, also provided Cork citizens with a mild sensation in this memorable summer of 1766. The Italian musician abducted his fifteen-year-old pupil, Dorothea Maunsell, from her sister's home in County Tipperary where she was visiting in company with her father, a Dublin councilman. The couple were married privately by a Roman Catholic priest in Cork on 19 August. Miss Maunsell by entering into matrimony with a man of alien faith and without parental blessing doubly scandalized her relatives and friends, many of them persons of prominence. *Faulkner's Dublin Journal* expressed their dismay in a brief but pointed statement: 'An amiable young lady has deserted her parents and thrown herself away upon an Italian singer; a most extraordinary matter of amazement, and no doubt a great distress to a very respectable family.'[1] Councillor Maunsell, like Barry and Busteed, resorted to the Cork court to assuage his resentment. On Thursday night, 28 August, Signor Tenducci was arrested at the Theatre Royal 'on an action of Damage, for having seduced and married a young lady of a good family and fortune'.[2] He had been advertised to sing the principal role in the new opera of *The Royal Shepard* for his benefit on the following Monday, but of course the performance had to be called off.[3] Upon his release from jail 'a very sick and confined condition' necessitated his absence from the bill of the rescheduled benefit on 11 September. Yet, with the right touch of pathos, Tenducci announced that he expected 'to be carried to the Playhouse . . .

[1] FDJ, 2 Sept. 1766.
[2] Ibid., 6 Sept. 1766.
[3] CCh, 28 Aug. and 4 Sept. 1766.

to be ready to offer any Entertainment in his Power . . . in the Exceptance [*sic*] of which the Audience may please to Honour him'.[1] Presumably the Signor recovered his strength as rapidly as talk of the abduction subsided. Two years afterwards he abandoned both Ireland and his stage-struck wife.

The contentious atmosphere which had pervaded the theatre in George's Street for a half-dozen years vanished with the termination of the Barry family management in the winter of 1767–8. Young Thomas fell ill and died at Dublin on 10 April 1768.[2] Meanwhile his father decided to give up the Dublin stage in favour of Drury Lane and Mrs. Dancer. Before Spranger Barry departed from Ireland in December 1767 he seems to have disposed of his rights in the Cork Theatre Royal to the Smock Alley manager, Henry Mossop, who at the same time took a lease on Barry's Crow Street Theatre. Consequently it was a united Dublin company that Mossop led to Cork in July 1768. The new manager revived Thomas Sheridan's policy of guest stars for a limited number of appearances. Mrs. Frances Abington and Tom King, old Cork favourites from Drury Lane, shared the limelight for six weeks in a series of outstanding comedies, such as *Rule A Wife*, *The Beaux' Stratagem*, *The Provok'd Wife*, and *The Clandestine Marriage*.[3] Around the middle of August Mrs. Elizabeth Fitzhenry, the noted Dublin-born *tragédienne*, commenced her second and last engagement in the city. She played Isabella in *Measure for Measure* with Mossop, a strong-voiced actor inclined to regal or tragic roles, as the Duke.[4] In *The Earl of Warwick*, a much-heralded production on account of 'an entire new set of Vandyke Dresses', these two stars performed Margaret of Anjou and the Earl.[5] Mossop closed his first Cork season on 23 September, acting Zanga in *The Revenge*, the part which raised him to fame twenty years before.[6] During the two months of his company's performing not a single controversy regarding plays or players had broken out. This remarkable change in local theatrical relations was largely the consequence of a tactful and conscientious attitude in the new George's Street régime.

Mossop undertook some renovation of the Theatre Royal

[1] Ibid., 8 Sept. 1766.
[2] FDJ, 12 Apr. 1768.
[3] CEP, 28 July–11 Aug. 1768.
[4] Ibid., 11 Aug. 1768.
[5] Ibid., 15 Aug. 1768.
[6] Ibid., 22 Sept. 1768.

before its tenth year began. 'Newly painted and decorated', it opened on Monday, 31 July 1769, with *The Beggar's Opera*, in which Mrs. Hester Jackson from Edinburgh starred as Polly.[1] She and her husband John were the important new faces in the Cork troupe. Performances started out on a Monday, Wednesday, Friday night schedule, but for the first two weeks they failed to attract audiences sufficiently large to pay expenses. Therefore, on Monday evening, 14 August, Mossop came forward to dismiss the small house. A choleric little major in the pit demanded that the curtain rise.[2] When the manager refused to comply, the major, leaping upon the stage, drew his sword on him and precipitated a duel. Mossop at last made a thrust into his antagonist's arm; the major in turn ran his weapon through the fleshy part of the manager's thigh. These wounds forced the duellists to call it quits. Mossop's injury did not incapacitate him for long. In spite of a report in the *Chronicle* that 'the present manager is determined not to act again',[3] he reopened the playhouse on Friday, 18 August,[4] and maintained regular production thereafter. He chose a comedy fresh from Drury Lane, *The School for Rakes*, to celebrate his benefit on Monday night, 20 September, the season's finale.[5] It turned out to be Mossop's last appearance on the Cork stage.

Reports from Dublin in regard to Mossop's financial difficulties during the winter of 1769–70 so much disturbed the 'Proprietors of Shares' in the Theatre Royal, George's Street, that they called a dinner meeting for three o'clock on Thursday, 8 March 1770, at Rugg's Tavern 'to take into consideration the present wretched state of the Playhouse, and come to some resolutions for securing the property of the subscribers, which is now becoming every day less in its value, and must soon be totally lost, if some effectual measure be not taken'.[6] Despite the alarm implied in the foregoing notice the conferees evidently agreed upon no formal action in March. During the late spring Tottenham Heaphy, a respected figure in Irish theatricals for twenty years past, purchased from the bankrupt Mossop the title and patent of the Cork theatre in conjunction with his opening of a new playhouse at Limerick. Heaphy designed for

[1] CEP, 24 and 27 July 1769.
[2] FJ, 19 Sept. 1769.
[3] CCh, 17 Aug. 1769.
[4] Ibid., 24 Aug. 1769.
[5] CEP, 18 Sept. 1769.
[6] HC, 5 Mar. 1770.

the summer touring a 'commonwealth' company, that is, one in which all the senior players had equal shares in the profits. On 30 May he wrote to Charles Macklin in London and invited him to join the venture as a sharer, but the noted comedian, dubious of his rewards on such a basis, promptly refused.[1]

Meanwhile the concern of the Theatre Royal subscribers about the future of their building persisted. The notice of a dinner meeting on Wednesday, 11 July, in the garden of Rugg's Tavern voiced their amusingly desperate intent 'to make one effort more to secure their property, before they are forever precluded, which in a few days more they must be, if some spirited measures are not resolved on'.[2] In response to the local anxiety the new proprietor hastened 'to assure the public that the Theatre Royal in this city will be opened at the ensuing [i.e. August] assizes'.[3] At the same time he requested the subscribers to confer with him at Rugg's Tavern on Wednesday, 22 August, 'as he has some matters to propose'.[4] The day following this conference brought a flowery statement from Manager Heaphy regarding the 'fate' of the George's Street playhouse:

> It will on Friday next [i.e. 24 August] be in perfect order for exhibition, and much more so than for some years. The rapid manner in which the repairs are executing, the natural encumbrances of the Theatre, and the other weighty expenses attending the removal of a whole company, wardrobe, &c., leave but a languid prospect of their being able to defray them [i.e. the expenses] in the course of eight nights' performances.
>
> The irretrievable ruin into which every part of that theatre must inevitably fall, if unoccupied and unrepaired this season; and the certainty there now is of uniting for the future the theatrical entertainment of the cities of Cork and Limerick under the same management, were the motives which induced Mr. Heaphy, and the company, for a very short time to attempt so arduous and expensive an undertaking.[5]

The statement concluded by directing the subscribers how to claim their annual right of four per cent. interest on their fifty-pound shares. They were 'to send to the box-keeper for the interest tickets of the year, and . . . to write their respective

[1] This letter of Heaphy to Macklin, endorsed on 7 June with Macklin's refusal, was described in Bertram Dobell's catalogue, Aug. 1936, item no. 1105.

[2] HC, 5 and 9 July 1770.

[3] CEP, 16 Aug. 1770.

[4] HC, 20 Aug. 1770.

[5] CEP, 23 Aug. 1770.

names on the back of each ticket in order to prevent the confusion which has frequently happened for want of that precaution'. The confusion arose from the fact that the subscribers could rent for any given season their silver tickets of permanent admission. For instance, Mr. John King of Sullivan's Quay advertised in July 1775: 'To be sold, during the theatrical season, the use of a Silver Ticket.'[1] If Mr. King found a taker, Heaphy had to recognize the right of the temporary holder to a subscriber's admission privileges. On the other hand, the proprietor had to see to it that Mr. King rather than the seasonal user of Mr. King's ticket got the year's dividend. Heaphy's innovation of countersigned interest certificates was planned to forestall both invalid and also multiple claims for payment.

The Cork Theatre Royal opened, as promised, on Friday evening, 24 August, with a rather unexciting group of performers drawn from the new Capel Street playhouse in Dublin as well as from Crow Street. Local interest naturally centred upon the Dublin young lady, Dorothea Maunsell, who four years before at Cork had entered into a notorious marriage with her Italian singing teacher. Now separated from Signor Tenducci, she had made her stage début in her native city a few months previous. On the opening night at George's Street she acted the pathetic Jane Shore and then, to demonstrate her versatility, appeared on the next evening as Cherry, the pert servant in *The Beaux' Stratagem.*[2] Her appeal to the Cork theatregoers evidently continued strong because the manager for his benefit on 3 September selected Miss Maunsell to play the sweetly sad Imoinda in *Oroonoko*.

The title role in Aphra Behn's tragedy was undertaken by 'a young gentleman who has had an university education, and who is also possessed of every other accomplishment necessary to form a capital Actor'.[3] This unidentified novice turned out to be a local youth, Frederick Pilon. His initial performance, according to a reviewer, betrayed 'poor voice and deportment', even though he had received platform training at the Castle Street house of the fashionable hairdresser, Tom Barrett, where the theatrically inclined assembled twice a week in a 'spouting

[1] HC, 10 July 1775. [2] CEP and CJ, 23 Aug. 1770.
[3] HC, 30 Aug. 1770.

room' on the first floor.[1] In spite of this inauspicious beginning Pilon did not at that time abandon his ambition for a stage career.

Three days after the *Oroonoko* production the George's Street season for 1770 ended, according to the newspaper notices, with *As You Like It.*[2] Just two years later Heaphy advertised the same play as the season's finale with the puff, 'not acted here in ten years'.[3] Usually, however, he displayed uncommon reliability as a theatre manager; for example, his adherence to the announced season of only eight nights. To be sure, the excitement in Limerick over the new theatre made business there probably more lucrative than at Cork for the time being. Before returning to the Munster capital, nevertheless, the manager took pains to settle all his company's accounts by calling for prompt presentation of bills, a practice that he yearly repeated: 'As there will not be any play this season after tomorrow evening, all artificers, traders, and others who have any demands unpaid, are desired to bring in their accompts . . . that they may be immediately discharged.'[4] The *Hibernian Chronicle*, commending Heaphy in 1772 for the 'decency and regularity' of his management, asserted that he owed 'not a penny' to any Cork tradesman when the curtain rang down at the Theatre Royal.[5] This persistent care in dealing with the business community surely had much to do with Heaphy's ultimate reputation as 'one of the most respectable characters that ever graced public or private life in Ireland'.[6]

The approach of the 1772 summer season provoked a typical fanfare of managerial rhetoric about sparing 'no necessary expence in the immediate repairs and decorations, in order to render the Theatre, for the future, as elegant as it appeared before it was lacerated and almost destroyed by occasionally renting it to *outré* and exotic exhibitions for which it was never originally intended'.[7] The Dublin curtain time of seven o'clock and the Dublin scale of prices—4*s*. for box seats, 3*s*. for pit, and 2*s*. for gallery—continued in force.[8] To discourage the increased sampling of the day's entertainment by the city bucks, Heaphy began to insert in his bills that no admission money would be

[1] Croker, ch. 9, pp. 24–25. [2] CEP, 3 Sept. 1770.
[3] HC, 22 Oct. 1772. [4] CEP, 5 Sept. 1771. [5] HC, 26 Oct. 1772.
[6] Hitchcock, i. 216. [7] HC, 11 May 1772. [8] Ibid., 17 Aug. 1772.

returned 'after the Curtain is drawn up'.[1] The regular schedule of performances rose to four nights a week on account of the growing attendance.

The larger audiences resulted from the presence of a scintillating stage couple. The ever-popular Charles Macklin at last had consented to join a summer tour and had brought along his protégée, Henrietta Leeson, the liveliest *ingénue* in Dublin, for her first appearance in Cork. They played Shylock and Portia on the opening night at George's Street—Wednesday, 19 August—and thereafter acted together in a half-dozen comedies, including Macklin's own *Love à la Mode*, *The True-Born Irishman*, and *The True-Born Scotsman*.[2] During this summer the middle-aged comedian felt more than a fatherly affection for Miss Leeson, but learned that he had a rival in a younger actor, William Thomas Lewis, whose handsome physique and spirited deportment much attracted the actress. One evening at the Theatre Royal the suspicious Macklin, making a sudden entrance into her dressing-room, discovered Lewis in the closet.[3] Mrs. Leeson quickly appeared to defend her daughter against Macklin's accusation of improper conduct. His jealousy, however, would not permit him to dismiss the incident from his mind. For years afterwards he took occasion to refer to Lewis as 'the man in the closet'.

Heaphy's troupe went to Limerick for the September assizes and then returned to Cork for a month largely filled with benefits and their accompanying novelties. On Wednesday, 23 September, Wren the boxkeeper elected to illuminate the house with wax tapers and to rail in the larger part of the pit with the adjoining front boxes 'for the better accommodation of the Ladies, after the same manner as the Opera House in the Haymarket, London'.[4] Two days later the programme on behalf of the South Infirmary included the first presentation of a farce, *The Siege of the Castle of Aesculapius*, by a Cork writer unnamed in the bills. A cabal against the author suddenly organized and hooted the piece off the stage.[5] One vociferous participant remarked that 'nothing gave him more pleasure

1 Playbill for 31 Aug. 1772, Shaw Collection, Harvard University Library.

2 Ibid.; HC, 17 and 27 Aug., 3 Sept. 1772.

3 William W. Appleton, *Charles Macklin: An Actor's Life* (Cambridge, Massachusetts, 1960), pp. 164–5.

4 HC, 21 Sept. 1772.

5 Ibid., 1 Oct. 1772.

(Never Acted in this City.)

As the Company are to perform but a Fortnight more here, until the Week on which the Assizes commence; they beg leave to acquaint the public, that there will be four Exhibitions in each Week, and that no piece will on any account be repeated unless by general desire.

By his Majesty's Company of Comedians.

By Permission of the Right Worshipful Mayor of CORK.

At the THEATRE-ROYAL.

On Monday next the 31st Inst. will be presented the last new Tragedy, call'd,

The Grecian Daughter.

As it is Acted at the Theatres Royal in London and Dublin, with uncommon Applause.

Evander, Mr. HEAPHY,
Dionysius, Mr. MAHON,
Philotas, Mr. KEEFE,
Melanthon, Mr. MARLTON,
Arcas, Mr. VANDERMERE,
Greek Herald, Mr. CHAPLIN,
Callipus, Mr. WALSH,
Officer, Mr. BURDEN,
Phocian, by Mr. LEWIS.
Erixene, Mrs. O'NEILL,
Euphrasia, by Mrs. BURDEN.
With proper Scenery and Decorations.

DANCING by Master WARD and Miss ARCHBOLD.

End of the Play, The Soldier Tir'd, by Mrs. SHEWCRAFT.

To which will be added Mr. MACKLIN's celebrated Comedy of two acts, call'd,

LOVE-ALA-MODE.

Sir Archy Macsarcasm, by Mr. MACKLIN,
(Being the fourth Night of six which he is engaged to performed here.)
'Squire Groom, by Mr. LEWIS,
Beau Mordecai, Mr. KEEFE,
Sir Theodore Goodchild, Mr. MARLTON,
Lawyer, Mr. CHAPLIN.
Sir Callaghan O'Bralaghan, (with a song in character) Mr. MAHON.
Charlotte, Mrs. O'NEILL.

Boxes 4s. 4d. Pit 3s. 3d. Gal. 2s. 2d. N. B. To begin precisely at Seven.

Places in the Boxes to be taken of Mr. Wren, Box-keeper, at the Theatre, every Day from Ten to Three o'Clock.

Tickets to be had at Mr. Reynold's in Fish-street.

N. B. No money will be return'd after the Curtain draws up.

CORK: Printed by P. BAGNELL and Comp.

Cork Playbill, Monday, 31 August 1772

than roasting an author'. Once more the latent crankiness of a formidable minority among the Cork theatre-lovers had manifested itself. The next night another local aspirant, Frederick Pilon, fared not too much better in an acting performance. As Castalio in Otway's *The Orphan* he won even less approbation than as Oroonoko two years before.[1] This second failure on the boards caused him to shift to playwriting, in which he subsequently attained a modest fame.

The recurrence of a hypercritical feeling towards local stage activities did not extend to the once irritable *Chronicle*. On the contrary, at the start of the 1773 season, it introduced a series of puffs relating to the Theatre Royal's affairs. Perhaps its action grew out of the manager's generous conduct in March when 'a Gentleman' asked for a lease of the playhouse 'to entertain with humorous and moral lectures' during Assize Week. The *Chronicle* expressed the hope that permission would be granted 'for this *rational* occasion'.[2] Heaphy in turn 'most cheerfully consented to such use of the Theatre Royal without any emolument whatever'.[3] The summer's opening performance on Thursday, 3 June (the earliest date on record for a Cork summer *première*), drew most flattering comments in the *Chronicle*: the decorations, 'very expensive'; the wardrobe, 'equal in richness and elegance to any in Great Britain'; the company, 'equal to any which has been in this Kingdom these seven years'.[4] A *tragédienne* new to Cork, Mrs. King from York, played the evening's star role of the Grecian Daughter and elicited praise for 'a majestic dignity of deportment that matched the striking elegance of her figure'.[4] The *Chronicle* also acclaimed Mrs. Richard Sparks on the subsequent night for 'exhibiting all the spirited elegance of fashionable life' as Lady Townley in *The Provok'd Husband*.[5] This glowing estimate differed considerably from William Smith's delineation of her in the following year: 'She is what may be called handsome, but clumsy, vulgar, and inanimate, and has the brogue very strong.'[6] Mrs. Sparks therefore may have been better suited for the part which she

[1] Ibid., 24 Sept. 1772; Croker, ch. 9, p. 25.
[2] Ibid., 18 Mar. 1773.
[3] Ibid., 22 Mar. 1773.
[4] Ibid., 7 June 1773.
[5] Ibid., 14 June 1773.
[6] *The Private Correspondence of David Garrick* (London, 1831–2), i. 644.

chose for her benefit on 23 July, namely, the hearty Irish Widow in Garrick's farce by that title.[1]

This same summer of 1773 saw the noted ex-manager of the Smock Alley Theatre, Thomas Sheridan, engage in his first tour to the south of Ireland. As always, he confined his repertory almost wholly to the leading characters of Shakespearian and established eighteenth-century tragedy, such as Brutus, Cato, Hamlet, Macbeth, Tamerlane, and Orestes in Ambrose Philips's *The Distrest Mother*.[2] He once deviated into comedy as Sir Charles Easy in Cibber's *The Careless Husband*.[3] His most unusual impersonation occurred on Friday, 9 July, when he portrayed King John in the first Irish production of that Shakespearian historical drama outside Dublin.[4] So successful did Sheridan's early appearances on tour prove that he contracted to stay with Heaphy's company all summer, going with it to Limerick for three weeks in August and coming back to Cork for another three weeks. For his return performance as Hamlet on 30 August the manager, expecting a tremendous crush of spectators, issued a polite but stern reiteration of the rule that Sheridan himself had originally introduced to the Irish stage: 'It is humbly hoped that no offence will be taken that the strictest directions are given to prevent any person whatsoever from coming behind the scenes, as it will be otherwise impossible to conduct the entertainment with that decorum and propriety which is due to the audience of this city.'[5] The season's only acting of *King Lear* on Monday, 13 September, completed the triumphal visit of the veteran tragedian.[6]

Though Sheridan as a guest star from England probably appeared for a guaranteed fee per night, the other members of Heaphy's troupe participated on a 'commonwealth' basis. The case of a young comedian from London, Thomas Wilks, well illustrated this kind of financial arrangement and its rewards in the current season. After a fatiguing ten days of sailing in a West Indiaman to cross from Bristol to Cobh, he underwent his Cork début at George's Street on 26 July.[7] For this night's perform-

[1] HC, 19 July 1773.

[2] Brutus, 25 June and 1 Sept.; Cato, 18 June; Hamlet, 11 June; Macbeth, 16 July; Tamerlane, 10 Sept.; Orestes, 5 July and 8 Sept.

[3] 12 July.

[4] HC, 5 July 1773.

[5] Ibid., 26 Aug. 1773.

[6] Ibid., 9 Sept. 1773.

[7] Snagg(e), p. 92.

ance of the foppish Jessamy in the comic opera of *Lionel and Clarissa* he received £7. 18*s*., which represented an equal share of the night's profits minus the fixed daily charge of £30 for company expenses.[1] His second Cork appearance on 28 July brought him only £6. 7*s*., though he played the more demanding role of the aristocratic fop, Lord Ogleby, in *The Clandestine Marriage*.[2] The three-week sojourn in Limerick during August netted him £34. 1*s*.[3] Then, back at Cork from 25 August to 22 September, he enjoyed, in addition to his share of the proceeds from the non-benefit evenings, the receipts from his benefit on 14 September when he acted Sir Harry Wildair in *The Constant Couple*.[4] The dozen or so profit-sharing days resulted in £1,193. 5*s*. of company revenue.[5] Since Wilks made a stage appearance probably on not more than half of those days, he was compensated accordingly. Even so, his share must have amounted to about £50. He therefore earned £115–£120 for two months of performing. It is no wonder that he felt well rewarded by his first tour in Ireland.

On the Wednesday and the Friday following the Tuesday benefit of Wilks, John Vandermere and John O'Keeffe enjoyed similar occasions. Each presented as special attraction an original interlude depicting the life and topography of Cork's environs. *The Humours of Cove; or, The Smugglers Return* offered 'an exact representation of the Town of Cove, the Harbour's Mouth, Ardbouling Island and Castle, painted by Mr. Vandermere'.[6] *Tony Lumpkin's Ramble Thro' Cork* by O'Keeffe contained scenic views of 'the Mall, Red-House Walk, Sunday's Well, Coffee-Houses, Taverns, &c.'.[6] This end-of-the-season appeal to local patriotism extended to Mrs. Heaphy's benefit on the last night, 22 September, when the programme included a fresh pantomime entitled *Medley; or, Harlequin's Vagaries in Munster*.[7] Of these three new works *Tony Lumpkin's Ramble* alone was ever revived anywhere. O'Keeffe put it on for his Cork benefit in the ensuing year and again in 1775, each time with additions of local scenes, such as Mallow Lane, the 'Change,

1 Ibid., p. 93; HC, 19 July 1773.
2 Snagg(e), p. 93; HC, 26 July 1773.
3 Snagg(e), p. 93.
4 HC, 6 Sept. 1773.
5 Snagg(e), p. 93.
6 HC, 13 Sept. 1773.
7 Ibid., 16 Sept. 1773.

the Riding School, the Fortune Teller, and the Adventures of a Sedan Chair.[1]

William ('Gentleman') Smith and his fellow player from Covent Garden, Mrs. Rosamond Hartley, supplanted Sheridan and Wilks as the guest attractions at Cork in 1774. On 10 July the London pair arrived 'with a large party for the Lake of Killarney'.[2] Three days later they turned their attention from the beauties of the south-of-Ireland landscape to stage business. Then for somewhat more than two weeks they carried out an exhausting schedule of classics: *Richard III*, *Hamlet*, *Macbeth*, *The Recruiting Officer*, *All for Love*, *Jane Shore*, *The Conscious Lovers*.[3] At the end of ten days Smith reported happily to Garrick in London that he had 'got more than all expenses, considerably'.[4] In ten more days the fatigue attendant upon his first visit to Ireland had so much soured his disposition that his next report to Garrick spoke of 'damned Cork' and of not one among his fellow actors as 'worth 10*s*. per week', the salary of an inexperienced or inferior stroller.[5] Fortunately city opinion did not view the current entertainers at the Theatre Royal with any such disdain. A *Chronicle* correspondent, observing the Dublin stage in the autumn of 1774, informed its readers that 'Mr. Heaphy gives Cork as good a set of Performers as he can possibly procure, or we can expect'.[6]

No outstanding players, however, brightened the summer of 1775 at the George's Street playhouse. In September, when the benefit nights came round, Robert Aldridge, a hornpipe dancer, sought local patronage by the novel claim that he received 'no certainty from Mr. Heaphy for his performance here', and 'no emolument whatever for dancing, except such as may arise from his benefit'.[7] Aldridge's example spurred John Vandermere in the next issue of the *Chronicle* to announce that he too had 'no other emoluments' for his summer's playing than the profits from his Cork and Limerick benefits.[8] Yet he was preparing at his own expense a new pantomime entitled *Harlequin Restored; or, A Trip to Killarney*, and was himself painting the scenes, which included 'some views near Cork and several of the Lake of Killarney'.

[1] HC, 8 Sept. 1774, 21 Sept. 1775.
[2] Ibid., 11 July 1774.
[3] Ibid., 11–25 July 1774.
[4] *The Private Correspondence of David Garrick*, i. 644.
[5] Ibid., i. 648.
[6] HC, 1 Dec. 1774.
[7] Ibid., 7 Sept. 1775.
[8] Ibid., 11 Sept. 1775.

The most elaborate of the season's benefits took place on Saturday, 16 September, in support of the Fund for Completing the Linen Hall, a brick-and-stone structure, considerably larger than the Theatre Royal, located west of the North Mall and built around a large open court. The Masonic Order with its strong mercantile interests felt a peculiar obligation to sponsor this new trading centre of a rapidly expanding industry in County Cork. For apparently the first time since Brother Heaphy had assumed his managership the local lodges conducted 'a grand Procession to the Theatre, attended by the Masters, Wardens, and Officers in their proper Cloathing and Jewells', and sat as a body in 'an Amphitheatre raised on the Stage'.[1] Farquhar's *The Recruiting Officer* and Murphy's *The Old Maid*, with Masons' songs between the acts, afforded the sponsors four hours of laughter over the antics of Irish character.

The wife of a Mason served as the theme for a unique Cork production in the succeeding year. On 14 October 1776, *The Clock Case; or, The Freemason's Wife's Curiosity*, a farce by an anonymous local author, had both its *première* and also its demise.[2] Richard Sheridan's farce, *St. Patrick's Day*, experienced a happier reception on its first Irish staging, 26 August.[3] The colourful pageantry appealed to the incipient nationalism of the moment. A long and motley procession of 'Hibernians', including 'Irish Kings, Milesians, Druids, Bards, Dermod Roderick O'Connor, Bryan Borro, Sitric O'Neal, Strongbow Earl of Pembroke', opened the performance, and a musical number 'Carolan the Irish Bard' by 'the full grand chorus of all the Characters' concluded it. Such patriotic extravagances did not diminish, however, Cork's esteem for the dignified acting of Richard Sheridan's father, Thomas, during that same summer. On this second and final visit to the south of Ireland the tragedian repeated his previous repertoire of Brutus, Cato, Hamlet, Lear, Macbeth, Richard III,[4] and then made his last appearance at Cork as the Earl of Essex for his benefit on Monday, 7 October.[5]

[1] Ibid., 14 Sept. 1775.

[2] Ibid., 7 Oct. 1776.

[3] Ibid., 19 Aug. 1776.

[4] Brutus, 4 Oct.; Cato, 22 July, 1 Oct.; Hamlet, 17 July, 25 Sept.; Lear, 2 Aug.; Macbeth, 19 Aug.; Richard III, 26 July.

[5] HC, 3 Oct. 1776, advertised 'The House to be illuminated with wax'.

For the 1777 season, Heaphy somewhat enlarged his 'commonwealth' company. Consequently, though the total profits from the Cork–Limerick tour rose to £3,705,[1] the summer incomes of the individual sharers did not increase. For instance, Thomas Wilks rejoined the troupe, after a four-year absence. Quite according to character, with his hairdresser as attendant, he drove 'a showy charger' in a gig down from Dublin and reached Cork via Kilkenny in four days.[2] Playing his parts of fop or rake steadily during the next three months, he ended with earnings of about £100,[3] a drop of at least fifteen per cent. from the income of his previous trip.

Unlike Wilks, Mrs. Ann Dancer Barry, an old favourite returning from a decade in London, performed under a guest contract at a stated fee per night. The enthusiastic press reaction to her opening performance as Belvidera in *Venice Preserved* on Friday, 25 July, demonstrated that she could still charm Cork. According to the *Chronicle* 'no play in the Cork Theatre for many years past has been so capitally acted, or more justly applauded'.[4] She proceeded to do a different role for six successive nights, Sunday excepted, before admiring audiences. At her benefit and last appearance a cry went up for more Barry performances.[5] A company spokesman stepped on stage to explain that her engagement could not be extended since she had already sent off her wardrobe. Then a gentleman in the boxes shouted: 'Well, have we no silk-weavers or mantua-makers in Cork?' This bit of waggery met with plaudits from the house but effected no extension of the actress's visit. She left the city, handsomely rewarded by some £300 for her week of exhibitions.[6]

In the wake of the glamorous Mrs. Barry the mediocre Dublin composer Michael Arne and his wife attempted for the first time in Cork a series of operatic productions, beginning on 6 August with Garrick's faded libretto of *Cymon* for which Arne had done the music.[7] Shortly thereafter the Theatre Royal closed for a week while the company participated in the Limerick Jubilee programme. This interruption evidently cooled for good whatever enthusiasm Cork might have developed for the Arne entertainments. On the first of September

[1] Snagg(e), p. 102. [2] Ibid., pp. 99–100. [3] Ibid., p. 102.
[4] HC, 28 July 1777. [5] O'Keeffe, i. 230. [6] Snagg(e), p. 102.
[7] HC, 4 Aug. 1777.

the composer publicly admitted 'his late disappointment at the Theatre, the receipts having fallen considerably short of the expenses charged for the House'.[1]

The unhappy experience of the Arnes pointed to the desirability of more robust amusement at the coming benefits. William Henry Moss offered on 13 October equestrian spectacles such as had not hitherto been shown in the theatres of the Irish county towns.[2] At the close of the performance of *The Miser*, Moss, in his role as the duped father, mounted an ass and rode upon the stage to deliver an original epilogue. This humorous antic may be traced back to the identical piece of stage business invented by the London comedian Joseph Haynes nearly a century before. The satiric appearance of Moss and his steed prepared the spectators for the next item on the evening's programme, a novel interlude entitled *Mallow Races*, which featured a sweepstake run for 100 guineas between two ponies ridden by 'young gentlemen'.[2] This kind of stunt apparently did not invade the Dublin stage until the Crow Street Theatre held pony races in the autumn of 1795.

Spectacular novelties of quite another sort highlighted John O'Keeffe's benefit on 9 September.[3] He undertook Garrick's operetta, *A Christmas Tale*, its only production in Ireland outside Dublin, and fitted it out with new 'magic deceptions', such as Negromanta's Burning Castle and 'the Giant in the Fiery Lake 20 feet high'. The complicated stage machinery broke down so often during the performance that O'Keeffe felt impelled to express thanks in the press for the audience's 'particular indulgence to the errors'.[4] The threat of further mechanical mishaps did not restrain him from advertising as the feature of his wife's benefit a month later 'a grand illumination of 500 various coloured lights . . . indisputably the finest and most beautiful ever seen in this Kingdom'.[5] He assured the public that this extraordinary piece of lighting was 'so constructed that no errors of Carpenters or Mechanics can possibly injure the Exhibition'. This bold claim, he added, should not be construed as 'a decoying puff'. O'Keeffe's confidence turned out to be well founded, and therefore the same illuminated stage set

[1] Ibid., 1 Sept. 1777.
[2] Ibid., 6 Oct. 1777.
[3] Ibid., 4 Sept. 1777.
[4] Ibid., 11 Sept. 1777.
[5] Ibid., 6 Oct. 1777.

reappeared as the major attraction at Mrs. Heaphy's benefit on Friday, 17 October, the last night of the season.[1]

By the summer of 1778 a mounting wave of patriotism and wartime prosperity had swept from the Cork stage such vapid sensationalism as animal stunts and magically lighted apparitions. The city with a current population of over 80,000[2] had become the provisioning centre for the British forces engaged in transatlantic conflict. At the same time the rebellion of the American colonies and the resultant threat of a French invasion of Ireland had stirred Cork's inhabitants to a feverish state of loyalty. The streets teemed not only with British seamen and soldiers, but also with the newborn Irish Volunteers, who were busily organizing themselves into a national defence corps. 'The town is all up in arms; every gentleman in the place wears a uniform and is under military rule', the English actor Willoughby Lacy wrote on 24 July to David Garrick.[3] The uniformed elements, feeling their importance to the full, would countenance no raillery from civilians. On Sunday, 12 July, the day before the Theatre Royal opened, one of its minor performers, Hollocombe, got into a broil for making remarks allegedly 'injurious to the Armed Societies'.[4] The latter therefore would not allow him to appear on the George's Street stage. Ten days after the incident he tried to regain his professional freedom by publishing a formal apology for his misconduct, but to no avail.[4] Two weeks later he apologized a second time in the press, entreated 'forgiveness' from the armed forces, and pleaded that they 'permit him to get his bread in the Theatre'.[5] Eventually, of course, Hollocombe secured their permission to go on the boards again. By then his case had served as a stern warning for the theatrical world not to trifle with the military.

The colourful martial activity on every side, coupled with the rising wealth, incited the Cork gentility to more elegance and show than ever. The *habitués* of the South Mall, now often called the Parade, were determined to 'preserve the Terrace as a safe and pleasant Walk'. Repeated newspaper notices requested 'persons of quality' not to ride on the Mall. The

[1] HC, 9 Oct. 1777.
[2] Richard Twiss, *A Tour in Ireland in 1775* (London, 1776), p. 135.
[3] *The Private Correspondence of David Garrick*, ii. 309.
[4] HC, 23 July 1778.
[5] Ibid., 6 Aug. 1778.

printed admonitions to the lower classes used far more severe language: 'Servants and mean persons found offending . . . will be treated as they deserve.'[1] The gallant Mr. Lacy observed with delight the city's 'very dressy' ladies promenading 'in full dress'.[2] Their finery exhibited the smartness that made Cork society answer 'every expectation' this Londoner had formed.

The growing ease and sophistication naturally promoted stronger inclinations towards theatrical diversion. Manager Heaphy, taking advantage of this fresh enthusiasm, put on sale 'a certain number' of untransferable season tickets at a figure not advertised, but no doubt attractive to the steady playgoer. Subscription tickets of this kind, though known to Dublin, had not previously been offered in Cork. The scheme evidently brought in sufficient profit to justify its continuation in subsequent years. The manager also introduced a mild tightening of the regulations as to the booking of seats in the boxes: (1) box accommodations had to be taken 'according to the London and Dublin fashion, first come, first placed'; (2) 'no preference' would be shown to anyone; (3) box places could be obtained each day from ten to two o'clock only; (4) places would be given out strictly 'in order of application'.[3] Heaphy would have done well if he also had set up some fresh rules for governing the feminine headgear worn in the boxes. Gentleman patrons, irritated by 'the enormous breadth as well as height of the Ladies' heads', were publicly threatening to adorn themselves with large 'Damian' or Greek-goddess hats and Grenadier-guardsman caps, to go early and sit on the front rows of the boxes, and thus to retaliate 'for the monopoly of seeing so long engrossed by the Ladies'.[4] At present, the gentlemen complained, it was 'impossible to get even a peep at the performance, except an occasional one, through the bore of some Ladies' curls'.

In anticipation of fervid and overflowing audiences a more impressive array of acting talent journeyed to the Capital of the South than had visited it for many years: Mrs. Sophia Baddeley, Mrs. Priscilla Brereton, Miss Elizabeth Young, and Willoughby Lacy, all from Drury Lane; Mr. and Mrs. Ward from Covent

[1] Ibid., 14 Feb. 1782.

[2] *The Private Correspondence of David Garrick*, ii. 309.

[3] HC, 9 July 1778.

[4] Ibid., 2 Aug. 1779.

Garden; Mr. and Mrs. Richards from Edinburgh; Miss Jane Barsanti and Robert Owenson, recent Dublin luminaries. Their individual engagements were spread with care over an unusually long season from mid-July to early November. Lacy performed during the latter part of July; Miss Young, 24 July to 24 August; Mrs. Baddeley, 17 July to 31 August; Miss Barsanti, 28 August to 2 November; Mrs. Brereton, mid-July to early September.[1] The starring visitors attempted a variety of then important roles: Lacy, Lord Townley in *The Provok'd Husband* and Hamlet; Miss Young, the Countess in *The Countess of Salisbury* and Rosamond in *As You Like It*; Mrs. Baddeley, Polly Peachum in *The Beggar's Opera* and Julia in *The Rivals*; Miss Barsanti, Belinda in *All in the Wrong* and Lady Teazle in the first Cork production of *The School for Scandal* on 9 September.

Of all the guest stars, Robert Owenson alone designed his entertainment to encourage the swelling Irishism of the times. Born a M'Owen of County Mayo in 1744, he early acquired a repertory of songs and lore in Irish, as well as an easy mastery of the language. His rich store of native culture, supported by a resonant voice and a remarkably handsome commanding presence—'six feet high in his petticoats'—marked him as a unique figure among the actors in eighteenth-century Ireland.[2] Possessed of a heartfelt but unreasoned national sentiment, quite divorced from politics, he specialized in Irish impersonations. In the higher class of Irish characters Owenson, according to a Dublin observer, 'looked well, but did not exhibit sufficient formal dignity: and in the lowest, his humour was scarcely quaint and original enough: but in what might be called the "middle class of Paddies" no man ever combin'd the look and manners with such felicity'.[3] In this, his first exhibition at Cork, he began with Major O'Flaherty in *The West Indian*, followed with Paddy O'Carrol in *The Register Office* and Captain O'Blunder in *The Brave Irishman*, and then played the musical Irishman in Bickerstaffe's operetta, *The Recruiting Serjeant*, a part which he embellished with Irish songs and an 'Irish Cry'.[4] Next, on 19 October, he acted the Irish apprentice, Jackiden, in the first

[1] HC, 6 July–19 Oct. 1778.

[2] Lady Morgan [Sydney Owenson], *Memoirs: Autobiography, Diaries, and Correspondence* (ed. W. H. Dixon, London, 1862), i. 83.

[3] Sir Jonah Barrington, *Personal Sketches of His Own Times* (London, 1827), ii. 219.

[4] HC, 9 and 23 July, 10 and 27 Aug. 1778.

performance in Ireland of Foote's farce, *The Tailors*.[1] All the participants in this piece wore, as a patriotic gesture, costumes of Irish manufacture. Owenson reserved the more original of his Irish roles, however, until the last days of his Cork sojourn. To raise the curtain at his own benefit on 26 October he came forward as a stroller Phelim O'Flanagan and sang, in Irish, Torlogh O'Carolan's saga of a feast.[2] Later in the evening he transformed himself into a local youth for the presentation of a comical medley 'Larry O'Shaughnessy's Tour through Dublin with His Return to Cork'. On 30 October at the benefit for the House of Industry—an affair of such civic importance that newspaper notices requested 'no Private Parties on the above night'—Owenson displayed his abilities at improvisation in the native Irish vein.[3] As Phelim O'Flanagan once more, he performed a dramatic prelude, written by himself, with the title 'Pleaharca na Rourcough' ('O'Rourke's Revelry'), and afterwards he sang an old tale, 'Drimmhuin Dhuh' ('My Black Beauty'). Thus he strove throughout his first appearance on the Cork stage to adhere to his dream of fostering by means of theatrical representations what he called the 'national mind'.[4]

News of the good business at George's Street in 1778 must have tempted a veteran itinerant actor, John Linegar Owens, in the following spring to challenge the Theatre Royal's long-standing monopoly and its manager's harsh pronouncement that 'no Strollers will be permitted to perform in this city'.[5] Owens, an alcoholic who was constantly losing employment, announced in the *Chronicle* that as 'a comedian from the Theatre Royal, Dublin' he would open 'the New Theatre, erected in the Tuckey-street Assembly Room', with *Venice Preserved* on Monday, 26 April.[6] Successive advertisements of *Venice Preserved* with Owens as Pierre and Mrs. Owens as Belvidera kept postponing the *première*.[7] Then they changed the location to the 'New Theatre, in Henry Street, near the Mayoralty House' on Hammond's Marsh in the north-west sector of the island city.[8]

Finally, 'Proprietor' Owens gave notice that the New Theatre in Henry Street would 'positively' be opened on Friday, 21 May, and that he had 'spared no expense to render it commodious

[1] Ibid., 12 Oct. 1778. [2] Ibid., 19 Oct. 1778. [3] Ibid., 29 Oct. 1778.
[4] Morgan, i. 65. [5] HC, 22 Nov. 1773. [6] Ibid., 22 Apr. 1779.
[7] Ibid., 26 Apr., 3, 6, and 10 May 1779. [8] Ibid., 13 and 17 May 1779.

for the Nobility, Gentry, and the Public in general'.[1] It contained boxes, pit, and one gallery, with seats priced at 3*s*., 2*s*., and 1*s*. respectively—the scale customary for the county towns but lower than the so-called 'Dublin' scale of the Theatre Royal in George's Street. Because of the 'extraordinary demand' for box places at the first performance, part of the pit was 'obliged to be railed in with the boxes'. By this enlargement of the *élite* section Owens was practising a rather common stratagem for stimulating advance ticket sales among the snobbish. No seats in the house, however, were individually numbered and reserved. Ladies who purchased box tickets, therefore, were 'most humbly requested to send Servants early' to hold for a seven-o'clock curtain the particular seats that the ticket holders wished to occupy. Despite arrangements to gratify the fashionably inclined citizens this fifth and newest Cork playhouse closed down after three weeks of production. The last advertised performance occurred on Monday, 14 June, when Mr. and Mrs. Owens, Sr., along with Mr. and Mrs. Owens, Jr., took the four leading parts in Dr. Brown's tragedy of *Barbarossa*.[2] By August the elder Owens concluded his Cork enterprise in debtors' prison.[3]

The fruitless venture in Henry Street had been all but forgotten by the time of the Theatre Royal's opening for the summer season on Monday, 5 July. For the first six weeks the audiences focused their attention upon the still attractive Mrs. Ann Dancer Barry, who now returned with a third husband, Thomas Crawford, a Dublin councillor infatuated with stage life. Mrs. Crawford's appearances as Belvidera, Lady Townley, Rosamond, and Zenobia went off most happily during July and through the strenuous Assize Week of 2–7 August.[4] When, however, she faced the acting of Beatrice in *Much Ado About Nothing* for the manager's benefit on 10 August, she succumbed to her former subterfuge of last-minute indisposition.[5] Mr. Crawford stepped before the curtain to offer apologies, saying that his wife was suffering from the over-exertion of performing

[1] HC, 20 May 1779.

[2] Ibid., 10 June 1779, advertised the performance to be the junior Mrs. Owens's stage début, and 'the House to be lighted with wax'.

[3] Ibid., 19 Aug. 1779.

[4] Ibid., 15, 22, and 26 July 1779.

[5] *The Hibernian Magazine*, Aug. 1779, p. 486.

on three successive nights and could not rehearse the role of Beatrice properly. Furthermore, he asserted, 'it was a notorious truth that *capital* performers were never obliged to play three nights running, not having the constitution to bear it, like the Pack horses of a theatre'. He then proposed that if Heaphy wished to try another benefit, Mrs. Crawford would do 'any part she was perfect in'. Mr. Crawford retired; Mrs. Heaphy came forward to show the audience Mrs. Crawford's contract 'with an endorsement whereby she was bound to play for the manager's benefit'. Mrs. Heaphy then claimed that the prospect of not collecting the usual twenty-guinea fee per night provoked Mrs. Crawford not to keep her contract. 'Overcome by Modesty at this point', Mrs. Heaphy departed amid applause from the house. Mr. Crawford, reappearing, offered to make affidavit that no contract about benefit playing existed; he also denied Mrs. Heaphy's insinuation about the twenty-guinea fee with the indignant comment: 'To any person acquainted with Mrs. Crawford's natural generosity and disinterestedness the accusation must appear futile and exceedingly uncandid.' Humility and the diffidence he entertained of his own abilities, he continued, caused him to withhold further argument and withdraw. The audience in reply murmured a loud discontent but failed to draw the actress from her dressing-room. This useless bickering consumed a valuable half-hour of entertainment, but, as the Cork reporter humorously observed, 'our theatrical folks have resolved to take example by the Bustle of the Times in commencing a War in their own little World'.[1]

In the latter half of the season Robert Owenson together with Mr. and Mrs. Richard Daly replaced Mrs. Crawford as the current attraction. 'Dashing Dick' Daly, a notorious Dublin buck, had recently commenced a stage career and married Jane Barsanti, whose maiden appearance at Cork had gone off very successfully in the preceding year. Daly's local début in no way foreshadowed his turbulent future as actor and manager in Dublin, Cork, and Limerick. The two Dalys formed a lively and handsome pair for polite comedy: Lord and Lady Townley in *The Provok'd Husband*, Wilding and Penelope in *The Gamesters*, Beverley and Belinda in *All in the Wrong*, Charles Surface and Lady Teazle in *The School for Scandal*.[2] Owenson, on the other

[1] Ibid. [2] HC, 30 Aug.–16 Sept. 1779.

hand, indulged not at all in genteel humour, but, as in the past, concentrated on broad and sentimentally patriotic pieces of comedy. For his benefit on 21 September he assumed his favourite character of a country player, Phelim Oguffnocarrolo Carney MacFrame, and revived his prelude in Irish, 'Pleaharca na Rourcough'.[1] Then he presented an original sketch entitled 'Irish Manufacture; or Darby Hoolughan's Description of Donnybrook Fair'; recited his medley, 'Larry O'Shaughnessy's Tour through Dublin with His Return to Cork'; and, between the acts of *The West Indian*, sang a love lyric in Irish, 'Sceala ni Counnolhan', as well as a new song in honour of the Cork armed societies, 'A Fig for the French and the Spanish; or, the Cork Legions Forever'.

The tensions of war and possible invasion continued in 1780 to inspire at the Theatre Royal occasional entertainment with strongly Irish coloration. John O'Keeffe composed for his wife's benefit on 23 August a revised *Tony Lumpkin's Frolics through Cork*, describing 'public edifices, streets, a tavern dinner, a dyke-house breakfast, . . . a masquerade, a fashionable drum, . . . Tony and Bet Bouncer at the Play'—a dramatic panorama of the goings-on in the southern metropolis.[2] The bill on Mrs. O'Keeffe's night also included a new Irish farce, *The Reprisals*, with an up-to-date documentary setting, namely, 'an exact representation of the ship Count D'Artois as boarded by H.M.S. Bienfaisant off Cork Harbour on the 13th instant'. A similar piece of wartime humour, *The French Flogged; or, British Sailors in America*, adapted to the moment by the Cork writer Frederick Pilon, had its *première* on 24 October, the last performance of the season.[3] Above all, Robert Owenson's offerings reflected a persistent appeal to racial pride. His benefit on 11 October consisted of 'plain wholesome Irish Fare', beginning with a medley of Irish 'lilts' and a dramatic recitation, 'The Humours of St. Patrick's Day, or Manus McWhackum's Journey to Cork and His Ramble to Mardyke Field to See the Review'. Later, as *entr'acte* repertoire, he sang 'Dublin Cries', 'Planxty Connor', and, in Irish, 'Drimmhuin Dhuh' ('My Black Beauty'). This evening's programme contained, Owenson

[1] HC, 16 Sept. 1779.
[2] Ibid., 17 Aug. 1780.
[3] Ibid., 16 Oct. 1780.

advertised, 'the three dishes . . . ever found at an Irish Entertainment, namely: mirth, good-humour, and a *keath meleh faltha* [i.e. a hundred thousand welcomes]'.[1]

The spirit of revolt and change now so deeply permeated affairs in Ireland that it could not long be restrained in the theatrical domain. As soon as the 1780 season at Cork closed, Mr. and Mrs. Daly withdrew from the Crow Street company in Dublin to set up at the Smock Alley playhouse a rival organization of equal merit. By the next summer the energetic new manager had negotiated an alliance with the ageing proprietor of the Cork and Limerick theatres, Tottenham Heaphy. The latter on 2 August 1781 informed the Cork public that he had entered into 'a coalition with Mr. and Mrs. Daly, who are Proprietors of the Dublin Theatre', and that henceforth the Cork productions would be carried on 'by the principal performers of that Theatre, and with the same decorations'.[2]

The inauguration of the joint management at George's Street attracted little public attention amid the general excitement of the times. After the Theatre Royal's opening week, 4–9 August, a *Chronicle* correspondent 'A. B.' deplored the thin audiences in the face of excellent performances.[3] Though the season never aroused the degree of interest that attached to its immediate predecessors, it did offer at intervals some unusual features. On 30 August West Digges, a notable actor, arrived at Cork direct from London to reside permanently in his native land;[4] soon he was appearing in such leading roles as Hamlet, Old Norval in *Douglas*, Cardinal Wolsey in *Henry VIII*, and Sir John Restless in Murphy's comedy of *All in the Wrong*.[5] On 12 October Owenson, as usual at his benefit, presented two new musical skits of patriotic content, 'Teague's Ramble to Blarney to See the Review' and 'The Dungarvan Aboard; Or, M'Grory's Invitation to Go Privateering', along with his perennial sketch in Irish, 'Pleaharca na Rourcough'.[6] Two days earlier Alexander Pope, a nineteen-year-old Cork artist, made an anonymous stage début as the dusky hero of *Oroonoko*.[6] He had to reveal his identity in order to enjoy a benefit on 24 October when he played Charles Surface in *The School for Scandal*.[1] Pope's

[1] Ibid., 9 Oct. 1780.
[2] Ibid., 2 Aug. 1781.
[3] Ibid., 13 Aug. 1781.
[4] Ibid., 30 Aug. 1781.
[5] Ibid., 10 and 20 Sept., 4 Oct. 1781.
[6] Ibid., 8 Oct. 1781.

début had followed the season's most festive night, 8 October, in support of the Charity Fund of Munster for Distressed Masons, Widows, and Orphans.[2] The Cork lodges, costumed in 'their proper Jewels', went through their long-established routine of marching to the playhouse and sitting on the stage in a body. This occasion proved to be Heaphy's farewell hospitality to his Masonic brothers. They had always given him the warmest support in the dozen years of his management at Cork and Limerick.

After the finish of the 1781 season in these two cities Daly pressed to take over completely Heaphy's managerial powers. On 27 December the *Freeman's Journal* in Dublin reported that Daly had assumed sole authority over the Cork Theatre Royal, but no public notice of that fact appeared in Cork until 15 July 1782. On this date Heaphy announced that 'the precarious state of his health' caused him to lease his two theatres to Daly for 'a certain number of years',[3] actually ten years as subsequent events disclosed. The elder manager struck a shrewd bargain with his junior. Both apparently kept the terms from public knowledge till the nineties.[4] First, Heaphy received a rental of £210 per year for the two playhouses. Secondly, he retained the right to use, during the six winter months of each year, both the Cork and Limerick buildings, including 'the scenery on the premises'. Thirdly, Daly had to honour all outstanding silver admission tickets to the aforementioned theatres. On 22 July the new manager issued an extravagant puff about his redecoration of the Cork Theatre Royal 'in the most elegant manner', including 'the new plan of stage illumination' now employed at Drury Lane, Covent Garden, and Smock Alley, Dublin.[5] This plan contained two innovations: (1) across the entire width of the stage apron on the audience side of the footlights, a solid tin shade high enough to shield the pit spectators from the glare; (2) hidden behind the proscenium in the sidewings, a set of wing-lights to brighten the upper stage. In addition, Daly advertised, he had, 'at a very great expence, entered into engagements with a number of the most capital

[1] HC, 22 Oct. 1781. [2] Ibid., 20 Sept. 1781. [3] Ibid., 15 July 1782.

[4] Memorandum enclosed in a letter of 6 Aug. 1797 from Daly to E. Cooke, and the reply of 8 Aug. 1797 from F. E. Jones to E. Cooke, in the case of *Daly* v. *F. E. Jones*. See note 2, p. 80.

[5] HC, 22 July 1782.

Performers . . . , likewise, with considerable difficulty, procured Copies of all the new Pieces, printed and in manuscript, lately produced at the London theatres, which he means to bring regularly forward'.[1]

The first of Daly's fifteen seasons as manager at George's Street opened on 29 July 1782 with a performance of *Hamlet* distinguished by the Cork *premières* of two London stars, John Philip Kemble in the title role and Mary Anne Hitchcock as Ophelia.[1] Kemble, twenty-five-year-old brother to Mrs. Sarah Kemble Siddons, displayed for so young an actor a remarkable repertoire of twenty different parts, and during the eight-week season paired with several leading ladies. Mrs. Jane Barsanti Daly, the manager's wife, acted Millamant to his Mirabel in *The Way of the World*.[2] Miss Elizabeth Young, back from Covent Garden for a second triumphal visit, played Hermione to Kemble's Orestes in *The Distrest Mother* and the Countess to his Count of Narbonne in Jephson's tragedy of that title.[3] Her strenuous schedule of eleven nights, plus a benefit, within three weeks enabled her to pocket the magnificent sum of £600 by 20 August when she departed for London.[4] Mrs. Charlotte Melmoth, from Smock Alley on her first tour to the south, performed Cleopatra to Kemble's Antony, and Lady Allworth to his Sir Giles Overreach in the famous Jacobean comedy of *A New Way to Pay Old Debts*, advertised as previously unacted at Cork.[5]

Daly's company also included another starring actress and vocalist, Anna Maria Phillips of Drury Lane, who at the age of nineteen was making her maiden trip to Ireland. Though Kemble never supported her on stage, he gave her manly support backstage one evening after she had exhibited her charms as the singing heroine of *Love in a Village*.[6] Several ecstatic officers from a Cork regiment decided to seek the honour of escorting Miss Phillips to her lodgings. 'They were rather more elevated

[1] Ibid.
[2] Ibid., 30 Sept. 1782.
[3] Ibid., 1 and 8 Aug. 1782.
[4] HJ, 23 Aug. 1782.
[5] HC, 5 Aug. and 7 Oct. 1782.
[6] M. J. Young, *Memoirs of Mrs. Crouch* [A. M. Phillips] (London, 1806), i. 186–9, mistakenly dated the episode in the summer of 1783 because Kemble did not visit the south of Ireland at that time. Michael Kelly, *Reminiscences* (London, 1826), ii. 148–50, erroneously located the incident at Limerick in 1783; Bernard, i. 154–6, placed it at Limerick in 1782.

than, perhaps, they might have been *before* dinner', she coyly observed in retrospect. They began a loud dispute among themselves outside her dressing-room. The young actress, in fright locked the door and asked them to leave, but she met only with refusals. Meanwhile word of her besieged situation reached Kemble. Sword in hand, he strode to her door and offered protection if she would come out. As she started to emerge, she saw the unruly admirers and hesitated. Kemble, however, took her by the hand, saying with theatrical dignity, 'Be under no apprehension, I am resolved to protect you from interruption'. One officer then moved to slash at Kemble, but an alert dresser, Judy Cameron, grabbed the officer's arm and snatched his sword. Kemble, turning towards Judy, quipped 'Well done, Euphrasia', for his actor's imagination at once had caught the likeness to the Grecian Daughter Euphrasia's interception of Dionysus' dagger when he lunged to stab her. The repulse of the officer's attack calmed the violent spirit of his companions, so that Kemble could conduct Miss Phillips out of the building without further disturbance. His gallant courtesy won from her a lifelong admiration.

John Kemble's younger brother, Stephen, also joined Daly's company for the summer's tour. On 2 August he made his Irish début by acting Pyrrhus in *The Distrest Mother.*[1] The part of Wellborn in *A New Way to Pay Old Debts* on 10 October[2] marked his most important assignment during this, the sole visit that he ever paid to Cork.

Another young player whom Daly recruited from England, John Bernard, was, like Stephen Kemble, undertaking his first stage appearance in Ireland. Bernard had a disturbing encounter with Daly on the evening of Tuesday, 10 September, when the manager was to do Millamour and Bernard to personate Dashwould in Arthur Murphy's comedy, *Know Your Own Mind.*[3] Daly regularly wore a pink suit for his stylishly genteel roles. In this suit, therefore, he arrayed himself as Millamour, all curled, powdered, and ruffled to the very height of fashion. Bernard, who owned a suit of the same cut and colour, forgot about the manager's favourite costume and put on his own pink outfit. The coincidence in dress of course startled and then irritated the two actors when they came together in the green-room before the

[1] HC, 1 Aug. 1782. [2] Ibid., 7 Oct. 1782. [3] Ibid., 9 Sept. 1782.

evening's performance.[1] They 'strutted by each other like a couple of cocks of the same feather'. Daly, always overbearing, rudely directed the hireling to change his clothes, but the latter refused because of the imminent rise of the curtain and walked out in anger. A few minutes later the manager sent his wife running up to Bernard's dressing-room with a coat from Daly's wardrobe. In the face of Mrs. Daly's gracious pleading Bernard relented, donned the new garment, 'settled his cravat', and descended for the opening cue. The sudden wrath between these two stage cocks soon faded to a coolness that never entirely vanished.

Bernard enjoyed other more amusing encounters in connexion with this 1782 tour, his only one to Cork. When the theatrical season closed on Monday, 14 October,[2] a half-dozen of the Theatre Royal troupe, including Mrs. Taplin, Bernard, and Kennedy the treasurer, formed a party to travel to Dublin.[3] At daybreak on the 15th they departed from Cork with their baggage heaped in a 'two-horse car' over and around Kennedy's trunk containing the receipts of the last night at George's Street. The tall, well-formed Mrs. Taplin, attired in a scarlet pelisse with fur trim and a fur cap with gold band, sat at the front of the car with all the dignity which she had displayed as the Queen in *Hamlet* on 27 September. The gentlemen took turns on the seat beside her, each one riding so many miles. On the second day, after the travellers had entered a dark and rocky pass, a dozen uncouth fellows rushed out of the woods with clubs in hand. The party of actors quickly had the wit to commence a pretended quarrel, shouting 'Lay on, Macduff', 'Renounce your claim', &c., and at the same time thrusting swords at one another around the car. Over its side Mrs. Taplin leaned, stretching down her hands, letting loose her hair, and crying out 'Spare him, spare him'. The threatening ruffians, put off by this sudden and violent combat, quietly withdrew from what now seemed a band of kindred rogues.

Meanwhile a man on horseback approached and asked what the uproar was all about. The waggish Robert Bowles pointed to the imposing fur-cloaked figure of Mrs. Taplin with an air of mystery, saying that she was the notorious Empress of Russia who had voyaged to Ireland to lead a rebellion. Her escort, he

[1] Bernard, i. 142–3. [2] HC, 10 Oct. 1782. [3] Bernard, i. 164–8.

added, was an official bodyguard who had taken custody of her at Cork and were conveying her to Dublin Castle. At this astonishing news the horseman dashed off to arouse the inhabitants of the next village. When the theatrical party arrived at the inn, the villagers instantly blocked the windows, doors, and passages to catch a glimpse of 'the Impariel Quane in the red thingumbob', who had meant to free Ireland, and of 'the Russian jontlemen who had cotched her in Cork, and were carrying her to Dublin Castle to be executed'. Fearing that local Irish heroes at any moment might be stirred to rescue the royal lady and beat up her captors, the players informed the landlord of their hoax and asked him to call off the crowd. In spite of the unpleasing denouement a large train of attendants waited on Mr. Daly's company of comedians at their quitting the hamlet. These wayfaring experiences of Bernard illustrate with what a merry swagger the majority of eighteenth-century actors carried on their rough and tedious journeys between the various Irish towns.

Manager Daly, imitating his predecessors Barry and Heaphy, had begun his Cork régime with a flourish of improvement in the company and the bills at the Theatre Royal. Yet Ireland's attainment of legislative independence in the winter of 1782–3 invigorated the theatrical life of the city more than did the new management in George's Street. An unprecedented rash of stage enterprises by amateurs broke out in January and lasted through March. The most ambitious set of ladies and gentlemen fitted up, on the Long Quay (now St. Patrick's Street), an 'elegant temporary' playhouse called the 'Gentlemen's Theatre' and directed by Mr. Doyle, an actor at the Theatre Royal in the summers.[1] This little theatre, lacking boxes, sold all seats at the one genteel price of 3*s*. Its group of performers, apparently in expectation of a larger audience, shifted to the Theatre Royal for the season's final production, *Venice Preserved*, on 31 March.[2] 'Crito' in the *Chronicle* adjudged it 'highly respectable', but dismissed the heroine's performance with this damning apostrophe: 'Pillowed on oblivion be thy head, fair Belvidera, and sleep undisturbed by criticism—or sensibility.'[3]

The increased enthusiasm for theatrical amusement in this year of Ireland's jubilation moved Daly to secure the top

[1] HC, 9 Jan. 1783. [2] Ibid., 27 Mar. 1783. [3] Ibid., 3 Apr. 1783.

attraction of the London stage, Mrs. Siddons, for her initial exhibition outside England. In the original agreement, apparently, she contracted to play in Dublin but nowhere else. Daly, an inveterate promoter, naturally wished to exploit her drawing power outside the capital. Through Joseph Lefanu, a prominent Dublin citizen and friend of Thomas Sheridan, he persuaded the venerable Irish actor, who had experienced gratifying receptions at Cork, to call upon Mrs. Siddons in May at her London residence and urge an extension of her tour as far as Cork. She rebuffed Sheridan at once 'by declaring that no consideration whatsoever should induce her to go to Cork'.[1] Perhaps the recommendation of her brother, J. P. Kemble, whom she joined in June at Smock Alley, may have determined her change of plans. At any rate, after six weeks in Dublin, she travelled down to the Theatre Royal in George's Street for ten performances in company with her leading man at Drury Lane, William Brereton. Opening on Monday, 11 August, in *Isabella*,[2] she played the Grecian Daughter, the Countess of Salisbury, Belvidera twice, Calista in *The Fair Penitent*, Zenobia in *The Mourning Bride*,[3] and closed her exclusively tragic series on Monday, 1 September, with the last of three representations of Jane Shore. During her three-week sojourn one unforeseen experience offstage much pleased her vanity. While staying at Miss Granahan's on the Grand Parade,[4] she sat for her portrait to the popular young local artist and actor, Alexander Pope. He selected, as the appropriate subject, a pose from her Cork *première*. On 29 August she reported with delight that Pope had 'made a small full length of me in Isabella, upon the first entrance of Biron—he has succeeded to admiration'.[5]

Mrs. Siddons found her first Irish visit so enjoyable and remunerative that Daly had little difficulty in arranging for her return in the summer of 1784. After performing at Smock Alley from mid-June to mid-August she fell ill, probably from exhaustion. This 'casual and melancholy event' postponed the opening of the Cork Theatre Royal to Monday, 1 September.[6]

[1] Letter of 1 May 1783 from Sheridan to Lefanu, Lefanu Papers, microfilm 2975, N.L.I.

[2] HC, 7 Aug. 1783.

[3] Belvidera, 13 and 23 Aug.; Calista, 22 Aug.; Countess of Salisbury, 30 Aug.; Grecian Daughter, 29 Aug.; Jane Shore, 15 and 29 Aug.; Zenobia, 27 Aug.

[4] HC, 28 Aug. 1783.

[5] Percy Fitzgerald, *The Kembles* (London, 1871), i. 140.

[6] HC, 30 Aug. 1784.

For the season's first night Mrs. Siddons chose the inexhaustibly satisfying part of Jane Shore, but on her next two evenings she played roles not seen on the 1783 visit, namely, Lady Randolph in *Douglas* and Sigismunda in *Tancred and Sigismunda*.[1] Continued weakness forced an abrupt shortening of her engagement at George's Street. Her third appearance on 10 September marked her permanent farewell to Cork. Thereafter the brilliance of the Theatre Royal season faded. To inject a last bright touch, however, the resourceful Daly suddenly put forward Miss Elizabeth Farren (later the celebrated Countess of Darby), a beautiful and promising actress whom he had just enticed from London for the coming winter in Dublin. On 30 September she made her unheralded Irish début as the sentimental heroine Olivia in Goldsmith's *The Good Natur'd Man*.[2]

Though the Cork manager had no exciting female figures like Mrs. Siddons or Miss Farren to enliven the 1785 season, in their stead he presented two male attractions from London: Mrs. Siddons's well-liked brother, J. P. Kemble, on his third Irish visit; and a new star from Covent Garden, Joseph Holman, aged twenty. The Theatre Royal opened on Tuesday, 23 August, with Kemble as Zanga in *The Revenge*.[3] For the other three nights of his limited engagement he impersonated Beverly of *The Gamester*, the Count of Narbonne, and Sir Giles Overreach, in that order.[4] Holman followed Kemble, also for four nights only. Still a Shakespearian novice but possessed of a 'naturally majestic bearing',[5] he displayed an already solid and versatile talent in his acting of Hamlet, Richard III, Benedict, and Romeo successively.[6] His departure on or about 9 September left the remaining three weeks of starless performances an anti-climax, one that was all the more disturbing because Daly and his wife, an entertaining comic pair, did not put in a stage appearance during the entire season.

The Theatre Royal subscribers now perceived that their manager had grown more concerned with the promotion of his summer seasons at Dublin than at Cork, and that he was prolonging the one in the capital and abbreviating the tour in the south of Ireland. In 1785 Cork had enjoyed only five weeks of

[1] HC, 2 and 9 Sept. 1784.
[2] Ibid., 23 Sept. 1784.
[3] Ibid., 22 Aug. 1785.
[4] Ibid., 25 and 29 Aug. 1785.
[5] *The Monthly Mirror*, v (1798), 131.
[6] 3, 6, 7, and 8 Sept. 1785.

entertainment. Yet this reduction was occurring at a time when the local public were showing a disposition for more rather than less theatrical amusement. Therefore, in the early autumn, the restive subscribers evidently made representations to Heaphy as well as Daly that the Theatre Royal should offer a winter season in accordance with the intention stated in the original leasing agreement between the two men. At a meeting on 2 November the subscribers received assurances from Heaphy that there would be during each year two periods of performance, a winter and a summer one; that the 'best' performers would be engaged; and that the playhouse would be kept at all times 'in the compleatest condition'.[1] These assurances resulted only in some evenings of solo entertainment by the itinerant comedian Lee Lewes during March and April 1786.[2] Then, on 1 May, Daly and Heaphy, as if embarking on a fresh policy, reiterated with sly ambiguity their original understanding that, since the Cork citizens wished winter as well as summer performances, Daly would leave to Heaphy's direction the winter season 'as often as a proper company can be engaged for that purpose'.[3] The subscribers could do nothing other than accept such an unexceptionable pronouncement.

The winter's agitation over the scheduling of stage entertainment perhaps moved Daly to lengthen Cork's season in 1786 despite the extension of his theatrical responsibilities to Waterford. For the first time he divided his summer forces into two divisions: the first and more talented he led in person to Waterford; the second he consigned to the care of his assistant, William Dawson, and arranged for it to open the Theatre Royal in George's Street on 1 August.[4] Thus the Cork public had the opportunity to attend two weeks of moderately good theatricals before Daly's first division arrived from Waterford and Limerick. This latter contingent included two dashing comedian-vocalists who were revisiting the city after a considerable lapse of time, Charles Bannister from Drury Lane and John Henry ('Jack') Johnston from Covent Garden.[5] A seventeen-year-old *tragédienne*, Anne Brunton, also from Covent Garden, surpassed

[1] HC, 3 Nov. 1785.

[2] Ibid., 2 and 30 Mar., 6 Apr. 1786.

[3] Ibid., 1 May 1786.

[4] Ibid., 31 July 1786.

[5] Bannister opened as Macheath in *The Beggar's Opera* on 17 Aug.; Johnston as Lubin in *The Quaker* on 18 Aug.

the appeal of both male visitors through the magic of her remarkably sweet voice and expressive eyes. As one more of the shrewd Daly's numerous 'discoveries', Miss Brunton made her Irish début on Monday, 14 August, in the role of Euphrasia, the Grecian Daughter.[1] Subsequently she impersonated noted stage heroines such as Monimia in *The Orphan*, Hermione in *The Distrest Mother*, and Horatia in *The Roman Father*.[2]

Another Covent Garden actress, Mrs. Frances Abington, thirty years older than Miss Brunton but, according to the Cork press, still 'an enchanting woman', reappeared after almost two decades to exhibit her skill in rendering 'the manners of high or polite life'.[3] On 28 October she brought her special engagement of eight nights to a brilliant climax as Millamant in *The Way of the World*, her last performance ever in Cork.[4] Two nights before she had shown her loyalty to an old colleague, West Digges, by playing in a special benefit to defray the costs of his prolonged illness.[5] On 11 November he died at the age of sixty-two in his Coal Quay lodgings[6] and was buried the following day near the north wall of St. Finbarr's churchyard.[7]

Covent Garden supplied one further attraction in the acrobatic actor Chalmers. He as Harlequin and George Dawson of Dublin as Clown constituted a pantomime team more exciting than Cork had ever before watched. They started with Messink's *The Island of Saints; or, The Institution of the Shamrock*, said to have cost Daly £1,000 for its original preparation at Dublin, and never undertaken in London.[8] Then they produced Chalmers's piece, *The Triumph of Mirth*, which presented an extraordinary variety of stage effects: 'a Fall of Snow', 'the Skeleton of a Gladiator', and 'a Lion's Leap over twelve Men's Heads'.[9] Dawson, who claimed that he would 'receive his entire summer emolument from his benefit', went to the expense of working up for the occasion a new pantomime, *Harlequin Foundling*.[10] In its climactic escapade Dawson flew from the very rear of the stage through the proscenium to the top of the gallery and then back to his starting-point. This spectacular flight was

[1] HC, 10 Aug. 1786.
[2] Ibid., 14–24 Aug. 1786.
[3] Ibid., 12 Oct. 1786.
[4] Ibid., 23 Oct. 1786.
[5] Ibid., 19 Oct. 1786. A copy of the playbill for this performance is in the Shaw Collection, Harvard University Library.
[6] HC, 13 Nov. 1786.
[7] *Notes and Queries*, Oct. 1886, p. 356.
[8] HC, 31 Aug. 1786.
[9] Ibid., 2 Oct. 1786.
[10] Ibid., 30 Oct. 1786.

repeated on 6 November to end the final performance in the Theatre Royal's unusually long schedule of twelve weeks.[1]

The season of 1787 lasted only half as long and contained few novelties. Michael Kelly, the Dublin singer who had just returned from a triumphal sojourn in Europe and London, exhibited his vocal powers in Cork for the first time on 30 July.[2] Mrs. Ann Crouch, the former Miss Phillips, accompanied him in a week of musical plays such as *The Beggar's Opera*, and *Lionel and Clarissa*.[3] The most publicized night of the summer, Thursday, 13 September, marked the benefit for a new local charity, the Cork Dispensary and Humane Society, dedicated to 'the Recovery of Persons apparently Drowned'.[4] Mr. and Mrs. Daly played Sir Charles Racket and his lady in *Three Weeks after Marriage*, a bright contrast to the heavy pathos of *Venice Preserved*, which had preceded with Joseph Holman and Mrs. Achmet in the leading parts. This charity performance Mr. Alexander Fitton 'humanely' provided with superior and unprecedented illumination by means of his 'patent reflecting lamps'.[5] The one-night installation of these improved oil lamps with cylindrical wicks and glass chimneys may have had some influence in persuading Daly to equip with the same or a similar type of patent lamp his Crow Street Theatre when he was refurbishing its interior during the winter of 1787–8. In September 1789 Mr. Fitton once again 'humanely' installed his patent lamps to illuminate a charity night,[5] but his repeated benefaction did not induce Daly to make the improved type of lighting permanent in the Cork playhouse.

Holman continued to be the most versatile male performer at George's Street, but in 1788 he acted with a new group of leading ladies, none of whom had ever before set foot on the Cork stage. His pupil and mistress, Maria Hughes, aged twenty-six, played Angelica to his Valentine in *Love for Love* and Charlotte Rusport to his Belcour in *The West Indian*.[6] Mrs. Harriet Esten, who at the age of twenty had recently made her Irish *première*, paired with Holman in *Macbeth* and *Much Ado About Nothing*.[7] The local public, however, looked upon Miss Harriet Westropp Atkins,

[1] Ibid., 2 Nov. 1786.
[2] Ibid., 26 July 1787.
[3] Ibid., 30 July–6 Aug. 1787.
[4] Ibid., 3 Sept. 1787.
[5] Ibid., 17 Sept. 1789.
[6] Ibid., 25 Aug. and 11 Sept. 1788.
[7] Ibid., 1 and 8 Sept. 1788.

a Munster belle, as his most captivating partner. Her professional début on Friday, 22 August, as Juliet, with Holman as Romeo, occasioned wide notice.[1] The *Leinster Journal* of Kilkenny, attributing her action to 'the theatric mania at present', expressed surprise that 'a lady of her beauty, connections, and situation in life, could condescend to risque the lash of the critic, or the possibility of the cannonade of the apple, or the hiss of the gallery'.[2] The *Journal*, however, had no cause for further concern, because the young lady gained immediate approbation in a succession of *ingénue* roles: Indiana in *The Conscious Lovers*, Maria in *The School for Scandal*, and Louisa in *The West Indian* on 15 September, the final night of the six-week season.[3]

Nevertheless Miss Atkins did not go to Dublin with Daly's company, but remained in Cork to become the stage heroine whom the gentlemen players had sorely needed to ensure the complete success of their productions. The local dramatic group at this time included Joseph D. Herbert as the principal male performer, and James Knowles (1759–1840), an elocutionist of some repute and the father of James Sheridan Knowles the actor and playwright.[4] Sir Henry Hayes, one of the supporting actors, used to entertain his fellow thespians with splendid dinners at his country villa. The new round of amateur theatricals started up at the Theatre Royal on 28 November and persisted until 1 June 1789.[5] Miss Atkins and Herbert took the leading parts in *The Orphan*, *The Gamester*, *Oroonoko*, and *Catherine and Petruchio*, among others. Miss Atkins's subsequent career never fulfilled the fine promise of her maiden year. She did not rejoin Daly's company at Cork in the summer of 1789, but she did perform with it once more two years afterwards. Whether by choice or by reason of insufficient talent she never appeared on the Dublin stage.

The amateur players had to give over the Theatre Royal for the month of March 1789 to the first 'winter' season of professional amusement ever offered there. The Sadler's Wells acrobats and dancers under the direction of 'the Little Devil'

[1] HC, 21 Aug. 1788.
[2] LJ, 23 Aug. 1788.
[3] HC, 1, 8, and 11 Sept. 1788.
[4] J. D. Herbert, *Irish Varieties* (London, 1836), pp. 175–6.
[5] HC, 17 and 27 Nov. 1788, 15 Jan., 23 Feb., 5 Mar., 6 Apr., 18 and 25 May 1789; CEP, 13 Apr. 1789.

gave exhibitions of pantomime, tumbling, and tight-rope walking, at country prices: 3*s*. in the boxes, 2*s*. in the pit, and 1*s*. in the gallery.[1] The bill of fare evidently pleased a considerable number of Cork citizens, because Daly arranged for the same troupe to reappear at George's Street in February 1790, when it featured a spectacular depiction of the recent storming of the Bastille.[2]

The violent commencement of the French Revolution had been first celebrated at the Cork Theatre Royal only two months after its occurrence by an entertainment, *The Triumph of Liberty; or, The Destruction of the Bastille*, given in London on 8 August 1789, and then secured post-haste for an Irish *première* at George's Street.[3] Though displaying up-to-date views of Paris and of the Bastille with its famous drawbridge, the piece apparently failed to rouse loud applause, for Daly never produced it at Dublin.

The brief and rather dull 1789 season presented one further, mildly notable, feature in the Cork début of James Middleton [Magan], a Dublin-born actor trained at Covent Garden. Though less experienced, he capably filled Holman's former position in Daly's summer casting and paired with Mrs. Esten in *Romeo and Juliet*, *Othello*, and *Venice Preserved*.[4] He returned to George's Street in September 1790 to support another Daly 'discovery', Maria Campion, whose prowess at the age of thirteen had astonished Dublin audiences during the past spring. At her first Cork appearance on 6 September she and Middleton took the leads in *Venice Preserved*, then acted in *The Orphan* and *Othello*, and concluded the local season with *Oroonoko* on 15 September.[5]

Except for the herculean performance of the teen-aged actress, the season of 1790 proved as ordinary as the preceding one. Manager Daly, preoccupied with the heavy attacks of journalists and political critics in the capital, was not attending too assiduously to the welfare of his playhouses elsewhere. Even so he dared an innovation by holding a benefit for 'Improving and Decorating the Cork Theatre Royal', and ventured to

1 HC, 26 Feb.–30 Mar. 1789.
2 CEP, 8 Feb. 1790.
3 HC, 14 Sept. 1789, advertised this spectacular entertainment for 16 Sept.
4 Ibid., 27 and 31 Aug., 10 and 14 Sept. 1789.
5 Ibid., 2, 9, and 13 Sept. 1790.

request the ladies and gentlemen of Cork to keep the night of Saturday, 4 September, free of private parties, so that the benefit might suffer no social competition.[1]

In view of this public solicitation some redecorating of the Theatre Royal might well have been expected, but no such activity was advertised in the ensuing winter or spring. In April 1791, however, the Theatre Royal's predecessor, located on the corner of George's and Prince's Streets, was reopened by Sir Vere Hunt's troupe from Limerick under the management of William Henry Moss.[2] One of the senior actors, Ezra Wells, later stopped playing after a dispute with Moss. Several young men and women were added from time to time to maintain the group's size at ten men and five women, of whom the manager, Mr. Brennan, and Mrs. Castelli were the leading performers. On Tuesday, 26 April, the curtain rose again after thirty-two years at the so-called 'New Theatre Royal, Prince's Street',[3] a deliberately misleading title since no official patent had been connected with the building since 1759. Because of Assize Week, 2–7 May, plays were acted almost every night for the first two weeks of the season. The receipts from eleven performances during this period totalled £203, an average of more than £18 per night as compared with £8 at Limerick around the time of the assizes there. To be sure, the Prince's Street playhouse was slightly larger than the one in Cornwallis Street, but essentially the contrast in receipts reflected the far stronger support of theatricals by all classes in Cork.

The surviving accounts of the company treasurer for this 1791 season at Prince's Street disclose housekeeping details of considerable interest. After three decades of disuse the playhouse needed new globes for the lamps at all three of its entrances—the stage door, the gallery door, and that to the pit and boxes. The lamplighter charged 1*s.* for installation and 9*s.* a week for watching over the lamps. Since the theatre's metal admission tickets had long since been lost, a new supply of 350—150 for the boxes, 100 for the pit, and 100 for the gallery—had to be bought at an expenditure of 7*s.* The three ticket collectors for the boxes,

[1] HC, 2 Sept. 1790. General Burgoyne's comic opera *The Lord of the Manor* and Milton's *Comus* composed the bill.

[2] Hunt MSS.: Account Books, 1790–1; Journal, 1781–1807.

[3] HC, 26 May 1791.

the pit, and the gallery, respectively, were furnished with bags made for 6*d.* apiece by the stage seamstress out of linen edged with cloth tape. The pit seats required a fresh covering of green baize; the material cost £2. 17*s.* 6*d.* The concession for women selling fruit in the theatre was assigned at a fee of 1*s.* an evening. The pantomime *The Death of Captain Cook,* which apparently proved as popular in Cork as in Ennis and Limerick, involved some amusing expenses: 4*s.* for Captain Cook's coffin, and £1. 9*s.* 6*d.* for eighteen private soldiers, one drummer, and two corporals to rehearse and then to perform one night. When 'no soldiers could be had', the band received an additional 7*s.* for taking their places.

Sir Vere Hunt's corps gave the last performance of its Cork season during the week of 13–18 June.[1] By this time Manager Moss, according to Sir Vere, had become rebellious.[2] No doubt wearied by the irritations of theatrical proprietorship, the baronet decided to discontinue his stage activities at once and to turn over all responsibility for the troupe's future to Ezra Wells. Reorganized probably as a 'commonwealth' and independent group of strollers, it moved under Wells's leadership to Youghall in early July.

Though Daly kept silence in respect to any renovation of the Theatre Royal for the summer season of 1791, he did not hesitate to proclaim that 'he had launched out into extraordinary and uncommon expenses in selecting the most capital Company in the British Dominions'.[3] His most capital performers, however, excelled in operas and other musical drama. He engaged from Covent Garden two of its foremost singers, Charles Incledon and Mrs. James Billington, 'the first vocal actress of the age, whose astonishing powers are the admiration of Europe'.[3] Two young vocalists with a considerable name in Dublin, Joe Kelly and Miss George, supported the stars from England. Mrs. Billington commanded £50 per night,[3] the top stage fee in eighteenth-century Ireland; Incledon received only £15 nightly if he got paid as in 1795.[4] These two eminent voices joined in eight musical performances, commencing with *Love*

[1] The last advertisement appeared in CEP, 13 June.
[2] Hunt MSS.: Account Books, 1790–1; Journal, 1781–1807.
[3] HC, 8 Aug. 1791.
[4] Mathews, i. 151.

in a Village as the season's *première* on 12 August and ending with *Orpheus and Eurydice* in its first Cork rendition on 26 August.[1] On every one of the eight evenings the Theatre Royal overflowed.[2] Charmed audiences demanded from both principals as many as five to eight repetitions of certain songs. Applause at George's Street during the eighteenth century perhaps never surpassed the ovations at the Billington–Incledon appearances. The overwhelming demand for admission caused the management to break a long-standing custom and suspend the privilege of reserving places in the boxes without advance payment. For 'the Billington nights' the nobility and gentry were 'respectfully requested to take tickets for the number they may have occasion for, as from the continued disappointment the Public have hitherto met with and the heavy loss the Theatre has sustained by Ladies giving up their Boxes on the very Nights of Performance, the Box-keeper cannot be answerable for any Places but those that Tickets are issued for'.[3] Despite the obvious advantages of the prepayment system to both the box customers and the management, the Cork Theatre Royal did not have the fortitude to maintain this temporary innovation.

The tremendous outpouring of admiration at these George's Street operas probably little affected Incledon's stage behaviour. A young actor who some years later saw much of him in Cork and Limerick reported that the famous singer was 'a very good-hearted fellow, as generous as a prince, with sense enough to conduct himself like a gentleman'.[4] Though 'without the advantage of a good education or polite introduction to the world', Incledon possessed a natural humility that never felt 'ashamed to mention his former situation . . . in a strolling company at half a guinea per week'.[4] On the other hand, the continual adulation of the Cork audiences apparently intensified Mrs. Billington's notorious arrogance. For the junior soloist, Miss George, accompaniment of the female star must have developed into a most trying contest of voices. A sympathetic older performer, when asked how well Mrs. Billington and Miss George collaborated on stage, replied that 'he could compare them to nothing but St. George and the Dragon'.[5]

[1] HC, 11–25 Aug. 1791.
[2] *The Diary*, 7 Sept. 1791.
[3] HC, 8 Aug. 1791.
[4] Mathews, i. 151.
[5] HC, 20 Oct. 1791.

For several decades one of Cork's oldest institutions, the Society for Relief and Discharge of Persons Confined for Small Debts, had been regularly allowed a benefit performance near the end of the Theatre Royal season. The Society in advertising its night usually did not publicize the details of its philanthropy, but in 1791 it prefixed to the advertisement of its benefit an annual report that unwittingly dramatized the grave irony in the social consciousness of eighteenth-century Ireland. On the one hand, a severe legal and economic inhumanity tended to hold down or crush the persons of small property without regard to race or creed: on the other hand, a paternalistic but genuine beneficence organized projects to relieve the effects of the inhumanity, projects to which the comfortable theatregoers were expected to contribute liberally every year. Their bounty to the Cork Relief Society, its report asserted, had not been dispensed 'in vain, or capriciously':

> Forty persons, whose Debts amounted to 390*l.*, have been restored to their Families at an expence of 60*l.*—6,720 weights of potatoes, 28*l.* worth of milk, 72 loads of straw, and 20 barrels of coal have been distributed to the poor, the naked, and the hungry in prison: add to this, that to promote Industry and encourage Manufacture, 1,170 Guineas were lent to 390 poor Tradesmen, interest free, which, from the attention of the Managers of the Loan, have been paid in by weekly Installments without the loss of a shilling.[1]

This efficacious charity, which, according to its sponsors, did 'honour to the national character', certainly merited a full house on Friday, 7 October, when Joe Kelly and Miss George sang the title roles in the operetta *Inkle and Yarico*.

The independent company managed by Ezra Wells occupied the renovated Dunscomb's Marsh playhouse in the spring of 1792 and again advertised it as 'the New Theatre Royal, Prince's Street'. The strolling scale of admission fees prevailed: 3*s.* to the boxes, 2*s.* to the pit, and 1*s.* to the gallery. Production started about mid-April with O'Keeffe's comedy, *Wild Oats*,[2] which had enjoyed its Irish début at George's Street on the closing night of the preceding summer. Performances at Prince's Street went on from April until at least 29 May, when 'a new

[1] Ibid., 3 Oct. 1791.

[2] CEP, 9 Apr. 1792, advertised the opening performance 'in the course of a few days'.

and beautiful Display of Fireworks' closed Mr. Cottrell's benefit and possibly the company's season.[1] Then in the winter of 1792–3 a strolling troupe, which during the autumn had performed at Galway under the leadership of Alexander Macartney, took up occupancy of the Prince's Street building and called it 'the Little Theatre, Prince's Street'. The last performance recorded in this venerable structure, a benefit for Mr. Macartney, took place on Monday, 18 February 1793,[2] almost fifty-seven years after its opening as the first theatre royal outside Dublin.

Meanwhile Richard Daly had renewed his lease of the Theatre Royal, George's Street, from Tottenham Heaphy, though at the beginning of the 1791 season Daly had referred to that season as 'the last of his retaining the Theatre'.[3] This deliberately provocative reference so alarmed the subscribers and the other permanent ticket holders that they called a meeting on 10 August 1791, at the Crown Tavern, for consideration of the manager's statement 'which they think is calculated to injure their Properties very materially'.[3] These ever anxious investors may have brought some undisclosed pressure to bear upon Daly. In any case, he decided to carry on and to put the Theatre Royal 'into elegant repair . . . under the immediate direction of Mr. Doyle',[4] whose 'jolly, deserving'[5] personality had been associated with local stage activities for twenty-five years. A typical Daly puff ushered in the season of 1792 on 1 August when 'Gentleman' Lewis played Vapid in *The Dramatist.* The manager claimed that he had 'considerably shortened the present season in Dublin' in order to present, after an absence of seven years, 'so favourite an Actor'.[6] Lewis's accomplished playing of a half-dozen sparkish heroes called forth the most extreme praise. Correspondents in the *Cork Evening Post* currently described him as 'one of the most beautiful and elegant performers in Europe', and as 'the first [i.e. finest] imitator of the many coloured Life that graces the Stage'.[7] After two decades of constant theatrical migration he apparently still retained his graceful wiry figure and polished mercurial movement. So urgent a plea arose for more performances by Lewis

[1] A copy of the playbill for this night is at the N.L.I.
[2] CEP, 14 Feb. 1793. [3] HC, 8 Aug. 1791. [4] CEP, 23 July 1791.
[5] Ibid., 26 Aug. 1793. [6] Ibid., 30 July 1792. [7] Ibid., 2 and 9 Aug. 1792.

that the Theatre Royal management persuaded him to return to the city on 27 August for a few additional nights prior to his departure for England.[1] After doing three of his best parts—Goldfinch in *The Road to Ruin*, Ranger in *The Suspicious Husband*, and the Copper Captain in *Rule a Wife*—he left on 4 September with the most flattering tribute from his Cork admirers: 'We may not in this Age have a Successor to Mr. Lewis.'[2]

During 1792 Daly had left affairs in Cork to his deputy, Mr. Doyle, but by the next summer the manager commanded so little in the way of distinguished personnel that he and his wife, who had not acted together on the George's Street stage since 1787, had to reappear there in a limited but entertaining repertoire of social comedy. A newspaper editorial, probably inserted at the manager's request, welcomed the return of the Dalys and paid 'a grateful tribute to their abilities, never beheld without delight and admiration'.[3]

The lack of any fresh attractions in Daly's company also caused him to resort to the uncommon pretence of elevating an ordinary pair of his Crow Street troupers to the status of guest stars on a limited engagement. Thus he advertised the opening of the Theatre Royal on Wednesday, 14 August 1793, as 'the First of Mr. and Mrs. Pope's Six Nights'.[4] Mr. Pope was Alexander Pope, the young actor and painter who in 1783 made the portrait of Mrs. Siddons at Cork and in 1785 married at Dublin a fellow performer, Elizabeth Younge. The Popes had appeared once before at Cork in 1788, but without any special notice.[5] Now they enjoyed top billing for two weeks, starting with the season's opening vehicle, *Democratic Rage; or, Louis the Unfortunate*, by the Dublin playwright William Preston. First acted at Crow Street in June, this drama on the violence and chaos of the French Revolution evidently was thought so very controversial that it neither had a revival at Dublin nor ever reached the London boards. It was, however, exported from Ireland to the United States for production at Boston and Charleston in 1794.

During the winter of 1793–4 Daly's situation as theatrical entrepreneur continued to deteriorate in consequence of his

[1] Ibid., 23 and 27 Aug., 3 Sept. 1792.
[2] Ibid., 9 Aug. 1792.
[3] Ibid., 22 Aug. 1793.
[4] Ibid., 12 Aug. 1793.
[5] HC, 4, 18, 25, and 28 Aug. 1788.

tactless and negligent conduct. Eventually he came to realize that for a profitable summer season at both Dublin and Cork he must invigorate his fading Crow Street forces with new blood. Amidst this state of affairs a stage novice, Charles Mathews, seventeen years old, arrived from London to try his fortune in Ireland under the Crow Street manager. Soon Mathews so impressed Daly that the young aspirant was put on a salary of one guinea a week and, contrary to custom, his expenses were paid when the company moved in August to Cork.[1]

The 'Capital of the South', though now containing well over 100,000 inhabitants,[2] still presented a peculiar mixture of cosmopolitan and provincial life. The spirited city belles took morning promenades on the Grand Parade in ultra-modish attire of green worsted petticoat, crimson wool jacket, blue yarn stockings, and stout Irish brogues.[3] At the same time beggars and pigs disfigured the near-by thoroughfares. Main Street, still the central artery of a swollen metropolis, remained dirty, noisome, and congested, blocked at the north as well as the south end by an ugly prison and, in the middle, by the protruding bulk of the Exchange. Living continued 'wonderfully cheap' in comparison with Dublin or London.[4] Mathews boarded at Mrs. Malony's for half a guinea per week. Bargaining in native fashion to win a heavy reduction in price, he finally bought a piece of brownish-yellow nankeen cotton for six shillings and had tailored from it two pairs of breeches. These he proudly wore when he acted 'genteel parts'.[5] In the shops, the markets, the taverns, and, of course, the streets, he heard the Irish language 'very much talked'.[6] To his patronizing English ear Irish seemed 'a very singular kind of language and very discordant'. The local English dialect exhibited what he termed 'a very strong brogue', derived in part from the Somerset speech of the immigrants whom Sir Walter Raleigh

[1] Mathews, i. 96, 106–7.

[2] Sir John Carr, *A Stranger in Ireland; or, A Tour in the Southern and Western Parts of that Country in the Year 1805* (London, 1806), p. 414, reported that Cork's population had increased by 10,000 in the last ten years and then totalled over 180,000. CG, 17 Oct. 1795, set a figure of 120,000.

[3] Dorothea Herbert, *Retrospections 1770–1798* (London, 1929), pp. 312–13.

[4] Mathews, i. 108–9.

[5] Ibid. i. 119.

[6] Ibid. i. 108–9.

and Sir Robert Boyle settled in south Munster. Two centuries later Corkmen were still commonly saying 'feace', 'neame', 'steage', and so on.

Mathews found the Theatre Royal in George's Street 'very handsome and very neatly built', with an 'immensely large' stage and, unlike its sister playhouse in Limerick, with a good number of dressing-rooms, so that even a novice could dress in company with only one other performer.[1] Daly turned into a conscientious taskmaster, calling rehearsals every morning, frequently at ten and never after eleven, and holding them until four in the afternoon.[2] The players then ate dinner and prepared for a seven o'clock curtain. Mathews as a minor actor usually went on the boards four nights a week and often six during the assizes or benefits. Quite justifiably he came to feel the summer schedule 'very tiresome' and deplored the little time for study of his roles.

This young comedian, of course, did not bear the London stamp which Daly now required to draw crowds to his theatres. As the perfect fulfilment of that requirement he engaged the vivacious Elizabeth Farren of Drury Lane, who had not visited the Cork Theatre Royal for ten years. Though she demanded £50 per night, she packed the house at each of her performances and thus brought in, according to Mathews, nearly £200 an evening,[3] a handsome return on the manager's 'very great expence'.[4] To hold down personnel costs Daly invited no male player of comparable popularity to come over with Miss Farren, but, rejuvenated by necessity, he elected himself as her stage partner. They must have formed a handsome and dashing pair in their forte of gay-mannered comedy, to which they adhered for all six nights of Miss Farren's Cork engagement and the three subsequent benefits.[5] Because her extraordinary success in Dublin, the first stop on her Irish tour, prolonged the summer performances there, it was not until Monday, 18 August, that the Daly–Farren combination raised the curtain on the George's Street season with *Know Your Own Mind* by Arthur Murphy, the noted Cork-born dramatist. A second Murphy comedy, *All in the Wrong*, on Friday, 5 September, afforded Miss Farren in the role of Belinda her final appearance before a Cork audience.

1 Ibid. i. 107. 2 Ibid. i. 117. 3 Ibid. i. 107.
4 CEP, 11 Aug. 1794. 5 Ibid., 11 Aug.–1 Sept. 1794.

A clever solo entertainment by Mathews also contributed to making Miss Farren's farewell a memorable occasion. Two weeks previous, at a rehearsal in the Theatre Royal green-room, he had amused the celebrated actress, the manager, and members of the rehearsing cast with his imitations of prominent London and Dublin actors.[1] His mimicry gave Daly vast amusement. Finally the manager ejaculated, 'By Jasus! Mathews, your fortune is made', and proceeded to arrange for a public exhibition by this unknown novice on Miss Farren's last night. Mathews, given 'plenty of room' on the forestage in clear view of the entire audience, brought down the house with his impersonations of such notables as J. P. Kemble, Joseph Munden, and, in particular, 'Sheepface' Wathen of the present George's Street troupe.[2]

To prevent a disastrous slump in attendance after Miss Farren's departure Daly imported direct from Drury Lane a bizarre stage couple, Mrs. Bateman and the Chevalier D'Eon, whose mysterious identities largely accounted for their current notoriety. Mrs. Bateman, a stage-struck Englishwoman, whose husband was said to be in India and to allow her £1,000 a year, had met in London this supposed 'chevalier', purportedly a woman, and had taken up company with her in addition to providing some support. Mrs. Bateman limited her performances to modest comic roles, but in Cork, according to Mathews, 'she was thought very little of as an actress'.[3] 'The most talkative woman I ever met with', he declared, 'and . . . great entertainment in the green-room.' Off stage she tried to sport the lady of fashion.

Mrs. Bateman's companion the Cork newspapers described as a person of incredible achievements:

> The history of human life . . . has never displayed a character more extraordinary than that of the lady before us—for the Chevalier is a female. In the manual exercises she is an adept; in elegant accomplishments a proficient; and in her mind we find a fund of classical, historical, and philosophical learning, elegantly polished by attentive study to the Belles Lettres. D'Eon has served as a soldier, bears three wounds as proof, and the Eroin de St. Louis as a reward of her military skill and courage. Her services in the field

[1] Mathews, i. 107. [2] Ibid. i. 111. [3] Ibid. i. 117.

have not been more conspicuous than her wisdom in the Cabinet. She has filled with the highest reputation, at the Courts of London and Petersburg, the arduous office of Minister Plenipotentiary from Versailles . . . .[1]

Yet the Chevalier's most incredible achievement must be counted her complete success in avoiding, despite numerous fruitful positions, any accumulation of subsistence, so that in 1793 she had to 'seek resource from indegency in her own abilities'.[1] Actually a man, of course, the Chevalier entertained with fencing exhibitions and, in Cork, employed as opponent 'a gentleman brot from England'.[2] At the Chevalier's début on the George's Street stage he walked on in a 'most ludicrous' fencing costume: 'a helmet, with a plume of feathers', capping a woman's hairdress; armour covering a body attired in a white satin petticoat; and female shoes on the feet. The outfit at once caused loud merriment among the 'gods' in the gallery, but the entire audience burst into laughter when the Chevalier, in doffing the helmet to acknowledge applause, inadvertently removed the female wig and exposed a bald head. This comical catastrophe apparently did not halt popular curiosity. The Chevalier continued to fence in pseudo-female costume and, at the benefit on 14 October, appeared in 'her' uniform of the Captain of Dragoons, which, according to Mathews, looked 'amazingly well'.[3] Since the ridiculous novelty connected with this pair of theatrical adventurers clearly gratified the Cork public, Daly took them to Dublin as the opening features of the autumn season at his Crow Street playhouse.

No such attractions as Miss Farren and the strange Chevalier D'Eon enlivened the regular summer season of the Theatre Royal in 1795. A December 'after-season', however, offered entertainment that Cork had not seen since the 'Mallow Races' of 1777. Handy's circus company, straight from Crow Street, converted 'the whole extent of the Stage and part of the Pit' into a George's Street race-course.[4] Overflowing audiences for three to four weeks viewed the ponies and their running. Handy exhibited a 'surprising little pony' only thirty inches high.[5] In the week of 14 December a weird combination of spectacles

[1] CEP, 6 Oct. 1794.
[2] Mathews, i. 117–18.
[3] Ibid. i. 118; CEP, 13 Oct. 1794.
[4] CG, 12 Dec. 1795.
[5] Ibid., 19 Dec. 1795.

greeted the attendants.[1] Indian chiefs, dressed in their 'proper Habits and Implements of War', conducted 'tomahawk exercises' as well as war dances and songs in between the pony races. Cork may have previously observed Indians in its streets, but had not, until now, watched them as theatrical performers. This kind of Indian stage show was just beginning to tour Ireland as a stirring and exotic response to a deepening interest in the North American continent.

Early in 1796 Daly, threatened with disaster at Dublin from the inroads of the Fishamble Street Theatre under Frederick E. Jones, sought to reverse the downward course of his theatrical business. For the first time since he had become the Cork manager, he provided the city with a so-called 'winter' season of fully professional dramatics. A Crow Street contingent, led by Mr. and Mrs. John Jackson whom Daly recently had engaged from Edinburgh, acted at Cork for three weeks in late March and early April.[2] Meanwhile, on 17 March, the Cork public heard important news: 'Mr. Daly . . . at very great expense to himself, and under the kind attention of Mr. Doyle, proposes during the next summer not only to repair but to decorate the Theatre Royal in a very elegant and superb style. The best artists from England are already engaged about the scenery; and some of the most skilful men have been sent to Cork to prepare the intended works.'[3] This would be the first extensive renovation in the thirty-five years of the Theatre Royal's existence. The manager also announced a thorough revision of the situation in respect to the free admission tickets. All holders of such tickets at once were to place evidence of their rights in the hands of a local attorney, Mr. John Franklin.[3] When he had certified a holder's title, that individual would be issued a *copper* ticket newly struck off. None of the existing *silver* tickets would thereafter be recognized as valid by the doorkeepers. Only the *copper* tickets would be accepted for admission.

The reconstruction of the playhouse progressed with such dispatch as to permit its opening on Saturday, 30 July.[4] An

[1] CG, 12 Dec. 1795. [2] HC, 24 Mar.–14 Apr. 1796.
[3] CEP, 17 Mar. 1796.
[4] CEP and HC, 25 July 1796. The bill was the opera of *Robin Hood* and the farce of *The Farmer*.

editorial in the *Cork Evening Post* expressed warm civic pride in the outcome of the undertaking:

> Upwards of £600 has been already spent on our Theatre Royal by the Manager, under the direction of Mr. Doyle, and with such attention and taste, that it is without exaggeration admitted to be the handsomest in Ireland. . . . Many connoisseurs have examined the [overhead] painting by Signor Zafarini, and confess that it is not only masterly but beautiful. . . . Almost the whole of the scenery is new, and upon a much admired plan—and it is with pleasure we add that the very ingenious Architect, Mr. Seymour, is a native of this City.[1]

The most interesting structural changes concerned the side-boxes, which up to the present had consisted of a lower or 'under' tier, and an upper tier called 'lettices'. These two tiers had been topped by open 'slips', which may have contained benches in line with the highest rows of the gallery. The 'slips' now underwent the same alteration as Daly had carried out at Crow Street Theatre in 1788. They were boarded off from the gallery and turned into a third tier of side-boxes termed 'green-boxes'.[1] In the 'lettices', now the middle box tier at George's Street, high wooden partitions, similar to those in the 'under-boxes', were installed in place of the former low railings.[1] Hereafter the 'lettices' offered the same privacy and cosiness as the boxes of the first tier. In these latter the elevation of the seats had been redesigned to allow as good a view from the rear as from the front of each compartment.[1] The many improvements in the box accommodations led to an increase of one shilling in the charge for box seats. The new price of 5*s.* applied, so the Theatre Royal advertisements stated, to 'Boxes, Lettices, Upper Boxes'.[2] At Dublin, however, only places in the first row of boxes cost 5*s.*; all other box seats, 4*s.* Daly rightly judged Cork high society to be more prodigal in its spending for theatrical entertainment. No downward revision of the regular summer season box fee seems to have taken place at George's Street before 1800.

Daly tried to match the new brilliance of his Cork theatre with a fresh look to his summer company. He introduced an attractive *ingénue* from Covent Garden, Miss Gough, and brought back two popular low comedians, Lee Lewes and Joseph Munden, neither of whom had appeared in Cork for

[1] CEP, 21 July 1796. [2] HC, 25 July 1796.

quite a long time.[1] Then he tempted the noted J. P. Kemble of Drury Lane, last seen at Cork in 1785, to play for eight nights at a stipend of £400.[2] The manager advertised this sum as 'far exceeding any hitherto given to any performer in this city', but he must have conveniently forgotten that he paid Mrs. Billington an identical amount for eight nights of opera in the summer of 1791. Kemble deviated from his standard repertoire by commencing his engagement with a recent Drury Lane comedy, *The Wheel of Fortune*, on 12 August.[2] Thereafter he fell back upon his perennial roles of Hamlet, Richard III, Count of Narbonne, and so on.[3] Daly's most interesting acquisition turned out to be Montague Talbot, a dashing fellow of twenty-one, who already was grooming himself as a successor to 'Gentleman' Lewis. Using the stage pseudonym of 'Mr. Montagu', he made his Cork début in *The Rivals* on Tuesday, 23 August, when he played Charles Surface to Miss Gough's Lady Teazle.[4] Just twenty years later Talbot came to the city as its theatre manager.

The eldest member of the present Cork Theatre Royal company, Lee Lewes, had been enjoying benefit nights all around Ireland for a third of a century, but the one in 1796 at George's Street inspired certainly the most unusual spectacle ever undertaken by his supporters. The Society of 'the gay, jolly Munster Druids', whose membership used the forms of address 'Bard' and 'Bardess', held its meetings at the tavern of 'Bard' Scraggs. From there, on the evening of 5 September, the benefit night of 'the venerable and humorous brother Lewes', the Druids proceeded to the Theatre Royal in 'a solemn druidical march accompanied by select pieces of ancient music'.[5] The 'Bards' were dressed in 'emblematical and antique' garb, prominently adorned with the sacred mistletoe. The 'fair Bardesses and little Togo's' wore green scarfs and ribbons. The flamboyant Irish fancifulness in this procession must have delighted the theatregoers as well as the sportive Lee Lewes. After the performance 'Bard' Scraggs probably served in the tavern ballroom a supper, with punch, at half a crown, just as he did for the Masons after their benefit procession and play four nights later.[6]

[1] HC, 28 July, 1 and 15 Aug. 1796.
[2] Ibid., 11 Aug. 1796.
[3] CEP, 15, 25, and 29 Aug. 1796.
[4] Ibid., 15 Aug. 1796.
[5] CG, 3 Sept. 1796.
[6] Ibid., 7 Sept. 1796.

In the enlargement and beautification of the Theatre Royal in George's Street Richard Daly had made a characteristic grand gesture to the public before the final curtain dropped on his managerial activities. Early in the summer of 1797 he began negotiations with his Dublin opponent, F. E. Jones, for the disposal of all the Daly theatrical property. On 12 August, Jones took over not only the Crow Street but also the Cork and Limerick playhouses.[1] Though Daly complained long and loudly about the harshness of the terms of his surrender, in truth he gained a remarkably generous settlement so far as it involved his Cork and Limerick investment.[2] Jones assumed responsibility for all Daly's present obligations, as lessee, to Tottenham Heaphy, the titleholder:

1. Annual rent for the Cork and Limerick theatres of £210 due on 1 November 1798.
2. Free use of the two theatres and of all scenery on the premises by Heaphy or his agent during the 'winter' months.
3. Acceptance of twenty-five certified free admission tickets in Limerick, and of fifty-seven such Cork tickets, forty of which call for four per cent. interest annually.
4. Payment of taxes and other charges levied on the theatre buildings.

In addition to the foregoing obligations, Jones had to pay Daly an annual profit rent of £300, beginning on 1 July 1798 and continuing for seven years. If in the face of the profits during this seven-year period the rent was adjudged excessive by a third party, later to be named, then the annual profit rent for the next seven years was to be reduced to £200. If after the second seven-year period Jones had not been the gainer by at least £100 per year, then he might give up the lease unconditionally.

The transfer of the legal control of the Theatre Royal in George's Street had no significant effect upon the conduct of its 1797 season. The local direction apparently was left, as in the preceding year, with Mr. Doyle. The actors quite overshadowed the actresses in the summer's performances. It was

[1] MS. 494/331296, Office of the Registry of Deeds, Dublin.

[2] See note 4, p. 116.

an interesting coincidence that J. P. Kemble, whose Cork début assisted in the inauguration of Daly's management in 1782, should also participate in the last days of Daly's régime fifteen years later.[1] The veteran 'Gentleman' Lewis and the rising Montague Talbot also starred.[2] And then Henry Erskine Johnston, 'the Scotch Roscius', nineteen years of age, made his first Cork appearance on 21 September in a Scottish tragedy, *Douglas*.[3] His benefit on 5 October evidenced that audiences at the end of the eighteenth century, as at the beginning, desired a very long and varied programme of entertainment. A surviving copy of Johnston's bill lists five kinds of performance in the following order: (1) a comedy, *The Way to Get Married*; (2) a violoncello concerto; (3) a musical interlude, *No Song, No Supper*; (4) a 'Scotch ballet'; (5) an operetta, *Children in the Wood*.[4] In addition, the evening certainly started with a prologue and ended with an epilogue. Such a programme, lasting considerably over four hours, would dismiss between eleven-thirty and midnight, so that playgoers from outside the city would be going home in the darkest and most dangerous hours. Therefore, on occasion, the Cork advertisements called attention to the fact that 'the Moonlight Nights afford Country People' an unusually good opportunity for coming to the theatre.[5]

Night travelling became not only very hazardous but also much restricted in the aftermath of the rebellion that broke out on 23 May 1798. English and Anglo-Irish military forces overran Cork and established a daily curfew. Fortunately for the Theatre Royal, Major-General Lake the commander-in-chief, as well as the other high-ranking officers, looked with warm favour upon stage amusements and were willing to modify the curfew regulations when the Cork theatre belatedly raised its curtain on Saturday, 15 September.[6] The management took care to advertise that 'the Patroles and Centries have received orders not to interrupt any persons till after eleven o'clock at night . . . excepting only bodies with arms'.[7] A week or two

[1] Kemble performed from 10 Aug. to 20 Sept. 1797.

[2] Lewis began on 4 Aug. and left on 26 Aug. 1797.

[3] HC, 18 Sept. 1797.

[4] Reeves Collection, Royal Irish Academy, Dublin, vol. 1796–1837, no. 12.s.7. In *The Way to Get Married* Johnston made his début in the role of Tangent, and Mrs. Johnston, as Julia Falkner, her second appearance on any stage.

[5] HC, 13 Mar. 1800.

[6] CEP, 13 Sept. 1798.

[7] Ibid., 17 Sept. 1798.

later General Lake ordered the curfew to be changed to twelve o'clock for the duration of the theatrical season.[1]

The George's Street company, now operating under Thomas Ludford Bellamy, Jones's deputy manager at Dublin, presented as its chief guest star for 1798 George Frederick Cooke from Covent Garden. On Monday, 17 September, he gave an exciting *première* in his favourite role of Shylock.[2] On Wednesday the 26th he played one of his most recent Covent Garden parts, Delaval in Thomas Holcroft's comedy *He's Much to Blame*, its only recorded production in eighteenth-century Ireland.[3] Three days afterwards the company suspended their Cork performances in order to act in Limerick during the autumn assizes. At six o'clock on Sunday morning, 30 September, Cooke, accompanied by eleven fellow players, set out in fine weather and clothes upon the overnight journey to the Munster capital.[4] The party of seven women and five men rode in four post-chaises, three to a carriage, with Mrs. Garvey, Rawlins, and Cooke gaily in the lead. At the pretty spa of Mallow, 'the Irish Bath',[5] they made a leisurely stop for breakfast and a promenade alongside the town's pleasant cascades.

On the same September date two years later Cooke concluded his next Cork appearances but staged quite another kind of colourful departure, which has not hitherto been published.[6] After the drop of the George's Street curtain on the final night he suddenly disappeared. Days of searching at last located him dead drunk in 'the Bulk', a cobbler's tenement adjoining the playhouse. Since all Cooke's money had gone, his theatrical associates gathered funds for his passage to England and deposited the cash as well as the actor in the safe keeping of a packet master. Cooke, 'as happy as a Lord' at embarkation on 13 October, found nothing inglorious in this exit.

The inward consequences of the 1798 Rebellion soon became manifest. An unsettled state of mind developed throughout Ireland and diminished interest in playgoing almost everywhere. During the winter of 1798–9 business fell off at the

[1] Ibid., 22 Oct. 1798.

[2] Ibid., 13 Sept. 1798, advertised Cooke's first performance for the 15th.

[3] HC, 24 Sept. 1798.

[4] William Dunlap, *The Life of George Frederick Cooke* (2nd ed., London, 1815), i. 125–7.

[5] Smith, i. 327–8.

[6] Croker, ch. 9, p. 32.

Dublin Theatre Royal by reason of not only public uncertainty but also Jones's lackadaisical management. The change from Daly to Jones had gained the Irish stage little or nothing. When the time for summer touring to the south of Ireland arrived in late July 1799, Jones sent down a truly starless company under the direction of his new deputy, Jacob Hammerton.[1] On Saturday, 7 September, a benefit for the Cork poor closed the most undistinguished season that the city had experienced in several decades.[2] The Theatre Royal's last bill of the century, composed of *The Merchant of Venice* and *The Adopted Child*, flattered its audience with no superlative display of art, but with a rather unctuous humanitarian sentiment. The *Hibernian Chronicle*'s report of this 'crowded and brilliant event' struck the final cloying note: 'What a pleasing reflection it must be to a virtuous mind, that while it is enjoying the most rational of all amusements, it is at the same time contributing to the relief of the afflicted, sweetening the bitter draught of wretchedness, and smoothing the straw, where want lies aggravated by all the sad variety of pain.'[3]

Before the end of 1799 Jones, dissatisfied with the condition of his entire theatrical empire, apparently became convinced for the moment that one avenue of betterment lay through the construction of a new playhouse at Cork as well as at Limerick. The extensive and careful redecoration of the Theatre Royal in George's Street only three years earlier seems to have been purposely disregarded in his estimate of need. In December, according to the *Freeman's Journal* of Dublin, Jones 'suffered an ejectment to take place upon the old Theatres in [Cork and Limerick], in order to be released from keeping them in his possession, as it appears they are in such a decayed and ruinous condition, that he estimates it would be much more advantageous to him to build new Theatres than repair the old'.[4] On 2 January 1800 the *Freeman's Journal* mentioned 'the elegant architectural plans that have been produced' for new theatres in Cork and Limerick, and also displayed on the centre of its front page the following advertisement: 'New Theatres, Cork and Limerick. Wanted, Ground in a central Situation in the City of Cork, whereon to erect a New Theatre; at least

[1] CA, 27 Aug. 1799, advertised a benefit for Hammerton as manager.
[2] HC, 5 Sept. 1799. [3] Ibid., 12 Sept. 1799. [4] FJ, 31 Dec. 1799.

60 feet in Front by 150 in Depth.—Also Ground in a Similar Situation, for the like purpose, in the City of Limerick: 50 feet in Front, by at least 130 in Depth.—Application to Mr. H. G. Manders, Esq.; Attorney at Law, Pitt-street, Dublin.' The dimensions specified for the desired lot of ground in Cork corresponded very closely to those of the existing playhouse site in George's Street. Evidently the new building that was being contemplated would exceed by little, if at all, the size of the existing Cork structure.

All the news reports, the advertisements, and the legal manœuvres of the scheming Frederick E. Jones resulted in no early actions for superseding the Theatre Royal in George's Street. At the opening of the nineteenth century it continued to stand as one of Cork's most impressive edifices with an exterior probably more handsome than that of any other Irish theatre. For forty years it had entertained Ireland's second city with plays and players that represented the capital's best fare. Occasionally, indeed, it had exhibited interesting plays and players that Dublin had not yet seen and, in some cases, to the latter's loss, never saw. Between 1760 and 1800 every notable luminary of the English stage who performed in Ireland played on the George's Street boards sooner or later. The eldest of the important Irish playhouses still in use at the time of the Union, the Theatre Royal at Cork faced the new century and the change in the national life with a record that placed it near the top of the English-speaking playhouses outside London and Dublin.

VI · WATERFORD

DURING the eighteenth century, thousand-year-old Waterford dominated the commercial and social life of south-east Ireland. In the amount and variety of its exports this city, lying seventeen miles up the River Suir from the Irish Sea, followed closely behind Limerick, though the number of Waterford's inhabitants before 1800 probably never exceeded two-thirds of the Munster port's population. Large quantities of butter and herring were traded to Spain in return for fruit and wines.[1] Butter was shipped to Holland; pork and linen to Canada; woollen yarn, linen, glass, hides, and tallow to England.[1] Local manufacture of white china, cut glass, and fine linens flourished especially in the last third of the century.[2] The very lush dairyland of County Waterford gave rise to a numerous country gentry and to many well-kept estates in the city's environs.

Waterford, unlike Limerick, did not spread much beyond its ancient walled limits before 1800. It remained largely a constricted aggregation of irregular blocks formed by crooked streets that generally allowed the passage of no more than one coach.[3] Hence coaches seldom appeared about town except in the large square before stately Christ Church.[4] There the Protestant Ascendancy of the region often assembled to exhibit themselves and their equipage. As late as the 1770's, when the city was claiming to be the third in Ireland 'for Trade and Opulence', the *Waterford Chronicle* was complaining that 'many of our Streets, Lanes, &c., are constantly overspread with Dirt in many Places'.[5] The street lighting had not yet been 'put on a sure and lasting Footing'. The lamentable want of street lamps, the newspaper warned, encouraged 'the Melancholy Occasion of Riots, Robberies, and numberless Accidents and Inconveniences'.

On the other hand, Waterford of that era possessed some very

[1] Pococke, p. 134. [2] Maxwell, p. 268. [3] Willes, pp. 32–34.
[4] Maxwell, p. 258. [5] WC, 15 Nov. 1771.

attractive features. In 1705 the corporation began the improvement of the harbour front by razing the old city walls and gate along the Suir, and by lengthening the quays. The river street, over half a mile in length, was widened to forty feet and paved with stone;[1] by mid-century it had become Waterford's most impressive sight. For a considerable distance rich gentlemen and merchants had lined it with handsome new houses facing 'the broad, clean river like the Thames at Lambeth'.[2] Near the mid-point of the quays stood the Exchange, a big hewn-stone edifice with an arched piazza similar to that of the Galway Tholsel.[3] Here the fashionable of town and country congregated for assemblies, balls, and drums from autumn to the end of spring.[4] Waterford society in time denoted the area from the Exchange eastwards to the Ring (now Reginald's Tower) as 'the Grand Parade', where ladies and gentlemen could take a dressy airing on foot in pleasant weather.[5] Persons of quality also gathered at the spacious Bowling Green on the river bank just to the east of the Tower, and promenaded behind the Green on the Mall.[6] This latter walk, though only an eighth of a mile long, was charmingly set out with double rows of elm trees, and stone walls.[7]

In addition to these amusements of the gentility, Waterford began to enjoy public stage entertainment in the 1730's when the Dublin troupes started to tour southwards as far as Cork. The earliest known reference to Waterford theatricals is to be found in the *Dublin News-Letter* of 25 June 1737, wherein it was announced that the Smock Alley company under their manager, Lewis Duval, was 'in a short time to set out for Waterford and to open there with *The Committee*, Teague [the original stage Irishman] to be perform'd by Mr. [John] Barrington'.[8] Three 'English Gentlemen', Messrs. Dennis Delane, Adam Hallam, and Bridgewater, from the London theatres, were to accompany the Dublin players as guest actors.

Waterford's earliest playhouse seems, therefore, to have been erected at about the same time as Cork's theatre on Dunscomb's

[1] P. Luckombe, *A Tour through Ireland in 1779* (London, 1780), p. 39.

[2] Willes, p. 32.

[3] Pococke, p. 133.

[4] WC, 10 Jan. 1771.

[5] O'Keeffe, i. 214.

[6] Charles Smith, *The Ancient and Present State of the County and City of Waterford* (2nd ed., Dublin, 1774), p. 192.

[7] Pococke, p. 133.

[8] DN, 25 June 1737.

Marsh. Like the latter, the Waterford structure was financed and owned by the estate of the deceased Dublin manager, Thomas Elrington.[1] A ruined monastic precinct was chosen, as in Limerick, for Waterford's first theatrical site. Occupied originally by the Dominican friary of St. Saviour and still called 'the Blackfriars', it lay to the north of High Street on the west side of Conduit Lane. The friary chapel had already been renovated to serve as the County Court House.[2] Alongside it on the north the playhouse was constructed—a building with the approximate dimensions of the later theatres in Artillery Lane, Derry, and Cornwallis Street, Limerick; that is, 80 feet in length by 40 feet in width.[3] Access to the 'snug playhouse within the Friary'[4] was gained by a long but commodious passage that ran northwards from High Street past the Court House, turned sharp to the right between the Court House and the theatre, and emerged at the latter's east end in a small yard before the main entrance.[5] No extant advertisements of Blackfriars performances mention boxes. If they existed, they could have been located only at the sides of a rectangular pit, because the rows of gallery seats ascended directly from the rear of the pit and, on special occasions, the first few rows were railed in with the lower area to provide added *élite* accommodations.[6] A Dublin tourist, observing Waterford's 'neat' stage in 1741, 'was surprised to find the Scenes so elegantly painted'.[7] In August of that year the scenery and costumes as well as the building were bought by the proprietors of the Theatre Royal in Aungier Street, Dublin.[8] They in turn offered the Waterford property for public sale at least twice during the 1740's.[9] Ultimately it appears to have been consolidated with other holdings of the Dublin Theatre Royal patent.

[1] Indenture of 11 Aug. 1741 between Frances Elrington, widow of Thomas Elrington, and Lord Mountjoy, trustee for the Dublin Theatre Royal proprietors. Office of the Registry of Deeds, Dublin, old vol. 106, p. 420.

[2] Smith, p. 180; Pococke, p. 133.

[3] 'A Map of the City and Suburbs of Waterford' (1764) by William Richards and Bernard Scalé. The dimensions have been calculated according to the scale of measurement accompanying the map.

[4] Lewes, i. 36.

[5] 'A Map of the City and Suburbs of Waterford' (1764).

[6] WC, 20 Sept. 1771.

[7] *A Tour through Ireland in Several Entertaining Letters*, p. 160.

[8] Indenture of 11 Aug. 1741 between Frances Elrington and Lord Mountjoy.

[9] FDJ, 26 Dec. 1741 and 8 Mar. 1747/8.

PLATE IX

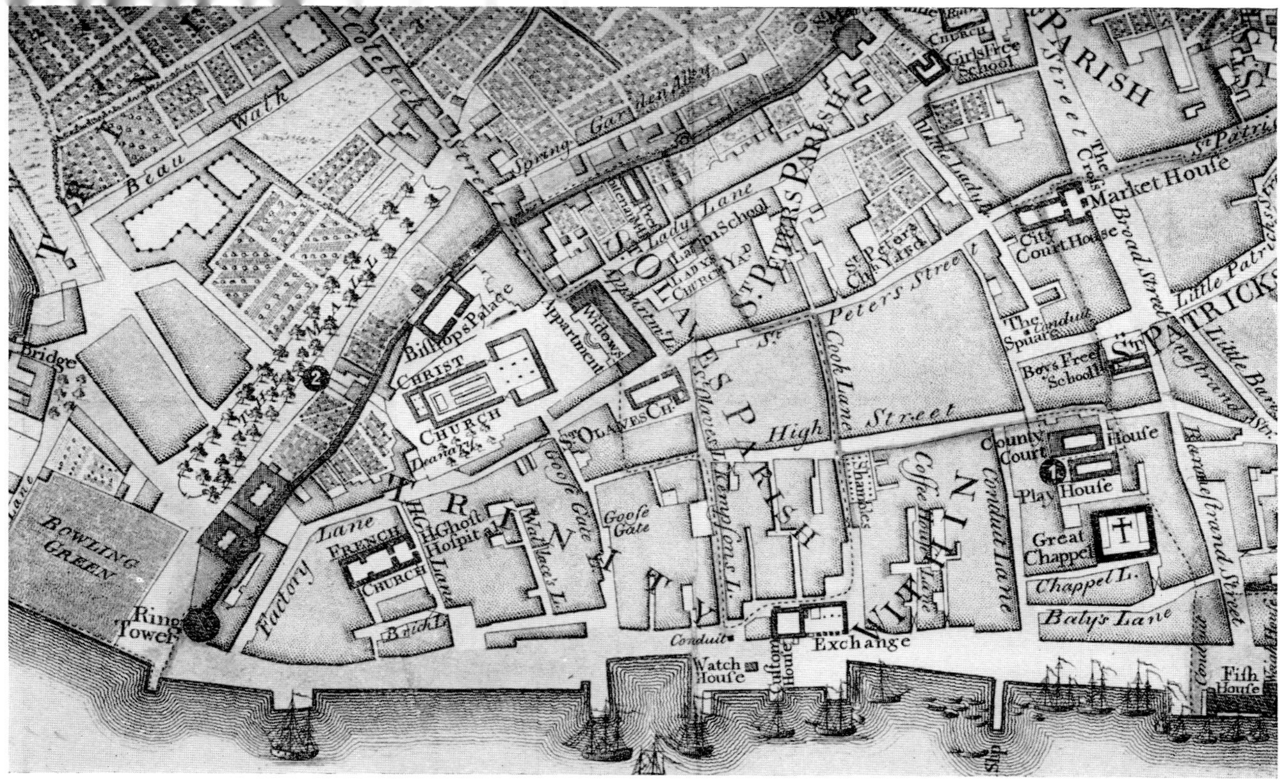

Waterford in 1764

Theatre Sites: (1) The Blackfriars; (2) The Mall

For half a century strolling actors or Dublin troupes on summer tour entertained at 'the Theatre in Blackfriars'. The existing records, however, are so meagre that they present only a patchwork of the theatrical activity there. Indeed, not until 1767 do even the patches start to assume definite form and colour. In late October of that year the veteran Dublin actor Thomas Ryder, who had just taken to the road as a manager, brought a good strolling company to Waterford for three weeks of performances. Ryder advertised as his outstanding attractions 'a fine set of scenery' and a new pantomime, *Harlequin in Waterford; or, The Dutchman Outwitted*, a piece intended to give a distinctive flair to his initial season in Waterford.[1] The scenes to the pantomime, said to have cost forty pounds (an unusually big expenditure to fit out a single play), depicted notable sights in the city and its suburbs on both sides of the Suir: 'a view of Tramore, the Quay of Waterford, Christendom Church and Churchyard, Form-yard, Tombs, Church, Pump, &c.' Ryder acted Dunderpate Dismal the Conjurer; the company's leading *ingénue* Miss Hern, Columbine; Logan, Harlequin; Binns, Mynheer Vanderflawken the Dutchman. This original entertainment was almost certainly the invention of Ryder's talented actor-friend John O'Keeffe, who had made his début as an author for the stage in Dublin eight months earlier. In 1768 O'Keeffe and Ryder, acting together at Derry, revised the pantomime as *Harlequin in Derry; or, The Dutchman Outwitted.* It was produced by Ryder at Kilkenny in 1767 under its first title and, under its second, at Belfast in 1770, but it was never staged at Dublin and therefore has gone unrecorded for two centuries. No doubt most of the Waterford audience found this harlequinade with its picturesque local settings the highlight of their brief theatrical season.

Four years later Ryder returned full of apologies and plans after his long absence:

> Mr. Ryder with infinite Pleasure informs the Ladies and Gentlemen of the City and County of Waterford, that he has obtained Permission from the present Worshipful Mayor, to open a Theatre in the said City. . . . He embraces this Opportunity of assuring them, that the highest Attention shall be paid to their Amusement and Entertainment in the Exhibition of the newest and most moral

[1] LJ, 21 Nov. 1767.

Theatrical Pieces that have been performed at the Theatres of London and Dublin the two last Winters. And as he had the ill Fortune to displease some of the Ladies and Gentlemen of Waterford by not coming at the former appointed Times, he declares in this Public Manner, it did not proceed from the want of a proper Respect, he ever did, and ever shall retain for them, but a Chain of concurring Disappointments which totally deprived him of the Means for undertaking so long a Journey, being then near 200 miles from Waterford [i.e. at Derry and Belfast]. He therefore hopes they will impute the Disappointment to the real Cause, his Misfortune not his Fault, for which he has not only severely suffered from the Displeasure, but also very considerably in his Property. He thought it his Duty to lay this true State of the Affairs before his Friends and once more begs leave to solicit their Protection and Encouragement.[1]

'Mr. Ryder's Company of Comedians', a combination of strollers and Smock Alley players, opened at the Theatre in Blackfriars about the third week of September 1771, and continued there into November. The first novelty of the season occurred on Wednesday, 25 September, in honour of the Friendly Brothers of the Knot of St. Patrick.[2] The manager railed in the first two rows of the gallery with the pit so that some of the Friendly Brothers could be accommodated there and yet could fraternize easily with their brethren in the pit. When the curtain rose, announced to be 'exactly at seven o'clock', Ryder stepped on stage and sang the 'Friendly Brothers' Song' accompanied by 'a full band and chorus'. The comedy of *The Conscious Lovers* and the farce of *The Apprentice* followed.

A second gala event took place on Wednesday, 9 October, when Ryder presented the *première* of *Love and Despair*, a tragedy written by an unnamed Waterford gentleman.[3] A friend of the author provided a prologue and epilogue spoken by Mr. and Mrs. Ryder respectively; and a former native of Waterford, the Dublin musician Charles Clagget (*c.* 1740–95), composed for the occasion 'a Procession with Music'. Seven men and three women, the best of Ryder's troupe, constituted the cast:

Ryder = Demetrius	L'Estrange = Cha-Zeba
Wilmot = Raphael	Mitchell = Orel-Kan

[1] WC, 9 Aug. 1771. [2] Ibid., 20 Sept. 1771. [3] Ibid., 4 and 8 Oct. 1771.

Duffy = Polybius	Mrs. S. Ryder = Theodosia
Owens = Hierome	Mrs. E. Brown = Eutropia
Hallion = Thyrsus	Miss Barry = Fideles

Despite an elaborate and careful production *Love and Despair* evidently did not impress and never graced any but the Waterford stage, so far as the records show.

The benefits toward the end of the company's stay suffered from bad weather and conflicting social engagements, the perennial enemies of the actors' livelihood. Mrs. Ryder, whose night was first scheduled for Monday, 28 October, had to postpone to the next evening a very lavish programme: a tragedy, *Douglas*; a dramatic romance, *Cymon*; a farcical skit, *Linco's Travels*; and two original musical recitations by Ryder, 'The Ramble through Dublin' (containing visits to St. Stephen's Green, the College Green, and the Music Hall in Fishamble Street) and 'A Lick at Modern O'Economy, with an address to the Ladies and Gentlemen of Waterford'.[1] Mrs. Brown and Mr. Wilmot fared so poorly that they dared to make a fulsome plea for support of a second joint benefit on Monday, 4 November: 'Mr. Wilmot and Mrs. Brown present their very respectful Compliments to the Ladies and Gentlemen of this City . . . for the Honour they did, and intended doing them at their former Benefit, but as the kind Intentions of the greater Part of their Friends were frustrated by the inclemency of the Weather and their pre-Engagements to several Drums that Evening, they humbly hope for their Patronage and Encouragement on the above Night.'[2]

In 1778 Ryder, now manager of the Crow Street Theatre, sent his deputy John Byron Vandermere with a contingent of Crow Street actors to Waterford after the Dublin summer season closed on 13 August. During this year volunteer defence corps, termed 'Independent Companies', had begun to form in the city and county to ward off a possible French invasion. Patriotic and martial feelings were stirring the populace. Members of the Independent Companies turned out to celebrate the opening night of the Waterford season and hear Vandermere address to them an original prologue written by Dr. Houlton, a local author. The piece voiced the customary

[1] Ibid., 25 and 29 Oct. 1771. [2] Ibid., 1 Nov. 1771.

managerial allegiance to the English Ascendancy, but also contained an amusing mixture of appeals:

To arms, to arms! th' inspiring drum invites,
'Tis Britain's voice, support her injur'd rights:
Rouse, rouse, Hibernia's sons, obey the call,
And join in vengeance on perfidious Gaul. . . .
And now ye gallant sirs, if I might dare,
Small things with things of moment to compare, . . .
I've rais'd an arm'd company of my own; . . .
But hark! a whisper says, dear Vandermere,
How stile you this detachment[1] quarter'd here?
Alas! so light our purses are, d'ye see,
We truly may be stiled *light infantry*!
But would you, ladies, be as kind as fair,
Often to grace our scene of action here,
And you, good sirs, deign frequent to review
The little corps I've solely rais'd for you,
Soon should I boast your generous acts to me,
Made mine an *independent Company*![2]

The local martial spirit expressed a slightly more nationalistic pride in another of Dr. Houlton's prologues spoken by one of the chief actors, Bennet, at his benefit. He pretended to be an Irish warrior conversing with Andromache in Elysium:

Madam, cried I, accept me your protector,
You'll find an Irishman as brave as Hector:
For tho' we fight not with such arms as he has,
We still have glorious weapons call'd shillelahs.
I've heard, said she, in courage and in love
You Irishmen can match e'en Mars or Jove.[3]

A woman's view of the present crisis came from young Miss Graham. Surrounded 'by near a hundred ladies and gentlemen on the stage', she brought her crowded benefit to a rousing end by delivering in military dress a castigation of current male effeminacy:

But now in scarlet coat, with sword, cockade,
I feel myself a mettlesome young blade,

[1] i.e. the detachment from the Crow Street Theatre.
[2] *Exshaw's Gentleman's and London Magazine*, Feb. 1779, p. 118.
[3] Ibid., p. 119.

So stout within; without, so bold my speech is,
That, faith, there's something magical in breeches. . . .
Ladies, a thought has struck me, pray attend
And if you like it, you'll my scheme befriend. . . .
Full many there are, I mean those darling honies,
Your petit-maitres, beaux, and macaronis,
Who ape our tender manners, lisp, and sigh,
Faint if they're frighten'd, and at operas die. . . .
What say you, ladies, shall we out of hand,
Like me equip'd, compose a female band,
To wage continual enmity with all those
Who, by their monkey-tricks, disgrace the small-cloaths:
Believe me, all the world will call that plan good,
Which bears such reptiles back to manhood.[1]

The foregoing speeches offer a fair sample of how the Waterford stage, like those all over Ireland, was responding to the fervour of the times.

The excitement over public affairs soon heightened the interest in theatrical entertainment throughout the country. The expansion of dramatic activities at near-by Kilkenny between 1780 and 1784 moved Waterford to emulation. A group of citizens set about the project of erecting a new theatre and eventually secured financial assistance from the Corporation. On 18 May 1784 the City Council took generous action: 'Resolved that the sum of £200 be granted by the Corporation for the purpose of carrying on the building of the new Play House and Assembly Rooms and that the Mayor be empowered to sign an Order for the same.'[2] Already, on 28 February 1784, the Kilkenny manager, John Vandermere, had announced his election as manager of 'the New Theatre, Waterford'.[3] These developments spelled the demise of the little theatre in Blackfriars and led to its ultimate demolition. The outer walls of the eighteenth-century County Court House and the passage which once led to the theatre from High Street still survive, but Woolworth's store, now extending from Barron Strand Street far back toward Conduit Lane, has obliterated all traces of Waterford's first playhouse.

[1] Ibid., p. 120.
[2] Corporation Minute Book, City Hall, Waterford.
[3] LJ, 28 Feb. 1784.

In contrast to its confined location its successor had a very convenient and fashionable site half-way along the north side of the Mall. The theatre formed the west end of the new 'public buildings' that later became known as the City Hall.[1] Waterford's second playhouse surpassed the Blackfriars structure in accommodations as well as size, for it contained not only lower and upper side-boxes, but also a row of boxes behind the pit.[2] A year after its completion it was selected as the handsomest edifice in which to hold the splendid civic reception in honour of the visit of the Lord-Lieutenant of Ireland and his wife, the Duke and Duchess of Rutland. 'The kitchen belonging to the new Public Buildings at the Mall' was made ready for this occasion at the expense of the Corporation,[3] and the theatre auditorium 'was, by order of the Mayor, most elegantly fitted up for a temporary ballroom'.[4]

Manager Vandermere directed his preparations so well that, even though he did not conclude his Kilkenny season until 9 June, he was able to raise the curtain of the new Waterford stage on Monday, 26 July 1784. Newspapers as far away as the *Belfast Mercury* welcomed 'the superb theatre . . . built by the inhabitants'.[5] The bill for the opening night consisted of a celebrational prologue delivered by Vandermere, Shakespeare's *As You Like It* (which also initiated Limerick's playhouse of 1790), Arthur Murphy's farce *The Citizen*, and special orchestral numbers with Charles Clagget of Dublin as conductor.[6] From various sources Vandermere had assembled a moderately good set of players, including probably Mr. and Mrs. Benjamin Barrett, Mr. and Mrs. Fielding Wallis, Jacob Hammerton, George Mitchell, and Mrs. O'Neill from his recent Kilkenny

[1] The following advertisement in WM, 9 Feb. 1818, is the earliest reference to describe precisely the location of the Theatre Royal in relation to the City Hall: 'To Be Let. The West End of the New Town Hall, as a Theatre, which, unless taken as such within three months from the date hereof, will be set by Public Auction for other Purposes, preserving, however, the Uniformity of the Building. By order of Council, Robert Cooke, Town Clerk.' R. H. Ryland in *The History, Topography, and Antiquities of the City and County of Waterford* (Waterford, 1824), p. 166, noted that 'under the same roof with the Town Hall is a very neat theatre'. Theatrical performances are still regularly staged in this playhouse, the oldest in Ireland, though it has been much altered since the eighteenth century.

[2] WH, 13 Mar. 1792; WM, 23 Dec. 1801.

[3] Corporation Minute Book, 26 Oct. 1785.

[4] HC, 28 Nov. 1785.

[5] BM, 6 Aug. 1784.

[6] DEP, 3 Aug. 1784; FJ, 5 Aug. 1784.

troupe, and from Dublin, Mr. and Mrs. John Bernard.[1] As top feature he engaged the glamorous vocalist Mrs. James Billington, whose Irish début had rocked Dublin a few months before. She delighted the Waterford public until her second benefit, when she became vexed at the lack of a crowded house and from the stage 'berated the audience like a common streetwalker'.[2]

Vandermere reigned as local manager for only two seasons, because death ended his career at Dublin in February 1786. Richard Daly, holder of the Dublin Theatre Royal patent, assumed charge of what he presently labelled the 'Theatre Royal Waterford', and for the next four years he played there with his Dublin company either before or after its Cork and Limerick summer seasons. On 18 July 1786 he began a two weeks' stay with an especially fine casting of *The Beggar's Opera*: Charles Bannister of Drury Lane, Macheath; Mrs. Charlotte Melmoth, Lucy; Miss Jameson, Polly.[3] The following year the Daly troupe performed during the month of October chiefly in such well-tried comedies as *The Suspicious Husband*, *The Constant Couple*, *The Beaux' Stratagem*, and *The School for Scandal*, together with a considerable repertory of humorous songs by the famous Irish comedians Andrew Cherry and Robert Owenson. The latter on occasion sang in Irish: for instance, 'Salhuin neen Wenugh; or the Munster Mantle' at the box-keeper O'Mara's benefit on 10 October; and, at his own night on 15 October, 'Carolan's Planxties'.[4] O'Reilly, another singing comedian, arranged for his benefit on 17 October a rich potpourri of entertainment: (1) a comedy, *He Would Be a Soldier*, interspersed with *entr'acte* songs and a finale, 'A Twiggle and a Friz in Modern Manner with some new Heads to work upon', by O'Reilly; (2) an interlude, *The Generous Tar*; (3) a farce, *Barnaby Brittle*; (4) a pantomime, *The Death of Harlequin and the Animation of Columbine*.[5] A strange mishap threw the ticket situation for this evening into much confusion. A day or two previously O'Mara had set off for Dublin, carrying with him by mistake the Waterford box book. Therefore O'Reilly had to

1 Bernard, i. 371, 377.
2 *Memoirs of Mrs. Billington* (London, 1792), p. 22.
3 HC, 20 July 1786.
4 WC, 9 and 12 Oct. 1787.
5 Ibid., 16 Oct. 1787.

issue a last-minute request that all those who had made reservations for his night should repeat their orders to him at the theatre in advance of the performance and thus avoid a great press at curtain time. His patrons must have been considerably irritated at this inconvenience of rebooking.

Daly's policy of varying from year to year the bill of fare in connexion with his summer theatres was well illustrated at Waterford in 1789. He dispatched direct to that city, instead of Cork, for an early summer season the better portion of his Dublin company together with the two visiting London celebrities, Mrs. Maria Phillips Crouch and John Philip Kemble. In late July and the first two weeks of August they played 'every night to great houses, half the pit rail'd in, *constantly*'.[1] Then, after acting at Cork, Daly and his troupe returned to Waterford to open on 3 October[2] an autumn season that concentrated largely on classic plays. James Middleton [Magan], a young Irishman fresh from Covent Garden on his first tour in Ireland, co-starred with Mrs. Esten in *Romeo and Juliet*, *As You Like It*, *Othello*, and *Venice Preserved*.[3] The Proprietor's Night, however, on 7 October called for the more timely entertainment of Pilon's *He Would Be a Soldier*.[4]

Between 1789 and 1793 Daly gave up any connexion with Waterford theatrical affairs, perhaps because his lease on the playhouse ran out and his heavy involvements in Dublin discouraged renewal of a not too lucrative adjunct. The newly installed Limerick proprietor, Sir Vere Hunt, proceeded to take over the Theatre Royal Waterford in 1790. About the first part of July the Hunt troupe under the management of Lawrence Clinch arrived to play for three or four weeks.[5] When Sir Vere withdrew from all theatrical directing in June 1791 he had no further interest in the Waterford outlet. By July local press notices were appearing in anticipation of summer theatricals under the management of the city's old friend Thomas Ryder.[6] By mid-September the report ran that the Theatre Royal would open soon, but that it could not be 'open,

[1] Hunt MSS.: Letter of 7 Aug. 1789 from Mr. Crouch.
[2] LJ, 3 Oct. 1789.
[3] WC, 2, 6, and 9 Oct. 1789.
[4] Ibid., 6 Oct. 1789.
[5] Hunt MSS.: Account Books, 1790–1; Journal, 1781–1807.
[6] WH, 21 July 1791.

at this time, longer than three weeks'.[1] Then, the Waterford performances were 'unavoidably postponed . . . since some of the principal performers had not yet arrived, tho' hourly expected'.[2] Next, the theatre could not be opened 'until after the Limerick Races [in October] on account of the unforeseen delay in the arrival of some of the principal performers'.[3] Finally, the illness of the venerable Ryder in October and his death on 26 November at Sandymount near Dublin stopped all talk of immediate stage entertainment in Waterford.

In January 1792, however, Sir Vere Hunt's former company, now an independent strolling group, turned up to play for two months. On their opening night, Monday, 30 January, they acted an entirely new pantomime, *The Witches of the Rocks; or, The Regions of Fancy*, with 'an elegant display of scenes, dresses, and decorations'.[4] According to an enthusiastic spectator, the first scene showed 'a grove so romantic and charming as to cause a burst of applause from the whole house—and the trees instantly transformed themselves into the weird sisters of Macbeth'.[5] Then Harlequin appeared in the churchyard 'in the likeness of Time, with a scythe, even like the sculptured marble of the Fitzgeralds, in Christ Church [at Waterford]'. At the end, after Hymen and Cupid had presented Columbine to Harlequin at the Temple of Hymen, the scene lighted up to disclose the Waterford Arms—an azure shield with three lions, *passant gardant*, in gold on the upper part, three ships in gold on the lower part, and the motto '*Urbs Intacta Manet*'. This harlequinade, though it excited favourable comment at its *première*, was never recorded elsewhere. On 15 February, McCrea, the company specialist, performed a second original pantomime, *The Enchanted Castle; or, Harlequin Conqueror*,[6] but, like *The Witches of the Rocks*, it too vanished from theatrical history. The next to the last night of the season, Wednesday, 28 March, featured a third *première*, that of an opera, *The Siege of Waterford*, written by a local figure, James St. John, M.D.[7] The author founded his lyrics chiefly upon 'the most approved Irish airs', and his plot upon King Diarmuid's capture of Waterford in 1170 with the aid of Strongbow and upon the

[1] Ibid., 13 Sept. 1791.
[2] Ibid., 15 Sept. 1791.
[3] Ibid., 20 Sept. 1791.
[4] Ibid., 28 Jan. 1792.
[5] Ibid., 2 Feb. 1792.
[6] Ibid., 9, 11, and 14 Feb. 1792.
[7] Ibid., 27 Mar. 1792.

latter's marriage to Diarmuid's daughter, Eva. Despite a review which praised the libretto as 'sublime, nervous, and animated' this opera tempted no producer to stage it outside its native city. Although none of these new pieces ever caught on, still the former Hunt troupe evidenced their superior ambition by avoiding the stereotyped repertory of the average strollers.

In the summer of 1792 another Kilkenny manager, John Davison, decided to follow the example of Vandermere and undertake the management of the Waterford theatre too. On 16 July he announced his intention with the assurance that his actors, who had been playing in Kilkenny for six months to 'crowded houses', would 'give satisfaction'.[1] The new director imitated the summer policy of managers in Dublin; he contracted for a rotation of star talent to perform for limited periods with his regular troupers. Starting on 23 July with Miss W. Brett, the noted Dublin vocalist, he concentrated on operettas: *The Beggar's Opera*, *The Woodman*, *The Romp*, *Robin Hood*, and *Inkle and Yarico*.[2] On 4 August he added West, the dancer from London and Dublin, to entertain with exhibitions of Irish song and dance.[3] West closed his engagement on 20 August in a spectacular pantomime, *The Elopement*, which opened with a transparent moonlight scene.[4] The melodramatic climax required that West as Harlequin 'fly across the stage out of one Balcony into the other' in pursuit of Columbine who has to 'elope from a balcony window in man's apparel'. On 13 August Mrs. Charlotte Melmoth from Dublin had her first night in connexion with Miss Brett's last night and benefit.[5] They combined their vocal skills in Cobb's *The Haunted Tower*, a work that, according to the *Waterford Herald*, 'rescued modern English opera from the oblivion into which it was about to be immerged [*sic*]'.[6] The *Herald* added that 'the refined taste and powerful execution' of the two ladies made the evening an 'extatic musical banquet'. Miss Brett's departure brought on Maria Ann Campion and James Middleton, both of the Dublin Theatre Royal. These two joined Mrs. Melmoth for a month in a radical change of Waterford's theatrical menu, namely, a repertory of tragedy and tragicomedy: *The Earl of Essex*, *The Fair Penitent*, *The*

[1] WH, 17 July 1792.
[2] Ibid., 19, 26, 28, 31 July, and 2 Aug. 1792.
[3] Ibid., 31 July, 4, 7, and 9 Aug. 1792.
[4] Ibid., 14 Aug., 1792.
[5] Ibid., 7 Aug. 1792.
[6] Ibid., 11 Aug. 1792.

Grecian Daughter, *Hamlet*, *Jane Shore*, *The Orphan*, *Percy*, *The Rival Queens*, *Romeo and Juliet*, *Theodosius*, and *Venice Preserved*.[1] The playing of Middleton and Miss Campion as Romeo and Juliet inspired a Waterford editor to speak of 'a delicious banquet when we witness the co-operation of these two ornaments of drama in the pathetic, the beautiful tragedy'.[2] In *The Fair Penitent* on 10 September Dr. St. John, author of the previous spring's opera *The Siege of Waterford*, strove to gain stage laurels as well by acting the role of Altamont. His impersonation drew faint praise from the local critic: 'No offensive symptom was manifested by the audience to any part of his performance.'[3]

When Davison closed his season on Tuesday, 18 September, he stated that he would open the Waterford playhouse again in time for the spring assizes.[4] Adhering to this declaration, he returned in February 1793 after a winter of managing theatricals at Wexford. His announcement of the first performance on Monday, 11 February, stressed the alluring fact that 'a constant Fire will be kept to air the Theatre'.[5] Monday, Wednesday, and Friday continued, as in the past, to be the days of playing, while the curtain, also as before, rose 'precisely at seven o'clock'.[6] On the three regular nights of performance the manager publicly asked the ladies to give no drums, because his company could not stay 'longer than the Assizes'.[6] In spite of that request Fullam and Mrs. Saunders were forced to change their benefit from Monday, 18 March, to Tuesday, 19 March, 'on account of several Parties being formed for Monday night'.[7] To be sure, Davison's present troupe included no very exciting personalities, though his advertisements puffed Thomas Betterton of Dublin, his son, and his daughter Julia as special attractions. Julia Betterton, hailed as 'a ten-year-old dramatic genius engaged at a considerable expense', presented scenes from *The Fair Penitent* and *Venice Preserved*, played the young girl in the farce *The Virgin Unmask'd*, and danced a court minuet with her brother.[8] Yet the Bettertons did not possess sufficient appeal to guarantee prosperity. Receipts so disappointed Manager Davison that on Monday, 11 March, he took a second

[1] Ibid., 14 Aug.–15 Sept. 1792.
[2] Ibid., 18 Aug. 1792.
[3] Ibid., 11 Sept. 1792.
[4] Ibid., 20 Sept. 1792.
[5] Ibid., 7 Feb. 1793.
[6] Ibid., 16 Feb. 1793.
[7] Ibid., 16 Mar. 1793.
[8] Ibid., 19 Mar. 1793.

benefit, though 'no circumstance but the very ill success he has experienced this Season, could induce him to trouble the Ladies and Gentlemen of Waterford again'.[1] Even after the second trial he still felt dissatisfied and appointed the last night of the season, Saturday, 23 March, as a third benefit for himself—certainly a desperate measure.[2]

As a result of this unhappy experience Davison withdrew from the Waterford management, and Richard Daly resumed the responsibility after a lapse of four years. His company, *en route* to Dublin after their Cork season, opened the Theatre Royal Waterford on Monday, 30 September 1793. Using the brevity of their month's visit as an excuse, the manager instituted a weekly schedule of four playing days: Monday, Wednesday, Friday, Saturday.[3] Then he persuaded the *Waterford Herald* to insert in every issue some kind of a puff regarding the Theatre Royal performances. Comment about the opening night lauded the acting of Mr. and Mrs. Daly in the leading parts of *The Jealous Wife* as 'chaste and perfect', and described their audience as 'fashionable and, considering the wetness of the evening, numerous'.[4] A few days later, 'every part of the House was full, except the pit, in which we perceived a few empty seats. The boxes were thronged with beauty and fashion'.[5] On another occasion, praise for the season's productions in general was bestowed because they were 'got up in better style than for several years'.[6] By these various stratagems, Daly, a very shrewd entrepreneur, hoped to encourage more frequent attendance from the playgoing portion of the city and county. The decade following the erection of the new theatre had indicated that stage entertainment in Waterford did not command as generous support as in Cork, Kilkenny, and Limerick.

For the last half-dozen years of the century only a few stray reports exist to throw any light on the Theatre Royal Waterford. Naturally its operations reflected the increasing political tensions. One day in May 1794 two persons in the pit refused to take off their hats when 'God Save the King' was played as usual at the end of the evening's bill.[7] An uproar ensued, and

[1] WH., 9 Mar. 1793. [2] Ibid., 21 Mar. 1793. [3] Ibid., 28 Sept. 1793.
[4] Ibid., 1 Oct. 1793. [5] Ibid., 3 Oct. 1793. [6] Ibid., 5 Oct. 1793.
[7] ClG, 17 May 1794.

rumours of further incendiary action arose. The Mayor promptly ordered the playhouse to be shut 'until measures could be taken to prevent the threatened outrage'. Two years later a somewhat similar incident occurred after all the actors had come on stage to join in the singing of 'God Save the King'. The house reverberated with shouts of 'Off with the hats' directed at those who had forgotten to doff them. A soldier struck one fellow, asleep in his gallery seat, and tossed his hat into the pit. The awakened man, howling from pain and surprise, roused the whole audience to noisy approbation of his punishment.[1] Thus the sentiments of the English Ascendancy sternly ruled the proceedings of Waterford's audiences as Ireland moved towards the Act of Union.

[1] DeLatocnaye, p. 65.

VII · KILKENNY

THE largest inland town in eighteenth-century Ireland and the centre of one of the island's most prosperous districts, Kilkenny lay on the Dublin–Cork coach road where it crossed the River Nore seventy miles from the capital and ninety miles from the southern port city. Kilkenny also maintained close communications with the adjoining county seats of Waterford, thirty miles to the south, and Wexford, fifty miles to the south-east. As early as the seventeenth century Kilkenny had gained distinction for its attractiveness and refinement.[1] With a strong Anglo-Protestant heritage, it took pride in cultivating an English town atmosphere. It encouraged 'extraordinary civility even from the meanest tradesman', and kept the often uncivil as well as unkempt 'natives' segregated in Irishtown to the north of its walled precincts, which dated from the twelfth century.[2] The 'native' boys who infiltrated the choir at historic St. Canice's Cathedral in Irishtown shocked eighteenth-century residents by reason of their bare legs and feet.[3]

Kilkenny's chief streets appeared neat and trim because they were paved with dark-grey marble from quarries only a mile distant and consequently could be swept clear of litter without difficulty. In the heart of the town many of the older houses and shops had been built with their fronts supported on pillars of local marble to form arcades for pedestrians.[4] The handsome Tholsel was constructed during the middle of the eighteenth century with a ground-floor portico which two hundred years later affords a quaint roofing of the sidewalk halfway along High Street. Clean inns matched the neat streets. Travellers especially praised the linen and food at the Wheat Sheaf, commonly abbreviated to the Sheaf.[5] When members of the Charitable Society embarked upon yearly theatricals in the

[1] See Clark, pp. 21, 109.

[2] *A Tour through Ireland in Several Entertaining Letters*, pp. 174, 181.

[3] Mark Elstob, *A Trip to Kilkenny* (Stockton, 1778), p. 153.

[4] Ibid., p. 163; O'Keeffe, i. 213; Pococke, p. 129.

[5] Maxwell, p. 300.

1780's, they made the Sheaf's wainscoted rooms their favourite meeting-place.[1] Its high-pitched gabled front faced Rose Inn Street, which ran easterly below the Ormonde Castle to St. John's Bridge over the Nore and afforded the principal exit towards Dublin.

The Ormonde Castle and its occupants had dominated Kilkenny for over five hundred years. This magnificent residence, at the south-east corner of the old walled town on an eminence overlooking the river, was in the eighteenth century one of Europe's show places, 'rich on every side with marble, and ornamented with many things so curious, that those who have seen it say that it surpasses many palaces of Italy'.[2] Its grounds, 'finer than the Privy-Garden in Whitehall', comprised 'Bowling Green, Gardens, Walks, Orchards and a delightfull Waterhouse adjoining to the Bowling Green'.[2] The high bluff, capped by medieval battlements and towers, provided a most picturesque background to Kilkenny's fashionable promenade, the 'Mall', that extended from St. John's Bridge for half a mile along the bank of the Nore.[3] The main gate of the Castle opened on the Parade, a broad esplanade bordered on its east side by the wall of the Castle garden.[3]

The Parade had only a northern exit into High Street, the town's main artery, which in turn led northwards to an extension called 'Coal Market'. Midway up the east side of Coal Market there still stands, set back from the street, the grey-marble County Court House and Jail completed during the 1750's.[4] This impressive edifice and the Tholsel in High Street resulted from a sharp rise in Kilkenny's trade and wealth. Even before the middle of the eighteenth century the manufacturing, at home or in small factories, of beaver hats, leather goods, linens, flannels, worsteds, and friezes began to expand rapidly in the county as well as in the town.[5] Four large fairs each year drew crowds of visiting buyers in addition to the cottars and farmers of the vicinity. These local folk brightened the streets with their coats, cloaks, and petticoats dyed in the famous county blue.

Kilkenny's High Street and Coal Market had witnessed

[1] LJ, 27 Dec. 1786. [2] See Clark, p. 109.
[3] See 'A Survey of the City of Kilkenny' (1758) by J. Rocque.
[4] Ibid.; Pococke, p. 129. [5] Maxwell, pp. 238, 247, 269.

dramatic entertainment before any other site in Ireland outside Dublin. There, for some eighty years before the Civil War in England, the staging of Corpus Christi plays had gone on annually under the supervision of the town corporation.[1] Then, for more than a century after the War, Kilkenny enjoyed theatrical amusement on very infrequent occasions. In the summer of 1698 the second Duke of Ormonde, a warm patron of the Theatre Royal in Dublin, persuaded its company to visit the town and perform, probably both at his castle and also in some public building like the old Tholsel at the northern junction of Pudding Lane and High Street.[2] This visit of 1698 marked the first tour within Ireland by an Irish professional troupe, but it did not bring about an early introduction of country-wide strolling. When Dublin players began to travel more or less regularly to Cork from 1736 onwards, they sometimes stopped by the River Nore to give a few performances.[3]

Definite records of Kilkenny's stage entertainment during the eighteenth century commenced with the first local newspaper, the *Leinster Journal*, founded in 1767. During November of that year Thomas Ryder, a veteran Dublin actor who had turned strolling manager, brought his company from Waterford to play at the County Court House in Coal Market. His stage carpenter and machinist, Mr. Geoghegan, from Smock Alley, transformed the assizes hall into 'a most regular little theatre' with the proper machinery for 'the new and elegant scenes'.[4] Similarly transformed over and over again, the Court House served as Kilkenny's chief theatrical site during the next quarter of a century. Since this temporary playhouse for the present had no box accommodations, Ryder adopted the very unusual procedure of selling pit and gallery seats in advance of the opening performance on Monday, 30 November.[5] Tickets for the pit at 2*s.* and for the gallery at 1*s.* could be procured from him at Widow Newman's in High Street. His early advertisements stressed a determination 'to have the business conducted with the utmost regularity'. The usual days of playing were to

[1] Clark, pp. 21–25.

[2] Ibid., pp. 108–10.

[3] FDJ, 16 Oct. 1744, reported that 'His Majesty's Company of Comedians intend speedily to entertain the city of Kilkenny with some of their best plays'. The same company visited Kilkenny in the summer of 1746 (Chetwood, p. 137) and again certainly in 1755 (Lewes, ii. 166).

[4] LJ, 21 Nov. 1767.

[5] Ibid., 25 Nov. 1767.

be Monday, Wednesday, and Friday. 'The Ladies and Gentlemen may depend on the Curtain being drawn up precisely at half an hour after six o'clock, to whatever company are then in the house.'[1] No one should 'take it ill' if the manager refused admittance behind the scenes. The first night's production of *The Clandestine Marriage* prompted 'Rusticus' to a brief word of praise in the *Leinster Journal*: 'I came to town last night . . . and was not more surprised at the propriety and decorum the Play was conducted with, than with the elegance of the scenes.'[2]

It was perhaps the excellence of the *décor* rather than of the acting that sustained the interest of the public through the winter. Except for Ryder and his wife, the company included no players of any repute. Geoghegan, however, proved himself an ingenious and enthusiastic producer of the stage spectacles to which the manager's taste often inclined. The elaborate and costly pantomime, *Harlequin in Waterford*, originally staged by Ryder and Geoghegan at that city in October, was performed in Kilkenny on 14 December for a delighted audience.[3] Then, on 15 January 1768, they presented Shakespeare's *Henry VIII* with a freshly painted set depicting the interior of Westminster Hall, London, and with coronation robes 'entirely new'.[4] These visual attractions gave an excuse for raising the gallery admission fee to 2*s*. Actually, however, Ryder 'laid the Pit and Gallery into one, in order to accommodate every person in the front of the house'. This unconventional arrangement mixed together the playgoers of high and low station to the discomfort of some 'persons of consequence'. Therefore the manager 'humbly hoped no Gentlemen will attempt coming upon the Stage' in order to avoid such discomfort. The same house accommodations and prices prevailed three days later for a production of *The Tempest* with 'entirely new' costumes for the Devils, Monsters, and Spirits, and 'new' scenes, especially 'a flying chariot, surrounded with clouds, in which Ariel [Mrs. Ryder] ascends singing'.[5] On 18 February *The Rival Queens* was acted with 'entirely new Grecian Trophies, Urns, Vases, Banners', and 'a car drawn by four captive Kings', all copied from the Crow Street Theatre properties.[6] For Mrs. Ryder's benefit on 29 February her husband wrote and put on a musical entertainment, *A Ramble*

[1] Ibid.
[2] Ibid., 2 Dec. 1767.
[3] Ibid., 12 Dec. 1767.
[4] Ibid., 13 Jan. 1768.
[5] Ibid., 16 Jan. 1768.
[6] Ibid., 13 Feb. 1768.

through Dublin, which described with scenes 'Stephen's-Green, the College, the College-Green, the Music Hall in Fishamble Street, with a lick at the Jew Jugglers, and a peep into Crow Street Theatre'.[1] The audience assisted in supplying the spectacle on 16 February, when the President and Brethren of the Friendly Brothers of St. Patrick, of the Principal Knot of the City of Kilkenny, sat on the stage 'in their formalities',[2] and again on 14 March, when the Masons occupied the same seats 'in their proper Cloathing'.[3]

After this Masonic night Ryder had to dismantle his theatre at the Court House on account of the spring assizes, but he did not wish to lose the profitable business which Assize Week in the Irish county seats usually afforded. He evidently discovered a small hall available in one of the buildings opposite the Castle, and so he 'fitted up commodiously' what he advertised as 'the Theatre in the Parade'.[4] At a uniform fee of 2*s*. for admission, it opened on Thursday, 24 March, with *The Clandestine Marriage*, the same play with which Ryder had commenced at the County Court House in the preceding autumn. The performances, which were to begin 'each night exactly at seven o'clock to whatever company is in the house', continued on 25 and 26 March;[5] then apparently they stopped. No further reference to this little playhouse ever appeared. Ryder did not return to the Court House but departed on a long tour to the west and north of Ireland.

The next strolling company to visit Kilkenny arrived at the beginning of June 1769 from Belfast and Newry under the management of James Parker. He installed boxes for the first time in the County Court House hall and priced seats in them at 3*s*. each.[6] Pit and gallery admission remained at the customary 2*s*. and 1*s*. respectively. Like Ryder, the present manager sold the lower-priced tickets as well as the box places in advance from his lodgings at Mr. Fennelly's in High Street.[7] Parker, however, proclaimed a different policy from his predecessor in respect to the raising of the daily curtain: 'As the former Comedians that performed here used to begin considerably

[1] LJ, 17 Feb. 1768.
[2] Ibid., 13 Feb. 1768.
[3] Ibid., 12 Mar. 1768.
[4] Ibid., 23 Mar. 1768.
[5] *Love in a Village* on Friday, and *Richard III* on Saturday.
[6] LJ, 3 June 1769.
[7] Ibid., 7 June 1769.

after the time advertised, the present Company think it proper to inform the Public, that the curtain will be drawn up exactly at SEVEN o'clock, to whatever company may be then in the house.'[1] Parker's troupe may not really have done better than Ryder's in prompt starting, but it must have surpassed the latter in the quality of its acting with such members as Michael Atkins, Brownlow Forde, Michael Fullam, Myrton Hamilton, James Stewart, Joseph Waker, and the sprightly singer Mrs. Mozeen.[2] All these at one time or another played acceptably at the Dublin Theatre Royal. Parker's repertoire lacked, however, the colourful show that Ryder often provided. The Friendly Brothers of St. Patrick furnished the one unusual spectacle of the season by sitting on the stage at the closing night, Thursday, 17 August.[3]

In September 1770 Ryder returned to Kilkenny from Belfast with much the same company as had visited the town two years before. It also contained three noteworthy additions: the versatile young comedian John O'Keeffe, the bumptious John Linegar Owens, and the scene-painter Whitmore. Ryder timed his troupe's arrival in Kilkenny to coincide with the autumn assizes when the local demand for amusement would be at its height. In so doing, however, he had to forgo the use of the County Court House and to set up his theatre in the Tholsel assembly room, which possessed no gallery but could be fitted out with side-boxes and, above them, lattices. Places in the boxes and lattices at 3*s.* each, and tickets for the pit at 2*s.* each, might be obtained in advance from the manager at Widow Waters's in Coal Market.[4] The constricted facilities of the new playhouse required more severe regulation of the public's behaviour than usual. Neither servants nor persons of quality were permitted to come early to hold pit seats for other individuals. Servants also were not admitted without payment, and no one was allowed 'behind the Scenes'.[4]

The performances at the Tholsel assembly room opened on Friday, 14 September, with Bickerstaffe's operetta of country romance, *Maid of the Mill*. Ryder, still adhering to his former policy of exploiting stage spectacle, chose the Bickerstaffe work for the first night, because it gave his pair of experts, Whitmore

[1] Ibid.
[2] Ibid., 3 June–16 Aug. 1769.
[3] Ibid., 16 Aug. 1769.
[4] Ibid., 12 Sept. 1770.

and Geoghegan, an exceptional chance to show their talents for scenic effect.[1] Whitmore painted an original set of scenes, comprising Miller Fairfield's House, the Mill at work, the Waterfall, and Lord Ainsworth's House with Gardens. Geoghegan constructed the watermill and its operating machinery. The interest in pictorial representation which this performance evidently aroused in local circles inspired John O'Keeffe, who fancied himself an artist of merit, to undertake a subscription series of four drawings on Kilkenny subjects: the town as viewed from Wind Gap Hill and also from Green's Bridge; the Castle; and St. Canice's Cathedral.[2] The actor-artist advertised for twenty subscribers at £1. 1*s*. for the unmounted set. He was prepared to furnish at £5. 5*s*. a single drawing glazed and framed suitably 'for a Nobleman or Gentleman'. How O'Keeffe fared in this novel project he never reported, though his public statement that it was 'very repugnant to his inclinations to quit this city immediately after his benefit on 12 November'[3] might have been prompted in part by a gratifying response to his pictorial art.

As soon as the assizes had come to a finish in late September, Ryder moved his theatre to the County Court House and accentuated scenic display. On 15 October Whitmore and Geoghegan collaborated to produce the pantomime of *Giant's Causeway; or, A Trip to the Dargle* with 'entirely new' machinery and sets, including the Causeway, the Dargle River, and the Waterfall at Powerscourt.[4] Nine days later they staged the one and only performance of the pantomime *Harlequin in Patagonia* with original scenes of that far-away wilderness and 'an exact representation of a Patagonian man and woman, brought from Patagonia by the Dolphin in her voyage around the world'.[5] The operetta of *Lionel and Clarissa* on 2 November had as a special feature a 'moonlight' setting.[6] *The Rival Queens* exhibited on 19 November a triumphal procession into Babylon with 'entirely new' *décor* by Whitmore and a 'royal car by Geoghegan, exactly after the much-admired one at the Theatre Royal in Crow Street'.[7] A week afterwards, for Mrs. Ryder's benefit, the front of the stage was 'entirely new decorated, the Decorations painted by Mr. Whitmore'.[8]

[1] LJ, 12 Sept. 1770.
[2] Ibid., 19 Sept. 1770.
[3] Ibid., 10 Nov. 1770.
[4] Ibid., 13 Oct. 1770.
[5] Ibid., 24 Oct. 1770.
[6] Ibid., 31 Oct. 1770.
[7] Ibid., 17 Nov. 1770.
[8] Ibid., 21 Nov. 1770.

Mr. Ryder's fellow players held benefits in steady succession throughout December, four or five nights a week, and knowingly placed a heavy strain upon Kilkenny's benevolence. Therefore they resorted to often amusing excuses for squeezing the community's purse. Mr. Fotteral issued a plea that his benefit, 'happening unfortunately the last Night in the Week, and there being six Plays that Week, causes him to have no dependence on his play; and therefore he relies solely on the Goodness and Humanity of the Ladies and Gentlemen of Kilkenny on this Occasion, as his entire dependence is on that Night'.[1] Mr. Remington and Mrs. Logan decided upon a joint benefit, explaining to the local ladies and gentlemen that 'as their stay in town will be but short, [the two actors] would not presume to trouble them singly'.[1] Mr. Owens announced that he would not try advance solicitation for his night on 5 December, 'as it is a Custom by some Persons to be extremely troublesome to Ladies and Gentlemen in disposing of Tickets'.[1] He attempted the innovation of preparing 'for this night only' box accommodations at 3*s.* per seat. Nevertheless the benefit brought him more expense than revenue, 'it being impossible for his friends to honour him with their company, on account of the inclemency of the night'.[2] Consequently, he advertised a second night for 19 December with this fresh argument: 'He has refused an advantageous engagement in Dublin, equal, if not superiour, to any of those persons who have deserted the Company (except Mr. Ryder), out of the respectful esteem he has conceived for the audience of Kilkenny, and in order to help the present Company.'[2] Once more he offered box places along with pit and gallery seats. Despite his effort to meet 'the desire of several Ladies who have Engagements that night' by promising a six-o'clock curtain and the completion of the tragedy 'very early',[3] an insufficient number of patrons turned out. Obstinately he went ahead with a third benefit on 29 December but abandoned the sale of box seats. His notice of this occasion contained an ingenious series of comments: 'As several of Mr. Owens's Tickets have been stolen and mislaid, his Tickets for Saturday next will be sealed. Mr. Owens having lost near ten pounds by the expences he went to for his Plays, as

[1] Ibid., 28 Nov. 1770.
[2] Ibid., 8 Dec. 1770.
[3] Ibid., 19 Dec. 1770.

they happened on Nights when most of his Friends had other Engagements, he most humbly hopes that no Lady will have a Drum or Entertainment against him that Night.'[1]

Two weeks later Mrs. Logan, dismayed over 'the great loss she sustained by her first benefit', took 'another chance', this time with Miss Barry.[2] Likewise Miss Hern ventured a second night on 13 December, since 'her first failed, she not having within ten pounds what she had herebefore; and what she cleared here by her Benefit did not more than defray her expences coming from Belfast'.[3] Messrs. Whitmore and Geoghegan for their evening on 15 December worked up the pantomime of *The Miraculous Miller* with a nice touch of local realism in the setting, namely, 'a view of Kilkenny Castle and Mr. Scott's Watermills at work' on the River Nore.[3] As an added novelty they were to exhibit 'an exact model of Mr. Moore's ingenious carriage, that moves by self-impelling powers, without the assistance of horses, executed by Mr. Geoghegan, who will sit in it himself and carry a black behind him several Times up and down the Stage, with surprising swiftness'.[3] This 'automobile', which had already delighted Belfast, attracted so large an audience that the two stage technicians sought no further patronage. Stewart, however, bid for a renewed benefaction on 28 December with a frank confession of bankruptcy: 'The motive for taking a second Night proceeds from an honest ambition of discharging the several debts contracted here, which the small return of the first benefit could not accomplish, the truth of which the worshipful Chief Magistrate of this city already knows, whose kind indulgence I have experienced, and shall ever gratefully remember.'[4] Exactly a week later the season as well as the benefits came to an end when the manager's brother, Samuel Ryder, enjoyed the privilege of a second performance on his behalf, because 'he lost considerably by his first, there being several Engagements that Evening'.[5] Ryder, gambling on a rush for admission to this final entertainment, invalidated the tickets given out but unused at his previous benefit. Then he made available a fresh issue printed in red rather than black ink for easy identification

[1] LJ, 26 Dec. 1770.
[2] Ibid., 5 Dec. 1770.
[3] Ibid., 8 Dec. 1770.
[4] Ibid., 22 Dec. 1770.
[5] Ibid., 2 Jan. 1771.

at the doors. Ryder's stratagem to ensure a maximum of friendly purchases concluded an uncommonly detailed record of the varied manœuvres employed in respect to eighteenth-century benefit performances on the Irish stage. When 'the harvest of an actor is his benefit', as the *Ennis Chronicle* so aptly phrased the case in Ireland before the Union,[1] he must be expected to press for a bumper harvest with habitual and devious persistence.

The lean returns from these four months in the winter of 1770–1 evidently discouraged the Ryder family from ever appearing again at Kilkenny. Brownlow Forde, who had acted there in 1769, led the next troupe to perform at the County Court House. His players included the well-known strollers Michael Fullam and Tobias Gemea, and Whitmore, the scene designer whose painting had already pleased the town. Fullam's grotesque street-knocker sort of face which required no making-up at once fascinated the Kilkenny spectators, as it did all other Irish audiences for over thirty years of comic impersonation. Forde's actors opened their season with *The West Indian* on 31 December 1772 and kept on playing until June 1773.[2] For the first time a ticket office was established in connexion with the temporary theatre at the County Court House; it sold box places daily, from 10 a.m. to 2 p.m., at 3*s*. each for regular nights and 4*s*. for charity or actors' nights. A surprising innovation was the sale, at least for the opening performance, of seats on the stage at 5*s*.[3] On benefit occasions Forde collected a manager's fee of £1, which for a charity affair he usually refunded.[4] All beneficiaries had to pay the house expenses of somewhat over £7 per day.[4]

After this half-year fling at management, Forde, like the Ryders, never returned to Kilkenny. James Parker, who introduced Forde to the town in 1769, came back, however, in the summer of 1776 at the head of a contingent from both the Crow Street and Smock Alley Theatres, whom he advertised as 'His Majesty's Company of Comedians'. Fitting up the County Court House 'in the most elegant manner', Parker opened with *The Rivals* on Monday, 17 June.[5] The prices of seats continued as in the past, but admission was more strictly regulated. The

[1] EC, 1 Apr. 1790.
[2] LJ, 30 Dec. 1772 and 5 June 1773.
[3] Ibid., 30 Dec. 1772.
[4] Ibid., 30 Jan. 1773.
[5] Ibid., 8 and 15 June 1776.

bills steadily reiterated 'no Person whatever can be admitted behind the Scenes' and 'no Person on any account to be admitted under full Price, during the whole Entertainment'.[1]

Mrs. Crosby took the first of the season's benefits on 22 July. In hopes of arousing more generous patronage her husband published a statement in regard to his difficult situation: 'Mr. Crosby's close Attendance on the Business of the Theatre in the double Capacity of Actor and Prompter, having rendered him utterly incapable of cultivating any Interest here in Private Life, . . . he takes no benefit himself.'[2] Mrs. Crosby provided a colourful finale to her programme by delivering an address in the striking blue uniform of a Kilkenny Ranger. Her impersonation, at the time an original bit of stage business, was catering to the martial excitement that had invaded this county, as it had others, after the outbreak of the American Revolution in the previous year.

The series of benefits was suspended in order to gain the utmost profit out of Race Week, 5–10 August, when merry-making reached its zenith. The actors' nights resumed on the 12th for two final weeks of performance. On 21 August, the next to the last day, a twenty-year-old Irishman, William M'Cready, enjoyed a benefit.[3] Apparently he had begun his stage career in this present summer at Kilkenny, but his début there won no notice even years later after he had attained fame as the father and trainer of the noted tragedian, William C. Macready.

When James Parker left Kilkenny following a command performance of *She Stoops to Conquer* on 24 August for Masonic Lodge 256,[4] he had done his last strolling. Soon overtaken by poor health, he died at Dublin in April 1778. His successors in providing theatricals at the County Court House were John Linegar Owens, who had played there under Ryder in 1770, and John L. Owens, Jr. These two directed a very mediocre set of strollers, for whom John, Jr., without experience, tried to function as manager.[5] The company must have arrived in the late autumn of 1777, because they started to hold benefits in January 1778.[6] The younger Owens tried one on 4 February, but the supposedly attractive bill of *The Orphan*, plus 'a grand

[1] LJ., 6 July 1776. [2] Ibid., 20 July 1776. [3] Ibid., 17 Aug. 1776.
[4] Ibid., 24 Aug. 1776. [5] Ibid., 28 and 31 Jan. 1778. [6] Ibid., 7 Jan. 1778.

new masquerade scene illuminated with one thousand lights' in the afterpiece of *The Duenna*, plus wax lighting throughout the house,[1] did not draw a large enough audience to bail the inexpert manager out of his financial troubles. Within a few days he issued an appeal for funds:

> Mr. Owens, Jr., hopes such Friends as served him by Tickets will please to consider his present Distressed Situation, and send the amount of them to him. And as envious Malice has been strongly levelled against him, by some ungrateful Persons, he purposes stating the whole of his Conduct the few months he has commenced Manager; and to the Candid and Impartial, will give himself up to Censure, requesting Pardon for troubling the Public with his Ill Fortune and Injuries.[2]

At least one prominent citizen made a prompt and generous response to this plea. The Countess of Carrick remitted £12. 12*s*. The young manager published in the *Leinster Journal* his thanks for her liberal aid to 'his distressed situation; through which humane assistance he shall soon obtain the invaluable blessing—liberty'.[2]

The officers of the Kilkenny garrison also undertook to alleviate the plight of Owens and his fellows. The military turned players and performed, in support of the 'Company of Comedians', the tragedies of *The Fair Penitent* and *Venice Preserved* on 5 and 30 January respectively.[3] For the two occasions only box and pit seats in the County Court House theatre were available at the uniform price of 3*s*. Servants of local ladies and gentlemen might hold places after 5 p.m. for a 7 p.m. curtain. On 17 January the same officers presented *The Beggar's Opera* on behalf of the Charitable Society.[4] None of the announcements offered a hint as to the identity of the actresses, whether professionals or local belles. In any case, these performances of 1778 established the precedent for the subsequent 'Gentlemen's Plays', the forerunners of the celebrated 'Kilkenny Private Theatre'. Though plays at the County Court House ceased in mid-March to make way for the spring assizes, the mendicant Owenses remained in town as late as 2 April 1778 to collect the proceeds from a benefit assembly.[5]

[1] Ibid., 4 Feb. 1778. [2] Ibid., 7 Feb. 1778.
[3] Ibid., 3 and 24 Jan. 1778.
[4] Ibid., 14 Jan. 1778. [5] Ibid., 25 Mar. 1778.

Still another theatrical manager new to Kilkenny appeared in the autumn of 1779. John Vandermere, who had been serving as Ryder's deputy at Waterford for the past two summers, opened the Court House stage on Monday, 27 September, with a performance of *The Beggar's Opera* and Colman's farce, *Polly Honeycombe*.[1] 'No care or expense had been wanting to render the Theatre clean and worthy of attention.'[1] Vandermere's small troupe, headed by Mr. and Mrs. Richard Sparks of the Dublin Theatre Royal, did sufficiently good business in the next six weeks to justify extending its season. On 10 November the manager announced that 'by particular Desire' the company would remain in town and 'humbly hoped no Lady [would] fix her Drum on a Play Night'.[2] On account of oncoming winter weather the curtain hour changed from 7.30 to 7 p.m., and 'good fires in the Pit' became the rule.[3] At the same time two well-known Crow Street singers, Robert Mahon and Miss Jameson, joined the local corps of performers for a final month of strongly musical entertainment.[4] For Mahon's benefit on Friday, 10 December, advertised as the company's last night, the operatic version of *The Tempest* and Garrick's operetta, *Cymon*, composed the bill by command of Colonel Thomas Butler and the Rangers.[5]

In the autumn following the visit of Vandermere's troupe, John Linegar Owens, Sr., returned to Kilkenny with a group of strollers and fixed up a playhouse in the Tholsel assembly room, which he advertised as 'the New Theatre in High Street'.[6] After conducting performances there from mid-October to mid-November 1780,[7] he departed for Dublin to join Ryder's company at Crow Street. Alexander Macartney, already experienced in management at Lisburn, evidently took over Owens's playhouse and his troupers. Describing himself 'a perfect stranger in this County, desirous of the protection of the generous public',[8] Macartney announced an extensive redecoration of the 'New Theatre', so that 'for the size, there was not a more elegant House in the Kingdom'.[9] Furthermore,

[1] LJ, 25 Sept. 1779.
[2] Ibid., 10 Nov. 1779.
[3] Ibid., 17 and 20 Nov. 1779.
[4] Ibid., 17 Nov. 1779.
[5] Ibid., 8 Dec. 1779.
[6] Ibid., 4 Oct. 1780.
[7] LJ, 8 Nov. 1780, advertised the last play under Owens's management as *The Merchant of Venice* to be acted on 10 Nov.
[8] Ibid., 8 Nov. 1780.
[9] Ibid., 25 Nov. 1780.

'the most eligible Company, the best Wardrobe, Scenery, etc., travelling in Ireland' now were established there. 'Constant Fires' assured a warm house at *She Stoops to Conquer* on 25 November, the opening night.[1] Despite the rather elaborate preparation of the 'New Theatre' the manager limited its season to the four weeks before Christmas and thus gave the buyers of season tickets at 21*s.* no great bargain.[2]

Macartney perhaps shortened the period of his venture on account of the appearance of a rival company, who began acting on 16 December at the County Court House.[3] Their manager, John Vandermere, had directed a different group at the same location during the autumn of 1779. For his present troupe he had recruited two former Crow Street couples, Mr. and Mrs. Richard Hurst, and Mr. and Mrs. Fielding Wallis, to fill the leading roles in *The Clandestine Marriage*, *The Rivals*, *The Suspicious Husband*, *Romeo and Juliet*, *Venice Preserved*, and similar dependable vehicles.[4] After Hurst and Wallis had enjoyed the final benefit nights of 5 and 7 April 1781, the little temporary theatre had to be 'pulled down' in order to prepare the Court House for the assizes.[5]

Meanwhile Owens, forced out of the Crow Street organization, had come back to Kilkenny in January and resumed management of the 'New Theatre in High Street', from which Macartney had withdrawn at Christmas.[6] The inferior Owens company braved the competition at the County Court House until 8 March when they closed their Tholsel playhouse with a benefit for the manager.[7] A notoriously brash character, he appropriately elected to play the King in Shakespeare's *Henry VIII* for this, his permanent farewell to the town.

Unlike Owens, Vandermere did not sever his ties with Kilkenny at this time, but for several years he gave up strolling around Ireland and passed his managerial mantle over to one of his former troupe, Fielding Wallis. With Mr. and Mrs. Remington, well known to the local citizens, and a Mr. and Mrs. Butler 'from England' as his principal colleagues, Wallis opened a theatre in the County Court House on 5 November

[1] Ibid.

[2] LJ, 23 Dec. 1780, advertised Macartney's benefit for that night with the bill consisting of an appropriate prelude, *The Manager in Distress*, and *Henry IV*.

[3] Ibid., 13 Dec. 1780.

[4] Ibid., 3 Jan.–28 Mar. 1781.

[5] Ibid., 31 Mar. 1781.

[6] Ibid., 6 Jan. 1781.

[7] Ibid., 7 Mar. 1781.

1782 with *The Earl of Essex*.[1] For this first night, seats on the stage were sold at 5*s*. in addition to box admission at 3*s*., pit at 2*s*., and gallery at 1*s*.

No person could buy a seat on the stage, however, for the benefit evening of the Charitable Society on 16 December.[2] Instead of the professional players, a 'Set of Gentlemen' performed *Othello* and thereby inaugurated the famous Kilkenny tradition of 'Gentlemen's Plays'. Prices for the boxes, pit, and gallery were fixed at 5*s*., 3*s*., and 2*s*., respectively, by a ticket committee whose chairman was Thomas Butler, Mayor of Kilkenny in 1781 and the Colonel of the Kilkenny Volunteers. The charity night's entertainment concluded with an epilogue of jovial apology to the resident company:

> How much better, then, my honest Fellow,
> Would Wallis and his Set have play'd Othello?[3]

Only five days later the *Othello* cast of gentlemen acted *The Clandestine Marriage* and *All the World's a Stage* for the benefit of the professional actors.[4] Manager Wallis soon demonstrated his appreciation by engaging at the start of 1783 a number of experienced actors from Dublin to enliven the current repertory. His outstanding recruit, John P. Kemble, who had prolonged his maiden visit to Ireland into a second year, made his Kilkenny *première* on Thursday, 13 February, in the tragedy of *Douglas*.[5] Later on he shifted to comic parts, such as Petruchio and Charles Surface,[6] and presumably continued to play till the final night of 18 March, a command affair for the Rangers and the Volunteers.[7] No player of comparable magnitude performed at Kilkenny before 1800, but the town, of course, could not foresee in 1783 that Kemble's appearances would stand as probably the finest exhibitions of acting on the local stage during the century.

Early in 1784, after an absence of almost three years, John Vandermere resumed management of the temporary theatre at the County Court House with quite a competent band of actors, notably Mr. and Mrs. James Swindal, Mr. and Mrs.

[1] LJ, 28 Sept. and 2 Nov. 1782.
[2] Ibid., 4 Dec. 1782.
[3] Ibid., 21 Dec. 1782.
[4] Ibid., 18 Dec. 1782.
[5] Ibid., 12 Feb. 1783.
[6] Ibid., 12 and 22 Feb. 1783.
[7] Ibid., 12 Mar. 1783.

Wallis, Jacob Hammerton, and Thomas King.[1] Improving upon his former rival Macartney's scheme of season tickets, Vandermere advertised subscription tickets to twelve first nights at 21*s.* for the pit and 31*s.* 6*d.* for the boxes, the total issue to be limited to thirty subscribers. The new manager also announced an unusual winter schedule of four playing nights a week (Tuesday, Wednesday, Thursday, Saturday), with a 7 p.m. curtain, surprisingly late for midwinter. Performances started on Tuesday, 17 February, with *The Count of Narbonne*, and lasted until the spring assizes approached. On 9 March, however, the amateur players of 1783 took over the theatre at the County Court House to perform *Percy* on behalf of the Charitable Society.[2] For the first time an orchestra of 'musical gentlemen' participated. Though the sponsors raised the price in the boxes to 10*s.* and in the pit to 5*s.*, these record figures did not cut down the attendance. The benefit resulted in almost £75 of collected admissions, but so great a crowd pressed for entrance that by no means all who gained admittance paid the doorkeepers for their tickets. A subsequent polite advertisement may have pricked the consciences of some persons to send their admission money belatedly to the Society's treasurer.[3] The leading patron of both amateur and professional dramatics in Kilkenny, Colonel Thomas Butler, assisted Vandermere's troupe by a command performance for the Volunteers on Monday, 29 March, and another for the Rangers on the following Saturday.[4] Thus encouraged, the troupe reopened its theatre in the County Court House on 21 April with a spring curtain hour of 7.30 p.m.[5] A benefit for the manager on 9 June ended not only the present season,[6] but also Vandermere's career on the local stage.

The rather considerable theatrical activity between the autumn of 1782 and the summer of 1784 evidently sharpened public concern for a regular playhouse in Kilkenny. Furthermore, the spirit of national autonomy aroused by the 1783 declarations of the Irish Parliament was inspiring the larger towns to schemes for enhancing their individual prestige. On 15 December 1784 the *Leinster Journal* announced a project of historic importance

[1] Ibid., 14 Feb. 1784. [2] Ibid., 18 Feb. 1784. [3] Ibid., 17 Mar. 1784.
[4] Ibid., 24 and 31 Mar. 1784. [5] Ibid., 21 Apr. 1784.
[6] Ibid., 5 June 1784.

to its community: 'The most respectable Inhabitants of this City being desirous of having a handsome Theatre erected, and a convenient Lot of Ground being offered at the Parade for the Purpose, at a very moderate Rent, the most favourable Opportunity now presents itself to execute a Design which will be as ornamental to the City as profitable to the Subscribers.' The intended site must have been the uncovered piece of land, 90 feet wide by 200 feet deep, on the west side of the Parade opposite the Castle gardens about one hundred yards from the junction with High Street.[1] This was the only available lot of sufficient dimensions to permit the erection of the unique building described in the *Journal* announcement:

> It is proposed to build two substantial handsome Houses as Wings to the Theatre; the Rent of which Houses will nearly repay, it is presumed, the Expence of the entire Building, and at all times insure an annual income to the Subscribers: And when it is considered that a Company of Players never performed here during the Lent and Summer Assizes, the Periods most beneficial to them, it is likewise to be presumed that the Profits arising to the Subscribers from the Rent of the Theatre, with that of the two Dwelling Houses, will produce an ample Compensation for the Money expended. The Gentlemen who patronize this new Theatre, and who have become Subscribers, propose to apportion the Profits into Shares.

The subscription book and the architect's designs for the theatre reposed at the office of the *Journal*, where any interested person might inspect them and signify the amount of his support. The *Journal* carried repeated notices of the playhouse proposal until 25 June 1785. Then the promoters apparently decided that the sum of the subscriptions warranted no further action, and all publicity ceased. Despite the manifest inferiority of the town's theatrical accommodations, the genteel citizens could not be persuaded to rally to this attractive commercial as well as civic investment.

Two years of stage inactivity followed the proposal for a permanent playhouse. Then, at the beginning of 1787, the former group of Kilkenny amateurs reopened the County Court House as a temporary theatre and advertised their bills for the first time as 'Gentlemen's Plays'. On 9 January they performed *Othello* and *The Apprentice* in behalf of the Charitable

[1] See 'A Survey of the City of Kilkenny'.

Society at the usual benefit scale of 5*s.* for box seats, 3*s.* for the pit, and 2*s.* for the gallery.[1] As an innovation, members of the Society offered to hold box places for attending ladies in order that the latter would not send servants early to keep seats. In spite of this precaution against drawing a rowdy element to the performances, disturbances did occur. 'Some ill-minded person threw a stone at one of the sentinels' posted at the entrance and fractured his skull.[2] Others, less violent, annoyed the performers from the Grand Jury gallery and from behind the scenes.[3] Consequently it was announced in connexion with the second 'Gentlemen's Play' for the Charitable Society that any intrusion of these stage precincts would lead to the lowering of the curtain.[3] On this second night, Monday, 5 February, *The Orphan* and *The Apprentice* made up the entertainment, supported by an 'Orchestra, as in the last Play . . . composed of Gentlemen, and the best Performers that can be had'.[4] For the first time the advertisements listed a cast: Henry Brodrick, Thomas Henry Mann, Eland Mossom, and Roth as the principal male characters, and Mrs. Wells, a professional actress well known to the Kilkenny public, as the heroine Monimia. The same gentlemen presented on Tuesday, 13 March, a third benefit programme of *The Fair Penitent* and *The Mayor of Garret*, with a Mrs. Vincent as Calista in the tragedy.[5] Their fourth and final charity performance six days later contained only comedy: *The Mayor of Garret* again, *The Recruiting Serjeant*, and *The Devil to Pay*.[6]

The 'brilliant and crowded' audiences at these 'Gentlemen's Plays' of 1787 evidently tempted Chalmers, the leading harlequin in the Smock Alley company, to try his hand at managing a summer season in the Kilkenny County Court House. Elaborating on Vandermere's subscription plan of 1784, Chalmers advertised not only subscription tickets for twelve first nights, but also transferable tickets for twelve performances other than first nights.[7] The latter sold at 23*s.* 6*d.* for the boxes, a one-quarter discount, and 18*s.* for the pit, a discount of one-third. At the season's opening on 14 July 1787 Chalmers's company included William Joseph Smithson,[8] but it lost him

[1] LJ, 6 Jan. 1787. [2] Ibid., 13 Jan. 1787. [3] Ibid., 24 Jan. 1787.
[4] Ibid., 3 Feb. 1787. [5] Ibid., 3 and 10 Mar. 1787. [6] Ibid., 17 Mar. 1787.
[7] Ibid., 16 June 1787. [8] Ibid., 12 and 16 July 1787.

in mid-season since he was not allowed, so he claimed in a *Leinster Journal* notice, to play the roles previously agreed upon.[1] The addition of the Smock Alley actress Mrs. Hitchcock and her daughter after the summer assizes offset Smithson's defection.[1] With a skilled harlequin as manager the Kilkenny troupe relied on frequent pantomimes to provide novelty. For the last night before the assizes Chalmers put on *Harlequin Fortunatus* and also his own act of leaping through a hogshead of blazing fire.[2] Similarly, on the final night of the season, 24 September, he exploited his talent in *Neck or Nothing; or, Harlequin's Flight from the Gods* by flying 'from the Back of the Gallery, Head foremost, over the Pit to the Back of the Stage'.[3]

Though Smithson on his first visit to Kilkenny had left in a huff, he had been disgruntled not with the town, but with the company management. Therefore it was not surprising that after a successful venture as strolling manager in Wexford during the winter of 1788–9, he should decide to test the theatrical possibilities of Kilkenny. On 1 April 1789 he announced that early in the month he would 'present a Company' at the County Court House and maintain 'a careful Watch in arranging the Characters so as to correspond with the Strength of the Company'.[4] At the same time he offered, cost unspecified, 'a few transferable Tickets for twelve nights' of the season, a subscription plan which his Kilkenny predecessor, Chalmers, had introduced. The Court House performances finally began on Friday, 24 April, with the doors open at six o'clock and the curtain rising at seven.[5] The prices of seats continued as in the past twenty years, namely, 3*s.* in the boxes, 2*s.* in the pit, and 1*s.* in the gallery. 'Nothing under full price', however, was accepted during the entire evening's entertainment. Smithson adhered to a steady Monday, Wednesday, Friday schedule of playing unless a charitable assembly on one of these days made a performance unprofitable.

The feature of the opening night, *Love in a Village*, exhibited the company's chief attractions, a pair of young vocalists, Mr. Power and Mrs. Castelli, the latter advertised as from the Theatres Royal at London and Dublin.[6] Their skill enabled

[1] LJ, 15 Aug. 1787.
[2] Ibid., 28 July 1787.
[3] Ibid., 22 Sept. 1787.
[4] Ibid., 1, 4 and 8 Apr. 1789.
[5] Ibid., 18 Apr. 1789.
[6] Ibid., 22 Apr. 1789.

Smithson to produce in the next twelve weeks a lively series of comic operas—*The Poor Soldier*, *Robin Hood*, *The Beggar's Opera*, and the like. A few classic tragedies and comedies, such as *Douglas*, *Othello*, *The Merchant of Venice*, and *The School for Scandal*, were occasionally interspersed among the musical pieces and farces. The very popular bill of *The Beaux' Stratagem* and *Rosina* on Friday, 22 May, drew a house of £42 for the Charitable Society benefit.[1] When the season came to a close on Monday, 13 July, with the manager's second night, Mrs. Castelli informed the local public that she intended to prolong her residence in Kilkenny and to teach French, Italian, and music, both instrumental and vocal.[2] As late as 8 December she was still in town to take the leading roles in a special programme of *Love in a Village* and *The Poor Soldier* in behalf of the Charitable Society.[3]

Smithson, apparently well satisfied by his first managerial experience at Kilkenny, returned there in 1790. An announcement of 1 September stated that 'by permission' a playhouse was to be opened in the County Court House on 6 October and that a few subscription tickets for twelve nights' admission were to be available.[4] The painting and the airing of the Court House, as well as 'some Capital Engagements' of performers, could not be completed by 6 October.[5] Indeed, the theatre's opening had to be postponed for another month, but 'constant fires' were kept in the building.[6] Smithson's troupe, mainly composed of his Wexford–Kilkenny group from the previous year, at last raised their first curtain on 8 November for a production of *The Dramatist*.[6] Performances stopped on 20 December and resumed after the Christmas holidays for nine weeks, ending on 7 March 1791.[7]

The renewal of Kilkenny's professional stage entertainment stirred 'persons of the first rank in the city and county' to revive the 'Gentlemen's Plays' after a lapse of four years. On 12 January 1791 'as numerous an audience as was ever seen in this city' attended the County Court House theatre to view the acting of *Percy* and *The Apprentice* for the benefit of the Charitable Society.[8] In the tragedy Walter Butler, Lord

[1] Ibid., 20 May and 3 June 1789. [2] Ibid., 11 and 18 July 1789.
[3] Ibid., 5 Dec. 1789. [4] Ibid., 1 Sept. 1790. [5] Ibid., 6 Oct. 1790.
[6] Ibid., 6 Nov. 1790. [7] Ibid., 18 Dec. 1790–5 Mar. 1791.
[8] Ibid., 5 and 15 Jan. 1791.

Thurles, son and heir of the Earl of Ormonde, filled the title role, while two actresses from Smithson's group, Mrs. Brennan and Mrs. Scott, played the female leads. Only three days later the Kilkenny gentlemen undertook a second bill, consisting of *Rule a Wife* and *Bon Ton*, in aid of 'the Company now Performing Here'.[1] For this night Manager Smithson, instead of the usual citizens' committee, handled the advance sale of box places at 5*s*., as well as tickets for the pit at 3*s*. and for the gallery at 1*s*.

Smithson went back to his playhouses in the west of Ireland, and another new manager, John Davison, tried out Kilkenny in the following year. His theatre at the County Court House opened on 23 February 1792 with *The Clandestine Marriage*.[2] Spring assizes interrupted the stage entertainment for the first two weeks of April.[3] When starting performances again, Davison placed on sale a new variety of subscription ticket, transferable and good for nine first-nights, at a cost of 21*s*. for box admission and 13*s*. 6*d*. for the pit.[4] By June the manager had to entice the playgoers with a variety of weekly attractions. On the 4th, the interlude of *The Maid of the Oaks*, a country romance, appeared with a new set painted by a local artist, Mr. Gibson—a flat—depicting a Kilkenny panorama of Patrick Street, the Parade, the Castle, Rose Inn Street, and the Sheaf Inn.[5] The stage was 'beautifully illuminated to display this Scene as it deserves'. On 11 June Mr. Field from Crow Street made his local début as Romeo.[6] Four days later William H. Moss of the same company introduced himself to the town in another Shakespearian part, Shylock.[7] Miss W. Brett, also from Crow Street, entertained her first Kilkenny audience on 18 June by impersonating Rosetta in *Love in a Village*.[7] Moss concluded his special engagement with a benefit on 2 July and presented, as the feature of his evening, a highly diverting recitation, 'The Mossonian Budget; or, A Post Haste Journey from Dublin to Kilkenny', which he spoke while 'riding on an Ass'.[8] A Masonic night, celebrated with a procession of the three Kilkenny lodges to the theatre and with musical airs by a military band during

[1] LJ, 12 Jan. 1791.
[2] Ibid., 22 Feb. 1792.
[3] Ibid., 28 Mar. 1792.
[4] Ibid., 11 Apr. 1792.
[5] Ibid., 2 June 1792.
[6] Ibid., 9 June 1792.
[7] Ibid., 13 June 1792.
[8] Ibid., 30 June 1792.

the evening, brought Davison's season to a lively close on Monday, 16 July.[1]

A veteran actor from the Kilkenny company of 1792, Michael Fullam, took the next turn at managing theatricals in the County Court House. The core of his troupe was composed of players who had been performing recently at Waterford and Wexford under the leadership of Thomas Betterton. The latter, who had not previously visited Kilkenny, opened the 1793 season on 5 June in the title role of *The West Indian*.[2] In connexion with this event Manager Fullam, imitating his predecessor, advertised a subscription ticket for nine nights at 21*s*. for a box place and 13*s*. 6*d*. for a seat in the pit. Betterton's fourteen-year-old daughter, Julia, did not appear on the first night, but subsequently she made several appearances, the last one as Moggy M'Gilpin in *The Highland Reel* for her benefit on 5 July.[3] After that evening the two Bettertons hastened to Galway and never revisited Kilkenny.

The summer assizes in the first week of August put an end not only to the performances at the County Court House, but also to Fullam's management. John Davison reassumed direction of Kilkenny's stage entertainment and changed its location as well as its repertory. The assembly room in the Tholsel was 'fitted up in the most commodious and theatrical style' and named the 'New Opera House'.[4] Admission fees adhered to the long-prevailing scale of 3*s*. for the boxes, 2*s*. for the pit, and 1*s*. for the gallery. Davison went to Dublin and engaged at least ten Crow Street players, most of them with musical skills. In consequence, the new theatre commenced on Wednesday, 14 August, with the operetta *Love in a Village*, and a superior orchestra led by Signor Bartoli of the Dublin Theatre Royal. The last week of August offered an especially varied selection of light opera—*The Duenna*, *Lionel and Clarissa*, *Maid of the Mill*, *Robin Hood*, and *Rosina*—to be performed, according to the advertisements, by 'the first opera company in the Kingdom'.[5] This interesting puff did not take into account the large and able troupe at the Capel Street Opera House, Dublin, in the winter of 1783–4.

The August operatic week gave prominence to a newcomer

[1] Ibid., 14 July 1792. [2] Ibid., 5 June 1793. [3] Ibid., 29 June 1793.
[4] Ibid., 14 Aug. 1793. [5] Ibid., 24 Aug. 1793.

on the Kilkenny stage, Robert Owenson, who since 1776 had been exhibiting his comic and vocal gifts in the west and south of Ireland as well as in the capital. Though he did not shine as manager of the Fishamble Street Theatre, Dublin, in 1784–5, he persisted in his desire for managerial responsibility. Now, at Kilkenny, the attractive, honey-tongued actor ingratiated himself with several influential persons who apparently fired his ambition. Though Davison did not close the 'New Opera House' until early October,[1] Owenson on 11 September declared his succession to the managerial office in Kilkenny.[2] In the future he would have 'the Honour of conducting its Theatrical Amusements, a Circumstance he much prides himself upon', so his 'Good Fortune ha[d] decreed'. What Owenson called his 'good fortune' was, according to the recollection of his daughter, Lady Sydney Morgan, a request from a committee of Kilkenny gentlemen, headed by Lord Thurles, that the actor should lead a project to build a playhouse of 'aristocratic respectability'.[3] The present awkward arrangement of fitting up temporary stages in the County Court House or the Tholsel assembly room did not befit 'the Versailles of Ireland'[3] with its population of between 20,000 and 25,000,[4] particularly since county seats of less size and wealth, such as Ennis, Galway, Newry, and Wexford, had already erected permanent theatres.

Lord Thurles's father, John Butler, 17th Earl of Ormonde, provided a site on the Parade across from the Castle,[5] almost certainly not the same ground, however, that was considered in 1784 for a new theatre. At present the Inland Revenue Office occupies the location.[6] The Earl of Ormonde also initiated the patron list with a subscription of £50. One-half of the funds for construction were to come from subscribing citizens, and an equal amount from Owenson. Yet, much to the latter's dismay, only certain members of the Ormonde

[1] LJ, 2 Oct. 1793, advertised *The Rivals* for 4 Oct., the next to the last night.

[2] Ibid., 11 Sept. 1793.

[3] Morgan, i. 114.

[4] Charles T. Bowden, *A Tour through Ireland in 1790* (Dublin, 1791), p. 124.

[5] Morgan, i. 115.

[6] E. T. Keane, *A Glimpse of the Days That are Over* (Kilkenny, 1910), p. 16. According to the *Irish Quarterly Review*, ix (1859), 410, all but a small portion of the playhouse on the Parade was pulled down in 1851. Perhaps the remains were incorporated into the Athenaeum, a public meeting hall that was later altered into the Inland Revenue Office.

family and a very few others proceeded to subscribe.[1] As with the building proposal of ten years before, the enthusiasm of a small, respected group could not overcome the parsimony of the Kilkenny gentry at large.

The inadequacy of the subscriptions delayed the completion of the playhouse, since Owenson naturally held up his expenditures in the hope that more subscribers would come forward. Finally, in order to cover the remainder of his costs, he was forced to secure loans from various individuals and a mortgage of £500 from a local lawyer.[1] Owenson first expected to open the new structure on 23 June 1794, and set about engaging performers in Dublin.[2] A few days before the June date, however, he called off the engagements, saying that he had been 'disappointed of his theatre in Kilkenny' and could not start operation before August.[3] This expectation also proved false, and in the end the curtain never rose on the new Kilkenny stage during 1794.

At last, on 8 August 1795, Owenson published in Kilkenny a notice to 'the Nobility, Gentry, and the Public in general of this City and its Vicinity, that the New Theatre on the Parade will be open in a few Nights, with entire new Scenery'.[4] The new building, about 50 feet in width by 90 feet in depth,[5] much surpassed the dimensions of the Limerick playhouse and approximated those of the first Theatre Royal in Cork at the corner of George's and Prince's Streets. Yet, unlike the latter, the Kilkenny structure possessed a row of boxes encircling the pit, and also a second tier of side-boxes which provided the local playgoers with their first opportunity, since 1770, to sit in 'lattices'.[6] Seats there were priced at 3*s.*, the same as in the lower boxes. Owenson, despite his unanticipated financial burden, did not raise the admission charges above the long-standing figures. The 'Box Room' sold tickets every day from 11 a.m. to 3 p.m.

After several postponements the curtain went up for the first performance at the 'New Theatre on the Parade' on Monday, 31 August. A humorous welcoming address by the manager,

[1] Morgan, i. 115. [2] Mathews, i. 86. [3] Ibid., i. 89.

[4] LJ, 8 Aug. 1795.

[5] These dimensions are based upon William Robertson's plan of the Kilkenny Theatre (1818), now in the possession of the Kilkenny Historical Society.

[6] LJ, 26 Aug. and 2 Dec. 1795.

in the character of an Irish wag named Paddy O'Carrol, preceded the acting of *The Rivals* and *The Citizen*. The *Leinster Journal*, reporting on this historic event, asserted that 'the beauty and neatness of the Theatre, Scenery, etc., far exceeded the most sanguine expectations of the public—nor shall we scruple to say that for its size it is not inferior to any theatre in this or the sister Kingdom'.[1] During the next four months Owenson's company, which included veteran strollers like the Michael Fullams and the Richard Hursts, as well as minor Crow Street players, entertained mostly with popular classics of the day, such as *The Fair Penitent*, *The West Indian*, *The Provok'd Husband*, *As You Like It*, *The Beggar's Opera*, *Miss in Her Teens*, *Maid of the Mill*, *The Wonder*, and *The Duenna*.[2] The manager for his benefit on 15 December chose the season's only unusual production, Cumberland's comedy of *The Natural Son*, which had no other recorded performance in Ireland outside Dublin.[3] The Masons observed with songs, but with no procession, the night of 11 November in honour of 'Brother' Fullam,[4] and the Charitable Society enjoyed a benefit on 7 December, when that part of the pit adjoining the lower boxes was 'railed in' to be sold as box accommodations.[5] No further special occasions took place before the first season of the 'New Theatre' came to an end on 21 December 1795.[6]

When Owenson began his second season at Kilkenny in late July 1796,[7] he introduced the policy, long in vogue at Cork and Limerick, of presenting a succession of star performers for limited engagements. The noted Dublin actress, Maria Campion, led off and made her first stage appearance under her married name of Mrs. Spencer. For her benefit on 17 August she played Monimia in *The Orphan* at the command of the New Theatre's chief patron, Lord Thurles,[8] who had now become the 18th Earl of Ormonde by reason of his father's death in 1795. The next celebrity, the low comedian Lee Lewes, took the part of Sheva in *The Jew* for his Kilkenny début on 16 September.[9] After acting Marplot in *The Busie Body* at the Earl of Ormonde's command on 28 September, Lewes finished

[1] LJ, 2 Sept. 1795. [2] Ibid., 2 Sept.–28 Nov. 1795.
[3] Ibid., 14 Dec. 1795. [4] Ibid., 14 Nov. 1795. [5] Ibid., 2 Dec. 1795.
[6] LJ, 19 Dec. 1795, advertised for the 21st a bill of *The Conscious Lovers* and *Captain Cooke*, a pantomime which 'many persons desired' to have repeated.
[7] Ibid., 27 July 1796. [8] Ibid., 13 Aug. 1796. [9] Ibid., 10 Sept. 1796.

his engagement with *A Bold Stroke for a Wife* on 3 October.[1] Miss Poole, a young London singer recently at Crow Street, succeeded Lewes as the featured entertainer. Her repertoire consisted wholly of roles in musical 'hits', starting on 17 October with Rosetta in *Love in a Village* and closing a week later with Lorenza in *The Castle of Andalusia*.[2] Then Mrs. George Dawson, the leading actress of the Fishamble Street Private Theatre in 1793, came to town as the season's final attraction. The Earl of Ormonde sponsored her benefit on 15 November when she elected to impersonate Mrs. Heidelberg in *The Clandestine Marriage*.[3] The Charitable Society's benefit on 28 November concluded the 1796 performances.[4] Since admission to the boxes and pit on that night cost only 3*s*. and to the gallery, 2*s*., the proceeds amounted to little more than £44.[5] Back in 1784, with much higher charges for box and pit seats, the Society's benefit netted as much as £68.[6] Enthusiasm for this time-honoured charity seemed to be declining.

Though 'a brilliant assemblage of beauty and the first fashion of the county'[7] had often crowded into the new Kilkenny playhouse between July and November of 1796, still the finish of its second season found Manager Owenson on the brink of financial disaster. Not only did 'huge' bills remain unpaid, but the holder of the £500 mortgage suddenly foreclosed.[8] Neither the Earl of Ormonde nor any gentleman friend came to Owenson's rescue. Therefore he left the scene precipitately,[8] never to return to the theatre which he had brought into existence. Its doors stayed shut for over two years. The grave misadventure of its founder caused prospective successors to approach the opportunity with caution.

At last, in the spring of 1799, William Smithson, who had conducted performances at the County Court House in 1790–1 and, since then, had managed the Ennis as well as the Galway theatre, decided to try his fortune again at Kilkenny. On 13 March he announced his intention to furnish entertainment at the 'New Theatre' after making 'some necessary alterations'.[9] In late May the public was informed of 'his efforts to obtain Novelty and render the Theatre comfortable', and of his aim

[1] Ibid., 28 Sept. 1796. [2] Ibid., 15–22 Oct. 1796. [3] Ibid., 12 Nov. 1796.
[4] Ibid., 26 Nov. 1796. [5] Ibid., 7 Dec. 1796. [6] Ibid., 17 Mar. 1784.
[7] Ibid., 1 Oct. 1796. [8] Morgan, i. 120. [9] LJ, 13 Mar. 1799.

'to select such parts of the Drama as may be found Moral and Instructive'.[1] Never before had a Kilkenny manager sounded a didactic note in his publicity. It must have been inserted to enlarge the support of the serious-minded, middle-class citizens who constituted the predominant business element. Smithson's second innovation took the form of a brief observation near the top of the daily playbills. The one of 5 June remarked of *A Cure for the Heart Ache* 'An Excellent Lesson to Mankind', and that of 10 June commented on *The Heir at Law*: 'No Comedy since *The School for Scandal* has been played with so much success, or brought such Crowded Houses.'[2] The new manager also broke precedents by delaying curtain time till 7.30 p.m. for the convenience of suburban gentry, and by selling transferable tickets for the entire season at £2. 2*s*.[3] Single admission continued at 3*s*. for the boxes and lattices, 2*s*. for the pit, and 1*s*. for the gallery. Admittance behind the scenes, as usual, was forbidden.

The 'New Theatre, Kilkenny' opened its third season on Wednesday, 29 May 1799, with the comedy of *Every One has His Fault*.[4] Indeed, humorous and musical plays composed almost the whole entertainment throughout the ensuing summer. The concentration on the lighter species resulted from the limited capacities of Smithson's performers, a much inferior group to the preceding two engaged by Owenson. Of the present troupe only Michael Fullam and his wife had previously appeared in Kilkenny. With Fullam an active and popular Mason like himself, Smithson could expect in this Masonic stronghold a large attendance at any performance honouring the Order. Therefore the 'New Theatre' held a Masonic night on Friday, 28 June, with an 'amphitheatre' on the stage for those brethren who marched to the playhouse 'in their proper Regalia'.[5] The amusements for the evening consisted of the unfailingly comic *The Wonder: A Woman Keeps a Secret*, the musical farce of *The Wicklow Mountains*, and the *entr'acte* rendering of Masonic songs. The sole melodrama to be staged during the summer, *The Castle Spectre*, served as the main novelty of the Charitable Society night on Tuesday, 6 August,[6] but it brought in only

[1] LJ, 25 May 1799.
[2] B.M. Playbills, vol. 291.
[3] LJ, 25 May 1799.
[4] Ibid., 29 May 1799.
[5] Ibid., 26 June 1799.
[6] Ibid., 3 Aug. 1799.

a trifle over £22,[1] a record low figure. Yet this benefit headed the performances of the gay Assize Week. Balls, drums, and other private parties must have provided too stiff competition.

The closing of the playhouse on the Parade on Saturday, 10 August,[1] marked the end of theatricals in Kilkenny until after the Union. The town's stage facilities and activities during the eighteenth century hardly measured up to its social and economic distinction. It had lagged well behind comparable Irish county seats in the building of a permanent theatre. The absence of such a structure over most of the century discouraged professional troupes, especially those of Dublin, from performing in Kilkenny. Furthermore, the necessity of using either the County Court House or the Tholsel made it impossible or very expensive to take advantage of the two yearly assize periods most profitable to theatrical business in the Irish county towns. Even when the construction of a playhouse was belatedly undertaken, Kilkenny withheld proper financial assistance. Its niggardly conduct may be attributed to peculiar community factors. A majority of the substantial merchants and shopkeepers apparently felt a puritanical indifference or even aversion to stage entertainment of a secular kind. On the other hand, the fashionable gentry, since they found access to Dublin easy, gravitated towards the social life and amusements of the capital. Local aspirants in the practice of the arts also travelled to the metropolis for possible recognition. Neither a play nor any other dramatic entertainment written by a Kilkenny resident was recorded as presented on the local stage before 1800. After the Act of Union and the break-up of the Irish parliamentary sessions, Kilkenny society no longer looked to Dublin, but began to exploit its own resources for culture and recreation. The town and county gentry together set about reviving the once vigorous tradition of annual gentlemen's plays for local charity. They took over the playhouse erected by Robert Owenson on the Parade, and by degrees carried out drastic alterations. Their elegant performances eventually made that playhouse famous on both sides of the Atlantic under the name of the 'Kilkenny Private Theatre'.

[1] Ibid., 7 Aug. 1799.

VIII · NEWRY

BEFORE the summer of 1736 the Smock Alley troupe had to relinquish the southern theatrical circuit—Cork, Waterford, and possibly Limerick as well as Kilkenny—to the rival Aungier Street company. In compensation the Smock Alley actors undertook the first tour by Dublin players to the north of Ireland. After travelling two-thirds of the hundred miles to Belfast in late June or early July, they probably broke their journey to perform at Newry, the largest town *en route* and the chief trading centre of County Down.[1] Certainly they stopped there in July 1741 to give plays at the outset of their summer trip to Belfast and Derry.[2]

In this latter year the completion of the canal from the Newry River to Lough Neagh linked the town to the heart of Ulster by water and thereby initiated Newry's growth as an important Irish port. Some twenty years later the deepening of the river channel and the construction of quays put the finishing touches to Newry's sea communication.[3] The export of butter and linen, and the supplying of nails, scythes, and shovels to rural Ulster, brought steady prosperity during the rest of the eighteenth century. A population of five to six thousand in the 1760's gradually increased to about ten thousand by 1800.[3]

Well before the 1760's Newry's occasional contacts with Dublin actors had been replaced by Belfast stage connexions. In 1758, for example, Sheriffe led his very competent 'company of comedians' from Belfast to Newry for performances during July and August.[4] The first regular playhouse in Newry was not established, however, until 1769. In January of that year James Parker, manager of a troupe that had been acting at Belfast for six months, took it to Newry and on Monday the 23rd opened 'the New Theatre in High Street'.[5] The venerable High Street continued to be the town's leading thoroughfare

[1] Hitchcock, i. 97, 101.

[2] Ibid., p. 114; FDJ, 11 July 1741.

[3] Maxwell, p. 230.

[4] *Letters . . . between Mr. West Digges . . . and Mrs. Sarah Ward, 1752–1759* (Edinburgh, 1833), p. 123.

[5] BNL, 20 Jan. 1769.

and a residential quarter for persons of quality. The theatre, probably a converted structure, was situated not more than two hundred yards east of the Old Market on the south side of High Street next to the Pope's Head Tavern and near the Post Office.[1] Like the latter, it stood to the rear of a house fronting on the street.[2] Both the tavern and the theatre were demolished around 1830 to make way for the Convent of the Order of the Poor Clares, which still occupies the site.[3]

In announcing the *première* of the High Street stage, Parker described his company of about twenty performers as 'Comedians from the Theatres Royal of London, Dublin, and Edinburgh', and his bill as two favourite pieces, Farquhar's *The Inconstant* and O'Hara's *Midas*.[4] He boldly promised for the O'Hara burletta 'all the Original Music, Machinery, Scenery, Dresses, and Decorations, as Performed at the Theatres of London and Dublin with universal Applause'. The new playhouse possessed no boxes and such limited accommodation back stage that the manager from the start ordered 'No Person whatever . . . admitted behind the Scenes'.[4] The standard out-of-Dublin prices prevailed: 2*s.* for the pit, 1*s.* for the gallery.

After the notice of the opening performance no further news of the High Street theatre's first season appeared, except an account of the benefit for 'distressed Freemasons' on Wednesday, 5 April.[5] Two comedies, *The Constant Couple* and *The Ghost*, formed the night's entertainment. Local Masons attended in full regalia and sat in an amphitheatre on the stage. 'A more brilliant audience was never seen on the like occasion in the North of Ireland', nor a more generous assembly, it may be added, for the evening's receipts amounted to the surprising figure of £50.[5]

One of the performers at Newry in 1769, Michael Atkins, became manager of the resident Belfast troupe in 1773. During the next ten years the Atkins company occasionally played on the High Street stage. In 1778 it began a two-month stay with *Julius Caesar* on Wednesday, 13 May.[6] In advance of this affair the manager dared to voice his hope that 'the Shortness of the

[1] 'A Plan of the Town of Newry' by John Rocque, 1760; P. Keenan, *Old Newry: Some Historical Notes* (Newry, 1945), p. 4.

[2] *The Newry Magazine* (Newry, 1815–16), i. 18 n.

[3] Keenan, p. 4.

[4] BNL, 20 Jan. 1769.

[5] Ibid., 11 Apr. 1769.

[6] NC, 11 May 1778.

Season and the Excellence of the Performers will procure him that Countenance and Politeness from the Inhabitants of Newry which he has so often experienced'.[1] At the end of the season on 13 July Atkins announced that he would reopen the theatre in November after repairing and redecorating it 'in the most elegant manner'.[2] Eighteen transferable tickets for the winter series of performances would be issued at 21*s*. each; ten had already been subscribed for.

Three days after Atkins's notice two dissident members of his company, Messrs. Hamilton and Pero, advertised that they intended to open a new playhouse at Newry in October, and that, in addition to 'an elegant Wardrobe' already purchased, their scenery was now being prepared by Messrs. Bamford and Jolly, painters to the theatres in Dublin.[3] Hamilton and Pero also offered transferable season tickets to the limit of twenty at 18*s*. each. Their scheme, however, soon evaporated: Hamilton assumed charge of the Belfast theatre in the autumn of 1778 and hired Pero to assist.

Atkins departed in August to act with the Crow Street troupe at Cork, but he appointed one of his experienced players, Mr. Wilmot, to carry out the announced winter theatricals in Newry. The veterans of Atkins's company—Mr. and Mrs. Richard Knipe, Mr. and Mrs. Richard Rowe, Mr. and Mrs. Tyrrell—joined Wilmot in preference to performing at Belfast under Hamilton. Charles Clagget, a musician of 'distinguished abilities', came up from Dublin to direct the orchestra and the operas, as in the past he had done at Kilkenny and Waterford.[4] The theatre in High Street, 'now repaired and ornamented', began its season on Thursday, 3 December 1778, with *The Rivals* and Bickerstaffe's comic opera, *The Padlock*.[4] When the curtain lifted for the opening scene of Sheridan's play, 'an extremely little man with a droll face' entered and spoke the first lines as Fag, the waggish servant of Captain Absolute. This was the stage début, hitherto unrecorded, of Andrew Cherry, a sixteen-year-old Limerick youth who matured into one of the century's leading comedians. Following his performance of Fag, he played the impertinent rogue, Mungo, in *The Padlock*. So quickly did he gain fame for his comic power during the

[1] NC, 11 May 1778. [2] Ibid., 13 July 1778.
[3] Ibid., 16 July 1778. [4] Ibid., 30 Nov. 1778.

winter in Newry and the ensuing summer in Derry that within a year Manager Ryder engaged him at Crow Street. Cherry had to wait four years, however, until his coming of age, before he could marry the attractive young actress, Miss Knipe, who impersonated Lydia Languish in *The Rivals* on the night of his début.

Crucial support for Newry's winter theatricals came from the Volunteers, though they had been organized but a few months.[1] On Monday, 4 January 1779, their first command performance drew 'a most numerous and polite audience' to enjoy a night of gay drama, *As You Like It* and *Polly Honeycombe*.[2] The actors' benefits started in March. The evening of Friday the 26th had to be allotted suddenly to Mrs. Knipe. Her husband, Richard William Knipe, died on the 24th 'after a short illness', bequeathing to his 'small family' nothing more tangible than 'a very fair character'.[3] Originally trained in the law and admitted to the King's Bench, Knipe had abandoned his legal career 'about thirty years ago', to gain modest repute as a stage comedian in Irish towns from Belfast to Cork.

On 4 April Manager Wilmot tried to fill the house by presenting the Newry *première* of *The School for Scandal*.[4] His advertisements contained two quite different appeals to the snobbish sentiments of his more opulent patrons. For this presentation of Sheridan's newest comedy 'a most Elegant and Correct Copy at very considerable Expence' had been procured. Furthermore, since no person could 'on any account be admitted behind the Scenes', admission to the gallery had been doubled in price to raise that area to the cost and therefore the prestige of the pit. Exactly three weeks after this fashionable affair Wilmot seems to have closed his season with a second benefit for Mr. and Mrs. Rowe.[5] With the humility affected by their profession they notified the public that 'nothing but *necessity* could induce them to solicit again'.

While Newry was amusing itself at the High Street playhouse during the foregoing season, there occurred an event that assumed considerable significance in theatrical history, local and otherwise. On Friday, 8 January 1779, Mrs. Thomas

[1] The Newry Volunteers held their first meeting on 5 October. NC, 5 Oct. 1778.
[2] Ibid., 7 Jan. 1779.
[3] Ibid., 25 and 29 Mar. 1779.
[4] Ibid., 1 Apr. 1779.
[5] Ibid., 26 Apr. 1779.

Betterton gave birth at Newry to a daughter who as Julia Betterton Glover attained fame on the English stage. Mr. and Mrs. Betterton, players of minor parts in Myrton Hamilton's company at Belfast, had been married in that city on 21 December 1778.[1] Family or friendly connexions must have prompted them to choose Newry as the birthplace of their first child. Here Betterton had 'spent the earliest part of his youth . . . as both citizen and soldier',[2] though he had been born in Dublin. Thither he subsequently returned to study dancing. Then he changed his vocation to acting and his name from Butterton to Betterton in remembrance of the noted Restoration actor Thomas Betterton, and made his début at the Fishamble Street Theatre early in 1777. Though handsome and graceful, he soon proved vain, extravagant, and too eager to manage. These disturbing traits finally caused him in the summer of 1783 to withdraw from the Crow Street company and go to Newry, where he believed an irresistible opportunity existed to set himself up in a theatre of his own. At this time Newry was displaying that strong craving for amusements and gaiety which swept over Ireland in the wake of the drive for legislative freedom. The *élite* among the town's 'genteel, dressy' young men belonged to the Snug Club and held dinner meetings at Bailey's Ship Tavern, Castle Street, under the leadership of Isaac Corry, Captain of the Volunteers and Member of Parliament from Newry.[3] Betterton interested this group, and other local enthusiasts for entertainment, in the erection of a theatre more suited to the town's prosperity and cultivation than the little fifteen-year-old structure off High Street. Cash subscriptions, purchases of season tickets, and loans came to hand so encouragingly that the bold promoter went ahead to finish his building as early as October or November 1783.[4]

The second Newry theatre, like the first, was located adjacent to a tavern, but in a thriving business section several blocks north of High Street and one block south of the river. The new building stood next to the Shakespeare Inn upon the ground occupied today by 71 and 73 Hill Street—an attractive site on the eastern side only a few doors from busy Margaret

[1] BNL, 25 Dec. 1778. [2] NC, 26 July 1792.
[3] The Drennan Correspondence, no. 66; NC, 23 July 1792.
[4] The Drennan Correspondence, no. 95; *The Newry Magazine*, i. 18.

Square towards Kildare Street.[1] Betterton's playhouse befitted the site; it was elegant and spacious, containing a row of boxes behind the pit in addition to lower and upper side-boxes.[2] The interior lighting followed the latest Dublin arrangement of chandeliers at the rear of the box compartments, so that the beauty of the female occupants might be clearly viewed![3] Since the building could be easily transformed into a 'showy' ball-room, one of Betterton's patrons gave it a most festive opening.[4] A guest afterwards described the occasion as 'a very magnificent Ball for the encouragement [of the builder] of this air-balloon'.[4] When stage performances got under way, the performers turned out to be 'a miserable set'. Even so, Newry citizens found it 'pleasant to pass an evening' at their luxurious theatre during the winter of 1783–4.[5]

Betterton scheduled his second season for the ensuing summer and therefore went down to Dublin to recruit some actors in June 1784. On the 25th he announced from the capital that he had fixed up the Newry theatre 'in a very elegant style' and had engaged Thomas Ryder, George Dawson, Mrs. Margaret Cornelys, and other able Crow Street players to act six nights there.[6] Neither this summer season nor any performances that Betterton may have presented in the winter of 1784–5 much reduced his heavy debts as builder and manager. Consequently he 'involved himself and his infant family in many distressing situations' before he fled from his creditors in the spring and sought a common actor's living in the English provinces.[7]

The dissolution of Betterton's venture tempted the mono-polistic Crow Street manager, Richard Daly, who already controlled the Cork, Limerick, and Waterford playhouses, to extend his authority northwards also. On 12 April 1785 he informed the public that he had purchased 'the New Theatre, Newry' for 'a considerable sum', and that he meant 'to keep it open during the summer months with an able company of comedians from the Theatre Royal, Dublin'.[8] Daly may have adhered to his plan of yearly summer performances at Newry,

[1] Keenan, p. 7; 'Newriensis', *A Historical Sketch of Newry* (Newry, 1876), p. 195.
[2] NC, 2 July 1792; *Newry Commercial Telegraph,* 24 Nov. 1818.
[3] BNL, 2 Nov. 1790.
[4] The Drennan Correspondence, no. 134.
[5] Ibid., no. 143.
[6] BNL, 25 June 1784.
[7] NC, 26 July 1792; *The Newry Magazine,* i. 18.
[8] BM, 12 Apr. 1785.

but the almost complete disappearance of the local newspapers for the remaining dozen years of Daly's régime leaves his conduct towards Newry uncertain. At least in 1792 he provided the town with a summer theatrical season of six weeks. William Dawson, deputy manager for Daly, brought from Dublin a good company of actors and vocalists, including the Covent Garden singer Charles Incledon, who was enjoying his first year of Irish applause.[1] Dawson scheduled popular operettas, such as *The Duenna*, *Rosina*, *Love in a Village*, and *The Deserter*, for the Mondays and Tuesdays of Incledon's three-week stay. 'Notwithstanding a very encreased expence attended the musical engagements' the manager fixed the admission prices at the 'usual' scale: 3*s.* for the boxes, 2*s.* for the pit, and 1*s.* for the gallery. *The Beggar's Opera*, starring Incledon as Macheath in company with the Ryder sisters as Lucy and Polly, opened the Theatre Royal in Hill Street on Monday, 18 June. The curtain was advertised to rise on that evening and thereafter at 'exactly 7 o'clock to avoid the Complaint of late Hours'.[2] The countryside gentry, an indispensable source of revenue, in many cases had to ride far and wished to start homewards well before midnight.

The surprising member of Dawson's troupe was Newry's unfortunate former manager, Thomas Betterton, now advertised to the town as 'a great theatrical treat from the Theatre Royal, Liverpool'.[3] Yet Betterton and his wife received from Dawson 31*s.* 6*d.* and 15*s.* per week respectively, second-rate salaries that quite belied this newspaper puff.[4] Julia Betterton, thirteen years old, accompanied her parents and presented *entr'acte* dances both with and without her father. At her benefit on Friday, 20 July, she made her Irish début as an actress, playing the young Prince Arthur in the murder scene from Shakespeare's *King John*.[5] The notice of the occasion appealed to Newry's 'generous' inhabitants for support of Miss Betterton's 'first attempt', since she 'has the Honour of boasting this Town gave her Birth'. At her father's benefit, she danced in the comedy of *Wild Oats* but did not take an acting role.[6]

[1] NC, 14 and 18 June 1792.
[2] Ibid., 25 June 1792.
[3] Ibid., 18 June 1792.
[4] HJ, 21 Jan. 1793.
[5] NC, 16 July 1792.
[6] Ibid., 26 July 1792.

In anticipation of Mr. Betterton's night on Wednesday, 1 August, a 'Friend to Justice' wrote to the *Newry Chronicle* to emphasize 'the distressing and embarrassing situation of our truly deserving Favourite', and to urge a patronage large enough for 'our late Manager to make a Compromise with his Creditors'.[1] Apparently the returns proved sufficient for him to proffer at least token restitution, because he escaped debtors' prison and proceeded to Crow Street for the winter. This benefit for Betterton not only rang down the curtain upon Newry's season of 1792, but also is, very appropriately, the last known event of the eighteenth century in the theatre born of Betterton's rash ambition—a pretentious edifice that more than any other in Newry before the Act of Union gained reputation for the town.[2]

[1] Ibid.

[2] See *The Hibernian Magazine*, Aug. 1792, p. 171.

IX · DERRY

Derry, Ireland's most northerly city and port, was visited for the first time by professional Irish players in 1741, if the Smock Alley troupe of Dublin carried out their intention of acting there in the late summer after performances at Newry and Belfast.[1] During the next thirty years Derry, like Newry, now and then saw touring companies, usually from Belfast. The group brought by Dublin-born Richard Elrington from England to Belfast for the winter season of 1754–5 moved to Derry in March 1755 and performed throughout the spring.[2] Late in 1769 a respected Irish manager, Thomas Ryder, appeared there for a stay of four or five months with a superior band of strollers that included the colourful singing comedian, John O'Keeffe.[3]

By the time of the Ryder company's visit the praise of travellers had established Derry's attractiveness as outstanding. 'Unexceptionably the cleanest, best built, and most beautifully situated of any town in Ireland', *Hibernia Curiosa* asserted.[4] O'Keeffe, an artist as well as a comedian, called it 'a model for pretty cities'.[5] Located about seventy miles north-west of Belfast and twenty miles from the ocean on the west bank of the River Foyle, Derry by the 1760's had grown to be an urban community of seven to eight thousand,[6] and had developed its deep, commodious harbour into a seaport with a rich trade in cattle and linen, a fleet of sixty vessels, and an annual customs revenue of £30,000.[7] The centre of the city lay at the summit of an oval-shaped hill, which the Irish Society had enclosed in 1614–18 with twenty-foot walls, pierced by four gates.[8] A

[1] FDJ, 11 July 1741, in reporting the Smock Alley itinerary referred to the city by the historic name of Derry, which was widely used in the eighteenth century. This usage has been followed throughout the present volume.

[2] BNL, 21 Mar. 1755.

[3] O'Keeffe, i. 190–3.

[4] *Hibernia Curiosa* (Dublin, 1769), p. 57.

[5] O'Keeffe, i. 190.

[6] *The Hibernian Magazine*, May 1777, p. 330, reported 1,500 houses. These have been estimated to contain 8,000–9,000 inhabitants.

[7] Maxwell, p. 231.

[8] O'Keeffe, i. 190; *Hibernia Curiosa*, p. 57.

PLATE X

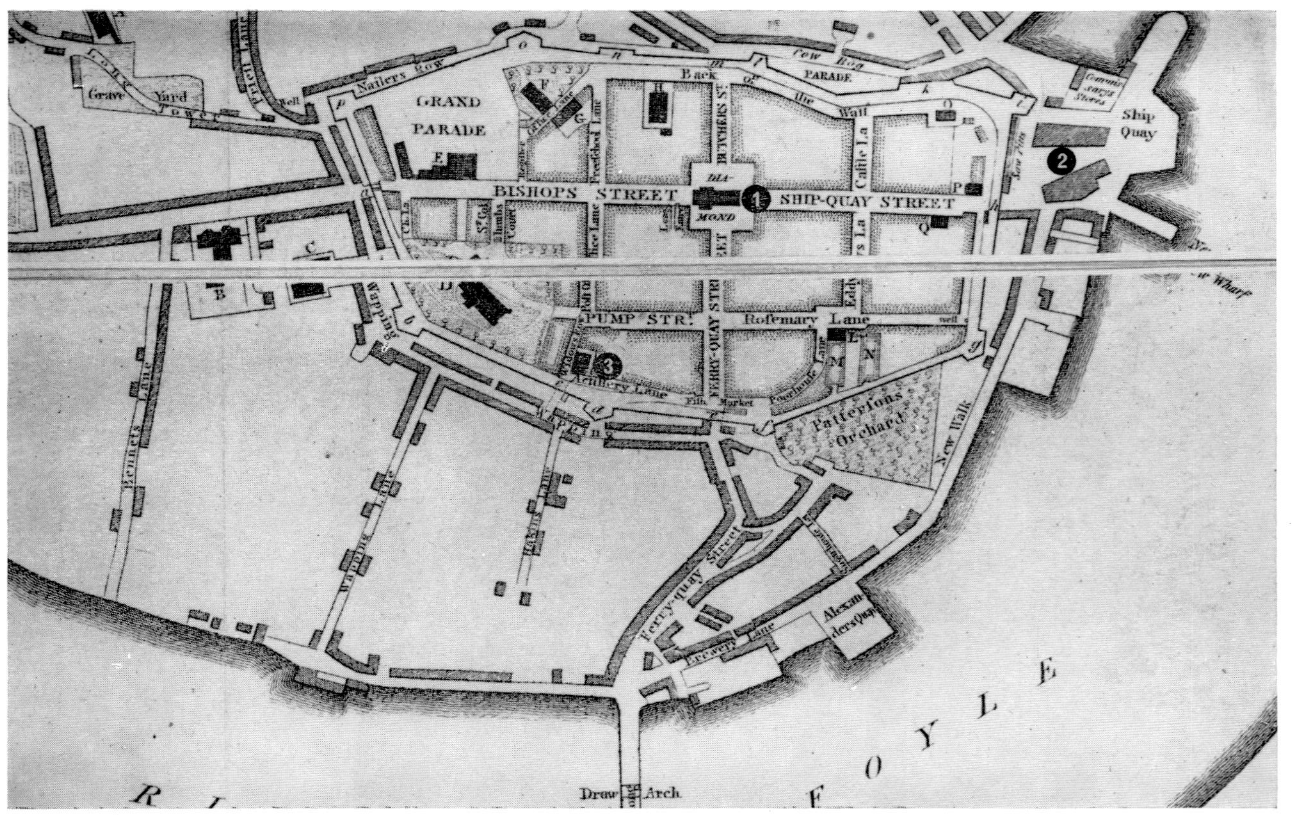

Derry in 1799

Theatre Sites: (1) The Diamond; (2) Ship Quay; (3) Artillery Lane

wide gravel walk ran on top of the walls and afforded during the warmer months a 'very pleasant' promenade.[1] During the colder periods of the year, however, its high and exposed position led to the Derry saying 'When the Wind blows strong at the North, you may hear the Grinding of the North Pole turning round its Axis'.[2] The seventeenth-century reconstruction of the old town laid out its centre as a large square, later named 'the Diamond' and lined with 'magnificent, spacious' houses.[3] From the four sides of this square the main streets radiated to the four wall gates. The streets, though comparatively broad and well paved, had a rather steep incline that made them difficult for both coaches and sedan chairs.[4]

A visitor, looking through any one of the four gates, could see in the middle of the Diamond a 'handsome' stone structure resting on 'piazzas', the Town House and Exchange presented by King William III in 1692.[5] The great hall on the upper floor of this building served as Derry's chief place of entertainment—assemblies, balls, civic celebrations, and, occasionally, theatricals.[6] Here a dancing master, Mr. Morris, once held an unusual ball.[7] Dancing began 'at six o'clock in the afternoon'. 'The Company [were] treated with tea, cakes, and cards.' Sometime after all the 'company' had gathered, Morris put on a performance of 'part of a play never before acted here by any of his occupation'. It was this same hall in the Town House that Ryder's actors used for their theatre during the winter of 1769–70. A local violinist conducted their orchestra and also proved a fine accompanist to O'Keeffe, whose songs were regularly billed as *entr'acte* attractions.[8] O'Keeffe also furnished one of the winter's dramatic novelties: a pantomime entitled *Harlequin in Derry; or, The Dutchman Outwitted*, which he adapted from his earlier *Harlequin in Waterford; or, The Dutchman Outwitted* by revising the locations of the scenes.

Five years after the stay of Ryder and his strollers the enterprising new Belfast manager, Michael Atkins, sought to improve theatrical business in Derry by the erection of a proper

[1] O'Keeffe, i. 190; Pococke, p. 42; DeLatocnaye, p. 198.
[2] Willes, p. 130.
[3] O'Keeffe, i. 190–1.
[4] Willes, p. 130.
[5] Pococke, p. 42; O'Keeffe, i. 191.
[6] O'Keeffe, i. 191.
[7] LDJ, 12 Sept. 1772.
[8] O'Keeffe, i. 192–3.

playhouse. A local builder, William Stewart, became interested in promoting the venture and proceeded to put up a small, insubstantial building (some years later described as 'a temporary erection'[1]) outside the north-east gate on the New Row, Ship Quay,[2] approximately the site of the present Guild Hall. During June 1774 repeated notices in the *Londonderry Journal* stated that by permission of the Worshipful Mayor a new theatre would be opened shortly and that the occupying company of players would be 'in many respects superior to any that have performed in this city for several years'.[3] Stewart followed up these notices by offering to 'any gentlemen' season subscription tickets, transferable before the benefits, for 42*s*., a price that indicated a prospective season of three months or more.[4] Purchasers were advised to be 'early in their application, as no more than twenty tickets will be disposed of'. These admitted to ordinary seats in the pit, since the new playhouse, like the first such structures at Belfast and Newry, contained no box accommodations.

The two promoters timed the opening of the theatre to coincide with the beginning of Derry's Race Week, Monday, 8 August, when the city was especially crowded and festive. Atkins reassembled most of his Belfast troupe of the previous winter, but he made up the loss of two veteran comedians, Knipe and Waker, by adding only one worthy substitute, Wilmot, who with Myrton Hamilton and the manager constituted the major actors. The *première* bill of *The Constant Couple* and *The Deuce is in Him* called for uniform admission at the top charge of 2*s*. with pit and gallery 'laid together'.[5] The heavy press for admittance expected from moneyed visitors on the opening night led to a warning that no gold coin would be changed at the door! This prohibition helped to seat the playgoers more promptly and therefore to ensure the start of the entertainment close to the advertised hour of seven o'clock. As the curtain rose on the Ship Quay stage for the first time, Wilmot came forward and delivered, in a fellow actor's flowery verse, the sentiments of 'the little tribe' behind the footlights.[6]

[1] Bernard, i. 227. [2] LDJ, 25 June 1782.
[3] Ibid., 10 and 28 June 1774.
[4] Ibid., 28 June–12 Aug. 1774.
[5] Ibid., 5 Aug. 1774. [6] Ibid., 9 Aug. 1774.

A few of the forty-four lines in the address refer directly to the local setting and occasion:

> Here, patriot honours, Truth has long decreed,
> And Fame, with thrilling trump, proclaim the deed: . . .
> Lur'd with such charms, unknowing and unknown,
> Behold our Leader dares attack your town; . . .
> Then spite of walls—or you in martial plight,
> E'er prompt for Life and Truth and Vict'ry to fight, . . .
> [The motto on Derry's coat-of-arms = '*Vita, Veritas, Victoria*']
> Back'd with our troop, in sock and buskins clad,
> He'll drive you from your posts—with laughter mad; . . .
> Each gate shall open to dramatic laws,
> And crowding hands shall greet us with applause!

True to the spirit of the foregoing prologue, Atkins's company amused Derry almost entirely with comedy and farce, not only every evening of the August Race Week but afterwards—on Mondays, Wednesdays, and Fridays—for four and a half months. The bill, however, in honour of the President and Friendly Brothers of the Knot of St. Patrick on Friday, 21 October, began with a tragedy, *The Brothers*, but then offset it with Murphy's frolicsome *The Apprentice*.[1] The 1774 season seems to have ended on 26 December with an appropriate combination of mirth: *As You Like It* and *Marriage à la Mode; or, What We Must All Come To*.[2] The night belonged to Myrton Hamilton, who, after an unsuccessful first benefit, implored patronage for this second affair. He felt it 'a duty incumbent upon him to undeceive the public' about the report, 'industriously propagated', that he was 'possessed of an independent fortune'. Nothing could be further from the truth; he had 'no other means of supporting himself and his family than what accrued from the theatre'.[2] The city was to hear more from this voluble and querulous stage figure.

Atkins and his troupe returned in 1775 to Derry for performances every evening of Race Week, 7–12 August,[3] and perhaps stayed longer. They may have returned again for the races in the summer of 1776;[4] certainly they were acting at the Ship

[1] Ibid., 18 Oct. 1774.
[2] Ibid., 20 and 23 Dec. 1774.
[3] Ibid., 11 July–4 Aug. 1775.
[4] LDJ, 20 Aug.–6 Sept. 1776, advertised 'public ordinaries, balls, or plays each night'.

Quay theatre during October and November.[1] Atkins on 6 November took a benefit, offering the same pair of humorous plays, *The Constant Couple* and *The Deuce is in Him*, as he had presented at the original opening of the theatre in 1774.[2] Announcements for the Derry races in 1777 and 1778 advertised 'plays each night'. Possibly, therefore, the Belfast actors visited the city at those times, but left no record.

After Atkins had gone in August 1778 to join the Crow Street company, Wilmot turned manager in his stead and took the cream of the Belfast players to Newry in December and then to Derry at the end of April 1779. Their repertory, depending largely on the talents of Andrew Cherry and Richard Rowe, inclined to comedy, but in a variety of types, such as *The Duenna*, *The School for Scandal*, *The Citizen*, and *The Merchant of Venice*.[3] Shakespeare's drama was presented at Mrs. Rowe's benefit on Monday, 16 August, with the serious and suggestive subtitle, 'The Inexorable Jew', a titling not on record elsewhere in eighteenth-century Ireland.[4] Two days later a benefit for Messrs. Cherry and Williams completed the season's entertainment. Though the audience no doubt considered *The Beggar's Opera* the main attraction of that evening, the most interesting feature historically was George S. Carey's comic interlude, *Three Old Women Weatherwise; or, A Cure for All Ills*, in its only known Irish performance.[5]

Between 1779 and 1782 Derry seems to have lacked any professional theatricals. Then in February and March 1782 the *Journal* carried side by side, for several issues, notices from the two recurrent adversaries, Michael Atkins and Myrton Hamilton. The latter announced from Coleraine that, by permission of Mayor Robert Fairly of Derry, he proposed to open 'a theatre' on 1 April.[6] Atkins proclaimed from Newry an intention to open 'his theatre' in June with 'the best company ever yet seen in the country [i.e. county towns] of Ireland', a leading member to be Mrs. Richard Sparks of Dublin, 'one of the most capital performers in the Kingdom'.[6] On the Tuesday

[1] LDJ, 15 Oct. 1776, contained a notice of Mr. Hamilton's benefit on 16 Oct.

[2] Ibid., 5 Nov. 1776.

[3] Ibid., 8 and 18 June, 13 Aug. 1779.

[4] Ibid., 13 Aug. 1779.

[5] Ibid., 17 Aug. 1779.

[6] Ibid., 26 Feb., 5 and 26 Mar. 1782.

of Race Week, 25 June, Hamilton finally started playing at the Ship Quay theatre, probably with a nondescript troupe.[1] The opening bill consisted of *The Merchant of Venice* and Dibdin's operetta, *The Quaker*. The curtain rose at seven o'clock on an audience that had paid 2*s*. to sit anywhere in the house. Within a month Hamilton had satisfied his managerial ego for the moment and made his last exit from Derry.

Late in July Atkins commenced to publicize the approach of his theatrical season.[2] Ladies and gentlemen could apply to Mrs. Atkins for the few subscription tickets available at 21*s*. each. About mid-August Atkins began performances on the Ship Quay stage with the strongest group of actors he had ever brought to the city. New faces from Dublin—Mr. and Mrs. George Day, Mrs. Sparks—supplemented the comic favourites, Messrs. Cherry and Rowe. The benefit nights, running from late October to early December, gave Derry playgoers a chance to enjoy a series of pieces never before on the local boards: Milton's *Comus* with the original music, Murphy's *Know Your Own Mind*, Mrs. Cowley's *The Runaway*, O'Beirne's *The Generous Impostor*, and Bickerstaffe's musical interlude, *The Recruiting Serjeant*. The last two works proved such a happy combination that they, along with the farce, *Flora; or, Hob in the Well*, appeared on two successive Wednesdays, 27 November and 4 December.[3] A week later, 11 December, the 1782 season closed with an unspecified bill for the benefit of the poorhouses and orphans. The Mayor as sponsor expressed the hope that ladies and gentlemen would keep themselves free from any other engagement, 'the more effectively to promote this charity'.[4]

In the summer of 1783 Atkins sent his Belfast company on tour with John Bernard as deputy manager. The troupe included Mr. and Mrs. Cherry, Mr. and Mrs. Rowe, Mr. and Mrs. Tyrrell, Mrs. and Miss Hoskins, and an eccentric hairdresser turned comedian, Geoffrey Galway, who gave an amusing distinction to small parts such as the Player King in *Hamlet*, the Murderer in *Macbeth*, and the Apothecary in *Romeo and Juliet*.[5] These plus a few other performers came to Derry

[1] Ibid., 25 June 1782.

[2] Ibid., 30 July–13 Aug. 1782.

[3] Ibid., 26 Nov. and 3 Dec. 1782.

[4] Ibid., 10 Dec. 1782.

[5] Bernard, i. 200–1.

probably about Race Week and played for a month to audiences so large that, despite the very limited capacity of the playhouse and the absence of box receipts, Atkins's share as manager amounted to £25 net.[1] The city, increased in population to at least nine thousand,[2] was more than ever bustling with overseas commerce and military defence activities. Throngs of Derry Volunteers enlivened the streets and benefited the theatre with their frequent attendance. The Volunteer Band contributed its services as the orchestra.[3] The most generous individual patron of the current theatricals proved to be the learned but singular Bishop of Derry, Lord Frederic Augustus Hervey, fourth Earl of Bristol, a supporter of the Volunteer Movement, a proponent of religious toleration and the civil emancipation of the Catholics, and a great *bon-vivant*, who spent liberally on good will and good living from a yearly income of at least £25,000, the highest reported for any contemporary ecclesiastic in Ireland.[4]

After their month of fine summer business Bernard and his group left to perform in Sligo awhile. When they arrived back at Derry in October, a report greeted them that a weak gallery beam rendered the theatre unsafe. A local carpenter, called in to test the suspected timber, on Monday, 27 October, pronounced it 'sound as the first hour it was formed for use'.[5] Upon this assurance Bernard went ahead with the opening of the playhouse two days later; he had already taken the precaution of making the building warm and comfortable by 'constant fires'. The winter repertory of 1783–4 displayed the usual predominance of comedy, but a less fresh and varied comic fare than that of the previous season. *The Busie Body* and *Who's the Dupe?* led off on 29 October;[5] *The Way to Win Him* and *The Way to Keep Him* offered balance of situations for the last bill, a benefit in behalf of the poor on 16 February 1784.[6] This year the Mayor, evidently expecting a more prosperous public, raised the charity admission fee to an unprecedented 2*s.* 6*d.* 'for every part of the house, and nothing less to be taken during the evening'.

[1] Bernard, i. 203.

[2] G. V. Sampson, *Memoir Explanatory of the Chart and Survey of the County of Londonderry, Ireland* (London, 1814), p. 185.

[3] Bernard, i. 221–4.

[4] Ibid.; DeLatocnaye, p. 201.

[5] LDJ, 28 Oct. 1783.

[6] Ibid., 10 Feb. 1784.

A week or two before the season's finale Andrew Cherry elected to try French rather than English humour at his benefit, but soon found that the performance of Molière's *The Miser* 'was not taking'.[1] On the spur of the moment he improvised some stage business in order to bring down the house. The drummer in the orchestra habitually turned his back to the stage when he was not playing, and assumed a commanding stance as if in contempt of the actors' abilities. After a time they discovered that the drummer wore a wig—a fact which Cherry now determined to turn to his advantage. In the last scene of Act IV the comedian in his role of Harpagon started to dash about, shouting 'Who's got my money?' Then, leaning over the edge of the stage, he pointed questioningly at several persons in the pit: 'Have you, Sir—or you—or you—got my money?' At length, fixing his eyes on the unobserving drummer directly beneath him, he cried out '*You* have got my money', pounced upon the top of his victim's head 'as an eagle would swoop on a sheep, seized the wig, and waving it aloft in triumph, exclaimed "Here is my money! I have got my money!"' Then the comedian ran off stage, 'leaving the astonished musician with his bald pate shining like the apex of Mont Blanc on a summer morning'. Of course pit and gallery alike laughed uproariously. By unexpected tricks of this sort the roguish Cherry endeared himself to the audiences of many Irish towns in the 1780's and 1790's.

The laughter over Cherry's coup rocked the Ship Quay playhouse 'to its very foundation', according to Manager Bernard,[2] and made more evident than ever the flimsiness of its construction. This fact, together with the opening of the Rosemary Lane Theatre in Belfast, whetted Atkins's desire for a new building at Derry. The first move in his campaign for local assistance took the form of an announcement on 14 September 1784 that 'a new theatre on an elegant plan is soon to be established in this city, in which a respectable company of comedians are to be exhibited at stated seasons under the direction of Mr. Atkyns'.[3] Public support appears to have developed very slowly, for nothing more was published concerning the project during 1784 and 1785, not even when

[1] Bernard, i. 226–7. [2] Ibid., i. 227.
[3] LDJ, 14 Sept. 1784.

Atkins returned to occupy the Ship Quay theatre near the end of the latter year. Early in November 1785 he printed a succession of notices in regard to the commencement of a winter theatrical season, embellishing them with verbal flourishes: 'all the new pieces that have appeared in London and Dublin for these two seasons past', 'fitting up of the house in a most elegant and comfortable manner', 'his hope to experience a participation of the candour of hospitality of the polite audience of Londonderry'.[1] Amid this barrage of words he offered for purchase twenty transferable tickets at 31*s.* 6*d.* each, good for the season of at least thirty nights but, as always, invalid for the benefits.[1] The season, in spite of the absence of newspaper advertising, must have gone well and extended into May 1786 because on the 22nd of that month the manager expressed his thanks 'for the very great encouragement he and his company had met with this year'.[2]

On this same date Atkins also issued a statement of progress regarding the erection of a Derry playhouse. His report, addressed in particular to the venture's subscribers, emphasized that 'he had begun to build an elegant and commodious new theatre which (when finished) will for its magnitude be equal in elegance to any house in the Kingdom'.[2] Then three years passed with no signs of continuing activity. Finally, in May 1789 Atkins sent off his company to perform on the Isle of Man while he took up residence in Derry to superintend the finishing of his theatre, 'which will be the first [i.e. finest] country playhouse in the Kingdom'.[3] In keeping with this boast he had secured a conspicuous and accessible site at the corner of Widow's Row (now London Street) and Artillery Lane (now Artillery Street) in the south-east sector of the city, close by St. Columb's Cathedral. This new Derry theatre, about 80 feet long by 40 feet wide,[4] approximated the size of the Limerick Theatre Royal, but it surely had more prepossessing frontage and entrances. It faced east on Artillery Lane with the gallery door evidently located on the north side and reached by a passage that still exists. In spite of drastic remodelling in the

[1] LDJ, 1, 8, and 15 Nov. 1785. [2] Ibid., 22 May 1786.

[3] FJ, 30 May 1789.

[4] Estimated dimensions based upon the area marked on Robert Porter's 'Plan of the City and Suburbs of Londonderry' (1799). Sampson, p. 200, mistakenly identifies this theatre with the earlier one of 1774.

nineteenth century, the shell of the eighteenth-century playhouse has partly survived in the building on the site, now used as the Church of Ireland diocesan office but formerly its synod house.[1]

The opening of the 'New Theatre' in Artillery Lane took place during the autumn of 1789. The first performance now on record, however, was a gala night at the beginning of January 1790 when the Derry Independent Volunteers in their new uniforms paraded to the playhouse and watched with peculiar interest the acting of *He Would Be a Soldier*.[2] The performers belonged to the largest and best company that Atkins had ever assembled at Derry. Mr. and Mrs. John Cornelys of Crow Street, Mr. and Mrs. Godfrey, Mr. and Mrs. James May, Mr. and Mrs. James Remington, Mr. and Mrs. Robinson were visiting the city for the first time. The actors' nights started towards the end of April and lasted over seven weeks.[3] The city must have been considerably drained of its benevolence in that period. Five or more of the players did not fare too well at their original benefit and therefore tried a second. Box returns traditionally provided the major source of benefit income. The old Ship Quay theatre had had no boxes, but the new theatre contained at least side-boxes[4] and therefore much improved the players' chances for benefit revenue. The Derry troupe presently initiated a most uncommon but sensible arrangement to promote the sale of box tickets by setting up a mid-town box office, open all day, at the book shop of George Douglas.[4] Comedies overshadowed the few stale tragedies, like *Douglas* and *The Brothers*, on the benefit bills. Remington's night on Wednesday, 26 May, concluded with the season's most spectacular entertainment, the pantomime of *Prometheus; or, Harlequin's Animation*.[5] Atkins himself had painted the flats for every one of its nine episodes: (1) the marble statue, (2) the lady's hat, (3) the gladiator, (4) the bookcase, (5) the pump and cobbler's stall, (6) the miraculous doctor, (7) the tailor's disaster or the dancing shop-board, (8) the dying, (9) the temple of Hymen. After 'an elegant piece

[1] See Robert Simpson, *The Annals of Derry* (Londonderry, 1847), p. 239; *Ordinance Survey, County of Londonderry* (Dublin, 1837), i. 118, 193.

[2] FJ, 5 Jan. 1790.

[3] LDJ, 4 May–15 June 1790.

[4] Ibid., 4 May 1790.

[5] Ibid., 25 May 1790.

of machinery' by degrees had transformed the stage into the final temple scene, all the pantomime characters entered to participate in a country dance amid the incongruous classical setting. A literary and less colourful novelty was presented at the company's last performance on Friday, 18 June, when Mrs. Cornelys, taking a second benefit, tried out 'at the request of several ladies and gentlemen' a comedy of her own making, *The Deceptions; or, Fashion and Folly*, its only known appearance outside Dublin.[1]

Derry's next theatrical season saw marked improvements and innovations. Manager Atkins had much strengthened his roster of actresses by the addition of Mrs. Courtney Melmoth, Mrs. Coates, and Mrs. Mason, all from Dublin. Their presence resulted in a more balanced repertory than the city had been offered for many years—a repertory that included a fair number of the established tragedies, such as *The Countess of Salisbury*, *Hamlet*, *Isabella*, *Jane Shore*, *The Mourning Bride*, and *The Orphan*. The ever popular tragedy of *Douglas* opened the season on Wednesday, 21 February 1791, and called forth the first theatrical criticism ever to be published in the city.[2] An unsigned criticism commended Mrs. Melmoth as Lady Randolph for 'her mellifluent and expressive tone of voice' that drew 'a profusion of tears in every part of the house'. The men of the troupe were urged by the critic to second more impressively the endeavours of the actresses. The seven o'clock curtain met approval along with 'dismissal at an early hour'.[2] Further critical comment on 4 March chastised the 'gentlemen' watching *The Way to Keep Him* for their loud laughs and vulgar jests.[3] This same comedy and *The Wonder: A Woman Keeps a Secret* amused 'a most brilliant and crowded audience' on Wednesday, 6 April, the first Masonic night recorded at a Derry theatre.[4] Orange Lodge No. 132, after gathering at six o'clock in their lodge room at Preston's, marched to the playhouse stage where 'a throne and an amphitheatre' permitted the brethren to sit by rank in 'their proper Cloathing, Jewels, etc.'. Brother May delivered the evening's prologue, Brother Atkins and others sang Masonic songs at intervals, and Sister Melmoth spoke the epilogue. She also, as the principal

[1] LDJ, 15 June 1790.
[2] Ibid., 22 Feb. 1791.
[3] Ibid., 8 Mar. 1791.
[4] Ibid., 5 Apr. 1791.

actress, had the honour of starting on 2 May the benefit performances that stretched over seven weeks.[1] A week later Mrs. Coates chose for her night the season's newest play, *Better Late Than Never*, fresh from Drury Lane. The presentation had to be postponed four days in order that the Andrews comedy might be 'performed with Propriety' on its first appearance in Ireland.[2]

By the end of the benefits on 22 June social life in Derry had arrived at an urbanity such as this city of nearly ten thousand inhabitants had never before exhibited. The splendid drawbridge, just constructed across the Foyle by an American engineering crew, afforded an ideal quarter-mile esplanade on the water. There the genteel citizens had lost no time in establishing what they called 'High Mall', on Sundays as well as on weekday evenings.[3] Music by the 64th Regiment Band regularly augmented the gaiety of the promenading. It was a most auspicious time for Atkins to announce his engagement of the first 'capital performer' ever to visit a Derry theatre. Tom King, the famous Drury Lane comedian, was to play six nights before going on to Belfast with the Atkins company.[4] 'Theatricus' on 21 June published an extravagant eulogy of King as 'almost absolute perfection in the first line of genteel comedy'.[5] Theatre parties were reported to be coming from the surrounding towns of Coleraine, Letterkenny, Newtown, and Strabane, for a view of this 'greatest Ornament of the Stage'.[5] The Derry manager, expecting a demand for seats much in excess of the supply, promulgated ticket regulations far more stringent than any hitherto in force.[6] Dublin prices of 5*s.* for the boxes, 3*s.* for the pit, and 2*s.* for the gallery were to prevail. 'Infants in the Arms' were not to be admitted to any part of the playhouse; 'children (and children only)' were to be allowed at half price. No servants might come early and hold box places. 'Any lady or gentleman' might take for any number of nights an entire box, or an entire row of seats (but no less) in a box. The tickets for the reserved box or box row must be picked up in advance of the day of performance. Rules as strict as these were not put into effect again at Derry during the eighteenth century.

[1] Ibid., 26 Apr.–21 June 1791.
[2] Ibid., 10 May 1791.
[3] Ibid., 21 June 1791.
[4] Ibid., 7 June 1791.
[5] Ibid., 21 June 1791.
[6] Ibid., 7 and 21 June 1791.

King elected to play Lord Ogleby in *The Clandestine Marriage* as his opening role on Wednesday, 27 June, in the presence of 'a very crowded and splendid audience', and, as his next role two days later, Sir Peter Teazle, the part he had taken in the *première* of *The School for Scandal* at Drury Lane.[1] The attendance of the gallery proletariat must have fallen off so gravely, after a brief excited curiosity, that the manager on 6 July reduced the gallery admission to the customary 1*s*. for King's fifth evening when he acted Sir John Restless in *All in the Wrong* and Sir John Trotley in *Bon Ton*.[2] His final performance on Monday, 11 July, terminated a long and memorable theatrical season, wherein Derry had had the honour to enjoy 'the first Comedian of the Present Age' before he showed his talents to the north of Ireland's largest metropolis.[2]

By September Atkins had become engrossed in the building of his new theatre at Belfast and consequently gave no further thought to the Derry stage for a whole year. Then in the autumn of 1792 he appointed James May to manage his 'Ulster Company of Comedians' and to undertake a season at the theatre in Artillery Lane.[3] For the opening on Thursday, 1 November, May had hoped to present a star actress, Maria Campion of Crow Street, but 'notwithstanding Miss Campion made a positive agreement with Mr. Atkins to appear on this stage and that money was sent to her at her own desire, she has since broken her engagement'.[4] The indignant manager assured the public that every possible effort would be made to procure 'an actress of equal merit and one who has learnt to abide by her agreement'. Eventually the city had to be content with a second-rate attraction from Crow Street, Richard Hurst. Yet, when he played Banks in *Wild Oats*, he was publicly thanked for condescending to appear in 'so subordinate a part', since he was said to possess 'some of the great master strokes of the immortal Garrick with whom he was in the constant habit of performing the part of Kent for fifteen years in London'.[5] This London association seems to have been the cause for Hurst's aspiring to the role of Lear in Derry. On 18 December it was reported that Shakespeare's tragedy was being rehearsed and

[1] LDJ, 28 June 1791.
[2] Ibid., 5 July 1791.
[3] Ibid., 9 Oct. 1792.
[4] Ibid., 30 Oct. 1792.
[5] Ibid., 27 Nov. 1792.

that the public eagerly awaited Hurst's performance of the King.[1] The 'long-expected' event at last occurred on Wednesday, 2 January 1793.[2] Hurst must have pleased the onlookers, because the Mayor asked to have *King Lear* repeated for the night on behalf of the city poor.[3]

Other novelties during the winter included the elaborate pantomime of *The Death of Captain Cook*, staged at least four times,[4] and a half-dozen very recent comedies from London: Bickerstaffe's *Spoil'd Child*, Holcroft's *The Road to Ruin* and *The School for Arrogance*, O'Keeffe's *Modern Antiques* and *Wild Oats*, Reynolds's *Notoriety*. No serious dramas were acted except the Shakespearian trio of *Hamlet*, *King Lear*, and *The Tempest*. The bill for Mr. Prior's night stood out among the benefits, because it concentrated on patriotic and martial items in keeping with the times: (1) an occasional address by Prior in the uniform of a Derry Volunteer; (2) the comedy of *The School for Wives; or, The Faithful Irishman*; (3) the interlude of *British Loyalty*; (4) the operetta of *The Poor Soldier*; (5) the ensemble singing of 'God Save the King'.[5] The 'uncommon overflow' of attendance forced Prior to the happy apology that 'he had it not in his power to accommodate all his friends'.[6] Those who held outstanding tickets for his benefit had to wait four weeks before he could arrange to have his tickets accepted for admission to some other benefit—in this case, that of Mr. King and Mrs. Hoskins.[7] In contrast to Prior's good fortune, *The School for Scandal* brought Mr. Lynch such poor returns on his first benefit that he attempted a second on 15 February 1793, the season's last performance, with a plea to 'the lovers of theatrical amusements' to show kindness to 'the cause of true merit and indefatigable industry'.[8] Like most of his contemporaries Lynch believed in the efficacy of the self-manufactured puff.

The School for Scandal, Lynch's experience to the contrary, generally proved a drawing-card. Therefore Atkins selected it along with *Three Weeks after Marriage* to form the bill for opening the next Derry season on Wednesday, 5 February 1794, with 'a respectable company of comedians'.[9] Early

[1] Ibid., 18 Dec. 1792. [2] Ibid., 1 Jan. 1793. [3] Ibid., 5 Feb. 1793.
[4] Ibid., 27 Nov., 4, 11, and 25 Dec. 1793. [5] Ibid., 8 Jan. 1793.
[6] Ibid., 22 Jan. 1793. [7] Ibid., 5 Feb. 1793. [8] Ibid., 12 Feb. 1793.
[9] Ibid., 28 Jan. and 4 Feb. 1794.

notices emphasized the curtain time as seven o'clock precisely. After several weeks the manager received warm public commendation for the prompt beginnings of the performances.[1] Though new pantomimes and spectacles were promised as soon as the scenes and decorations could be got ready,[2] none was forthcoming. Instead, a dull mediocrity characterized the repertory and the acting up to the completion of the benefits in mid-June.

Suddenly, on 17 June, Atkins announced a summer theatrical season for Derry, its first one, with distinguished guest players and with no rise in admission fees.[3] The season's *première* on Wednesday, 9 July, offered an evening of truly glamorous entertainment. Maria Campion of Crow Street as the lovely and regal Elwina in *Percy, Earl of Northumberland*, made a pleasing contrast to the animated Mrs. M'George of Bath as young Rosina in the operetta of that name.[4] Two days later Miss Campion acted another beautiful and pathetic heroine, Juliet. A Derry critic said of her Elwina that 'with the purest pronunciation and the most dignified action she exhibited all the deep agonizing distress which the author attaches to that part'.[5] In similar unrestraint he praised the 'enchanting' Miss Campion for 'a complete representation of the lovesick, the unfortunate Juliet'. The Crow Street actress towards the end of her stay shifted to less serious impersonations and played Lady Amaranth in *Wild Oats* for her farewell role on Friday, 25 July.[6]

James Middleton from Covent Garden, who succeeded Miss Campion as the starring figure, commenced with *Othello* on Monday, 4 August.[7] His performance of the title part in *Alexander the Great* furnished Atkins with an opportunity to indulge in two scenes of long-promised spectacle: Alexander's triumphal entry into Babylon, and a grand banquet in the royal palace.[8] Not to be outdone by Miss Campion's Juliet a few weeks earlier, Middleton elected to play Romeo for his final appearance on 20 August.[9] His youthful exhibition of the romantic Shakespearian hero provided a satisfying culmination

[1] LDJ, 25 Feb. 1794.
[2] Ibid., 18 Feb. 1794.
[3] Ibid., 17 June and 1 July 1794.
[4] Ibid., 8 July 1794.
[5] Ibid., 15 July 1794.
[6] Ibid., 22 July 1794.
[7] Ibid., 5 Aug. 1794.
[8] Ibid., 12 Aug. 1794.
[9] Ibid., 19 Aug. 1794.

to a lively summer season that would not be repeated before 1800.

In 1795 Manager Atkins reversed his schedule of theatrical activity at Derry. Waiting till the autumn, he presented the incomparable Andrew Cherry as an opening attraction for two weeks prior to the actor's winter engagement at Crow Street. After *The School for Scandal* on Monday, 30 September, Cherry performed two leading roles each night in a variety of comedies, farces, and musical entertainments.[1] For his benefit and last performance on Monday, 12 October, he exerted himself to the limit, singing *entr'acte* songs in addition to taking three major parts: Solus in Mrs. Inchbald's comedy *Every One has His Fault*, Tom Grogg in the interlude of *The Generous Tar*, and the Apothecary in *The Prize*, a musical farce previously unacted at Derry.[2]

Benefits, starting on 16 November, continued for ten weeks until 25 January 1796, two weeks longer than the regular subscription season which preceded them.[3] The veteran Mrs. Hoskins abjectly called upon the local inhabitants to 'rescue their poor old favourite from the greatest misery and distress, and enable her to support herself in her latter days without soliciting charity which her spirit had hitherto prevented her from'.[4] At the other extreme of affectation Miss Duncan, whose first benefit failed because of inclement weather, boldly claimed in the notice of her second that 'her admirable character and manners and promising abilities' would very shortly elevate her to be 'one of the first ornaments of her profession'.[5] Mrs. Hall adopted another approach, confessing that she hoped 'to extricate herself and her husband from the embarrassing situation into which an unavoidable debt has thrown them'.[6] James Remington described himself as 'a favourite performer ... whose conduct in private life has been uniformly exemplary'.[7] On the evening of 16 December he delivered a lengthy 'farewell' poem written by a local gentleman. After addressing 'the peerless and angelic fair' in the boxes, and 'the descendants of a valiant strain who fought for freedom on the crimson plain'

[1] Ibid., 29 Sept. and 6 Oct. 1795.
[2] Ibid., 6 Oct. 1795.
[3] Ibid., 10 Nov. 1795–18 Jan. 1796.
[4] Ibid., 24 Nov. 1795.
[5] Ibid., 15 Dec. 1795.
[6] Ibid., 12 Jan. 1796.
[7] Ibid., 15 Dec. 1795.

in the pit, the actor turned to the gallery commoners with a concluding patriotic exhortation:

May 'prentice Boys among you still be found
To fight the battles of this sacred ground.[1]

Remington, however, stayed on to welcome his brother Masons with a prologue at their command performance on Wednesday, 6 January 1796. It had been almost five years since the Derry brethren had marched 'in their proper cloathing and jewels' from their lodge rooms to the Artillery Lane stage and sat in 'an amphitheatre formed for their reception'. Once again Brother Atkins rendered several Masonic songs and entertained them with their staple comedy, *The Wonder: A Woman Keeps a Secret*.[2]

Soon after the finish of this 1795–6 season conditions in Belfast and in Ulster generally grew unsettled to the point of violence. The disorder persisted until late in 1799. The city of Derry, however, by reason of its large garrison and its heavily pro-English sentiment, remained undisturbed during these years. Therefore Atkins, unwilling to risk performances in his Belfast theatre, employed the undistinguished remnant of his troupe at Derry for two successive January–May seasons in 1798 and 1799. In both years Cumberland's comedy, *The Wheel of Fortune*, seems to have raised the curtain on the Artillery Lane stage, but in 1798 the officers from the local barracks undertook the principal male parts.[3] The mixed casts of army and professional actors, which recurred at frequent intervals, encouraged, of course, lucrative patronage by the military elements in the vicinity of Derry.[4] Because of personnel limitations and the somewhat changed complexion of the audiences, Atkins attempted little innovation. Yet on 28 February at the benefit of Remington, now the leading figure in the diminished company, a new and anonymous interlude, fetchingly entitled *Just Arrived in L'Derry; or, The Thespian from Ennishoen*, had its only known performance, interspersed with songs by a lady and gentleman 'lately arrived from America'.[5] The most festive night of the season was held on 20 April in

[1] LDJ, 22 Dec. 1795. [2] Ibid., 29 Dec. 1795. [3] Ibid., 9 Jan. 1798.
[4] LDJ, 27 Feb. 1798, announced participation by officers of the garrison in forthcoming performances on 2 and 5 March. [5] Ibid., 27 Feb. 1798.

aid of the Derry Volunteer Cavalry, who attended in full uniform. A local patriot, inspired by his 'virgin city proud on a hill', composed for this event a fervid prologue with its theme drawn from the present danger:

> But sure at such a time as this when France
> Shakes furious against the world her poison'd lance . . .
> How can I doubt while I this circle view
> That Derry's sons will to themselves be true?

Officers and gentlemen of the city combined with members of Atkins's troupe to perform *The Beaux' Stratagem* and *No Song, No Supper*. 'Filled with the spirit of loyalty and patriotism, the most brilliant audience ever witnessed in this place' sang at the close of the evening 'Rule, Britannia!' and 'God Save the King'.[1]

The city's fervour had perceptibly declined when Atkins returned with his players at the beginning of 1799. The military forces no longer sought to be involved in stage activities, though 'the French Band of the Somerset Regiment' contributed musical numbers occasionally.[2] The Derry audiences were treated to a few pieces of entertainment which they had not previously seen: two melodramas, Lewis's *The Castle Spectre* and Morton's *Zorinski*, and a musical play by Birch, *The Adopted Child*. These met so enthusiastic a reception that they appeared again and again before the end of the season on 15 May.[3] Thus Michael Atkins, a proprietor of modest foresight, saw to it that this northern outpost of the Anglo-Irish theatrical world cultivated in its small way the changing dramatic fare at the close of the eighteenth century. As a result the little Derry theatre in Artillery Lane commanded a lively public support for its future after the Union.

[1] Ibid., 24 Apr. 1798.

[2] Ibid., 22 Jan. 1799.

[3] LDJ, 9 Apr.–7 May 1799, announced *The Castle Spectre* on 10 and 22 Apr. and 1 May; *Zorinski* on 15 April; *The Adopted Child* on 19 Apr., 1 and 13 May.

X · BELFAST

UNTIL well past the middle of the eighteenth century no visitor to Belfast would have imagined that before the century's end its residents would call it 'the Athens of the North'. Up to about 1760 Belfast remained a backward town unattractively located near the confluence of the River Lagan and Belfast Lough, and largely owned by an absentee landlord, the titled Chichester family, Earls of Donegall.[1] A long broad thoroughfare, High Street, ran from Mill Street Gate on the west to the Lagan waterside on the east.[2] One block to the north, Wern (now Waring) Street paralleled High Street. These two main thoroughfares and the lanes leading from them encompassed the well-built core of the town, chiefly brick houses and shops two or three stories high. Elsewhere the buildings were 'low thacht dwellings of a mean appearance'.[2] The streets and lanes had little or no paving, no sidewalks, no lighting, but abounded in night-time ruffians, who continued to commit assaults freely even after the population had grown from a few thousand in the early 1700's to nine thousand in 1760.[3]

Though generally unprogressive, Belfast possessed a playhouse in or before 1730,[4] one which only the playhouses of Dublin and Cork antedated. The original Belfast structure seems to have been the same as that in use twenty years later when its location was identified as 'at the Vaults'. This curiously named building had once contained spacious wine vaults[5] which, probably during the 1720's, had been converted into a suitable theatre with a pit and a gallery but without boxes. It was situated apparently in Weigh-house Lane,[6]

[1] *Town Book of the Corporation of Belfast* (1613–1816) (ed. R. M. Young, Belfast, 1892), p. xii.

[2] See 'A Plan of the Town of Belfast, 1757'.

[3] BNL, 4 Jan. 1782; *Town Book*, p. xii. Population in the first census of 1757 was 8,549.

[4] The Funeral Register of the First Presbyterian Church under the date of 18 June 1731 contains this entry: 'Mrs. Johnes, play howse.' Cited in George Benn, *A History of the Town of Belfast* (London, 1877), p. 507.

[5] Lewes, i. 144.

[6] BNL, 13 Apr. 1795, advertised for leasing 'that well situated Tenement in Weigh-house Lane, denominated the Old Vaults—with the stores thereon'.

which ran south from High Street, between Church Lane and Princes Street, to the present Marlborough Street. The site, though in the vicinity of the 'English' (now St. George's) Church, was on the edge of the warehouse and shipping district, and therefore could not ever have been very inviting. The construction of the new and wide Victoria Street wiped out all traces of the lane over a century ago.

The playhouse 'at the Vaults' presumably accommodated the Smock Alley company when it came north in the summer of 1736 to present the first theatricals definitely recorded at Belfast. The hundred-mile journey from Dublin by horseback or by cart must have severely taxed the players' spirits. Even in the 1750's the Dublin–Belfast stage coach, pulled by six horses, took three days for the trip, so rough was the road.[1] The Smock Alley troupe opened its season with an 'exceedingly' good performance of *The Beaux' Stratagem* on Friday, 16 July, before a large turnout of nobility and gentry, including such notables as the Earls of Antrim and of Hillsborough.[2] Five summers later the Smock Alley troupe returned with two starring performers: the dancer and harlequin Thomas Phillips, and Ireland's first female Hamlet, Mrs. Elizabeth ('Fanny') Furnival.[3] They departed in mid-September, 1741, after a stay of unknown duration.[4]

Almost a decade passed without the record of any further stage activity. Then, on 2 January 1749/50, the *News-Letter* published the first extant Belfast theatrical notice:

> By Permission of the Worshipful Sovereign of Belfast. On Wednesday the 3rd of January 1749/50 (for the Benefit of Mr. Dugan and Miss Quin) will be Acted a Tragedy call'd, *The London Merchant, or The Tragedy of George Barnwell.* The Part of Touchwood by Mr. Dougon [*sic*]. The Part of Millwood by Miss Quin. The rest of the Parts by Young Gentlemen who never appeared on a Public Stage. To which will be Added a Ballad Opera call'd *Flora.* With several Entertainments of Singing and Dancing between the Acts. We humbly hope that kind Benefactors will honour us with their Company. N.B. A Prologue on the Occasion. To begin exactly at 6 o'clock.

[1] *Town Book*, p. xii.

[2] *Weekly Oracle* (Dublin), 24 July 1736. Reported without source in Hitchcock, i. 97.

[3] Hitchcock, i. 114; FDJ, 11 July 1741.

[4] FDJ, 12 Sept. 1741.

This detailed announcement obviously was not publicizing a benefit night connected with the current season of any professional troupe. The principals, Mr. Dugan and Miss Quin, would seem to have been local professionals striving to eke out a living by occasional performances such as the foregoing. The young lady, after that January appearance, vanished for ever from Irish stage history. Dugan, however, turned up thirteen years later as a member of a strolling troupe at the Vaults.[1] Here also he must surely have played on that dual benefit evening in 1750, since no other place of performance in Belfast at this date would have been so well known that a newspaper advertisement would omit mention of the location.

In the winter of 1751–2 a company of experienced strollers, headed by James Love, acted at the Vaults. Love encouraged attendance by selling tickets at his lodgings in near-by Forest's Lane. Admission to the pit cost 2*s.*, and to the gallery, 1*s.* The performance on Wednesday, 18 December, 'to begin exactly at 7 o'clock', presented the customary double bill, Rowe's tragedy of *Jane Shore* and Fielding's ballad opera, *The Virgin Unmask'd*.[2] Mr. and Mrs. Tobias Gemea, Mr. and Mrs. William Lewis, a younger brother Philip Lewis, Mr. and Mrs. Love, Mr. and Mrs. Tyrer, took the leading parts. Gemea had appeared at Smock Alley back in 1739 and later married Richabella, daughter of the well-known Smock Alley prompter, W. R. Chetwood. On another evening two comic items, *The Honest Yorkshire-Man* and *The Merry Wives of Windsor*, comprised the bill.[3] Love played Falstaff, the role which subsequently brought him a modest fame, while 'Master' Lewis served him as the page boy, Robin. This was very possibly the stage début of William Thomas Lewis (then aged five or six), who later became the comedian 'Gentleman' Lewis renowned on both the London and Dublin stages.

The nucleus of this 1751–2 troupe at the Vaults—Mr. and Mrs. Gemea, Mr. and Mrs. Tyrer, Philip Lewis, Mrs. William Lewis (called 'Widow' at her benefit) and her young son—returned in the summer of 1753 with good reinforcements: William Dawson, Mr. and Mrs. Sheriffe, two former Smock

[1] BNL, 21 Jan. 1763.
[2] Playbill, Shaw Collection, Harvard University Library.
[3] Undated playbill, Shaw Collection.

[By PERMISSION.]
By a Company of COMEDIANS from the THEATRES OF *LONDON* and *DUBLIN.*

At the VAULTS in BELFAST.

ON *Monday* Evening, will be Presented, A COMEDY, call'd,

The Merry WIVES of WINDSOR.

(Written by *Shakespear.*)

The Part of Sir *JOHN FALSTAFF*, by *Mr.* LOVE.
Sir *HUGH EVANS*, by *Mr.* LEWIS.
SLENDER, by *Mr.* GEMEA.

Mr. Ford,	by	*Mr.* Phillipson.	*Simple,*	by	*Mr.* Bushby.
Mr. Page,		*Mr.* Brown.	*Rugby,*		*Master* Sennet.
Host,		*Mr.* Tyrer.	*Robin,*		*Master* Lewis.
Fenton,		*Mr.* Howard.	*Anne Page,*		*Mrs.* Love.

JUSTICE SHALLOW, by *Mr.* P. LEWIS.
The Part of Doctor *CAIUS*, by *Mr.* GUITAR.
Mrs. QUICKLY, by *Mrs.* GEMEA.
Mrs. *PAGE*, by *Mrs.* TYRER.
And the Part of *Mrs. FORD*, by *Mrs.* LEWIS.

With a FARCE, call'd,

The Honest YORKSHIRE-MAN.

The Part of *GAYLOVE*, by *Mr.* LEWIS.
SAPSCULL, by *Mr.* TYRER.

Muckworm,	by	Mr. *P. Lewis.*	Blunder,	by	Mr. *Love.*
Slango,		Mr. *Gemea.*	Servant,		Mr. *Bushby.*

COMBRUSH, by *Mrs.* GEMEA.
And the Part of *ARABELLA*, by *Mrs.* LOVE.

Pit 2*s.* 2*d.* Gallery 1*s.* 1*d.* To begin exactly at Seven o'Clock

TICKETS to be had at Mr. LOVE's Lodgings at Mrs. *Gibson's*, in *Forest's* Lane; and at the Crown.

N. B. *No Children or Servants will be admitted without paying.*

N. B. It is hoped, NO GENTLEMAN will attempt to come behind the CURTAIN, or into the D[illegible] ROOM this Night, on any Account whatever; the Play being so extremely full of Business, that but the Presence of a SINGLE PERSON behind the Scenes must greatly disconcert the REP[illegible]

Belfast Playbill, *c.* 1751

Alley players Mr. Maurice and Mrs. Robert Layfield, and, as prompter, W. R. Chetwood, now retired from that post at Smock Alley. They opened a three-month season with *The Fair Penitent* and *Tom Thumb* on a festive Monday, the 4th of June, the anniversary of the Prince of Wales's birthday.[1] Beginning on 15 June the newspaper advertisements referred to the place of performance as 'the Theatre in Belfast', or 'The Theatre, Belfast', rather than 'The Vaults', and for at least a half-dozen years the more quaint name was discontinued. The repertory in 1753 included no recent plays or other novelties, but represented a balanced selection of standard Dublin favourites: in tragedy, *Earl of Essex*, *Hamlet*, *The Mourning Bride*, *Oroonoko*, *The Revenge*, *Richard III*, *Romeo and Juliet*, *Tamerlane*, *Venice Preserved*; in comedy, *As You Like It*, *The Careless Husband*, *The Miser*, *Sir Harry Wildair*, *The Spanish Fryar*, *The Suspicious Husband*; in farce, *The Anatomist*, *The Honest Yorkshire-Man*, *The Lying Valet*, *Miss in Her Teens*, *What D'Ye Call It*; in ballad opera, *Flora*, *The Virgin Unmask'd*. After only six weeks the benefits commenced and extended over the next six or seven weeks to the season's conclusion in early September.[2] William Dawson had his turn at a benefit night on Tuesday, 14 August, the earliest record in his forty years of acting and managing in Ireland.[3] The same night marked the second known performance of Master William T. Lewis, who had acted at the Vaults the preceding year. Now six or seven years of age, he took the role of the young Duke of York in Shakespeare's *Richard III*. The widowed mother of Master Lewis married William Dawson not very long after this Belfast summer visit.

Another strolling troupe, headed by Richard Elrington, youngest son of the noted Dublin actor Thomas Elrington, occupied the Vaults during the winter of 1754–5. In the previous winter Elrington, then the manager of a company touring around the English Midlands, had been on the point of opening the newly built Manchester theatre when he provoked the indignation of the local authorities and had to leave the city.[4] This misfortune ultimately caused him and some of his company

[1] BNL, 1 June 1753.

[2] Ibid., 13 July–7 Sept. 1753.

[3] Ibid., 14 Aug. 1753.

[4] Lewes, i. 136–43; J. L. Hodgkinson and Rex Pogson, *The Early Manchester Theatre* (London, 1960), p. 18.

to sail back to Ireland, whence they had come. After an appearance or two at Smock Alley in early October 1754, Elrington decided to lead a group of players northwards and try his fortune first at Belfast. His wife, the notorious Betty Martin, his elder brother Joseph,[1] his sister Nancy and her husband Thomas Ward, composed the strong family base to his corps. Three former Dublin performers—the versatile Mr. Longfield, the singer Mrs. Mozeen, the dancer and harlequin George Pitt—reinforced the Elrington contingent. The resulting combination of talents made possible a season of the most varied stage entertainment that Belfast had yet seen. *The Fair Penitent*, as in 1753, was billed for the opening performance on Monday, 18 November 1754, when 'the Ladies and Gentlemen [might] depend upon the Curtain being drawn up precisely at seven o'clock'.[2] Within a month thereafter, the youngest member of the Elrington clan, Master Richard, Jr., appeared twice on the boards, as a page boy in *Love Makes a Man* and then in *The Orphan*, on 11 and 17 December respectively,[3] the only instances of his acting in Ireland other than at the Smock Alley benefit for his father and himself in May 1750.

In observance of the New Year miming tradition Manager Elrington staged on Friday, 3 January 1755, Belfast's first pantomime, *Harlequin Amazed; or, Fairy Friendship*, an anonymous work never again presented.[4] The local public, however, must have indicated a liking for their first taste of harlequinade, because four days later the bill at the Vaults included a second pantomime, which exhibited 'the surprising Escape of Harlequin into a Quart Bole [Bowl]'.[5] This bit of magic spectacle was to follow, by a strange managerial choice, the tragic dignity of *Hamlet*. Three other Shakespearian productions formed benefit attractions: *Julius Caesar* on 27 January, *Romeo and Juliet* on 28 February, and *Henry IV, Part I*, on 14 March.[6] The manager

[1] 'Joe' Elrington during the winter of 1754–5 journeyed between Belfast and Dublin a number of times in order to play at both the Vaults and Smock Alley. According to the Belfast and Dublin theatrical advertisements, his shifts in location were sometimes incredibly swift, and sometimes his appearances directly conflicted —as on 22 Nov. 1754 his Cassio in *Othello* at Smock Alley and his Bellmour in *Jane Shore* at the Vaults, and on 3 Jan. 1755 his Phoenix in *The Distrest Mother* at Smock Alley and his Sir John Bevil in *The Conscious Lovers* at the Vaults.

[2] BNL, 15 Nov. 1754.

[3] Ibid., 10 and 17 Dec. 1754.

[4] Ibid., 3 Jan. 1755.

[5] Ibid., 7 Jan. 1755.

[6] Ibid., 24 Jan., 25 Feb., and 14 Mar. 1755.

assigned himself Hamlet, Brutus, and Romeo; Longfield did Cassius, Falstaff, and the King in *Hamlet*; Pitt impersonated Antony, Mercutio, and the Ghost in *Hamlet*.[1] Mrs. Elrington and her husband repeated their roles of Juliet and Romeo for the final benefit night at the Market House of the near-by town, Lisburn,[2] where the company acted intermittently between 19 February and 5 March. Soon after mid-March Elrington moved his personnel from Belfast to perform at Derry.[3]

For almost three years the stage at the Vaults remained dark. Then early in 1758 Sheriffe, who had visited Belfast in 1753 and now managed 'the Drogheda Company of Comedians', came to town with his troupe, of whom only Mr. and Mrs. Gemea were known to the local public. Sheriffe, however, had collected some promising youthful players who ultimately attained a measure of fame in the Dublin and London theatres: Francis and James Aickin, Rosetta Comerford who became Mrs. Thomas Ryder, Mrs. William Hopkins, John ('Shane') O'Neill. The Drogheda company opened its season with a gay bill of *The Inconstant; or, The Way to Win Him* and *The Virgin Unmask'd* on Monday, 6 February 1758, at the early hour of six.[4] Admission continued, as in the past, at 2*s.* for the pit and 1*s.* for the gallery. On Wednesday the 8th John O'Neill so delighted the audience with his impersonation of Captain O'Blunder, 'the brave Irishman', that he repeated the characterization on several subsequent nights.[5] For occasional novelty Sheriffe attempted elaborate stage effects: a masquerade, a formal dance, a dirge, and a funeral procession in *Romeo and Juliet* on 15 March; 'a grand procession according to the Manner of the Ancient Romish Church' in *Theodosius* on 10 April.[6] *The Tempest*, however, on 24 April surpassed these previous displays 'with a set of new Scenes and all decorations as represented in London and Dublin'.[7] The manager hoped that his 'great expense and trouble' would receive from the town 'proper encouragement'. Perhaps the town did not respond adequately, because no further performance of *The Tempest* was

[1] 'Joe' Elrington was advertised to act Horatio in *Hamlet*, and Julius Caesar, his roles at Smock Alley also.

[2] BNL, 4 Mar. 1755.

[3] Pitt announced in BNL, 21 Mar. 1755, that he would teach dancing at Derry 'during his stay in that town'.

[4] BNL, 3 Feb. 1758.

[5] Ibid., 7 and 24 Feb. 1758.

[6] Ibid., 14 Mar. and 7 Apr. 1758.

[7] Ibid., 21 Apr. 1758.

advertised. Sheriffe also tried to curry the favour of the Belfast theatregoers with Irish *premières* for two very new London plays:[1] on 12 April, a 1757 comedy by Tobias Smollett, *The Reprisal; or, The Tars of Old England*; on 14 April, John Home's tragedy, *Agis*, done at Covent Garden only two months earlier and never recorded elsewhere in Ireland. It is remarkable that an Irish manager outside Dublin could have secured the script of a London piece within a month after its first performance, as must have been the case with this tragedy by Home. Mrs. Sheriffe too provided a bold innovation by daring to be the first actress to play in male attire on the Belfast stage.[2] At her benefit on Wednesday, 24 May, she appeared 'by desire' as Sir Harry Wildair in *The Constant Couple*; she doubtless caused an admiring stir among the gentlemen present. The Drogheda company offered no other special attractions before it lowered the final curtain at the Vaults on Monday, 12 June,[3] and prepared for a summer stay at Newry.

Another three years of darkness descended upon the Vaults. Then, exactly twenty summers after the last troupe from Dublin, a company which called itself 'His Majesty's Servants from the Theatre in Dublin' arrived in Belfast for an opening performance on Wednesday, 1 July 1761.[4] The advertisements for its curtain raiser, *The Beaux' Stratagem*, and for subsequent bills, disclosed that ten of the major players—Mr. and Mrs. William Dawson, Miss Dillon, Thomas Kniveton, Robert Mahon, Mr. Reed, Isaac Sparks, Mr. and Mrs. Howard Usher, John Vernel—did come direct from Dublin, but that the company also relied heavily on a half-dozen strollers—the perennial Mr. and Mrs. Gemea, Mr. Longfield, Mr. and Mrs. Trevillian, Miss Willis. The Irish capital's most talented low comedian, Isaac Sparks, quickly proved on this, his only trip to the north of Ireland, an outstanding attraction, as he had already done at Cork. His rough joviality excelled at the moment in the portrayal of Falstaff, of Young Hob in *Flora; or, Hob in the Well*, of the Irish boatswain Patrick O'Monaghan in *The Wapping Landlady*, and of Captain O'Blunder in *The Brave Irishman*, which Thomas Sheridan had written especially for him.[5]

[1] BNL, 7 and 14 Apr., 1758.
[2] Ibid., 23 May 1758.
[3] Ibid., 9 June 1758.
[4] Ibid., 30 June 1761.
[5] Ibid., 3, 7, 28, and 31 July 1761.

The two sons of Mrs. William Dawson (formerly Mrs. William Lewis) added a distinct interest to several performances. Master William T. Lewis, aged fifteen, appeared on 17 July and 28 August as Squire Richard in *The Provok'd Husband*, and on 29 July as the Duke of York in *Richard III*.[1] Master George Dawson, aged five, made his stage début on Monday, 24 August, as Young Sifroy in Dodsley's tragedy of *Cleone*,[2] its only presentation in Ireland outside Dublin. Addison's *Cato* and Carey's *The Honest Yorkshire-Man* furnished a conventional balancing of solemnity and mirth for the Dublin troupe's closing night, Friday, 4 September.[3]

The next group to inhabit the Vaults had the courage to open the theatre in midwinter. Perhaps Mr. Dugan, because he had last appeared at the Vaults in January 1750, persuaded the small itinerant band that January was a propitious month. Their first performance took place on Friday, 14 January 1763, with the doors open at six and the curtain up at seven.[4] To encourage purchase in advance, Mr. Bloomer of the company sold tickets, for the pit at 2*s*. and for the gallery at 1*s*., at his lodgings in near-by Church Lane. Subsequently admission tickets could be bought at the Castle House in High Street, the King's Arms in Broad Street, and at Joy the Printer's. Though this troupe showed more initiative than its predecessors in setting up agencies around town, it was surely much inferior in acting talent. None of its members ever achieved future theatrical notice except Mr. and Mrs. James Remington, who were just beginning a long career on the stages of both Dublin and the Irish towns. Mr. Bloomer played Lothario on the opening night's bill of *The Fair Penitent* and *The Virgin Unmask'd*, but thereafter had no leading role. A French dancer, Monsieur Soucadan, directed frequent *entr'acte* features, such as 'a grand Statue Dance' on 21 January, a Pierrot–Pierrette dance on 15 February, and 'a new grand ballet' on 28 February and 14 March.[5] The benefit bills, which as usual started about halfway through the season, resulted in some interesting notices. Mr. and Mrs. Parks on 3 March offered the first Masonic entertainment to appear on the Belfast stage: a prologue in

[1] Ibid., 17 and 28 July 1761.
[2] Ibid., 21 Aug. 1761.
[3] Ibid., 4 Sept. 1761.
[4] Ibid., 14 Jan. 1763.
[5] Ibid., 21 Jan., 15 and 25 Feb., 11 Mar. 1763.

the character of a Master Mason by Parks and an epilogue in the character of a Master's Wife by Mrs. Parks, as well as Masonic songs and choruses by the two.[1] Mrs. Bloomer on 9 March advertised herself to speak a humorous epilogue in 'boy's clothes', surely a most incongruous transformation for an actress who had just finished the part of Hermione in *The Distrest Mother*.[2] In connexion with the benefit for the poor on 25 March, the sponsors urged that those 'well disposed Persons' who could not attend should buy tickets to give away, since with provisions 'now dear' the poor stood in great need.[3] The season's finale on Monday, 4 April, belonged to Edward Hinde, who had the temerity to sound the note of an expectant pensioner even though he was accompanied by a performing adolescent son and daughter.[4] He appealed for benefaction from 'the Worthy Inhabitants of Belfast . . . to enable him to become a Residenter in the Town', so that 'a whole family's enjoying the comforts of an agreeable retirement' might be effected! No hint of the brash Mr. Hinde's fate was ever reported.

The last tenants of the theatre at the Vaults took up occupancy in the autumn of 1765. An itinerant troupe, directed by the Dublin and Cork comedian Richard W. Knipe, commenced on Monday, 7 October, with *Othello* and *High Life Below Stairs*.[5] Two nights later the Countess of Donegall, queen of Belfast society, occasioned the town's first command performance, a bill comprised of *Love in a Village* and *Miss in Her Teens*,[6] two of the most amusing current favourites. During the local season *Love in a Village* was acted on at least five nights, as were *The Citizen* and *The Virgin Unmask'd*.[7] Even though Knipe repeated at least once almost every piece in his repertory, his audiences evidently supported the repetitions, including the popular Shakespearian tragic quartet of *Macbeth*, *Othello*, *Richard III*, and *Romeo and Juliet*.[8] *Hamlet*, however, was presented only on Friday, 28 February 1766, for Mrs. Knipe's benefit, when she interpolated between the acts 'a Variety of Songs now in

[1] BNL, 1 Mar. 1763.
[2] Ibid., 8 Mar. 1763.
[3] Ibid., 25 Mar. 1763.
[4] Ibid., 1 Apr. 1763.
[5] Ibid., 4 Oct. 1765.
[6] Ibid., 8 Oct. 1765.
[7] Ibid., 11, 22, and 25 Oct., 8 and 19 Nov., 20 and 31 Dec. 1765; 3, 10, and 28 Jan., 11 Feb. 1766.
[8] Ibid., 1 and 29 Nov., 20 and 24 Dec. 1765; 7 and 31 Jan., 7 and 21 Feb. 1766.

Vogue, never Sung on this Stage before'.[1] The evening's principal novelty consisted of a two-act ballad farce, *The Humours of Belfast*, 'never performed before in any place'. Its failure to be revived anywhere would suggest that the burlesque did not at all entertain the spectators at the *première*. Mr. Knipe had enjoyed a benefit five weeks earlier, but none the less he sought to exploit Mrs. Knipe's night for his own as well as his wife's profit. He therefore issued an elaborate expression of thanks to the ladies and gentlemen who had proposed his taking a second benefit 'as he had the worst benefit in the whole company'. He begged leave, however, to decline and 'entreated their Protection for Mrs. Knipe's Night, which he will ever remember with the highest Sense of Gratitude'.[1]

The customary evening dedicated to the aid of the poor was, for the first time, scheduled before the actors' benefits and carried out with factual publicity. The occasion, renamed a benefit for 'Reduced Housekeepers' and arranged for Monday, 9 December, offered a conventional bill, *Douglas* and *The Devil to Pay*, at the pit fee of 2*s*. for the whole house.[2] As a further innovation Knipe's company refrained from playing on the preceding Friday, so that the solicitors might have 'sufficient Time to carry this laudable Scheme into Execution'. All receipts were to be 'laid out in Coals, to be bought on the best Terms, and delivered out to reduced House Keepers'. Those who disposed of ten tickets or more had 'the Nomination of Objects for the Distribution, to the Value of the Tickets they respectively took'. Manager Knipe wrote and delivered a prologue which with sentimental unction expounded the interrelation of the city's philanthropy and trade:

> Tonight you save the infant and the old,
> From the keen pangs of winter's piercing cold . . .
> From hence you traffic with foreign lands
> And bind the distant world in Commerce's bands.[3]

Four days after the benefit the income had been spent with admirable economy and dispatch: total receipts, £49. 16*s*.; total disbursements, 75 tons of coal @ 13*s*. per ton = £48. 15*s*., plus delivery @ £1; 350 poor housekeepers each received at least

[1] Ibid., 25 Feb. 1766. [2] Ibid., 6 Dec. 1765. [3] Ibid., 13 Dec. 1765.

two bags of coal.[1] Knipe was as careful to assist Belfast's piety as its charity; he called off performances during the first week of Lent 'in accordance with the Law and Custom of this Town re this Solemn Occasion'.[2] Then he concluded his season on Monday, 10 March, in order to be gone before Easter Week.[3]

The Vaults, by now presumably the oldest Irish playhouse still in use, had become intolerably drab and primitive in its accommodations. Therefore, when James Parker, a leading Irish itinerant manager, made his first visit to Belfast in the summer of 1768, he fixed up a small unpretentious theatre near the junction of Mill and Castle Streets at the ancient town wall, an area then called Mill Gate. Today the area is close to the intersection of Chapel Lane, Castle, Mill, and Queen Streets. 'The New Theatre in Mill Street' (alternatively denoted as 'the Theatre, Millgate') opened on Tuesday, 23 August, with a performance of *The Beggar's Opera* and *The Miller of Mansfield* by command of the Countess of Donegall.[4] Parker's playhouse, like its predecessor, contained no boxes. Tickets for the pit and gallery, at the usual rates of 2*s.* and 1*s.* respectively, could be purchased from the manager at Nelson the Tobacconist's in the Market Place, High Street. The rise of the curtain was announced for seven o'clock with the prohibition, new to Belfast, 'No person whatever can be admitted behind the Scenes'. After the command opening on a Tuesday, the regular days of performance were Monday, Wednesday, and Friday.

The company, though advertised as the 'Comedians from the Theatres Royal of London, Dublin, and Edinburgh', included no one directly from London, only John Jackson from Edinburgh, and but three couples from Dublin—Mr. and Mrs. Brown, Mr. and Mrs. Michael Fullam, Mr. and Mrs. Joseph Waker. Among those who had recently been travelling under Parker's management Michael Atkins, aged twenty-one, the son of a minor Drury Lane actor, exhibited the most promise. In this, his first extended appearance in an important Irish town, he played a variety of major roles, such as Richard III, Romeo, Young Bevil in *The Conscious Lovers*, and Colonel Rivers in *False Delicacy*.[5] More important, his maturing skill as harlequin, machinist, and scene designer influenced Parker

[1] BNL, 13 Dec. 1765. [2] Ibid., 11 Feb. 1766. [3] Ibid., 7 Mar. 1766.
[4] Ibid., 23 Aug. 1768. [5] Ibid., 26 Aug., 2 and 6 Sept., 25 Oct. 1768.

to indulge in more spectacle as the season advanced. On 23 November Atkins certainly had a large hand in the costly staging of *The Rival Queens*, especially 'the Bower of Semiramis with new Trophies, Standards, Banners, etc., painted for the Occasion'.[1] In November also he must have been chiefly responsible for two new pantomimes: (1) *The Genii; or, Harlequin Restored*, performed at no other time or place; (2) *Harlequin in the Shades*, presented again here in 1771 and once at Smock Alley during Atkins's sojourn there in 1774.[2] It was most probably he who worked up a third original pantomime, *The Escape; or, Harlequin Victorious*, for a unique production at Mill Street on 6 January 1769.[3] In this work Atkins incorporated the episode of the Flying Tailor from *Harlequin Sorcerer*, an old harlequinade doubtless known to him in his London youth.

Manager Parker had started his season with a conventional command night, but in November he was obliged to put on a special request performance that had no precedent in Belfast. The 'Gentlemen of the Musical Society' evidently wished to display their allegiance to the Ascendancy at the same time that they raised funds for their organization. They therefore arranged with Parker to imitate the Dublin stage custom of observing King William III's birthday with the acting of Rowe's *Tamerlane*.[4] Tickets, printed especially for this anniversary occasion on Saturday, 5 November, cost only 1*s.* and yet admitted to the pit as well as the gallery. Perhaps because this low price attracted the casual and thrifty playgoers, the house was filled comfortably. The sponsors of the benefit for the poor on Friday, 20 January 1769, sold their tickets of general admission at the higher figure of 2*s.*[5] The Sovereign (i.e. the Mayor) of Belfast honoured the event by coming to 'receive' the tickets when the doors opened at six o'clock. With this charitable affair Parker ended his season, apparently so well remunerated that he took pains to publish an effusive valedictory:

The uncommon Hospitality and genteel Treatment my Company and Self have received since we have had the Honour of performing in Belfast, calls for the warmest Acknowledgements; but as no Words can sufficiently express my Obligations, I shall beg leave to assure the two worthy Magistrates who have presided

[1] Ibid., 22 Nov. 1768.
[2] Ibid., 11 and 25 Nov. 1768.
[3] Ibid., 6 Jan. 1769.
[4] Ibid., 4 Nov. 1768.
[5] Ibid., 20 Jan. 1769.

since my Arrival, and the Town in general, that it will ever be my Study to merit a Continuance in their Favour.[1]

By 1770 Belfast was displaying fresh monuments to its urban development. Along with a deepening of the Lagan channel the first permanent quay had been constructed at the eastern terminus of High Street to accommodate overseas shipping.[2] A long-needed Exchange, a rectangular brick edifice, had been built in the square formed by the junction of North, Linenhall (now Donegall), and Wern (now Waring) Streets.[2] The city's growth soon attracted the most able of the current Irish strolling managers, Thomas Ryder, who for several years had been conducting performances in Waterford, Kilkenny, Drogheda, Sligo, and recently in Derry. To make certain of a welcome from the Belfast authorities he first sought the customary permission from the Sovereign to act in the city, and in December 1769 sent as emissary from Derry his gayest player, John O'Keeffe. An avowed dandy, O'Keeffe rode into Belfast on Christmas night, wearing a large blue-cloth hussar cloak lined with scarlet and a little gold-laced cocked hat, and carrying a long cane.[3] He put up at the best inn, the Donegall Arms in Castle Place, where he ordered for his Christmas dinner six Carrickfergus oysters on 'nine-inch shells, each looking like a little boiled chicken'. In spite of his Frenchified manners he established cordial relations with the city fathers and procured for his troupe the desired privilege.

Soon after Ryder arrived at Belfast in late March or early April 1770 he informed the public that he had not been able to find a place of 'sufficient Dimensions for his Scenery'.[4] He therefore contracted with a carpenter 'to erect a Place, on such a Plan, as will not only be extremely commodious to the Audience, but will also leave him proper Room to shew, to the utmost Advantage, his entire Set of Scenes'. These preparations would seem to indicate that Ryder did not take over, as he might have been expected to do, Parker's playhouse of the preceding year. Moreover, the *Belfast News-Letter* on 20 April reported that 'the Theatre which Mr. Ryder is erecting in Mill Gate, is going forward with the utmost Expedition'. Yet it is

[1] BNL, 20 Jan. 1769.
[2] *Town Book*, p. xii.
[3] O'Keeffe, i. 197, 200–1.
[4] BNL, 13 and 17 Apr. 1770.

a tantalizing coincidence that both Parker's and Ryder's buildings were located in the rather confined section of Mill Street known as 'Mill Gate', and that both possessed no box seats. If, indeed, Ryder was doing no more than enlarging and refurbishing Parker's former stage, his publicity continued to conceal the fact even in the announcement of the opening performance on Monday, 30 April.[1] The location was advertised as 'Mr. Ryder's New Theatre in Mill Gate'. There he proposed to enforce some strict regulations: 'No Person will be admitted behind the Scenes or to a Rehearsal. . . . Places cannot be had in the Pit, nor Servants admitted without payment. [Performances] to begin exactly at seven o'clock.' Like previous Belfast managers, Ryder sold both pit and gallery tickets at his lodgings in the Seven Stars Entry, High Street. When his benefit introduced the six-week period of actors' nights on 4 July, two of his regulations had to be amended 'on account of the length and variety of entertainments' connected with most of the benefit bills.[2] The rise of the curtain had to be advanced a half-hour to six-thirty o'clock in order that the audiences might be dismissed about eleven, the conventional time in Belfast to depart homewards. An appreciable number of playgoers evidently would have liked to attend only a portion of these more protracted performances at a reduced price. Such an arrangement, however, would have diminished the actors' receipts materially. Therefore the rule of 'nothing under full price' was inserted again and again in the benefit notices.

Ryder stressed visual and musical features at Belfast, just as he had done previously in Waterford, Kilkenny, and Derry, mainly because his company contained a superior combination of skills in scenic and lyric artistry: Whitmore the scene painter, Geoghegan the machinist, Logan the harlequin, and O'Keeffe the creator of pantomimes, songs, and light humoresques. This quartet staged as its first undertaking an adaptation of O'Keeffe's *Harlequin in Waterford; or, The Dutchman Outwitted* (1767), entitled *Harlequin in Derry; or, The Dutchman Outwitted* and substituting views of the north of Ireland. To get the intricate machinery 'entirely ready' necessitated a last-minute postponement from 7 to 9 May.[3] O'Keeffe's pantomime *The*

[1] Ibid., 24 Apr. 1770.
[2] Ibid., 3 July 1770.
[3] Ibid., 4 and 8 May 1770.

Giant's Causeway; or, A Trip to the Dargle was presented for the first time outside Dublin on 25 May with 'entirely new scenes and machinery including an elegant View of the Giant's Causeway, the Dargle, and the Waterfall of Powerscourt'.[1] *The Rival Queens* on 15 June exhibited Whitmore's scene paintings of Alexander the Great's entry into Babylon, and the conqueror's 'Triumphal Car' executed by Geoghegan.[2] These particular items of *décor* had already been admired at Waterford and Kilkenny. For another tragedy, *Theodosius*, on 7 August, the stage was 'grandly illuminated' to display Whitmore's impressive set of 'a stately Temple, with an Altar, shewing the Christian Religion in its first Magnificence, then but lately established at Rome and Constantinople'.[3] On the next evening Geoghegan took his benefit and demonstrated 'an exact model of Mr. Moore's famous and ingenious Carriage, that moves by Self-Impelling Power'.[3] The machinist, directing it himself, rode, 'with a Black behind, several times up and down and around the Stage'. Apparently the Belfast spectators expressed so much delight over this spectacle that Geoghegan gave the identical demonstration at Kilkenny in the ensuing December.

The summer gaiety of Belfast society, led by the Earl and Countess of Donegall, caused two benefits to be changed from Friday to Saturday, since the actors particularly depended upon these two generous patrons and their coterie. A genial young comedian, 'Jemmy' Fotteral, shifted his night from 13 to 14 July 'on account of a Ball being given at Carrickfergus by the Right Honourable the Earl of Donegall', but even so he failed to gain a satisfactory return and tried a second time together with the manager's brother, Samuel Ryder, on 2 August.[4] A more brash newcomer, John Linegar Owens, who made much ado about his writing and speaking a prologue to the ladies, moved his benefit from 27 to 28 July because of a large ball in town.[5] He too felt that he must arrange another benefit for 11 August 'as he had lost considerably by his first'.[6] O'Keeffe, however, created an irresistible appeal for the Donegalls' patronage of his night on Thursday, 26 July, by composing a new pastoral, *Colin's Welcome*, and dedicating it

[1] BNL, 25 May 1770.
[2] Ibid., 15 June 1770.
[3] Ibid., 7 Aug. 1770.
[4] Ibid., 10 and 31 July 1770.
[5] Ibid., 24 and 27 July 1770.
[6] Ibid., 10 Aug. 1770.

to the Countess.[1] Airs by Purcell, Arne, and Tenducci provided O'Keeffe with the accompaniments for his songs. One of them, 'Hibernia! Happy Isle', became an immediate hit and for some years enjoyed preference over 'Rule, Britannia!' among many patriotic Irishmen. The young author, a capable artist as well, had been enjoying the services of the Earl of Donegall's carriage and footmen for sketching expeditions.[2] In token of his gratitude he presented his benefactor with two views of Belfast. Then, on 31 July, he advertised to do a copy of each of these two drawings and raffle them off, provided that he could secure twenty subscribers at 10*s.* 6*d.* each.[3] Three days later, in the hope of accelerating responses, he promised to glaze and frame the views 'in the most elegant Manner' at his own expense. This enlarged offer drew no full subscription, though the deadline was postponed twice, finally to 12 August.[4] Even the Donegall influence could not elevate the dapper comedian to fashionability in the face of Belfast's aesthetic conservatism. Thus O'Keeffe concluded his sole visit to the north of Ireland mildly disappointed as artist, but much encouraged as stage performer.

Manager Ryder brought his first Belfast stay to a close on 15 August with a second benefit for himself.[5] The evening's bill consisted of Farquhar's *The Constant Couple* and Foote's farce, *The Orators*, its only recorded Irish appearance outside Dublin. During the fifteen weeks of his company's season Ryder performed the heavy duties not only of management but also of leading actor in a most varied repertoire. His parts ranged from the heroic tragedy of Hamlet, Lear, and Lee's Alexander the Great to the high comedy of Shylock, Young Bevil in *The Conscious Lovers*, and Ranger in *False Delicacy*—to the farcical Mock Doctor, and Mungo in *The Padlock*—to the Conjurer in *Harlequin in Derry*. Ryder also often 'turned a tune' in *entr'acte* medleys as well as in more serious pieces such as *Comus* and his own 'Panegyric on King William III'.[6] These multifarious accomplishments in evidence on his maiden visit to Belfast explain why a contemporary, well acquainted with both English and Irish players, rated Thomas Ryder 'as universal an actor

[1] Ibid., 24 July 1770.
[2] O'Keeffe, i. 36.
[3] BNL, 31 July 1770.
[4] Ibid., 3 and 7 Aug. 1770.
[5] Ibid., 10 Aug. 1770.
[6] Ibid., 18 May and 3 July 1770.

as ever graced the boards'.[1] Unfortunately his remarkable versatility was not to entertain a Belfast audience again for two decades, and then only as an ailing veteran in a few appearances some weeks before his death.

Though Ryder never returned as a manager, his immediate predecessor James Parker came back in the summer of 1771 with a considerably stronger company than the one under his management two years earlier. From Ryder's troupe he had taken over James Fotteral and Mrs. Tobias Gemea; from the Dublin theatres he had recruited Mr. and Mrs. Burden, Mr. and Mrs. George Day, Mr. and Mrs. Brownlow Forde, and John Kane, a native of Belfast. Michael Atkins continued to be a mainstay in the company, and on 18 October married a Belfast young lady, Catherine Hutton, the daughter of a goldsmith.[2] The first hint of an impending visit by Parker appeared in the 16 July issue of the *Belfast News-Letter*, which reported that 'the Theatre in Mill Street is repairing'. This must surely have been the playhouse built by Parker in 1768, though his announcement of the 1771 *première* on Friday, 2 August, bore only the indefinite heading 'Theatre, Belfast'.

Macbeth 'with all the original Music and accessory Decorations' provided refreshing variation from past opening bills.[3] Atkins, the company's specialist in stage *décor*, probably suggested the choice. On 18 December he staged the first performance of *The Magical Soldier; or, Harlequin's Mouth Opened*.[4] Two weeks later, for the Burdens' benefit, he put on *Harlequin Skeleton*, its single presentation outside Dublin.[5] He also had a major share in one of the season's two original dramatic productions. On Friday, 15 November, Parker by managerial prerogative held the first of the benefits and hopefully introduced as a local attraction a two-act comedy written by a County Down gentleman and entitled *The Mentalist; or, Doctor of the Passions*.[6] Then, on Wednesday, 22 January 1772, *Love in a Bog*, a comic opera by the Belfast physician, Dr. Thomas Maryat, was performed with music by Michael Atkins.[7] Neither of these native compositions apparently ever received a second hearing.

[1] Snagg(e), p. 110.

[2] Register of the Old Parish Church, High Street. Cited in W. J. Lawrence, 'Michael Atkins: A Noted Belfast Actor-Manager', *Irish Life*, 14 Nov. 1913.

[3] BNL, 2 Aug. 1771. [4] Ibid., 17 Dec. 1771. [5] Ibid., 31 Dec. 1771.

[6] Ibid., 12 Nov. 1771. [7] Ibid., 14 Jan. 1772.

Parker showed interest in encouraging not only new local stage compositions but also new local theatrical traditions. In 1768 the Belfast Musical Society had persuaded him to give a special performance observing the anniversary of King William III's birthday. Now in 1771 Parker, apparently on his own initiative, celebrated the anniversary, Monday, 4 November, by an unsponsored playing of *Tamerlane* in accordance with London and Dublin custom.[1] Then on Friday, 29 November, he arranged for John Kane to lead his fellow Masons among the Mill Street actors in Masonic songs on stage 'in the same Manner as the Grand Lodge do in the Theatre Royal in Dublin'.[2] The occasion constituted an initial step towards a Masonic lodge night at the Belfast theatre. Near the end of the 1771–2 season Parker for two consecutive weeks published newspaper notices to 'those who have any demand upon the Company' that they should furnish bills at once since the players would be departing in the near future.[3] This was the first such public notification by a Belfast manager and appeared at a time when the practice had not yet become usual with troupes visiting the Irish towns. Parker's fruitful contributions to the Belfast stage terminated for ever with the closing performance at his Theatre in Mill Street on Friday, 24 January 1772.[4]

Michael Atkins in 1773 succeeded Parker as manager at Belfast. The new leader introduced an epoch-making change in the city's theatrical situation. For the rest of the eighteenth century Belfast was to be the home base of an acting company that would go out on yearly tours, of considerable duration sometimes, to north-of-Ireland towns. Atkins inherited from Parker a corps of competent veterans: Myrton Hamilton, Mr. and Mrs. Thomas Farrell, Mr. and Mrs. Richard Knipe, Mr. and Mrs. Pye, Mr. and Mrs. Joseph Waker. To this group young Mr. and Mrs. Kenna from Smock Alley contributed a little fresh talent. Mrs. Kenna and Atkins played the leading roles in *Douglas* on the opening night, Monday, 6 September, at the Mill Street playhouse, which all advertisements henceforth identified merely as 'Theatre, Belfast'.[5] Two nights later

[1] Ibid., 1 Nov. 1771.
[2] Ibid., 29 Nov. 1771.
[3] Ibid., 14 and 21 Jan. 1772.
[4] Ibid., 21 Jan. 1772.
[5] Ibid., 3 Sept. 1773.

the manager put his wife on stage for the first time in the comic opera of *Lionel and Clarissa*; he evidently possessed much confidence in her vocal as well as acting ability to assign her the part of Clarissa.[1]

A number of plays experienced local débuts during the 1773–4 season. *She Stoops to Conquer*, less than six months on the London boards, had its *première* at Mill Street on Friday, 17 September.[2] In the ensuing two months Atkins, whose forte continued to be pantomime, worked up two original pieces with new dresses, machinery, music, and scenery: *The Hermit; or, Harlequin Victorious* on Wednesday, 13 October; *The Witches; or, Harlequin's Vagaries* on Friday, 19 November.[3] Though a good deal of expense attended their preparation, their producer never seems to have revived them in subsequent years. On 3 December loud applause greeted G. A. Stevens's operatic farce, *A Trip to Portsmouth*,[4] first staged at London in the previous August. Similar to the harlequinades in scenic and musical emphasis, but catering more directly to the growing patriotic fervour, it culminated in 'a grand view of the British fleet'. The loyal sentiments of an aroused Belfast public demanded seven performances within six weeks.[5] For these bills with a broad popular appeal Atkins was obliged to apply strictly the well-known but often bypassed regulations that children and servants would not be admitted without paying, and that nothing under the full price of admission would be accepted during the entire performance. Enforcement of such justifiable rules came no easier in Belfast than in any other Irish town. The new manager also maintained the long-established policy of closing the season with a benefit for the poor, an all-Garrick programme of *Isabella* and *The Guardian*, on Friday, 18 February 1774.[6]

For the next year and a half Atkins kept his company performing mostly at the new playhouse in Derry. When the troupe finally returned to open the theatre in Mill Street on Wednesday, 22 November 1775,[7] it displayed some interesting additions: Mr. and Mrs. Wilmot, formerly at Smock Alley; Mr. and Mrs. Booth, Mrs. Burdett, all three vocalists of modest

[1] BNL, 7 Sept. 1773.
[2] Ibid., 16 Sept. 1773.
[3] Ibid., 12 Oct. and 19 Nov. 1773.
[4] Ibid., 3 Dec. 1773.
[5] Ibid., 14 Jan. 1774.
[6] Ibid., 18 Feb. 1774.
[7] Ibid., 21 Nov. 1775.

attainments; and a mysterious John Barron, who on 23 February 1776 undertook a specially advertised appearance as the Brave Irishman, Captain O'Blunder, 'for this night only'.[1] He seems to have been a Belfast Mason and a novice actor who aspired to the comic skills of Charles Macklin and Isaac Sparks. At his benefit on Wednesday, 3 April, he elected to play Matthew Mog in Foote's *The Mayor of Garret* and, in Colman's *The Jealous Wife*, the jovial Irish countryman O'Cutter 'with Brogue-ancrean Songs in character'.[2] Though Barron himself gained no further notice in Irish theatrical annals, his benefit made Belfast stage history since it brought about the first local observance of a full-fledged Masons' Night. In imitation of the procedure at the Dublin and Cork theatres a throne was erected on the Mill Street stage for the Worshipful Master, and tiers of seats for the Wardens and Brethren, all of whom came in 'their proper Cloathing'. At intervals they joined Barron and other performers in Masonic songs. The unprecedented programme occasioned a newspaper announcement: 'On account of the extraordinary Length of the Entertainment the Doors will be opened at half an hour after Six, and the Curtain will rise precisely at half an Hour past Seven o'clock, to whatever company shall be then in the House.'[2] A week after this historic event the benefit of the poor once more ended the season with the pit and gallery, as usual, 'thrown into one, and nothing under the full price' of 2*s.*[3]

After another lapse of a year and a half, at least partly spent in Derry, the Atkins company resumed performances at Mill Street about 24 October 1777. For the first time in Belfast an advertisement of season tickets appeared, but the phrase 'at the usual Price' in the newspaper notice would indicate that the sale of season subscriptions had been carried on in the past.[4] The Mill Street repertory did not begin to exhibit new productions until the winter had set in. Then, on 14 December, an Irish historical tragedy by Francis Dobbs, *The Patriot King; or, Irish Chief*,[5] perhaps stirred nascent racial loyalties a little, but provoked no more admiration for its dramatic artistry than at its single Dublin showing in 1773. Music and spectacle intensified after the New Year. On 7 January *Macbeth* came

[1] Ibid., 23 Feb. 1776. [2] Ibid., 2 Apr. 1776. [3] Ibid., 9 Apr. 1776.
[4] Ibid., 17 Oct. 1777. [5] Ibid., 11 Dec. 1777.

out with 'the original music, scenery, sinkings, and flyings'.[1] A week afterwards *The Governess*, Thomas Ryder's pirated version of Sheridan's *The Duenna*, had its first presentation outside Dublin and so delighted the Belfast playgoers with the 'Airs, Songs, Catches, Glees, Duettes, and Choruses' that it was repeated at least three times within a month.[2] On the last occasion, 11 February, an original pantomime, *The Spell; or, Harlequin's Funeral*, with new dresses, machinery, music, and scenery, followed. This, like most of the earlier harlequinades arranged by Atkins, seems not to have been revived after the current season.

The benefit period in April 1778 brought forth several novel offerings. Mrs. Wilmot on her night, Friday the 10th, acted Miss Hoyden in the Irish *première* of John Lee's comedy, *The Man of Quality*, adapted from Vanbrugh's *The Relapse*.[3] The Lee play was subtitled, at this performance only, *A Trip to Scarborough* in a blatant appropriation of title from Sheridan's competing adaptation. Mrs. Wilmot daringly advertised for her benefit 'a moonlight night', the earliest instance of such a promissory notice outside Dublin. A second *première* occurred on Monday, 20 April, when Mr. Pero and his wife of a month, the Belfast actress Widow Villars, introduced at their benefit an interlude, *Twiss in Ireland; or, The Fop in Disgrace*, 'written by a Trinity College Dublin Gentleman'.[4] This original comic sketch never entertained another audience. An interlude drawn from Foote's comedy, *Taste*, and entitled *Lady Pentweazel of Blow Bladder Street*, featured the last actors' benefit, that of Mr. and Mrs. Richard Cox Rowe, on Friday, 24 April.[5] Rowe, Atkins's most notable recruit from Dublin, impersonated Lady Pentweazel with extraordinary success and thereby launched himself as Belfast's stage idol for the remaining fifteen years of his life. The annual performance on behalf of the poor completed on 27 April 1778 the third season under Atkins's management.[5] So far he had made no visible efforts to remove the handicap of a very small and inelegant playhouse, and in general he had not yet shown distinction in his theatrical leadership.

[1] BNL, 6 Jan. 1778.
[2] Ibid., 13, 16, and 27 Jan., 10 Feb. 1778.
[3] Ibid., 10 Apr. 1778.
[4] Ibid., 17 Apr. 1778.
[5] Ibid., 24 Apr. 1778.

By 1778 Belfast was gaining rapidly in social and political prestige among the Irish towns, though its population amounted to no more than 12,000. Through the munificence of the Earl of Donegall an Assembly Hall, scarcely less elegant and spacious than the much admired one at Limerick, had just been constructed as the second story of the Exchange.[1] Its completion quickly encouraged Belfast society to a more avid and urbane pursuit of amusement. At about this same time the city gave birth to the movement for a local volunteer defence corps,[2] a movement that within a few months spread across an Ireland filled with rumours of a French invasion. The ardour of the city's Volunteers at once sought an outlet in entertainment, particularly that which stage performances could furnish. A Belfast theatre manager, therefore, had to face the prospect of larger and more sophisticated audiences who would soon call for accommodations superior to those at the playhouse in Mill Street.

Manager Atkins, however, was not disposed to get involved in the erection of a new theatre, at least partly because a major rift developed in his company during its stay at Newry in the early summer of 1778. Myrton Hamilton, who had acted along with Atkins since their first appearance together at Belfast in 1768, now set himself up as a rival leader and threatened to oppose Atkins's future engagements whether at Newry or elsewhere. The latter, no doubt much disgusted by this revolt, found it a good cause for cutting loose from his Belfast stage connexions. In August he joined Thomas Ryder's Crow Street performers at Cork and continued with them for the regular Dublin season. With his departure the ambitious Mr. Hamilton proceeded to take up the role of Belfast manager and to set about the opening of a new playhouse. He reconstructed a building that was located somewhere in Ann (formerly Bridge) Street, a broad thoroughfare which, one block south of High Street, ran parallel to it and connected the market district with the 'Long Bridge' over the Lagan. The playhouse site may have been, as tradition stated, at the corner of Church Lane and

[1] Maxwell, p. 243.

[2] The first Belfast Volunteer company held its initial parade on 28 June 1778 in its new uniforms: 'scarlet turned up with black velvet, white waistcoat and breeches.' *Town Book*, p. xiii.

Ann Street, but more likely it was further westwards between Crown Entry and Wilson's Entry (now Wilson's Court) on the north side of Ann Street. A visiting English actor in 1783 remembered the theatre as 'small, infirm, and inconvenient'.[1] Evidently it did not represent much of an advance over its Mill Street predecessor in size or comfort, but it did offer box accommodations for the first time in Belfast's half-century of stage entertainment.[2] The fee set for the box seats, 3*s*., followed the price then prevailing in all Irish towns except Cork.

The 'New Theatre in Ann Street' opened on Friday, 23 October 1778, with Love's version of John Fletcher's comedy *Rule a Wife*, followed by Garrick's farce, *The Guardian*.[3] At the rise of the curtain Manager Hamilton stepped forward dressed as a sailor and delivered a prologue which chided the former manager for desertion and praised the new incumbent for his generous assumption of the captaincy:

> Lo! the old brig in which I lately sail'd,
> Tho' long o'er threat'ning dangers she prevail'd,
> At length struck on a rock—What's to be done?
> The Captain [i.e. Atkins] trembling to the long-boat run,
> And as the bending oars he eager ply'd,
> Loud hail'd the crew—hop'd they'd ride out the tide—
> And he'd return anon and be their future guide.
> 'Hey day, good Captain,' warmly I reply'd,
> 'If *you*, in *duty*, won't the storm abide,
> 'Who will? Each moment lost our danger's greater,
> 'Self-preservation's the first law of nature.' . . .
> Thus situate, I agreed
> To serve myself and messmates (now in need)
> By venturing my *all*,—the toil of years—
> To build a little frigate—See she appears!—
> Mark she outrides each wave—braves every blast—
> Eager to moor in safety at Belfast;
> Where she no storms need dread, nor privateers,
> Nor plundering hands of treach'rous Monsieurs,
> While guarded by brave Belfast Volunteers.[4]

This closing compliment to the Volunteers paid quick dividends in a command performance for the Belfast corps on Wednesday,

[1] Bernard, i. 199. [2] BNL, 27 Oct. 1778. [3] Ibid., 23 Oct. 1778.
[4] *The Hibernian Magazine*, Appendix, 1778, p. 751.

4 November, the anniversary of the birth of King William III 'of glorious and immortal memory'.[1] The Volunteers had chosen William as the conqueror symbol for the campaign which they had just recently initiated to free Ireland from civil and economic repression by the English government. On this festive night admittance did not commence until six-thirty o'clock, but the curtain rose at the customary time of seven. 'A numerous and splendid audience'[2] enjoyed the double bill of *Tamerlane*, the usual anniversary play, and *Catherine and Petruchio*. The performers, labelled 'the Belfast Comedians', included a few members of Atkins's last troupe—Mr. and Mrs. Booth, Mr. and Mrs. Pero, Mr. and Mrs. Pye; a few former Belfast players returning from Dublin—Mr. and Mrs. Day, Mr. and Mrs. Farrell, Mr. Kane; and a few newcomers from Dublin—Mr. and Mrs. Thomas Betterton, Mr. and Mrs. William Richards.

The Richards couple soon impressed the city with their lively acting and singing in popular operettas: as Captain Macheath and Polly in *The Beggar's Opera*, as Lionel and Diana in *Lionel and Clarissa*, as Mungo and Leonora in *The Padlock*, as Wally Cockney and Priscilla Tomboy in *The Romp*.[3] On 4 December Mrs. Richards as Miss Lucy in *The Virgin Unmask'd* so delighted 'a frequent auditor at the New Theatre' that in a note to the *Belfast News-Letter* he declared her 'the best local performer in this Kingdom'.[4] Her husband observed his benefit on Friday, 12 February 1779, by acting Sir Peter Teazle in the Belfast *première* of *The School for Scandal*.[5] To enhance the brilliance of the occasion the theatre was illuminated with wax tapers instead of the conventional tallow, the first advertised instance of special 'house' lighting at Belfast. Exactly a month later Mrs. Richards also employed wax illumination at her benefit.[6] Playing the season's first Rosetta in *Love in a Village*, she sang 'My Bonnie Jemmy O!' as her featured musical number, one which Belfast was said never to have heard. The six-year-old daughter who accompanied Mr. and Mrs. Richards already was being trained to become a singing *comédienne* like her mother. Elizabeth Rebecca Richards chose the title role in *The*

[1] BNL, 3 Nov. 1778.
[2] Ibid., 6 Nov. 1778.
[3] Ibid., 4, 8, and 11 Nov. 1778; 12 Mar. 1779.
[4] Ibid., 4 Dec. 1778.
[5] Ibid., 12 Feb. 1779.
[6] Ibid., 12 Mar. 1779.

Romp and the part of Cupid in the operatic romance of *Cymon* for her benefit on 24 March, the last night advertised in that spring.[1] All in all, the Richards family made the outstanding contribution to the pronounced gaiety of Hamilton's maiden season at Ann Street.

During the summer of 1779 the Belfast Comedians acquired two most important patrons, John O'Neill, Esq., and his wife, the former Henrietta Frances Boyle, who resided at Edenduffcarrick Castle on the north-east corner of Lough Neagh, eighteen miles west of Belfast and three miles west of Antrim. For the past several years they had been redecorating and enlarging the ancestral seat, traditionally known as Shane's Castle and, before its present renovation, described as 'a most dreary old mansion . . . four storeys high with corner towers . . . [which] might inspire veneration but was by no means calculated to inspire delight'.[2] The O'Neills, who shared a great fondness for the drama, invited the Belfast Comedians, before the regular city season, to entertain them at near-by Antrim with two performances. The first, on Friday, 1 October, presented a pair of current favourites, *She Stoops to Conquer* and *The Honest Yorkshire-Man*; the second, on the following Monday, consisted of an equally popular combination, *The Rivals* and *Polly Honeycombe*.[3] The general public could gain admission for 2*s*., presumably a price high enough to keep out any curious Antrim proletariat. This foretaste of dramatic entertainment hastened the O'Neills to finish their private stage at Edenduffcarrick and start their own amateur theatricals. On Monday night, 24 January 1780, they opened their castle playhouse with a professional-like double bill of *Much Ado About Nothing* and Jackman's farce, *All the World's a Stage*.[4] Mr. O'Neill led off with a prologue written by his wife, and she in turn concluded the entire programme with an epilogue of her own. She also took the most prominent feminine role of the evening, Beatrice in *Much Ado*. A newspaper reporter, whose judgement may well have been distorted by the magnificent supper after the plays, remarked of his hostess and her talents that 'to the improved

[1] BNL, 23 Mar. 1779.

[2] J. C. Pilkington, *The Real Story of John Carteret Pilkington* (London, 1760), pp. 126–7.

[3] BNL, 28 Sept. 1779.

[4] Ibid., 28 Jan. 1780.

possession of hereditary genius, she had combined the power of critical erudition'.[1]

Meanwhile other patrons had engaged the Belfast Comedians in command performances at the theatre in Ann Street. The Volunteers called for the anniversary tragedy of *Tamerlane* on Thursday, 4 November, William III's birthday.[2] This year, however, perhaps to assure a packed house, admission prices were cut by one-quarter to one-third with the result that seats in the boxes cost only 2*s.* 3*d.*; in the pit, 1*s.* 6*d.*; in the gallery, 9*d.* The admission arrangements also changed to conform to the more cityfied hours of seven o'clock for opening the doors and of seven-thirty for raising the curtain. Then the officers of the 36th Regiment requested an all-Sheridan bill of *The School for Scandal* and *The Duenna* for Wednesday, 17 November.[3] The regimental band furnished the orchestral accompaniment for the singing in both pieces. The Comedians, by way of complimenting their numerous supporters among the local military regulars and volunteers, gave on Friday, 26 November, the Irish *première* of Sheridan's new musical entertainment with a martial theme, *The Camp; or, A Trip to Cox-Heath.*[4] Since the Sheridan feature was to follow *The Beaux' Stratagem*, Hamilton showed good managerial foresight in issuing an implied warning to those who might be planning to view only the exciting finale that no admission under full price would be available on account of the expense of the *première.*

As a last novelty before the commencement of the actors' benefits Hamilton produced on Monday, 14 February 1780, Bickerstaffe's opera, *The Maid of the Mill*, with colourfully romantic sets and lighting.[5] The scenic display not only caused 'several ladies and gentlemen' to desire a second performance at once, but also drew from 'a Frequenter of the Theatre' the first newspaper comment on a Belfast stage production.[5] The pioneer critic thought 'the illuminations displayed the most beautiful colours' and 'the transparency [of the moon] well executed'. Nature's moonlit scene rather than the theatre's copy was heralded as a strong attraction for Mr. and Mrs. Best's benefit on Wednesday, 15 March.[6] A homely quatrain

[1] Ibid., 8 Feb. 1780.
[2] Ibid., 2 Nov. 1779.
[3] Ibid., 16 Nov. 1779.
[4] Ibid., 26 Nov. 1779.
[5] Ibid., 18 Feb. 1780.
[6] Ibid., 14 Mar. 1780.

accompanying the notice of their double bill, *The Way to Keep Him* and *The Romp*, pictured the outdoor enticement:

> The season now invites
> Each nymph and swain for mirth to roam;
> And when you're sated with delights,
> Bright Cynthia's beams will light you home.

The pageantry of historical realism was supposed to lure the public to Mrs. Day's benefit on Monday, 27 March, when the first and only eighteenth-century Belfast performance of *Henry VIII* exhibited the coronation of Anne Boleyn including 'the Ceremony of the Champion on Horseback in full Armour, as performed at the coronation of his present Majesty in Westminster Hall'.[1] This unique show, the last of the season to be advertised, also marked the last record of Hamilton's activity on the Belfast stage. After two apparently successful years of steering his 'little frigate' in Ann Street, he relinquished command to his former captain, Michael Atkins, and reverted to the status of ordinary actor at Smock Alley, Dublin.

Atkins delayed almost a year in recommencing his stage activities at Belfast. On 20 March 1781 he offered 'a few' subscription tickets to a forthcoming season at 31*s*. 6*d*. each. Three days later the first local performance of Dibdin's opera, *The Quaker*, celebrated the apparent reopening of the theatre in Ann Street.[2] Atkins, perhaps for reasons of economy, employed hardly any newspaper advertisements in the subsequent season. One of its most festive occasions must have been the Masons' Night on Wednesday, 9 May.[3] The brethren of Orange Lodge 257, starting from their lodge quarters at six o'clock, marched to the playhouse stage and occupied a specially erected amphitheatre with the Master's throne in the centre. A senior actor, Brother Wilmot, dressed as a Knight Templar, spoke a prologue written by Amyas Griffith, who in 1780 had arrived from Dublin as Excise Surveyor and already was becoming a conspicuous figure in the city's cultural life. He had joined the Philharmonic Society, a weekly club of melody and mirth, and the Adelphi, a small literary group to which Atkins and several of his company belonged.[4] Griffith's stock of original ideas and his great fluency in expressing them soon established him as the

[1] BNL, 21 Mar. 1780. [2] Ibid., 20 Mar. 1781. [3] Ibid., 8 May 1781.
[4] See frontispiece portrait of the Adelphi members in 1783.

critical sovereign of Belfast.[1] Many called him the 'modern Æsop' because his back and both of his legs were badly misshapen. Yet these bodily deformities always provoked him to jesting rather than rancour. Following the Griffith prologue Atkins's troupe played Mrs. Centlivre's old comedy of *The Wonder: A Woman Keeps a Secret*, and then Bickerstaffe's opera, *Daphne and Amintor*, its sole Belfast presentation. Between the acts the brethren on stage entertained themselves and the audience with Masonic songs. Mrs. Wilmot rang down the curtain with an epilogue as a Mason's Wife.

The Belfast Comedians presumably discontinued playing at Ann Street from May to October 1781. The reappearance of their advertisements in the *News-Letter* towards the end of October suggested a recent resumption of performances. On Wednesday, 7 November, the local *première* of Hannah Cowley's new and sparkling comedy of manners, *The Belle's Stratagem*, provoked immediate enthusiasm.[2] The Belfast Battalion requested that it be repeated for the third time on their special night, 14 November.[3] Two days later the Volunteers attended a command performance of Addison's heroic tragedy, *Cato*.[4] Between the acts the 49th Regiment Band played martial airs, and Atkins, supported by Tyrrell, a newcomer, rendered patriotic songs. The Belfast Musical Society sponsored the final bill of the season on Friday, 25 January 1782, as a benefit for Byrne, the theatre's head musician.[5] After the production of *Love in a Village* the company's vocalists, assisted by Byrne's instrumental accompaniment, entertained with catches and glees. This *entr'acte* musical programming for most of the performances helped to divert attention from the generally unimpressive acting of the Ann Street personnel.

Atkins, since his return to the north of Ireland two years before, had shown little enterprise in his management of the Belfast Comedians. A city of over 13,000 inhabitants,[6] now entering upon a boom period, would soon be demanding from him, however, a more spirited exercise of theatrical responsibility. Upon the conclusion of the season at his Derry playhouse

[1] Bernard, i. 195–6. According to Bowden, p. 236, Griffith revived the inactive Orange Lodge 257 after he came to Belfast in 1780.

[2] BNL, 6 Nov. 1781.

[3] Ibid., 13 Nov. 1781.

[4] Ibid., 16 Nov. 1781.

[5] Ibid., 25 Jan. 1782.

[6] Population in the second census of 1782 was 13,105. BNL, 4 Jan. 1782.

in December 1782, he finally responded to the expanding situation with fresh vigour. He dispatched a genial young deputy, Andrew Cherry, to recruit players in Dublin for a spring season at Ann Street.[1] Cherry's mission resulted in a notable addition of experienced talent to the Belfast company: Mr. and Mrs. John Bernard, Mr. Garvey, Mrs. Charles Hoskins, Miss Hoskins, John Kane, Mr. Kennedy, William M'Cready, John O'Neill. On Friday, 24 January 1783, Atkins announced that he had procured 'at great expense and trouble some capital performers'.[2] One of those he listed, Miss Jameson, 'the best public singer in Ireland', if she came to Belfast at all, could have stayed for no more than two or three weeks, since she appeared at Smock Alley again on 25 February. The Bernards, who had toured to Cork and Limerick without excessive discomfort, found the trip to the north over rutty and stony roads, 'diversified by ponds of water', as arduous an adventure as had the Smock Alley troupers of a half-century earlier. 'A "buggy" was our conveyance (which, in the vermin it contained, seemed to justify its designation)', related Bernard, 'drawn by a nondescript collection of bones and hairs termed in Ireland, with some humour, a "horse". The driver used a wisp of hay in his hand to induce the beast to go forward and bite it (wearing out whips being expensive).'[3]

The nine Dublin recruits joined about the same number of actors from Atkins's recent Derry company, which had included Andrew Cherry, Miss Knipe (Mrs. Andrew Cherry later in the spring), Jacob Hammerton, Mr. and Mrs. Richard Rowe, Mr. and Mrs. Tyrrell. The much-strengthened corps at Ann Street opened the theatre around the beginning of February with a 'well and elegantly attended' performance of *The School for Scandal*.[4] Bernard impersonated Charles Surface; M'Cready, Joseph Surface; Rowe, Sir Peter Teazle; Mrs. Bernard, Lady Teazle; Cherry, Crabtree; and Garvey, Careless. Of all this strong cast Garvey, a former cavalry captain who had chosen the stage, exhibited, according to Bernard, the 'most imposing' character. Handsome, tall, graceful, possessed of infinite good humour and 'a sufficient measure of that impudence which is called ease and is enveloped by an air of fashion',

[1] Bernard, i. 189.
[2] BNL, 24 Jan. 1783.
[3] Bernard, i. 189–90.
[4] Ibid., i. 195.

he portrayed the Irish ideal of a fine fellow.[1] Because of his mellow voice he had the solo part in the drinking song, 'Here's to the Maiden!' (Act III, Scene 3). The audience called upon him for encore after encore: 'The Olympian [i.e. gallery] ladies were in ecstasies; and if they could have had their will, they would have given up the play for the song. "Give it us again, Captain Garvey, you jewel! Let us have your own swate pipe."—"There's a leg, Judy! and there's a back!"—"Oh, he's a nate son of a sod!"'[2]

No advertisement of the opening or of any ordinary night appeared during the season. The announcement of Masons' Night on Friday, 14 March, informed the public about the seven o'clock curtain, the *entr'acte* Masonic songs, and the double bill of Sophia Lee's comedy, *The Chapter of Accidents*, and Dibdin's musical farce, *Poor Vulcan*,[3] but it contained no reference to the fact that both works were being given their Belfast *premières*. Bernard's brief notice of his benefit on Monday, 21 April, did state, however, that the second item on his bill, Sheridan's burlesque of *The Critic*, had never before been acted in the city.[4] Mrs. Bernard's expression of thanks to the Earl of Donegall for his support of her evening on Monday, 19 May, concluded the newspaper record of the spring's theatricals.[5] Despite the manager's very sparse advertising the vastly improved company at Ann Street attracted throughout the season larger audiences than ever.

Atkins therefore was experiencing such prosperity that he decided the time had come to put up a new theatre. His persistent rival, Myrton Hamilton, heard in Armagh of his intention and tried to create opposition by announcing in the *Belfast News-Letter* of 17 June 1783 that, since the theatre in Ann Street was 'at times too small', he proposed to enlarge it and solicited subscriptions for that purpose with the following conditions:

1. The theatre to be made 10 feet wider and 5 feet higher, and to be 'bound round like Smock Alley with a box-room in the front for servants to wait in'.
2. Subscription money to be paid to one of the subscribers as treasurer.

[1] Ibid., i. 190–2. [2] Ibid., i. 195. [3] BNL, 11 Mar. 1783.
[4] Ibid., 18 Apr. 1783. [5] Ibid., 23 May 1783.

3. No more than twenty subscribers to be accepted.
4. Each subscriber to pay £10. 10*s.* and to receive one transferable ticket admitting to the pit for each performance (except benefits) for ten years.

Atkins's prestige kept his rival's project from gaining any appreciable support. Soon Hamilton, convinced at last that he could never defeat the established manager, went off to England. The Ann Street playhouse consequently underwent no renovation, but now and then housed amateur theatricals or other entertainment for at least a couple of years.[1] Meanwhile Atkins carried forward his venture with cordial assistance from Belfast citizens. By mid-June 1783 John Ewing and John Holmes had agreed to build for a certain rent the shell of the new theatre and to leave the finishing of the inside to Atkins.[2] The latter had secured from other 'respectable gentlemen' enough subscriptions to finance the construction of the interior and the lease of a desirable site.[3] On 20 June the manager disclosed that he had 'taken a lot of ground in Rosemary Lane [now Street], an excellent and central situation'.[3] This lot, formerly called 'the garden' and located to the south of Rosemary Street, was connected to that street by a passage almost opposite the First Presbyterian Church.[4] The passage, marked by a gate later known as the 'Old Playhouse Gate', formed the entrance-way to the theatre and led to its east side, probably the front of the structure.[5] Today the playhouse site lies behind the 'Castle Chambers' (36–40 Rosemary Street) and to the rear of the Union-Ulster Club in Royal Avenue.

While the Rosemary Lane theatre was being erected, Atkins sent his players under John Bernard to perform in Derry and Sligo. Finally, on Wednesday, 3 March 1784, he opened the new building with special admission arrangements, but customary prices: boxes, 3*s.*; pit, 2*s.*; gallery, 1*s.*[6] Ladies and gentlemen with box tickets were to send their servants at six o'clock to

[1] The last recorded advertisement in BNL, 29 July 1785, announces 'at the Theatre, Ann Street' a lecture on electricity. 'Pit, 2*s.* Gallery, 1*s.* No person admitted to the Boxes.'

[2] The Drennan Correspondence, no. 85, dated 17 June 1783.

[3] BNL, 20 June 1783.

[4] S. Shannon Millin, 'Arthur Street Theatre', *Belfast Telegraph*, 21 Apr. 1938.

[5] See 'A Map of the Town of Belfast' (1788) by John Mulholland.

[6] BNL, 2 Mar. 1784.

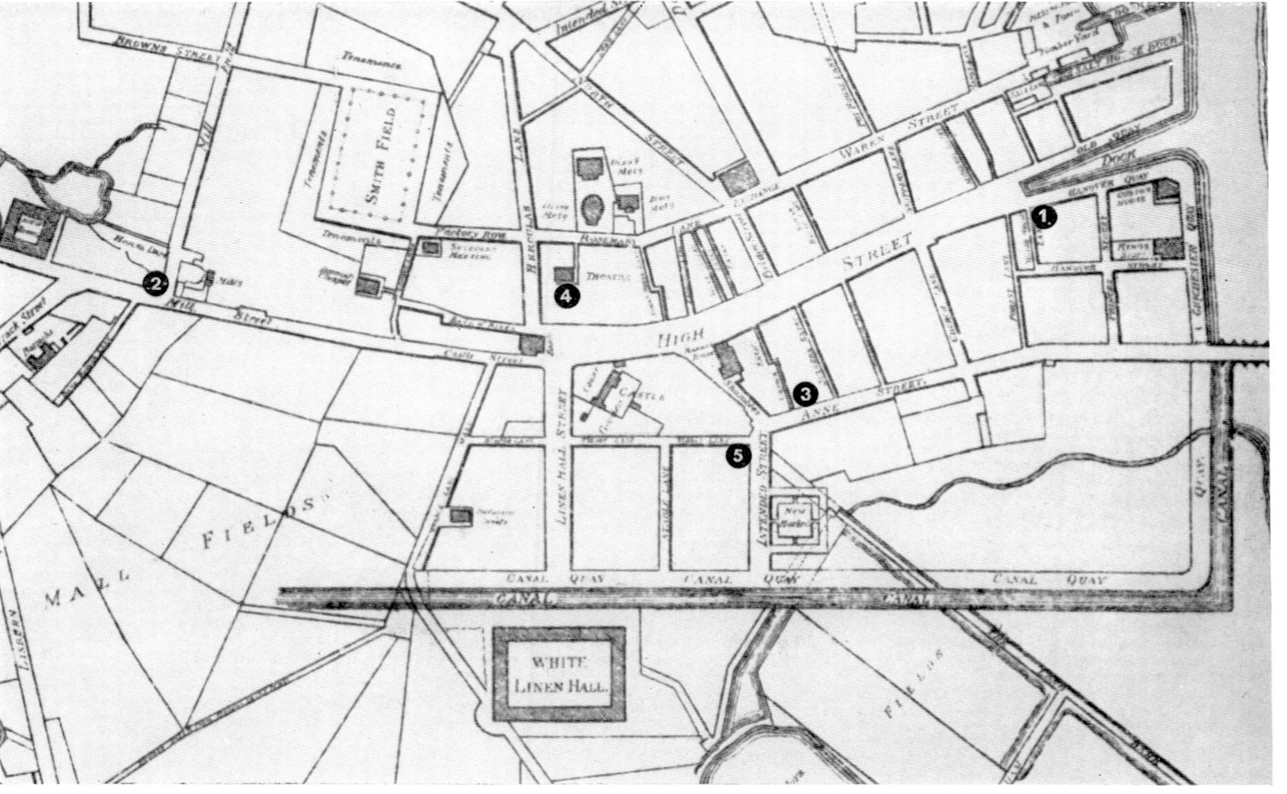

Belfast in 1788

Theatre Sites: (1) The Vaults; (2) Mill Gate; (3) Anne Street; (4) Rosemary Lane; (5) Arthur Street

hold their places. The servants, when relieved, were to be admitted into the gallery that they might be 'always ready to answer the commands of their respective Masters and Mistresses'. Admittance to the house after nine o'clock would be allowed at half-price, but no admittance, on any account, behind the scenes. The entertainment on this first night commenced with an 'elegant address', which, according to the *Belfast Mercury*, Atkins wrote and delivered.[1] John Bernard, however, remembered Mrs. John O'Neill as the author and himself as the speaker.[2] The initial lines disclose the expansive mood of Belfast's citizens, who were currently excited over the opening of the first mill in Ireland to manufacture calico and muslin out of imported cotton:

> Rais'd by the bounty of our Patrons here,
> In a new Theatre we now appear;
> A structure wish'd for by this polished Town
> To worth and opulence by virtue grown.[3]

This prologue was followed by Cumberland's sentimental classic, *The West Indian*, and O'Keeffe's operatic farce, *The Son-in-Law*. In the performance of *The West Indian* an anonymous Belfast critic complimented Mr. and Mrs. Bernard for the 'great propriety and ability' of their Belcour and Charlotte, John Kane for his 'reverend' Old Dudley, and Andrew Cherry for his 'original and facetious' elderly lawyer.[3] The critic especially singled out for praise the Major O'Flaherty of Timothy Duncan, a veteran stroller who was making his first local appearance: 'It is usual to represent the Major as a vulgar brogueineering Irishman; but Duncan with true propriety, tho' he still retained the Irish characteristics in his terminations, showed O'Flaherty the man of travel, of Mars, of the world.'

In reviewing the opening night the *Belfast Mercury* lauded the elegance of the new playhouse's auditorium and stage: 'The Theatre when lit up has a beautiful appearance; a delicate taste is displayed in the ornamental panels around the audience part of the house; but the scenery and the stage finishing exceeds . . . anything of the kind the city of Dublin can at present exhibit and does Mr. Atkins, who planned and principally executed the whole, the greatest honour.'[3] Here spoke the pride of an adolescent metropolis keen to establish its coming

[1] BM, 5 Mar. 1784. [2] Bernard, i. 228. [3] BM, 5 Mar. 1784.

of age. The much older *Belfast News-Letter*, on the other hand, took care to point out two structural defects: 'The entrance is not as convenient as might be wished, and there is only one passage thro' the pit, and *that* one too narrow for the present mode of female dress.'[1] The newspaper went on to say that the 'ingenious' manager should rectify these flaws in design by opening a second passage through the pit as well as widening the existing one. At the time, however, Atkins did not choose to undertake any improvements.

Hardly any news of Rosemary Lane stage activities came out during the first seven weeks of its maiden season. Then O'Keeffe's operatic farce, *The Dead Alive*, was reported as performed on Wednesday, 28 April, for the first time in Belfast 'with great applause before a splendid audience'.[2] The next Wednesday evening, 5 May, saw an 'uninteresting' production of *The Fair Penitent*, but the exciting local *première* of Sheridan's pantomime, *Robinson Crusoe; or, Harlequin Friday*.[3] The 'admirable' scenery, which at the start depicted Crusoe in Defoe costume at his island hut and, later, his man Friday's romance in Spain with Pantaloon's daughter, caused Atkins so much expense that he would permit 'nothing under full price during *Robinson Crusoe*'s representation this season'. The critic in the *Belfast Mercury* acclaimed the current harlequinade as 'far superior, in every point of view, to any pantomime ever attempted in this Town'.[4] Two days after the first display of the Crusoe saga the Masons of Orange Lodge 257 enjoyed a very different kind of performance. They watched the acting of their usual exemplary drama, *Cato*, while they sat in their 'proper Cloathing' on the stage amphitheatre 'raised for their reception'.[4]

After the Masonic celebration the benefits commenced, and each player tried to offer some unusual attraction. On 4 June Tyrrell floated 'an Air Balloon' between the second and third acts of Dibdin's comic opera, *The Deserter*.[5] This exhibition of a balloon on the Belfast stage seems to have antedated any similar feature in a Dublin bill; it was inspired by the introduction of balloons into pantomimes at Drury Lane and Covent Garden during November 1783 and the subsequent winter

[1] BNL, 5 Mar. 1784.
[2] BM, 30 Apr. 1784.
[3] Ibid., 4 and 7 May 1784.
[4] Ibid., 7 May 1784.
[5] Ibid., 4 June 1784.

months. All these theatrical 'flights' grew out of the widespread excitement over French experiments with manned aerial bags in the summer and autumn of 1783. Mrs. Duncan's night on 23 June included two novelties: John Delap's tragedy of *The Royal Suppliants*, its first and only Irish showing outside Dublin; and, of more historical significance, a new song, 'The Gift of the Gods; or, Establishment of Irish Freedom', written by Mr. Duncan and intended to be 'applicable to the Times'.[1] Two days later John Kane's benefit, which presented Dryden's operatic version of *The Tempest* as its feature, brought about an encounter that typified both the tense feeling and also the fellowship backstage on such occasions.[2] Kane expected the mere fact of his being a Belfast man to draw a crowd, but, on peeping out at the rise of the curtain, he was horrified to discover a very small audience. Before long Garvey observed Kane with a mirror in his hand, trying to make up his face while wiping the tears from his eyes, 'the big drops cutting out curious channels through the black and red paint, and his cuff carrying away with every wipe half the rouge he put on'. When Garvey approached to console Kane, John Bernard overheard this dialogue:

Garvey: Come, come, Jack! be a man; don't snivel like a girl!

Kane: Like a girl! ay, ay, Mr. Garvey, it's all mighty fine talking; don't you see I shall be ruined by my benefit! not enough people to pay the candles! and to sarve me so! Jack Kane, their own Belfast boy! och, the Divil fly away with such patronage, say I.

Garvey: Well, Jack, be patient; if you lose your benefit now, you may get one hereafter!

Kane (mistaking the allusion): Pogh, pogh, Mr. Garvey! benefit hereafter; haven't I always had a benefit *before*?

The first season of Rosemary Lane theatricals was drawing such good business that Atkins extended the performances into midsummer. The Volunteers crowded the playhouse on Tuesday, 13 July, for the playing of Colman's *The Jealous Wife* and O'Keeffe's *The Agreeable Surprise*.[3] When their guest of honour, the Earl of Charlemont, Commander-in-Chief of the Ulster Volunteers, entered the 'front' box, the one in the centre

[1] Ibid., 11, 18, and 22 June 1784.

[2] Ibid., 22 June 1784; Bernard, i. 230–1.

[3] Ibid., 20 July 1784.

of the box circle behind the pit, he received loud applause for five minutes. Then a self-appointed master-of-ceremony in the gallery began to call out the names of public characters or groups for the audience, especially that in his section, to approve or condemn. It clapped and cheered for George Washington, but hissed and groaned at the mention of 'the Aristocracy of Ireland'. Many personages were introduced and treated 'in such style as the Gods [i.e. the gallery occupants] deemed adequate to their several deserts'. That boisterously patriotic occasion made the concluding night of the season, the benefit for the poor on 19 July, seem an anticlimax.[1] The charity evening was, however, a far more proper affair than the Volunteers' Night for the twenty-two young ladies of William Ware's select boarding school, who sat together in box seats, guarded by their headmaster and his wife.[2]

Though John Bernard might have been right in thinking Atkins 'not a clever manager'[3] during their professional alliance from January 1783 to July 1784, Atkins certainly developed more and more initiative under the growing prosperity and prestige bestowed upon him by the new playhouse. When he learned in the spring of 1784 that the most recent idol of the London theatregoers, Mrs. Sarah Siddons, after performing at Edinburgh, was coming to play at Dublin and Cork in the summer, he sent her an offer of £100 to act three nights at Belfast.[4] Through Dr. Alexander Haliday, a warm supporter of the local stage, he enlisted the aid of Mrs. John O'Neill in urging acceptance of his offer upon Mrs. Siddons, who owed her first engagement at Drury Lane to Mrs. O'Neill's recommendation and influence. On 15 June Mrs. Siddons passed through Belfast on her way to Dublin from Edinburgh, where she had received between £800 and £1,000 for three weeks of acting.[5] In addition to £1,050 for twenty performances at Dublin, she was to enjoy a benefit there and an after-season at Cork, so that her total proceeds in Ireland were expected to approximate £2,000.[6] The *Belfast Mercury* remarked with sly

[1] BNL, 16 July 1784.

[2] Ware entered in his Cash Book (still extant) on 17 July 1784: 'To Mr. Atkins and Bernard—£3. 19. 7½.' This amount paid for twenty-four seats in the boxes plus one seat in the gallery for the servant in attendance on the party.

[3] Bernard, i. 190.

[4] The Drennan Correspondence, no. 100.

[5] BM and BNL, 18 June 1784.

[6] BM, 18 June 1784.

irony, 'Mrs. Siddons surely cannot call the times bad'.[1] Her presence in the city, though brief and clandestine, incited the lovers of the drama to feverish adulation and expectancy. To prick their extravagant sentiments a humorist on 18 June inserted the following notice in the *Mercury*: 'A Gentleman, by great pains and assiduity, has obtained about a quart of the very scarce *Siddonic tincture* extracted from a *Sherridanean vase*, which he will dispose of, to Theatrical Ladies and Gentlemen, by the drop or thimblefull, *at a very low price*.' Anticipation turned to disappointment on 23 July when, according to the *Belfast News-Letter*, it was thought that the city would be 'deprived of seeing Mrs. Siddons this season'. Six days later joy replaced disappointment because the same newspaper reported that through the friendly attention of Mrs. O'Neill, at the moment a patron of Mrs. Siddons's Dublin performances, the latter was 'positively engaged to act three nights at £100 in the beginning of September'.[2] Then on 17 August gloom descended upon the followers of the local stage at the announcement that a 'late indisposition' in Dublin left Mrs. Siddons unable to play at either Cork or Belfast.[3] This heartbreaking cancellation did not diminish in the least the public demand to view the celebrated English actress. The Belfast manager had to persist in his efforts to bring her to Rosemary Lane at a later time.

With the disappearance of all hope for presenting the Drury Lane star at an early autumn opening of the city's 1784–5 theatrical season, Atkins transferred his company in August to the handsome Market House of near-by Lisburn and fixed up its second-floor ballroom as a theatre. Performances were held there until mid-November.[4] Then, just as the company was on the point of returning to Rosemary Lane for the winter, a report spread around Belfast that a windstorm had badly damaged the playhouse roof. One feminine theatregoer hastened to inform her brother in Newry that 'part of our Playhouse having fallen, there cannot be any acting for some time—if Mrs. Siddons had come it wou'd have been Tragedy in perfection'.[5] Atkins immediately requested two local architects, Dunlap and Mulholland, to examine the walls as well as the

[1] Ibid. [2] BNL, 29 July 1784. [3] Ibid., 17 Aug. 1784.
[4] BM, 3 Aug.–12 Nov. 1784.
[5] The Drennan Correspondence, no. 122.

roof of his Rosemary Lane building. They certified on 15 November the entire fabric to be 'perfectly secure'.[1] The manager, however, delayed production for three weeks in order to carry out a few improvements of the interior. He constructed one more lattice on each side of the house in addition to making 'the stage decorations . . . richer and better disposed than heretofore'.[2]

A 'thin, but select and discerning audience' attended the opening night on Wednesday, 8 December 1784.[3] Attention centred upon the accomplishments of two Dublin actresses who were appearing for the first time in the north. Mrs. James Swindal, in spite of 'an unprepossessing figure (to a degree, *l'embonpoint*)', gave a forceful interpretation of the title part in *Isabella*. Mrs. George Dawson proved acceptable as Venus in Dibdin's musical burlesque, *Poor Vulcan*. 'Cordial applause' greeted Atkins, Cherry, Rowe, Tyrrell, and 'Old Jack Kane the best of *bon compagnons*'. Two nights later Miss Usher, the daughter of a well-known London actor, celebrated her Irish début by playing the heroine in *The Grecian Daughter*.[4]

During the remainder of the season Atkins announced in the newspapers only three occasions: the Masons' Night on 19 January 1785;[5] the Belfast *première* of Holcroft's latest comic success, *The Follies of the Day; or, The Marriage of Figaro*, on 28 March;[6] and the Volunteers' Night on Monday, 11 April.[7] At this last affair the auditors in the upper regions took fire from the sentiments which Rowe enunciated in his acting of Cato. When the curtain dropped after the tragedy, the 'gallery gods' commenced an interlude similar to that in which the Volunteers had joined at their previous Rosemary Lane gathering. The Captain of the Volunteers, Waddell Cunningham, was clapped and cheered. 'The Aristocracy' along with 'agents and Hacks' received three groans. The 'Constitution Club', 'the Liberty of the Press', and 'the American Congress' each brought forth three cheers. Between the outbursts of partisan feeling the musicians were called on to play the 'Volunteers March', 'Liberty Hall', 'Patrick's Day', and other patriotic airs. The nationalistic cause had now invaded Belfast's

[1] BM, 16 Nov. 1784. [2] Ibid., 10 Dec. 1784. [3] Ibid., 7 and 10 Dec. 1784.
[4] Ibid., 10 Dec. 1784. [5] BM and BNL, 18 Jan. 1785.
[6] BM, 24 Mar. 1785. [7] Ibid., 15 Apr. 1785.

theatricals to a far greater extent than anywhere else outside Dublin.

As the summer of 1785 approached, other causes besides nationalism roused the north of Ireland's capital to an unprecedented outburst of activity. The extraordinarily fine weather during May stimulated the 16,000 inhabitants[1] to participate more vigorously than ever before in 'the wonderful strides'[2] which their city was making. The spring opening of the spacious, new White Linen Market on the site of the later City Hall was drawing in not only the countrymen of Ulster, but also buyers from Dublin, England, and Scotland.[3] And, at last, the long-awaited Mrs. Siddons was really coming for her Belfast début, according to Manager Atkins, at a fee of £30 per night plus a benefit clear of all house charges.[4] After Atkins had announced on 27 May that her intended repertoire of only 'first-rate' characters would reveal 'all the amazing powers of a great actress',[4] the *Belfast Mercury* published a stirring editorial in regard to her engagement:

> This promises to be the gayest, most bustling, money-making, money-spending summer ever remembered in this quarter of the Kingdom. The *Siddons* leads up the ball, and when she winks, all the world will follow. There is scarce a genteel lodging in town not engaged, or in treaty, for the months of June and July next. The fame of Mrs. Siddons is great enough to attract a throng of fashionable company; but when there is an opportunity of combining business with pleasure, a still greater inducement must be owned.[5]

Mr. and Mrs. Siddons, and the latter's younger sister, Anne Kemble, finally arrived from Scotland by way of Portpatrick and Donaghadee on Saturday, 4 June,[6] just two days in advance of the advertised first appearance on stage. For all the Siddons appearances Atkins, well aware of the current prosperity, set ticket prices much higher than Belfast ever had previously paid: boxes, 6*s.*; pit, 5*s.*; gallery, 3*s.* Furthermore, he would give 'no credit for tickets' to any purchaser.[7] The female sex were admonished 'not to wear hats, bonnets, or feathers . . . so that the Ladies who have places in the second or

[1] *Town Book*, p. xiii; BM, 28 June 1785.
[2] The Drennan Correspondence, no. 170.
[3] *Town Book*, p. xiii; BM, 31 May 1785.
[4] BM, 27 May 1785.
[5] Ibid., 31 May 1785.
[6] Ibid., 7 June 1785.
[7] Ibid., 27 May 1785.

back seats of the Boxes will see equally well with those in the front'.[1] Gentlemen and ladies alike had to heed another special regulation in force during the Siddons performances: 'Servants who keep places in the Boxes cannot be admitted (as usual) into the Gallery gratis.'[2] The manager expended some of his anticipated revenue on minor redecoration of the playhouse. It emerged, according to local report, 'vastly handsomer than many of the Dublin Theatres'.[3] A similar refurbishing should be given to Belfast's dirty thoroughfares, so one indignant citizen thought, and 'the Sovereign (i.e. the Mayor) should perambulate the streets in order to their being decent, at a time when so many strangers are expected'.[4]

Nobility and gentry from as far away as Kilkenny and Selkirk, Scotland, crowded Rosemary Lane Theatre on Monday evening, 6 June, to view the *première* of 'the inimitable Siddons' in *Venice Preserved*.[5] Perhaps the most delighted observer of this historic occasion was that dean of Belfast critics, Amyas Griffith, who by reason of his recent dismissal from the Excise Office boasted of not being 'worth a sou on earth'.[6] Consequently the Rosemary Lane actors, gratefully recalling his past services in their behalf, 'obliged him to accept of seven box tickets for the seven nights'[6] of the London star's paid appearances. Another enthralled spectator, Mrs. Martha McTier, wrote a vivid account of 'Mrs. Siddons' siren tongue working wonders' in her initial role of Belvidera:

> No one was disappointed, even the old bigots to Mrs. Cibber and Garrick. Dr. Haliday swelled, Mother [i.e. Mrs. Thomas Drennan] snivelled, Major Leslie cried and damned the play, W. Cunningham [Captain of the Volunteers] rubbed his legs and changed his posture, a Miss Aderton was really taken out in convulsions, and Miss Lewis, now Mrs. Britt, left the house and is at present in danger of a miscarriage. Yet many Ladies besides these were much affected ... —Margaret Jones who restrained her tears for a long time but at length they burst forth with an unwilling sob, and particularly one of the Miss Fords, who appeared to enjoy the soft sorrow, forgetful of all around her.[7]

[1] BM, 3 June 1785. [2] Ibid., 27 May 1785.
[3] Ibid., 7 June 1785. [4] Ibid., 31 May 1785. [5] Ibid., 7 June 1785.
[6] Amyas Griffith, *Miscellaneous Tracts* (Dublin, 1788), p. 42.
[7] The Drennan Correspondence, no. 163.

After playing Zara in *The Mourning Bride* on Wednesday the 8th and Jane Shore in Rowe's tragedy on Friday the 10th, Mrs. Siddons went by carriage with her devoted patrons, Mr. and Mrs. John O'Neill, to spend the week-end at Shane's Castle.[1] There she found herself in the midst of 'an Arabian Night's Entertainment' with lords and ladies riding on horseback around a 'terrestrial paradise' or sailing about the lough in a pleasure boat.[2] These noble guests feasted on 'profuse and elegant' repasts. At dinner they were entertained by a fine band of musicians and afterwards they strolled into a superb conservatory to pick their dessert from trees bearing the 'most exquisite' fruits. The lavishness of the O'Neill hospitality surpassed anything in the actress's experience hitherto.

Meanwhile the gentility of Belfast were doing 'everything in their power to accommodate with places those Ladies and Gentlemen who have come from the Country to attend the plays'.[3] A large party from Derry, including 'the lady of General Stewart who was in the late American war as an *American* general', helped to fill the theatre on Monday, 13 June, when Mrs. Siddons did the Grecian Daughter.[3] She took the part of Mrs. Beverly in *The Gamester* on Wednesday, and then brought her second week to a close with a portrayal of Isabella in *The Fatal Marriage* on Friday.[4] In this last impersonation 'her powers of exciting horror' provoked admiring comment in the *Belfast News-Letter* from its publisher's son, Henry Joy, Jr.[5] He deemed 'her distracted embrace of the child' and 'the torturing scene of madness' as 'perfect studies from nature'. Mrs. McTier expressed equally warm praise for the Isabella characterization. Therein she adjudged Mrs. Siddons 'to have reached the heights of human powers'.[6]

Yet, at the same time, Mrs. McTier, who also possessed a good deal of the historian's detachment, set down other, rather less subjective memories of *The Fatal Marriage* performance:

> Five ladies were taken out fainting in the last act, and hardly a man could stand it. Sam [i.e. Samuel McTier, her husband] cried for half an hour after he went to bed, and many others who

[1] BM, 7, 10, and 14 June 1785.
[2] Percy Fitzgerald, *The Kembles* (London, 1871), i. 194–5.
[3] BM, 14 June 1785.
[4] Ibid., 14 and 17 June 1785.
[5] BNL, 21 June 1785.
[6] The Drennan Correspondence, no. 165.

withstood it in the house gave up to tears after they went home. . . . As for myself I can wonder, admire, be chilled, thrilled, etc., but cannot cry, not that I *feel* too much for tears, but she [i.e. Mrs. Siddons] does not melt me. I believe she is too great, . . . I drop a tear, but it's almost a single one. I am therefore at ease enough to criticize—I see all her perfections, perhaps several little unassuming modest beauties not attended to by others; many, I daresay, have spoken a speech as well and in great places been as great, but in the delicate minutiae of character expressed by a bend, a look, in all those little decencies and graces which are so charming in life that they are prized above virtue—or are they not rather the essence of it—in all these she is perfect, and affords a pleasure to an attentive observer that perhaps was never equalled on the stage, unless by Garrick, but in a fine woman they have a finer effect. . . . She sings charmingly—her sister joins with more judgement but not so sweet a voice.[1]

This perceptive Belfast lady's observations more or less coincided with the views of Atkins's recent deputy, John Bernard, who called Mrs. Siddons 'the matron of the stage' and asserted that she 'claimed the dominion of the dignified, the vehement, the maternal, and the intellectual'.[2] Some Belfast theatregoers, however, who were strong admirers of the Dublin *tragédienne* Mrs. Ann Dancer Barry Crawford (though they had never seen her on the local stage), looked upon the present adulation of Mrs. Siddons as a 'new superstition, which staunch and orthodox Crawfordites should reckon no better than a rank and damnable Heresy'.[3] On the other hand, Bernard, refusing to rate the two celebrated actresses in order of merit, named Mrs. Crawford 'the lover', whose dominion extended over 'the tender, the confiding, and the impassioned'.[4] Such judicious estimation did not, of course, still the rage of the controversy.

At the end of her second week Mrs. Siddons again visited the O'Neills at Shane's Castle, but returned to town on Monday, the 20th, to act Lady Randolph in *Douglas*.[5] She chose to repeat Belvidera for her benefit on Wednesday, the 22nd, when 'the greatest assemblage of elegant company that were probably ever drawn together upon any occasion in this part of the Kingdom attended'.[6] For Miss Kemble's benefit two days later

[1] The Drennan Correspondence, no. 165. [2] Bernard, i. 172.

[3] Original Correspondence of James, late Earl of Charlemont, iii (2nd series), no. 17.

[4] Bernard, i. 172. [5] BM, 21 June 1785. [6] Ibid., 24 June 1785.

the older sister appeared a second time as Isabella.[1] However, for the benefit of the poor on Monday, the 27th, Mrs. Siddons added to her Belfast repertoire by impersonating Lady Macbeth, a role which the *Belfast Mercury* believed 'by no means adapted to her great powers', since only the banquet and sleep-walking scenes permitted her abilities 'sufficient scope'.[2]

The *Macbeth* production concluded the most lucrative as well as the most exciting series of theatrical entertainments presented in the north of Ireland before the Union. The gross receipts for the ten nights ran as follows:[3]

June	6: £64. 7*s.* 6*d.*		June	17: £130. 0*s.* 0*d.*	
,,	8: £83. 7*s.* 6*d.*		,,	20: £100. 9*s.* 0*d.*	
,,	10: £116. 12*s.* 0*d.*		,,	22: £113. 13*s.*	(benefit)
,,	13: £101. 18*s.* 6*d.*		,,	24: £98. 17*s.* 6*d.*	,,
,,	15: £120. 0*s.* 6*d.*		,,	27: £106. 0*s.* 0*d.*	,,

Of £716. 15*s.* 0*d.* taken in during Mrs. Siddons's engagement, she received £210 or almost 30 per cent. The harvest of £113 from her benefit raised her total remuneration to £323 for the three weeks of performing. Quite rightly a letter-writer in the *Belfast Mercury* viewed these handsome financial returns to both the actress and the local manager as 'a vindication of the commercial urbanity' which Belfast had attained.[4]

A day or two after the Siddons finale at Rosemary Lane, the city's leading physician, Dr. Alexander Haliday, 'met this Enchantress Siddons posting up, in a black chariot, dragg'd along by four black Drughidee [Drogheda] divils of Horses'.[5] No doubt she was on her way to Shane's Castle where she was to stay a week before setting out for Edinburgh on 7 July.[6] Her departure did not stop the summer season at Rosemary Lane, because theatregoing continued brisk in connexion with the annual gathering of all the Belfast Volunteer Corps. During the week of 11–16 July 3,000 Volunteers conducted manœuvres in the daytime and sought amusement in town at night. Atkins's troupe gave daily performances, beginning on Wednesday the 13th with *The Recruiting Officer* and *Rosina.*[7] With the passing

[1] Ibid.
[2] Ibid., 1 July 1785.
[3] Ibid., 28 June 1785.
[4] Ibid., 17 June 1785.
[5] Original Correspondence of James, late Earl of Charlemont, iii (2nd series), no. 17.
[6] BM, 1 and 8 July 1785.
[7] BNL, 12 July 1785.

of the Review Week it presumably soon left off playing until it settled in Derry for the winter of 1785–6.

Since the Rosemary Lane stage remained dark throughout the early autumn of 1785 and promised to stay so a long time, the play-loving O'Neills determined to hold a magnificent theatrical fête at their 'Mahometan Paradise of Shane's Castle'.[1] Invitations went out to the *élite* of Belfast and vicinity to attend on Monday, 28 November, an evening programme of plays, ball, and supper. The Sunday just before this brilliant event Dr. Haliday reported that the invited guests were 'pouring in from all parts . . . to be at hand, and my own house is filling fast with Sabbath-breakers—for the hairdressers are at work'.[2] On the next night, in the Edenduffcarrick Theatre, these gay ladies and gentlemen were first treated to the acting of *Cymbeline* and, thereafter, Murphy's farce, *The Upholsterer*.[3] In Shakespeare's drama the dashing Isaac Cory, prominent M.P. from Newry, played Iachimo; Mr. O'Neill, Posthumus; Mrs. St. Leger, Imogen; and Mrs. O'Neill, the Queen. This the *Belfast News-Letter* considered 'a most unfavourable part' for Mrs. O'Neill, and applauded 'her good humour and condescension in taking it up'. The *News-Letter* then described in an ecstatic sentence her appearance in the *Cymbeline* epilogue, which she wrote the very morning of the fête and delivered in the attire of a Sylph: 'The *légèreté* of her beautiful figure was the very thing that the poet fancied.'[3] Dr. William Drennan, Mrs. McTier's brother, recorded a far less favourable impression of the Shane's Castle hostess and her performing: 'It is really singular that she should like playing when she is so totally devoid of all theatrical power. . . . Her manners are those of a finished Courtesan.'[4]

When the dramatic entertainment concluded a little before midnight, the playhouse, designed like 'a superb palace . . . to be converted instantaneously into a ball-room',[5] was cleared and given over to dancing until six in the morning.[6] At that hour the dancers sat down to a sumptuous breakfast in the conservatory amid 'a profusion of flowering shrubbery—in the centre,

[1] The Drennan Correspondence, no. 168.

[2] Original Correspondence of James, late Earl of Charlemont, iii (2nd series), no. 52.

[3] BNL, 6 and 9 Dec. 1785.

[4] The Drennan Correspndence, nos. 198, 206.

[5] Bowden, pp. 233–4.

[6] BNL, 6 and 9 Dec. 1785.

a large spreading rose tree in full blow and filled with lights'. Eighteenth-century Belfast never again witnessed so spectacular a display of luxury. 'The enormous expense bore heavily on the minds' of a few thoughtful guests, such as Dr. Haliday,[1] who could not forget the severe economic and political oppression which ruled the lives of a majority of their countrymen.

The widespread excitement created by the incomparable Mrs. Siddons and the equally incomparable Edenduffcarrick theatrical fête had quite subsided when Atkins raised the curtain again at Rosemary Lane in the autumn of 1786. His first notice of the coming season proclaimed that, as regards his actors, 'there never was such a company in point of merit yet seen in the North of Ireland'.[2] This daring puff grew out of his recruitment of two celebrated players who had not hitherto performed in Belfast: Lee Lewes and Mrs. Achmet, 'the first female ornament of the Irish Stage' according to Atkins's billing.[3] They opened the theatrical season on Monday, 23 October, in the famous old comedy of *Rule a Wife*. The manager expected so large a house that he announced no entering or leaving to be allowed at half-price 'during the whole performance'.[3]

Mrs. Achmet for her first benefit on Friday, 11 November, sought to attract especially the male playgoers by appearing in breeches as Sir Harry Wildair, after many decades still the favourite part of Irish actresses bent on sex appeal. She anticipated enough patronage to justify 'railing in part of the Pit as Boxes'.[4] Her co-star, Lewes, delayed his first benefit until Wednesday, 20 December, and then used the occasion for his wife's stage début.[5] As Rosalind in *As You Like It*, 'she acquitted herself tolerably well', the *Belfast News-Letter* reported, 'but her person and voice threaten to be insuperable bars to her arriving at eminence in the profession'.[6] Her husband chose to play Touchstone when he should have left the role to Richard Rowe, the *News-Letter* believed, since he spoke the famous poetic passages with such 'languor' that the audience listened

[1] Original Correspondence of James, late Earl of Charlemont, iii (2nd series), no. 54.

[2] BNL, 3 and 6 Oct. 1786.

[3] Ibid., 20 Oct. 1786.

[4] Ibid., 14 and 17 Nov. 1786.

[5] Ibid., 12 and 15 Dec. 1786.

[6] Ibid., 22 Dec. 1786.

to him without emotion. Nevertheless Lewes thought the response so warm and generous as to render 'his refusing a *permanent* engagement at Covent Garden Theatre very light and easy to him'.[1]

Though Mrs. Achmet concluded her intended appearances with a second benefit on New Year's Night, 1787, she generously agreed to perform for the benefit of the Poor House and the Infirmary on 15 January.[2] It proved, however, a less than festive finale for the Dublin actress. The playhouse was by no means well filled despite the fact that the ladies and gentlemen of the city had been urged to 'suffer no private engagements to interfere'. The *News-Letter* subsequently chastised the Belfast public for its unworthy support: 'It would be becoming, in an enlightened community, to make even the luxury of the age conducive to the purposes of humanity! Every benefit play for the Poor, ill attended, is a satire on the depravity of the Times.'[3] The bills for this night had announced a minuet by Mrs. Achmet, but on the evening of the benefit neither the play nor the farce included a dance.[4] Consequently 'an universal stamping' arose from every section of the theatre. Mrs. Achmet at last came forward and delivered 'a very genteel and faithful apology'. Yet, when in due time no dancers presented themselves, 'the irritation of the audience continued in an alarming degree'. Finally, 'a gentleman, in the interests of gallantry to the lady, and of politeness to the audience, offered his services, and gave Mrs. Achmet an opportunity, in the graceful movement of the minuet, of displaying once more that elegance of form which has, this season, so frequently been the admiration of every person of taste in this place'. The unhappy circumstances of this farewell appearance evidently left no deep unpleasantness in Mrs. Achmet's memory, because a year afterwards her biographer wrote of the Belfast tour in nothing but glowing retrospect: 'This favourite of Nature soon became a favourite of the [people] also. Her Estifania, Euphrasia, Polly, Juliet (particularly capital), Sigismunda, Sir Harry Wildair, Calista, and Monimia did . . . all that could be wished: both her name and her purse derived consequence from the expedition.'[5]

[1] BNL, 22 Dec. 1786. [2] Ibid., 12 Jan. 1787. [3] Ibid., 23 Feb. 1787.
[4] Ibid., 19 Jan. 1787. [5] *The Hibernian Magazine*, May 1788, p. 285.

Andrew Cherry succeeded Mrs. Achmet as the visiting celebrity from Smock Alley. His characterizations of Sir Pertinax MacSycophant in *A Man of the World* and of Lingo in *The Agreeable Surprise* on Friday, 19 January, gave rise to some pointed comment in the *Londonderry Journal* by 'Atticus'. This keen observer disliked the popular young comedian's 'extravagant gestures and buffoonish tricks', by which 'he principally exerts himself to gratify the gross ideas of the spectators in the Upper Regions'.[1] His Sir Pertinax came off 'by no means so happy in his pronouncing of the Scotch dialect as could have been wished'.[2] As Lingo, Cherry inserted into many situations most absurd business: 'Not content with Cowslip pulling his wig a little to one side, he, to make himself look still more ridiculous, must turn it entirely around. . . . In the scene with Mrs. Cheshire his violent manner of forcing her into a chair and throwing the cloak over her head were highly unnatural and improper.'[2] These antics brought down 'roars of applause' from the gallery, but, for 'the judicious persons' present, his impersonations suffered in comparison with Richard Rowe's 'habitual chasteness of acting'.

'Atticus' also criticized the tasteless staging in *The Agreeable Surprise*.[2] A 'highly improper' set of 'columns' had appeared as side-scenes to both the 'street' and the 'chamber' flats. 'Atticus' recommended that the theatre should acquire a couple of additional sets of wing-flats suitable to those two much-employed scenes. Another facet of managerial economy earlier in the winter had incited a Belfast playgoer to complain about the poor illumination of the boxes: 'A great number of ladies do not prefer the elevated box seats at the expense of their beauty, which is certainly not a little diminished by the gloom that the boxes, for want of lights, and of proper colours for reflection, diffuse over the features.'[3] The deplorable situation, the plaintiff argued, could be easily remedied by installing additional chandeliers and by draping the box interiors with 'those colours which have been found by experience to be favourable to the complexion'.

These criticisms of house and stage *décor* at Rosemary Lane seemed to indicate that Atkins was giving less attention to physical conditions than to the dramatic repertory. In the

[1] LJ, 30 Jan. 1787. [2] Ibid., 23 Jan. 1787. [3] BNL, 22 Dec. 1786.

course of the 1786–7 season he staged four London comedies new to Belfast: Murphy's *The Upholsterer* on 20 December; Andrews's *Reparation* on 23 February, its only known eighteenth-century Irish performance; MacNally's *Fashionable Levities* on 26 February; R. B. Sheridan's *A Trip to Scarborough* on 9 and 21 March.[1] The season ended with the début of a new opera, *The World*, by Mr. Eccles, a local citizen who 'for upwards of thirty years [had] filled a very useful department in the education of the youth of this town'.[2] Two days after the opera's 'well attended' *première* on Wednesday, 25 April, its author enjoyed a benefit marked by 'generous applause'.[3] The approbation, however, secured the work no further performances at home or elsewhere.

Belfast's initial summer theatricals, thanks to the magnetic presence of Mrs. Siddons, had so richly succeeded that Atkins decided to repeat the venture in 1787 with an actress of eighteen, Anne Brunton, whom the managers of Covent Garden and Smock Alley were publicizing as the 'growing rival' of Drury Lane's first lady.[4] Though the Rosemary Lane manager originally announced on 24 July raised prices of 6*s.* for the boxes, 4*s.* for the pit, and 2*s.* for the gallery during Miss Brunton's engagement, he apparently discovered the demand for box and pit seats not as great as he had hoped, and therefore, a week later, lowered the figures to 5*s.* and 3*s.* respectively.[5] Miss Brunton selected for her north-of-Ireland *première* on Friday, 3 August, her favourite roles of Horatia in *The Roman Father* and Rosina in Mrs. Brooke's comic opera.[6] Her performance elicited from the *News-Letter* critic a warm eulogy 'of her rare sweetness of modulation, expressive face, and elegant taste in dress'.[7] The same commentator, after her portrayal of Euphrasia in *The Grecian Daughter* on the following Monday, dared to say that 'in tenderness of look and mild intonation the towering talent of Mrs. Siddons falls short of Excellence, whereas Miss Brunton excels, tho' she does not attempt as bold a flight'.[8]

The eighteen-year-old actress's third night showed 'her theatric powers peculiarly suited to Juliet', according to the

[1] BNL, 15 Dec. 1786; 23 Feb., 6 and 20 Mar. 1787. [2] Ibid., 24 Apr. 1787.
[3] Ibid., 27 Apr. 1787. [4] Ibid., 10 Aug. 1787. [5] Ibid., 31 July 1787.
[6] Ibid., 3 Aug. 1787. [7] Ibid., 7 Aug. 1787. [8] Ibid., 10 Aug. 1787.

News-Letter.[1] Mrs. McTier felt that 'she was really Shakespeare's', a very high tribute since Mrs. McTier confessed to be 'sick of this tragedy after having seen it so long that I know each Ha and Oh by heart'.[2] Miss Brunton's repertoire also included such conventional leading characters as Calista in *The Fair Penitent*, Beatrice in *Much Ado*, Perdita in *Florizel and Perdita*, and Monimia in *The Orphan*.[3] With this last part she concluded her advertised engagement of ten nights on Friday, 24 August, and made her permanent farewell to Belfast. Atkins did not extend the young star's appearances, perhaps because they actually had been, as Mrs. McTier reported, 'ill-attended'[4] by the city's theatregoers, who may well not yet have recovered from the spellbinding effect of Miss Brunton's older rival.

After this second venture with a summer season the Rosemary Lane troupe retired for fourteen months behind a curtain of newspaper silence in respect to its Belfast doings. Reports, however, did appear of its acting at Derry during the early spring of 1788. In October of that year Atkins announced the imminent opening of the Belfast playhouse again with the assertion that his company deserved 'the countenance and protection of the judicious and polite audience' of the city.[5] He singled out for especial mention 'our old favourite Rowe'; Mrs. Francis Molloy, whose 'first-rate musical abilities' were to be displayed on this, her initial visit to Belfast; lastly, Mr. and Mrs. James Chalmers of Covent Garden and Smock Alley on their maiden tour to the north of Ireland.[6] Chalmers, long famous for his roles in pantomime, made the mistake of attempting 'heavy' parts to prove himself a versatile actor to the Belfast spectators. When he performed Othello on 10 November, 'Dennis' the *News-Letter* critic found the play 'stripped of every beauty for which it has been celebrated' and Chalmers's talents 'never intended for the Moor's role'.[7] This criticism in print may have been the influence that caused him to desist from further 'heroic' exhibitions and to return to his forte. On 16 January 1789 he starred as Harlequin in *Prometheus; or, Harlequin's Animation*, which Atkins staged with fresh scenery

[1] Ibid. [2] The Drennan Correspondence, no. 238.
[3] BNL, 10, 14, 17, and 24 Aug. 1787.
[4] The Drennan Correspondence, no. 239.
[5] BNL, 3 Oct. 1788. [6] Ibid., 10 Oct. 1788. [7] Ibid., 11 Nov. 1788.

of his own invention.[1] The spectacular moment of this pantomime occurred when Chalmers 'leaped through a brilliant Sun of variegated Fire', the flaming chariot wheel by means of which Prometheus the magician transformed him from a motionless figure into a living Harlequin. He repeated the same feat at his benefit on 26 January, and then did a similar leap through fire and water amid a brilliant sun in *Harlequin Gard'ner* at his wife's benefit on 11 February.[2] His second benefit and final appearance on 18 March presented *Neck or Nothing; or, Harlequin's Flight from the Gods*, in which he carried out a sensational exhibition of flying from the back of the stage to the top of the theatre auditorium over the gallery, and of returning thence, head foremost, to the starting point.[3] Chalmers appealed for a particularly generous patronage on this occasion because he received a salary 'no larger than that of any average member of the company, although he combined the offices of actor and of Harlequin.'

The very next evening after Chalmers's failure as Othello on 10 November the veteran comedian, Tom King, *en route* from London to Dublin, made his first Belfast appearance in eighteen years and scored a great success in his favourite role, Lord Ogleby in *The Clandestine Marriage*. 'Time had tended only to mature his judgements, . . . and his person, tho' hardly of the middle size, was still genteel and fashionable.'[4] The *News-Letter* then went on to commend the clarity of his speech, 'thoroughly audible even in the lowest tones'. The audience delighted in King's impersonation of 'a gay old debilitated debauchee of fashion, whose formal dress of pink and silver, with a silver tissue waistcoat, was well fancied and tasty'.

Closely following Tom King and also heading for Dublin, there came two other 'capital performers', Joseph Holman and Maria Hughes, both in their twenties and both strangers to Belfast audiences. Atkins's 'great expense' in engaging them required the same raised prices for tickets to their nights as to Miss Brunton's the previous year: 5*s*. for the boxes, 3*s*. for the pit, and 2*s*. for the gallery.[5] Subscribers' tickets were accepted for free admittance, but no half-price admissions were permitted.

[1] BNL, 20 Jan. 1789.
[2] Ibid., 23 Jan. and 6 Feb. 1789.
[3] Ibid., 17 Mar. 1789.
[4] Ibid., 18 Nov. 1788.
[5] Ibid., 11 Nov. 1788.

The starring guests began their engagement on Wednesday, 19 November, with *Hamlet*.[1] Holman, according to Mrs. McTier, acted 'just the elegant young Prince'.[2] The *News-Letter* described his manner as 'spirited and chaste'.[3] Though the newspaper somewhat objected to 'the liberty taken (we believe universally) of omitting the admirable instructions of Polonius to Laertes', it strongly deprecated the feeble expression of applause, which, it intimated, had now become habitual with the local theatregoers: 'The admiration on this occasion was, *as usual*, to be discovered rather by the universal silence that prevailed.' However lackadaisical the city's initial response, Holman and Miss Hughes carried on without deviation their announced repertory of *The Provok'd Husband* on 21 November, *Romeo and Juliet* on the 24th, and *Tancred and Sigismunda* on the 26th.[4] At this point Manager Atkins grew distressed at the unorthodox behaviour of some playgoing ladies who were being seen in the gallery instead of the pit or the boxes. Therefore, at his behest, no doubt, the *News-Letter* published an admonition that 'this practice had a tendency to injure the receipts of the house at the time when the Manager has had extraordinary expenses to bring actors of eminence to the theatre'.[5]

After a break on account of Mrs. Molloy's final night and benefit, the young couple resumed their performing on Monday, 1 December, in *The West Indian*. As Charlotte, Miss Hughes, though 'elegant in figure', demonstrated an unevenness in the quality of her interpretation, 'the inevitable consequence of inexperience'.[6] The 'unexpected neglect' of *The Distrest Mother* on Wednesday the 3rd did not remain unnoticed by the bitterly disappointed Miss Hughes, who seemed to have considered the occasion her first benefit, though not so advertised. She issued a petulant statement: 'She was at a loss to account for so poor a house: it must have proceeded from some mistaken idea.'[6] The bill of the 3rd was repeated on Monday the 8th, and announced as a benefit for Miss Hughes.[6] She acted Belvidera in *Venice Preserved* at Holman's benefit on the 15th.[7] Then the pair, to celebrate their farewell to Belfast for ever, attempted on Wednesday the 17th a more unusual programme with Moore's *The*

[1] Ibid., 18 Nov. 1788.
[2] The Drennan Correspondence, no. 276.
[3] BNL, 21 Nov. 1788.
[4] Ibid., 18 Nov. 1788.
[5] Ibid., 28 Nov. 1788.
[6] Ibid., 5 Dec. 1788.
[7] Ibid., 12 Dec. 1788.

Gamester and Milton's *Comus*.[1] After their departure the special engagements ceased, and the season proceeded in a generally uneventful fashion until the last performance on Monday, 27 April 1789.[2]

For well over a year thereafter Manager Atkins occupied himself with constructing and opening a new playhouse in Derry to the neglect of Belfast theatricals. Meanwhile the city was advancing 'rapidly in size, improvement, and prosperity'.[3] The population had risen to 18,000, with eighty-four citizens possessing an income of £5,000 or more per annum.[4] Rents had become very high and housing so scarce that in 1790 three hundred new buildings were being erected.[5] A mail coach was now running regularly between Belfast and Dublin.[6] In spite of all this advancement Atkins undertook no moves to beautify the Rosemary Lane interior before he reopened it in October 1790 with the latest Dublin star, Mrs. Elizabeth Coates, as the attraction.[7] Even her glamorous presence could not blind the senses of the genteel spectators to the manager's inattention to 'ornament, decency, or cleanliness' in the pit and boxes.[8] One theatregoer at last expostulated in a lengthy bill of complaints:

> It is impossible for Ladies to go in full or half dress without the chance of their cloathes being soiled or totally destroyed by the quantities of dirt and dust which are suffered to remain for months. The chandeliers are too few, and so contrived that the tallow runs out of them. The gallery is so ill ceiled that quantities of punch and other liquors fall in copious showers on the unoffending heads in the boxes. The seats consist of ill planed boards, destitute of covering. In short, everything in the boxes is finished in the shabbiest style, and in a manner the most unfriendly to the appearance of female beauty; the boxes being a number of dark caverns without any illumination from the rear (not as those in Newry and other theatres) and hung with some dirty stuff the colour of which is no longer to be ascertained. . . . These faults act as so many effectual bars against the attendance of many a female party that would otherwise more generally grace the theatre with their presence.

[1] BNL, 12 Dec. 1788.
[2] Ibid., 24 Apr. 1789.
[3] Original Correspondence of James, late Earl of Charlemont, v (2nd series), no. 75.
[4] Population in the third census of 1791 was 18,320. *Town Book*, p. xiii.
[5] Bowden, pp. 235–6.
[6] *Town Book*, p. xiii.
[7] BNL, 19 Oct. 1790.
[8] Ibid., 2 Nov. 1790.

The communication closed, however, with a compliment to the manager's excellent scenery and general good sense.[1]

Atkins could not well ignore so devastating a citation, and quickly promised that 'the hint . . . concerning the boxes shall be attended to and the alterations required made as speedily as possible'.[2] After this reply the *News-Letter* correspondent directed his critical remarks to the Rosemary Lane players. In the performance of 8 November, James May as Hamlet 'never sunk below mediocrity'; Stewart as the Ghost 'might have whined less in some of the least impassioned of the Poet's lines'; Rowe unhappily omitted '*as usual*' Polonius's speech of advice; Mrs. Coates as Ophelia 'acquitted herself with singular propriety'.[3] Her exhibition in *Jane Shore* on the 10th was thought 'remarkable for chastity and correctness'.[3] She drew no comment, however, for her Lady Rutland in *The Earl of Essex* at her benefit and last night on the 12th.

While Mrs. Coates was playing for six weeks at Crow Street, Dublin, Mrs. Mason (formerly Mrs. Booth) became the leading lady. Her characterization of Euphrasia in *The Grecian Daughter* on 3 December did not please the *News-Letter* critic, because both she and 'all our present actresses too closely imitate Mrs. Siddons's tones in her most impassioned scenes, instead of following the native bent of their genius'.[4] Mrs. Mason gave precedence back to Mrs. Coates when she rejoined the company at Rosemary Lane, on 31 December, as Laetitia Hardy in *The Belle's Stratagem*.[5] Mrs. Coates for her second benefit on 26 January 1791 acted Lady Teazle in *The School for Scandal*.[6] Mrs. Mason at her benefit on 17 January presented, instead of a popular classic, the first Irish performance of John Philip Kemble's farce, *The Pannel*.[7] Repeated on 7 February, the next to the last night, it had the distinction of being the only new play in the undistinguished season of 1790–1. Throughout the winter the Rosemary Lane manager had persistently risked diminishing his audiences by very little innovation in either repertory or house refurbishing, since he had had his mind set on a fresh theatrical enterprise.

Before Atkins began to execute his project, however, he

[1] Ibid. [2] Ibid., 5 Nov. 1790. [3] Ibid., 12 Nov. 1790.
[4] Ibid., 7 Dec. 1790. [5] Ibid., 31 Dec. 1790. [6] Ibid., 25 Jan. 1791.
[7] Ibid., 14 Jan. 1791.

conducted one more summer season in Belfast, its last before 1800. For these special summer entertainments the Dublin ticket scale prevailed: 5*s*. for the boxes, 3*s*. in the pit, 1*s*. in the gallery.[1] Half-price admission applied to 'Children *and Children only*'.[2] Nothing less than a whole row of seats could be purchased in a box.[2] Atkins, who formerly lived on Ann Street, now sold box places from his residence in Arthur Street.[3] The season's outstanding attraction was advertised as 'that great ornament of the English and Irish Stages', namely, Tom King the comedian.[4] He managed to play Lord Ogleby in *The Clandestine Marriage* for the summer's opening night, Monday, 18 July 1791, before he had to discontinue performances during the remainder of the week on account of the Maze Races at Hillsborough, fourteen miles south of Belfast.[5] When the curtain rose again at the start of the following week, King acted Sir Peter Teazle in *The School for Scandal* on Monday the 25th, Marplot in Mrs. Centlivre's *The Busie Body* on Wednesday, and Shylock on Friday.[6] Performances had to be suspended again on Monday, 1 August, by reason of the Grand Review of the Volunteers at Armagh.[7] Two days afterwards King took for his benefit part Sir John Restless in Murphy's *All in the Wrong*, repeated Lord Ogleby on Friday, impersonated Touchstone on the next Monday, and, as Ranger in *The Suspicious Husband*, generously participated 'without emolument' in Mrs. Coates's benefit on Wednesday, 10 August, his final stage appearance in Belfast and the last night of the special season.[8]

The summer performances had been ended precisely four weeks when Atkins unveiled his splendid theatrical design to public view. Previously, from leading citizens, such as Samuel McTier, Henry Joy the *News-Letter* publisher, and Dr. Alexander Haliday, he had collected individual subscriptions of £100 each in return for a silver ticket of permanent admission to the boxes.[9] Dr. Haliday summed up the community view of the undertaking with dramatic brevity: 'Religion and luxury with us go

[1] BNL, 12 July 1791.
[2] Ibid., 8 July 1791.
[3] Ibid., 12 July 1791.
[4] Ibid., 8 July 1791.
[5] Ibid., 22 July 1791.
[6] Ibid., 22, 26, and 29 July 1791.
[7] Ibid., 22 July 1791.
[8] Ibid., 2, 5, and 9 Aug. 1791.
[9] W. J. Lawrence in 'The Old Belfast Stage: Its Glories and Romances', *The Irish News*, 21 Nov. 1895, first reported these details of public subscription, but cited no source.

on, hand in hand, no ordinary partnership. We are building a new meetinghouse [i.e. the Fourth Presbyterian Church] and a new theatre, bane and antidote together!'[1] Once assured of the financing, Atkins had selected for the playhouse site the plot of ground at the south-west corner of Castle Lane and Arthur Street, where the pleasure garden of ancient Belfast Castle had existed up to its burning in 1708 and where, subsequently, 'a meadow and pasture' or 'a private garden' had continued for over eight decades.[2] In 1791 no large number of buildings stood in immediate proximity to the chosen site, and to the south-east a broad area of open land, known as Cromac Wood, stretched to the River Lagan. On Wednesday, 7 September, the cornerstone of Atkins's new theatre was laid.[3] The *News-Letter* reported the location as 'excellent, the front of the building to be in Arthur Street, extending sixty feet and containing two very handsome entrances for the box and pit audiences'.[3] The doors to the gallery and the stage were to be in Castle Lane, along which the theatre was to extend eighty-four feet. Thus the entrances and exits of the 'various classes' would be kept properly separate, the *Belfast Northern Star* remarked, and the approach for carriages in Arthur Street would seem 'extremely convenient'.[4]

While the new playhouse was being constructed, stage activities continued to be carried on at Rosemary Lane. To enliven the autumn opening, Atkins persuaded that much-travelled Irish trouper, Thomas Ryder, and his two daughters, to visit the north of Ireland for the first time in twenty years. 'Admired for their comic and musical powers', the Ryder family commenced the Belfast season on Wednesday, 14 September, in *All in the Wrong* and *Rosina*, with Miss E. Ryder undertaking her Irish stage début as Belinda in the comedy and Rosina in the opera.[5] After a series of successful performances in their favourite dramatic genres, the Ryders had to cut short their engagement on 10 October because of the father's mortal illness.[6]

[1] Original Correspondence of James, late Earl of Charlemont, v (2nd series), no. 75, dated 27 Aug. 1791.

[2] S. Shannon Millin, 'Arthur Street Theatre', *Belfast Telegraph*, 21 Apr. 1938.

[3] BNL, 13 Sept. 1791.

[4] BNS, 6 Feb. 1793.

[5] BNL, 16 Aug. and 13 Sept. 1791.

[6] Ibid., 7 Oct. 1791. Ryder died at Sandymount, Co. Dublin, on 26 Nov. 1791.

Within the week Mrs. Charlotte Melmoth from Dublin took the place of the Ryders as the chief attraction.[1] On 2 November, in the first Belfast performance of Holcroft's very recent comedy, *The School for Arrogance*, she roused a considerable outcry, especially from the gallery, because she played Mrs. Peckham, 'a complete Mrs. John Bull, who believes that there is no place in all the world but England' and who steadily browbeats the simple-hearted, honest Irishman M'Dermot.[2] Soon Mrs. Melmoth had to share female 'leads' with Mrs. Coates for the rest of the season. The latter made a great hit as Lady Amaranth in O'Keeffe's comedy, *Wild Oats*, which had its initial Belfast production on 15 February 1792, and was repeated at least thrice within the next month.[3] A second O'Keeffe comedy, *Modern Antiques*, entertained local audiences for the first time on 2 March.[4] Two other plays new to the city, Mrs. Inchbald's *Next Door Neighbours*, and R. B. Sheridan's prelude of *Regions of Accomplishment* in its only Irish performance, celebrated the last night of the Rosemary Lane Theatre on Friday, 30 March 1792.[5]

Several months before the close of the season 'a dangerous indisposition' compelled the comedian Richard Cox Rowe to give up acting. Atkins generously arranged a benefit for him on 19 March.[6] By that date Rowe was wholly confined and eventually died on Monday, 7 May 1792, of a 'dropsical complaint'.[7] Born at Dublin in 1753 and 'destined by his parents for a mechanical employment',[8] he joined instead the Belfast company at the age of twenty-four and never thereafter left the north-of-Ireland stage. 'Neither vain nor ostentatious',[8] he soon established himself as the most beloved actor in eighteenth-century Belfast. The following homely, elegiac lines of a Derry admirer expressed the affectionate esteem felt by all classes of theatregoers:

> The curtain's dropp'd—the act of life is past;
> Poor Dick is gone where all must go at last.
> That tongue which set the audience in a roar
> Shall charm the Derry spectators no more.

[1] BNL, 14 Oct. 1791.
[2] Ibid., 4 Nov. 1791.
[3] BNS, 11, 15, and 25 Feb., 7 Mar. 1792.
[4] Ibid., 29 Feb. 1792.
[5] Ibid., 24 Mar., and BNL, 30 Mar. 1792.
[6] BNS, 14 Mar. 1792.
[7] Ibid., 9 May 1792.
[8] LJ, 22 May 1792.

From busy scenes the valued actor's fled,
And Thalia mourns in Rowe a favourite dead.[1]

Popular subscriptions placed over his grave in the churchyard at Newtownbreda, County Down, a headstone inscribed 'Public Gratitude erected this stone. . . to a celebrated comedian', the first public memorial to an actor in Ireland.

No sooner had Atkins finished his Belfast season than he journeyed to Dublin and conferred with the Castle authorities in order to protect his theatrical properties against a rumoured invasion by Richard Daly. The acquisitive manager of the Theatres Royal at Cork, Dublin, Limerick, Newry, and Waterford supposedly was threatening to extend his influence and control to Belfast. Therefore Atkins prepared and took with him to Dublin 'a petition back'd by the most respectable people' that he might be granted official recognition of his rights in the form of a patent.[2] On 26 April Dr. Haliday, the spokesman for the subscribers to the new Belfast theatre, wrote to urge the Earl of Charlemont to use his influence on behalf of Atkins's mission: '[Mr. Daly] is a Tyrant eager to invade foreign Territories; the other [i.e. Mr. Atkins] is a mild Monarch tender of his Subjects, and wishes only to defend himself—he has been known among us for a length of years and is universally esteem'd as a good and just man, and a humane, liberal manager—if your Lordship can help him and us in this business, I need not solicit you to do it.'[2] In the end Atkins seems to have procured no formal patent, but his representations fully headed off whatever designs Daly might have intended.

These Dublin consultations and manœuvrings did not halt the construction of the playhouse. Unfortunately, however, the pace of erection did not make it possible to have the building ready for any entertainment while the crowds gathered in Belfast for the Volunteer Review and Celebration of the French Revolution during the second week of July. On Friday the 13th the Volunteers held their grand procession with the flags of various nations 'borne by boys dressed in the national uniform

[1] Ibid.
[2] Original Correspondence of James, late Earl of Charlemont, vi (2nd series), no. 16.

of Ireland with blue sashes'.[1] The mottoes on the flags read as follows:

> Ireland—'Unite and be free.'
> America—'The Asylum of Liberty.'
> France—'The Nation, The Law, and the King.'
> Great Britain—'Wisdom, Spirit, and Liberality to the People.'
> Poland—'We will support it.'[1]

One group of marchers wore green ribbons and laurel leaves in their hats, and carried a green flag saying 'Our Gallic brother was born July 14, 1789; alas! we are still in embryo', and, on the reverse, 'Superstitious jealousy the cause of the Irish Bastille; let us unite and destroy it!'[1] After the procession five thousand citizens assembled at a rally of United Irishmen and Volunteers in the White Linen Hall.[1]

The high tide of patriotic demonstration had receded when in August the shell of the new Arthur Street Theatre was completed. On the 21st, Michael Atkins, 'comedian', proceeded to sign with the builders, John Ewing and John Holmes, the same kind of contract as he had concluded with them years earlier for the Rosemary Lane Theatre.[2] He leased for seventy-eight years from 1 May 1792 'the new messuage or tenement, then lately erected, the same . . . intended for a Playhouse and Theatre and Dressing Rooms and other Apartments', at a yearly rental of £66. 9*s*. 3*d*. plus 'four Passes or Tickets to the Play on every night of entertainment during the said term, or in default of rendering the said Passes or Tickets, at the yearly rent of £100'.[2]

Now in possession of the bare fabric, Atkins had to go about decorating and furnishing the interior. On 1 February 1793 he announced that the new theatre would be opened 'in the course of a few days'.[3] From the 11th, tickets for the season subscribers might be picked up at his house in Arthur Street, and box places at the theatre box office between 11 and 3 o'clock.[4] The local newspapers had an opportunity to view and report on the inside of the 'very handsome' edifice. 'Glass lustres' provided

[1] NC, 16 July 1792.
[2] S. Shannon Millin, 'Arthur Street Theatre', *Belfast Telegraph*, 21 Apr. 1938.
[3] BNL, 1 Feb., and BNS, 2 Feb. 1793.
[4] BNS, 20 and 23 Feb. 1793.

the lighting.[1] 'An entire new style' characterized 'the paintings and ornaments of the house'.[1] The semicircular amphitheatre permitted from the uppermost seat in the gallery as good a view as from the front of the boxes or pit.[1] The latter section was 'admirably contrived' in respect to entrance: 'On the most crowded night, persons on the first seat cannot be prevented from seeing by others standing before them, as the passage by the orchestra is considerably below the platform or floor which contains the seats.'[2] The circular row of front boxes appeared 'elegant and commodious', the stage or side-boxes 'roomy and comfortable'.[3] The geometrical staircases to the lattices or upper boxes were 'very handsome and convenient',[3] but the one stair to the front boxes seemed 'quite too narrow' and therefore a second one desirable.[4] The backstage area contained eight dressing-rooms and a 'large, convenient Green-Room'.[5] The scenery and machinery promised to give 'ample scope for the display of Mr. Atkins' pencil'.[5] In contrast to the foregoing compliments on the internal arrangements, the exterior of the Arthur Street structure called forth no comments at this time. The silence suggests that the early viewers might well have agreed with the city's first historian, who thirty years later described the outside of the theatre as 'not only unornamented, but heavy and disagreeable'.[6]

The Arthur Street playhouse opened for the first time to 'a very brilliant audience' on Monday night, 25 February 1793.[7] One of the senior actors, James May, delivered a special prologue written by a young Ulsterman and lawyer, Hugh George Macklin, who in conventional flowery rhetoric strove to express the civic and national pride that should be associated with so important a cultural occasion:

> And have not here our souls with Freedom glow'd;
> Has she not here long fix'd her lov'd abode?
> Yes—and old time shall yet, with glad surprize,
> View in Belfast a second Athens rise: . . .
> In this new structure (and we'll proudly boast
> So fair has never grac'd Ierne's coast)

[1] Ibid., 6 Feb. 1793.
[2] BNL, 13 Sept. 1791.
[3] BNS, 6 Feb. 1793.
[4] BNL, 26 Mar. 1793.
[5] Ibid., 13 Sept. 1791.
[6] George Benn, *The History of the Town of Belfast* (Belfast, 1823), p. 99.
[7] BNS, 2 Mar. 1793.

He, in whose friendly cause I thus appear,
Bids me present his thanks—immense—sincere.[1]

Then the orchestra played 'God Save the King'. The officers in the audience clapped, and '*all* the house did the same'.[2] When the time came for the second musical number, however, 'the gallery and a few voices in the pit'[2] began calling for the then current French national song, '*Ah! ça ira, ça ira, ça ira!*' Finally silenced, these persons contented themselves with obtaining and clapping the 'Volunteer March'. The gallery 'growled' during the first play, but thereafter 'a few gentlemen' went up and sat in the upper regions, and all was quiet.[2] Mrs. McTier, and probably many other attendants on that night, had 'much feared'[2] that serious disturbance might break out, so strong were the partisan sentiments running in the city.

The great agitation caused in early March by the Government's orders to disarm and disperse the Belfast Volunteers led to a suspension of stage performances during that month. Atkins employed the interim to recruit from Dublin James Middleton, and Mr. and Mrs. Richard Hurst, none of whom had previously appeared in the north. Hurst, a performer of the second rank with forty years' experience, was 'induced to quit the respectable and profitable situation of Deputy Manager of the Theatre Royal in Dublin from the very flattering account of the attention paid to Theatrical Amusements at Belfast'.[3] Twenty-five-year-old Middleton provided a far stronger attraction than Hurst when the curtain rose again at Arthur Street on Monday, 1 April.[4] For the next six weeks he acquitted himself with equal and considerable ability in two standard roles of tragedy, Romeo and Alexander the Great, and in light comic parts, such as Irwin in Mrs. Inchbald's *Every One has His Fault*, which had its first local production at Middleton's benefit on 10 May.[5]

The season's new play of outstanding interest, however, was an historical tragedy, *The Guillotine; or, The Death of Louis XVI*,[6] written by a Belfast clergyman, the Reverend Dr. Bambridge. He intended it to portray the French monarch's disaster as a

[1] Ll. 13–16, 43–46, of the fifty-four lines in the prologue. BNS, 2 Mar. 1793.
[2] The Drennan Correspondence, no. 391 A.
[3] BNS, 18 May 1793.
[4] Ibid., 30 Mar. 1793.
[5] Ibid., 4 May 1793.
[6] Ibid., 22 May 1793.

consequence of royal disregard for popular grievance. In view of the current tension Atkins braved serious trouble in putting so controversial a play on stage. As soon as the performance began on Monday, 27 May, cries of 'Off, off!' came from the pit and the boxes, while the gallery shouted 'Go on!'[1] Confusion instantly spread throughout the theatre, and 'the ladies got out as fast as possible'. The manager came forward, begged the audience to consider 'the very great losses he had already sustained this season', and asserted that continued disorderly conduct would result in 'his total ruin'. He offered to entertain with a farce 'in ten minutes' time' but the gallery remained discontented and noisy. At last Lynch directly addressed that section, suggested that he do a hornpipe dance, was accepted, and thereby restored calm to the entire house. Two days later an editorial in the politically liberal *Northern Star* adjudged the interrupted drama 'imprudent and rather tending to keep up those animosities which have so much prevailed at the theatre this last year'.[1] The near-riot at Arthur Street stopped once and for all the stage career of Dr. Bambridge's historical tragedy and brought a speedy close to the 1793 season on 31 May.[1]

Faced with persisting disturbed conditions in Belfast, Atkins did not attempt to open his new playhouse during the autumn or winter of 1793–4, but in the following spring and summer employed his troupe at Derry where less unrest existed. By September 1794 he had returned to Belfast to busy himself with 'retouching and adding to the decorations of his beautiful theatre'.[2] An announcement in the *Northern Star* expressed the hope that 'the revival of this elegant entertainment will not be attended with any of those rude intrusions, which, during the residence of *certain strangers*,[3] interrupted every pleasurable and social meeting, and that the inhabitants of this united place shall in future have an additional opportunity of coming together, as they have always done, with harmony and good humour'.[4] To lessen the possibility of agitation at the performances, the manager decided to take the control of the orchestra entirely into his own hands, and thus to ensure that no tune

[1] Ibid., 29 May 1793.

[2] Ibid., 22 and 25 Sept. 1794.

[3] Thomas Russell and Theobald Wolfe Tone were the two leading 'strangers' who came to Belfast to promote the organizing of the United Irishmen.

[4] BNS, 22 and 25 Sept. 1794.

which might be called for would be played.[1] Certainly 'the well-known candour and good sense of the Belfast audience' would approve this procedure. As a further precaution against disturbance, Atkins ordered that from the opening night on Monday, 13 October, 'no boys of any description whatever' should be admitted to the gallery.[2]

For the past decade the Belfast manager had been accustomed to get the season off to a lively start by presenting a performer of some distinction and of not too recent local appearance. This autumn Andrew Cherry, who had last visited the city seven years before, was secured and commenced a limited engagement on Friday, 24 October, as Lazarillo in Jephson's farce, *The Hotel*, and as Trudge in *Inkle and Yarico*, Colman's comic opera.[3] On his third and again on his sixth night Cherry shifted to a somewhat higher vein of comedy and acted Sheva in Cumberland's *The Jew*.[4] The casting of parts in support of the star actor apparently provoked some discontent that reached the public ear, because the *Northern Star* advised the manager: 'Little jealousies of superior merit or precedence among the performers [must not] prevent the audience from being deprived of their abilities, however trifling the character assigned to them. They are in a discerning town.'[5] Cherry put on a rich display of fresh entertainment at his benefit and last appearance in Belfast before the Union: Sir David Dunder in the first local performance of Colman's *Ways and Means;* Shelty the Piper in O'Keeffe's *The Highland Reel*, likewise a local *première;* and lastly, a new musical recitation of his own making, *Poor Darty's Trip to Belfast*, 'a serio-comic ballad descriptive of the town, public places, prevailing modes and fashions, etc.'.[6] This festive occasion on Friday, 7 November, drew 'the greatest audience ever known in the North of Ireland' and resulted in 'an overflow from every part of the House'.[7] Though the ordinary prices of 3*s*. for the boxes, 2*s*. for the pit, and 1*s*. for the gallery prevailed, the benefit netted Cherry the astonishing figure of £87.[7] Even Mrs. Siddons, after the prices had been tripled in the gallery and doubled elsewhere, had taken away benefit receipts of only £113.

[1] BNS, 6 Oct. 1794.
[2] BNL, 10 Oct. 1794.
[3] Ibid., 27 Oct. 1794.
[4] BNS, 27 Oct. and 3 Nov. 1794.
[5] Ibid., 23 Oct. 1794.
[6] Ibid., 3 Nov. 1794.
[7] Ibid., 10 Nov. 1794.

The amphitheatre on Cherry's night became so extremely crowded that 'the flooring of a great part of the Pit gave way and sank to the level of the ground. . . . Happily no limbs were broken though the risque was great. . . . The audience chiefly remained in their places'.[1] Soon after the mishap the *News-Letter* recommended improvements in the playhouse's interior:

> The passages leading to the boxes and gallery, as well as the door into the pit, should as far as possible be widened, as a press of people, in cases of alarm, might have serious consequences. . . . We cannot entertain a doubt that the pit will be rebuilt in such a manner as forever to prevent a similar disaster; and we would think it advisable for the manager, after the rebuilding is done, to publish the opinion of an architect as to the strength of it and of the galleries, for the purpose of doing away with the fears of any who will not themselves examine them.—It is alleged that the present gloom of the boxes might be removed by sinking the chandeliers some inches lower than their present stations.[1]

About three weeks later Atkins gave public assurance that all repairs were being made 'for the future security of the building' and that 'the lowering of the Lustres added particularly to the Brilliancy of the Amphitheatre'.[2] At the same time two architects, Roger Mulholland and Hugh Dunlap, published an affidavit: 'Being called upon to inspect into the security of the Belfast Theatre, and to give such instructions as we could see necessary for the safety of the Audience, we now, on second examination, find everything done according to the directions given.'[2]

Meanwhile performances had been recommenced with Mrs. Coates the leading actress. As Lady Macbeth on 26 November she aroused the *News-Letter* to comment sharply that 'her manner and her voice are as happily suited to comedy as they are totally unfit for tragedy'.[3] Yet on 15 December the *Northern Star* praised her Juliet as 'a finished piece which rendered the audience incapable (more than once) of withholding the tear of sensibility'.[4] The veteran comedian Lee Lewes joined Mrs. Coates in top billing for the month of December, but shortly thereafter both players completed their Belfast engagement. Of Lewes in *Henry IV* on 8 December the *Northern Star* observed

[1] BNL, 10 Nov. 1794. [2] BNS, 1 Dec. 1794.
[3] BNL, 28 Nov. 1794. [4] BNS, 18 Dec. 1794.

that though he kept 'the chastity of soliloquy' in his characterization of Falstaff, 'he must soften the *contour* a little'.[1] When Lewes acted the Copper Captain and Mrs. Coates Estifania, in *Rule a Wife* on 17 December, both Belfast newspapers expressed irritation at the bill for quite different reasons. The *News-Letter* believed that managerial censorship should have been exercised in respect to the text of Fletcher's Jacobean comedy:

> Many of our old plays, some of them calculated for the dissolute age of Charles II, and replete with humour, indulge a loose and indecent vein, which can never fail in representation to hurt the feelings of a modest audience. The Manager who with his pen would expunge such expressions as are exceptionable, would deserve the thanks of every auditor. . . . The performance of Wednesday last, in certain passages, required his correction.[2]

The *Northern Star*, on the other hand, chided the manager because of a last-minute change in the farce on that night:

> These sudden indispositions of performers may be put up with occasionally, but the public wont bear to be frequently tricked in this Manner. . . . The Manager should not permit the *pique* or *huff* of an individual to disappoint the audience; and, finally, to injure the company, as well as himself.[3]

Between the political sensitivity of the theatregoers and the rigorous judgements of the newspaper critics Atkins experienced a difficult winter of appeasement, although the early months of 1795 brought no more strictures in the press or misadventures in the playhouse. The season arrived at a gratifying climax with the first Belfast appearance of twenty-year-old Maria Campion, the lovely *tragédienne* of Crow Street, and, for the moment, 'the First Female Ornament of the Irish Stage'.[4] Her engagement started on Monday, 13 April, with a brilliant success in *Romeo and Juliet*, in which her physical gifts supremely qualified her for the heroine's role: 'Her conversation in the Balcony and her anxious solicitude at the return of the Nurse must have pleased everyone that has a taste for the simplicity of nature. In the tomb scene the wild disorder of the senses, and returning recollections, were justly expressed.'[5] On Friday, 18 May, Miss

[1] BNS, 15 Dec. 1794. [2] BNL, 19 Dec. 1794. [3] BNS, 18 Dec. 1794.
[4] BNL, 10 Apr. 1794. [5] Ibid., 14 Apr. 1795.

Campion closed her sole visit to the city with her benefit.[1] At this final performance of the 1794–5 season she dared to lay herself open to direct comparison with Mrs. Siddons by acting for the first time in her career Mrs. Siddons's favourite part of Isabella in *The Fatal Marriage*.

Since Atkins had afforded the Arthur Street theatregoers the sight of an eminent performer in the spring, he felt little incentive to undertake a similar exhibition for the summer or autumn of 1795, especially in view of the uncertainty of the times. Therefore he led his troupe off to Derry. At the beginning of 1796 the situation in Belfast promised to remain for a while sufficiently quiet to permit the reopening of the playhouse. A French visitor at this period reported the city's inhabitants 'perfectly calm' and talking 'mostly about the prices of sugar or linen, the sale of muslin, and the buying of wine'.[2] The Atkins company, returning from Derry at the end of January, held their first performance on Wednesday, 17 February.[3] As usual, the manager had engaged special talent to lure good audiences early in the season. Miss Maria Rebecca Duncan, aged sixteen, from Crow Street, made her Belfast début on the opening night as the heroine in *Inkle and Yarico*. Her 'fine figure, graceful and dignified action, and powerful voice' charmed 'a respectably attended' house.[3] Two weeks later she was joined by a second very youthful star from Crow Street, Henry Erskine Johnston, 'the celebrated Scotch Roscius', nineteen years of age.[4] At his Belfast *première* on 2 March in *Douglas* he acted Young Norval, and Miss Duncan, Lady Randolph.[5] The *Northern Star* thought that in the first act Johnston 'burst upon us too rapidly'.[6] Throughout the play 'his face and eyes turned up too much'. Moreover, he needed 'a little more temperance in the tempest; and perhaps a less frequent use of the raging pitch' in his voice. He may well have read and taken to heart these perspicuous observations. In any case, when he repeated his Young Norval on the 10th, the *News-Letter* stated: 'We never saw his superior.'[7] After doing Hamlet with 'much grace and spirit' on the 4th,[8] he played Zaphne in *Mahomet the Impostor* (its first and only Belfast performance) on the 11th, Macbeth on the 14th, and

[1] Ibid., 4 May 1795.
[2] DeLatocnaye, p. 222.
[3] BNS, 18 Feb. 1796.
[4] Ibid., 25 Feb. 1796.
[5] Ibid., 29 Feb. 1796.
[6] Ibid., 3 Mar. 1796.
[7] BNL, 11 Mar. 1796.
[8] Ibid., 7 Mar. 1796.

Tancred on the 16th for his benefit.[1] This occasion, according to the *Northern Star*, attracted 'as brilliant an assemblage as ever Belfast witnessed'.[2] The receipts amounted to £92. 12*s*., exceeding by a little Cherry's remarkable benefit in 1794. However, £20 in admissions had to be turned away. Therefore Johnston on Friday the 18th acted Hamlet as an extra performance, without reward, in order to allow the numerous persons who held outstanding benefit tickets an opportunity to use them.[3] After that act of generosity the *Northern Star* sped him on his way to Edinburgh the next morning with extravagant praise: 'Few players at so early a period of life, and in so short a space of time, have ever acquired so great a degree of theatrical reputation.'[4]

After 'the Scotch Roscius', young Miss Gough of London and Dublin appeared as the special attraction at Arthur Street. Her first Belfast appearance occurred on Thursday, 21 April, as Calista in *The Fair Penitent*.[5] Taking the cue for all her repertoire from her famous predecessors in the city, Mrs. Siddons, Miss Brunton, and Miss Campion, she chose to portray Mrs. Beverly in *The Gamester* on the 25th, Alicia in *Jane Shore* on the 27th, Hermione in *The Distrest Mother* on the 29th, and, for her last night on 2 May, Isabella in *The Fatal Marriage*, a maiden attempt of that role.[6]

The youngest of all the performing talent during the 1796 season, eight-year-old Henry Brown, 'The Child of Promise',[7] received prominent billing in May when the season commenced to wane. His recitation, *New Brooms; or, Birch from Parnassus*, at his mother's benefit on Monday, 16 May, caused the box receipts to total 'more than was ever known without railing in the Pit',[8] though the *News-Letter* did not support this claim with any figures. 'The Child of Promise' celebrated his own benefit on Wednesday, 1 June, with the two amusing, boyish parts of Mungo in Bickerstaffe's opera *The Padlock*, and the Page in Cross's melodrama *The Purse*. The feature of the evening, however, was 'a serio-tragic-comic operatic epilogue' in which Master Brown impersonated Hamlet, Romeo, Scrub, Justice

[1] BNS, 10 and 14 Mar. 1796.
[2] Ibid., 17 Mar. 1796.
[3] Ibid., and BNL, 18 Mar. 1796.
[4] BNS, 17 Mar. 1796.
[5] Ibid., 18 Apr. 1796.
[6] BNL, 22 Apr., and BNS, 25 and 28 Apr. 1796.
[7] BNL, 30 May 1796.
[8] Ibid., 20 May 1796.

Woodcock, and others unnamed.[1] The fact that the stage actions of this youngster should command so much local interest revealed the deteriorating level of theatrical entertainment in Belfast as the season drew to a close on 13 June 1796.[2]

By September the city's quiet had disappeared. The quasi-military government had taken over a good deal of local authority. Arrests of United Irishmen, suspected of conspiring for armed rebellion and attack from outside, took place almost daily.[3] After the French fleet appeared off Bantry Bay in December, fears of invasion mounted. The next month the Belfast Yeomanry, both infantry and cavalry, were organized to assume the protective duties of the now disbanded Volunteers.[4] Suspicion and anxiety and political antagonisms rent the community. It grew dangerous to wear either orange or green.[5] For thoughtful citizens, such as the theatre-loving Mrs. McTier, 'the right path became complex', because it proved equally unpalatable either to swear support of the present government or to decline arming against a foreign enemy.[6] Murders and seizures of suspects increased with the advent of spring. On 19 May 1797 militia wrecked the offices of the *Northern Star*[7] and thus ended the life of that 'liberal' newspaper. All this recurring disorder and violence prevented Atkins from conducting any theatricals at Arthur Street in 1797.

Conditions changed, if at all, for the worse as the winter and spring of 1798 passed. With the great number of soldiers and sailors in the city, it grew 'infested with abandoned females', singing 'the most shocking songs', striking the chair-men and their lanterns. 'All ladies must give up going out at night, except in chairs', Mrs. McTier reported.[8] On 27 May the Government declared martial law in anticipation of the actual hostilities that broke out at Antrim on 7 June.[9] Imprisonments and executions made a veritable 'Reign of Terror' out of the summer and early autumn. Yet by late November the powers of the Government had brought in a forced peace. The Belfast citizens, pent up for two years, broke out with 'parties, dances,

[1] BNS, 27 May 1796.
[2] Ibid., 6 June 1796.
[3] The Drennan Correspondence, no. 629.
[4] *Town Book*, p. xiii.
[5] The Drennan Correspondence, no. 648.
[6] Ibid., no. 645.
[7] Ibid., no. 661.
[8] Ibid., no. 685.
[9] *Town Book*, p. xiii.

and coteries'.[1] On 3 December Atkins sponsored at the Arthur Street Theatre a concert with his daughter as one of the soloists.[2]

Mrs. McTier consequently expected the manager to start stage performances almost at once,[3] but instead he went to Derry and opened his theatre there. Finally, on Monday, 9 December 1799, he raised the curtain at Arthur Street after having taken care to have the house 'well-air'd'.[4] Since the assizes were to be in session that week, plays were given every evening. Atkins still feared disturbance and therefore announced: 'N.B. Boys of any description will not be admitted to the Gallery; nor any Person, on any account whatever, behind the scenes.'[4] The interval of two and a half years had considerably changed the complexion of Atkins's company. Both his son and his daughter (now Mrs. Boucheron) belonged to the corps. The only surviving veteran, Lynch, died the day after his benefit on 12 February 1800.[5] The two leading recruits were the peripatetic Lee Lewes and Joseph Herbert, a Crow Street actor who got his start in amateur theatricals at Cork a decade before. During early February the comedian well known for his grotesque countenance, Michael Fullam, and his wife, came up from Dublin for a week's engagement. On Monday, 3 February, Mrs. Fullam played Juliet; Herbert, Romeo; and Lewes, Mercutio.[6] The following Monday Fullam at his benefit took the part of Sir Benjamin Dove in Cumberland's *The Brothers*,[7] which had not been seen in Belfast since 1789.

Atkins had good reason to be anxious about the behaviour of his audience, particularly of the arrogant English officers, who exhibited an almost sadistic urge to assert their authority over the native civilians in the theatre as well as on the streets. Mrs. McTier witnessed one of their displays at Arthur Street on Monday evening, 24 February 1800:

> Our Play House, it is probable, will be shut up as last night two Officers of the Horse, who not having been noticed, seemed bent on insult, jumped over the box, while 'God Save the King' was playing, and both most magnanimously horsewhipp'd a Captain of a ship,

[1] The Drennan Correspondence, no. 725. [2] BNL, 30 Nov. 1798.
[3] The Drennan Correspondence, no. 725. [4] BNL, 6 Dec. 1799.
[5] Ibid., 7 Feb. 1800. [6] Ibid., 28 Jan. 1800. [7] Ibid., 7 Feb. 1800.

sitting in the Pit with his hat *off*—most of the Ladies left the house except Mrs. Mattear, who, filled with involuntary indignation and pity, cried out, but in vain, to the whippers that she saw the man take off his hat—the answer was, he was not on his feet—do not be frightened, Mrs. Mattear, we will be in yr box immediately—no, not in *my* Box, said she, the Gallery is the fittest place for you, and before I come here again, I shall enquire where you are engaged—he redden'd and said a lady was privileged to say anything— . . . The Man [i.e. the ship's captain] bore it as well as he cou'd, left the House . . .—the Man proves to be a most loyal subject, a stranger here—not perhaps blessed with a quick ear and wishing to be amused at a play, he paid for it.[1]

Other incidents of unruly manners often marred the performances, but the manager could not afford to close the theatre except under extreme provocation.

Nevertheless these 'riots', to use Mrs. McTier's rather extravagant term,[2] deterred Atkins from undertaking any considerable number of new or unusual productions. He did stage, however, two notable Belfast *premières* of famous melodramas, Lewis's *The Castle Spectre* and R. B. Sheridan's *Pizarro*, each so long and so elaborate in its scene shifts that no farce followed on the evening's bill.[3] As further innovation, each ran originally for three successive nights, Monday, Wednesday, Friday, 10, 12, 14 March and 14, 16, 18 April, respectively, the first times in Belfast theatrical history that the bill remained the same for an entire week. For *Pizarro* Atkins, Sr., painted the architectural features on the flats, including 'a magnificent tent and pavilion, and a Temple of the Sun'; Atkins, Jr., the landscape portions, including 'Rocky Reefs with a Cascade over a Precipice and falling Bridge'; and Herbert (a portrait painter as well as actor), the human figures.[4] By distracting the spectators with such exotic stage *décor* the Arthur Street manager perhaps hoped to cover up the deficiencies of a weak and dull troupe. Yet in a month or so the novelty of the sets had so much worn off that the last performance of *Pizarro* on 23 May had to advertise 'Half Price in the Pit at the usual hour'.[5]

Mr. Kelly, one of the newcomers to the local company,

[1] The Drennan Correspondence, no. 837.
[2] Ibid., no. 839.
[3] BNL, 7 Mar. and 8 Apr. 1800.
[4] Ibid., 8 Apr. 1800.
[5] Ibid., 20 May 1800.

thought to enliven the appeal of his benefit on 25 April by an original 'divertisement' entitled 'A Ramble through Belfast':

I. Description of the Academy and the Church, Donegall Street—Arts, Sciences, etc.
II. The Poor House—Blessings arising from Charity, etc.
III. The Exchange on a business day—Traffic, etc.
IV. Rooms on a coterie night—Music, Taste, etc.
V. The Quay—Benefits arising from Shipping and Commerce.
VI. The Linen Hall and Manufactory—The staple wealth of Ireland and the comforts of industry.
VII. A Peep into the Playhouse—Actors, critics, etc.
VIII. A Tavern scene and the nightly adventures of a Buck.
IX. Conclusion—A eulogy on the Town, Trade, and Commerce of Belfast.[1]

This sketch by Kelly promised to be an entertaining directory of the city's institutions and manners, but, in fact, it did not greatly amuse the playgoers. Though the author for his wife's benefit on 9 May advertised that he would repeat the 'Ramble' and would give away printed copies at the doors of the theatre,[2] he failed to entice a sufficient audience to make Mrs. Kelly's night a success. As a result she was allowed a second benefit on 'positively the Last Night of this Season', Monday, 9 June 1800.[3] Mr. Kelly did not brave a third trial of his 'Ramble'!

Like Kelly, Manager Atkins doubtless had found to his discomfiture that Belfast, as the *Northern Star* once said, was 'a discerning town', rarely taken in by an excessive self-pride. Indeed, it sometimes showed not enough pride: to cite a minor instance, it refrained from any action until the end of the century to enforce a regular public sweeping of the main streets. With all its expanding commerce and wealth in the 1780's and 1790's, Belfast still contained but 19,000 inhabitants in the year of the Union[4] and, as yet, had not evolved into a true metropolis. Therefore, in the patronage of the arts and especially of the drama, 'the Athens of the North' should not have been expected to compare too favourably at that time with

[1] BNL, 22 Apr. 1800. [2] Ibid., 6 May 1800.
[3] Ibid., 3 and 6 June 1800.
[4] According to the *Town Book*, p. xiii, the population in 1793 was 19,133, and in 1802, 19,001.

its big and urbane counterpart at the other extremity of the island. The Cork Theatre Royal in George's Street, though built as far back as 1760, much surpassed in size and elegance the most recent of the Belfast playhouses, the Arthur Street Theatre of 1793. For half a century Cork had enjoyed yearly seasons of the Dublin Theatre Royal company and its guest stars from England—always *summer* visits, however. Belfast, on the other hand, during the thirty years since 1770, had supported twenty *winter* seasons of three to nine months each. Since 1773 these seasons had been provided by a *resident* company. In the hey-day of the company from 1785 to 1792, it imitated the theatrical custom of the 'Capital of the South' and presented four summer seasons with outstanding guest performers, but ones that Cork had already viewed. Thus Cork's manager, Richard Daly, granted that he possessed the superior material resources, still must be judged to have outmatched Atkins in aggressiveness and acumen.

Yet from 1792 onwards the Belfast manager was compelled to contend with adversities much more baffling than those which Daly encountered at Cork. The Ulster area, and Belfast in particular, developed an intensity of nationalistic and revolutionary sentiment that far outstripped the political feeling around Cork and that kept the Ulster city in constant turmoil up to 1800. For Atkins the running of a playhouse there turned into a hazardous and often losing enterprise. It was to the glory of 'the Athens of the North' that so many of her citizens, high in station and distinguished in talent, absorbed themselves in the movements for emancipation, liberation, or even revolution, during the nineties, but this patriotic absorption and activity gradually transformed Belfast's theatre into an amusement dominated by military aliens and governmental outsiders, a definitely impermanent audience. Therefore Atkins, always a supporter of the Ascendancy like most of the successful theatre managers of eighteenth-century Ireland, looked upon the Act of Union as an act for stability and the recovery of his personal fortune.

XI · THE REPERTOIRE IN RETROSPECT

THE account that the preceding chapters have given of stage activities in the Irish county towns of the eighteenth century indicates that the dramatic repertoire enjoyed by them from year to year followed pretty closely the Dublin trends. During the last third of the century the increased visiting of the larger towns by star performers who had appeared in the capital helped to accentuate Dublin fashions in the country at large. The noted players tended, especially in tragedy, to perpetuate the stage life of long-established works in which a single role or two provided the chance for virtuoso display. Of the fifteen most performed tragedies, only three were written after 1750: John Home's *Douglas*, Edward Moore's *The Gamester*, and Mrs. Hannah More's *Percy*. Shakespeare led all the tragedians with five perennial favourites: *Hamlet*, *Macbeth*, *Othello*, *Richard III*, *Romeo and Juliet*. Thomas Otway with *The Orphan* and *Venice Preserved*, and Nicholas Rowe with *The Fair Penitent* and *Jane Shore*, came next. Edward Young's *The Revenge*, and Ambrose Phillips's *The Distrest Mother* complete the list.

Somewhat less conservatism was evidenced in comedy. Again Shakespeare headed the roll of popular authors with three pieces: *As You Like It*, *Henry IV*, *The Merchant of Venice*. Mrs. Susannah Centlivre's *The Busie Body* and *The Wonder: A Woman Keeps a Secret*, Colley Cibber's *The Provok'd Husband*, George Farquhar's *The Beaux' Stratagem*, David Garrick's *The Lying Valet*, Benjamin Hoadly's *The Suspicious Husband*, and Richard Steele's *The Conscious Lovers* were early eighteenth-century plays that held their popularity to the end of the century. The later social comedy of *The Clandestine Marriage* by George Colman the Elder and of *The West Indian* by Richard Cumberland kept its appeal indefinitely. After 1750 a quartet of Irish comedians came to the fore: Oliver Goldsmith in *She Stoops to Conquer*, Arthur Murphy in *All in the Wrong*, John O'Keeffe in *Wild Oats*, R. B. Sheridan in *The Rivals* and *The School for Scandal*. The outstanding success of these five plays in the Irish towns depended to no appreciable extent upon the birthplace of the authors.

No matter whether a tragedy or a comedy was the main item on the night's bill at the town playhouse, the bill also included one or more afterpieces in the form of a farce, an operatic farce, a ballad opera, a comic opera, a burletta, or, less often, a pantomime. Of the most popular farces Murphy wrote two, *The Apprentice* and *The Citizen*; Garrick, also two, *Catherine and Petruchio* and *Miss in Her Teens*; Thomas Sheridan and James Townley, one apiece, *The Brave Irishman* and *High Life Below Stairs* respectively. Lloyd's *The Romp*, McNamara Morgan's *The Sheep-Shearing*, and O'Keeffe's *The Agreeable Surprise* stood out among the operatic farces. Though the ballad opera antedated all other species of musical low comedy, five specimens, *The Beggar's Opera* by John Gay, *The Devil to Pay* by Charles Coffey, *Flora; or, Hob in the Well* by John Hippisley, *The Honest Yorkshire-Man* by Henry Carey, and *The Virgin Unmask'd* by Henry Fielding, retained strong popularity up to 1800. Isaac Bickerstaffe reigned pre-eminent in comic opera with *Lionel and Clarissa*, *Love in a Village*, *Maid of the Mill*, and *The Padlock*. Mrs. Frances Brooke's *Rosina*, Charles Dibdin's *The Deserter*, and O'Keeffe's *The Poor Soldier* also enjoyed frequent performance in the last quarter of the century. Another Irishman, Kane O'Hara, outdid all other composers of burlettas with his *Midas*. The spectacular pantomime of *The Death of Captain Cook*, though it did not come on the Irish stage until 1790, surpassed every earlier example of this genre in the number of town productions before 1800.

Even if the popular items in the repertoire at the playhouses of the country towns did not differ notably from the Dublin 'hits', those playhouses also produced a not inconsiderable body of original dramatic entertainment.[1] Only a small portion of this output ever reached the stages of the capital. O'Keeffe's pastoral, *Colin's Welcome* (Belfast, 1770); his farce, *The Comical Duel* (Cork, 1775); and his interlude, *The Generous Tar* (Waterford, 1787), ultimately appeared at the Crow Street Theatre. It too staged an anonymous tragedy, *The Royal Captive* (Cork, 1760); two anonymous farces, *The Fashionable Wife* (Belfast,

[1] Appendix A includes a complete list of all the entertainment originating in the county towns.

1768) and *The Reprisals* (Cork, 1778); two interludes, *The Taylor and the Undertaker* (Wexford, 1793) and Thomas Ryder's *The Gates of Calais* (Drogheda, 1749). Samuel Foote's interlude, *The Disappointment* (Kilkenny, 1768); Brownlow Forde's farce, *The Miraculous Cure* (Newry, 1771); and George Stayley's interlude, *Mimickry Expos'd* (Cork, 1758), all were presented later at Smock Alley. In addition, two anonymous interludes, *The Swaddling Shopkeeper* (Kilkenny, 1770) and *Modern Matrimony* (Cork, 1780); a prelude, *The New Register Office* (Cork, 1781); and a pantomime, *Harlequin in The Shades* (Belfast, 1768), found their way to the boards there. On the other hand, Dublin never saw Eccles's opera, *The World* (Belfast, 1787); Thomas Betterton's entertainment, *A Touch of the Times* (Wexford, 1793); Joseph Waker's pastoral, *Love in a Cottage* (Waterford, 1781); three anonymous comedies, *The Mentalist* (Belfast, 1771), *The School for Ladies* (Belfast, 1784), *The Siege of the Castle of Aesculapius* (Cork, 1772); an anonymous tragedy, *Love and Despair* (Waterford, 1771); two anonymous farces, *The Magical Tale* (Cork, 1786) and *The Vintner Tam'd* (Belfast, 1765); and nearly one hundred other entertainments, interludes, and pantomimes by unknown Irish authors.

The foregoing survey makes evident that the repertoire of the town theatres was by no means confined to the fare suggested by Dublin. Nevertheless the managers outside the capital did not pursue an avowed policy for the encouragement of local playwriting. Like the first of their tribe, Joseph Ashbury of Dublin, they also held no positive convictions about the role of the stage in cultivating loyal sentiments towards Ireland as a nation. Their primary concern, like Ashbury's, was always to keep in the good graces of official authority and to avoid occasioning any stoppage of performance. As for the actors and writers, worthwhile fame and fortune depended finally upon success in London, just as at the beginning of the eighteenth century. Therefore all parties concerned with theatricals anywhere in Ireland usually gave tacit support to the English Ascendancy or, at best, when patriotic passions were at their peak from 1778 to 1798, expressed a romantically neutral Hibernianism on occasion. As a result the companies in the county towns only sporadically tried to appeal to their audiences with works of Irish content.

Many of the pieces with Irish titlings presented little more than an amusing depiction of local settings and manners. John O'Keeffe showed the way by composing brief dramatic sketches or pantomimes with regional colour: *Harlequin in Waterford* (Waterford, 1767), *Harlequin in Derry* (Belfast, 1770), *Giant's Causeway* (Belfast, 1770), *Tony Lumpkin's Ramble thro' Cork* (Cork, 1773), *Tony Lumpkin's Frolics thro' Cork* (Cork, 1780). Various short-lived efforts exhibited a similar descriptive intent: *The Humours of Belfast* (Belfast, 1766), *The Humours of Cove* (Cork, 1773), *Mallow Races* (Cork, 1777), *The Rakes of Mallow* (Cork, 1778), *The Diamond Mine of Cork* (Cork, 1778), *Tony Lumpkin's Rambles thro' Cork in 1796* (Cork, 1796), *Just Arrived in L'Derry* (Derry, 1798), *Poor Darty's Trip to Belfast* (Belfast, 1794), *Rambles through Belfast* (Belfast, 1800). The appearance of these humorous travelogues during the last third of the century was only one manifestation of an increasingly conscious, but usually superficial, patriotism in both producers and audiences.

Rather more substantial in the treatment of native life and character was a small group of comic dramas that made their débuts in Ireland between 1720 and 1800: Thomas Sheridan's *The Brave Irishman* (Dublin, 1737; Belfast, 1755), Charles Macklin's *The True-Born Irishman* (Dublin and Cork, 1762), R. W. Knipe's *The Wexford Wife* (Wexford, 1764), the anonymous *Connaught Wife* (Kilkenny, 1769), Dr. Maryat's *Love in a Bog* (Belfast, 1772). The three comedies first performed outside Dublin apparently were not of sufficient dramatic stature to gain them either publication or production in the capital. The two farces by Sheridan and Macklin became immensely popular throughout the country and also won high praise in London. Their portrayal of the gay and swaggering male Hibernian contributed a good deal to the establishment of this important stereotype on the English-speaking stage.

A serious rather than a humorous view of Irish personality and aspiration led Francis Dobbs to historical tragedy in *The Patriot King; or, The Irish Chief* (Dublin, 1773; Lisburn, 1775), and Dr. James St. John to historical opera in *The Siege of Waterford* (Waterford, 1792), the lyrics of which were said to be drawn from the 'most approved' native airs. Neither playwright, however, had the genius to dramatize forcefully the country's troubled past, and therefore these stage utterances were quickly extinguished. Two other writers dared in the same year, 1793, to imply their views on Ireland's explosive situation in terms of contemporary French affairs. William Preston of Dublin in *Democratic Rage; or, Louis the Unfortunate* (Dublin, June; Cork, August) took a monarchist position and pictured the tragic excesses of popular revolt, while the more liberal Rev. Dr. Bambridge of Belfast in *The Guillotine; or, The Death of Louis XVI* (Belfast, May) presented the King's catastrophe as the result of royal indifference to human want and indignation. Both plays, though of no great artistic merit, stirred immediate partisan agitation. Consequently the ever-cautious managers would not repeat performance for fear of incurring the wrath of the Establishment.

The one figure who made a sustained effort in the playhouses of the county towns to build up an honest sentiment of Irish confraternity was Robert Owenson, an actor with the unique ability to perform in the Irish language. As he strolled through the west and south of Ireland in the years following the start of the Volunteer Movement, he devoted much attention to dramatic and musical entertainment based on native materials. In the character of a simple country player, named either Darby Mulroney or Phelim O'Flanagan or Phelim Ouffnocarrolocarney MacFrame, he charmed town audiences with his large store of 'cries' and 'lilts', and with his Irish as well as English renderings of 'planxties' by Ireland's famous bard, Carolan. He liked especially to recite in Irish two dramatic poems, 'Drimmhuin Dhuh' ('My Dark Beauty') and 'Salhuin neen Wenugh' ('The Munster Mantle'). His most ambitious composition in Irish, a prelude entitled 'Pleahàrca na Rourcough' ('O'Rourke's Revelry'), dramatized with bardic humour a splendid Irish feast.

Owenson's prelude, first performed at Cork in 1778 and often repeated in subsequent years, remained the sole recorded contribution to eighteenth-century dramatic literature in the Irish language. In English the contributions resulting from the extensive theatricals in the county towns were, as has been noted, fairly numerous but, for the most part, of slight substance or inept craftsmanship and therefore not literarily memorable. Even so, an unmistakable, though mild, strain of cultural

Irishism developed in the towns' dramatic entertainment between 1720 and 1800. Thus modestly oriented towards an incipient nationalism, the stage activity of this period founded a strong, country-wide taste for the theatre amongst an instinctively gifted people who had had no folk heritage in that art.

APPENDIX A

PLAYS ACTED IN IRELAND OUTSIDE DUBLIN 1720–1800

All plays whose authorship is known are listed under their respective authors. Plays of unknown authorship are at the end of the list and are grouped in four categories: (1) plays, (2) preludes, (3) pantomimes, (4) entertainments and musical interludes.

Each title is preceded by one of the following contractions to indicate the type of composition:

T.	Tragedy	M.D.	Melodrama
C.	Comedy	Int.	Interlude
T.C.	Tragi-comedy	M. Int.	Musical Interlude
F.	Farce	Ent.	Entertainment
M.	Masque	M. Ent.	Musical Entertainment
O.	Opera	P.	Pantomime
C.O.	Comic Opera	B.	Burlesque
B.O.	Ballad Opera	Burl.	Burletta
O.F.	Operatic Farce	Past.	Pastoral
D.	Drama	Prel.	Prelude

Symbols that in many cases precede the foregoing contractions have designations as follows:

* originated in Ireland outside Dublin
† not performed in Dublin
‡ not performed in London
§ not recorded in A. Nicoll's *A History of English Drama: 1660–1900*

The date in parentheses after the title is that of the earliest known production in Dublin or London. If production occurred first in Dublin and later in London, the London date is also inserted. The contractions preceding the date or dates indicate Dublin and London theatres as follows:

1. *Dublin*

A.S.	Aungier Street	F.S.	Fishamble Street
Cap. S.	Capel Street	R.S.	Rainsford Street
C.S.	Crow Street	S.A.	Smock Alley

2. *London*

B.F.	Bartholomew Fair	H.[2]	The Little Theatre in the Haymarket
C.G.	Covent Garden	L.[1]	Lincoln's Inn Fields (*ante* Apr. 1705)
D.G.	Dorset Garden	L.[2]	Lincoln's Inn Fields (*post* Nov. 1714)
D.L.	Drury Lane	R.C.	Royal Circus
G.F.	Goodman's Fields	R.G.	Royal Grove
H.[1]	The King's Theatre (Opera House) in the Haymarket		

Beneath each title the record of known performances outside Dublin is listed by years, the towns being indicated thus:

1. *Principal Towns*

B.	Belfast		
C.	Cork	K.	Kilkenny
D.	Derry (Londonderry)	L.	Limerick
E.	Ennis	N.	Newry
G.	Galway	W.	Waterford

2. *Minor Towns*

Ant.	Antrim	Col.	Coleraine
Ath.	Athlone	Dr.	Drogheda
Ba.	Ballymena	Du.	Dundalk
Car.	Carrick-on-Suir	Ennc.	Enniscorthy
Carf.	Carrickfergus	F.	Fethard
Carl.	Carlow	Lis.	Lisburn
Cash.	Cashel	Sl.	Sligo
Cast.	Castlebar	Tr.	Tralee
Cav.	Cavan	Wex.	Wexford
Cl.	Clonmel		

ADDISON, JOSEPH

T. Cato (D.L. 14/4/1713).

1749: Dr. 7/12. **1756:** Tr. 15/3. **1761:** B. 4/9. **1766:** C. 15/6. **1770:** B. 20/6. **1773:** C. 18/6; L. 6/8. **1776:** C. 22/7, 1/10. **1781:** B. 16/11, 5/12. **1782:** C. 9/8. **1784:** B. 7/5; Lis. 1/11. **1785:** B. 11/4. **1789:** L. 21/12. **1791:** B. 30/11.

ANDREWS, MILES PETER

† C.O. Belphegor; or, The Wishes (D.L. 16/3/1778).

1782: K. 28/9.

† C. Better Late Than Never (D.L. 17/11/1790).

1791: D. 13/5. **1792:** B. 20/2.

† C. Reparation (D.L. 1784).

1787: B. 23/2.

C.O. Summer Amusement; or, An Adventure at Margate . . . assisted in writing by W. A. Miles (H.[2] 1/7/1779).

1781: C. 7/9, 12/10. **1786:** C. 31/8.

ARNE, DR. THOMAS AUGUSTUS

C.O. Artaxerxes (C.G. 2/2/1762).

1766: C. 13/10. **1777:** C. 19/8, 10/9. **1783:** C. 14/8, 19/8. **1792:** C. 13/8, 15/8, 17/8.

† O.F. Cooper [s], The (H.[2] 10/6/1772).

1777: C. 15/10.

ATKINSON, JOSEPH

‡ C. Mutual Deception, The (S.A. 2/3/1785).

1787: K. 24/9.

BAKER, THOMAS

C. Tunbridge-Walks; or, The Yeoman of Kent (D.L. 27/1/1703).

1756: Tr. 30/4. **1759:** Ba. 27/9. **1768:** B. 11/11.

BAMBRIDGE, REV. DR.

*†‡§ T. The Guillotine; or, The Death of Louis XVI.

1793: B. 27/5.

BANKS, JOHN

T. Albion Queens, The; or, The Death of Mary Queen of Scotland (D.L. 6/3/1704). [An alteration of *The Island Queens* by the same author.]

1775: C. 31/7.

T. Unhappy Favourite, The; or, The Earl of Essex (D.L. *c.* Sept. 1681).

1768: B. 21/10. **1776:** B. 6/3.

BATE, REV. HENRY

C.O. Flitch of Bacon, The (H.[2] 17/8/1778).

1780: C. 4/8, 9/8, 22/8. **1783:** C. 8/9. **1784:** C. 1/9. **1789:** Wex. 16/2. **1790:** C. 17/8, 2/9; E. 24/8. **1791:** C. 16/8, 28/9. **1792:** C. 17/8. **1793:** Wex. 18/1. **1795:** C. 2/11. **1798:** C. 23/10. **1799:** L. 2/8.

INT. Henry and Emma; or, The Nut Brown Maid (C.G. 13/4/1774).

1774: C. 27/7. **1776:** B. 29/3; C. 26/8, 22/9.

C.O. Rival Candidates, The (D.L. 1/2/1775).

1776: C. 28/8, 4/10. **1777:** C. 1/10. **1779:** C. 22/9. **1783:** C. 18/3. **1787:** C. 20/9. **1788:** C. 28/11. **1791:** D. 18/5.

C.O. Woodman, The (C.G. 26/2/1791).

1791: C. 26/9. **1792:** K. 4/7; Wat. 30/7, 1/8; Wex. 26/10. **1795:** C. 8/9.

BEAUMONT, F., and FLETCHER, J.

C. Rule a Wife, and Have a Wife.

1740: Dr. 25/8. **1759:** Ba. 28/9. **1765:** C. 20/9. **1766:** C. 29/9. **1768:** C. 17/8. **1770:** B. 1/8. **1776:** K. 24/6.

[An Adaptation by James Love (D.L. 14/2/1776).]

1778: C. 12/10; B. 23/10. **1780:** C. 30/9. **1782:** C. 13/9. **1783:** C. 8/9. **1784:** K. 21/4; C. 21/9. **1786:** C. 20/10; B. 23/10. **1787:** C. 18/9. **1791:** K. 15/1. **1792:** C. 4/9. **1793:** G. 21/8. **1794:** C. 27/8; B. 17/12. **1796:** B. 4/5.

BEHN, MRS. APHRA

F. Emperor of the Moon (D.G. *c.* Mar. 1686/7).

1760: C. 11/10. **1775:** C. 21/9.

BETTERTON, THOMAS

T.C. King Henry IV, Part I, with the Humours of Sir John Falstaff (L.[1] *c.* Apr. 1700).

1755: B. 14/3. **1756:** Tr. 6/3. **1758:** C. 25/8. **1761:** B. 3/7; C. 6/7. **1765:** C. 13/8, 26/9. **1770:** K. 29/11. **1771:** B. 25/10. **1776:** B. 7/2. **1777:** B. 21/11. **1779:** C. 23/7. **1780:** C. 4/8; K. 23/12. **1783:** C. 12/3, 2/9; L. 8/10. **1784:** C. 11/3. **1785:** C. 22/9. **1794:** B. 8/12. **1796:** B. 22/4; K. 23/9. **1797:** C. 13/11.

BETTERTON [originally BUTTERTON], THOMAS

*†‡§ ENT. Touch of the Times, A; or, Dame Nature in a Frolic.

1793: Wex. 18/4; G. 26/8.

BICKERSTAFFE, ISAAC

F. Absent Man, The (D.L. 21/3/1768).

1768: C. 29/7; L. 13/10. **1769:** B. 13/1.

C.O. Daphne and Amintor (D.L. 8/10/1765).

1766: C. 18/10. **1776:** C. 5/10. **1778:** C. 31/7. **1781:** B. 9/5. **1786:** C. 14/9.

C. Doctor Last in his Chariot (H.[2] 21/6/1769).

1772: C. 10/9.

INT. Ephesian Matron, The (H.[2] 31/8/1769).

1773: L. 17/8. **1774:** C. 8/8. **1775:** Lis. 6/10. **1776:** K. 31/8. **1777:** C. 8/10. **1778:** K. 4/2. **1779:** D. 16/8. **1780:** C. 30/9, 7/10. **1782:** B. 25/1.

C. Hypocrite, The (D.L. 17/11/1768). [An alteration of C. Cibber's *The Non-Juror*.]

1773: B. 10/12, 22/12. **1774:** B. 2/2. **1776:** B. 20/3. **1778:** C. 7/9, 30/10; B. 11/12. **1779:** C. 24/9, 11/10. **1782:** C. 26/9. **1786:** C. 26/10. **1787:** Wat. 19/10. **1789:** B. 30/1. **1790:** L. ?/11. **1795:** B. 8/4.

C.O. Lionel and Clarissa; or, A School for Fathers (C.G. 25/2/1768).

1770: K. 2/11, 7/11, 14/11. **1771:** B. 11/10; L. 29/10. **1772:** B. 3/1, 17/1; L. 3/8; C. 27/8, 8/9, 9/10. **1773:** C. 16/6, 26/7, 9/9, 21/9; B. 8/9, 3/12; Lis. 4/10. **1774:** C. 23/7. **1776:** K. 15/7; C. 5/8, 14/8, 21/8. **1777:** C. 18/7, 23/7; L. 14/8. **1778:** C. 12/8; B. 9/12, 30/12. **1779:** N. 15/3; C. 4/10; K. 16/12. **1780:** C. 26/9. **1782:** C. 10/8. **1786:** C. 2/11. **1787:** B. 1/1; L. 16/7; C. 31/7; Wat. 16/10. **1788:** B. 28/11. **1789:** C. 1/6. **1790:** C. 12/4, 7/9; En. 23/9. **1791:** L. ?/3; C. 25/4; B. 10/10. **1792:** C. 25/8; Wex. 26/11, 10/12; D. 5/12, 12/12, 26/12. **1793:** K. 26/8. **1795:** C. 19/8, 5/9. **1796:** B. 28/3; C. 16/8; Dr. 10/10; K. 19/10. **1797:** C. 9/10. **1798:** D. 30/4.

C.O. Love in a Village (C.G. 8/12/1762).

1765: C. 16/8, 19/8, 29/8, 16/9; B. 9/10, 8/11. **1766:** B. 3/1, 29/1; C. 24/9. **1768:** K. 25/3. **1769:** K. 31/7; C. 2/8, 30/8. **1770:** B. 4/5. **1772:** L. 15/7. **1775:** Lis. 18/10; B. 8/12. **1776:** C. 24/7, 16/8, 12/10; K. 14/8. **1777:** C. 10/9. **1778:** C. 2/9. **1779:** B. 12/3; C. 10/9; K. 17/11. **1780:** C. 12/8, 22/8, 1/9. **1782:** B. 25/1. **1786:** L. 31/7. **1787:** K. 16/8. **1788:** L. 19/7; C. 5/8; Wex. 26/12. **1789:** K. 24/4; C. 18/4, 12/9. **1790:** E. 26/4; C. 8/5, 17/8, 31/8; L. 13/8. **1791:** L. ?/3; C. 11/8, 28/9; B. 3/10. **1792:** K. 18/6; N. 19/6; Wat. 23/7; G. 3/9; C. 11/9; Wex. 15/10, 28/11. **1793:** D. 23/1; K. 14/8; C. 11/9. **1795:** C. 17/8; Car. ?/10; D. 23/12. **1796:** B. 26/2, 3/6; C. 2/8; K. 17/10. **1797:** E. 17/4. **1798:** C. 8/9, 25/9.

C.O. Maid of the Mill (C.G. 31/1/1765).

1765: C. 18/9. **1768:** K. 6/1, 11/1; B. 26/9. **1769:** C. 11/9. **1770:** K. 12/9, 17/10. **1771:** B. 29/11. **1775:** Lis. 20/9. **1776:** C. 23/8. **1777:** C. 4/10. **1778:** K. 10/2. **1779:** C. 6/10. **1780:** B. 14/2, 18/2. **1786:** C. 10/8, 25/8; L. 15/8. **1787:** B. 30/3. **1789:** Wex. 4/2. **1791:** B. 23/9, 27/9. **1792:** W. 2/8; Wex. 29/10; D. 22/11. **1793:** K. 27/8. **1795:** K. 4/11. **1796:** B. 10/6; C. 5/8.

C.O. Padlock, The (D.L. 3/10/1768).

1769: C. 12/9. **1770:** B. 16/5, 23/5, 14/7; K. 19/9. **1771:** B. 6/9, 4/10. **1772:** C. 11/9, 2/10. **1773:** C. 23/6, 2/9; B. 15/10. **1774:** B. 7/1. **1775:** Lis. 22/9. **1776:** B. 7/2; K. 22/7, 19/8; C. 26/7, 15/10. **1777:** B. 14/11. **1778:** K. 21/1, 31/1; B. 27/4; C. 28/8, 16/10; N. 3/12; B. 11/12. **1779:** B. 12/2; N. 4/4; C. 7/7. **1780:** B. 10/3; C. 26/9. **1781:** B. 14/11. **1782:** L. 31/8. **1783:** C. 23/8. **1786:** C. 6/11. **1788:** C. 12/9. **1789:** Wex. 28/1. **1790:** E. 25/3. **1791:** C. 19/8. **1792:** B. 17/2; W. 30/7; Wex. 28/11; D. 13/12. **1793:** D. 9/1. **1795:** K. 7/12. **1796:** B. 1/6; Dr. 12/10. **1799:** D. 24/4; K. 5/6.

C. Plain Dealer, The (D.L. 7/12/1765). [An alteration of Wycherley's *The Plain Dealer*.]

1773: C. 15/9.

INT. Recruiting Serjeant, The (D.L. 1770).

1772: L. 3/8; C. 8/9. **1774:** L. 24/8. **1776:** C. 28/8, 7/10. **1777:** C. 12/9.

1778: C. 2/9. **1779:** B. 5/3; N. 15/3. **1780:** B. 8/1; C. 1/9, 6/10. **1781:** C. 10/10. **1782:** D. 27/11, 4/12. **1787:** K. 19/3. **1788:** C. 11/9. **1795:** C. 3/9.

F. Spoil'd Child, The (D.L. 22/3/1790).

1793: D. 18/1. **1794:** C. 26/9. **1795:** B. 4/3; C. 20/8. **1796:** E. 26/5. **1800:** B. 4/5.

O.F. Sultan, The; or, A Peep into the Seraglio (D.L. 12/12/1775).

1778: C. 14/10, 2/11. **1779:** B. 19/3; C. 13/9, 17/9, 29/9. **1781:** C. 17/8, 24/8, 7/9; B. 16/11. **1782:** C. 12/7. **1783:** C. 19/9. **1786:** C. 20/10. **1787:** B. 1/1. **1790:** E. 24/9. **1791:** C. 5/10. **1792:** W. 13/8; Wex. 31/12. **1793:** L. 25/7.

INT. Thomas and Sally (C.G. 28/11/1760).

1761: C. 28/9. **1765:** C. 24/9. **1768:** K. 1/2; B. 7/9. **1769:** C. 2/8. **1770:** L. 14/4. **1771:** L. 24/9. **1776:** C. 14/7; K. 12/8. **1777:** C. 30/7; B. 11/12. **1778:** B. 7/1; C. 12/10. **1779:** B. 22/1; C. 14/6. **1780:** C. 17/10. **1785:** B. 10/6. **1791:** C. 4/10. **1792:** B. 15/2.

BIRCH, SAMUEL

M.D. Adopted Child, The (D.L. 1/5/1795).

1799: D. 19/4, 1/5, 7/5; C. 7/9.

BOADEN, JAMES

M.D. Fontainville Forest (C.G. 25/3/1794).

1794: D. 23/7.

BROME, R.

B.O. Jovial Crew, The (D.L. 8/2/1731). [An adaptation by Matthew Concanen, Roome, and Sir William Yonge.]

1761: C. 2/10. **1770:** B. 26/7.

BROOKE, MRS. FRANCES

C.O. Rosina (C.G. 31/12/1782).

1783: C. 29/8, 6/9. **1785:** L. 1/3. **1786:** C. 1/8. **1787:** B. 3/8, 10/8, 17/8. **1788:** C. 25/8; B. 12/11. **1789:** Wex. 23/1, 23/2; B. 9/2; K. 22/5, 24/6; C. 1/6. **1790:** C. 16/8. **1791:** D. 16/5; B. 14/9. **1792:** B. 6/2; N. 25/6; C. 25/8; Wex. 2/11; D. 21/11. **1793:** C. 16/8; K. 26/8; W. 30/9; G. 9/10. **1794:** D. 9/5, 9/7. **1795:** B. 25/3. **1796:** B. 2/3. **1797:** E. 31/3. **1799:** K. 16/6; C. 31/8.

BROOKE, HENRY

T. Earl of Essex, The (S.A. 7/5/1750; D.L. 3/1/1761).

1755: B. 7/3. **1758:** B. 5/5. **1766:** B. 10/1.

‡ T. Gustavus Vasa, The Deliverer of his Country (S.A. 3/12/1744).

1779: B. 27/1.

BROWN, DR. JOHN

T. Barbarossa (D.L. 17/12/1754).

1758: B. 1/3. **1760:** C. 26/9. **1769:** C. 12/9. **1770:** B. 28/7; K. 5/12. **1779:** C. 14/6. **1780:** C. 23/8.

BULLOCK, CHRISTOPHER

† F. Adventures of Half an Hour, The (L.[2] 19/3/1716).

1766: B. 29/1.

F. Cobler of Preston, The (L.[2] 17/1/1716).

1742: G. n.d. **1753:** B. 14/9. **1756:** Tr. 5/5. **1763:** B. 3/3. **1766:** C. 15/9.

C. Woman's Revenge; or, A Match in Newgate (L.[2] 24/10/1715).

1740: Dr. 25/8.

BURGOYNE, JOHN

C. Heiress, The (D.L. 14/1/1786).

1786: C. 11/9, 11/10. **1787:** C. 21/9; W. 18/10. **1789:** B. 4/2, 9/3. **1790:** D. 5/5. **1791:** B. 10/1. **1792:** B. 29/2, 26/3. **1794:** C. 3/9.

C.O. Lord of the Manor, The (D.L. 27/12/1780).

1781: C. 17/8. **1782:** C. 16/8. **1786:** C. 12/8, 15/8. **1790:** C. 4/9. **1793:** Wex. 4/1; D. 11/1, 25/1.

C.O. Maid of the Oaks, The (D.L. 5/11/1774).

1777: C. 10/10. **1782:** C. 15/8, 3/10. **1784:** C. 22/9. **1786:** C. 24/10. **1788:** C. 1/9. **1790:** D. 21/5. **1792:** K. 4/6; Wex. 9/11.

CAREY, GEORGE SAVILLE

M. Shakespeare's Jubilee. [Ptd. 1769.]

1772: C. 1/9, 8/9. **1773:** C. 15/9. **1776:** C. 8/10. **1782:** C. 3/10.

INT. Three Old Women Weatherwise; or, A Cure for All Ills (D.L. 1770).

1779: D. 18/8.

CAREY, HENRY

F. Contrivances, The; or, More Ways Than One (D.L. 9/8/1715).

1759: C. 22/8. **1760:** C. 30/9. **1763:** B. 14/3. **1765:** C. 15/8, 26/9; B. 27/11. **1766:** B. 3/1, 7/2. **1768:** K. 5/2, 12/2; B. 30/12. **1771:** B. 18/9. **1776:** B. 27/3. **1778:** C. 31/8. **1787:** B. 24/8.

B.O. Honest Yorkshire-Man, The (H.[2] 15/7/1735).

1751: B. n.d. **1753:** B. 3/7. **1756:** Tr. 25/4. **1760:** C. 2/10. **1761:** B. 4/9. **1765:** B. 16/10. **1767:** K. 26/12. **1768:** K. 8/1; B. 2/12. **1770:** K. 17/9. **1771:** B. 2/8, 22/11. **1772:** B. 17/1; C. 4/9. **1773:** C. 30/6, 27/8; B. 1/10, 31/12. **1774:** D. 9/8. **1778:** K. 4/2; B. 24/4. **1779:** Ant. 1/10. **1780:** B. 8/1; C. 12/8. **1791:** B. 31/1; E. 11/11.

B.T. Tragedy of Chrononhotonthologos, The (H.[2] 22/2/1734).

1756: Tr. 11/3. **1765:** B. 8/11. **1766:** B. 8/1, 15/1. **1770:** B. 4/8; K. 21/11. **1778:** B. 16/1. **1783:** C. 27/9. **1784:** C. 11/3. **1794:** D. 23/5. **1795:** B. 6/4.

B.O. Wonder, A; or, An Honest Yorkshire-Man (G.F. 6/8/1735). [A pirated edition of *The Honest Yorkshire-Man.*]

1741: C. n.d. **1783:** C. 12/9.

CENTLIVRE, MRS. SUSANNAH

C. Bold Stroke for a Wife, A (L.[2] 3/2/1718).

1758: B. 24/2; C. 4/9. **1763:** B. 3/3. **1765:** B. 11/12. **1768:** K. 16/2. **1770:** K. 5/11. **1772:** C. 16/10. **1773:** C. 22/10. **1779:** K. 30/10. **1791:** K. 7/3. **1793:** Wex. 14/1; G. 9/9. **1796:** K. 3/10.

C. Busie Body, The (D.L. 12/5/1709).

1756: Tr. 7/5. **1759:** C. 22/8. **1762:** C. 30/10. **1763:** B. 26/1, 25/3. **1765:** Dr. 26/8; C. 6/9; B. 27/11. **1766:** C. 5/9, 18/10. **1768:** Car. 19/10. **1771:** K. 2/1; B. 16/10, 27/12. **1773:** K. 20/2; B. 15/12. **1775:** Lis. 15/9, 22/9. **1778:** C. 31/10. **1780:** C. 14/8. **1783:** D. 29/10. **1784:** B. 14/5; C. 3/9. **1786:** C. 2/8, 5/8. **1788:** Wex. 29/12. **1789:** K. 28/4. **1790:** C. 30/8. **1791:** B. 27/7. **1792:** G. 28/2. **1796:** B. 9/5; E. 27/6; K. 28/9. **1799:** K. 26/6.

C. Gamester, The (L.[1] *c.* Jan. 1704/5).

1770: K. 28/11.

C. Wonder, The: A Woman Keeps a Secret (D.L. 27/4/1714).

1759: C. 24/8. **1768:** C. 12/8. **1770:** B. 25/7. **1772:** C. 13/10. **1773:** C. 31/8. **1774:** D. 10/8. **1775:** B. 22/11. **1776:** K. 17/7; C. 19/7. **1777:** C. 1/10. **1781:** B. 9/5. **1784:** B. 30/4. **1788:** L. 29/7. **1789:** Wex. 13/2; C. 28/9. **1790:** E. 24/8; L. ?/11. **1791:** B. 9/2; D. 6/4; C. 11/5; E. 7/10. **1792:** K. 16/7. **1793:** G. 9/7; C. 9/9. **1794:** C. 25/8; L. ?/9. **1795:** C. 21/8; K. 7/12. **1796:** D. 6/1; Dr. 12/10. **1800:** B. 28/4.

CHALMERS, JAMES

‡§ P. Triumph of Mirth, The; or, Harlequin Animation (S.A. 9/4/1785).

1786: C. 6/10, 3/11. **1787:** K. 20/7.

CIBBER, COLLEY

C. Careless Husband, The (D.L. 7/12/1704).

1753: B. 7/9. **1761:** B. 5/8. **1769:** B. 6/1. **1773:** C. 12/7. **1776:** K. 22/7.

B.O. Damon and Phillida (H.[2] 16/8/1729).

1753: B. 6/7. **1754:** B. 18/11, 22/11. **1755:** Lis. 3/3, 5/3. **1756:** Tr. 9/3, 21/4, 23/4; C. 30/8. **1758:** B. 13/2, 2/6. **1761:** B. 12/8; C. 26/9. **1765:** C. 13/8; B. 13/11. **1775:** L. 13/10; B. 13/12. **1776:** B. 29/3.

C. Double Gallant, The; or, The Sick Lady's Cure (H.[1] 1/11/1707).

1757: C. 5/8. **1771**: C. 6/9. **1790**: C. 27/8. **1792**: K. 23/5.

C. Lady's Last Stake, The; or, The Wife's Resentment (H.[1] 13/12/1707).

1779: C. 5/10.

C. Love Makes a Man; or, The Fop's Fortune (D.L. 13/12/1700).

1754: B. 11/12. **1758**: C. 13/9. **1761**: B. 14/8. **1768**: K. 10/2. **1770**: B. 20/7; K. 21/11. **1772**: C. 19/10. **1773**: L. 18/8; C. 25/8. **1774**: B. 9/2; C. 3/8; D. 24/8. **1776**: B. 28/2. **1778**: B. 1/4. **1780**: C. 23/10. **1792**: C. 31/8. **1794**: D. 9/5, 14/5.

C. Love's Last Shift; or, The Fool in Fashion (D.L. Jan. 1695/6).

1773: C. 27/8. **1776**: K. 31/7. **1777**: C. 7/10.

C. Provok'd Husband, The; or, A Journey to London (D.L. 10/1/1728). [An alteration of Vanbrugh's *The Journey to London.*]

1755: B. 31/1; Lis. 19/2. **1756**: Tr. 6/4. **1758**: B. 26/5; C. 26/9. **1760**: C. 2/10. **1761**: B. 17/7, 28/8. **1762**: C. 28/9. **1763**: B. 21/1, 4/4. **1765**: C. 19/9; B. 16/10. **1766**: B. 1/1; C. 15/9. **1768**: K. 25/1. **1769**: B. 13/1. **1770**: K. 21/11. **1771**: L. 15/8; B. 2/10. **1773**: C. 4/6, 20/9. **1774**: B. 7/1; D. 31/8; C. 6/9. **1775**: C. 12/7; Lis. 17/11. **1777**: L. 13/8; C. 20/8. **1778**: C. 27/7. **1779**: C. 11/8; L. 17/8; C. 1/9. **1781**: C. 5/10. **1782**: C. 9/10; D. 23/10; K. 7/11. **1786**: C. 17/10. **1788**: C. 30/8; B. 21/11. **1789**: C. 8/9. **1790**: D. 4/6. **1791**: B. 4/2. **1792**: B. 19/3; Wex. 19/11. **1793**: Ennc. 8/3; W. 8/3; G. 10/7, 12/7; K. 2/10. **1794**: D. 19/2; C. 29/8. **1795**: K. 23/9. **1796**: E. 24/6.

C. Refusal, The; or, The Ladies Philosophy (D.L. 14/2/1721).

1772: L. 13/7; C. 11/9.

F. School-Boy, The; or, The Comical Rival (D.L. 24/10/1702).

1768: K. 4/3. **1775**: B. 27/1.

C. She Wou'd and She Wou'd Not; or, The Kind Impostor (D.L. 26/11/1702).

1758: C. 6/9. **1761**: B. 12/8. **1773**: C. 21/7, 26/8; L. 17/8. **1783**: C. 24/9.

CIBBER, MRS. SUSANNA-MARIA

M. Oracle, The (C.G. 17/3/1752).

1758: B. 27/2, 5/4, 19/5; C. 14/8. **1759**: C. 1/10. **1763**: B. 21/1.

COBB, JAMES

O.F. Doctor and the Apothecary, The (D.L. 25/10/1788).

1789: C. 12/9. **1792**: C. 15/9; Wex. 7/11, 14/12.

F. First Floor, The (D.L. 13/1/1787).

1787: W. 20/10.

C.O. Haunted Tower, The (D.L. 24/11/1789).

1791: C. 27/9. **1792**: W. 13/8; G. 14/9; Wex. 12/11, 14/12. **1798**: L. 6/10.

COFFEY, CHARLES

B.O. Beggar's Wedding, The (S.A. 24/3/1729; H.[2] 29/5/1729).

1755: Lis. 24/2.

B.O. Devil to Pay, The; or, The Wives Metamorphos'd (D.L. 6/8/1731).

1754: B. 11/12. **1755**: B. 31/1. **1756**: Tr. 8/4. **1758**: B. 17/3, 31/3. **1759**: Ba. 25/9. **1761**: C. 30/7. **1763**: B. 19/1, 29/3. **1765**: C. 14/8; B. 18/10, 9/12. **1768**: K. 29/2. **1769**: K. 5/6, 17/8. **1770**: K. 28/11. **1771**: B. 16/8, 13/12; W. 4/11. **1775**: Lis. 20/10. **1776**: K. 19/6, 14/8; C. 2/8, 9/8, 1/10. **1777**: C. 14/10. **1778**: K. 19/1. **1786**: C. 5/8. **1787**: B. 30/3; C. 17/9. **1788**: L. 25/7. **1789**: B. 18/2. **1790**: C. 13/9. **1791**: B. 12/1, 30/11. **1792**: Wex. 12/10. **1793**: G. 26/7, 29/7; C. 3/9. **1796**: D. 4/1.

COLMAN, GEORGE, *the Elder*

C. Clandestine Marriage, The (D.L. 20/2/1766). [Wr. in collaboration with David Garrick.]

1766: C. 20/8, 1/9. **1767**: K. 30/11. **1768**: K. 24/3; C. 29/7; B. 14/9, 30/9. **1769**: K. 17/8. **1770**: B. 10/5. **1772**: B. 23/1. **1773**: C. 28/7, 11/9; L. 10/8; B. 1/10. **1774**: B. 14/1. **1775**: C. 1/9. **1776**: C. 11/10. **1777**: C. 26/8. **1778**: C. 16/10. **1779**: K. 11/10. **1781**: K. 4/1. **1782**: K. 21/12. **1783**: C. 25/9. **1788**: C. 13/9; B. 11/11. **1791**: B. 18/7, 5/8. **1792**: K. 23/2; W. 31/7; Wex. 17/12. **1793**: W. 18/2. **1796**: K. 15/11.

M. Comus. [See John Milton.]

F. Deuce is in Him, The (D.L. 4/11/1763).

1768: B. 7/10. **1771**: B. 23/10, 30/10. **1773**: B. 6/10. **1774**: D. 8/8. **1776**: D. 6/11. **1777**: C. 8/10. **1778**: C. 17/7; B. 30/10. **1780**: C. 14/10. **1787**: K. 24/9. **1792**: W. 18/2; N. 2/7. **1793**: Wex. 14/1. **1800**: B. 9/5.

C. English Merchant, The (D.L. 27/2/1767).

1768: K. 1/2. **1773**: B. 29/10. **1790**: D. 24/5.

C. Jealous Wife, The (D.L. 12/2/1761).

1768: B. 21/11, 23/12. **1771**: B. 8/11. **1773**: B. 1/12. **1775**: C. 20/9. **1776**: B. 3/4. **1777**: B. 14/11. **1782**: B. 16/1. **1784**: D. 9/1; B. 13/7; C. 20/9. **1786**: C. 6/11. **1787**: B. 2/3; C. 2/8, 28/8. **1788**: C. 12/9. **1791**: D. 27/5. **1792**: C. 30/8. **1793**: D. 4/2; C. 26/8; W. 30/9. **1796**: K. 26/11.

PREL. Manager in Distress, The; or, The Theatre in An Uproar (H.[2] 30/5/1780).

1780: K. 23/12. **1782**: C. 26/9, 12/10. **1794**: C. ?/9. **1796**: E. 27/6.

C. Man of Business, The (C.G. 29/1/1774).

1774: L. 17/8; C. 12/9.

F. Musical Lady, The (D.L. 6/3/1762).

1765: C. 2/10.

PREL. New Brooms; or, Birch from Parnassus (D.L. 21/9/1776).

1796: B. 16/5.

PREL. Occasional Prelude, An (C.G. 21/9/1772).

1778: C. 14/10. **1779:** C. 20/9.

F. Polly Honeycombe (D.L. 5/12/1760).

1763: C. 7/9, 21/9. **1764:** C. 3/10. **1766:** B. 31/1. **1770:** B. 18/6; K. 30/11. **1772:** B. 22/1. **1773:** B. 12/11. **1779:** N. 4/1; K. 27/9; Ant. 4/10.

C. Spanish Barber, The; or, The Fruitless Precaution (H.[2] 30/8/1777).

1782: C. 26/9.

C. Tit for Tat (H.[2] 29/8/1786). [An alteration of Atkinson's *Mutual Deception.*]

1788: C. 2/9, 11/9. **1789:** K. 10/6, 26/6. **1791:** D. 2/5; B. 30/9; E. 3/10, 7/10. **1793:** G. 21/8.

T. Virtue in Distress; or, The Invasion of Britain with the Fall of Bonduca, British Queen. [= *Bonduca* (H.[2] 30/7/1778).]

1782: C. 3/10.

COLMAN, GEORGE, *the Younger*

M.D. Battle of Hexham, The (H.[2] 11/8/1789).

1792: W. 14/9; Wex. 17/12. **1793:** W. 19/3; G. 7/10.

INT. British Loyalty; or, A Squeeze for St. Paul's (D.L. 30/4/1789).

1789: C. 11/9. **1793:** D. 14/1.

C. Heir at Law (H.[2] 15/7/1797).

1798: C. 21/9, 28/9, 19/10, 23/10. **1799:** K. 10/6, 12/6. **1800:** E. 10/2.

C.O. Inkle and Yarico (H.[2] 4/8/1787).

1788: C. 3/9, 10/9; B. 19/12. **1789:** Wex. 6/3; K. 3/6; C. 4/9. **1790:** L. 13/8; E. 13/9. **1791:** D. 4/5; B. 30/9; C. 7/10. **1792:** D. 2/1; K. 4/7; W. 2/8; Wex. 22/10, 30/11. **1793:** D. 6/2; C. 7/9. **1794:** B. 24/10. **1796:** B. 17/2, 6/6; Dr. 10/10. **1797:** C. 26/8. **1800:** B. 25/4.

M.D. Mountaineers, The (H.[2] 3/8/1793).

1795: C. 2/11. **1797:** C. 3/5, 15/8, 8/9. **1798:** D. 5/3. **1800:** B. 22/1, 27/3.

M.D. Surrender of Calais, The (H.[2] 30/7/1791).

1793: B. 13/5, 29/5. **1795:** K. 26/10.

C. Ways and Means; or, A Trip to Dover (H.[2] 10/7/1788).

1794: B. 7/11. **1795:** D. 7/10. **1796:** B. 25/4.

CONGREVE, WILLIAM

C. Double Dealer, The (D.L. Oct. 1693).

1738: Dr. 27/10. **1755:** B. 24/2. **1758:** C. 8/9. **1772:** C. 25/9. **1780:** C. 30/8. **1783:** C. 23/9. **1787:** C. 10/9.

C. Love for Love (L.[1] Apr. 1695).

1742: C. and W. n.d. **1755:** B. 21/2. **1756:** Tr. 10/4. **1759:** Ba. 26/9, 27/12; Col. 17/12. **1768:** K. 8/2. **1770:** B. 4/7, 9/7. **1771:** L. 25/9. **1777:** C. ?/9. **1784:** K. 29/3. **1788:** C. 27/8. **1791:** L. ?/3.

T. Mourning Bride, The (L.[1] 20/2/1697).

1753: B. 6/6. **1758:** B. 3/5. **1760:** C. 19/9. **1761:** C. 31/7. **1763:** C. 14/9. **1766:** C. 27/9. **1768:** B. 14/11. **1770:** B. 14/7; K. 1/12. **1771:** B. 20/9. **1775:** C. 29/9. **1783:** C. 27/8. **1785:** B. 7/6. **1791:** B. 12/1; D. 25/5.

C. Old Batchelour, The (D.L. Mar. 1692/3).

1740: Dr. 3/10.

C. Way of the World, The (L.[1] Mar. 1699/1700).

1756: C. 22/9. **1758:** C. 7/8, 4/10. **1763:** C. 28/9. **1777:** C. 8/10. **1782:** C. 4/10. **1786:** C. 28/10.

CORNELYS, MRS. MARGARET

‡ C. Deceptions, The; or, Fashion and Folly (C.S. 14/3/1781).

1790: D. 18/6.

COWLEY, MRS. HANNAH

C. Belle's Stratagem, The (C.G. 22/2/1780).

1781: C. 10/10, 15/10, 20/10; B. 7/11, 14/11. **1782:** B. 4/1; C. 5/8, 11/10. **1786:** C. 6/10. **1787:** K. 20/7. **1788:** C. 1/9. **1789:** Wex. 23/2. **1790:** B. 31/12. **1791:** C. 3/6. **1793:** D. 9/1; W. 19/3; K. 3/7; C. 5/9. **1796:** B. 30/4. **1800:** B. 23/4.

C. Bold Stroke for a Husband, A (C.G. 25/2/1783).

1783: C. 18/9. **1784:** C. 1/10. **1792:** C. 26/5.

† C. More Ways than One (C.G. 6/12/1783).

1789: B. 6/2. **1791:** D. 10/6.

C. Runaway, The (D.L. 15/2/1776).

1776: K. 23/8; C. 26/8. **1782:** D. 19/11.

C. Which is the Man? (C.G. 9/2/1782).

1783: C. 4/9, 16/9. **1784:** C. 25/9. **1791:** B. 17/1; D. 15/6; E. 11/11; B. 2/12. **1792:** B. 23/1; W. 20/8; Wex. 19/12. **1793:** C. 6/9.

F. Who's the Dupe? (D.L. 10/4/1779).

1781: C. 14/9. **1782:** K. 5/11. **1783:** D. 29/10. **1798:** L. 6/10.

CROSS, JAMES

M.D. Purse, The; or, The Benevolent Tar (H.[2] 8/2/1794).

1795: B. 27/2. **1796**: D. 13/1; B. 1/6.

CUMBERLAND, RICHARD

T. Battle of Hastings, The (D.L. 24/1/1778).

1778: C. 7/8.

C. Brothers, The (C.G. 2/12/1769).

1770: L. 14/4. **1772**: C. 1/9. **1773**: C. 30/6; L. 14/8. **1774**: D. 21/10. **1776**: K. 19/8. **1777**: C. 15/10. **1781**: K. 24/3. **1789**: B. 18/2. **1790**: D. 7/5, 14/5, 26/5. **1796**: K. 2/11. **1800**: B. 10/2.

T. Carmelite, The (D.L. 2/12/1784).

1785: C. 17/9, 24/9. **1791**: D. 20/5, 14/10.

† C. False Impressions (C.G. 23/11/1797).

1799: D. 24/4.

C. Fashionable Lover, The (D.L. 20/1/1772).

1772: L. 6/7, 19/9. **1773**: C. 2/9; B. 24/9, 29/9, 15/10, 12/11. **1774**: D. 9/8; L. 28/9. **1775**: B. 29/12. **1776**: C. 31/7. **1778**: C. 3/11; B. 20/11. **1781**: B. 30/5. **1787**: C. 12/9. **1793**: G. 9/10. **1795**: B. 9/3. **1796**: D. 25/1. **1800**: B. 6/6.

C. Impostors, The (D.L. 26/1/1789). [An alteration of Farquhar's *The Beaux' Stratagem.*]

1789: B. 27/4.

C. Jew, The; or, The Benevolent Hebrew (D.L. 8/5/1794).

1794: C. 15/10; B. 29/10, 5/11. **1795**: D. 30/9. **1796**: K. 16/9. **1797**: E. 23/3.

T. Mysterious Husband, The (C.G. 28/1/1783).

1788: C. 25/8.

C. Natural Son, The (D.L. 22/12/1784).

1795: K. 14/12.

F. Note of Hand, The; or, A Trip to Newmarket (D.L. 9/2/1774).

1774: C. 8/8; L. 19/8.

C.O. Summer's Tale, The (C.G. 6/12/1765).

1777: C. 12/9.

C. West Indian, The (D.L. 19/1/1771).

1771: Cav. n.d. [Acted in the author's presence]; B. 28/8, 27/11; L. 22/10; W. 4/11. **1772**: L. 7/7; C. 26/8, 6/10. **1773**: C. 23/6; B. 17/12. **1774**: D. 26/8. **1775**: C. 28/9; Lis. 3/11. **1776**: B. 2/2. **1778**: C. 14/7. **1779**: C. 21/9. **1780**: C. 10/8. **1782**: L. 2/8; C. 17/9. **1784**: B. 3/3; C. 29/9. **1785**: C. 2/9. **1787**: C. 15/9; W. 20/10. **1788**: Ath., Cast., and Sl. n.d.;

C. 15/9; B. 1/12, 5/12. **1789:** C. 16/9. **1790:** E. 18/1, 24/9; C. 1/9. **1791:** D. 16/3; C. 4/10. **1792:** B. 1/2; N. 20/7; Wex. 28/9. **1793:** Wex. 11/1; W. 11/2; K. 5/6, 13/6, 16/8. **1794:** C. 14/10. **1795:** K. 2/9; C. 9/9; D. 4/11. **1796:** C. 9/9. **1797:** E. 21/4. **1800:** E. 1/4; B. 14/5.

C. Wheel of Fortune, The (D.L. 28/2/1795).

1795: K. 12/10; D. 9/11. **1796:** B. 4/4; C. 8/4, 12/8, 30/8. **1797:** Dr. 7/4. **1798:** D. 10/1. **1799:** D. 23/1.

DALTON, DR. JOHN

M. Comus. [See John Milton.]

DELAP, JOHN

T. Royal Suppliants, The (D.L. 17/2/1781).

1784: B. 23/6.

DELL, HENRY

C. Frenchified Lady Never in Paris, The (C.G. 23/3/1756). [An alteration of Cibber's *Comical Lovers*.]

1762: C. 28/9.

DENT, JOHN

ENT. Bastille, The (R.C. 19/10/1789).

1790: C. ?/2. **1792:** C. 27/10.

DIBDIN, CHARLES

C.O. Deserter, The (D.L. 2/11/1773).

1774: C. 5/8; L. 22/8. **1776:** B. 25/1; K. 1/7, 3/7, 8/7; C. 7/8. **1778:** C. 7/8, 4/9. **1779:** B. 8/1, 26/2; C. 23/7. **1780:** C. 28/8. **1781:** K. 6/2. **1782:** D. 23/10. **1784:** B. 4/6. **1787:** B. 19/2; C. 31/7. **1788:** C. 8/8. **1789:** Wex. 9/1, 20/3; B. 2/3; K. 15/5, 25/5; C. 28/8, 8/9. **1790:** E. 9/4; D. 5/5; C. 3/9. **1791:** C. 3/5. **1792:** B. 20/2; N. 2/7; C. 12/9; Wex. 16/11. **1793:** Ennc. 8/3.

BURL. Poor Vulcan (C.G. 4/2/1778).

1781: C. 10/10. **1783:** B. 14/3. **1784:** Lis. 1/11; B. 8/12. **1785:** B. 15/6. **1787:** C. 9/8. **1788:** B. 28/11. **1796:** B. 20/4.

C.O. Quaker, The (D.L. 7/10/1777).

1779: C. 30/7, 3/8, 11/8; L. 20/8. **1780:** C. 23/10. **1781:** B. 23/3, 5/12; C. 5/10. **1782:** D. 25/6; L. 26/7. **1784:** D. 9/1. **1785:** C. 2/9. **1786:** L. 3/8; C. 18/8, 21/8. **1789:** Wex. 13/2. **1791:** C. 13/5; B. 25/7. **1792:** N. 4/7; C. 4/9; D. 23/11; Wex. 21/12. **1793:** D. 16/1. **1795:** C. 21/8. **1796:** B. 10/5. **1799:** C. 2/9.

† C.O. Rose and Colin (C.G. 18/9/1778).

1780: C. 28/8.

B.O. Waterman, The; or, The First of August (H.[2] 8/8/1774).

1777: C. 6/8, 13/10; B. 21/11. **1779:** B. 19/2; N. 1/3; C. 21/9. **1780:**

C. 10/10. **1783:** C. 15/8. **1786:** C. 28/8. **1789:** Wex. 26/1, 30/1. **1790:** C. 12/4. **1791:** C. 25/4, 26/5; D. 6/5. **1792:** C. 15/8; G. 22/10; Wex. 5/12. **1796:** B. 6/5.

C.O. Wedding Ring, The (D.L. 1/2/1773).

1774: C. 25/7; L. 23/8.

C.O. Wives Revenged, The (C.G. 18/9/1778).

1781: C. 14/9, 3/10.

DIBDIN, THOMAS JOHN

C. Birth-Day, The (C.G. 8/4/1799). [An alteration of Kotzebue's *Fraternal Enmity*.]

1799: C. 5/9.

C. Five Thousand a Year (C.G. 16/3/1799).

1800: E. 3/3.

F. Jew and the Doctor, The (C.G. 23/11/1798).

1799: C. 3/9. **1800:** B. 30/4.

DOBBS, FRANCIS

‡ T. Patriot King, The; or, The Irish Chief (S.A. 26/4/1773).

1775: Lis. 27/10. **1777:** B. 14/12.

DODSLEY, ROBERT

B.O. Blind Beggar of Bethnal Green, The (D.L. 3/4/1741).

1762: C. 28/10.

T. Cleone (C.G. 2/12/1758).

1761: B. 24/8.

C. King and the Miller of Mansfield, The (D.L. 29/1/1737).

1758: B. 21/4. **1765:** B. 22/11.

C. Miller of Mansfield, The [= *The King and the Miller of Mansfield.*]

1753: B. 29/6. **1756:** Tr. 1/4. **1763:** B. 9/3; C. 27/9. **1766:** C. 2/10. **1767:** K. 23/12. **1768:** B. 23/8. **1770:** B. 20/6. **1771:** B. 13/9. **1774:** B. 11/2; D. 24/8, 26/8. **1775:** B. 22/12.

C. Toy Shop, The (C.G. 3/2/1735).

1787: W. 22/10.

DOWNING, GEORGE

† O.F. Volunteers, The; or, Taylors, to Arms! (C.G. 19/4/1780).

1780: C. 16/10.

DRYDEN, JOHN

T. All for Love; or, The World Well Lost (D.L. Dec. 1677).

1760: C. 13/10. **1762:** C. 25/10. **1765:** C. 30/9. **1774:** C. 25/7. **1782:** C. 6/8.

O. King Arthur; or, The British Worthy (D.G. *c.* May 1691).

1766: C. 10/9. **1779:** C. 11/10. **1786:** C. 9/10, 13/10.

C. Spanish Fryar, The; or, The Double Discovery (D.G. Mar. 1679/80).

1753: B. 29/6, 24/8. **1758:** B. 27/2. **1763:** B. 14/3. **1768:** B. 18/11. **1771:** B. 13/11.

C. Tempest, The; or, The Enchanted Island (L.[1] Nov. 1667). [An alteration of Shakespeare's *The Tempest.*]

1758: B. 24/4. **1768:** K. 18/1. **1770:** K. 24/10. **1773:** C. 17/9. **1774:** L. 22/8. **1780:** C. 20/10. **1784:** B. 25/6. **1793:** D. 16/1, 28/1. **1796:** B. 6/5.

ECCLES, —

*†‡§ O. World, The.

1787: B. 25/4, 27/4.

EYRE, EDMUND JOHN

T. Maid of Normandy, The; or, The Death of the Queen of France (Wolverhampton, 1794).

1794: C. 26/9.

FARQUHAR, GEORGE

C. Beaux' Stratagem, The (H.[1] 8/3/1707).

1736: B. 16/7. **1755:** B. 17/1. **1756:** Tr. 11/3, 17/4, 10/5. **1758:** B. 3/3. **1761:** B. 29/6; C. 30/7. **1763:** C. 25/7. **1766:** C. 4/10, 14/10. **1768:** K. 13/1; C. 6/8. **1769:** B. 20/1. **1770:** C. 25/8; K. 26/9. **1771:** F. 22/3; B. 4/9, 13/12. **1773:** B. 20/10. **1774:** B. 3/1. **1775:** B. 6/12. **1776:** C. 12/7. **1778:** K. 19/1; C. 19/10; B. 28/10. **1779:** B. 19/3, 26/11. **1781:** K. 10/1; C. 13/10. **1783:** C. 6/9. **1784:** C. 28/9. **1786:** C. 12/9. **1787:** K. 14/7; W. 11/10. **1789:** Wex. 23/1, 20/3; K. 22/5. **1790:** E. 30/1. **1791:** K. 4/3. **1792:** K. 18/4; D. 3/11. **1793:** Wex. 21/1. **1794:** L. 20/1. **1798:** D. 20/4. **1800:** B. 1/5, 26/5.

C. Constant Couple, The; or, A Trip to the Jubilee (D.L. Nov. 1699).

1754: B. 25/11. **1756:** Tr. 28/4. **1758:** B. 24/5. **1766:** B. 27/1. **1767:** K. 26/12. **1769:** N. 5/4. **1770:** B. 15/8; K. 15/10. **1771:** B. 15/11. **1772:** B. 24/1. **1773:** C. 2/7, 14/9; L. 20/8; B. 24/11. **1774:** D. 8/8. **1776:** B. 13/1; D. 6/11. **1780:** C. 6/10. **1786:** B. 17/11. **1787:** W. 16/10.

C. Inconstant, The; or, The Way to Win Him (D.L. Feb. 1701/2).

1758: B. 6/2. **1766:** B. 10/3. **1768:** K. 12/2. **1769:** N. 23/1. **1770:** K. 31/12. **1771:** B. 4/12. **1773:** K. 5/6; B. 6/10. **1778:** C. 2/11. **1780:** C. 2/8. **1784:** D. 16/2. **1789:** B. 2/3. **1790:** D. 12/5. **1794:** C. 20/8. **1796:** E. 27/4, 22/6. **1797:** C. 3/10.

C. Love and a Bottle (D.L. *c.* Dec. 1698).

1758: C. 14/8, 27/9.

c. Recruiting Officer, The (D.L. 8/4/1706).

1754: B. 6/12. **1756:** Tr. 1/4. **1758:** B. 10/2. **1759:** C. 5/10. **1763:** C. 18/8. **1765:** B. 13/11. **1767:** K. 23/12. **1768:** C. 16/9. **1774:** C. 22/7. **1775:** C. 16/9; B. 15/12. **1776:** D. 16/10. **1778:** C. 26/10. **1780:** C. 10/10. **1785:** B. 13/7. **1789:** C. 22/9. **1791:** E. 3/10. **1792:** C. ?/8, 11/9. **1795:** C. 14/9.

c. Sir Harry Wildair: Being the Sequel of the Trip to the Jubilee (D.L. *c.* Apr. 1701).

1753: B. 2/8.

F. Stage Coach, The (L.[1] *c.* Jan. 1703/4).

1756: Tr. 15/3, 19/4.

c. Twin-Rivals, The (D.L. 14/12/1702).

1753: B. 9/8. **1761:** B. 24/7. **1773:** K. 12/4. **1774:** C. 15/9. **1780:** C. 11/10. **1781:** B. 21/11.

FIELDING, HENRY

c. Don Quixote in England (H.[2] 5/4/1734).

1795: K. 9/11.

F. Intriguing Chambermaid, The (D.L. 15/1/1734).

1755: B. 7/2; Lis. 1/3. **1756:** Tr. 12/4. **1758:** B. 21/2. **1768:** K. 27/1. **1770:** B. 28/7; K. 26/9. **1775:** C. 1/9. **1777:** C. 25/7. **1779:** C. 28/7. **1782:** C. 4/10, 11/10. **1790:** C. 15/9. **1791:** B. 10/10.

B.O. Lottery, The (D.L. 1/1/1732).

1755: B. 17/1. **1758:** B. 15/3. **1768:** C. 5/8. **1770:** B. 16/7. **1774:** L. 15/8. **1776:** B. 19/1. **1778:** B. 1/4. **1781:** B. 21/11.

c. Miser, The (D.L. 17/2/1733).

1753: B. 22/8. **1763:** B. 23/2. **1770:** B. 18/7; K. 30/11. **1771:** B. 13/9, 20/12. **1773:** B. 22/9. **1774:** B. 11/2. **1776:** B. 10/4; K. 21/8. **1777:** C. 19/7, 13/10. **1778:** B. 30/10. **1780:** C. 24/10. **1785:** C. 20/9. **1786:** C. 18/8, 3/11. **1789:** Wex. 20/2; C. 29/9. **1791:** B. 5/1, 2/2; D. 15/6. **1792:** Wex. 7/12. **1793:** K. 23/7. **1796:** K. 27/7.

B.O. Mock Doctor, The; or, The Dumb Lady Cur'd (D.L. 23/6/1732).

1755: B. 5/2. **1756:** Tr. 17/3, 16/4. **1758:** B. 10/2, 3/3. **1765:** C. 13/9; B. 30/10. **1768:** B. 23/12. **1770:** B. 30/4; C. 24/8. **1771:** B. 11/9. **1773:** B. 6/9. **1774:** C. 24/6. **1775:** Lis. 29/9, 27/10. **1776:** K. 21/8. **1780:** B. 8/1. **1781:** B. 30/5. **1788:** L. 14/7. **1789:** L. 9/10. **1791:** C. 26/5.

B. Tom Thumb the Great (H.[2] 25/4/1730).

1753: B. 4/6, 6/6. **1756:** Tr. 10/4, 26/4; C. 22/9. **1758:** C. 22/9. **1770:** B. 1/8.

B.O. Virgin Unmask'd, The (D.L. 6/1/1735). [= *An Old Man Taught Wisdom; or, The Virgin Unmask'd.*]

1751: B. 18/12. **1753:** B. 24/8. **1754:** B. 27/11, 6/12. **1756:** Tr. 3/4.

1758: B. 6/2, 12/6. **1759:** C. 24/8. **1761:** B. 26/8. **1763:** B. 14/1, 26/1. **1765:** C. 1/10; B. 23/10, 20/12. **1766:** B. 10/1, 19/2; C. 3/10, 11/10. **1768:** C. 12/8. **1770:** C. 25/8; K. 13/12. **1772:** B. 23/1. **1775:** Lis. 4/10; B. 29/12. **1778:** B. 4/12. **1779:** C. 10/5, 21/5. **1780:** C. 26/7, 28/7. **1792:** Wex. 5/12. **1793:** W. 21/3; Wex. 1/5; G. 12/7. **1795:** C. 4/9; G. 22/9. **1796:** B. 18/3.

FOOTE, SAMUEL

C. Author, The (D.L. 5/2/1757).

1758: B. 12/5; C. 8/8, 11/9. **1763:** C. 28/9. **1776:** K. 5/8. **1777:** C. 17/10. **1778:** C. 24/10. **1791:** B. 10/8.

INT. Devil upon Two Sticks, The (H.[2] 30/5/1768).

1777: C. 10/9. **1786:** C. 1/9. **1790:** D. 21/5. **1793:** D. 1/2.

*‡§ INT. Disappointment, The; or, An Old Woman with a Colt's Tooth (S.A. 6/5/1771).

1768: K. 1/2. **1770:** B. 16/7, 28/7. **1772:** L. 12/8.

ENT. Diversions of the Morning, A Dish of Foote's Tea; or, The Player's Looking Glass (H.[2] 22/4/1747).

1756: Tr. 28/4. **1758:** C. 6/9. **1765:** Dr. 26/8.

*† F. Doctor Last's Examination (H.[2] 14/8/1787). [Fr. Foote's *The Devil upon Two Sticks.*]

1778: C. 13/10.

C. Englishman in Paris, The (C.G. 24/3/1753).

1758: C. 18/8. **1760:** C. 25/7.

§ INT. Lady Pentweazel of Blow-Bladder St. (D.L. 1758/9). [An alteration of Foote's *Taste,* Act I.]

1762: C. 15/10. **1770:** K. 26/11, 3/12. **1778:** B. 24/4. **1779:** N. 1/3. **1792:** Wex. 21/11, 30/11.

C. Lyar, The (C.G. 12/1/1762).

1771: L. 22/10. **1772:** C. 16/10. **1773:** C. 5/7; L. 10/8. **1774:** L. 11/8. **1782:** C. 7/8, 10/9. **1783:** C. 4/9. **1786:** C. 16/9. **1787:** K. 16/8; W. 12/10. **1792:** B. 15/2; K. 23/2; W. 17/8; C. 31/8; Wex. 24/9. **1796:** B. 27/4.

C. Mayor of Garret, The (H.[2] 20/6/1763).

1765: C. 21/9, 30/9. **1766:** B. 21/2; C. 4/10. **1768:** K. 2/3. **1770:** B. 26/7. **1771:** B. 27/11. **1772:** L. 6/7. **1773:** C. 11/6. **1775:** C. 3/7, 21/7, 12/9. **1776:** B. 3/4. **1777:** C. 23/7. **1778:** C. 14/7. **1779:** N. 15/3; B. 19/11. **1787:** K. 13/3, 19/3. **1792:** D. 17/12. **1793:** Wex. 25/1. **1800:** B. 21/4.

C. Minor, The (C.S. 28/1/1760; H.[2] 28/6/1760).

1762: C. 27/10. **1768:** K. 10/2.

C. Nabob, The (H.[2] 29/6/1772).

1773: C. 19/8.

C. Orators, The (H.[2] 30/8/1762).

1770: B. 15/8.

INT. Piety in Pattens (H.[2] 15/2/1773).

1774: C. 25/7; L. 22/11.

† F. Tailors, The (H.[2] 2/7/1767). [Nicoll, iii. 345, lists as anonymous.]

1778: C. 19/10. **1786:** C. 30/10.

F. Taste (D.L. 11/1/1752).

1760: C. 29/9. **1768:** K. 8/2. **1771:** L. 27/9. **1783:** C. 5/9. **1790:** E. 2/10.

INT. Trial of the Cock Lane Ghost [Fr. Foote's *The Orators.*]

1762: C. 27/10.

FORDE, BROWNLOW

*‡§ F. Intriguing Footman, The; or, The Humours of Humbug (C.S. 10/2/1776).

1769: K. 14/8. **1771:** B. 25/10. **1773:** K. 28/1. **1774:** D. 31/8. **1775:** B. 24/11. **1776:** B. 18/3; C. 11/10. **1782:** B. 25/1.

*‡ F. Miraculous Cure, The; or, The Citizen Outwitted (S.A. 22/1/1781). [An alteration of C. Cibber's *Double Gallant.*]

1771: B. 9/10, 11/10. **1782:** C. 22/10.

FRANCKLIN, THOMAS

T. Earl of Warwick (D.L. 13/12/1766).

1768: K. 7/3; C. ?/8. **1771:** B. 7/8. **1782:** C. 31/7.

T. Matilda (D.L. 21/1/1775).

1778: C. 24/8.

FRANKLIN, ANDREW

‡ M. INT. Hypochondriac, The (S.A. 4/1/1785).

1786: C. 27/10.

GARRICK, DAVID

F. Bon Ton; or, High Life Above Stairs (D.L. 18/3/1775).

1776: B. 28/2, 22/3; C. 24/7, 2/8, 14/8. **1777:** C. 6/8, 4/10. **1778:** B. 28/10. **1779:** C. 13/10. **1782:** C. 29/7. **1790:** E. 1/10. **1791:** K. 15/1; D. 16/3, 6/7; B. 3/8, 16/9. **1792:** W. 7/9; Wex. 22/9.

F. Catherine and Petruchio (D.L. 21/1/1756).

1758: B. 7/4, 3/5; C. 23/8, 13/9. **1761:** B. 24/8. **1762:** C. 24/9. **1765:** Dr. 26/8. **1768:** B. 25/11. **1772:** C. 23/10. **1773:** C. 18/6; B. 15/12. **1774:** C. 22/7. **1776:** B. 13/1. **1778:** B. 4/11. **1779:** C. 26/7. **1780:** B. 3/3. **1782:** C. 16/8, 9/10. **1783:** K. 15/2. **1785:** C. 8/9. **1786:** L. 31/7; C. 15/8. **1787:** C. 2/8. **1788:** L. 19/7; C. 30/8; B. 1/12, 3/12, 8/12, 15/12. **1789:** C. 28/1,

18/12. **1790:** C. 11/9. **1791:** C. 11/8. **1792:** W. 22/8; D. 28/11. **1795:** C. 3/9. **1796:** B. 16/3; C. 26/8, 10/9. **1797:** C. 21/8. **1800:** B. 27/1.

C. Chances, The (D.L. 7/11/1754).

1759: C. 31/8. **1765:** C. 11/9. **1766:** C. 17/9. **1779:** C. 16/7; L. 20/8. **1782:** C. 8/8. **1784:** C. 24/9. **1786:** C. 4/9. **1787:** C. 19/9.

ENT. Christmas Tale, A (D.L. 27/12/1773).

1777: C. 9/9.

C. Clandestine Marriage, The. [See George Colman, *the Elder.*]

C. Country Girl, The (D.L. 25/10/1766). [An alteration of Wycherley's *The Country Wife.*]

1792: G. 16/8. **1795:** B. 27/2. **1798:** C. 30/10.

O. Cymon (D.L. 2/1/1767).

1771: C. 6/9; L. 27/9; B. 23/10; W. 28/10. **1772:** L. 5/8; C. 26/8, 13/10. **1774:** L. 28/9. **1776:** C. 12/10. **1777:** C. 6/8. **1778:** C. 5/8. **1779:** B. 24/3; C. 16/7, 15/9; K. 10/12. **1780:** B. 1/3. **1792:** W. 21/12. **1793:** B. 13/5.

C. Every Man in His Humour (D.L. 29/11/1751).

1770: K. 3/12.

INT. Farmer's Return from London, The (D.L. 20/3/1762).

1770: K. 5/12.

C. Gamesters, The (D.L. 22/12/1757). [An alteration of Shirley's *The Gamester.*]

1779: C. 15/9. **1784:** C. 23/9. **1786:** C. 24/10.

F. Guardian, The (D.L. 3/2/1759).

1760: C. 15/10. **1768:** K. 9/3. **1769:** K. 30/10. **1771:** B. 20/9, 2/10, 4/12. **1774:** B. 18/2; D. 10/8; L. 27/9. **1775:** C. 20/9; B. 22/11. **1777:** C. 8/9. **1778:** B. 14/1, 28/1, 23/10. **1779:** B. 1/1. **1781:** C. 10/9.

P. Harlequin's Invasion (D.L. 31/12/1759).

1772: C. 3/9. **1792:** C. 26/5. **1796:** B. 4/5.

F. High Life Below Stairs. [See J. Townley.]

C. Irish Widow, The (D.L. 23/10/1772).

1773: C. 2/7, 23/7, 31/8, 7/9, 21/9; L. 14/8; B. 22/9, 24/9. **1774:** B. 5/1; C. 23/7. **1775:** Lis. 15/9. **1777:** B. 24/10, 19/11. **1779:** C. 24/9. **1781:** C. 19/10. **1783:** C. 19/9. **1786:** C. 7/8, 28/10. **1789:** Wex. 2/1. **1790:** E. 5/4, 2/10. **1792:** K. 12/7; Wex. 26/9. **1799:** D. 6/5.

T. Isabella; or, The Fatal Marriage (D.L. 2/12/1757). [An alteration of Southerne's *The Fatal Marriage.*]

1766: C. 11/10. **1773:** C. 19/7. **1774:** B. 5/1, 18/2. **1776:** B. 8/3. **1783:** C. 11/8. **1784:** B. 8/12. **1785:** B. 17/6, 24/6. **1787:** W. 9/11. **1788:** C.

29/8. **1790:** B. 20/12. **1791:** D. 2/5. **1795:** B. 8/5. **1796:** D. 4/1; B. 2/5. **1797:** C. 3/10.

INT. Jubilee, The (D.L. 14/10/1769).

1780: B. 27/3. **1789:** B. 28/1. **1791:** D. 20/5; C. 26/9. **1792:** C. 10/9. **1793:** D. 25/1. **1795:** B. 16/3. **1797:** C. 3/10.

M. King Arthur (D.L. 13/12/1770). [An alteration of Dryden's *King Arthur; or, The British Worthy.*]

1780: C. 29/9, 16/10.

INT. Linco's Travels (D.L. 6/3/1767).

1768: C. 15/8. **1769:** C. 9/2; K. 14/8, 17/8. **1770:** B. 15/6, 18/7; K. 17/9. **1771:** L. 22/10; W. 28/10. **1772:** C. 26/9, 2/10. **1773:** K. 20/2. **1774:** B. 28/1. **1776:** B. 28/1; C. 2/8, 4/10. **1777:** C. 20/8. **1778:** C. 19/10. **1782:** L. 17/7.

C. Lying Valet, The (C.G. 30/11/1741).

1753: B. 8/6, 22/8. **1754:** B. 13/12. **1755:** Lis. 19/2. **1756:** Tr. 30/3; C. 24/9. **1758:** B. 5/5, 12/5, 26/5; C. 27/9. **1759:** C. 17/8. **1761:** B. 3/7; C. 6/7. **1763:** B. 23/2. **1768:** B. 14/9; Carf. 21/10. **1770:** B. 25/7. **1771:** B. 25/9. **1773:** L. 20/8. **1775:** C. 12/7; Lis. 29/11; B. 1/12. **1776:** B. 10/4; K. 15/7, 24/8. **1777:** B. 7/11. **1778:** C. 5/8, 4/11. **1779:** K. 17/11. **1781:** C. 20/8. **1785:** C. 23/8. **1789:** K. 8/6. **1791:** B. 27/7; E. 30/9. **1792:** N. 18/6; W. 24/7. **1793:** W. 13/3, 23/3. **1794:** C. 20/8. **1798:** C. 25/9. **1800:** B. 10/2, 26/5.

O.F. May-Day; or, The Little Gypsy (D.L. 28/10/1775).

1777: C. 7/10.

F. Miss in Her Teens; or, The Medley of Lovers (C.G. 17/1/1747).

1753: B. 23/7, 7/9. **1754:** B. 25/11, 29/11. **1755:** B. 24/1; Lis. 22/2; B. 7/3. **1756:** Tr. 4/4; C. 17/9. **1758:** B. 8/3; C. 25/9. **1760:** C. 10/10. **1762:** C. 29/10. **1763:** B. 15/2. **1765:** C. 16/9, 19/9; B. 9/10, 27/12. **1767:** K. 7/12. **1768:** Carf. 19/10. **1769:** K. 31/7. **1770:** B. 18/5; K. 7/11. **1775:** Lis. 20/9. **1786:** C. 10/10. **1791:** D. 17/6. **1793:** K. 19/6; G. 17/7, 22/7. **1795:** K. 23/9.

B. Peep Behind the Curtain, A; or, The New Rehearsal (D.L. 23/10/1767).

1774: C. 1/8. **1790:** C. 27/8. **1792:** B. 29/2, 9/3.

T. Romeo and Juliet. [See Shakespeare.]

GARRICK, MRS. DAVID

F. Lethe; or, Aesop in the Shades (D.L. 15/4/1740).

1753: B. 13/7. **1754:** B. 17/12. **1755:** B. 10/1. **1756:** Tr. 23/3. **1758:** B. 14/4. **1761:** B. 5/8. **1767:** K. 21/12. **1770:** K. 2/10. **1777:** C. 13/8. **1778:** C. 31/10. **1779:** C. 13/8. **1780:** C. 11/8. **1783:** C. 8/1, 31/3, 27/8. **1785:** C. 6/7, 22/9. **1788:** C. 30/8.

GAY, JOHN

B.O. Beggar's Opera, The (L.[2] 29/1/1728).

1728: Dr. 13/6. **1754:** B. 29/11. **1755:** Lis. 26/2. **1756:** Tr. 16/4; C. 24/9. **1758:** B. 8/3, 27/3; C. 6/10. **1760:** C. 25/7. **1761:** B. 9/7. **1763:** B. 28/1, 15/2. **1765:** C. 17/8, 21/10; B. 15/11. **1767:** K. ?/12. **1768:** C. 6/8, 13/8, 17/9; B. 23/8. **1769:** K. 5/6, 12/8; C. 31/7. **1770:** B. 1/6, 6/7; K. 29/10. **1771:** B. 20/11. **1772:** L. 27/7. **1773:** K. 28/1. **1775:** Lis. 29/9. **1776:** C. 10/7, 30/8, 8/10, 15/10; K. 2/8. **1777:** C. 16/7, 10/10. **1778:** K. 17/1, 24/2; C. 17/7; B. 4/12. **1779:** B. 24/2; D. 18/8; K. 27/9. **1780:** C. 29/7, 18/8. **1782:** L. 31/8; Dr. 9/10. **1783:** L. 15/3; C. 9/8, 12/8. **1786:** C. 17/7, 1/9; W. 18/7. **1787:** C. 3/8. **1788:** L. 26/7; B. 12/11. **1789:** Wex. 2/1; B. 18/3; K. 8/6; C. 28/8. **1792:** N. 8/6; K. 20/6; W. 27/7; C. 12/9; Wex. 19/10. **1793:** D. 18/1; L. 29/7; G. 7/10. **1795:** C. 20/8; K. 5/10. **1796:** B. 8/6; K. 22/10. **1797:** C. 13/10.

BURL. What D'Ye Call It, The (D.L. 23/2/1715).

1753: B. 27/7. **1755:** B. 28/2. **1756:** Tr. 28/4. **1763:** C. 24/9. **1770:** B. 20/7; K. 3/12. **1786:** C. 23/10.

GENTLEMAN, FRANCIS

‡ O. Orpheus and Euridice (S.A. 5/1/1784).

1791: C. 25/8, 26/9.

C. Tobacconist, The (Edinburgh, *c.* 1760; H.[2] 22/7/1771). [An alteration of Ben Jonson's *The Alchemist.*]

1772: L. 15/7. **1775:** C. 28/9 [called *The Alchymist; or, The Fighting Tobacconist*]. **1785:** C. 27/9, 30/9 [called *Abel Drugger*]. **1792:** C. 29/5; Wex. 10/10.

GOLDSMITH, OLIVER

C. Good Natur'd Man, The (C.G. 29/1/1768).

1773: C. 6/7. **1776:** K. 19/8. **1777:** B. 7/11. **1784:** C. 30/9.

C. She Stoops to Conquer; or, The Mistakes of a Night (C.G. 15/3/1773).

1773: C. 29/6, 7/9; L. 14/8, 16/8; B. 17/9, 29/12. **1776:** B. 17/1; K. 26/6, 24/8; Lis. 30/10. **1777:** C. 9/9. **1778:** C. 27/10; B. 13/11. **1779:** C. 7/6, 7/7, Ant. 1/10; K. 5/11. **1780:** C. 17/10; K. 25/11. **1784:** C. 27/9. **1785:** C. 30/9; L. 7/11. **1786:** C. 5/9, 4/11. **1789:** B. 16/1; K. 20/5. **1791:** L. ?/1; C. 15/6. **1792:** Wex. 21/11. **1793:** W. 23/3. **1794:** C. 6/9. **1797:** E. 30/5; C. 19/6, 28/6.

GRIFFITH, MRS. ELIZABETH

C. School for Rakes, The (D.L. 4/2/1769).

1769: C. 20/9. **1771:** B. 27/9. **1777:** C. 3/10.

HARTSON, HALL

T. Countess of Salisbury, The (C.S. 2/5/1765; H.[2] 31/8/1767).

1765: C. 13/9, 25/9. **1766:** C. 24/9. **1770:** B. 9/5; 10/10. **1774:** D. 2/12.

1775: Lis. 27/9. **1776:** B. 23/2. **1778:** C. 24/7. **1783:** C. 30/8. **1786:** C. 1/8. **1791:** B. 7/2; D. 3/6, 8/6.

HAVARD, WILLIAM

T. King Charles the First (L.[2] 1/3/1737).

1782: C. 7/10.

HAWKESWORTH, JOHN

C. Amphitryon; or, The Two Sosias (D.L. 15/12/1756). [An alteration of Dryden's *Amphitryon.*]

1772: C. 10/9.

ENT. Edgar and Emmeline (D.L. 31/1/1761).

1779: C. 4/10.

HILL, AARON

T. Alzira (L.[2] 18/6/1736).

1763: C. 21/9, 29/9.

T. King Henry V; or, The Conquest of France, By the English (D.L. 5/12/1723).

1758: B. 3/4. **1760:** C. 10/10. **1771:** B. 6/9.

T. Meropé (D.L. 15/4/1749).

1766: C. 22/10.

T. Tragedy of Zara, The (D.L. 12/1/1736).

1766: C. 21/10. **1777:** C. 14/7. **1782:** C. 7/8.

HIPPISLEY, JOHN

B.O. Flora; or, Hob in the Well (L.[2] 18/4/1729).

1750: B. 3/1. **1753:** B. 19/7. **1756:** Tr. 28/4. **1761:** B. 29/7, 28/8. **1763:** C. 14/9, 16/9. **1765:** C. 27/9. **1768:** K. 25/1. **1770:** K. 8/10. **1774:** C. 3/8. **1780:** C. 21/8, 6/10. **1782:** D. 27/11, 4/12. **1783:** C. 26/8. **1790:** E. 3/2, 3/5; D. 19/5. **1791:** B. 28/1; K. 31/1. **1792:** B. 30/1; Wex. 31/12. **1793:** G. 9/7; L. 29/7. **1796:** E. 1/6.

HITCHCOCK, ROBERT

C. Macaroni, The (York, Feb. 1773).

1774: C. 14/9.

HOADLY, DR. BENJAMIN

C. Suspicious Husband, The (C.G. 12/2/1747).

1753: B. 8/6; C. 23/6. **1755:** B. 24/1; Lis. 1/3. **1758:** B. 17/3, 31/3; C. 28/9. **1760:** C. 18/9. **1761:** C. 26/9. **1765:** B. 30/10. **1766:** C. 22/9. **1767:** K. 14/12. **1768:** B. 10/10, 14/10. **1769:** K. 12/7. **1770:** B. 30/4; K. 19/9. **1771:** L. 24/9. **1772:** C. 30/9. **1773:** C. 28/8; B. 22/10. **1776:** C. 7/8. **1778:** C. 14/10. **1779:** C. 29/9. **1781:** K. 6/2; C. 28/8. **1784:** K. 3/4; C. 14/9. **1786:** C. 1/11. **1787:** C. 9/8; W. 10/10. **1790:** C. 30/8.

1791: D. 23/5, 1/6; B. 10/8. **1792:** B. 28/3; C. 29/8; Wex. 24/9. **1793:** K. 7/6; G. 25/10.

HOADLY, JOHN

T. Mahomet, The Impostor. [See Rev. James Miller.]

HOARE, PRINCE

O.F. Lock and Key (C.G. 2/2/1796).

1799: L. 22/7.

O.F. My Grandmother (H.[2] 16/12/1793).

1796: C. 8/4. **1800:** B. 1/5, 14/5.

O.F. No Song, No Supper; or, The Shipwreck (D.L. 16/4/1790).

1791: C. 26/9, 3/10. **1792:** W. 19/3; Wex. 31/12. **1793:** D. 4/1; B. 8/5, 15/5, 29/5; G. 7/10. **1795:** D. 9/12. **1796:** B. 23/5. **1797:** L. 4/9; C. 5/10. **1798:** D. 20/4. **1800:** B. 6/5.

O.F. Prize, The; or, 2, 5, 3, 8 (H.[1] 11/3/1793).

1794: C. 30/9. **1795:** D. 12/10. **1800:** B. 28/4.

HOLCROFT, THOMAS

C. Deserted Daughter, The; or, The Child of Providence (C.G. 1795).

1795: C. 10/9; K. 14/10. **1797:** E. 24/3, 19/4, 26/4.

C. Duplicity (C.G. 13/10/1781).

1790: D. 19/5.

C. Follies of a Day, The; or, The Marriage of Figaro (C.G. 14/12/1784).

1785: B. 28/3; C. 19/9. **1786:** C. 9/9. **1790:** C. 24/8, 9/9. **1793:** D. 11/2. **1794:** C. 4/9.

† C. He 's Much to Blame (C.G. 13/2/1798).

1798: C. 26/9.

C. Road to Ruin, The (C.G. 18/2/1792).

1792: N. 4/7; W. 4/8, 9/8; C. 27/8; Wex. 2/10; D. 7/12, 14/12. **1793:** Wex. 18/1; W. 22/2; G. 2/8. **1794:** B. 19/12. **1796:** D. 20/1; B. 20/4, 21/7; E. 25/5. **1797:** C. 21/8.

C. School for Arrogance, The (C.G. 4/2/1791).

1791: B. 2/11. **1792:** W. 10/8; Wex. 22/11; D. 3/12. **1793:** D. 21/1.

HOLMAN, JOSEPH GEORGE

C.O. Abroad and at Home (C.G. 19/11/1796).

1797: C. 10/10.

HOME, DR. JOHN

† T. Agis (D.L. 21/2/1758).

1758: B. 14/4.

T. Douglas (C.G. 14/3/1757).

1758: B. 21/2, 10/3, 12/4, 2/6. **1759:** C. 17/8. **1760:** C. 9/10. **1761:** B. 22/7, 31/7; C. 2/10. **1763:** B. 19/1; C. 26/8. **1765:** B. 6/11, 9/12. **1768:** K. 4/3; Carf. 17/10; B. 30/12. **1769:** C. 4/8. **1770:** B. 10/8; C. 27/8. **1771:** W. 29/10. **1772:** C. 28/8, 22/10. **1773:** B. 6/9. **1776:** C. 16/10. **1779:** L. 27/8. **1780:** K. 11/10; C. 14/10. **1781:** C. 3/10. **1783:** K. 13/2; G. 8/8. **1784:** C. 4/9. **1786:** C. 7/8. **1789:** Wex. 19/1; K. 24/6. **1790:** E. 25/3; D. 17/5; B. 19/11. **1791:** D. 21/2. **1796:** B. 10/3. **1797:** C. 21/9, 30/9. **1799:** L. 2/8; Car. ?/12. **1800:** B. 16/5.

HOOLE, JOHN

T. Cyrus (C.G. 3/12/1768).

1773: C. 14/7.

HOWARD, SIR ROBERT

C. Committee, The; or, The Faithful Irishman (T.R. in Vere St. *c.* Nov. 1662).

1737: W. ?/6. **1756:** Tr. 17/3. **1778:** C. 4/9. **1780:** C. 26/7, 28/7.

HUGHES, JOHN

T. Siege of Damascus, The (D.L. 17/2/1720).

1762: C. 2/11. **1770:** B. 16/5. **1790:** Car. ?/4.

HULL, THOMAS

T. Edward and Eleonora (C.G. 18/3/1775). [An alteration of James Thomson's *Edward and Eleonora.*]

1777: C. 8/9.

T. Henry II; or, The Fall of Rosamund (C.G. 1/5/1773).

1775: Lis. 13/9.

† C. Perplexities, The (C.G. 31/1/1767).

1773: K. 18/2.

INCHBALD, MRS. ELIZABETH

F. Animal Magnetism (C.G. 29/4/1788).

1789: K. 18/5, 20/5, 25/5; C. 1/9, 18/9, 25/10; W. 3/10.

D. Child of Nature, The (C.G. 28/11/1788).

1789: C. 4/9. **1790:** C. 10/9. **1797:** E. 25/3.

C. Every One has His Fault (C.G. 29/1/1793).

1793: B. 10/5; C. 21/8; G. 11/10. **1794:** C. 10/10, 17/10. **1795:** D. 12/10. **1798:** D. 9/5. **1799:** K. 29/5.

C. I'll Tell You What (H.[2] 4/8/1785).

1786: C. 14/9; L. 18/9.

D. Lover's Vows (C.G. 11/10/1798).

1799: K. 15/7, 31/7; L. 22/7; C. 31/8. **1800:** B. 13/1; E. 3/2.

F. Midnight Hour, The; or, War of Wits (C.G. 22/5/1787).

1787: C. 6/9, 22/9. **1788:** C. 27/8. **1789:** B. 2/2; C. 7/9. **1791:** D. 25/5. **1792:** B. 27/2; C. 29/5; G. 28/9; D. 5/12. **1793:** Wex. 4/1; D. 6/2; G. 4/9. **1800:** B. 23/4.

F. Next Door Neighbours; or, The World As It Goes (H.[2] 9/7/1791).

1792: B. 30/3; Wex. 19/11.

C. Such Things Are (C.G. 10/2/1787).

1787: C. 7/8, 30/8. **1789:** Wex. 26/1; B. 27/2. **1790:** L. ?/12. **1791:** C. ?/5. **1792:** C. 29/5, 14/9. **1793:** D. 4/1; B. 31/5; C. 3/9. **1795:** B. 25/3.

† F. Widow's Vow, The (H.[2] 20/6/1786).

1790: D. 12/5.

C. Wives as they Were and Maids as they Are (C.G. 4/3/1797).

1797: L. 4/9. **1798:** C. 19/8.

JACKMAN, ISAAC

F. All the World's a Stage (D.L. 7/4/1777).

1777: C. 12/9. **1778:** C. 2/9; B. 13/11. **1779:** C. 21/7. **1780:** B. 24/1; C. 17/8. **1782:** C. 24/9; K. 21/12. **1783:** G. 8/8; C. 25/9; L. 11/10. **1788:** C. 5/9. **1789:** Wex. 4/2; K. 3/6. **1792:** B. 8/2; D. 2/11, 22/11. **1793:** Wex. 11/1; G. 2/8. **1794:** B. 13/10. **1795:** K. 2/9. **1796:** B. 10/6.

O.F. Divorce, The; or, Fashionable Folly (D.L. 10/11/1781).

1785: L. 16/8. **1788:** Wex. 26/12. **1789:** Wex. 9/2; K. 24/4. **1790:** E. 30/1, 2/8. **1791:** E. 14/10. **1792:** Wex. 19/12 [subtitled *The Fortunate Irishman*]. **1794:** C. 25/8. **1797:** C. 4/8.

JACKSON, JOHN

*†‡§ F. Tony Lumpkin's Rambles thro' Cork in 1796.

1796: C. 10/9.

JEPHSON, ROBERT

T. Count of Narbonne, The (C.G. 17/11/1781).

1782: C. 12/8, 19/8. **1784:** K. 17/2. **1785:** C. 30/8. **1792:** W. 30/1. **1796:** C. 26/8.

‡ F. Hotel, The; or, The Servant with Two Masters (S.A. 8/5/1783). [An alteration of Vaughan's *The Hotel; or, The Double Valet.*]

1783: C. 12/8. **1787:** C. 7/8, 15/9. **1788:** C. 9/9. **1794:** B. 24/10, 5/11. **1798:** C. 18/9, 30/10.

F. Two Strings to Your Bow (C.G. 16/2/1791).

1797: E. 17/4. **1800:** E. 1/4.

JOHNSON, CHARLES

C. Country Lasses, The; or, The Custom of the Manor (D.L. 4/2/1715).

1755: B. 10/1. **1759**: Ba. 25/9. **1772**: C. 21/10.

JONES, HENRY

T. Earl of Essex, The (C.G. 21/2/1753).

1753: B. 27/7. **1762**: C. 18/10. **1769**: C. 18/9. **1772**: L. 18/9; C. 2/10. **1774**: L. 23/8. **1775**: C. 19/7, 12/9. **1776**: C. 7/10. **1782**: C. 2/10, 12/10; K. 5/11. **1790**: B. 12/11. **1791**: B. 19/10. **1792**: W. 7/9; Wex. 12/10. **1793**: C. 16/8.

KELLY, HUGH

T. Clementina (C.G. 23/2/1771).

1773: B. 19/11. **1774**: B. 7/7. **1775**: Lis. 18/9. **1780**: C. 2/10.

C. False Delicacy (D.L. 23/1/1768).

1768: C. 15/8; B. 31/10. **1771**: B. 6/12.

C. Romance of an Hour, The (C.G. 2/12/1774).

1775: C. 31/7. **1776**: K. 24/6, 17/7. **1787**: W. 22/10.

C. School for Wives, The (D.L. 11/12/1773).

1774: L. 15/8. **1776**: B. 27/3. **1786**: C. 5/10. **1790**: E. 3/5. **1791**: B. 14/1; D. 18/5. **1793**: D. 14/1. **1795**: B. 23/2; K. 30/9; D. 9/12.

C. Word to the Wise, A; or, All for the Best (D.L. 3/3/1770).

1779: B. 1/1, 8/1. **1781**: B. 23/3. **1783**: B. 21/4.

KEMBLE, JOHN PHILIP

F. Farmhouse, The; or, The Female Duellist (D.L. 1/5/1789).

1791: B. 5/1.

T. King Henry V; or, The Conquest of France (D.L. 1/10/1789). [An alteration of Shakespeare's *Henry V*.]

1791: C. 20/9.

† F. Pannel, The (D.L. 28/11/1788).

1791: B. 17/1, 7/2; D. 4/5.

T.C. Tempest, The; or, The Enchanted Island . . . with Additions from Dryden (D.L. 13/10/1789). [An alteration of Shakespeare's *The Tempest*.]

1800: B. 31/1.

KING, THOMAS

F. Wit's Last Stake (D.L. 14/4/1768).

1769: C. 4/8. **1771**: B. 18/12. **1773**: K. 5/6. **1779**: C. 11/10.

KNIPE, R. W.

*†‡§ F. Wexford Wife, The; or, The True-Born Irishwoman.

1764: Wex. 12/6.

LANGFORD, ABRAHAM

B.O. Lover his own Rival, The (G.F. Feb. 1735/6).

1760: C. 26/9.

LEE, HARRIET

C. New Peerage, The; or, Our Eyes may deceive us (D.L. 10/11/1787).

1788: C. 5/9.

LEE, JOHN

F. Country Wife, The (D.L. 26/4/1765). [An alteration of Wycherley's *The Country Wife*.]

1766: C. 11/9.

F. Man of Quality, The (C.G. 27/4/1773). [An alteration of Vanbrugh's *The Relapse*.]

1778: B. 10/4. **1796:** B. 25/5.

LEE, NATHANIEL

T. Rival Queens, The; or, The Death of Alexander the Great (D.L. 17/3/1677).

1760: C. 15/9. **1762:** C. 24/9. **1768:** K. 18/2; B. 23/11. **1770:** B. 15/6; K. 19/11. **1771:** B. 11/9, 18/12. **1772:** W. 31/8. **1774:** L. 16/8. **1775:** B. 22/12.

T. Theodosius; or, The Force of Love (D.G. *c.* Sept. 1680).

1753: B. 29/6. **1756:** Tr. 3/5. **1758:** B. 10/4. **1761:** C. 28/9. **1765:** C. 4/9; B. 14/10. **1767:** K. 7/12. **1768:** K. 3/2. **1770:** B. 7/8. **1772:** W. 17/9. **1773:** K. 7/1. **1774:** C. 8/8; L. 19/8. **1777:** B. 12/11. **1786:** C. 29/8.

LEE, SOPHIA

C. Chapter of Accidents, The (H.[2] 5/8/1780).

1781: C. 22/10. **1783:** B. 14/3. **1788:** Cash. 10/9. **1789:** B. 28/1; Wex. 16/2; K. 15/5; C. 15/9. **1790:** C. 8/9; K. 15/12. **1792:** B. 2/3. **1793:** B. 8/5. **1794:** D. 12/5.

LEWIS, MATTHEW GREGORY

M.D. Castle Spectre, The (D.L. 14/12/1797).

1799: D. 10/4, 22/4, 1/5; K. 1/7, 6/8; C. 5/9. **1800:** E. 31/1, 17/2, 31/3; B. 10/3, 12/3, 14/3.

LILLO, GEORGE

T. Fatal Curiosity (H.[2] 27/5/1736).

1770: K. 7/12.

T. London Merchant, The; or, The History of George Barnwell (D.L. 22/6/1731).

1750: B. 3/1. **1756:** Tr. 8/4. **1758:** B. 12/6. **1768:** C. 20/9. **1770:** K. 29/12 [as *The London 'Prentice*]. **1778:** C. 20/10; B. 11/11. **1789:** B. 13/4. **1791:** D. 17/6.

LLOYD, —

O.F. Romp, The (Cap. S. 23/1/1771; C.G. 28/3/1778). [An alteration of Bickerstaffe's *Love in the City*.]

1772: C. 22/10. **1773:** C. 29/6, 25/8; L. 16/8. **1774:** C. 8/7; L. 17/8; C. 15/9. **1775:** C. 4/8. **1776:** K. 26/6, 31/7. **1779:** B. 12/3. **1780:** B. 15/3; C. 30/8. **1781:** B. 25/10. **1782:** B. 4/1. **1790:** C. 31/8. **1791:** K. 4/3. **1792:** W. 27/7; G. 16/8; Wex. 19/10, 30/11; D. 7/12. **1793:** B. 1/4; K. 14/8; W. 2/10. **1796:** D. 25/1. **1797:** C. 20/9. **1798:** D. 4/5. **1800:** B. 9/6.

LOVE, JAMES [JAMES DANCE]

C.O. Ladies' Frolick, The (D.L. 7/5/1770). [An alteration of Brome's *The Jovial Crew*.]

1794: D. 7/5.

§ C. New Way to Pay Old Debts, A (S.A. 10/12/1781). [An alteration of Massinger's *A New Way to Pay Old Debts*.]

1782: C. 10/10. **1785:** C. 31/8.

C. Rule a Wife, and Have a Wife. [See Beaumont and Fletcher.]

MACKLIN, CHARLES

F. Love à la Mode (D.L. 12/12/1759).

1762: C. 8/10. **1772:** L. 27/7, 31/7; C. 31/8, 9/10. **1777:** C. 3/10. **1779:** B. 3/3. **1784:** K. 29/3; C. 23/9. **1785:** C. 17/9. **1789:** Wex. 20/2. **1790:** E. 26/4, 30/4. **1793:** G. 30/8. **1796:** B. 9/5. **1799:** K. 28/6. **1800:** E. 31/3.

C. Man of the World, The (C.G. 10/5/1781). [An alteration of *The True-Born Scotsman*, infra.]

1786: C. 16/9; L. 19/9. **1787:** B. 19/1; K. 30/7; C. 20/9. **1795:** B. 2/3; D. 2/10. **1799:** D. 6/5.

C. True-Born Irishman, The (C.S. 14/5/1762). [= *The Irish Fine Lady* (C.G. 28/11/1767).]

1762: C. 27/9, 6/10. **1770:** C. 6/9. **1772:** L. 22/7, 3/8; C. 28/8, 17/10. **1785:** C. 26/9. **1789:** B. 27/4, 18/9. **1796:** B. 17/2, 6/6.

‡ C. True-Born Scotsman, The (S.A. 10/7/1764). [Later altered to *The Man of the World*, supra.]

1772: L. 12/8; C. 4/9.

MACNALLY, LEONARD

C. Fashionable Levities (C.G. 2/4/1785).

1787: B. 26/2.

F. Retaliation, The (C.G. 7/5/1782).

1782: C. 10/8, 13/9.

C.O. Robin Hood; or, Sherwood Forest (C.G. 17/4/1784).

1786: C. 2/9. **1787**: B. 13/4. **1788**: C. 4/8, 23/8. **1789**: K. 10/6, 26/6; C. 7/9. **1790**: E. 30/4, 2/8; C. 1/9. **1791**: C. 8/10. **1792**: W. 1/8; Wex. 22/10, 10/12. **1793**: B. 17/5; K. 28/8; C. 14/9. **1794**: Cl. 23/7. **1795**: D. 30/12. **1796**: E. 13/6; L. 18/7; C. 30/7. **1799**: C. 4/9. **1800**: B. 30/4.

M'CREADY [MCCREADY, or MACREADY], WILLIAM C.

C. Bank Note, The; or, Lessons for Ladies (C.G. 1/5/1795).

1796: C. 9/4; K. 29/9. **1797**: E. 27/3, 31/3. **1799**: K. 16/6.

F. Irishman in London, The; or, The Happy African (C.G. 21/4/1792).

1792: C. 30/8, 14/9. **1793**: G. 11/10. **1796**: B. 15/4; En. 22/6. **1799**: D. 23/1.

F. Village Lawyer, The (H.[2] 28/8/1787).

1794: C. 26/8, 29/8; L. 8/9. **1795**: D. 7/10. **1800**: B. 31/1, 27/3.

MARYAT, DR. THOMAS

*†‡§ C.O. Love in a Bog.

1772: B. 22/1.

MENDEZ, MOSES

M. ENT. Chaplet, The (D.L. 2/12/1749).

1758: C. 18/9. **1765**: C. 23/9. **1771**: B. 27/12. **1773**: K. 18/2; B. 17/11. **1774**: B. 9/2. **1776**: C. 23/8. **1782**: C. 19/8; L. 31/8.

MESSINK, JAMES

‡§ P. Enchanted Lady, The; or, Justice Triumphant (C.S. 24/2/1766).

1766: C. 12/9.

‡§ P. Island of Saints, The; or, The Institution of the Shamrock (S.A. 27/1/1785).

1786: C. 4/9, 9/9, 12/9, 11/10, 13/10.

‡ P. Mercury Harlequin in Ireland; or, The Rape of Columbine (C.S. 16/5/1763).

1765: C. 4/9, 9/9, 25/9.

MILLER, REV. JAMES

T. Mahomet, The Impostor (D.L. 25/4/1744). [In collaboration with Dr. John Hoadly.]

1776: C. 28/8. **1788:** C. 28/11. **1796:** B. 11/3; C. 28/3.

MILTON, JOHN

M. Comus (D.L. 4/3/1738). [An alteration by Dr. John Dalton.]

1765: C. 24/9. **1766:** C. 10/10, 17/10. **1767:** K. 16/12. **1770:** B. 18/5.

M. Comus (C.G. 16/10/1773). [An alteration by George Colman, *the Elder*.]

1774: C. 14/9. **1776:** C. 12/7, 19/7, 4/10. **1778:** C. 14/8. **1779:** C. 6/10. **1780:** C. 1/9. **1782:** D. 30/10. **1783:** C. 22/9. **1786:** C. 29/8. **1787:** C. 10/8. **1788:** B. 17/12. **1790:** C. 4/9. **1792:** K. 12/7; W. 6/8; Wex. 12/11. **1793:** B. 31/5.

MOORE, EDWARD

C. Foundling, The (D.L. 13/2/1748).

1758: B. 19/5. **1770:** K. 12/11. **1773:** C. 23/7. **1776:** K. 1/7. **1779:** C. 8/9. **1781:** B. 25/10. **1782:** K. 7/11. **1787:** C. 6/9. **1788:** C. 4/9. **1789:** Wex. 12/1, 16/1. **1791:** E. 30/9, 17/10. **1792:** B. 13/1, 25/1; W. 19/3; D. 7/11. **1796:** B. 23/5.

T. Gamester, The (D.L. 7/2/1753).

1753: B. 3/7, 6/7. **1775:** Lis. 13/10. **1777:** B. 24/10. **1781:** C. 24/8. **1785:** B. 15/6; C. 27/8. **1788:** B. 17/12. **1789:** Wex. 28/1; C. 3/3. **1790:** D. 21/5; E. 2/10. **1791:** B. 21/1; C. ?/5. **1792:** Wex. 12/12. **1793:** G. 24/7. **1794:** C. 16/10. **1795:** B. 2/1. **1796:** B. 25/4. **1799:** C. 2/9.

MORE, MRS. HANNAH

T. Percy, Earl of Northumberland (C.G. 10/12/1777).

1778: K. 24/2; B. 20/4. **1779:** N. 1/3; C. 26/7. **1783:** K. 15/2. **1784:** K. 9/3; B. 12/4. **1785:** C. 6/7. **1789:** C. 18/12. **1791:** K. 12/1; C. 5/10. **1792:** B. 10/2; W. 17/8; G. 22/10; C. 23/11. **1793:** K. 19/6; G. 31/7. **1794:** D. 9/7.

MORGAN, MCNAMARA

PAST. Sheep-Shearing, The; or, Florizel and Perdita (C.G. 25/3/1754).

1756: Tr. 6/4, 10/5; C. 13/9. **1757:** C. 5/8. **1758:** B. 29/2, 10/3; C. 21/8, 28/9. **1759:** Ba. 26/9. **1760:** C. 15/9, 13/10. **1770:** B. 30/5; K. 1/10, 29/12. **1771:** W. 9/10; B. 29/11. **1776:** C. 9/10. **1778:** B. 2/12. **1787:** B. 20/8. **1789:** C. 14/9. **1790:** D. 2/6. **1791:** B. 19/1; E. 14/11. **1792:** B. 24/2, 26/3; W. 24/8. **1794:** D. 14/5, 23/7.

MORTON, THOMAS

INT. Children in the Wood, The (H.[2] 1/10/1793).

1794: C. 27/9, 13/10; B. 19/11, 29/12. **1795:** B. 8/4; Dr. 17/8; D. 2/10.

1796: E. 13/6. **1797**: C. 5/10. **1798**: D. 28/2. **1799**: K. 31/7. **1800**: B. 6/6.

M.D. Columbus; or, A World Discovered (C.G. 1/12/1792).

1793: C. 7/9.

C. Cure for the Heart-Ache, A (C.G. 10/1/1797).

1797: C. 11/8, 16/8. **1798**: D. 23/1. **1799**: E. 3/6, 5/6.

† C. Secrets Worth Knowing (C.G. 11/1/1798).

1799: C. 3/9. **1800**: B. 27/1.

C. Way to Get Married, The (C.G. 23/1/1796).

1797: C. 5/10.

M.D. Zorinski (H.[2] 20/6/1795).

1799: D. 15/4.

MURPHY, ARTHUR

C. All in the Wrong (D.L. 15/6/1761).

1766: C. 3/9. **1768**: K. 26/2. **1770**: B. 30/5; K. 1/10. **1771**: B. 18/9. **1774**: B. 28/1. **1777**: C. 6/9. **1778**: K. 21/1; C. 28/8, 21/10. **1779**: C. 20/9. **1781**: C. 8/10. **1783**: C. 5/9. **1784**: B. 4/6. **1786**: C. 23/10. **1787**: B. 19/2; C. 11/9. **1789**: B. 20/2. **1791**: L. ?/1; C. 20/5; D. 6/7; B. 3/8, 14/9. **1793**: W. 2/10. **1794**: C. 5/9. **1795**: K. 16/11.

F. Apprentice, The (D.L. 2/1/1756).

1758: B. 24/5; C. 11/8, 26/9. **1768**: K. 13/1. **1770**: C. 27/8; K. 12/11. **1771**: W. 25/9. **1772**: C. 19/10. **1773**: C. 21/7; L. 19/8; B. 29/10. **1774**: D. 21/10. **1778**: K. 2/2; B. 30/12. **1780**: K. 4/10. **1784**: C. 30/9. **1787**: K. 9/1, 3/2. **1791**: K. 12/1; D. 3/6, 10/6. **1792**: W. 31/8. **1793**: B. 17/4; G. 9/9. **1794**: D. 13/8.

F. Citizen, The (D.L. 2/7/1761).

1765: C. 30/8; B. 14/10, 25/10, 20/11. **1766**: B. 1/1. **1768**: K. 8/2; C. 15/8; B. 30/11. **1770**: B. 11/8; K. 21/11. **1771**: B. 27/9, 8/11, 6/12. **1773**: C. 6/7; B. 20/10. **1775**: C. 5/7; Lis. 11/9. **1776**: B. 5/1; L. 18/7; K. 26/7. **1778**: C. 21/10; B. 9/12. **1779**: B. 5/3; D. 16/8. **1781**: C. 13/10, 24/10. **1782**: C. 27/9. **1785**: B. 24/6; C. 27/9. **1787**: C. 10/9; W. 16/10. **1788**: C. 4/8. **1789**: C. 3/3, 14/4. **1790**: C. 8/9; E. 23/9; B. 12/11; K. 13/12. **1791**: C. 11/5. **1792**: N. 28/6; C. 29/8; D. 12/12. **1793**: K. 10/6; G. 5/7, 15/7. **1794**: C. 27/8, 3/9. **1795**: K. 31/8. **1796**: B. 26/2, 29/4, 8/6; C. 2/8.

T. Grecian Daughter, The (D.L. 26/2/1772).

1772: L. 31/7; C. 31/8. **1773**: C. 3/6; B. 13/10, 8/12. **1774**: B. 16/2. **1783**: C. 29/8. **1784**: B. 10/12. **1785**: B. 13/6. **1786**: C. 14/8. **1787**: B. 6/8. **1790**: B. 3/12. **1792**: W. 27/8; Wex. 3/10. **1795**: C. 4/9, 11/9.

C. Know Your Own Mind (C.G. 22/2/1777).

1778: C. 23/10. **1779**: B. 3/3; C. 13/9, 1/10. **1780**: C. 16/8. **1781**: C. 8/8. **1782**: C. 10/9; D. 30/10. **1784**: B. 5/3, 6/9. **1794**: C. 18/8; L. 8/9. **1795**: B. 4/3. **1796**: B. 18/5.

F. Marriage à la Mode. [Another title for *What We Must All Come To*, infra.]

1773: C. 14/7, 28/8. **1774:** B. 19/1; L. 16/8; D. 26/12. **1776:** K. 2/8, 12/8

C. Old Maid, The (D.L. 2/7/1761).

1765: B. 2/12, 11/12, 18/12. **1767:** K. 30/11. **1768:** K. 20/1; Carf. 17/10. **1770:** K. 29/10. **1771:** B. 4/9, 20/12. **1772:** B. 15/1; C. 19/8. **1773:** B. 1/12. **1775:** C. 26/7, 16/9. **1776:** B. 8/4. **1778:** K. 12/1; C. 30/10. **1779:** B. 24/2. **1780:** C. 20/10. **1782:** C. 30/7. **1783:** C. 9/8. **1786:** C. 30/10.

T. Orphan of China, The (D.L. 21/4/1759).

1783: C. 27/9.

F. Three Weeks after Marriage; or What We Must All Come To (C.G. 30/3/1776). [An alteration of *What We Must All Come To*, infra.]

1777: C. 8/8, 5/9. **1780:** C. 2/10. **1781:** C. 3/10. **1782:** C. 19/8; L. 4/9; C. 7/10. **1787:** C. 13/9. **1788:** L. 22/7. **1789:** B. 30/1. **1794:** D. 5/2. **1795:** G. 3/9; C. 4/9.

F. Upholsterer, The; or What News? (D.L. 30/3/1758).

1758: C. 4/9. **1760:** C. 18/9, 6/10. **1786:** C. 10/4; B. 20/12.

C. Way to Keep Him, The (D.L. 24/1/1760).

1762: C. 15/10. **1766:** C. 10/10. **1768:** K. 24/2. **1770:** B. 8/8. **1775:** C. 29/9. **1777:** C. 29/9, 6/10. **1778:** C. 23/10. **1779:** C. 20/9. **1780:** B. 15/3. **1782:** C. 2/10. **1784:** D. 16/2. **1786:** L. 3/8; C. 10/10. **1789:** B. 18/3. **1790:** B. 31/12. **1791:** D. 4/3, 6/4. **1792:** B. 1/2.

F. What We Must All Come To (C.G. 9/1/1764).

1766: B. 10/3.

T. Zenobia (D.L. 27/2/1768).

1776: C. 9/10. **1778:** C. 21/8. **1779:** C. 30/7.

NOVERRE, JEAN GEORGES

ENT. Chinese Festival (D.L. 8/11/1755).

1758: C. 6/9. **1759:** C. 22/8.

O'BEIRNE, THOMAS LEWIS

C. Generous Impostor, The (D.L. 22/11/1780).

1782: D. 27/11, 4/12.

O'BRIEN, WILLIAM

F. Cross Purposes (C.G. 5/12/1772).

1773: C. 19/7, 26/8. **1778:** B. 11/11. **1786:** C. 10/4. **1788:** L. 29/7; C. 29/8.

O'HARA, KANE

BURL. Golden Pippin, The (C.G. 6/2/1773).

1777: C. 10/9. **1779:** C. 5/10.

BURL. Midas; or, The Assembly of the Gods (C.S. 22/1/1762; C.G. 22/2/1764).

1765: C. 1/10. **1768:** B. 23/9, 30/9, 14/10, 5/11, 18/11. **1769:** B. 20/1; N. 23/1. **1770:** B. 10/5; K. 10/11. **1771:** L. 25/9, 29/10. **1772:** B. 1/1; L. 7/7, 13/7. **1773:** K. 16/2; B. 29/9. **1774:** B. 2/2. **1775:** B. 15/12. **1776:** B. 2/3; C. 31/7, 16/10. **1777:** C. 20/8. **1778:** C. 21/8. **1779:** N. 26/4. **1780:** C. 11/10. **1782:** L. 17/7; Dr. 9/10; D. 19/11. **1786:** C. 4/11. **1787:** B. 22/8; W. 18/10. **1790:** E. 1/3; C. 20/8, 7/9; B. 29/12. **1791:** C. 6/10. **1793:** D. 2/1; K. 16/8. **1794:** Cl. 25/7; C. 6/9.

F. Tom Thumb the Great (C.G. 3/10/1780). [An alteration of Henry Fielding's *Tom Thumb*.]

1782: K. 28/9.

O'KEEFFE, JOHN

O.F. Agreeable Surprise, The (H.[2] 3/9/1781).

1782: C. 8/8, 13/8, 6/9, 17/9, 1/10, 12/10; K. 28/9. **1783:** C. 10/2. **1784:** B. 13/7; C. 21/9. **1785:** L. 31/1, 4/2; B. 22/6; C. 21/9. **1786:** C. 9/8. **1787:** B. 19/1, 13/4; C. 11/9, 19/9. **1788:** C. 15/9. **1789:** Wex. 7/1; K. 29/5; C. 11/9, 22/11. **1791:** C. 29/9; B. 3/10. **1792:** Wex. 15/10. **1793:** D. 28/1; B. 26/4; G. 24/7, 23/8. **1794:** C. 6/9; B. 17/12. **1800:** B. 29/1, 28/2.

O.F. Beggar on Horseback, A (H.[2] 16/6/1785).

1786: C. 31/8. **1796:** E. 27/6. **1797:** E. 26/4.

C.O. Castle of Andalusia, The (C.G. 2/11/1782).

1783: C. 26/8. **1789:** C. 11/9. **1790:** C. 2/9. **1792:** Wex. 14/12. **1796:** C. 10/8, 3/9; K. 24/10. **1798:** L. 8/10.

*‡ PAST. Colin's Welcome (C.S. 24/2/1772).

1770: B. 26/7, 11/8; K. 12/11. **1772:** C. 19/10.

*‡ F. Comical Duel, The; or, The Good Boy (C.S. 21/5/1776).

1775: C. 29/9. **1776:** C. 9/10.

O.F. Dead Alive, The (H.[2] 16/6/1781).

1782: C. 5/8, 20/9, 30/9, 14/10. **1784:** B. 28/4, 30/4; C. 23/9. **1785:** C. 16/9. **1788:** Cash. 8/9. **1790:** B. 19/11. **1791:** B. 5/8.

C.O. Farmer, The (C.G. 31/10/1787).

1788: C. 4/9. **1789:** Wex. 30/3; K. 11/5, 13/5, 25/5. **1790:** E. 18/1. **1792:** N. 1/8; Wex. 29/10. **1793:** D. 30/1; G. 19/8. **1795:** B. 4/3. **1796:** L. 18/7, 20/7; C. 30/7.

C.O. Fontainbleau; or, Our Way in France (C.G. 16/11/1784).

1786: C. 4/10. **1791:** C. 24/8. **1792:** Wex. 5/12. **1793:** W. 11/3. **1797:** C. 22/8.

*‡§ INT. Generous Tar, The (C.S. 22/2/1788).

1787: W. 17/10. **1789:** C. 22/9. **1795:** D. 12/10.

§ P. Giant's Causeway; or, A Trip to the Dargle. [Probably

an adaptation of *A Trip to the Dargle* (C.S.15/12/1762) and of *Giant's Causeway* (S.A. 2/2/1763).]

1770: B. 25/5, 4/7, 6/8; K. 15/10, 17/10.

*†‡§ P. Harlequin in Derry; or, The Dutchman Outwitted.

1770: B. 9/5, 6/7.

*†‡§ P. Harlequin in Waterford; or, The Dutchman Outwitted.

1767: W. 28/10; K. 14/12. **1768:** K. 3/2.

C.O. Highland Reel (C.G. 6/11/1788).

1789: C. 10/9, 23/9. **1790:** E. 22/2, 8/3. **1791:** B. 7/1, 19/1, 16/9. **1792:** W. 6/8; C. 15/9; Wex. 26/10, 26/11; D. 17/12. **1793:** D. 11/2; B. 20/5; K. 5/7, 21/8; G. 19/7, 25/10. **1794:** D. 7/5, 6/6; B. 7/11. **1795:** B. 18/3. **1796:** D. 13/1; K. 27/7. **1798:** D. 2/3. **1800:** B. 13/2.

C. London Hermit, The; or, Rambles in Dorsetshire (H.[2] 29/6/1793).

1793: C. 11/9.

INT. Lord Mayor's Day; or, A Flight to Lapland (C.G. 25/11/1782).

1783: C. 23/9.

F. Modern Antiques; or, The Merry Mourners (C.G. 14/3/1791).

1791: C. 29/9; E. 14/11. **1792:** B. 2/3, 5/3; Wex. 28/9; D. 29/11.

C.O. Patrick in Prussia; or, Love in a Camp (C.G. 17/2/1786).

1786: C. 5/9.

C.O. Peeping Tom of Coventry (H.[2] 6/9/1784).

1785: B. 7/6; C. 19/9, 30/9. **1786:** C. 7/9, 4/10, 17/10; L. 18/9. **1787:** K. 14/7; C. 30/8; W. 10/10. **1789:** Wex. 12/1, 16/1, 6/2; K. 6/5. **1790:** E. 27/1. **1791:** B. 24/1; L. 18/5; C. 13/10. **1792:** Wex. 5/10. **1793:** D. 8/2. **1794:** B. 29/10. **1795:** D. 30/9.

C.O. Poor Soldier, The (C.G. 4/11/1783).

1784: C. 20/9, 23/9, 29/9. **1785:** L. 25/1, 5/3, 15/3; B. 28/3, 17/6. **1786:** C. 5/10. **1787:** C. 28/8, 12/9. **1788:** C. 23/8; B. 19/11; Wex. 29/12. **1789:** Wex. 19/1, 6/2; B. 2/3; K. 28/4; C. 29/9; L. 17/11. **1791:** B. 14/1. **1792:** D. 14/1; W. 4/8; C. 10/9; Wex. 10/10. **1793:** D. 23/1; W. 20/2, 4/10. **1794:** L. 20/1; C. 14/10, 22/10. **1795:** K. 30/9. **1796:** E. 24/6; L. 21/7. **1797:** E. 19/4. **1798:** C. 20/9. **1799:** K. 10/6, 12/6.

F. Positive Man, The (C.G. 16/3/1782).

1782: C. 30/9.

F. Prisoner at Large, The (H.[2] 2/7/1788).

1789: C. 16/9. **1791:** C. 4/5. **1797:** E. 6/5.

‡ F. She Gallant, The; or, Squaretoes Outwitted (S.A. 14/1/1767).

1774: C. 12/9.

O.F. Son-in-Law, The (H.[2] 14/8/1779).

1781: C. 8/8. **1782**: K. 28/8. **1783**: C. 18/9. **1784**: B. 3/3. **1792**: N. 2/7. **1793**: D. 1/2.

C.O. Sprigs of Laurel; or, British Bravery (C.G. 11/5/1793).

1793: C. 5/9. **1794**: Cl. 30/6. **1795**: Dr. 14/8; D. 7/10. **1796**: L. 25/7. **1797**: C. 13/11.

*†‡§ F. Tony Lumpkin's Frolics thro' Cork.

1780: C. 4/10.

*†‡§ F. Tony Lumpkin's Ramble thro' Cork.

1773: C. 17/9. **1774**: C. 12/9. **1775**: C. 29/9.

C.O. Wicklow Gold Mines, The; or, The Lads of the Hills (C.G. 13/4/1796).

1798: L. 8/10. **1799**: L. 3/8.

C.O. Wicklow Mountains, The (C.G. 7/10/1796).

1798: D. 28/2. **1799**: K. 26/6, 28/6.

C. Wild Oats; or, The Strolling Gentleman (C.G. 16/4/1791).

1791: C. 13/10. **1792**: B. 15/2, 17/2, 27/2, 9/3; K. 29/2, 15/4; C. ?/4; N. 30/6, 1/8; G. 14/9; Wex. 8/10, 12/11; D. 21/11, 29/11. **1793**: W. 13/3; K. 19/6; G. 3/7, 17/7; C. 19/9. **1794**: Cl. 30/6; D. 25/7; C. 27/9. **1795**: Dr. 14/8. **1796**: D. 22/1.

C. Young Quaker, The (H.[2] 26/7/1783).

1784: C. 11/9, 22/9. **1790**: C. 9/9, 3/10. **1792**: C. 13/9. **1793**: B. 15/5, 27/5. **1794**: C. 30/9.

OTWAY, THOMAS

F. Cheats of Scapin, The (D.G. *c.* Dec. 1676).

1758: C. 20/9, 4/10. **1766**: B. 27/1. **1767**: K. 2/12. **1768**: K. 18/1. **1770**: B. 4/5; K. 22/9. **1780**: C. 7/10. **1791**: B. 23/9.

T. Orphan, The; or, The Unhappy Marriage (D.G. *c.* Mar. 1679/80).

1754: B. 27/11, 17/12. **1755**: B. 5/2. **1756**: Tr. 30/3. **1758**: B. 12/5; C. 18/8. **1760**: C. 21/7. **1765**: B. 2/12. **1766**: B. 5/2. **1767**: L. summer. **1768**: K. 4/5; B. 3/10; Carf. 21/10. **1769**: C. 9/2, 25/4. **1770**: B. 11/8; C. 24/10. **1772**: C. 26/9. **1775**: C. 14/9. **1776**: C. 5/8. **1778**: K. 4/2. **1781**: C. 17/10. **1783**: C. 10/2. **1785**: L. 1/3. **1786**: C. 19/8. **1787**: K. 5/2; B. 24/8. **1789**: C. 28/1. **1790**: E. 9/4; C. 10/9. **1791**: D. 22/6. **1792**: W. 29/8. **1793**: G. 22/7. **1796**: K. 17/8.

T. Venice Preserved (D.G. 9/2/1682).

1753: B. 15/6. **1755**: B. 7/2. **1760**: C. 17/9. **1765**: C. 23/9; B. 22/11. **1766**: B. 19/2. **1768**: B. 2/12. **1770**: K. 22/9. **1772**: L. 22/7; C. 23/9. **1775**: Lis. 18/9. **1777**: C. 25/7. **1779**: C. 26/4, 10/5, 21/5, 19/7. **1781**:

K. 6/1; C. 19/10. **1782:** C. 13/8. **1783:** C. 31/3. 13/8, 23/8. **1785:** L. 25/1; B. 6/6, 22/6. **1787:** C. 13/9. **1788:** C. 8/8; B. 15/12. **1789:** Wex. 13/3; C. 18/9; L. 17/11. **1790:** E. 27/1; C. 6/9. **1792:** W. 24/8. **1793:** W. 21/3; G. 17/7. **1794:** B. 29/12. **1795:** G. 3/9. **1796:** C. 9/4.

OULTON, WALLEY CHAMBERLAINE

‡ INT. Haunted Castle, The (Cap. S. 18/12/1783).

1786: C. 2/11.

PHILLIPS, AMBROSE

T. Distrest Mother, The (D.L. 17/3/1712).

1756: Tr. 12/4. **1758:** B. 21/4; C. 14/7. **1761:** C. 29/7, 16/9. **1763:** B. 9/3; C. 7/9. **1765:** B. 18/10, 25/10. **1768:** B. 7/10. **1770:** K. 27/11. **1771:** B. 16/8. **1773:** C. 5/7, 8/9. **1775:** C. 26/7. **1778:** B. 3/12, 8/12. **1780:** C. 11/8. **1782:** C. 2/8. **1786:** C. 28/8.

PHILLIPS, EDWARD

B.O. Mock Lawyer, The (C.G. 27/4/1733).

1740: Dr. 3/10.

PIGUENIT, D. J.

† ENT. Don Quixote (C.G. 1774).

1795: K. 9/11.

PILON, FREDERICK

† F. Barataria; or, Sancho Turn'd Governor (C.G. 29/3/1785).

1786: C. 2/9.

F. Deaf Lover, The (C.G. 2/2/1780).

1781: C. 8/10. **1786:** C. 11/9. **1791:** C. 20/5, 15/6.

*†‡§ C. French Flogged, The; or, British Sailors in America. [An alteration of G. Alexander Stevens's farce, *The French Flogged* (C.G. 20/3/1760).]

1780: C. 24/10.

C. He Would be a Soldier (S.A. 2/1/1786; C.G. 18/11/1786).

1787: C. 17/9; W. 17/10. **1789:** Wex. 7/1; K. 6/5; C. 21/9; W. 7/10. **1790:** D. ?/1; E. 3/2. **1791:** C. 13/5. **1792:** B. 30/1; Wex. 9/11; D. 6/12, 13/12. **1793:** G. 5/7. **1796:** L. 25/7. **1799:** D. 19/4; K. 22/7. **1800:** B. 29/1.

PREL. Illumination, The; or, The Glazier's Conspiracy (C.G. 12/4/1779).

1779: C. 4/10.

F. Invasion, The; or, A Trip to Brighthelmstone (C.G. 4/11/1778).

1779: C. 10/8.

† F. Liverpool Prize, The (C.G. 22/2/1779).

1779: L. 27/2; C. 10/9.

† O.F. Siege of Gibraltar, The (C.G. 25/4/1780).
1781: C. 12/10.

PRESTON, WILLIAM

‡ T. Democratic Rage; or, Louis the Unfortunate (C.S. 14/6/1793).
1793: C. 14/8, 22/8; G. 30/8.

RAMSEY, ALLAN

PAST. Gentle Shepherd, The (Edinburgh, 1725).
1768: B. 25/11. **1777:** C. 11/10. **1779:** B. 19/11. **1790:** D. 17/5.

RAVENSCROFT, EDWARD

C. Anatomist, The; or, The Sham Doctor (L.[1] 14/11/1696).
1753: B. 6/8, 31/8. **1756:** Tr. 13/3. **1758:** B. 27/3. **1759:** Ba. 28/9. **1765:** B. 20/1; C. 11/9, 22/9. **1766:** B. 5/2; C. 27/8, 1/9. **1768:** K. 6/1, 11/1, 22/2. **1772:** B. 3/1, 24/1. **1773:** B. 22/12. **1774:** B. 7/2. **1775:** C. 14/7. **1776:** B. 6/3. **1777:** C. 16/7. **1783:** C. 5/9, 16/9.

REDIGÉ, PAUL

‡ P. Hermit of the Rocks, The; or, Harlequin's Folly (C.S. 3/11/1788).
1789: C. 2/4.

REED, JOSEPH

F. Register Office, The (D.L. 25/4/1761).
1778: C. 24/7, 7/9, 28/9, 20/10. **1779:** C. 1/9, 1/10. **1780:** C. 2/8, 16/8. **1781:** C. 10/8, 15/8. **1785:** C. 13/9. **1791:** D. 8/6, 29/6; B. 18/7. **1793:** C. 5/9. **1800:** B. 16/5.

C.O. Tom Jones (C.G. 14/1/1769).
1771: B. 30/10, 1/11.

REYNOLDS, FREDERICK

C. Cheap Living (D.L. 21/10/1797).
1799: D. 13/5. **1800:** B. 21/4.

C. Dramatist, The; or, Stop Him who Can! (C.G. 15/5/1789).
1790: C. 16/8, 20/8; E. 18/8; K. 8/11; L. ?/12. **1792:** B. 22/2; N. 28/6; C. 1/8. **1793:** B. 29/5; G. 19/8. **1797:** C. 4/8.

C. Fortune's Fool (C.G. 29/10/1796).
1797: C. 9/8.

C. How to Grow Rich (C.G. 18/4/1793).
1793: C. 4/9. **1794:** Cl. 25/7. **1795:** K. 11/11. **1796:** E. 26/5.

C. Notoriety (C.G. 5/11/1791).
1793: D. 30/1; B. 26/4. **1795:** B. 6/4.

C. Rage, The; or, Frailties of Fashion (C.G. 23/10/1794).
1795: B. 11/3; Dr. 17/8; C. 3/9; D. 9/10.

T. Sorrows of Werther, The. [=Werther (Bath 25/11/1785).]
1786: C. 27/10. **1787:** K. 1/9; W. 25/10. **1788:** C. 28/8. **1790:** L. ?/8.

C. Speculation (C.G. 7/11/1795).
1796: B. 25/5.

C. Will, The (D.L. 19/4/1797).
1799: K. 19/7. **1800:** B. 28/2.

REYNOLDS, G. N.

† M. INT. Bantry Bay (C.G. 20/2/1797).
1797: L. 4/9.

RICH, JOHN

P. Fair, The (C.G. 7/2/1750).
1762: C. 30/10.

P. Necromancer, The; or, Harlequin Dr. Faustus (L.[2] 20/12/1723).
1769: C. 15/9, 20/9.

RICHARDSON, JOSEPH

† C. Fugitive, The (H.[1] 20/4/1792).
1792: C. 31/5.

ROSS, ANNA

‡ C.O. Cottagers, The; or, The Female Metamorphosis (C.S. 19/5/1789).
1796: B. 16/5, 1/6.

ROWE, NICHOLAS

T. Fair Penitent, The (L.[1] *c.* May 1703).
1753: B. 4/6. **1754:** B. 18/11. **1755:** Lis. 22/2. **1756:** Tr. 25/3; C. 17/9. **1758:** B. 8/2. **1760:** C. 6/8. **1761:** C. 29/9. **1762:** C. 4/10. **1763:** B. 14/1. **1765:** B. 4/12. **1768:** L. 13/10; B. 17/10. **1770:** B. 4/8; K. 13/12. **1771:** B. 25/9. **1776:** B. 16/2. **1778:** K. 5/1; B. 2/12. **1779:** N. 26/4. **1780:** C. 5/8. **1782:** C. 15/8. **1783:** C. 8/1, 22/8. **1784:** B. 5/5. **1786:** G. ?/5. **1787:** K. 13/3; B. 10/8. **1790:** E. 8/3. **1792:** W. 10/9. **1793:** W. 21/3; G. 12/7. **1795:** G. 22/9; K. 29/9. **1796:** B. 21/4; C. 10/9. **1800:** B. 4/5.

T. Jane Shore (D.L. 2/2/1714).
1751: B. 18/12. **1754:** B. 22/11. **1755:** B. 15/1. **1756:** Tr. 13/3. **1758:** C. 30/8. **1760:** C. 29/9. **1763:** C. 24/9. **1766:** C. 22/8. **1768:** L. 27/10. **1770:** B. 8/8; C. 24/8. **1771:** B. 9/10. **1774:** C. 27/7. **1775:** C. 14/7. **1776:** B. 5/1; C. 9/8. **1777:** L. 15/8. **1778:** B. 10/4; C. 31/7. **1781:** C. 21/8. **1782:** L. 17/7. **1783:** C. 15/8, 1/9. **1784:** C. 1/9. **1785:** B. 10/6. **1790:** E. 5/4; B. 10/11. **1791:** D. 4/3; B. 17/10. **1792:** W. 18/9; Wex. 26/9. **1794:** B. 19/11. **1796:** B. 27/4.

T. Tamerlane (L.[1] *c.* Dec. 1701).

1753: B. 13/7. **1754:** B. 13/12. **1762:** C. 27/10. **1765:** B. 10/11. **1768:** B. 5/11. **1771:** B. 4/11. **1772:** B. 1/1. **1773:** C. 10/9; B. 31/12. **1775:** B. 24/11. **1776:** B. 25/1. **1778:** B. 4/11. **1779:** B. 19/2, 4/11. **1797:** C. 22/8.

RYDER, THOMAS

*‡§ INT. Gates of Calais, The; or, The Roast Beef of Old England (C.S. 1/6/1769).

1765: Dr. 26/8. **1770:** K. 27/11.

‡ C.O. Governess, The (C.S. 2/2/1777). [A pirated adaptation of Sheridan's *The Duenna.*]

1778: B. 14/1, 16/1, 28/1, 11/2. **1779:** B. 13/1; D. 21/6. **1780:** C. 18/10.

C. Like Master, Like Man (S.A. 30/4/1766; H.[2] 21/9/1767). [An alteration of Vanbrugh's *The Mistake.*]

1770: B. 1/6; K. 1/12. **1776:** C. 17/7, 21/8. **1777:** C. 18/7. **1779:** C. 4/6.

*‡§ ENT. Ramble through Dublin, A. (S.A. 6/5/1771).

1768: K. 29/2. **1770:** B. 4/7. **1771:** W. 28/10.

ST. JOHN, DR. JAMES

*†‡§ O. Siege of Waterford, The.

1792: W. 29/3.

SHAKESPEARE, WILLIAM

C. As You Like It.

1753: B. 23/7. **1762:** C. 29/10. **1770:** C. 6/9. **1772:** C. 23/10. **1774:** D. 20/12. **1776:** B. 22/3. **1777:** C. 30/7; B. 11/12. **1778:** C. 14/8. **1779:** N. 4/1; B. 5/3; C. 28/7. **1780:** B. 3/3; C. 9/8. **1784:** W. 26/7. **1785:** C. 27/9. **1786:** C. 30/10; B. 20/12. **1787:** W. 22/10. **1789:** Wex. 9/2; C. 17/9. **1790:** L. 31/1; E. 22/2; L. ?/11. **1791:** K. 31/3; B. 8/8. **1792:** C. 22/9. **1795:** K. 2/11, 30/11. **1798:** D. 4/5.

T. Cymbeline.

1773: C. 7/7. **1774:** C. 8/7. **1785:** B. 28/11. **1795:** B. 20/3.

T. Hamlet, Prince of Denmark.

1740: Dr. 17/9. **1741:** B. spring. **1753:** B. 6/8. **1755:** B. 7/1. **1756:** Tr. 9/3. **1758:** C. 20/9. **1759:** C. 4/10. **1760:** C. 8/8, 30/9. **1765:** C. 12/8. **1766:** B. 28/2. **1767:** K. 21/12. **1768:** C. 5/8; B. 23/9. **1770:** B. 10/6, 2/8. **1772:** L. 27/9. **1773:** C. 11/6, 30/8; L. 11/8. **1774:** C. 15/7; L. 19/9. **1775:** Lis. 6/10; B. 13/12. **1776:** C. 17/7, 25/9; K. 12/8; W. ?/8. **1778:** K. 31/1; C. 22/7. **1779:** K. 6/11. **1781:** C. 11/9. **1782:** C. 29/7, 27/9. **1785:** C. 3/9. **1787:** B. 9/4; C. 10/8. **1788:** B. 19/11. **1789:** C. 25/8. **1790:** B. 8/11. **1791:** B. 28/1; D. 16/5. **1792:** B. 5/3; K. 14/7; W. 15/8; D. 23/11. **1793:** G. 19/7. **1794:** D. 23/5. **1795:** D. 16/12. **1796:** B. 4/3, 18/3; C. 17/8. **1797:** C. 9/9. **1800:** B. 2/6, 9/6.

T. Henry VIII.

1738: C. 27/4. **1759:** Col. 18/12; Ba. 28/12. **1762:** C. 6/10. **1768:** K. 15/1, 20/1. **1770:** K. 8/10. **1780:** B. 27/3. **1781:** K. 8/3; C. 4/10. **1782:** C. 3/8. **1785:** C. 26/9.

T. Julius Caesar.

1755: B. 27/1. **1758:** C. 18/9. **1762:** C. 13/10. **1773:** C. 25/6, 1/9; L. 19/8. **1774:** L. 27/9. **1776:** C. 4/10.

T. King John.

1773: C. 9/7. **1781:** K. 6/3. **1782:** C. 20/9. **1792:** N. 20/7.

T. King Lear.

1759: C. 1/10. **1768:** K. 22/2. **1770:** B. 18/6; K. 9/11, 17/11. **1772:** L. ?/6. **1773:** C. 13/9. **1776:** C. 2/8. **1778:** C. 4/11. **1779:** B. 26/2, 13/8. **1784:** K. 4/6. **1791:** L. ?/3. **1792:** Wex. 7/12. **1793:** D. 2/1, 8/2. **1795:** K. 21/9.

T. Macbeth.

1756: Tr. 5/5. **1759:** C. 27/8. **1760:** C. 11/10. **1762:** C. 15/10. **1765:** C. 27/8; B. 27/12. **1766:** B. 8/1; C. 1/10. **1768:** K. 24/2, 2/3. **1771:** B. 2/8. **1773:** C. 16/7. **1774:** C. 20/7, 30/8. **1776:** C. 19/8. **1778:** B. 7/1, 27/4. **1780:** B. 1/3. **1782:** L. 4/9. **1785:** B. 27/6. **1787:** C. 8/9. **1788:** C. 9/9. **1791:** B. 31/1; K. 21/2. **1794:** D. 30/5; B. 26/11. **1796:** B. 14/3. **1797:** C. 19/8.

C. Measure for Measure.

1758: C. 16/8. **1768:** C. 16/8.

C. Merchant of Venice, The.

1756: Tr. 14/4. **1758:** B. 19/4; C. 21/8. **1765:** C. 5/9. **1766:** C. 11/9. **1769:** K. 24/7. **1770:** B. 16/7. **1771:** B. 22/11. **1772:** C. 19/8. **1773:** Dr. late summer; B. 17/11. **1775:** Lis. 11/9. **1778:** K. 2/2; C. 13/10. **1779:** B. 22/1; C. 21/7; D. 16/8. **1780:** K. 10/11. **1782:** D. 25/6. **1785:** C. 13/9. **1789:** Wex. 30/3; K. 11/5, 29/5. **1790:** E. 1/3; B. 29/12. **1791:** C. 2/5; B. 29/7. **1792:** K. 13/6. **1793:** G. 4/9. **1796:** C. 15/4. **1798:** C. 15/9; L. 1/10. **1799:** C. 7/9. **1800:** B. 6/5.

C. Merry Wives of Windsor, The.

1751: B. ?/12. **1756:** Tr. 27/3. **1766:** C. 3/10. **1780:** C. 21/8. **1794:** B. 22/12.

C. Much Ado About Nothing.

1765: C. 14/8. **1766:** C. 16/8. **1778:** B. 25/11. **1779:** C. 10/8. **1780:** B. 10/3. **1785:** C. 7/9. **1787:** B. 15/8, 22/8. **1788:** C. 2/9. **1789:** B. 11/2. **1794:** C. 22/8.

T. Othello, The Moor of Venice.

1756: Tr. 3/4. **1760:** C. 23/7, 7/10. **1761:** B. 8/7, 15/7. **1762:** C. 27/9. **1765:** C. 9/9; B. 7/10, 29/11. **1766:** C. 27/10. **1768:** K. 27/1. **1769:** K. 12/8. **1772:** L. 5/8; C. 3/10. **1775:** C. 5/7; Lis. 20/10. **1776:** B. 29/3. **1778:** K. 12/1; B. 28/12. **1779:** C. 22/9. **1780:** C. 7/8. **1782:** K. 16/12.

1783: C. 19/9; L. 11/10. **1787:** K. 9/1. **1788:** C. 21/8; B. 10/11. **1789:** Wex. 30/1; K. 18/5; C. 1/9, 14/9. **1790:** C. 11/9. **1793:** C. 19/8. **1794:** D. 4/8. **1799:** L. 3/8.

T. Richard III.

1753: B. 14/8. **1756:** Tr. 20/3; C. 30/8. **1758:** B. 13/2. **1760:** C. 15/10. **1761:** B. 29/7. **1763:** B. 28/2. **1765:** B. 1/11. **1766:** B. 31/1, 7/2. **1767:** Carl. 10/7. **1768:** K. 8/1, 26/3; C. 1/8; B. 7/9. **1769:** C. 11/8. **1772:** B. 15/1; L. ?/6. **1774:** B. 19/1; C. 13/7. **1775:** B. 1/12. **1776:** B. 8/4; C. 26/7. **1777:** C. 6/10. **1778:** K. 28/1. **1779:** C. 3/8. **1780:** C. 31/7. **1782:** C. 6/9. **1785:** C. 6/9. **1786:** C. 25/10. **1791:** B. 24/1. **1792:** Wex. 30/10. **1793:** B. 22/5. **1796:** C. 31/8.

T. Romeo and Juliet.

1753: B. 22/6. **1755:** B. 28/2; Lis. 5/3. **1756:** Tr. 26/4; C. 13/9. **1758:** B. 15/3, 20/3; C. 11/8, 22/9 [Garrick's version]. **1760:** C. 11/8. **1761:** C. 10/7; B. 26/8. **1762:** C. 20/8. **1763:** B. 29/3. **1765:** C. 2/9; B. 20/12. **1766:** B. 21/2; C. 25/8. **1767:** L. summer. **1768:** B. 2/9. **1771:** B. 4/10. **1773:** B. 5/11. **1774:** C. 24/6. **1775:** C. 3/7; Lis. 29/11. **1776:** K. 8/7, 5/8; C. 14/7. **1778:** C. 24/10. **1781:** K. 8/2. **1785:** L. 16/8; C. 8/9. **1787:** B. 8/8, 17/8. **1788:** C. 22/8; B. 24/11, 5/12. **1789:** C. 29/8, 24/9; W. 3/10. **1790:** E. 21/9; L. ?/12. **1791:** B. 5/1; C. 16/8. **1792:** K. 11/6; W. 22/8; Wex. 16/11. **1793:** B. 1/4; G. 15/7, 26/7, 29/7. **1794:** D. 11/7, 20/8; B. 15/12. **1795:** B. 12/4, 29/4. **1796:** B. 7/3. **1800:** B. 3/2; E. 10/3.

SHERIDAN, MRS. FRANCES

C. Discovery, The (D.L. 3/2/1763).

1781: C. 10/9.

SHERIDAN, RICHARD BRINSLEY

‡ B.O. Beggar's Opera Reversed, The (C.S. 12/5/1779). [An alteration of Gay's *The Beggar's Opera*. Nicoll, iii. 399, lists as anonymous.]

1782: L. 2/8. **1784:** C. 5/10. **1786:** C. 1/9. **1791:** B. 21/9. **1794:** C. 11/10.

F. Camp, The; or, A Trip to Cox Heath (D.L. 15/10/1778).

1779: B. 26/11. **1780:** C. 29/9. **1794:** D. 12/5.

B. Critic, The; or, A Tragedy Rehearsed (D.L. 30/10/1779).

1781: C. 28/8. **1783:** B. 21/4. **1784:** B. 12/4. **1786:** C. 5/9. **1787:** B. 23/2. **1789:** B. 27/2. **1791:** D. 27/5; B. 29/7, 8/8. **1792:** W. 10/8, 14/9. **1793:** D. 7/1; Wex. 9/1. **1794:** D. 2/6.

C.O. Duenna, The; or, The Double Elopement (C.G. 21/11/1775).

1777: C. 8/8, 5/9, 13/9, 29/9, 17/10; L. 16/8. **1778:** K. 4/2; C. 10/10. **1779:** B. 10/11, 17/11. **1785:** L. 31/1. **1788:** L. 14/7, 22/7. **1790:** C. 24/8, 3/9. **1791:** C. 19/8. **1792:** N. 25/6; Wex. 2/11, 7/11. **1793:** K. 29/8. **1795:** K. 28/10; D. 20/11.

*†‡§ PREL. Pantheon, The.

1781: C. 13/10.

T. Pizarro (D.L. 24/5/1799).

1800: E. 2/4; B. 14/4, 16/4, 19/5, 23/5.

*†‡§ PREL. Regions of Accomplishment.

1792: B. 30/3.

C. Rivals, The (C.G. 17/1/1775).

1775: C. 21/7, 28/7; B. 27/12. **1776:** B. 19/1; K. 17/6, 3/7; C. 5/10. **1777:** C. 14/10. **1778:** B. 24/4; C. 31/8; N. 3/12. **1779:** Ant. 4/10; C. 13/10. **1780:** C. 13/10. **1781:** K. 18/1. **1782:** L. 26/7. **1785:** C. 21/9. **1786:** C. 9/8, 7/9. **1788:** Cash. 8/9. **1789:** B. 2/2, 9/2. **1790:** K. 29/11. **1791:** C. 7/10; E. 14/10. **1792:** W. 20/2; K. 30/3; N. 9/7; Wex. 5/10. **1793:** Wex. 25/1; G. 23/8; K. 4/10. **1794:** C. 4/9. **1795:** K. 31/8. **1796:** B. 16/5; C. 2/9; K. 14/9. **1799:** D. 29/4. **1800:** B. 9/5.

P. Robinson Crusoe; or, Harlequin Friday (D.L. 29/1/1781).

1783: C. 22/9. **1784:** B. 5/5, 14/5. **1795:** D. 6/11; C. 21/12. **1797:** E. 25/5, 30/5.

F. Saint Patrick's Day; or, The Scheming Lieutenant (C.G. 2/5/1775).

1776: C. 26/8. **1777:** C. 26/8. **1782:** K. 28/9. **1783:** C. 23/9.

C. School for Scandal, The (D.L. 8/5/1777).

1778: C. 9/9, 28/9. **1779:** B. 12/2; N. 4/4; D. 9/6; C. 17/9; B. 10/11, 17/11. **1780:** C. 28/8. **1781:** C. 22/8, 24/10. **1783:** B. 27/1; C. 9/9. **1785:** C. 16/9. **1787:** C. 22/9; W. 12/10. **1788:** C. 11/9. **1789:** Wex. 9/1; K. 5/6. **1790:** D. 2/6; K. 13/12. **1791:** B. 26/1; D. 6/5, 29/6; B. 25/7; C. 6/10. **1792:** K. 9/5; W. 24/7; Wex. 10/10. **1793:** D. 7/1, 1/2; K. 10/6; L. 25/7; W. 4/10. **1794:** D. 5/2; B. 13/10. **1795:** D. 28/9. **1796:** B. 18/4; C. 23/8.

*‡§ ENT. Tears of the Muses (S.A. 13/11/1780). [An elegy to Garrick, entitled in Dublin *Monody on Garrick.*]

1780: C. 2/10.

C. Trip to Scarborough, A (D.L. 24/2/1777).

1781: C. 14/9. **1787:** B. 9/3. **1789:** B. 26/1.

SHERIDAN, THOMAS

F. Brave Irishman, The; or, Captain O'Blunder (A.S. 21/2/1737; G.F. 31/1/1746).

1753: C. 23/6. **1755:** B. 15/1; Lis. 26/2. **1756:** Tr. 6/3, 27/3; C. 27/10. **1758:** B. 8/2, 24/2. **1761:** B. 8/7, 17/7, 14/8. **1762:** C. 20/8. **1765:** C. 5/9. **1766:** C. 15/8. **1771:** F. 22/3. **1776:** B. 23/2. **1778:** C. 12/8, 9/9. **1781:** C. 21/8. **1787:** C. 12/9; W. 12/10. **1789:** Wex. 6/3; L. 21/12. **1792:** C. 23/11. **1793:** D. 4/2; K. 21/8. **1795:** K. 12/10.

T. Coriolanus; or, The Roman Matron (S.A. 29/2/1752;

C.G. 10/12/1754). [An alteration of Shakespeare's *Coriolanus.*]

1758: C. 11/9.

SHIRLEY, WILLIAM

T. Edward the Black Prince; or, The Battle of Poictiers (D.L. 6/1/1750).

1779: C. 8/10.

SIDDONS, HENRY

M.D. Sicilian Romance, The; or, The Apparition of the Cliffs (C.G. 28/5/1794).

1796: B. 4/5.

SMOLLETT, TOBIAS

C. Reprisal, The; or, The Tars of Old England (D.L. 22/1/1757).

1758: B. 12/4, 19/4, 28/4. **1770:** B. 18/7, 2/8. **1771:** B. 20/11. **1775:** Lis. 13/9.

SOUTHERNE, THOMAS

T. Fatal Marriage, The; or, The Innocent Adultery (D.L. *c.* Feb. 1693/4).

1766: C. 11/10.

T. Oroonoko; or, The Tragedy of the Royal Slave (D.L. Dec. 1695).

1753: B. 19/7, 22/7. **1755:** B. 3/3. **1756:** Tr. 23/4. **1760:** C. 1/8. **1761:** B. 7/8. **1765:** B. 23/10. **1766:** B. 20/1. **1768:** K. 5/2. **1770:** C. 3/9. **1780:** C. 4/10. **1781:** C. 10/10. **1782:** C. 24/9. **1789:** C. 14/4. **1790:** C. 15/9. **1792:** N. 16/7. **1796:** E. 1/6. **1797:** C. 7/10.

STAYLEY, GEORGE

‡ INT. Mimickry Expos'd (S.A. 28/4/1758). [Entitled in Dublin *The Chocolate Makers; or, Mimickry Expos'd.*]

1758: C. 30/8, 8/9, 13/9.

STEELE, RICHARD

C. Conscious Lovers, The (D.L. 7/11/1722).

1755: B. 3/1. **1756:** Tr. 23/3. **1758:** B. 7/4; C. 25/9. **1760:** C. 6/10. **1761:** B. 3/8. **1762:** C. 28/10. **1764:** C. 3/10. **1765:** C. 2/10. **1766:** C. 10/9, 16/9. **1768:** B. 26/8. **1769:** C. 30/8. **1770:** B. 23/5; K. 26/11. **1771:** W. 25/9. **1772:** C. 17/10. **1773:** K. 16/2. **1774:** C. 29/7. **1780:** B. 27/3; C. 31/8; K. 14/12. **1788:** L. 25/7; C. 6/9. **1790:** C. 13/9. **1792:** W. 3/9. **1793:** Wex. 9/1.

C. Funeral, The; or, Grief à la Mode (D.L. *c.* Dec. 1701).

1768: K. 9/3. **1774:** C. 1/8; L. 24/8.

C. Tender Husband, The; or, The Accomplish'd Fools (D.L. 23/4/1705).

1760: C. 3/10. **1774:** C. 5/8; L. 11/8.

STEVENS, GEORGE ALEXANDER

C. French Flogged, The; or, British Sailors in America. [See Frederick Pilon.]

O.F. Trip to Portsmouth, The (H.[2] 11/8/1773).

1773: B. 3/12, 8/12, 10/12, 17/12. **1774:** B. 14/1; L. 24/8. **1775:** B. 27/12.

STUART, CHARLES

O.F. Gretna Green (H.[2] 28/8/1783).

1784: C. 27/9.

TATE, NAHUM

F. Duke and No Duke, A (D.L. 3/11/1684).

1756: Tr. 7/5. **1761:** C. 31/7. **1773:** C. 17/9. **1775:** C. 8/9. **1776:** C. 16/8.

THOMPSON, BENJAMIN

D. Stranger, The (D.L. 24/3/1798). [An alteration of Kotzebue's *Menschenhass und Reue.*]

1799: D. 10/5. **1800:** B. 17/2, 26/2.

THOMSON, JAMES

T. Tancred and Sigismunda (D.L. 18/3/1745).

1762: C. 8/10. **1763:** C. 27/9. **1765:** C. 9/10. **1766:** C. 23/9. **1784:** C. 10/9. **1788:** C. 20/8; B. 26/11. **1794:** C. 26/8. **1796:** B. 16/3.

TICKELL, RICHARD

PAST. Gentle Shepherd, The (D.L. 29/10/1781). [An alteration of Allan Ramsey's *The Gentle Shepherd.*]

1795: B. 23/2.

TOWNLEY, REV. JAMES

F. High Life Below Stairs (D.L. 31/10/1759).

1760: C. 1/8, 6/8. **1761:** B. 22/7, 24/7; C. 29/9. **1762:** C. 13/10. **1763:** B. 28/1, 28/2; C. 29/9. **1765:** B. 7/10, 29/11. **1766:** C. 19/8, 27/8. **1767:** K. 16/12. **1768:** C. 17/8. **1769:** K. 24/7. **1770:** K. 9/11. **1771:** B. 1/11. **1772:** C. 26/9. **1773:** C. 14/9. **1774:** B. 28/1, 16/2. **1775:** C. 28/7. **1776:** B. 8/3; C. 30/8, 7/10. **1778:** K. 5/1; C. 24/8. **1780:** C. 16/10. **1784:** C. 25/9. **1785:** C. 6/9. **1786:** C. 23/10. **1787:** B. 15/8. **1788:** C. 21/8. **1790:** C. 8/5. **1791:** B. 26/1; D. 13/5; C. 3/6, 8/10. **1792:** N. 11/7; Wex. 21/11; D. 3/12. **1793:** B. 10/5; G. 3/7. **1794:** C. 5/9. **1795:** B. 2/1; D. 16/12.

VANBRUGH, SIR JOHN

C. Confederacy, The; or, The City Wives Confederacy (H.[1] 30/10/1705).

1738: Dr. 11/9. **1740:** Carl. 22/9. **1758:** C. 23/8. **1766:** C. 25/9.

C. Provok'd Wife, The (L.[1] *c.* May 1697).

1756: Tr. 21/4. **1760:** C. 1/10. **1766:** C. 27/8. **1768:** C. 3/8. **1775:** C. 22/9. **1780:** C. 7/10.

C. Wrangling Lovers, The (H.[2] 27/12/1705). [= *The Mistake; or, The Wrangling Lovers.*]

1759: Ba. 27/9. **1768:** B. 16/11. **1775:** Lis. 8/9. **1792:** Wex. 2/10. **1800:** B. 3/2.

VANDERMERE, JOHN

*†‡§ P. Harlequin Restored; or, A Trip to Killarney.

1775: C. 11/9.

VILLIERS, GEORGE, DUKE OF BUCKINGHAM

B. Rehearsal, The (T.R. in Bridges St. 7/12/1671).

1765: C. 15/8, 30/8. **1766:** C. 14/8, 27/10.

WAKER, JOSEPH

*†‡ PAST. Love in a Cottage; or, Rosina.

1781: W. n.d. **1783:** L. 14/10. **1785:** B. 13/7. **1787:** B. 9/3, 21/3.

WALDRON, FRANCES

C. Heigh ho! For a Husband (H.[2] 14/1/1794).

1794: C. 13/10. **1795:** B. 11/3, 16/3; K. 19/10.

WARD, HENRY

F. Vintner Trick'd, The (A.S. 27/1/1743; D.L. 9/4/1746).

1758: C. 8/9. **1761:** B. 31/7. **1765:** B. 1/11. **1770:** K. 29/11. **1780:** K. 11/10. **1789:** Wex. 6/2.

WHITEHEAD, WILLIAM

T. Roman Father, The (D.L. 24/2/1750).

1773: C. 28/6; L. 13/8. **1777:** B. 19/11. **1786:** C. 21/8. **1787:** B. 3/8, 20/8.

C. School for Lovers, The (D.L. 10/2/1762).

1775: C. 4/8.

F. Trip to Scotland, A (D.L. 6/1/1770).

1772: C. 21/10. **1773:** B. 8/9, 29/12.

WOODBRIDGE, ROBERT

F. Pad, The; or, British Fashions (C.G. 27/5/1793).

1793: C. 5/9.

WOODFALL, WILLIAM

T. Sir Thomas Overbury (C.G. 1/2/1777). [An alteration of Savage's *The Tragedy of Sir Thomas Overbury.*]

1777: C. 11/10.

WOODWARD, HENRY

*‡§ P. Cupid's Frolick; or, Mid-Summer Mirth.

1761: C. 29/7.

*‡§ P. Fairies, The (C.S. 3/12/1760). [Probably an alteration of Woodward's *Fairy Friendship; or, The Triumph of Hibernia.*]

1760: C. 8/10.

P. Harlequin Dr. Faustus (A.S. 13/11/1750; C.G. 18/11/1766).

1787: B. 2/3.

P. Harlequin Fortunatus (D.L. 26/12/1753).

1787: K. 30/7.

F. Marplot in Lisbon (D.L. 20/3/1755). [An alteration of Mrs. Centlivre's *Marplot.*]

1760: C. 8/10.

WORSDALE, JAMES

B.O. Cure for a Scold, A (D.L. 25/2/1735).

1742: G. n.d. **1755:** B. 21/2.

YARROW, JOSEPH

F. Trick Upon Trick; or, The Vintner Outwitted (York 1742).

1756: Tr. 20/3.

YOUNG, EDWARD

T. Revenge, The (D.L. 18/4/1721).

1753: B. 31/8. **1756:** C. 27/11. **1758:** B. 28/4. **1764:** Wex. ?/6. **1765:** B. 13/12, 18/12. **1766:** B. 15/1. **1768:** K. 29/2; C. 27/7, 23/9. **1769:** C. 15/9. **1770:** B. 25/5, 6/8; K. 17/9, 10/11. **1776:** B. 18/3. **1778:** K. 10/2. **1779:** C. ?/5, 4/6. **1780:** K. 4/10. **1781:** K. 20/1. **1783:** C. 18/3. **1785:** L. 4/2, 5/3; C. 23/8. **1787:** W. 6/11. **1789:** L. 9/10. **1792:** B. 10/2.

UNKNOWN AUTHORS

I. Plays

T. Alexander the Great [An alteration of Lee's *The Rival Queens.*]

1775: C. 21/9. **1776:** C. 14/10. **1782:** C. 30/9, 14/10. **1783:** C. 22/9; L. 14/10. **1791:** B. 2/2. **1793:** B. 17/4. **1794:** D. 15/8. **1796:** B. 10/3. **1797:** C. 19/9.

F. Barnaby Brittle. [An alteration of Betterton's *The Amorous Widow*: probably the same as (1) *Barnaby Brittle; or, A Wife at her Wit's End* (C.G. 18/4/1781); and (2) *The Fashionable Wife*, infra.]

1765: C. 18/9. **1768:** K. 15/1. **1770:** K. 27/11. **1775:** C. 28/9. **1783:** C. 4/9. **1785:** C. 3/9. **1787:** C. 18/9; W. 17/10. **1788:** C. 5/8, 13/9.

1789: C. 18/4. **1792:** B. 13/1, 23/1; C. 21/9; D. 3/11, 7/11. **1794:** D. 30/5.

*†‡§ INT. Catechism, The.

1773: C. 21/7.

† INT. Clock Case, The; or, The Freemason's Wife's Curiosity. [Wr. by 'a Cork Gentleman': probably the same as *The Clock Case; or, Female Curiosity* (C.G. 2/5/1777).]

1776: C. 14/10.

C. Connaught Wife, The; or, The Honest Munster Man (S.A. 19/1/1767). [An alteration of Hippisley's *A Journey to Bristol*: attributed to Thomas Ryder.]

1768: K. 7/3. **1770:** B. 9/7.

‡§ INT. Death of General Wolfe, The.

1799: C. 2/9, 3/9.

*†‡§ INT. Disappointed Old Woman, The.

1789: Wex. 6/2.

† INT. Disguises, The.

1778: C. 20/10.

INT. Farmer's Return from the Coronation, The. [Probably an alteration of Garrick's *The Farmer's Return from London* (D.L. 20/3/1762; C.S. 10/5/1762).]

1762: C. 28/9.

§ F. Fashionable Wife, The. [Probably an alteration of Betterton's *The Amorous Widow*. See *Barnaby Brittle*, supra.]

1768: B. 2/9. **1775:** C. 19/7; B. 8/12 (subtitled *Barnaby Brittle*). **1779:** D. 18/8 (subtitled *The Humours of Barnaby Brittle*).

‡§ INT. Female Volunteer, The; or, The Humours of Loughrea (C.S. 27/4/1780).

1780: C. 16/10.

F. Fondlewife and Laetitia (C.S. *c.* 1767: H.[2] 14/8/1767). [An alteration of Congreve's *The Old Batchelour.*]

1775: Lis. 17/11.

C. Ghost, The (S.A. 2/12/1767; D.L. 10/4/1769). [An alteration of Mrs. Centlivre's *The Man Bewitched.*]

1768: B. 21/10. **1770:** K. 19/11. **1773:** B. 22/10, 5/11. **1774:** B. 3/1. **1775:** Lis. 18/9, 18/10; B. 6/12. **1778:** C. 10/10; B. 20/11. **1785:** C. 27/8.

*†‡§ INT. Happy Interposition.

1786: C. 2/9.

*†‡§ F. History of John Gilpin, The. [An adaptation of William Cowper's poem *John Gilpin*.]

1786: C. 10/4.

*†‡§ INT. Honest Deception, The.

1790: C. 15/9.

*†‡§ F. Humours of Belfast, The.

1766: B. 28/2.

*†‡§ INT. Humours of Cove, The; or, The Smugglers Return. [Wr. by 'a Cork Gentleman'.]

1773: C. 15/9.

*†‡§ INT. Irish Haymaker, The.

1786: C. 7/9.

*†‡§ INT. Just Arrived in L'Derry; or, The Thespian from Ennishoen.

1798: D. 28/2.

*†‡§ T. Love and Despair. [Wr. by 'a Waterford Gentleman'.]

1771: W. 9/10.

*†‡§ F. Magical Tale, The.

1786: C. 25/8.

*†‡§ INT. Mallow Races, The.

1777: C. 13/10.

*†‡§ C. Mentalist, The; or, Doctor of the Passions. [Wr. by 'a Co. Down Gentleman'.]

1771: B. 15/11.

*†‡§ INT. Merry Funeral, The.

1790: C. 11/9.

*‡§ INT. Modern Matrimony (S.A. 27/5/1782).

1781: C. 24/8, 8/10.

*†‡§ INT. Peep into the Kingdom of Mirth, A.

1782: C. 10/10.

O.F. Poor Sailor; or, Little Bob and Little Ben (C.G. 12/5/1795).

1796: Dr. 12/10.

*†‡§ B. Rehearsal, The; or, A Peep behind the Scenes of the Cork Theatre. [An alteration of Garrick's *A Peep behind the Curtain* (D.L. 23/10/1767).]

1786: C. 25/10.

*‡§ F. Reprisals, The (C.S. 16/4/1779).

1778: C. 26/10. **1780**: C. 23/8.

‡ O. Revenge of Athridates, The; or, Pharnaces (S.A. 12/12/1765). [An alteration of Hull's *Pharnaces*.]

1766: C. 15/8, 21/8, 12/9.

*‡§ B. Rival Queans, The; or, The Death of Alexander the Little. [Possibly an adaptation of *Alexander the Little* (C.G. 1764), or of C. Cibber's *The Rival Queans*, with the *Humours of Alexander the Great* (H.[1] June 1710).]

1784: C. 28/9.

*‡§ T. Royal Captive, The (C.S. 27/4/1761). [Wr. by an Irishman and based on Southerne's *Oroonoko*.]

1760: C. ?/10.

† INT. Scheming Valet, The; or, Brother and Sister.

1800: En. 2/4.

† C. School for Ladies, The; or, The Levee of Lovers (H.[2] 5/4/1780).

1784: B. 23/6.

*†‡§ INT. Scrub's Travels. [Possibly an adaptation of Francis Gentleman's *Scrub's Trip to the Jubilee*.]

1788: C. 25/9.

*†‡§ C. Siege of the Castle of Aesculapius, The. [Wr. by 'a Cork Gentleman'.]

1772: C. 25/9.

*‡§ INT. Swaddling Shopkeeper, The (S.A. 6/5/1771).

1770: K. 3/12. **1777:** C. 9/9.

*‡§ INT. Taylor and the Undertaker, The (C.S. 26/2/1796).

1793: Wex. 4/1.

*†‡§ INT. Taylor Without the Head, The.

1783: C. 27/9.

‡§ INT. Thurot's Trip to Carrickfergus (C.S. 15/6/1761).

1761: C. 31/7.

*†‡§ INT. Twiss in Ireland; or, The Fop in Disgrace. [Wr. by 'a T. C. D. Gentleman'.]

1778: B. 20/4.

† F. Two Knights from the Land's End.

1758: C. 16/8.

† F. Vintner in the Suds, The (D.L. 25/4/1740).

1753: B. 22/6.

*†‡§ F. Vintner Tam'd, The.

1765: B. 4/12.

*‡§ C. Wanton Wife, The; or, The Glassman Outwitted (S.A. 20/1/1762). [Perhaps an alteration of Betterton's *Amorous Widow*.]

1762: C. 18/10. **1765:** B. 6/11, 15/11, 13/12.

B.O. Wapping Landlady, The; or, The Humours of the Navy (C.S. 28/11/1758). [Probably *The Sailor's Wedding; or, The Humours of Wapping* (G.F. 21/4/1731).]

1759: Col. 27/12. **1761:** B. 3/8, 7/8.

‡§ INT. Wedding of Baltimore, The; or, Irish Hospitality (C.S. 27/4/1779).

1780: C. 2/10, 17/10.

II. Preludes

*†‡§ Auld Robin Gray; or, Jamie's Return.

1788: C. 4/9.

*†‡§ British Tars, The; or, Waterford Gambols.

1787: W. 18/10.

*†‡§ Candidates, The. [Wr. by 'a Cork Gentleman'.]

1783: C. 5/9.

Foote, Weston, and Shuter in the Shades (H.[2] 10/8/1784).

1786: C. 2/9.

*†‡§ Free Trade.

1780: C. 14/10.

‡§ Mad Actor, The (S.A. 19/5/1786).

1786: C. 7/9.

*‡§ New Register Office, The; or, Paddy O'Carrol in High Life (S.A. 10/5/1782).

1781: C. 12/10.

*†‡§ Rodney's Glory.

1780: C. 24/10.

True Blue (S.A. 11/5/1774; Royalty 1787). [An alteration of Henry Carey's *Nancy*.]

1782: C. 15/8.

III. Pantomimes[1]

Animation of Columbine, The.

1787: W. 17/10.

Birth of Harlequin, The.

1768: K. 6/12. **1792:** Wex. 10/12.

[1] Unless preceded by the sign ||, all titles in this list are previously unrecorded pantomimes presented only in Ireland outside Dublin.

Clown Triumphant.

1789: C. 29/9.

|| Death of Captain Cook, The (C.G. 21/9/1789).

1790: L. ?/8; E. 27/9, 28/9, 1/10. **1791:** L. 3/1, 5/1, 10/1, 24/1, ?/3; C. 4/5, 12/5, 14/5, 3/6, 10/6. **1792:** B. 25/1, 28/3, 30/3; D. 28/11, 6/12, 14/12, 26/12. **1793:** B. 29/5. **1795:** B. 9/3; K. 30/11, 19/12.

|| Death of Harlequin, The (D.L. 1716; S.A. 1/1/1750).

1787: W. 17/10.

|| Deserter of Naples, The (D.L. 2/6/1788; C.S. 21/5/1794).

1789: C. 23/9. **1796:** B. 18/5.

|| Don Juan; or, The Libertine Destroy'd (Royalty 23/6/1788).

1789: C. 10/9. **1795:** B. 20/3. **1797:** E. 21/4, 3/5.

|| Elopement, The; or, A Trip to the Dargle (D.L. 8/9/1768).

1792: W. 20/8.

Enchanted Castle, The; or, Harlequin Conqueror.

1792: W. 15/2.

Enchanted Peasant, The.

1758: C. 21/8, 6/9.

Enchantress, The; or, Harlequin Triumphant.

1775: L. 30/10, 3/11.

Escape, The; or, Harlequin Victorious.

1769: B. 6/1.

Fairy of the Rock, The.

1787: B. 2/3.

Fricasse, La.

1763: C. 4/9. **1789:** B. 13/4.

Genii, The; or, Harlequin Restored.

1768: B. 11/11.

Harlequin.

1790: E. 9/4, 24/9.

Harlequin Amazed; or, Fairy Friendship.

1755: B. 3/1.

|| Harlequin Foundling (Wakefield 11/9/1784).

1786: C. 1/11, 6/11.

Harlequin Gard'ner.

1789: B. 11/2. **1792:** C. 29/10.

Harlequin in Patagonia.

1770: K. 24/10.

Harlequin in the Shades (S.A. 4/5/1774).

1768: B. 25/11. **1771:** B. 22/11, 13/12.

Harlequin Pilgrim.

1796: Dr. 10/10.

Harlequin Shepherd; or, The Regions of Fancy.

1792: Wex. 8/10. **1796:** E. 24/6.

Harlequin Skeleton (S.A. 23/12/1771).

1772: B. 1/1.

|| Harlequin Sorcerer (Tottenham Court Aug. 1741).

1792: Wex. 10/10.

Harlequin Turned Buck.

1777: C. 7/10.

Harlequin's Choice.

1792: C. 13/9.

Harlequin's Statue.

1776: C. 14/10. **1777:** C. 11/10.

|| Harlequin's Vagaries; or, The Clown in Jeopardy. [Probably the same as *The Sorcerer; or, Harlequin's Vagaries.*]

1793: C. 7/9.

Hermit, The; or, Harlequin Victorious.

1773: B. 13/10.

Magical Soldier, The; or, Harlequin's Mouth Opened.

1771: B. 18/12. **1776:** C. 11/10.

Medley, The; or, Harlequin's Vagaries in Munster.

1773: C. 22/9.

Miraculous Miller, The.

1770: K. 15/12.

Neck or Nothing; or, Harlequin's Flight from the Gods.

1787: K. 24/7. **1789:** B. 18/3.

Passage Landlady, The.

1777: C. 15/10.

Power of Magic, The; or, Harlequin Freemason.

1795: C. 14/9.

|| Prometheus; or, Harlequin's Animation (C.G. 26/12/1775).

1789: B. 16/1, 26/1. **1790:** D. 26/5.

Proteus; or, The Adventures of Harlequin.

1800: B. 26/2.

Revels, The; or, Harlequin Villager.
1776: B. 16/2; D. 15/10.

|| Siege of Quebec, The (R.G. 31/5/1784).
1792: C. 30/8.

|| Sorcerer, The; or, Harlequin's Vagaries (C.S. 21/4/1762).
1762: C. 4/10. **1787:** C. 19/9 [Subtitle only].

Sorcerers, The; or, Harlequin Wizard.
1791: B. 2/12.

Spell, The; or, Harlequin's Funeral.
1778: B. 11/2.

|| Sylphs, The (C.G. 31/1/1774).
1774: C. 1/8; L. 24/8.

Tarantula; or, The Merry Bedlamites.
1786: C. 25/10, 4/11.

Tartars, The.
1758: C. 14/7.

|| Tavern Bilkers, The; or, Harlequin's Shaft (C.S. 23/11/1795). [A new second act to Sheridan's *Robinson Crusoe.*]
1795: C. 14/12.

Vauxhall Champêtre; or, Easter Gambols.
1790: E. 9/4.

Witches, The; or, Harlequin Salamander.
1778: C. 27/10. **1784:** C. 5/10 [Subtitle only]. **1796:** D. 20/1; B. 3/6.

Witches, The; or, Harlequin's Vagaries.
1773: B. 19/11, 24/11.

Witches, The; or, Harlequin Victorious.
1774: D. 2/12.

Witches of the Rock, The; or, The Regions of Fancy.
1792: W. 30/1.

IV. Entertainments and Musical Interludes[1]

ENT. Benjamin Bolus; or, The New Castle Apothecary.
1800: B. 27/1.

ENT. Comic Mirror, The; or, Folly and Fashion.
1794: D. 31/12. **1795:** D. 2/1, 5/1.

ENT. Debating Society, The.
1773: L. 19/8.

[1] Unless preceded by the sign ||, all titles in this list are previously unrecorded entertainments and interludes, presented only in Ireland outside Dublin.

ENT. Diamond Mine of Cork, The; or, A Scene from Mallow Lane. [Wr. by 'a Cork Gentleman'.]

1778: C. 13/10.

M. INT. Grenadier, The.

1777: C. 6/9, 3/10.

M. INT. Half an Hour in Turkey.

1778: C. 31/8.

M. INT. Irishman in Naples, The.

1800: E. 14/11.

ENT. Irish Simplicity.

1791: E. 14/11.

M. INT. Irish Volunteer, The; or, Country Courtship.

1783: L. 14/10.

ENT. Jacob Gawkey's Rambles from Somersetshire to London.

1792: N. 16/7.

ENT. Jobson and Nell.

1795: C. 28/12.

M. INT. Jovial Feast, The.

1778: C. 2/9.

M. INT. King Henry the Eighth.

1800: C. 14/3.

M. INT. Ladies Catch-Club, The.

1792: Wex. 31/12. **1793**: Wex. 9/1.

ENT. Larry O'Shaughnessy's Tour through Dublin with his Return to Cork.

1778: C. 26/10. **1779**: C. 21/9.

ENT. Magical Ring, The; or, A Peep into a Lodge of Free and Accepted Masons.

1791: E. 14/11.

ENT. Mirror, The; or, The World As It Goes.

1800: B. 25/4.

ENT. Mossonian Budget; or, A Post Haste Journey from Dublin to Kilkenny.

1785: C. 20/9. **1792**: K. 30/6.

ENT. National Spirit Roused.

1779: C. 8/10.

M. INT. New Love in a Village. [Wr. by 'an Irish Templar'.]

1785: C. 20/9.

M. INT. Nice and Thirsis.

1763: C. 29/9.

M. INT. Parting Lovers, The; or, Recruits for the Army. [Wr. by 'a Cork Gentleman'.]

1784: C. 5/10.

ENT. Poor Darty's Trip to Belfast.

1794: B. 7/11.

ENT. Rakes of Mallow, The.

1778: C. 4/10.

M. INT. Rambles through Belfast.

1800: B. 25/4, 9/5.

M. INT. Savoir Vivre, The.

1780: C. 23/10.

M. INT. School of Harmony, The.

1789: B. 4/2.

|| ENT. School of Shakespeare, The; or, Humours and Passions (H.[2] 7/8/1781).

1781: C. 15/10.

ENT. Shuter's Description of a Poste Haste Journey to Paris.

1782: C. 16/9.

|| ENT. Triumph of Liberty, The; or, The Destruction of the Bastille (R.C. 18/8/1789).

1789: C. 16/9. **1791:** K. 4/3.

ENT. Twiggle and a Frizze, A.

1786: C. 29/8, 2/9, 5/9, 6/11. **1787:** W. 17/10. **1789:** C. 25/9.

ENT. Will o' the Wisp; or, Blue Beard.

1795: B. 18/3.

APPENDIX B

ACTORS AND ACTRESSES IN IRELAND OUTSIDE DUBLIN: 1720–1800

THE year of début at Dublin and London, whenever known, is listed in addition to the recorded appearances in Irish towns.

The contractions used for the towns as well as for the Dublin and London theatres follow the tables in the headnote to Appendix A.

If two dates are inserted for the same town after a given year, they represent the first and last performances on record.

Abington, Mrs. James [*née* Frances Barton] (1737–1815). D.L. 1756. S.A. 1759. **1760:** C. 25/7, 10/10. **1768:** C. 3/8, 17/8. **1786:** C. 10/10, 28/10. **1793:** L. 25/7.

Achmet, Mrs. [*née* Catherine Ann Egan] (1766–97). S.A. 1784. C.G. 1789. **1786:** B. 23/10. **1787:** B. 15/1; C. 8/9, 20/9; W. 16/10, 17/10. **1790:** L. 9/8, 8/11; E. 13/9, 2/10. **1791:** L. 10/1.

Acres, Mr. **1791:** E. 14/10.

Adams, Mr. **1769:** C. 15/9.

Adams, Mrs. **1777:** C. 14/10.

Adamson, Mr. **1790:** L. 9/8, 8/11; E. 6/9, 2/10. **1791:** L. 7/2. **1792:** Wex. 12/10, 21/11. **1793:** Ennc. 8/3.

Adcock, William. C.S. 1760. D.L. 1765. **1760:** C. 11/8, 9/10. **1761:** C. 6/7. **1762:** C. 20/8, 24/9.

Adcock, Mrs. William [*née* Mary Palmer] (d. 1773). C.S. 1761. D.L. 1765. **1760:** C. 25/7, 8/10. **1761:** C. 6/7, 10/7. **1762:** C. 20/8, 28/9.

Adcock, Miss Sarah Maria (*see* Mrs. Richard Wilson).

Addison, John (*c.* 1766–1844). F.S. 1796. **1798:** C. 19/9; L. 1/10.

Addison, Mrs. John [*née* Willems]. F.S. 1796. C.G. 1796. **1798:** C. 18/9; L. 1/10. **1799:** L. 2/8; C. 31/8, 4/9. **1800:** C. 15/8.

Aecey, Mrs. M. S.A. 1781. **1781:** C. 8/8, 20/8. **1782:** C. 16/8; L. 31/8. **1783:** C. 6/9.

Aickin, Francis (1736–1812). S.A. 1756. D.L. 1765. **1756:** Tr. 9/3, 10/5. **1758:** B. 13/2, 12/6. **1780:** C. 5/8, 31/8. **1781:** C. 21/8, 24/8. **1783:** C. 13/8, 29/8. **1785:** C. 27/8, 2/9.

Aickin, Mrs. Francis (Mary) (d. 1786). **1758:** B. 8/3, 12/6.

Aickin, James (1735–1803). S.A. 1762. D.L. 1767. **1758:** B. 6/2, 26/5.

Aldridge, Robert (*c.* 1739–93). S.A. 1758. **1755:** K. summer. **1757–8:** Dr. n.d. **1760:** C. 21/7, 15/10. **1761:** C. 6/7, 7/10. **1775:** C. summer.

Allis, Mr. **1765:** B. 7/10.

André, Miss. S.A. 1783 (*fr.* Haymarket). **1787:** C. 28/8, 22/9.

Archbold, Miss. Cap. S. 1770. **1768:** C. 15/8. **1770:** C. 24/8. **1771:** L. 22/10. **1772:** L. 6/7, 31/7; C. 19/8, 17/10. **1773:** C. 15/9. **1774:** C. 14/9 (*see also* Mrs. Ward).

Archer, Mr. C.S. 1795. D.L. 1798. **1782:** C. 7/10 (Master Archer). **1794:** B. 21/10. **1795:** B. 20/3.

Archer, Mrs. C.S. 1795. **1795:** B. 20/3.

Arionelli, Mr. **1792:** N. 2/7.

Arne, Michael (*c.* 1741–86). C.S. 1776. **1777:** C. 19/8.

Arne, Mrs. Michael [*née* Ann Venables]. D.L. 1772. S.A. 1774. **1777:** C. 6/8, 19/8. **1779:** C. 11/10.

Arnold, Mr. **1786:** C. 29/8.

Arnold, Mrs. (*see* Miss Jameson).

Ashmore, Miss Frances (*see* Mrs. Richard Sparks).

Ashmore, Miss (*see* Mrs. Richard Cox Rowe).

Astley, Philip (1742–1814). Cap. S. 1773. **1800:** C. 3/3, ?/4.

Atkins, Austin. **1789:** C. 18/12. **1790:** W. ?/7; L. ?/8; E. 13/9, 2/10. **1791:** L. 7/2.

Atkins, Miss Harriet Westropp. **1788:** C. 22/8, 28/11. **1789:** C. 3/3, 14/4. **1790:** W. ?/7; L. 31/7, ?/11; E. 6/9, 24/9. **1791:** L. 18/3; C. 15/5, 16/8. **1792:** W. 19/3; C. 26/5.

Atkins, Michael (1747–1812). S.A. 1762. **1768:** B. 26/8, 3/12. **1769:** N. 23/1; K. 3/6, 17/8. **1771:** B. 16/8, 13/11. **1772:** B. 17/1. **1773:** B. 6/9. **1774:** B. 28/1; D. 8/8, 7/12. **1775:** D. 7/8; B. 22/11. **1776:** B. 6/3; D. 16/10, 15/11. **1778:** B. 10/4; C. 31/8, 27/10. **1779:** D. ?/6, ?/8. **1781:** B. 23/3, 16/11. **1782:** D. ?/8, 11/12. **1783:** B. 24/1, ?/9. **1784:** Lis. 3/8, 26/10; B. 8/12. **1785:** B. ?/6; D. ?/11. **1786:** D. ?/5; B. ?/10. **1787:** B. 21/3, 22/8. **1788:** B. 12/11, 17/12. **1789:** B. 27/4. **1790:** D. 5/5, 26/5; B. 12/11. **1791:** B. 26/1, 19/12; D. 6/4, 1/6. **1792:** B. 5/1, 27/2. **1793:** B. 8/5. **1794:** D. 16/5, 25/7; B. 2/10, 1/12. **1795:** B. 9/3; D. ?/9. **1796:** D. 25/1; B. 2/5. **1798:** D. 28/2, 26/3. **1799:** D. 23/1, 15/5. **1800:** B. 10/3, 14/5.

Atkins, Mrs. Michael [*née* Catherine Hutton]. **1773:** B. 8/9. **1774:** D. 8/8. **1776:** B. 20/3. **1778:** C. 2/9, 19/10. **1779:** D. 12/8. **1783:** B. ?/1. **1798:** D. 23/4.

Atkins, Michael, Jr. **1800:** B. 10/3, 14/4.

Atkins, Miss [*dau. of* Michael Atkins, Sr.] (*see* Mrs. Boucheron).

Austin, Joseph (1735–1821). D.L. 1760. C.S. 1761. **1761:** C. 28/10. **1762:** C. 20/8, 30/10. **1764:** C. 3/10. **1765:** Dr. 26/8.

Austin, Mrs. Joseph. C.S. 1789 (*fr.* C.G.). **1765:** Dr. 26/8.

Baddeley, Mrs. Robert [*née* Sophia Snow] (1745–86). D.L. 1765. S.A. 1778. **1778:** C. 17/7, 31/8.

Baker, David Erskine (1730–67). S.A. 1742. **1758:** B. 28/4, 12/5.

Baker, Miss Mary (*see* Mrs. Thomas King).

Baker, Thomas (*c.* 1764–1801). Cap. S. 1783. D.L. 1789. **1784:** C. 30/9.

Bannister, Charles (1741–1804). H.[2] 1762. C.S. 1764. D.L. 1767. **1769:** C. 31/7, 20/9. **1786:** W. 18/7; L. 31/7, 15/8; C. 17/8, 1/9.

Barnes, Mrs. S.A. 1784 (*fr.* C.G.). **1785:** C. 23/8, 24/9.
Barnett, Mr. **1782:** C. 16/8.
Barnett, Mrs. **1782:** C. 30/7, 9/8.
Barnshaw, Jack. F.S. 1777 (*fr.* C.G.). **1780:** C. 1/9, 24/10. **1781:** C. 20/8, 13/10.
Barre, Mrs. [*née* Grace]. S.A. 1770. **1771:** L. 22/10. **1772:** L. 6/7, 3/8; C. 22/10.
Barrett, Benjamin. C.S. 1782. **1784:** K. 17/2. **1788:** C. 4/8.
Barrett, Mrs. Benjamin. C.S. 1782. **1784:** K. 17/2. **1788:** C. 4/8.
Barrett, Giles Leonard (1744–1809). C.S. 1788 (*fr.* Norwich). R.C. 1790. **1789:** W. 10/10.
Barrett, Patrick (*c.* 1737–1825). C.S. 1781. **1771:** Cav. n.d.; Fet. 22/3. **1786:** L. 3/8; C. 29/8, 24/10.
Barrington, John (1715–73). R.S. 1735. C.G. 1745. **1737:** W. ?/6.
Barron, John. **1776:** B. 23/2, 3/4.
Barry, Spranger (1719–77). S.A. 1744. D.L. 1746. **1760:** C. 21/7, 15/10. **1761:** C. 10/7, 29/9. **1762:** C. 20/8, 2/11. **1763:** C. 25/7, 7/9. **1764:** C. 14/9. **1765:** C. 19/8, 12/10.
(1) Barry, Mrs. Spranger (d. *c.* 1767). C.S. 1763. **1762:** C. 24/9, 25/10. **1763:** C. 27/9. **1765:** C. 12/9.
(2) Barry, Mrs. Spranger [*form.* Mrs. William Dancer; *later* Mrs. Thomas Crawford; *née* Anne Street] (1734–1801). C.S. 1758. H.[2] 1766. D.L. 1767. (as Mrs. Dancer) **1760:** C. 1/8, 15/10. **1761:** C. 10/7, 2/10. **1762:** C. 20/8, 2/11. **1763:** C. 26/8, 29/9. **1764:** C. 14/9. **1765:** C. 14/8, 12/10. (as Mrs. Barry) **1770:** C. 25/8. **1777:** C. 25/7, 1/8. (as Mrs. Crawford) **1779:** C. 19/7, 11/8.
Barry, Miss. **1770:** K. 29/10, 31/12. **1771:** W. 9/10.
Barry, Thomas (d. 1768). C.S. 1761. H.[2] 1767. **1761:** C. 2/10. **1762:** C. 8/10. **1763:** C. 26/8, 21/9. **1765:** C. 11/9, 9/10. **1766:** C. 28/7, 27/10.
Barsanti, Miss Jane (*see* Mrs. Richard Daly).
Barton, Mr. **1761:** C. 26/9.
Bateman, Mrs. C.S. 1794 (*fr.* D.L.). **1794:** C. 25/9, 14/10.
Bath, Mr. **1758:** B. 1/3, 2/6.
Beatty, Mr. **1772:** K. 31/12. **1773:** W. n.d.
Beaumont, Mr. **1790:** W. ?/7; L. 31/7, 11/9; E. 13/9. **1796:** D. 4/1.
Beaumont, Mrs. **1796:** D. 4/1.
Beck, Mr. **1766:** C. 11/10.
Bellamy, Thomas Ludford (1770–1843). D.L. 1791. F.S. 1795. **1798:** C. 15/9, 18/9; L. 8/10. **1799:** L. 2/8.
Bengough, Mr. **1799:** D. 24/4.
Bengough, Mrs. **1799:** D. 24/4.
Benn, Mr. **1792:** K. 23/2; W. 24/7, 24/8; Wex. 12/10, 7/12. **1793:** Wex. 18/1; W. 8/3, 23/3.
Bennet, Mr. C.S. 1779. **1778:** W. autumn.
Berford, Mr. **1777:** C. 11/10.
Bernard, John (1756–1828). Cap. S. 1782–83. C.G. 1787. **1782:** L. 31/8; C. 27/9, ?/10. **1783:** B. 24/1, 21/4; Sl. summer; D. 29/10. **1784:** D. 16/2; B. 3/3, 19/7; W. ?/7, ?/8.

Bernard, Mrs. John [*form.* Mrs. Cooper; *née* Roberts] (1750–92). Cap. S. 1782–3. C.G. 1787. **1782:** L. 31/8; C. ?/9, ?/10. **1783:** B. 24/1, 19/5; Sl. summer. **1784:** W. ?/7, ?/8.

Bernard, Mrs. [*later* Mrs. Tayleure]. **1793:** B. 17/4, 13/5. **1794:** D. 6/5.

Berry, Francis. F.S. 1777. **1765:** B. 7/10. **1766:** B. 10/3. **1772:** B. 15/1.

Berry, Mrs. Francis. **1765:** B. 7/10, 18/10.

Best, Mr. **1780:** B. 15/3.

Best, Mrs. [*née* Russell]. **1780:** B. 15/3.

Betterton, Thomas (*c.* 1752–1834). F.S. 1777. C.G. 1799. **1779:** B. 12/2, 19/3. **1780:** B. 1/3. **1783:** N. autumn. **1784:** N. 25/6. **1792:** N. 21/6, 1/8; Dr. 8/10, 2/11. **1793:** W. 8/3, 13/3; Wex. 18/4, 1/5; K. 5/6, 19/6; G. 10/7, 7/10.

Betterton, Mrs. Thomas [*form.* Mrs. Palmer] (d. 1793). Cap. S. 1782. **1779:** B. 12/2. **1792:** N. 20/7.

Betterton, Master John. **1792:** N. 1/8. **1793:** W. 21/3; G. 12/7, 7/10.

Betterton, Miss Julia [*later* Mrs. Samuel Glover] (1779–1850). C.S. 1793. C.G. 1797. **1792:** N. 4/7, 20/8. **1793:** W. 21/3; Wex. 18/4, 1/5; K. 19/6, 5/7; G. 10/7, 28/8.

Bevan, Mr. **1800:** B. 14/4, 30/4.

Bevan, Mrs. **1800:** B. 14/4.

Bew, Mr. **1792:** B. 8/2.

Biddy, Mr. **1800:** B. 10/3, 6/6.

Billington, Mrs. James [*née* Elizabeth Weichsell] (1768–1818). S.A. 1783. C.G. 1786. **1784:** W. ?/9. **1791:** C. 11/8, 29/9; L. ?/9.

Bindon, Miss Emily Coates [*later* Mrs. Montague Talbot] (b. 1779). C.S. 1799. **1799:** C. 30/8.

Binns, Mr. C.S. 1769. **1767:** K. 12/12. **1768:** K. 15/1, 2/3.

Blackler, Mr. F.S. 1784. **1761:** B. 29/6, 17/7.

Blakes, Miss. **1787:** K. 5/2.

Blanchard, Mrs. Thomas. C.S. 1797. **1798:** L. 1/10.

Bland, Mr. **1769:** C. 15/9.

Blank, Mrs. **1765:** C. 21/9, 30/9.

Bloomer, Mr. **1763:** B. 14/1, 9/3.

Bloomer, Mrs. **1763:** B. 14/1, 9/3.

Boland, Mr. **1765:** C. 27/9.

Booth, Mr. **1770:** C. 25/8. **1775:** B. 1/12. **1776:** B. 28/2. **1778:** B. 30/10. **1779:** B. 12/2.

Booth, Mrs. [*later* Mrs. Mason]. (as Mrs. Booth) **1776:** B. 28/2, 8/3. **1778:** B. 10/4, 23/10. **1779:** B. 19/3. (as Mrs. Mason) **1790:** D. 14/3; B. 3/12. **1791:** B. 17/1, 19/10; D. 4/5, 22/6.

Boucheron, Mrs. [*née* Atkins] (d. 1807). (as Miss Atkins) **1798:** D. 28/2, 18/4. **1799:** D. 22/4. (as Mrs. Boucheron) **1800:** B. 10/3, 1/5.

Bourne, Mr. **1760:** C. 10/10.

Bowden, Wright (1752–1823). C.S. 1788 (*fr.* C.G.). **1788:** L. 7/7, 19/7; C. 23/8. **1790:** L. 13/8; C. 17/8, 2/9. **1796:** L. 18/8; C. 3/9.

Bowles, Robert (d. 1806). C.S. 1780. **1782:** L. 31/8; C. 27/9.

Bowles, Miss. C.S. 1794. **1796:** B. 20/5.

Boynton, Willoughby. **1792:** W. 24/7, 4/8; Wex. 12/10, 28/11. **1793:** K. 10/6.

Boynton, Mrs. Willoughby. **1792:** W. 24/7, 4/8; Wex. 28/9, 28/11. **1793:** Wex. 18/1; K. 10/6.

Brennan, Mr. Cap. S. 1783. **1788:** Cash. ?/8, ?/9; Car. ?/10; Wex. 26/12. **1789:** Wex. 6/3; K. 24/4, 13/7. **1790:** K. 8/11. **1791:** L. 23/2, 18/3; C. 26/4, 18/6. **1792:** C. 29/5. **1793:** G. 7/10.

Brennan, Mrs. **1789:** K. 24/4, 13/7. **1790:** E. 22/2; K. 8/11. **1791:** K. 12/1; L. 23/2, 18/3; C. 26/4, 18/6. **1792:** C. 29/5.

Brereton, William (1751–87). D.L. 1768. C.S. 1775. **1775:** C. 16/9. **1776:** C. 12/7, 28/8. **1778:** C. 27/7, 4/9. **1783:** C. 11/8, 29/8.

Brereton, Mrs. William [*later* Mrs. John Philip Kemble; *née* Priscilla Hopkins] (1758–1845). D.L. 1775. C.S. 1778. **1778:** C. 6/7.

Brett, William (d. 1795). C.S. 1769. C.G. 1782. **1792:** Wex. 31/12.

Brett, Miss W. [*later* Mrs. Chapman]. C.S. 1788. C.G. 1798. (as Miss Brett) **1789:** C. 25/9; W. 12/10. **1791:** Dr. ?/9. **1792:** K. 18/6, 12/7; W. 27/7, 13/8; G. 3/9, 14/9; Wex. 15/10, 31/12. **1793:** Wex. 4/1; L. 25/7, 29/7; C. 12/9, 16/9. **1794:** C. 6/9, 11/10. **1795:** C. 20/8, 22/10; Car. ?/10. (as Mrs. Chapman) **1797:** C. 15/8, 5/10.

Bridges, Mr. S.A. 1762. **1761:** C. ?/10.

Bridges, Mrs. C.S. 1760. **1761:** C. ?/10. **1768:** K. 12/2, 2/3. **1770:** B. 30/4, 7/8. **1792:** K. 23/2; W. 24/7, 27/7; Wex. 15/10, 28/11. **1793:** W. 8/3, 23/3.

Bridges, Miss. **1770:** B. 1/8. **1792:** K. 23/2; W. 24/7, 4/8; Wex. 12/10, 28/11. **1793:** Wex. 8/1.

Bridgewater, Roger (d. 1754). D.L. 1723. S.A. 1737. **1737:** W. ?/6.

Brown, Henry (d. 1770). D.L. 1753. S.A. 1757. **1759:** C. 17/8, 31/9. **1765:** C. 14/8, 20/9. **1766:** C. 14/8, 2/10. **1768:** B. 23/8. **1769:** N. 3/1; K. 3/6; C. 15/9, 29/9.

(1) Brown, Mrs. Henry. **1765:** C. 12/9, 16/9.

(2) Brown, Mrs. Henry [*née* E. Slack]. S.A. 1765 (*fr.* D.L.). (as Miss E. Slack) **1766:** C. 1/9, 13/10. (as Mrs. Brown) **1769:** C. 4/8, 20/9. **1771:** W. 9/10, 4/11. **1775:** C. 16/9.

Brown, Miss Hester (*see* Mrs. John Jackson).

Brown, Mr. J. (d. 1818). C.S. 1776. $H.^2$ 1783. **1776:** C. 5/10. **1779:** C. 10/9, 20/9. **1790:** L. 1/8, 4/9; E. 6/9, 2/10. **1795:** B. 18/3.

Brown, Mrs. J. [*form.* Mrs. Ross; *née* Mills] (d. 1823). C.S. 1779. C.G. 1785. **1779:** C. 10/9, 29/9. **1790:** E. 13/9. **1795:** B. 9/3, 25/3. **1796:** D. 25/1; B. 17/2, 1/6.

Brown, Master Henry [son of Mr. and Mrs. J. Brown] (b. *c.* 1788). **1795:** B. 27/2, 18/3. **1796:** B. 16/5, 1/6.

Brown, Matthew. C.S. 1779 (*fr.* Edinburgh). **1779:** C. 11/8, 11/10.

Browne, Campbell. Cap. S. 1782. $H.^2$ 1787. **1789:** C. 29/8, 25/9; W. 2/10, 12/10.

Brunton, Miss Anne [*later* (1) Mrs. Robert Merry, (2) Mrs. Thomas Wignell, (3) Mrs. William Warren] (1769–1808). C.G. 1785. S.A. 1787. **1786:** C. 14/8, 28/8. **1787:** B. 16/8, 24/8.

Buchanan, Mr. **1785:** L. 5/3.

Buckler, Mr. **1792:** K. 23/2; W. 24/7, 4/8.

Buckler, Mrs. C.S. 1789. **1792:** K. 23/2; W. 30/7, 20/8.

Bullock, Mr. **1768:** B. 26/8. **1769:** K. 3/6.

Bullrer, Mr. **1768:** B. 23/8.

Burden, Mr. Cap. S. 1770. **1768:** L. 13/10. **1770:** C. 25/8. **1771:** B. 4/9, 20/11. **1772:** B. 1/1; L. 6/7, 10/7; C. 19/8.

Burden, Mrs. [*née* Kitty White] C.G. 1760. S.A. 1762. **1768:** L. 13/10. **1769:** C. 4/4, 30/4. **1770:** C. 24/8, 3/9. **1771:** B. 20/11, 29/11. **1772:** B. 24/1; L. 10/7, 18/9; C. 2/10, 23/10.

Burdett, Mrs. **1772:** K. 31/12. **1773:** K. 16/2; W. n.d. **1775:** B. 8/12. **1776:** B. 5/1.

Burk, Mr. **1793:** Wex. 26/12.

Burk, Mrs. **1792:** C. 29/5; Wex. 19/10.

Burn, Mr. **1769:** K. 31/7.

Butler, Mr. S.A. 1782 (*fr.* England). **1782:** K. 28/9, 28/12. **1783:** K. 8/2.

Butler, Mrs. **1783:** K. 8/2.

Callan, Joseph. C.S. 1793. **1796:** C. 10/9; Dr. 10/10, 12/10. **1797:** C. 9/9, 5/10.

Calvert, Charles (1754–97). C.S. 1771. H.[2] 1784. **1772:** C. 23/9. **1773:** C. 3/6, 17/9. **1774:** C. 14/9.

Campion, Miss Maria Ann [*later* (1) Mrs. Spencer, (2) Mrs. Alexander Pope] (1775–1803). C.S. 1790. C.G. 1797. (as Miss Campion) **1790:** C. 1/9, 10/9. **1791:** C. 4/10, 5/10. **1792:** W. 17/8, 18/9. **1793:** G. 22/7, 4/9. **1794:** D. 9/7, 25/7; C. 26/8, 16/10. **1795:** B. 12/4, 8/5. (as Mrs. Spencer) **1796:** K. 17/8.

Carlton, Mr. **1800:** B. 10/3, 14/3.

Carmichael, Thomas. A.S. 1737. **1760:** C. 25/7, 15/10.

Carroll, Mr. **1761:** C. ?/10.

Carroll, Mrs. **1769:** C. 15/9.

Carroll, Miss. **1769:** C. 31/7.

Carthy, Mr. (*see* McCarthy).

Castelli, Mr. **1790:** K. 8/11.

Castelli, Mrs. S.A. 1787 (*fr.* Norwich). **1788:** L. 14/7; C. 4/8; Wex. 18/12. **1789:** Wex. 7/1, 6/3; K. 24/4, 13/7. **1790:** E. 26/4, 24/8; G. 25/8, 12/9. **1791:** L. 23/2, 18/3; C. 26/4, 18/6.

Cately, Miss Anne (1745–89). C.G. 1762. S.A. 1763. **1765:** C. 16/8, 19/8.

Caulfield, Mr. **1790:** D. ?/5. **1798:** D. 4/5.

Caulfield, Mrs. **1798:** D. 4/5.

Cecil, Mrs. **1796:** E. 26/5.

Chadduck, Mr. **1784:** Y. 20/12.

Chalmers, James (d. 1810). C.G. 1783. S.A. 1784. **1786:** W. 18/7; L. 31/7, 18/9; C. 2/8, 1/11. **1787:** K. 20/7, 24/9. **1788:** B. 10/10, 17/12. **1789:** B. 23/1, 11/2.

Chalmers, Mrs. James [*née* Mills] (d. 1792). C.G. 1783. S.A. 1786–7. **1786:** W. 18/7; L. 31/7, 18/9; C. 2/8, 3/11. **1787:** K. 20/7, 24/9. **1788:** B. 10/10, 17/12. **1789:** B. 26/1, 11/2.

Chambers, Mr. C.S. 1797. **1797:** C. 5/10.

Chaplin, Mr. [*or* Chaplain]. C.S. 1772. **1772:** L. 6/7, 18/7; C. 19/8. **1774.** C. 14/9.

Chapman, Mrs. (*see* Miss W. Brett).

Chapman, Miss. **1797:** C. 5/10.

Cherry, Andrew (1762–1812). C.S. 1779. D.L. 1802. **1778:** N. 3/12. **1779:** N. 1/3; D. 18/8. **1782:** D. 4/12. **1783:** B. ?/1, ?/5; Sl. summer; D. ?/5, ?/10. **1784:** D. ?/2; B. ?/3, 8/12. **1787:** B. 19/1; C. 10/9; W. 10/10, 17/10. **1788:** C. 21/8, 15/9. **1789:** C. 14/9, 18/9; W. 12/10, 13/10. **1792:** B. 24/10. **1794:** C. 11/8, 15/10; B. 24/10, 7/11. **1796:** Dr. 17/8.

Cherry, Mrs. Andrew [*née* Knipe]. S.A. 1786. (as Miss Knipe) **1766:** B. 5/2. **1778:** N. 3/12. **1783:** B. 24/1, 19/5. (as Mrs. Cherry) **1784:** Lis. 20/10. **1787:** B. 19/1; W. 17/10. **1788:** C. 21/8. **1789:** C. 15/9; W. 13/10.

Chute, Miss. S.A. 1780. **1780:** C. 10/10.

Clare, Mr. **1790:** W. ?/7; L. 31/7, 8/11; E. 6/9, 2/10. **1791:** L. 18/3; C. 26/4, 18/6.

Clark, Mrs. **1761:** C. ?/10.

Clinch, Lawrence (d. 1812). C.S. 1768. D.L. 1772. **1769:** C. 4/8, 20/9. **1770:** C. 24/8. **1774:** C. 24/6, 8/8; L. 23/8. **1776:** C. 25/9, 14/10. **1783:** C. 15/8, 23/9; L. 11/10. **1784:** C. 1/9, 30/9. **1786:** W. 18/7; C. 1/8, 28/10. **1787:** C. 17/9. **1788:** L. 25/7; C. 7/8, 4/9. **1790:** L. 31/1, 4/9; W. ?/7.

Clinton, Mr. C.S. 1780. **1778:** C. 19/10.

Coates, Miss. **1790:** K. 1/12, 15/12. **1792:** N. 11/7.

Coates, Mrs. Elizabeth. C.S. 1789. C.G. 1797. **1790:** C. 1/9, 8/9; B. 8/11, 31/12. **1791:** B. 5/1, 10/8; D. 9/5, 16/5; C. 4/10; L. 16/11. **1792:** B. 1/2, 28/3; N. 20/7. **1793:** G. 1/7, 19/7. **1794:** B. 7/11, 15/12. **1795:** B. 2/1.

Collins, John (1742–1808). S.A. 1764 (*fr.* Edinburgh). **1776:** B. 2/2, 7/2. **1781:** B. 30/5. **1790:** C. 30/7, 1/9.

Collins, Mrs. **1787:** B. 13/4. **1792:** K. 23/2, 11/6; W. 24/7, 6/8; Wex. 12/10, 7/12. **1793:** W. 8/3, 23/3. **1795:** G. 22/9.

Colthurst, Mr. C.S. 1790. **1791:** C. 4/10. **1792:** N. 16/7.

Comerford, Miss Rosetta (*see* Mrs. Thomas Ryder).

Comerford, Mr. **1789:** Wex. 6/3; K. 24/4, 13/7.

Connell, Mr. F.S. 1795. **1800:** C. 4/3.

Connor, Mr. **1799:** K. 5/6, 31/7.

Connor, Mrs. **1799:** K. 31/7.

Connor, Master. **1799:** K. 16/6, 31/7.

Cook, Mr. **1792:** N. 20/7.

Cooke, George Frederick (1756–1811). H.[2] 1777. C.S. 1794. **1798:** C. 13/9, 20/9; L. 1/10. **1799:** L. 2/8. **1800:** C. 30/9.

Cooper, Mr. C.S. 1788. **1790:** L. 22/11. **1791:** L. 18/3.

Cornelys, John. C.S. 1768. H.[2] 1791. **1781:** C. 8/8, 13/10. **1785:** C. 27/9. **1786:** W. 18/7; C. 2/8. **1787:** C. 1/8, 6/9. **1788:** L. 14/7; C. 4/8, 12/9. **1790:** D. 4/6.

Cornelys, Mrs. John (Margaret) (1723–97). C.S. 1780. **1781:** C. 10/9. **1784:** N. ?/6. **1785:** C. 27/9. **1787:** C. 3/8, 11/9. **1788:** L. 14/7; C. 4/8, 12/9. **1790:** D. 21/5, 18/6.

Corry, Isaac. Cap. S. 1784. **1788:** B. 10/10. **1796:** K. 23/9.

Corry, Robert. Cap. S. 1745. **1756:** C. 30/8, 24/9. **1758:** C. 7/8, 14/9.

Cottrell, Mr. **1790:** C. 4/9. **1792:** C. 29/5; W. 22/8; Wex. 10/10, 10/12. **1793:** Wex. 18/1; K. 10/6.

Cottrell, Mrs. **1792:** C. 29/5; Wex. 12/10, 12/12. **1793:** K. 10/6.

Coughlan, Mr. **1763:** B. 14/1, 14/3.

Courtney, Mrs. Patrick. **1799:** K. 5/6, 28/6 (*fr.* C.G.). **1800:** E. 13/1.
Cranford, Miss. **1792:** D. 20/11. **1793:** D. 16/1; B. 17/4, 15/5.
Crawford, Thomas (1750–94). C.S. 1778. C.G. 1779. **1779:** C. 19/7, 11/8. **1792:** K. 23/2, 4/6; W. 24/7, 27/7; Wex. 15/12, 21/12. **1793:** Wex. 18/1.
Crawford, Mrs. Thomas (*see* (2) Mrs. Spranger Barry).
Cremonini, Signora. S.A. 1764 (*fr.* H.[2]). **1766:** C. 1/9, 15/10.
Cresswell, Mrs. John. C.S. 1798. **1799:** C. 31/8.
Crosby, Mr. S.A. 1774. **1775:** C. 16/9. **1776:** K. 17/6.
Crosby, Mrs. **1775:** C. 16/9. **1776:** K. 17/6, 22/7.
Cross, Miss. F.S. 1777. **1778:** K. 16/2.
Crouch, Mrs. Rollings Edward [*née* Anna Maria Phillips] (1763–1805). D.L. 1780. S.A. 1782. (as Miss Phillips) **1782:** C. 30/7, 16/8; L. 31/8. **1783:** C. 9/8. (as Mrs. Crouch) **1787:** L. 16/7; C. 30/7, 10/8. **1789:** W. 9/8, ?/10; C. 28/8, 11/9.
Crow, Mr. **1768:** L. 29/10.
Crow, Mrs. [*née* Báptist]. **1768:** L. 29/10.
Cubitt, William. Cap. S. 1782. **1783:** C. 6/9.
Cunningham, Thomas. **1790:** E. 3/2, 9/4; K. 8/11. **1791:** E. 11/11. **1792:** C. 29/5. **1793:** G. 21/8.
Curtis, Mr. C.S. 1797. **1799:** K. 5/6, 12/6. **1800:** E. 13/1.
Cushon, Miss. **1779:** K. 16/12.

Dalton, Mr. Cap. S. 1770. **1778:** N. 3/12. **1779:** N. 26/4.
Daly, Mr. **1756:** Tr. 9/3, 10/5.
Daly, Mrs. **1756:** Tr. 9/3, 10/5.
Daly, Richard (*c.* 1758–1813). C.G. 1779. C.S. 1779. **1779:** L. 17/8; C. 1/9, 20/10. **1780:** C. 2/8, 1/10. **1781:** C. 8/8, 1/10. **1782:** C. 19/8, 1/10. **1783:** C. 9/8, 27/9; L. 11/10. **1784:** C. 6/9, 1/10. **1786:** W. 18/7; L. 3/8, 19/9; C. 16/9, 23/10. **1787:** C. 2/8, 22/9; W. 10/10, 12/10. **1793:** L. 25/7; C. 26/8, 1/9; W. 30/9, 4/10. **1794:** C. 18/8, 30/9; L. 8/9, 14/9; **1795:** C. 20/8.
Daly, Mrs. Richard [*form.* Mrs. John Richard Kirwin Lyster; *née* Jane Barsanti] (d. 1795). C.G. 1772. C.S. 1776. (as Miss Barsanti) **1778:** C. 28/8, 14/10. (as Mrs. Lyster) **1779:** L. 17/8; C. 1/9, 13/10. (as Mrs. Daly) **1780:** C. 2/8, 2/10. **1781:** C. 8/8, 14/9. **1782:** C. 19/8, C. 14/10; L. 4/9. **1783:** C. 4/9, 23/9. **1784:** C. 6/9, 5/10. **1786:** W. 18/7; C. 2/8; L. 3/8. **1787:** C. 9/8, 6/9; W. 10/10, 12/10. **1793:** C. 26/8, 5/9; W. 30/9, 4/10.
Dancer, Mrs. Ann (*see* (2) Mrs. Spranger Barry).
Darrington, Mr. **1790:** E. 13/9.
Davenport, George Gosling (1758–1814). C.S. 1792 (*fr.* Exeter). C.G. 1794. **1792:** N. 20/7.
Davenport, Mrs. George Gosling [*née* Mary Ann Harvey] (1759–1843). C.S. 1792 (*fr.* Exeter). C.G. 1794. **1792:** N. 20/7.
Davis, Mr. **1800:** C. ?/3; B. 10/3, 7/5.
Davison, John. **1790:** C. 4/9. **1792:** K. 23/2, 11/4; W. 24/7, 17/9; Wex. 22/9, 26/12. **1793:** Wex. 25/1; W. 8/3, 23/3; K. 13/7, 14/8.
Dawson, George (*c.* 1756–87). S.A. 1764. (as Master Dawson) **1761:** B. 24/8. **1768:** L. 13/10. **1770:** B. 18/7, 28/7. **1771:** L. 22/10. **1772:** L. 6/7.

(as Mr. Dawson) **1783:** C. 4/9, 22/9. **1784:** N. 25/6. **1785:** L. 16/8; C. 2/9, 26/9. **1786:** W. 18/7; C. 2/8, 1/11; L. 18/9.

Dawson, Mrs. George. C.S. 1778. **1784:** B. 8/12. **1787:** B. 12/3. **1788:** L. 14/7, 29/7; C. 4/8. **1789:** W. 12/10. **1790:** C. 4/9. **1791:** C. 7/10. **1793:** G. 24/7, 9/10.

Dawson, William (d. 1796). S.A. 1760. **1753:** B. ?/7, 14/8. **1756:** Tr. 1/4, 30/5. **1759:** Ba. 28/9, 27/12. **1761:** B. 29/6, 14/8. **1766:** C. 1/9, 10/9. **1767:** L. summer. **1770:** B. 28/7; C. 24/8, 25/8. **1772:** L. 6/7; C. 10/8, 6/10. **1788:** L. 16/7. **1789:** L. 17/8, 22/8; C. 16/9. **1792:** N. 4/7, 20/7. **1795:** Car. ?/10. **1796:** E. 7/6, 24/6.

Dawson, Mrs. William [*form.* Mrs. William Lewis]. S.A. 1760. (as Mrs. Lewis) **1753:** B. 3/7, 6/8. (as Mrs. Dawson) **1756:** Tr. 9/3, 7/5. **1761:** B. 29/6, 26/8. **1766:** C. 25/8. **1771:** L. 22/10. **1772:** L. 10/7, 18/9; C. 19/8, 3/9.

Dawson, Mr. **1790:** L. 22/11. **1791:** L. 18/3; C. 26/4, 28/5.

Day, George. S.A. 1770 (*fr.* C.G.). **1771:** L. 22/10; B. 30/10, 18/12. **1772:** B. 17/1. **1773:** K. 16/2. **1778:** B. 28/12, 30/12. **1779:** B. 12/2. **1782:** D. 23/10. **1794:** C. 20/8.

Day, Mrs. George. S.A. 1770 (*fr.* C.G.). **1771:** B. 30/10, 18/12. **1772:** B. 24/1. **1773:** K. 16/2. **1780:** B. 27/3. **1782:** D. 25/6. **1798:** L. 1/10. **1800:** C. 4/3.

Day, Miss. **1798:** L. 1/10.

Decoursey, Mr. **1792:** Wex. 12/11.

Delane, Dennis (d. 1750). S.A. 1729. C.G. 1735. **1735:** Carl. early summer; C. summer. **1737:** W. ?/6.

Dempsey, Mr. **1790:** W. ?/7; L. 31/7, 8/11; E. 6/9, 2/10. **1791:** L. 18/3; C. 26/4, 18/6.

Dennisson, Miss. **1753:** B. 23/7.

D'Eon, Chevalier. C.S. 1794. **1794:** C. 15/8, 14/10.

Desaw, Mr. S.A. 1771. **1775:** Lis. 1/12.

De Volney, Mrs. C.S. 1797. **1798:** L. 1/10.

Dexter, John (1726–64). D.L. 1752. S.A. 1753. **1756:** C. 30/8, 13/9. **1758:** C. 18/8. **1760:** C. 23/7, 29/9. **1761:** C. 21/7, 15/10. **1762:** C. 28/9.

Dexter, Mrs. John. C.S. 1762. **1760:** C. 17/9.

Digges, West Dudley (1720–86). S.A. 1749. H.[2] 1777. **1767:** L. summer. **1774:** C. 6/9; L. 19/9, 27/9 (*fr.* Edinburgh). **1781:** C. 1/9, 15/10. **1782:** C. 2/8, 3/10; L. 4/9. **1783:** C. 1/9, 27/9.

Dillon, Miss. S.A. 1760. **1761:** B. 28/6, 17/7.

Donavan, Mr. **1771:** L. 22/10.

Doyle, Mr. F.S. 1777. **1776:** C. 5/10. **1777:** C. 8/9. **1778:** C. 19/10. **1782:** C. 29/7, 10/10. **1783:** C. 31/3, 24/9. **1784:** C. 30/9, 1/10. **1785:** C. 22/9. **1786:** W. 18/7; C. 2/8, 5/10; L. 3/8, 15/8. **1787:** C. 6/9, 15/9. **1788:** C. 15/9. **1789:** C. 3/3, 21/9. **1790:** C. 24/8, 9/9. **1791:** C. 11/8, 4/10. **1792:** C. 23/7, 11/9. **1793:** C. 9/9, 16/9. **1794:** C. 6/9. **1795:** C. 20/8, 5/9. **1796:** C. 30/7. **1797:** C. 4/8, 3/10.

DuBellamy, Charles Clementine (d. 1793). C.G. 1774. C.S. 1777 (*fr.* C.G.). **1778:** C. 10/10, 16/10.

Duffy, Peter. S.A. 1771. C.G. 1789. **1768:** K. 1/2, 2/3. **1770:** B. 30/4, 18/7; K. 14/9, 21/12. **1771:** W. 9/10. **1778:** K. 18/2. **1786:** W. 18/7; C. 1/8,

2/11. **1787:** C. 9/8, 20/9; W. 10/10, 23/10. **1788:** C. 4/8, 4/9. **1795:** Car. ?/10.

Dugan, Mr. (*or* Dougan). **1750:** B. 3/1. **1763:** B. 21/1, 23/2.

Duncan, Timothy (d. 1801). S.A. 1766. **1768:** L. 13/10. **1784:** B. 3/3, 21/7. **1789:** C. 15/9 (*fr.* Newcastle); W. 13/10. **1791:** Dr. autumn. **1795:** D. 9/12. **1796:** B. 17/2, 9/5.

Duncan, Mrs. Timothy. **1784:** B. 5/3, 21/7.

Duncan, Miss Maria Rebecca [*later* Mrs. John Davison] (1780–1858). C.S. 1790. D.L. 1804. **1795:** D. 20/11. **1796:** B. 17/2, 13/6.

Dunne, Mr. **1796:** C. 28/3.

Duval, Lewis (d. 1766). R.S. 1733. **1737:** W. ?/6. **1738:** Dr. summer.

Dwyer, Mr. **1792:** Wex. 18/1 (*fr.* York). **1793:** K. 2/10.

Dyer, Michael (d. 1774). C.G. 1733. S.A. 1739. **1741:** C. n.d. **1742:** C. and W. n.d.

Dynan, Miss. C.S. 1791. **1789:** C. 22/9.

Eaton, Miss. S.A. 1766. **1770:** B. 30/4; K. 17/9, 31/12.

Edwards, John. S.A. 1781 (*fr.* D.L.). **1781:** C. 22/8. **1782:** L. 2/8.

Edwin, John, Sr. (1749–90). S.A. 1765. **1766:** W. ?/10.

Edwin, Mrs. John, Jr. (*see* Miss Richards).

Egerton, Mrs. [*form.* Mrs. Kelf; *née* Ambrose] (b. 1739). S.A. 1761. D.L. 1771. (as Mrs. Kelf) **1762:** C. 24/9, 15/10. **1765:** Dr. 26/8. **1766:** C. 16/8, 16/9. (as Mrs. Egerton) **1785:** L. 16/8; C. 2/9.

Ellard, Thomas. S.A. 1760. **1761:** C. 6/7, 1/10. **1762:** C. 20/8, 30/10. **1763:** C. 29/9.

Ellard, Mrs. Thomas. S.A. 1758. **1761:** C. 26/9, 1/10. **1764:** C. 14/9.

Elliot, Mr. **1778:** K. 18/2.

Elliot, Mrs. C.S. 1782. **1778:** K. 18/2.

Elrington, Francis (1692–1746). S.A. 1714. **1746:** K. summer.

Elrington, Joseph (d. 1755). S.A. 1731. **1754:** B. 18/11, 17/12. **1755:** B. 3/3.

Elrington, Richard (d. 1770). S.A. 1729. C.G. 1750. **1754:** B. 18/11, 13/12. **1755:** B. 10/1, 14/3.

Elrington, Mrs. Richard [*form.* (1) Mrs. Barnes, (2) Mrs. Christopher ('Betty') Martin; *later* (1) Mrs. Workman, (2) Mrs. Richard Wilson; *née* Elizabeth Grace] (b. 1716). R.S. 1733. C.G. 1733. **1754:** B. 18/11, 17/12. **1755:** B. 3/1, 7/3.

Elrington, Master [Richard]. S.A. 1750. **1754:** B. 11/12, 17/12.

Elrington, Thomas (1688–1732). D.L. 1709. S.A. 1712. **1728:** Dr. 13/6.

Emerson, Miss. S.A. 1780 (*fr.* Bath). **1781:** C. 8/8. **1784:** K. 17/2.

Esten, Mrs. Harriet Pye [*née* Bennett] (1768–1868). S.A. 1788 (*fr.* Bath). C.G. 1790. **1788:** C. 27/8, 2/9. **1789:** C. 29/8, 18/9; W. 2/10, 13/10.

Fairborn, Master. **1800:** B. 14/5.

Farce, Mrs. **1796:** E. 24/6.

Farrell, Thomas. Cap. S. 1747. **1768:** B. 2/9, 23/12; Ca. 15/10, 21/10. **1769:** B. 6/1; N. 23/1; K. 3/6. **1770:** B. 30/4. **1771:** B. 30/10, 27/12. **1772:** B. 23/1. **1773:** B. 6/9. **1774:** B. 2/2. **1779:** B. 22/1, 19/3.

Farrell, Mrs. Thomas (Elizabeth). Cap. S. 1747. **1768:** B. 23/8. **1769:** B. 6/1; N. 23/1; K. 3/6, 14/7. **1771:** B. 16/8, 27/12. **1772:** B. 17/1.

Farrell, the Misses. **1768:** Ca. 15/10 (*fr.* Edinburgh). **1771:** B. 27/12. **1772:** B. 23/1. **1773:** B. 6/12. **1774:** B. 2/2; D. 8/8. **1779:** B. 12/2, 19/3.

Farren, Miss Elizabeth (1759–1829). H.[2] 1777. C.S. 1784. **1784:** C. 30/9. **1794:** C. 18/8, 5/9; L. 8/9, 14/9.

Farren, George. *c.* **1768:** Sl. n.d.

Farrol, Mr. **1769:** C. 15/9.

Faulkner, Mr. **1800:** E. 13/1.

Fenner, Mrs. **1792:** B. 24/2; D. ?/12. **1793:** D. 7/1.

Field, Mr. C.S. 1792. **1792:** K. 6/6, 14/7. **1795:** K. 9/11.

Fisher, Alexander. C.S. 1759. **1765:** B. 7/10. **1766:** B. 31/1.

Fisher, Mrs. Alexander. **1766:** B. 19/2.

Fisher, Master, **1765:** B. 7/10.

Fitzgerald, Mr. C.S. 1766. **1762:** C. 4/10.

Fitz-Harris, Miss. C.S. 1796. **1797:** C. 5/10.

Fitzhenry, Mrs. Edward [*form.* Mrs. John Gregory; *née* Elizabeth Flannigan] (d. 1790). C.G. 1754. S.A. 1754. **1764:** C. 14/9. **1768:** C. 11/8, 19/8.

Fleetwood, Charles, Jr. (d. 1784). D.L. 1759. C.S. 1760. **1774:** L. 19/9.

Fleming, Miss. **1755:** B. 15/1, 7/3.

Flurry, Mr. **1761:** C. ?/10.

Forde, Brownlow. C.S. 1767. **1769:** K. 12/8, 17/8. **1771:** B. 13/11, 4/12. **1772:** K. 31/12. **1773:** K. 16/2, 20/2; W. ?/4. **1776:** C. 12/7, 11/10. **1777:** C. 18/7, 14/10. **1778:** C. 14/7, 19/10.

Forde, Mrs. Brownlow. **1771:** B. 13/11.

Forde, Master. **1773:** K. 5/6. **1777:** C. 14/10.

Fotteral, James. S.A. 1770. H.[2] 1777. **1769:** C. 15/9. **1770:** B. 14/7, 2/8; K. 14/9, 17/12. **1771:** B. 16/8, 30/10. **1772:** B. 17/1. **1775:** C. 16/9. **1781:** C. 8/8, 22/10. **1783:** C. 6/9. **1785:** C. 16/9, 30/9. **1787:** B. 9/4.

Francis, Miss Dorothea [*later* Mrs. Jordan; *née* Bland] (1761–1816). C.S. 1779. **1780:** C. 1/9, 14/10. **1781:** C. 8/8, 13/10.

Francis, Miss Hester. C.S. 1779. **1781:** C. 13/8, 7/9.

Franklin, Mr. **1796:** B. 6/6.

Freeman, Mr. **1788:** B. 17/12. **1789:** B. 2/3.

Freeman, Mrs. **1788:** B. 12/11. **1789:** B. 2/3.

Frodsham, Miss Sarah [*later* (1) Mrs. Reilly, (2) Mrs. George Inchbald] (b. 1761). C.S. 1778. H.[2] 1783. **1778:** C. 14/7, 24/8.

Fullam, Michael. C.S. 1767. **1768:** B. ?/12. **1769:** B. ?/1; N. 23/1; K. 3/6, 14/8. **1771:** L. 22/10. **1772:** K. 31/12. **1773:** K. 16/2. **1792:** K. 23/2, 11/6; W. ?/7, 14/9. **1793:** W. 8/3, 23/3; K. 5/6, 2/10. **1795:** K. 16/11. **1796:** K. 16/9, 2/11. **1798:** L. 1/10. **1799:** K. 5/6, 19/7; L. 2/8. **1800:** B. ?/2.

Fullam, Mrs. Michael. C.S. 1771. **1768:** B. 23/8. **1769:** B. 20/1; N. 23/1; K. 3/6, 14/8. **1772:** K. 31/12. **1773:** K. 16/2. **1779:** K. 5/6, 19/7. **1800:** B. 31/1, 10/2.

Fullamon, Mr. **1792:** K. 23/5.

Fuller, Mr. **1795:** K. 20/11.

Fulmer, Mr. **1772:** K. 31/12.
Fulmer, Mrs. **1772:** K. 31/12.
Furnival, Mrs. Thomas (Elizabeth, 'Fanny'). D.L. 1737. S.A. 1739. **1741:** B. 1/7.

Gain, Mrs. C.S. 1778. **1772:** K. 31/12. **1773:** K. 16/2. **1778:** C. 16/10. **1779:** C. 11/8, 29/9. **1780:** C. 28/8. **1782:** C. 1/10.
Gain, Miss. C.S. 1778. **1780:** C. 13/10.
Galway, Geoffrey. **1772:** K. 31/12. **1779:** N. 26/4. **1783:** D. ?/7, ?/10; Sl. summer. **1784:** D. ?/2.
Gardiner, Mr. **1795:** K. 25/11. **1796:** K. 14/9.
Gardiner, Mrs. **1796:** K. 16/9.
Garvey, Mr. Cap. S. 1782. **1783:** B. 24/1, 19/5; D. ?/7, ?/10; Sl. summer. **1784:** D. ?/2; B. 3/3, 19/7. **1792:** W. 28/3; G. 22/10.
Garvey, Mrs. C.S. 1797. **1792:** G. 16/8, 22/10. **1798:** C. 15/9. **1800:** B. 10/3, 26/5.
Gaudry, Richard. Cap. S. 1773. C.G. 1784. **1776:** K. 22/7, 14/8.
Gemea, Tobias. S.A. 1739. **1751:** B. 18/12. **1753:** B. 15/6, 31/8. **1761:** B. 8/7, 15/7. **1770:** B. 30/4, 28/7. **1773:** W. n.d.; K. 16/2.
Gemea, Mrs. Tobias [*née* Richabella Chetwood]. S.A. 1746. **1753:** B. 29/6, 7/9. **1758:** B. 24/2. **1759:** Ba. 25/9, 29/9. **1761:** B. 15/7, 17/7. **1770:** B. 25/7. **1771:** B. 16/8.
Gemea, Miss. **1770:** B. 30/4, 25/7. **1771:** B. 30/10.
Gemea, W. S.A. 1759. **1781:** C. 8/8. **1782:** C. 29/7; L. 31/8. **1783:** C. 23/8.
Gemea, Mrs. W. S.A. 1781. **1781:** C. 10/8. **1782:** L. 31/8. **1784:** C. 29/8, 30/9. **1785:** C. 27/8.
Gemea, Master. S.A. 1781. **1781:** C. 10/8. **1782:** C. 7/10. **1786:** C. 24/10.
Geoghegan, Mr. **1767:** K. 19/11. **1770:** B. 7/5, 8/8; K. 14/9, 15/12. **1792:** N. 20/7.
George, Miss. H.[2] 1783. C.S. 1788. **1790:** L. 13/8; C. 17/8, 31/8. **1791:** C. 19/8, 8/10.
Gerry, Thomas. **1766:** C. 3/10. **1768:** C. 17/9.
Giffard, Henry (1699–1772). S.A. 1716. L.I.F. 1717. **1735:** Carl. 7/7; C. summer. **1738:** Carl. ?/8; Dr. 11/9, 27/10.
Gilbert, Miss. **1768:** K. 22/2, 2/3; L. 13/10.
Glassington, Miss. C.S. 1769. **1769:** C. 20/9.
Glenvil, Philip. C.S. 1761. **1761:** C. 6/7, 28/10. **1762:** C. 3/10, 4/10. **1764:** C. 3/10. **1765:** C. 30/9. **1766:** C. 16/8. **1767:** L. summer. **1768:** L. 13/10. **1776:** K. 17/6.
Glover, William Frederick. S.A. 1756. **1757:** C. 5/8. **1758:** C. 14/8. **1759:** C. 7/8. **1760:** C. 25/7, 15/10. **1761:** C. 6/7, 24/9. **1762:** C. 3/10, 27/10. **1763:** C. 21/9, 29/9. **1764:** C. 14/9, 3/10. **1765:** C. 16/8, 1/10. **1766:** C. 27/8, 11/9.
Glover, Mrs. William Frederick (Elizabeth) (d. 1789). S.A. 1758. **1758:** C. 4/9. **1759:** C. 17/8. **1761:** C. 10/7. **1762:** C. 20/8, 29/10. **1763:** C. 29/9. **1764:** C. 14/9, 3/10. **1765:** C. 1/10. **1766:** C. 25/8, 1/10.
Godfrey, Mr. **1791:** B. 31/1; D. 6/6.

Godfrey, Mrs. **1790:** D. 5/5. **1791:** B. 14/1, 19/8; D. 30/5. **1792:** B. 27/2.
Godwin, Mrs. **1758:** C. 7/8, 4/10.
Golding, Mr. **1773:** K. 10/4.
Gotley, Mr. **1790:** W. ?/7; L. 31/7, 8/11; E. 6/9, 2/10. **1791:** L. 18/3; C. 26/4, 18/6. **1792:** C. 29/5.
Gough, Miss [*later* Mrs. Galindo]. F.S. 1793. C.G. 1795. **1796:** B. 21/4, 2/5; C. 15/8, 30/9. **1797:** C. 5/10. **1799:** L. 2/8; C. 29/8.
Grace, Mr. C.S. 1791 (*fr.* H.[2]). **1792:** K. 23/2, 16/5; N. 16/7, 20/7.
Graham, Mr. C.S. 1769 (*fr.* H.[2]). **1781:** C. 8/8, 14/9. **1782:** C. 29/7, 27/9.
Graham, Miss. **1778:** W. autumn.
Grant, James (*see* James Grant Raymond).
Grant, Miss. **1796:** E. 27/4, 22/6.
Gray, Mr. **1800:** C. 4/3.
Gray, Miss. **1800:** C. 4/3.
Greville, Mrs. **1779:** C. 16/7, 4/10.
Griffin, Mr. **1796:** Dr. 10/10.
Griffith, Thomas (1680–1744). S.A. 1698. **1728:** Dr. 13/6. **1735:** Carl. 7/7, 14/7.
Griffith, Mr. **1791:** B. 21/1; L. 16/5, 20/6. **1792:** B. 6/2, 5/3; D. ?/12. **1793:** D. 16/1. **1794:** D. 30/5. **1795:** C. 14/9. **1796:** D. 22/1; B. 9/5, 30/5. **1798:** D. 28/2, 9/4.
Griffith, Mr., Jr. **1792:** B. 6/2.

Hall, Mr. C.S. 1771. **1768:** K. 1/2. **1771:** Cash. 25/2; F. 22/3. **1778:** C. 19/10. **1785:** L. 1/3. **1788:** Cash ?/8, ?/9; Car. ?/10. **1789:** Wex. 7/1, 6/3; K. 24/4, 13/7. **1790:** E. 9/4; K. 8/11.
Hall, Mrs. [*née* Griffy]. **1788:** Wex. 26/12. **1789:** Wex. 7/1, 13/3. **1795:** D. 15/1.
Hallam, Adam (d. 1768). S.A. 1707. D.L. 1731. **1737:** W. ?/6.
Hallion, Mr. S.A. 1771. **1771:** W. 9/10. **1781:** C. 10/8.
Hamilton, Myrton. S.A. 1729. G.F. 1732. **1756:** C. 24/9. **1760:** C. 25/7, 15/10. **1761:** C. 6/7. **1762:** C. 20/8, 30/10. **1763:** C. 29/9. **1764:** C. 14/9. **1765:** C. 21/9, 30/9. **1768:** B. 23/8, 30/12. **1769:** N. 23/1; K. 3/6. **1771:** B. 4/9, 20/12. **1772:** B. 17/1. **1773:** B. 6/9. **1774:** B. 14/1. **1776:** B. 20/3; D. 16/10. **1778:** B. 1/4, 23/10; N. 16/7. **1779:** B. 1/1, 4/11. **1780:** B. 10/3. **1781:** C. 8/8. **1782:** D. 1/4. **1783:** B. 14/6.
Hamilton, Mrs. Myrton. S.A. 1729. G.F. 1732. **1761:** C. 31/7.
Hamilton, William. **1779:** B. 19/3 (*fr.* C.G.).
Ham[m]erton, Jacob (b. 1759). F.S. 1784. **1783:** B. ?/1, ?/5. **1784:** K. 17/2, 4/6. **1785:** C. 27/8, 24/9. **1787:** W. 17/10, 22/10. **1788:** C. 4/8. **1789:** W. 13/10. **1790:** C. 4/9. **1799:** C. 28/8.
Hanford, Mr. **1761:** B. 29/6, 26/8.
Hannam, Mr. **1786:** C. 29/8.
Hannam, Mrs. Cap. S. 1782. **1785:** C. 27/8. **1787:** W. 17/10. **1788:** C. 4/8.
Hardy, Mr. **1781:** C. 10/8.
Hargrave [Snow], Mr. C.S. 1793. C.G. 1796. **1794:** C. 11/8, 16/10. **1796:** C. 28/3, 8/4.

Hartley, Mrs. 'Rosamond' [*née* Elizabeth White] (1750–1824). C.G. 1772. S.A. 1774 (*fr.* C.G.). **1774:** C. 20/7, 29/7.

Hawkins, Mrs. **1800:** B. 14/4.

Hawtrey, Mr. C.S. 1761–2. **1762:** C. 20/8.

Hawtrey, Mrs. [*née* Macneil]. S.A. 1762. **1769:** C. 31/7, 15/9.

Haydon, Mr. **1797:** C. 2/10, 5/10.

Hayes, Mr. S.A. 1758. **1760:** C. 11/8, 15/10. **1761:** C. 6/7, 1/10.

Heaphy, Miss Mary (*see* Mrs. O'Keeffe).

Heaphy, Tottenham. Cap. S. 1749. **1757:** C. 5/8. **1758:** C. 14/7, 18/9. **1760:** C. 21/7, 15/10. **1761:** C. 6/7, 26/9. **1762:** C. 20/8, 2/11. **1763:** C. 7/9, 29/9. **1764:** C. 14/9, 3/10. **1765:** C. 13/8, 27/9. **1766:** C. 16/8, 11/9. **1769:** C. 2/8, 20/9. **1770:** L. summer; C. 24/8, 3/9. **1771:** L. 24/9, 22/10. **1772:** L. 6/7, 5/8; C. 19/8, 23/10. **1773:** C. 3/6, 21/9; L. 16/8. **1774:** C. 24/6, 25/7; L. 11/8, 28/9. **1775:** C. 3/7, 14/9. **1776:** 10/7, 4/10; L. 1/9, 21/9. **1777:** C. 25/7, 6/10; L. 13/8. **1778:** C. 17/7, 12/10. **1779:** C. 10/8. **1780:** C. 28/8, 30/9. **1781:** C. 10/9.

Heaphy, Mrs. Tottenham [*née* Alice Mason] (b. *c.* 1736). Cap. S. 1747. (as Miss Mason) **1757:** C. 5/8. **1758:** C. 14/7, 11/9. **1760:** C. 25/7, 15/9. **1761:** C. 26/9. **1762:** C. 20/8, 29/10. (as Mrs. Heaphy) **1771:** L. 22/10. **1772:** L. 6/7, 19/9; C. 6/10, 23/10. **1773:** C. 3/6, 22/9; L. 14/8. **1775:** C. 3/7, 21/9. **1776:** C. 24/7, 5/10. **1777:** C. 16/7, 17/10. **1778:** C. 14/7, 10/10. **1779:** C. 11/8, 13/10. **1780:** C. 11/8, 20/10. **1781:** C. 8/8, 19/10. **1782:** L. 31/8; C. 4/10. **1783:** C. 9/8, 25/9; L. 11/10. **1786:** L. 3/8, 15/8; C. 5/9, 30/10. **1788:** L. 14/7; C. 27/8, 15/9.

Heatton, Michael. S.A. 1760. **1761:** C. 6/7. **1762:** C. 20/8, 3/10. **1764:** Wex. ?/6; C. 3/10.

Heatton, the Misses E. and R. **1761:** C. summer. **1762:** C. 4/10. **1764:** C. 3/10.

Henderson, John H. (1747–85). H.[2] 1777. C.S. 1778. **1779:** C. 16/7, 13/8; L. 20/8.

Heney, Mr. **1788:** Cash. summer; Car. autumn. **1789:** Wex. 7/1, 6/3; K. 24/4, 13/7. **1799:** K. 5/6. **1800:** E. 13/1.

Heney, Master. **1799:** K. 31/7.

Henry, John (1746–94). D.L. 1762. S.A. 1774. **1761:** B. 7/8.

Herbert [Dowling], Joseph (1762–1837). C.S. 1799. C.G. 1804. **1789:** C. 14/4, 18/4. **1799:** L. 2/8. **1800:** B. 3/2, 26/5.

Hern, Miss. S.A. 1765. **1766:** C. 25/9. **1767:** K. 30/11, 26/12. **1768:** K. 8/1, 24/3; L. 13/10. **1770:** B. 30/4, 11/8. **1771:** L. 22/10.

Heslop, Mrs. **1797:** C. 2/10, 5/10.

Hilmer, Mr. **1799:** B. ?/12. **1800:** B. 10/3, 4/5.

Hinde, Edward. **1763:** B. 21/1, 4/4.

Hinde, Mrs. Edward. **1763:** B. 14/1, 21/1.

Hinde, Master. **1763:** B. 21/1, 14/3.

Hinde, Miss. **1763:** B. 21/1, 29/3.

Hitchcock, Robert (d. 1809). H.[2] 1781. S.A. 1781. **1794:** C. 13/9, 13/10. **1795:** C. 17/8, 22/10. **1798:** C. 23/10, 29/10. **1799:** C. 29/8, 3/9. **1800:** C. 16/9.

Hitchcock, Mrs. Robert (Sarah). H.[2] 1777. S.A. 1781. **1782:** C. 29/7, 19/8;

L. 31/8. **1783:** C. 9/8, 6/9. **1786:** W. 18/7; C. 1/8, 6/11; L. 18/9. **1787:** K. 15/8. **1788:** C. 4/8, 4/9; W. 3/10. **1789:** C. 15/9; W. 12/10. **1790:** C. 4/9, 13/9. **1791:** C. 28/9, 13/10. **1792:** C. 13/9. **1793:** C. 11/9. **1794:** C. 13/10. **1795:** C. 10/9. **1796:** C. 28/7, 23/8; Dr. 14/10. **1797:** C. 2/10, 9/10. **1798:** C. 13/9, 23/10. **1799:** C. 3/9.

Hitchcock, Miss Mary Anne [*later* Mrs. Jonas Greene] (1766–1854). H.[2] 1781. S.A. 1781. **1782:** C. 29/7, 7/10. **1786:** W. 18/7; C. 1/8, 24/10; L. 18/9. **1787:** K. 15/8, 1/9.

Hitchens, Mr. **1768:** K. 1/2, 2/3.

Holden, Mr. **1792:** C. 27/10.

Holland, Mr. **1756:** Tr. 6/3, 16/4. **1759:** C. 4/10.

Hollocombe, Mr. S.A. 1766. **1769:** C. 31/7, 15/9. **1770:** C. 16/8. **1771:** L. 22/10. **1772:** L. 6/7, 10/7; C. 19/8, 6/10. **1773:** C. 17/9. **1775:** C. 16/9. **1776:** C. 5/10, 15/10. **1777:** C. 20/8, 11/10. **1778:** C. 23/7, 31/10. **1779:** C. 2/8, 24/9.

Hollocombe, Mrs. **1769:** C. 15/9.

Holman, Joseph George (1764–1817). C.G. 1784. S.A. 1785. **1785:** L. 15/8, 16/8; C. 3/9. **1787:** C. 6/9, 8/9. **1788:** C. 27/8, 15/9; B. 19/11, 17/12.

Hopkins, William (d. 1780). S.A. 1757. D.L. 1761. **1758:** B. 6/2, 12/6; C. 8/9, 22/9.

Hopkins, Mrs. William (Elizabeth) (1731–1801). S.A. 1757. D.L. 1763. **1758:** B. 6/2, 1/3; C. 11/8, 8/9.

Hoskins, Mrs. Charles. Cap. S. 1770 (*fr.* D.L.). **1771:** L. 22/10. **1776:** C. 5/10. **1779:** K. 22/10. **1783:** B. 24/1, 19/5. **1788:** B. 17/12. **1789:** B. 28/1. **1790:** D. 19/5. **1791:** B. 5/1, 26/1; D. 20/5. **1792:** B. 10/2; D. ?/12. **1793:** D. 11/2. **1794:** D. 9/6. **1799:** D. 13/5.

Hoskins, Miss. C.S. 1778. **1779:** L. 22/10. **1783:** B. 24/1, 19/5. **1786:** B. 23/10. **1787:** B. 13/4. **1788:** B. 17/12. **1789:** B. 23/2. **1790:** D. 30/4.

Howard, Mr. **1787:** K. 20/7.

Huddart, Thomas (d. 1831). C.G. 1798. C.S. 1799. **1799:** L. 2/8, 3/8; C. 2/9.

Hughes, Miss Maria [*later* Mrs. John Scott-Waring] (1761–1812). C.S. 1788. **1788:** L. 7/7, 25/7; C. 7/8, 15/9; B. 21/11, 17/12.

Humphries, Mr. **1791:** E. 17/10.

Hunter [Hunt], Mrs. [*née* Maria Cooper]. C.G. 1774. S.A. 1775. **1775:** C. 12/7, 20/9.

Hurst, Richard (d. 1805). C.G. 1754. S.A. 1755. **1757:** C. 5/8. **1758:** C. 15/8, 6/9. **1759:** C. 17/8, 27/8. **1780:** C. 28/8; K. 16/12. **1781:** K. 7/3; C. 8/8. **1784:** C. 30/9. **1785:** C. 27/8. **1790:** W. ?/7; L. 31/7, 8/11; E. 6/9, 2/10. **1791:** L. 18/3; C. 26/4, 11/6. **1792:** D. 23/10. **1793:** D. 4/1; B. 22/5; W. 30/9. **1795:** K. 30/11.

Hurst, Mrs. Richard. C.S. 1781. **1780:** C. 9/8, 28/8; K. 16/12. **1790:** E. 13/9; L. 8/11. **1791:** L. 18/3. **1792:** D. 23/10. **1793:** D. 25/1; B. 22/5. **1795:** K. 2/11, 21/12.

Hutton, Mr. **1776:** B. 18/3. **1778:** N. 3/12. **1779:** N. 26/4.

Incledon, Charles Benjamin (1763–1826). C.G. 1790. C.S. 1791. **1791:** C. 8/8, 25/8. **1792:** N. 18/6, 4/7; C. 13/8, 12/9. **1795:** C. 20/8, 3/9.

Jackson, John (1730–1806). D.L. 1762. S.A. 1766. **1768:** B. 23/8. **1769:** C. 4/8. **1787:** C. 10/9. **1796:** C. 14/4, 15/4.

Jackson, Mrs. John [*née* Hester Sowdon; *original Dublin stage name* Miss Brown] (1750–1806). S.A. 1767. C.G. 1775. **1769:** C. 31/7 (*fr.* Edinburgh), 12/9. **1796:** C. 9/4, 10/9.

Jackson, Thomas (1741–98). S.A. 1772 (*fr.* H.[2]). **1773:** C. 3/6, 17/9. **1775:** C. 3/7, 16/9.

Jagger, Mr. S.A. 1764. **1767:** K. 26/12. **1768:** K. 12/2.

Jameson, Miss [*later* Mrs. Arnold]. S.A. 1775 (*fr.* C.G.). (as Miss Jameson) **1779:** C. 16/7, 6/10; K. 17/11, 10/12. **1780:** C. 28/8, 4/10. **1783:** B. 24/1; C. 12/8, 27/9. **1786:** W. 18/7; L. 31/7, 15/8; C. 2/8. (as Mrs. Arnold) **1786:** C. 24/10.

Jarrett, Miss. D.L. 1772. C.S. 1780. **1784:** C. 22/9.

Jefferson, Thomas (1732–1807). H.[2] *c.* 1747. D.L. 1753. C.S. 1758. **1760:** C. 1/8, 1/10. **1761:** C. 6/7, 29/9.

Jefferson, Mrs. Thomas [*née* Elizabeth May] (d. 1766). D.L. 1753. C.S. 1758. **1760:** C. 23/7, 15/10. **1761:** C. 6/7, 26/9.

Jenkinson, Mr. **1792:** C. 10/10.

Johnson, Mr. S. S.A. 1759. **1758:** B. 24/5.

Johnston, Henry Erskine (1777–1845). C.S. 1795 (*fr.* Edinburgh). C.G. 1797. **1792:** N. 20/7. **1796:** B. 2/3, 18/3. **1797:** C. 21/9, 5/10.

Johnston, Mrs. Henry Erskine [*née* Nanette Parker] (b. 1782). C.S. 1797. C.G. 1797. **1797:** C. 5/10.

Johnstone, John Henry (1749–1828). S.A. 1775. C.G. 1783. **1776:** C. 5/8, 5/10. **1777:** C. 19/8. **1779:** K. 25/10. **1780:** C. 26/9, 18/10. **1781:** C. 10/8, 22/10. **1786:** W. 18/7; L. 31/7, 15/8; C. 2/8, 31/8. **1788:** L. 14/7, 29/7; C. 4/8, 25/8. **1792:** N. 20/7.

Johnstone, Mrs. John Henry [*née* Maria Ann Poitier] (d. 1784). C.S. 1776. C.G. 1783. (as Miss Poitier) **1777:** C. 16/7, 15/10. (as Mrs. Johnstone) **1780:** C. 26/9, 18/10.

Jones, Mr. Cap. S. 1749. **1756:** Tr. 6/3, 30/4. **1759:** C. 1/10.

Jones, Mr. S.A. 1770. **1770:** C. 25/8. **1776:** C. 15/10. **1784:** Y. 20/12.

Jordan, Mrs. [*see* Miss Dorothea Francis).

Kane, John. C.S. 1768. **1769:** C. 31/7, 20/9. **1771:** B. 30/10, 29/11. **1775:** C. 16/9. **1776:** C. 5/10. **1778:** C. 19/10; B. 2/12. **1779:** B. 19/3. **1780:** C. 28/8. **1782:** C. 29/7; L. 31/8. **1783:** B. 24/1, 19/5; C. 23/8, 5/9. **1784:** B. 25/6. **1799:** D. 29/4.

Keeffe, John (*see* O'Keeffe).

Keegan, Mr. **1769:** C. 15/9.

Kelf, Mrs. (*see* Mrs. Egerton).

Kelly, Joseph (d. 1817). C.S. 1789. **1790:** L. 13/8; C. 17/8, 7/9. **1791:** C. 11/8, 7/10.

Kelly, Michael (*c.* 1762–1828). F.S. 1777. D.L. 1787. **1787:** L. 16/7; C. 30/7. **1789:** L. 17/8, 22/8; C. 28/8, 12/9; W. ?/10.

Kelly, Mr. **1788:** Cash. ?/8, ?/9; Car. ?/10. **1790:** W. ?/7; L. 31/7, 8/11; E. 6/9, 2/10. **1791:** L. 7/2.

Kelly, Mrs. **1790:** E. 13/9 (*fr.* L.).

Kelly, Mr. (b. London). C.S. 1792. **1799:** D. 19/4; K. 5/6, 16/6. **1800:** B. 10/3, 25/4.

Kelly, Mrs. **1799:** D. 6/5. **1800:** B. 10/3, 9/6.

Kelly, Mr. [*later* O'Kelly]. **1781:** C. 8/8. **1782:** C. ?/9, ?/10.

Kelly, Mrs. **1782:** C. 27/9 (*fr.* Bath).

Kelly, William. S.A. 1746 (as Master Kelly). **1756:** Tra. 6/3, 19/4. **1769:** C. 4/8, 15/9.

Kemble, Anne Julia (d. 1838). S.A. 1783. **1785:** B. 3/6, 24/6.

Kemble, John Philip (1757–1823). S.A. 1781 (*fr.* Edinburgh). D.L. 1783. **1782:** C. 22/7, 7/10. **1783:** K. 13/2, 27/2. **1785:** C. 23/8, 31/8. **1796:** C. 12/8, 31/8. **1797:** C. 15/8, 20/9.

Kemble, Stephen (1758–1822). Cap. S. 1782. C.G. 1783. **1782:** C. 2/8, 12/10.

Kenna, Mr. S.A. 1771. **1773:** B. 6/9, 8/9. **1774:** B. 5/1; D. 8/8.

Kenna, Mrs. S.A. 1771. **1773:** B. 6/9, 8/9. **1774:** D. 8/8.

Kenna, Master. **1774:** B. 7/2.

Kennedy, Lawrence (1720–86). S.A. 1737. G.F. 1744. **1756:** C. 22/9. **1757:** C. 5/8. **1758:** C. 14/8, 13/9. **1762:** C. 13/10. **1779:** C. 22/9. **1783:** B. ?/1, ?/5 (*fr.* D.L.).

Kennedy, Mrs. Lawrence [*née* Elizabeth Orfeur] (d. 1774). G.F. 1745. S.A. 1747. **1756:** C. 30/8, 13/9. **1757:** C. 5/8, 11/9. **1758:** C. 30/8. **1762:** C. 3/10. **1763:** C. 7/9, 28/9. **1764:** C. 3/10.

Kennedy, Master. S.A. 1755. **1756:** C. 22/9. **1758:** C. 30/8, 22/9. **1762:** C. 3/10. **1763:** C. 28/9. **1764:** C. 3/10.

Kennedy, Mrs. Morgan Hugh [*form.* Mrs. Farrell; *née* Margaret Doyle] (d. 1793). C.G. 1776. C.S. 1789. **1780:** C. 18/8, 1/9.

Kennedy, Mr. C.S. 1791. **1792:** C. 14/9. **1796:** B. 4/5. **1797:** C. 5/10.

Kennedy, Mrs. C.S. 1791. **1792:** C. 14/9. **1793:** L. 9/7; C. 6/9. **1795:** D. 16/11. **1796:** D. 18/1; B. 16/3, 20/4. **1797:** C. 15/8, 5/10.

Kennedy, Miss (b. *c.* 1788). C.S. 1793. **1796:** B. 20/4. **1797:** C. 5/10.

Kenny, Mr. **1778:** C. 19/10.

Keys, Mrs. Simon. **1793:** K. 4/10.

Keys, Miss [*later* Mrs. Mills]. C.S. 1792. C.G. 1798. **1793:** K. 14/8, 26/8.

Kiking, Master. **1763:** C. 29/9.

King, E. S.A. 1787. **1788:** C. 4/8. **1790:** C. 4/9. **1791:** C. 5/10. **1796:** K. 23/9. **1798:** L. 1/10.

King, Mrs. E. **1798:** L. 1/10.

King, G. S.A. 1787. **1790:** C. 4/9.

King, Thomas (1730–1805). D.L. 1748. S.A. 1750. **1757:** C. 5/8. **1758:** C. 16/8, 26/9. **1768:** C. 29/7, 15/8. **1788:** B. 11/11. **1791:** D. 27/6, 11/7; B. 18/7, 10/8.

King, Mrs. Thomas [*née* Mary Baker] (1730–1813). G.F. 1747. S.A. 1750. (as Miss Baker) **1757:** C. 5/8. **1758:** C. 14/7, 6/9.

King, Mr. **1784:** K. 17/2. **1786:** C. 24/10. **1788:** B. 17/12. **1789:** B. 4/3. **1792:** D. 21/11. **1793:** D. 11/2; B. 10/5, 24/5; K. 26/8.

King, Mrs. C.S. 1772 (*fr.* York). **1773:** C. 3/6, 19/7.

Kingston, Miss. F.S. 1793. **1793:** K. 14/8.

Knipe, Richard William (d. 1779). C.S. 1759. **1760:** C. 25/7, 9/10. **1761:** C.

6/7, 2/10. **1762:** C. 3/10. **1764:** Wex. ?/6; C. 3/10. **1765:** B. 7/10. **1766:** B. 28/2. **1769:** C. 31/7, 15/9. **1772:** K. 31/12. **1773:** W. n.d. **1778:** N. 3/12.

Knipe, Mrs. Richard William. C.S. 1758. **1760:** C. 25/7, 15/10. **1761:** C. 6/7, 28/10. **1762:** C. 3/10. **1764:** Wex. 26/3; C. 3/10. **1765:** B. 7/10. **1766:** B. 28/2. **1769:** C. 31/7, 15/9. **1774:** B. 19/1. **1779:** N. 26/3.

Knipe, Miss (*see* Mrs. Andrew Cherry).

Kniveton, Thomas (d. 1775). S.A. 1760. C.G. 1769. **1759:** Ba. 27/12. **1761:** B. 29/6, 28/8.

La Croix, Mrs. **1758:** C. 4/10.

Lacy, Willoughby (1749–1831). D.L. 1775. S.A. 1785. **1778:** C. 6/7.

Lahfe, Samuel. **1792:** Wex. ?/1.

Lamon, Mrs. C.S. 1776. **1776:** C. 9/8, 4/10.

Lane, Mr. (d. 1782). S.A. 1781. **1781:** C. 8/8.

Layfield, Lewis. L.[1] 1704. S.A. 1717. **1735:** Carl. 7/7, 14/7.

Layfield, Mrs. Robert. A.S. 1744. **1753:** B. 27/7, 10/8.

Layton, Mr. Cap. S. 1773. **1774:** D. 8/8.

Lebrun, Antony. S.A. 1780. **1779:** B. 12/2, 19/3; C. 11/8, 29/9. **1780:** C. 1/9.

Lee, Mr. C.S. 1767. **1769:** C. 15/9. **1774:** B. 16/2.

Lee, Mr. Samuel. S.A. 1774. **1774:** C. 1/8; L. 24/8.

Lee, Mrs. Samuel [*form.* Mrs. Jefferies; *née* Grantham]. C.G. 1762. S.A. 1764. **1771:** L. 22/10. **1774:** C. 8/7; L. 23/8. **1775:** C. 16/9.

Lee, Thomas. **1791:** B. 5/1, 7/2; D. 20/6. **1792:** Wex. 10/10, 31/12. **1798:** L. 1/10.

Leech, Mr. **1754:** B. 25/11, 13/12. **1755:** B. 27/1.

Leeson, Miss Henrietta Amelia [*later* Mrs. William T. Lewis] (1751–1826). C.S. 1771. C.G. 1775. **1772:** L. 10/7, 12/8; C. 19/8, 3/10.

Leonard, Mr. **1796:** Dr. 10/10. **1799:** K. 5/6.

Leslie, Mrs. S.A. 1750. **1756:** Tr. 3/4, 7/5; C. 27/10.

L'Estrange, Joseph. S.A. 1770 (*fr.* D.L.). **1771:** W. 9/10. **1774:** G. summer.

Lewes, Charles Lee (1740–1803). C.G. 1763. S.A. 1771. **1784:** C. 6/9. **1786:** C. 13/3, 11/9; W. 18/7; B. 23/10. **1787:** B. 2/3. **1794:** B. 8/12, 22/12; D. 31/12. **1795:** D. 2/1. **1796:** B. 25/4, 20/5; Dr. ?/6; K. 18/7, 20/7; C. 2/8. **1797:** C. 10/8. **1800:** B. 27/1, 10/2.

Lewes, Mrs. Catherine Maria [3rd wife of Lee Lewes] (d. 1796). **1786:** B. 20/12. **1787:** B. 2/3.

Lewis, Philip (d. 1791). S.A. 1757. C.G. 1763. **1751–2:** B. n.d. **1753:** B. 6/6, 31/8. **1756:** Dr. n.d. **1757:** Dr. n.d. **1758:** Dr. n.d.

Lewis, William (d. *c.* 1753). **1751–2:** B. n.d.

Lewis, Mrs. William (*see* Mrs. William Dawson).

Lewis, William Thomas (*c.* 1746–1811). S.A. 1761. C.G. 1773. (as Master Lewis) **1751–2:** B. n.d. **1753:** B. 14/8. **1756:** Tr. 6/3, 7/5. **1761:** B. 17/7, 3/8. (as Mr. Lewis) **1765:** Dr. 26/12. **1766:** C. 20/8, 8/10. **1770:** C. 25/8, 3/9. **1771:** L. ?/8, 22/10; C. 6/9. **1772:** L. 6/7, 18/9; C. 19/8, 19/10. **1773:** C. 21/7, 23/10; L. 10/8, 19/8. **1774:** C. 24/6, 1/8; L. 23/8, 24/8. **1790:** C. 15/8, 1/9. **1792:** C. 1/8, 31/8. **1797:** C. 4/8, 26/8; L. 4/9.

Lings, Mr. **1776:** K. 17/6.

Logan, Mr. S.A. 1772. **1767:** K. 2/12, 12/12. **1768:** K. 2/3. **1770:** B. 30/4, 16/7; K. 15/10, 5/12. **1773:** C. 17/9.

Logan, Mrs. S.A. 1772. **1766:** C. 14/8. **1767:** K. 2/12. **1768:** K. 2/3. **1770:** B. 30/4, 28/7; K. 14/9, 10/12. **1773:** C. 15/9. **1776:** C. 5/10. **1779:** C. 11/8, 29/9. **1780:** C. 1/9.

Longfield, Mr. S.A. 1751. **1754:** B. 18/11, 17/12. **1755:** B. 7/1, 14/3. **1761:** B. 29/6, 17/7.

Lonsdale, Mr. **1791:** E. 17/10.

Lord, Mr. **1772:** C. 2/10. **1773:** C. 20/9. **1781:** K. 10/1. **1783:** C. 10/3. **1784:** Y. 20/12.

Love [Dance], James (1722–74). G.F. 1745. S.A. 1754. **1751:** B. 18/12. **1752:** B. n.d. **1754:** L. ?/7 (*fr.* Edinburgh). **1756:** Tr. 9/3, 10/5.

Love [Dance], Mrs. James [*née* Hooper] (d. 1807). S.A. 1754. D.L. 1764. **1751–2:** B. n.d. **1756:** Tr. 5/3, 10/5.

Lyddel, Miss Esther [*later* (1) Mrs. George Bland, (2) Mrs. John Hamilton, (3) Mrs. Sweeny] (d. 1787). S.A. 1727. C.G. 1742. **1728:** Dr. 13/6.

Lynch, Mr. (d. 1800). S.A. 1780. **1771:** B. 16/8, 30/10. **1778:** K. 21/1. **1780:** C. 4/10. **1781:** C. 8/8. **1782:** C. 29/7; L. 31/8. **1783:** C. 23/8, 6/9. **1784:** C. 30/9. **1786:** C. 24/10. **1788:** B. 10/10, 17/12. **1789:** B. 20/2, 13/4. **1790:** D. 12/5. **1791:** B. 5/1, 2/11; D. 6/5, 22/6. **1792:** B. 27/2; D. 21/11. **1793:** D. 15/2; B. 20/5, 27/5. **1794:** D. 19/5; B. 24/10. **1795:** B. 2/1, 11/3; D. 14/12. **1796:** B. 17/2, 27/5. **1798:** D. 28/2, 2/3. **1799:** Car. ?/12.

Lynch, Mrs. **1782:** L. 31/8. **1788:** B. 17/12. **1789:** B. 13/4. **1790:** D. 28/5. **1791:** B. 9/2; D. 22/6. **1792:** B. 2/3; D. ?/11. **1793:** D. 21/1. **1795:** B. 8/4; D. 30/11. **1796:** B. 13/6. **1798:** D. 30/3.

Lynch, Miss. **1791:** D. 22/6. **1792:** D. ?/11. **1793:** D. 21/1. **1794:** D. 19/5, 6/6. **1795:** B. 11/3, 14/12. **1796:** D. 13/1; B. 18/5, 13/6. **1798:** D. 28/2.

Lyster, Mrs. (*see* Mrs. Richard Daly).

Macaddon, Mr. **1784:** K. 17/2.

Macartney, Alexander. **1775:** Lis. 18/9, 1/12. **1780:** K. 4/11, 23/12. **1781:** K. 8/3. **1782:** L. 26/7, 4/9. **1792:** G. 10/9, 5/11. **1793:** C. 18/2. **1795:** G. 3/9, 22/9.

McCarthy, Mr. **1761:** B. 7/8. **1768:** K. 10/2. **1769:** K. 3/6. **1770:** B. 30/4, 28/7. **1800:** G. summer.

MacCormick, James (d. 1768). **1768:** Sl. n.d.

McCormick, Mr. **1789:** Wex. 7/1; K. 24/4, 13/7. **1790:** K. 8/11.

McCourtney, Mr. **1790:** L. 9/8, 11/9; E. 13/9, 18/9.

M'Crea, Mr. C.S. 1792. **1790:** W. ?/7; L. 31/7, 8/11; E. 6/9, 2/10. **1791:** L. 18/3; C. 26/4, 18/6. **1792:** W. 30/1, 23/3.

M'Crea, Mrs. **1792:** W. 30/1, 29/2.

M'Cready, William C. (*or* McCready) (1755–1829). C.S. 1783. C.G. 1786. **1776:** K. 21/8. **1781:** K. 28/3. **1783:** B. 24/1, 19/5. **1784:** C. 30/9. **1792:** C. 9/8, 30/8. **1793:** C. 15/8, 7/9.

McCulloch, Mr. **1779:** N. 26/4. **1787:** K. 20/7, 24/9. **1790:** W. ?/7; L. 31/7, 8/11; E. 6/9, 2/10. **1791:** L. 7/2.

McCulloch, Mrs. **1790:** L. 4/12. **1795:** K. 28/10.

McCulloch, Master. **1795:** K. 28/10.
McGeorge, Horatio Thomas. S.A. 1760. H.[1] 1766. **1794:** D. 1/7 (*fr.* Bath).
McGeorge, Mrs. Horatio Thomas. H.[1] 1766. **1794:** D. 17/6, 9/7 (*fr.* Bath). **1795:** B. 25/3. **1796:** B. 9/5, 23/5.
Macklin, Charles (*c.* 1700–97). L.[2] 1730. D.L. 1733. S.A. 1748. **1762:** C. 27/9, 8/10. **1765:** Dr. 24/8, 26/8. **1772:** L. 10/7, 12/8; C. 19/8, 25/8.
Macklin, Mr. **1790:** E. 27/1, 1/3; K. 8/11, 27/11. **1791:** K. 21/2; E. 14/10. **1800:** B. 10/3, 14/4.
Macnamara, Mr. **1796:** E. 1/6.
McOwens, Mr. **1787:** W. 18/10, 9/11.
McShane, Mr. **1782:** Mal. n.d.
Madden, Mr. **1770:** C. 25/8.
Maguire, Mr. **1767:** K. 30/11. **1768:** K. 2/3, 24/3; L. 13/10.
Maguire, Mrs. **1767:** K. 30/11 (*fr.* D.L.). **1768:** K. 24/3; L. 13/10.
Maguire, Master. **1768:** K. 10/2, 2/3.
Maher, Mr. (d. 1782). C.S. 1776. **1776:** K. 17/6, 29/7. **1779:** K. 21/10. **1780:** C. 1/9.
Mahon, Mrs. Gilbraith [*née* Gertrude Tilson] (b. 1752). C.G. 1780. S.A. 1784. **1795:** K. 23/9, 14/10.
Mahon, Robert (1734–99). S.A. 1750. C.G. 1769. **1759:** K. 17/11, 10/12. **1760:** C. 25/7, 15/10. **1761:** B. 29/6, 24/8; C. 6/7, 26/9. **1762:** C. 20/8, 29/10. **1763:** C. 27/9. **1764:** C. 14/9. **1765:** C. 13/8, 17/10. **1766:** C. 29/9, 10/10. **1767:** L. summer. **1771:** L. 27/9, 22/10. **1772:** L. 15/7, 12/8; C. 19/8, 8/9. **1774:** C. 23/7, 14/9. **1779:** C. 16/7, 4/10; L. 27/8. **1781:** C. 8/8, 10/10.
Mahon, Mrs. Robert (d. 1768). S.A. 1760. **1760:** C. 26/9. **1761:** C. 29/7. **1762:** C. 4/10. **1763:** C. 7/9.
Mahony, Kane. **1761:** C. 26/9.
Malone, Mr. S.A. 1783. **1783:** C. 23/8. **1786:** C. 24/10. **1792:** B. 24/2.
Manwaring, Mr. **1761:** B. 15/7. **1765:** B. 7/10. **1766:** B. 21/2.
Mara, Madame Samuel Delaval [*née* Gertrude Elizabeth Scheneling]. D.L. 1788. C.S. 1792. **1792:** C. 13/8.
Marlton, Mr. C.S. 1771. **1771:** L. 22/10. **1772:** L. 18/9; C. 6/10.
Martin, Mr. **1784:** Y. 20/12.
Martin, Mrs. **1784:** Y. 20/12.
Martyr, Mrs. [*née* Margaret Thornton] (d. 1807). C.G. 1781. C.S. 1796. **1796:** L. 18/7, 18/8; C. 30/7, 5/8.
Mason, Miss Alice (*see* Mrs. Heaphy).
Mason, Mrs. Michael. S.A. 1747. **1765:** C. 3/10.
Mason, Mr. **1791:** B. 2/2.
Mason, Mrs. (*see* Mrs. Booth).
Massey, Mr. C.S. 1766. **1766:** C. 1/9.
Mathews, Charles (1776–1835). C.S. 1794. H.[2] 1803. **1792:** Wex. 16/11. **1794:** C. 15/8, 5/9; L. 7/9, 13/9. **1795:** C. 17/8, 14/9.
Ma[u]nsell, Miss Dorothea [*later* (1) Mrs. G. F. Tenducci, (2) Mrs. William F. Farren, (3) Mrs. Thomas Orton, (4) Mrs. Bell] (1748–1820). C.S. 1770. D.L. 1772. **1770:** C. 24/8, 3/9.
Maurice, Mr. S.A. 1750. **1753:** B. 22/6, 7/9.

Maxwell, Mrs. C.S. 1759. **1762:** C. 28/9. **1763:** C. 27/9. **1768:** B. 23/8. **1769:** N. 23/1; K. 3/6, 17/8. **1770:** B. 30/4, 7/5. **1772:** L. 6/7. **1779:** C. 13/9.

May, James. **1790:** B. 8/11. **1791:** B. 28/1, 14/10; D. 4/3, 22/6. **1792:** B. 27/2, 9/10. **1793:** D. 30/1; B. 25/2, 29/5. **1794:** B. 9/5. **1795:** D. 18/5; K. 26/10, 11/12.

May, Mrs. James. **1791:** B. 5/1, 26/1; D. 3/6, 22/6. **1792:** B. 6/2. **1793:** D. 2/1; B. 29/5.

Meadows, William. C.S. 1782 (*fr.* Manchester). C.G. 1785. **1783:** C. 9/8, 27/9. **1793:** C. 11/9.

Meadows, Miss. C.S. 1793. **1794:** C. 27/9.

Melmoth, Courtney [Samuel Jackson Pratt] (1749–1814). S.A. 1773. C.G. 1774. **1773:** Dr. summer.

Melmoth, Mrs. Charlotte [Mrs. Samuel Jackson Pratt] (1749–1823). S.A. 1773. C.G. 1774. **1773:** Dr. summer. **1782:** C. 3/8, 11/10; L. 4/9. **1785:** L. 1/3. **1786:** W. 18/7; L. 31/7, 15/8; C. 2/8, 24/10. **1790:** B. 12/11, 20/12. **1791:** B. 14/1, 2/11; D. 4/3, 16/5. **1792:** B. 6/2; W. 13/8, 18/9.

Merry, Mrs. Robert (*see* Anne Brunton).

Messink, James (1721–89). S.A. 1749. D.L. 1767. **1757:** C. 5/8. **1758:** C. 14/8, 8/9. **1760:** C. 1/8. **1761:** C. 6/7, 2/10. **1762:** C. 20/8, 4/10. **1763:** C. 29/9. **1764:** C. 14/9. **1765:** C. 4/9. **1766:** C. 23/9.

Middleton [Magan], James (*c.* 1769–99). C.G. 1788. C.S. 1789. **1789:** C. 29/8, 14/9; W. 2/10, 12/10. **1790:** C. 6/9, 15/9. **1791:** C. 16/8. **1792:** W. 14/8, 14/9. **1793:** B. 1/4, 10/5. **1794:** D. 4/8, 20/8.

Mitchell, George (d. *c.* 1799). S.A. 1771. **1771:** W. 9/10. **1773:** C. 3/6, 17/9. **1777:** C. 3/10. **1779:** C. 11/8, 27/9. **1782:** C. 29/7; L. 31/8. **1784:** K. 17/2. **1787:** W. 17/10. **1788:** C. 21/8, 4/9; Cash. ?/8, ?/9; Car. ?/10; Wex. 26/12. **1789:** Wex. 6/3; K. 24/4, 13/7.

Mitchell, Mrs. George. **1773:** W. n.d.

Molloy, Mrs. Francis [*née* Eliza Wheeler] (d. 1794). Cap. S. 1783 (as Miss Wheeler). C.G. 1786. **1788:** B. 10/10, 28/11.

Montague, Mr. (*see* Montague Talbot).

Montague, Mrs. F. S.A. 1780. **1781:** C. 10/8, 19/10.

Moore, Thomas (1779–1852). **1793:** Wex. 1/5.

Moore, William. **1790:** L. 8/11. **1791:** L. 7/2.

Morgan, Mrs. **1778:** K. 28/1, 2/3.

Morris, James (d. 1767). S.A. 1734. C.G. 1746. **1760:** C. 1/8, 11/8. **1761:** C. 6/7. **1762:** C. 24/9. **1763:** C. 29/9.

Moss, William Henry (1751–1817). H.[2] 1768. F.S. 1776. **1777:** C. 19/7, 13/10. **1778:** C. 14/7, 4/11. **1779:** C. 23/7, 29/9. **1780:** C. 24/10. **1782:** Dr. 9/10. **1785:** C. 23/8, 20/9. **1786:** W. 18/7; C. 6/8. **1790:** L. 8/11, 18/12. **1791:** L. 23/2, 18/3; C. 26/4, 11/6. **1792:** K. 13/6, 2/7. **1793:** K. 3/7, 21/8; W. 30/9.

Moss, Mrs. William Henry. **1790:** L. 8/11, 18/12. **1791:** L. 23/2, 18/3; C. 26/4, 11/6. **1793:** G. 9/9, 7/10.

Mossop, Henry (1729–74). S.A. 1749. D.L. 1751. **1766:** W. summer. **1768:** C. 27/7; L. 29/10. **1769:** C. 31/7.

Mountain, Mrs. John [*née* Rosemond Wilkinson] (1768–1841). C.G. 1786. C.S. 1789. **1790:** L. 13/8; C. 23/8, 4/9.

Mozeen, Mr. [son of Thomas Mozeen]. **1768:** B. 7/9.

Mozeen, Mrs. Thomas [*née* Edwards]. D.L. 1740. S.A. 1748. **1754:** B. 18/11. **1755:** B. 14/3. **1756:** C. ?/1. **1768:** B. 23/8. **1769:** B. 13/1; N. 23/1; K. 3/6, 17/8.

Munden, Joseph Shepherd (1758–1832). C.G. 1790. C.S. 1793. **1793:** C. 6/9. **1796:** L. 18/7, 25/7; C. 30/7, 10/8.

Murphy, F. C.S. 1778. **1772:** K. 31/12. **1773:** K. 16/2; W. n.d. **1778:** C. 19/10. **1779:** C. 13/9, 29/9. **1781:** C. 7/9. **1782:** C. 29/7; L. 31/8. **1783:** C. 23/8. **1796:** B. 8/6.

Murray, Mr. C.S. 1791. **1788:** Cash. ?/8, ?/9; Car. ?/10. **1789:** Wex. 7/1, 9/1. **1797:** C. 5/10.

Murray, Mrs. C.S. 1791. **1790:** L. 22/11. **1791:** L. 18/3; C. 26/4, 18/6.

Mynitt, William. S.A. 1743. **1756:** C. 13/9. **1757:** C. 5/8. **1758:** C. 14/8, 20/9. **1760:** C. 25/7, 30/9. **1762:** C. 27/10. **1764:** C. 14/9. **1765:** C. 26/9.

Mynitt, Mrs. William (d. 1761). S.A. 1743. **1756:** C. 13/9. **1757:** C. 5/8, 23/8. **1760:** C. 30/9.

Neagle, Mr. **1792:** G. 3/9, 10/9; Wex. 15/10. **1793:** Wex. 18/1; W. 18/2, 21/3; K. 10/6, 26/8. **1794:** Cl. 30/6, 23/7.

Neil, Mr. S.A. 1771. **1761:** C. ?/10.

Nicolle, Miss. **1800:** E. 27/3.

Nugent, Mr. **1770:** B. 7/5. **1788:** C. 1/9.

O'Brien, William (d. 1815). D.L. 1758. S.A. 1763. **1763:** C. 25/7.

O'Brien, Mr. **1797:** C. 5/10.

O'Connor, Mr. **1800:** E. 13/1.

O'Keeffe, John [Keeffe until 1774] (1747–1833). S.A. 1766. **1768:** L. 13/10. **1769:** D. autumn and winter. **1770:** B. 30/4, 11/8; K. 14/9, 12/11. **1771:** L. 22/10. **1772:** L. 6/7, 3/8; C. 31/8, 23/10. **1773:** C. 17/9. **1774:** C. 8/7, 14/9; L. 23/8. **1775:** C. 3/7, 29/9. **1776:** C. 14/7, 12/10. **1777:** C. 16/7, 7/10. **1779:** C. 16/7, 13/10. **1780:** C. 17/9, 23/10.

O'Keeffe, Mrs. John [*née* Mary Heaphy] (1757–1813). S.A. 1774. C.G. 1778. (as Miss Heaphy) **1766:** C. 16/8. (as Mrs. O'Keeffe) **1775:** C. 3/7, 29/9. **1776:** C. 14/7, 14/10. **1777:** L. 12/8, 13/8; C. 26/8, 7/10. **1779:** C. 16/7, 11/10; L. 20/8, 27/8. **1780:** C. 2/8, 7/10.

Oliver, Mr. C.S. 1761. **1758:** C. 14/8, 11/9. **1760:** C. 11/8. **1761:** C. 6/7.

O'Neill, John 'Shane' (d. 1798). Cap. S. 1782. **1758:** B. 8/2, 10/2. **1765:** B. 7/10. **1766:** B. 27/1. **1768:** Ca. 17/10, 21/10. **1783:** B. ?/1; Sl. n.d. **1786:** C. 29/8. **1790:** Du n.d. **1795:** C. 4/4; Car. n.d.

O'Neill, Mrs. C.S. 1767. **1771:** L. 22/10. **1772:** L. 6/7, 18/9; C. 19/8, 9/10. **1773:** C. 15/9, 17/9. **1776:** C. 5/10, 7/10. **1784:** K. 31/5. **1785:** L. 16/8; C. 30/9. **1786:** L. 1/3, 3/8.

O'Neill, Miss. **1791:** D. 17/6.

O'Reilly, William [Reilly after 1790]. S.A. 1782 (*fr.* Edinburgh). **1782:** C. 29/7, 27/9; L. 31/8. **1783:** C. 9/8, 23/9; L. 11/10. **1784:** C. 27/9, 28/9. **1787:** L. 16/7; C. 2/8, 21/9; W. 10/10, 17/10. **1788:** L. 14/7, 29/7; C. 4/8, 13/9; B. 11/11. **1789:** C. 11/9, 29/9. **1790:** K. 8/11. **1791:** K. 7/3. **1793:** G. 4/9. **1796:** B. 6/6.

O'Reilly, Mrs. William. S.A. 1782 (*fr.* Edinburgh). **1782:** C. 15/8; L. 31/8. **1783:** C. 9/8, 6/9. **1784:** C. 28/9. **1787:** C. 28/8; W. 17/10. **1788:** L. 14/7.

Osborne, Miss Jane [*later* Mrs. William Barry] (d. 1771). C.S. 1759. D.L. 1766. **1760:** C. 6/8, 15/10. **1761:** C. 28/10.

Osmond, Mr. **1763:** C. 29/9.

Owen, Mr. **1754:** B. 11/12. **1755:** B. 24/2.

Owens, John Linegar, Sr. S.A. 1771. **1770:** B. 28/7, 11/8; K. 24/9, 29/12. **1771:** W. 9/10. **1778:** K. 21/1, 2/4. **1779:** C. 26/4, 21/5. **1780:** C. ?/9. **1781:** K. 10/1, 8/3; C. 10/8. **1783:** C. 5/9.

Owens, Mrs. John L., Sr. **1778:** K. 12/1, 2/3. **1779:** C. 10/5, 7/6.

Owens, John L., Jr. F.S. 1777. **1778:** K. 21/1, 24/2. **1779:** C. 14/6.

Owens, Mrs. John L., Jr. Cap. S. 1783. **1779:** C. 14/6.

Owenson, Robert (1744–1812). C.G. 1771. C.S. 1776. **1778:** C. 14/7, 26/10. **1779:** C. 21/9, 13/10. **1780:** C. 28/8, 11/10. **1781:** Ath., Sl., Cast. n.d.; C. 10/8, 12/10. **1782:** G. ?/10. **1783:** G. ?/8. **1785:** L. 16/8; C. 23/9. **1786:** C. 2/8, 7/9; L. 18/9. **1787:** C. 12/9; W. 10/10, 15/10. **1788:** Ath., Cast., Sl. n.d. **1792:** C. 17/9. **1793:** K. 16/8, 6/9. **1794:** C. 17/10. **1795:** K. 8/8, 15/12. **1796:** K. 31/9; C. 10/10. **1797:** C. 3/10.

Packenham, Mrs. S.A. 1750. **1758:** C. 23/8, 4/10. **1761:** C. summer. **1762:** C. 4/10. **1763:** C. 27/9.

Palmer, William (d. 1797). C.S. 1764. H.[2] 1776. **1765:** C. ?/8, ?/10. **1766:** C. 1/4, 13/10. **1783:** C. 9/8, 6/9; L. 14/10. **1789:** C. 23/9; W. 12/10, 13/10. **1791:** Dr. ?/9. **1792:** C. 7/8, 15/9.

Palmer, Mrs. William. C.S. 1782. **1783:** L. 14/10.

Parker, George (1732–1800). H.[2] 1755. **1769:** N. 23/1.

Parker, James (d. 1778). **1756:** Tr. 6/3, 10/5. **1768:** B. 23/8, 30/11. **1769:** N. 23/1; K. 14/8. **1771:** B. 30/10, 15/11. **1772:** B. 17/1. **1776:** K. 17/6, 19/8.

Parker, Mrs. James. **1776:** K. 17/6, 19/8.

Parker, Mrs. (*see* Mrs. James Augustus Whiteley).

Parks, Mr. **1763:** B. 14/1, 29/3.

Parks, Mrs. **1763:** B. 21/1, 3/3.

Parsons, Mr. S.A. 1744. **1769:** C. 15/9.

Parsons, Miss. C.S. 1762. **1765:** C. 26/9.

Patten, Mr. C.S. 1794 (*fr.* Edinburgh). **1795:** Car. ?/10.

Paulet, Mr. F.S. 1784. **1786:** W. 18/7; C. 1/8, 29/8. **1787:** W. 17/10, 19/10.

Peacan, James. **1778:** K. 31/1.

Pearson, Mr. S.A. 1765. **1767:** Carl. 10/7.

Pearson, Master. **1791:** E. 17/10.

Peile, Mr. **1779:** C. 30/7, 22/9.

Perenini, Signor. **1765:** C. 23/9.

Pero, William (d. 1803). **1778:** B. 10/4, 20/4; N. 16/7. **1779:** B. 27/1, 3/3.

Pero, Mrs. William (*see* Mrs. Villars).

Pero, Miss. M. **1778:** B. 20/4. **1779:** B. 12/2.

Phillips, Miss Anna Maria (*see* Mrs. Crouch).

Phillips, Miss M. (d. 1782). S.A. 1756. **1759:** C. 17/8.

Phillips, Thomas. S.A. 1722. C.G. 1744. **1741:** B. ?/7.

Phillipson, Mr. **1753:** B. 9/8.

Pilon, Frederic (1750–88). **1770:** C. 3/9. **1772:** C. 26/9.

Pitt, George. S.A. 1730. C.G. 1741. **1754:** B. 18/11. **1755:** B. 28/2.

Poitier, Miss Maria Ann (*see* Mrs. John Henry Johnstone).

Poole, Miss Martha Frances Caroline [*later* Mrs. Peter Dickons] (*c.* 1770–1833). C.G. 1793. C.S. 1795. **1795:** C. 17/8, 8/9. **1796:** L. 18/7, 24/10; C. 28/7, 8/9.

Pope, Alexander (1763–1835). C.G. 1785. S.A. 1785. **1781:** C. 10/10, 24/10. **1784:** C. 30/9. **1788:** C. 6/8, 1/9. **1793:** C. 12/8, 26/8.

Pope, Mrs. Alexander [*née* Elizabeth Younge] (1740–98). S.A. 1755. C.G. 1762. (as Miss Younge) **1761:** C. 30/9. **1778:** C. 24/7, 24/8. **1782:** C. 31/7, 15/8. (as Mrs. Pope) **1788:** C. 21/8, 1/9. **1793:** C. 12/8, 4/9.

Pope, Miss. F.S. 1777. **1778:** C. 17/7, 19/10.

Powell, William (d. 1812). Cap. S. 1770. **1769:** K. 14/6, 14/8. **1771:** Cash. 25/2; F. 22/3.

Power, Mr. **1788:** C. 25/8; Wex. 26/12. **1789:** Wex. 6/3; K. 24/4, 13/7. **1790:** W. ?/7; L. 31/7, 8/11; E. 6/9, 2/10. **1791:** L. 7/2. **1792:** W. 30/1, 20/2. **1798:** D. 30/4.

Power, Mrs. **1789:** Wex. 7/1, 30/1; K. 24/4, 13/7. **1790:** W. ?/7; L. 31/7, 8/11; E. 6/9, 2/10. **1791:** L. 7/2; E. 11/11. **1795:** K. 11/11.

Price, Mrs. [*née* Brewer]. Cap. S. 1770. **1768:** L. 13/10. **1770:** C. 24/8, 25/8.

Prior, Mr. **1782:** L. 17/7, 2/8. **1791:** D. 22/6. **1792:** D. 21/11. **1793:** D. 27/2.

Prior, Mrs. S.A. 1780. **1778:** C. 19/10. **1779:** C. 11/8. **1782:** L. 17/7, 2/8. **1789:** K. 24/4, 13/7. **1790:** E. 5/4.

Prior, Miss. **1789:** K. 24/4, 13/7. **1790:** E. 5/4.

Purcell, Mrs. **1779:** C. 11/10.

Pye, Mr. **1768:** B. 23/8. **1769:** N. 23/1; K. 3/6, 17/8. **1771:** B. 16/8, 13/12. **1772:** B. 17/1. **1773:** B. 6/9. **1774:** D. 8/8, 2/12. **1776:** B. 22/3. **1777:** B. 24/10. **1779:** B. 12/2. **1780:** B. 3/3. **1788:** B. 17/12. **1789:** B. 18/2. **1790:** D. 7/5, 4/6. **1791:** B. 7/1; D. 15/6.

Pye, Mrs. (d. 1774). S.A. 1753. **1757:** C. 5/8. **1758:** C. 14/8. **1768:** B. 23/8, 30/11. **1769:** N. 23/1; K. 3/6, 17/8. **1771:** B. 16/8, 22/11. **1772:** B. 17/1. **1774:** B. 7/1.

Pye, Master. S.A. 1754. **1768:** B. 23/8. **1769:** N. 23/1; K. 3/6.

Quigley, Mr. **1790:** K. 8/11.

Quin, James (1693–1766). S.A. 1714. D.L. 1715. **1738:** Carl. ?/8. **1741:** C. summer.

Quin, Mr. **1779:** B. 12/2. **1799:** K. 5/6, 28/6.

Quin, Mrs. **1779:** B. 12/2, 26/2. **1799:** K. 5/6, 16/6.

Quin, Miss. **1750:** B. 3/1.

Randall, Mr. **1776:** W. ?/8.

Rawlin[g]s, George. C.S. 1797. **1798:** L. 1/10.

Rawlin[g]s, Mrs. George. **1799:** K. 5/6, 26/6.

Raymond [Grant], James (1768–1817). C.S. 1792. D.L. 1799. **1792:** N. 19/7, 20/7. **1794:** D. 14/5. **1795:** D. 17/11. **1796:** C. 28/3. **1797:** C. 15/8, 7/10.

Reddish, Samuel (1735–85). S.A. 1759. D.L. 1767. **1762:** C. 24/9, 15/10. **1763:** C. 12/9. **1777:** C. 9/7, 6/10.

Reddish, Mrs. Samuel [*née* Polly Hart] (d. 1799). S.A. 1765. D.L. 1767. **1777:** C. 14/7, 8/9.

Reed, Mr. C.S. 1758. **1760:** C. 23/7, 8/10. **1761:** B. 29/6, 17/7.

Reed, Mrs. **1792:** Wex. 12/10, 28/11 (*fr.* H.[2]).

Remington, James. S.A. 1764. **1763:** B. 19/1, 29/5. **1766:** W. ?/10. **1767:** K. 26/12. **1768:** K. 7/1, 4/3. **1770:** K. 14/9, 29/11. **1779:** K. 16/12. **1781:** K. 24/5. **1785:** C. 24/9. **1788:** B. 17/12. **1789:** B. 13/4. **1790:** D. 14/3; B. 12/11. **1791:** B. 26/1, 14/10; D. 6/5, 22/6. **1792:** B. 9/3; D. 21/11. **1793:** D. 4/1; B. 31/5. **1794:** D. 9/5; B. 8/12. **1795:** B. 16/3; D. 16/12. **1796:** D. 18/1; B. 17/2, 25/5. **1797:** C. 5/10. **1798:** D. 28/2. **1799:** D. 15/4.

Remington, Mrs. James. C.S. 1776. **1763:** B. 14/1, 23/2. **1770:** K. 14/9, 1/12. **1783:** K. 8/2. **1784:** Y. 20/12. **1788:** B. 17/12. **1789:** B. 6/3. **1790:** D. 26/5; B. 31/12. **1791:** B. 5/1; D. 27/5. **1792:** B. 6/2, 24/2; D. ?/11. **1793:** D. 28/1. **1794:** D. 2/6. **1795:** B. 6/4. **1796:** B. 9/5, 3/6. **1797:** C. 5/10. **1799:** D. 1/5.

Remington, Miss. **1797:** C. 5/10.

Reynolds, Mr. **1759:** C. 4/10. **1762:** C. 28/10. **1765:** C. 27/9. **1766:** C. 17/9. **1769:** C. 18/9. **1772:** C. 30/9. **1773:** C. 26/8. **1774:** C. 3/8.

Richards, William Talbot (d. 1813). C.S. 1779. **1778:** C. 12/8, 3/11 (*fr.* Edinburgh); B. 4/12, 9/12. **1779:** B. 19/3; C. 13/9, 29/9. **1792:** B. 24/2, 30/3; D. 21/11. **1793:** D. 18/1; B. 17/4, 27/5. **1794:** D. 23/5.

Richards, Mrs. William Talbot (Sarah), (d. 1820). C.S. 1779. **1778:** C. 7/8, 3/11; B. 4/12. **1779:** B. 19/3; C. 23/7, 6/10. **1794:** D. 12/5.

Richards, Miss Elizabeth Rebecca [*later* Mrs. John Edwin, Jr.] (b. 1773). C.S. 1780. H.[2] 1792. **1778:** C. 3/11. **1779:** B. 12/2, 24/3.

Richardson, Mr. C.S. 1768. **1769:** C. 15/9.

Rivers, Mr. **1791:** L. 23/2, 18/3; C. 26/4, 30/4.

Robinson, Mr. S.A. 1772. **1773:** C. 17/9. **1775:** C. 16/9. **1790:** D. 17/5.

Robinson, Mrs. **1775:** C. 16/9. **1790:** D. 17/5. **1791:** C. 2/5, 21/5.

Robinson, Mrs. [*later* (1) Mrs. William Perkins Taylor, (2) Mrs. Benjamin Wrench; *née* Hannah Henrietta Pritchard]. H.[2] 1778. S.A. 1786. **1786:** W. 18/7; C. 1/8, 30/10.

Robinson, Miss and Miss M. **1786:** C. 25/10, 30/10.

Roche, Mrs. **1761:** C. 28/10.

Roe, Mr. **1773:** K. 16/2.

Rogers, Mr. **1792:** Wex. 31/12.

Rosco, Miss. C.S. 1759. **1760:** C. 25/7, 15/10.

Ross, David E. (1728–90). S.A. 1748. D.L. 1751. **1775:** C. 5/7, 29/9.

Rowe, Richard Cox (1754–92). C.S. 1776. **1775:** C. 16/9. **1776:** C. 5/10. **1778:** B. 24/4; N. 3/12. **1779:** N. 1/3, 26/4. **1782:** B. 4/1; D. 19/11. **1783:** B. 24/1, 19/5; Sl. summer. **1784:** D. 30/1; B. 3/3, 8/12; L. 1/11. **1785:** B. 11/4. **1786:** B. ?/12. **1787:** B. 19/3, 3/8. **1788:** B. 10/10. **1789:** B. 19/2; D. 29/5. **1790:** D. ?/5; B. 2/11. **1791:** B. 3/1, 14/10; D. 16/5, 22/6.

Rowe, Mrs. Richard Cox [*née* Ashmore]. S.A. 1774 (as Miss Ashmore). **1778:** B. 24/4; N. 3/12. **1779:** N. 1/3, 26/4; D. 16/8.

Rusport, Mr. **1792:** N. 20/7.
Rusport, Miss. **1778:** C. 14/7.
Rutley, Mr. **1795:** Car. ?/10.
Ryan, Mrs. C.S. 1768. **1769:** C. 31/7.
Ryder, Miss E. C.G. 1790. C.S. 1791. **1791:** B. 14/9, 10/10. **1792:** N. 18/6, 25/6; C. 7/8, 22/9. **1793:** K. 27/8; W. 30/9. **1794:** Cl. 30/6, 25/7.
Ryder, Miss Rose [*later* Mrs. Pendred] (d. 1801). C.G. 1790. C.S. 1792. **1791:** B. 14/9, 10/10. **1792:** N. 18/6, 1/8; C. 1/8, 22/9. **1793:** K. 26/8; W. 30/9. **1794:** Cl. 30/6, 25/7. **1795:** K. 28/9, 4/11.
Ryder, Samuel (1738–71). **1770:** B. 30/4, 2/8; K. 14/9, 7/12. **1771:** K. 4/1.
Ryder, Mrs. Samuel. **1770:** B. 2/8. **1771:** K. 2/1; W. 9/10.
Ryder, Thomas (1735–91). S.A. 1757. C.G. 1786. **1765:** Dr. 26/8. **1767:** W. 28/10; K. 30/11. **1768:** K. 23/3. **1769:** Sl., G., D. n.d. **1770:** B. 30/4, 15/8; K. 14/9, 17/12. **1771:** W. 19/9, 28/10. **1780:** C. 31/7, 3/10. **1783:** C. 26/8, 26/9; L. 11/10. **1784:** N. 26/7. **1791:** B. 16/8, 10/10.
Ryder, Mrs. Thomas [*née* Rosetta Comerford] (d. 1794). S.A. 1752. (as Miss Comerford) **1758:** B. 10/2, 19/5. (as Mrs. Ryder) **1767:** K. 2/12, 26/12. **1768:** K. 8/1, 29/2. **1770:** B. 30/4, 16/7; K. 14/9, 7/12. **1771:** W. 9/10, 28/10.

St. Leger, Miss (*see* Miss Williams).
Saunders, Mrs. F.S. 1795. **1792:** K. 29/2; W. 24/7, 31/8; Wex. 12/11. **1793:** Wex. 18/1; W. 8/3, 23/3; K. 5/6, 17/7. **1795:** B. 4/3; K. 30/9, 16/11. **1796:** K. 6/8.
Schreven, Mr. **1782:** C. 16/8; L. 31/8.
Scott, Mr. **1790:** E. 8/3, 24/4; K. 8/11.
Scott, Mrs. **1791:** K. 12/1.
Second, Mr. **1787:** C. 19/9.
Seymour, Mr. **1794:** L. 8/9, 14/9. **1796:** C. 21/7.
Sharp, Mr. **1758:** C. 27/9.
Shaw, Mr. S.A. 1760. **1759:** C. 4/10.
Shepherd, Charles (d. 1768). S.A. 1761. **1764:** Wex. ?/6. *c.* **1768:** Sl. n.d.
Sheridan, Thomas (1719–88). S.A. 1743. D.L. 1744. **1773:** C. 11/6, 13/9; L. 6/8, 13/8. **1776:** C. 11/7, 7/10; L. 1/9, 21/9.
Sheridan, Mr. (as Master Sheridan) **1789:** K. 24/4, 13/7. (as Mr. Sheridan) **1790:** E. 27/1, 25/3. **1800:** B. 10/2, 26/5.
Sheriffe, Mr. S.A. 1758. **1753:** B. 6/6, 7/9. **1756:** Dr. n.d. **1757:** Dr. n.d. **1758:** Dr. n.d.; B. 6/2, 5/5; N. ?/8.
Sheriffe, Mrs. S.A. 1758. **1753:** B. 6/6, 7/9. **1758:** B. 6/2, 24/5.
Shewcraft, Miss [*later*, second wife of George Mitchell]. S.A. 1770. **1772:** L. 6/7, 3/8; C. 26/9, 17/10. **1773:** C. 17/9. **1774:** C. 25/7.
Shuter, Edward (*c.* 1728–76). C.G. 1744. C.S. 1760. **1761:** C. 6/7, 31/7.
Siddons, Mrs. William [*née* Sarah Kemble] (1755–1831). D.L. 1775. S.A. 1783. **1783:** C. 11/8, 30/8. **1784:** C. 1/9, 10/9. **1785:** B. 6/6, 27/6.
Simpson, George. C.S. 1791. **1789:** W. 12/10. **1790:** C. 4/9.
Sinclair, Mrs. **1794:** B. 24/10. **1795:** B. 2/3.
Skyddard, Miss. S.A. 1762. **1764:** Wex. ?/6.
Slack, Miss E. (*see* Mrs. H. Brown).

Smith, J. **1768:** Carf. 17/10, 21/10 (*fr.* Edinburgh).
Smith, William 'Gentleman' (1730–1819). C.G. 1753. C.S. 1774. **1774:** C. 13/7, 29/7.
Smith, Mr. & Mrs. **1768:** Carf. 17/10, 21/10 (*fr.* Edinburgh).
Smith, Mr. **1769:** C. 15/9.
Smith, Mr. C.S. 1776 (*fr.* Edinburgh). **1776:** C. 5/10. **1777:** C. 8/9, 3/10. **1778:** C. 21/8, 3/11. **1779:** C. 11/8, 8/10; W. 12/10.
Smith, Mrs. [wife of Mr. Smith *fr.* Edinburgh; *form.* Mrs. Scarce of Bath]. C.S. 1777. **1777:** C. 14/10. **1778:** C. 19/10, 3/11. **1779:** B. 5/3; C. 11/8, 8/10.
Smith, Mr. **1796:** Dr. 10/10.
Smith, Miss. **1800:** C. 4/3.
Smithson, William Joseph. F.S. 1784. **1787:** K. 20/7, 15/8. **1788:** Cash. ?/8, ?/9; Car. ?/10; Wex. 26/12. **1789:** Wex. 30/3; K. 24/4, 13/7; E. 31/12. **1790:** E. 7/1, 2/8; G. 25/8, 12/9; K. 8/11, 29/12. **1791:** K. 29/1, 7/3; E. 7/10, 14/11. **1792:** G. 27/8, 25/10. **1793:** G. 2/8, 11/10. **1796:** E. 26/3, 27/6. **1797:** E. 3/5, 20/5. **1799:** K. 5/6, 22/7. **1800:** E. 24/2, 5/4.
Smithson, Mrs. William J. **1800:** E. 10/3.
Snow, Miss. C.S. 1771. **1781:** K. 10/1.
Somerville, Mrs. **1782:** D. 1/4.
Sowdon, John (d. 1789). C.G. 1747. S.A. 1752. **1761:** C. 6/7. **1762:** C. 24/9, 2/11.
Sparks, Isaac (1719–76). R.S. 1736. A.S. 1738. D.L. 1745. *c.* **1736:** Sl. n.d. **1755:** C. summer. **1757:** C. 5/8. **1758:** C. 25/8, 26/9. **1761:** B. 29/6, 28/8. **1762:** C. 20/8, 30/10. **1763:** C. 14/9. **1765:** C. 13/8, 19/9. **1766:** C. 1/9. **1768:** L. ?/10. **1771:** L. 25/9. **1773:** C. 3/6, 17/9. **1774:** C. 22/7.
Sparks, Richard. C.S. 1771. D.L. 1798. **1771:** L. 22/10. **1776:** K. 17/6, 19/8. **1779:** K. 20/10. **1783:** C. 27/8. **1800:** B. 28/2, 27/3.
Sparks, Mrs. Richard [*née* Frances Ashmore] (b. *c.* 1749). S.A. 1765. D.L. 1798. (as Miss Ashmore) **1769:** C. 30/8, 15/9. **1770:** B. summer. (as Mrs. Sparks) **1773:** C. 4/6, 21/9; L. 14/8, 17/8. **1774:** C. 24/6, 5/8; L. 23/8, 28/9. **1776:** K. 17/6, 23/8. **1779:** K. 11/10. **1782:** D. 30/10, 19/11. **1783:** C. 19/8, 23/9; L. 11/10. **1797:** Carl. 14/10.
Spencer, Mrs. (*see* Miss Campion).
Spiletta, Signora. S.A. 1764. **1765:** C. 25/9, 1/10.
Stageldoir, Mr. **1760:** C. 10/10. **1761:** C. 28/10. **1762:** C. 4/10.
Stageldoir, Mrs. **1761:** C. 28/10. **1762:** C. 4/10.
Stanley, Mr. **1796:** K. 1/8.
Stanton, Mr. C.S. 1776. **1777:** C. 14/10. **1778:** C. 24/8, 19/10.
Stayley, George (b. 1727). S.A. 1752. **1757:** C. 5/8. **1758:** C. 14/7, 8/9. **1759:** C. 19/8, 5/10.
Stevens, Mr. C.S. 1778. **1780:** C. 28/8, 16/10.
Stewart, James Beatty. C.S. 1775. **1767:** K. 26/12. **1768:** K. 5/2, 24/2. **1769:** K. 12/8. **1770:** B. 7/5, 28/7; K. 24/9, 28/12.
Stewart, Mrs. James Beatty [*née* Griffith]. **1770:** K. 28/11.
Stewart, Mr. C.S. 1794. **1790:** B. 8/11, 29/12. **1791:** D. 20/6. **1792:** B. 24/2, 7/3. **1799:** L. 2/8, 3/8. **1800:** C. 4/3.
Stewart, Mrs. C.S. 1792 (*fr.* Edinburgh). **1792:** C. 13/8; D. ?/10. **1793:** D. 23/1; B. 17/4, 26/4.

Stewart, Miss. **1796:** E. 9/6, 22/6.

Storer, Charles (d. *c.* 1765). S.A. 1746. C.G. 1747. **1757:** C. 5/8. **1759:** C. 17/8, 31/8.

Storer, Mrs. Charles [*née* Elizabeth Clark] (d. 1767). S.A. 1742 (*fr.* C.G.). **1756:** C. 30/8, 24/9. **1757:** C. 5/8. **1759:** C. 17/8.

Storer, the Misses Fanny, Nancy, and Ann. **1756:** C. 17/9. **1759:** C. 1/10.

Stuart, Mr. C.S. 1792. **1792:** C. 29/5.

Sullivan, Mr. **1784:** Y. 20/12. **1792:** W. 24/7, 20/8; Wex. 28/9, 2/10.

Swendall, James [Swindall in Ireland]. C.S. 1780. Roy. 1787. **1783:** K. 13/2. **1784:** K. 17/2; C. 30/9. **1786:** W. 18/7; C. 2/8.

Swendall, Mrs. James. **1783:** K. 13/12. **1784:** K. 17/2; C. 30/9; B. 8/12.

Talbot, Montague [*stage name* Mr. Montague until 1798] (1774–1831). C.G. 1794. C.S. 1795. **1795:** C. ?/9. **1796;** C. 23/8, 10/9. **1797:** C. 15/8, 5/10.

Taplin, Mrs. [*née* Harriet Dyer]. S.A. 1776. **1781:** C. 8/8, 14/9. **1782:** C. 29/7, 27/9. **1783:** C. 9/8, 6/9; L. 11/10.

Tayleur, Mr. **1783:** K. 27/2.

Temple, Mr. **1780:** C. 1/9, 14/10. **1789:** Wex. 7/1, 6/3.

Temple, Mrs. **1789:** Wex. 7/1, 9/1.

Templeton, Mr. **1796:** C. 28/3.

Tenducci, Guisto Ferdinando (b. *c.* 1736). S.A. 1764 (*fr.* H.[2]). **1766:** L. 28/8; C. 11/9. **1767:** W. 21/11. **1783:** C. 14/8, 20/9.

Thompson, Mr. **1796:** K. 12/10.

Thompson, Mrs. **1796:** K. 12/10.

Thompson, Mrs. [*form.* Mrs. Joseph Vernon; *née* Jane Poitier] D.L. 1755. C.S. 1776 (as Mrs. Vernon). **1777:** C. 18/7, 16/10. **1780:** C. 29/7, 16/10.

Thompson, Master. **1780:** C. 6/10.

Tisdall, Mrs. (d. 1779). S.A. 1774. **1775:** C. 16/9, 29/9. **1778:** B. 30/12. **1779:** B. 22/1.

Toms, Mr. C.G. 1795. **1792:** W. 30/1, 21/3 (*fr.* Edinburgh).

Tone, Theobald Wolfe (1763–98). **1783:** G. 8/8.

Townsend, Edward Evans (1766–1809). C.G. 1793. **1796:** C. 30/7 (*fr.* C.G.); L. 18/7, 20/7.

Trevillian, Mr. **1759:** Ba. 27/12. **1761:** B. 28/8.

Trevillian, Mrs. **1761:** B. 29/6, 26/8.

Turner, Mr. **1768:** K. 1/2, 2/3.

Turpin, Mr. S.A. 1787. **1787:** W. 17/10.

Tyrer, Samuel. Cap. S. 1770. **1751:** B. 18/12. **1753:** B. 29/6, 24/8. **1756:** Tr. 6/3, 10/5.

Tyrer, Mrs. Samuel. **1751:** B. ?/12. **1753:** B. 24/8. **1756:** Tr. 11/3, 10/5.

Tyrrell, Mr. C.S. 1771. **1771:** L. 22/10. **1772:** K. 31/12. **1773:** K. 16/2. **1776:** C. 5/10. **1778:** N. 3/12. **1779:** N. 26/4. **1781:** B. 16/11, 21/11. **1782:** D. 19/11. **1783:** B. 24/1, 19/5. **1784:** D. 9/1, 10/2; B. 4/6, 8/12. **1787:** B. 2/3, 9/3. **1788:** B. 28/11, 17/12.

Tyrrell, Mrs. F.S. 1784. **1776:** K. 26/7, 19/8. **1778:** N. 3/12. **1779:** N. 26/4.

Urbani, Signor. S.A. 1782. **1783:** C. 14/8, 23/9.

Usher, Howard (d. 1802). D.L. 1744. S.A. 1758. **1761:** B. 17/7, 4/9. **1765:** C. 26/9, 2/10. **1766:** C. 10/9, 17/10.

Usher, Mrs. Howard. S.A. 1760. **1761:** B. 29/6, 4/9. **1765:** C. 9/9, 26/9. **1766:** C. 20/8, 27/10.

Usher, Miss. **1784:** B. 10/12. **1790:** E. 27/1, 15/3.

Vandermere, John Byron (1743–86). H.[2] 1768. C.S. 1771. **1772:** L. 6/7, 12/8; C. 3/8, 23/10. **1773:** C. 3/6, 15/9; L. 18/8. **1775:** C. 3/7, 29/9. **1776:** K. 17/6, 19/8. **1778:** W. ?/8. **1779:** K. 27/9. **1780:** K. 13/12. **1781:** K. 18/1. **1784:** K. 21/4, 9/6; W. 26/7.

Vandermere, Miss. S.A. 1766. **1767:** K. 2/12, 26/12. **1768:** K. 1/2, 2/3.

Vernel, John (1741–70). S.A. 1760. **1761:** B. 29/6. **1763:** C. 27/9. **1764:** C. 14/9. **1765:** C. 19/9, 9/10. **1766:** C. 11/9. **1768:** L. 13/10. **1769:** C. 2/8, 20/9.

Vernon, Joseph (*c.* 1738–82). D.L. 1754. C.S. 1758. **1761:** C. 6/7, 26/9.

Villars, Mr., Jr. C.S. 1797. **1799:** K. 5/6, 28/6.

Villars, Mrs., Jr. C.S. 1797. **1799:** K. 5/6, 28/6.

Villars, Mrs., Sr. [*later* Mrs. Pero]. S.A. 1774. (as Mrs. Villars) **1772:** K. 31/12. **1773:** K. 16/2. **1776:** B. 27/3, 8/4. (as Mrs. Pero) **1778:** B. 20/4. **1779:** B. 12/2; K. 5/6, 28/6.

Waddy, John (1751–1814). S.A. 1774. C.G. 1796. **1775:** C. 3/7, 22/9. **1776:** K. 17/6, 12/8.

Waker, Joseph. S.A. 1759. **1768:** B. 23/8. **1769:** N. 23/1; K. 3/6, 17/8. **1772:** L. 6/7, 10/7. **1773:** B. 8/9. **1774:** B. 3/1, 11/2. **1778:** K. 19/1. **1781:** W. n.d. **1782:** Mal. n.d.

Waker, Mrs. Joseph (d. 1776). **1768:** B. 23/8. **1769:** N. 23/1; K. 3/6. **1773:** B. 23/8.

Walker, R. C.S. 1795. **1795:** K. 5/10, 16/11. **1796:** B. 28/3.

Wallack, Mrs. William. F.S. 1795. **1800:** C. 4/3.

Wallis, Fielding (1754–1817). C.S. 1778. **1781:** K. 5/3, 5/4. **1782:** K. 28/9. **1783:** K. 8/2.

Wallis, Mrs. Fielding [*née* Jane Miller] (1750–85). C.S. 1778. **1781:** K. 8/2, 6/3. **1783:** K. 8/2. **1784:** K. 21/4, 9/6.

Wallis, Miss Tryphosa Jane [*later* Mrs. James Elijah Campbell] (1774–1848). C.S. 1778. C.G. 1789. **1783:** K. 8/2. **1784:** K. 26/5. **1795:** C. 21/8, 11/9.

Walpole, Miss Charlotte [*later* Mrs. Edward Atkyns] (*c.* 1758–1836). C.S. 1776. D.L. 1777. **1776:** C. 10/7, 12/10.

Walsh, Mr. Cap. S. 1770. **1770:** C. 25/8. **1771:** L. 22/10. **1772:** L. 6/7, 18/9; C. 19/8, 31/8; K. 31/12. **1773:** K. 16/2; C. 17/9. **1777:** C. 14/10. **1780:** B. 10/3.

Walsh, Mrs. **1770:** C. 25/8.

Ward, Mr. C.S. 1764. C.G. *c.* 1777. (as Master Ward) **1768:** C. 15/8. **1770:** C. 24/8, 27/8. **1771:** L. 22/10. **1772:** L. 6/7, 31/7; C. 19/8, 16/10. **1773:** C. 17/9. (as Mr. Ward) **1774:** B. 9/2. **1776:** K. 17/6, 24/8. **1778:** C. 6/7, 20/10.

Ward, Mrs. [*form.* Miss Archbold? *q.v.*]. C.S. 1777 (*fr.* C.G.). **1778:** C. 6/7, 20/10.

Ward, Mrs. **1787:** B. 19/2, 9/4. **1798:** D. 28/2, 5/5.
Ward, Mrs. Henry [*née* Sarah Achurch] (*c.* 1727–71). C.G. 1748. S.A. 1752. **1753:** C. ?/6, ?/9.
Ward, Thomas. **1754:** B. 18/11, 17/12. **1755:** B. 7/1, 28/2.
Ward, Mrs. Thomas [*form.* Mrs. Wrightson; *née* Nancy Elrington] (d. 1764). S.A. 1731. **1754:** B. 18/11, 17/12. **1755:** B. 7/1, 28/2.
Waterhouse, Mr. Cap. S. 1783. **1785:** C. 27/8.
Waters, Mr. **1778:** C. 24/10. **1781:** C. 17/10. **1792:** Wex. 12/10, 28/11.
Wathen, George (1762–1849). C.S. 1792. H.[2] 1795. **1794:** C. 6/9, 6/10.
Webb, Miss. **1790:** W. ?/7; L. ?/8; E. 13/9, 2/10.
Webster, Anthony (d. *c.* 1785). C.G. 1776. C.S. 1776. **1776:** C. 10/7, 30/8. **1777:** C. 18/7, 4/10. **1778:** C. 17/7, 2/9.
Webster, Mrs. Anthony [Mrs. Jonathan Battishill]. C.S. 1776 (*fr.* C.G.). **1776:** C. 22/7, 8/10. **1777:** C. 16/7, 10/10.
Wells, Ezra. Cap. S. 1782. **1783:** K. 15/2 (*fr.* Bristol). **1787:** K. 20/7. **1790:** W. ?/7; L. 31/7, 8/11; E. 6/9, 2/10. **1791:** L. 18/3; C. 26/4, 13/5. **1792:** W. 30/1, 2/3; C. 29/5. **1793:** W. 30/9.
Wells, Mrs. Ezra. Cap. S. 1782. **1783:** K. 15/2 (*fr.* Bristol). **1787:** K. 5/2, 20/7. **1790:** E. 2/10. **1791:** L. 4/2; C. 13/5. **1792:** W. 30/1; C. 29/5. **1793:** W. 30/9.
West, Mrs. **1773:** K. 16/2; W. n.d.
Weston, Thomas (1737–76). H.[2] 1759. S.A. 1760. **1760:** C. 10/10.
White, Mr. **1754:** B. 18/11. **1755:** Lis. 1/3; B. 14/3. **1762:** C. 4/10. **1766:** C. 23/9.
White, Mrs. S.A. 1775. **1776:** K. 17/6, 26/7. **1777:** C. 20/8, 14/10.
Whit[e]ley, James Augustus (*c.* 1724–81). **1742:** G. n.d. **1746:** Carl. n.d.
Whit[e]ley, Mrs. [*form.* Mrs. Cassandra Parker]. **1742:** G. n.d. **1746:** Carl n.d.
Whitmore, Samuel (?) (d. 1819). S.A. 1770. C.G. 1802. **1770:** B. 13/4, 8/8. **1771:** K. 14/9, 15/12. **1773:** K. 6/1. **1790:** W. ?/7; L. 31/7, 8/11; E. 6/9, 2/10. **1791:** L. 7/2.
Whitmore, Mrs. **1770:** B. 7/5.
Whitmore, Miss. **1770:** K. 17/9, 31/12.
Whiton, Mr. **1769:** C. 15/9.
Whittaker, Mr. **1768:** Carf. 17/10, 21/10.
Wilder, James (b. 1724). C.G. 1749. S.A. 1756 (*fr.* Edinburgh). **1758:** C. 14/8, 18/9. **1759:** C. 7/8.
Wilder, Mrs. James (Sarah). S.A. 1756 (*fr.* Edinburgh). **1757:** C. 5/8. **1758:** C. 14/8, 8/9. **1759:** C. 24/8.
Wilder, Miss. **1758:** C. 14/9, 18/9. **1759:** C. 24/8.
Wilkinson, Tate (1739–1803). C.G. 1757. S.A. 1757. **1792:** C. 29/5.
Wilks [Snagge], Thomas (1746–1812). D.L. 1768. Cap. S. 1770. **1773:** C. 26/7, 14/9; L. 10/8, 20/8. **1777:** C. 18/7, 8/10.
Williams, James (d. 1768). S.A. 1749. **1760:** C. 10/10.
Williams, Mrs. James. C.S. 1764. **1761:** C. 28/10.
Williams, Mr. and Mrs. **1769:** C. 15/9.
Williams, Mr. **1770:** K. 19/12, 21/12. **1778:** N. 3/12. **1779:** N. 26/4; D. 18/8.
Williams, Mrs. **1783:** K. 15/2. **1796:** E. 3/6.

Williams, Mr. **1792:** C. 29/5.
Williams, Miss [*later* Mrs. St. Leger]. C.S. 1794. **1795:** K. 29/9.
Willis, Mr. **1761:** B. 29/6, 17/7.
Willis, Miss. C.S. 1758. **1761:** B. 29/6, 12/8. **1762:** C. 4/10.
Willoughby, Mrs. **1798:** D. 2/4.
Willoughby, Miss. **1798:** D. 2/4.
Wills, Mr. **1769:** C. 15/9.
Wilmot, Mr. S.A. 1771. **1770:** K. 29/10, 21/12. **1771:** W. 9/10, 4/11. **1774:** D. 8/8. **1776:** B. 29/3. **1778:** B. 2/3, 24/4; N. 13/5, 3/12. **1779:** N. 22/4. **1781:** B. 9/5.
Wilmot, Mrs. **1770:** K. ?/11. **1776:** B. 29/3. **1778:** B. 10/4; N. 3/12. **1779:** N. 26/4. **1781:** B. 9/3.
Wilmot, Miss. **1776:** B. 29/3.
Wilson, Richard (1744–96). H.[2] 1774. S.A. 1786. **1786:** W. 18/7; L. 31/7, 23/9; C. 2/8, 25/10.
Wilson, Mrs. Richard [*form.* Mrs. Thomas Weston; *née* Sarah Maria Adcock] (1752–86). C.S. 1761. H.[2] 1774. (as Miss Adcock) **1760:** C. 10/10. **1761:** C. 10/7. (as Mrs. Wilson) **1786:** C. 2/9.
Wilson, Mr. **1768:** Carf. 17/10, 21/10. **1770:** B. 28/7, 4/8. **1792:** Wex. 12/10, 28/11.
Withington, Mr. S.A. 1781. **1779:** C. 22/9, 29/9. **1781:** C. 7/9. **1782:** C. 29/7; L. 31/8. **1783:** C. 23/8. **1784:** C. 30/9.
Wood, Charles. H.[2] 1780. S.A. 1781. **1784:** C. 30/9. **1785:** C. 30/9. **1786:** W. 18/7; C. 1/8, 6/11; L. 18/9.
Wood, Mrs. Charles [*née* Mucklow]. S.A. 1781. **1786:** C. 24/10.
Wood, Miss. H.[2] 1781. S.A. 1781. **1789:** C. 18/4, 18/12. **1790:** C. 12/4. **1791:** L. 14/3, 18/3; C. 26/4, 3/6.
Woods, Charles (d. 1783). **1772:** K. 31/12.
Woodward, Henry (1714–77). G.F. 1731. S.A. 1739. **1760:** C. 11/8, 10/10. **1761:** C. 29/7, 1/10.
Wright, Mr. S.A. 1770. **1769:** N. 20/1, 23/1.
Wright, Mrs. C.S. 1768. **1768:** B. 23/8. **1769:** K. 3/6.

Yates, Thomas. H.[2] 1794. **1797:** C. 2/10, 9/10.
Yates, Mrs. Thomas (Sarah). H.[2] 1794. C.S. 1797. **1797:** C. 9/9, 3/10.
Young, Mr. C.S. 1780 (*fr.* Bristol). **1779:** C. 27/8 (*fr.* Bristol); K. 6/11.
Young, Thomas. C.G. 1761. S.A. 1780. **1780:** C. 29/7, 2/10.
Younge, Miss Elizabeth (*see* Mrs. Alexander Pope).

BIBLIOGRAPHY[1]

I. *Manuscripts*

CHARLEMONT, EARL OF, 'Original Correspondence of James, late Earl of Charlemont', Royal Irish Academy, Dublin.

CROKER, THOMAS C., 'Recollections of Cork', MS. 1206, Trinity College Library, Dublin.

CROSSLE, DR. FRANCIS, Crossle Papers, Free Public Library, Newry.

DALY, RICHARD, *v.* F. E. JONES, 'Official Papers, 2nd Series, 1790–1831', carton no. 511, 47/17, Record Tower, Dublin Castle.

'The Drennan Correspondence', Public Record Office, Belfast.

GARRICK, DAVID, 'Original Letters to and from Garrick', Forster MS. 213, Victoria and Albert Museum, London.

HUNT, SIR VERE, MSS.: 'Account Books, 1790–1'; 'Journal, 1781–1807'; 'Letters to Hunt', City Public Library, Limerick.

LAWRENCE, WILLIAM J., 'Notebooks for a History of the Irish Stage', University of Cincinnati Library, Cincinnati, Ohio.

—— MS. 'Annals of the Old Belfast Stage, 1731–1820'; typescript in the possession of William Smith Clark.

'Lefanu Papers', Microfilm 2975, N.L.I.

TONE, THEOBALD WOLFE, MS. 'Autobiography', Trinity College Library, Dublin.

'Waterford Corporation Minute Books', City Hall, Waterford.

WILLES, CHIEF JUSTICE (BARON) EDWARD, 'Original Letters', Additional MS. 29252, B.M.

II. *Maps*

Plans of the principal towns . . . in Ireland, [*1751*]. (B.M.)

Belfast:

A Plan of the Town of Belfast, 1757 [Belfast, 1888]. (B.M.)

A Plan of the Town of Belfast, John Mulholland, 1788. (B.M.)

A Map of the Town and Environs of Belfast, 1791. (B.M.)

A New Plan of the Town of Belfast, 1819. (B.M.)

Cork:

A Survey of the City and Suburbs of Cork, J. Rocque, 1759, with all the new improvements to 1771. (B.M.)

A Map of the City and Suburbs of Cork, J. Connor, 1774. (B.M.)

A Plan of the City and Suburbs of Cork, W. Beauford, London, 1801. (B.M.)

[1] Abbreviations used throughout: B.M. = British Museum, London; COL. = Colindale Annex, British Museum; N.L.I. = National Library of Ireland, Dublin.

Derry:

A Plan of the City and Suburbs of Londonderry, with the Waterside, R. Porter, 1799. (B.M.)

Kilkenny:

A Survey of the City of Kilkenny, J. Rocque, 1758. (B.M.)

A Plan of the City of Kilkenny, S. Byron, [1795]. (B.M.)

Limerick:

A Plan of the City of Limerick, John Ferrar, 1786. (In Ferrar's *The History of Limerick to the Year 1787*.)

Newry:

A Plan of the Town of Newry, J. Rocque, 1760. (B.M.)

Waterford:

Waterford, C. Smith, 1745. (B.M.)

A Plan of the City and Environs of Waterford, William Richards and Bernard Scalé, 1764. (B.M.)

A Map of the City of Waterford and Its Environs, P. Leahy and Sons, 1834. (N.L.I.)

III. *Newspapers*[1]

Belfast Mercury; or Freeman's Chronicle [BM]: 1784–5 (N.L.I.); 1784–6 (COL.).

Belfast News-Letter [BNL]: 1738–55, 1760–1800 (Linen Hall Library, Belfast); 1757–9 (N.L.I.).

Belfast Northern Star [BNS]: 1792–4 (COL.); 1795–7 (N.L.I.).

Clonmel Gazette [ClG]: 1788–95 (N.L.I.).

Connaught Journal [CJ]: 1792 (Private Library, Galway); 1793, 1795 (N.L.I.).

Cork Advertiser [CA]: 1799–1800 (N.L.I.).

Cork Chronicle; or Universal Register [CCh]: 1764–9 (Cork City Public Library).

Cork Courier [CC]: 1794–5 (N.L.I.).

Cork Evening Post [CEP]: 1757–63, 1769, 1782, 1787–1800 (N.L.I.); 1768 (Cork City Public Library); 1770–1 (University College, Cork, Library).

Cork Gazette and General Advertiser [CG]: 1790–7 (N.L.I.).

Cork Journal [CJ]: 1756–62 (Private Library, Newcastle West, Co. Limerick); 1770–1 (University College, Cork, Library).

Covent-Garden Journal [CGJ] (Dublin): 1752–6 (COL.).

Dickson's Dublin Intelligence [DDI]: 1720–4, 1726–31 (N.L.I.); 1725 (COL.).

Drogheda Journal [DJ]: 1793–1800 (N.L.I.).

Dublin Daily Post, and General Advertiser [DDP]: 1739–40 (N.L.I.).

Dublin Evening Post [DEP]: 1732–6, 1757, 1788–1800 (N.L.I.); 1737–41 (COL.).

[1] The bracketed letters after the titles are the abbreviations used throughout the footnotes in this volume.

Ennis Chronicle [EC]: 1789–1800 (N.L.I.).

Faulkner's Dublin Journal [FDJ]: 1725 (B.M.); 1726–7, 1729–65, 1767–8, 1773–1800 (N.L.I.); 1737–8 (Linen Hall Library, Belfast); 1741–6 (Marsh's Library, Dublin); 1766 (COL.).

Freeman's Journal [FJ] (Dublin): 1763–1800 (N.L.I.).

Hibernian Chronicle [HC] (Cork): 1769–1800 (N.L.I.).

Hibernian Journal [HJ] (Dublin): 1771–82, 1784, 1786–1800 (N.L.I.); 1783 (COL.).

Leinster Journal [LJ] (Kilkenny): 1767–76, 1778–88, 1790–1800 (N.L.I.); 1789 (*Kilkenny Journal* office, Kilkenny).

Limerick Chronicle and General Advertiser [LC]: 1768–70, 1777 (COL.); 1771–3, 1779, 1794 (N.L.I.); 1774, 1794 (Limerick City Public Library); 1782–6, 1788–9, 1791–3, 1796–1800 (*Limerick Leader* office, Limerick).

Londonderry Journal [LDJ]: 1772–3, 1798–1800 (Magee University College Library, Derry); 1773–88, 1790–6 (Private library, Molenan, Co. Derry).

The Medley (Cork): 1738 (Cork City Public Library).

Munster Journal [MJ] (Limerick): 1749–51 (N.L.I.); 1761, 1767, 1777 (COL.).

Newry Chronicle and Universal Advertiser [NC]: 1778–9, 1792–3 (Free Public Library, Newry).

Reilly's Dublin News-Letter: 1737–43 (N.L.I.).

Volunteer Journal [VJ] (Cork): 1782–7 (N.L.I.).

Waterford Chronicle [WC]: 1771–2 (COL.); 1787, 1789, 1791, 1793 (N.L.I.).

Waterford Herald [WH]: 1791–3 (N.L.I.); 1793–6 (COL.).

Waterford Mirror [WM]: 1801–20 (Waterford City Public Library).

Weekly Oracle (Dublin): 1735–6 (COL.).

Wexford Herald [WxH]: 1788–9, 1792–4 (N.L.I.).

IV. *Playbills*

Belfast:

18 Dec. 1751. *Jane Shore + The Virgin Unmask'd.*

— Dec. 1751 (?). *Merry Wives of Windsor + An Honest Yorkshire-Man.*

(Shaw Collection, Harvard University Library.)

Cork:

31 Aug. 1772. *The Grecian Daughter + Love à la Mode.*

2 Aug. 1776. *King Lear + The Devil to Pay.*

24 Aug. 1780. *The Double Dealer + The Romp.*

28 Oct. 1786. *The Way of the World + The Irish Widow.*

4 Aug. 1788. *Robin Hood + The Citizen.*

(Shaw Collection, Harvard University Library.)

5 Oct. 1797. *The Way to Get Married + No Song, No Supper + Children in the Wood.*

(Reeves Collection, Royal Irish Academy, Dublin.)

Galway:

8 Aug. 1783. *Douglas + All the World's A Stage.*

(University College, Galway, Library.)

Kilkenny:

5 June 1799. *A Cure for the Heart Ache + The Padlock.*
10 June 1799. *Heir at Law + Poor Soldier.*
12 June 1799. *Heir at Law + Poor Soldier.*
17 June 1799. *Bank Note + Rosina.*
26 June 1799. *The Busie Body + Wicklow Mountains.*
28 June 1799. *The Wonder: A Woman Keeps a Secret + Wicklow Mountains.*
31 July 1799. *Lover's Vows + Children in the Wood.*
(B.M. Playbills, vol. 291.)

Tralee:

6 Mar. 1756. *King Henry IV + Captain O'Blunder.*
9 Mar. 1756. *Hamlet, Prince of Denmark + Damon and Phillida.*
11 Mar. 1756. *The Beaux' Stratagem + Chrononhotonthologos.*
13 Mar. 1756. *Jane Shore + The Anatomist.*
15 Mar. 1756. *Cato + The Stage Coach.*
17 Mar. 1756. *The Committee; or, The Faithful Irishman + The Mock Doctor.*
20 Mar. 1756. *King Richard III + Trick Upon Trick.*
23 Mar. 1756. *The Conscious Lovers + Lethe; or, Aesop in the Shades.*
25 Mar. 1756. *The Fair Penitent + The Honest Yorkshire-Man.*
27 Mar. 1756. *The Merry Wives of Windsor + The Brave Irishman.*
30 Mar. 1756. *The Orphan + The Lying Valet.*
1 Apr. 1756. *The Recruiting Officer + The Miller of Mansfield.*
3 Apr. 1756. *Othello + The Virgin Unmask'd.*
6 Apr. 1756. *The Provok'd Husband + The Sheep-Shearing.*
8 Apr. 1756. *The London Merchant + The Devil to Pay.*
10 Apr. 1756. *Love for Love + Tom Thumb.*
12 Apr. 1756. *The Distrest Mother + The Intriguing Chambermaid.*
14 Apr. 1756. *The Merchant of Venice + Miss in Her Teens.*
16 Apr. 1756. *The Beggar's Opera + The Mock Doctor.*
17 Apr. 1756. *The Stratagem + The Stage Coach.*
19 Apr. 1756. *King Henry IV + Captain O'Blunder.*
21 Apr. 1756. *The Provok'd Wife + Damon and Phillida.*
23 Apr. 1756. *Oroonoko + Damon and Phillida.*
26 Apr. 1756. *Romeo and Juliet + Tom Thumb.*
28 Apr. 1756. *The Constant Couple + A Dish of Tea.*
30 Apr. 1756. *Tunbridge-Walks + Flora; or, Hob in the Well.*
3 May 1756. *Theodosius + What D'Ye Call It.*
5 May 1756. *Macbeth + The Cobler of Preston.*
7 May 1756. *The Busie Body + Duke or No Duke.*
10 May 1756. *The Stratagem + The Sheep-Shearing.*
(Folger Shakespeare Library, Washington, D.C.)

Youghal:

20 Dec. 1784. *The Beaux' Stratagem + The Busie Body.*
(B.M. Playbills, vol. 291.)

V. *Books and Printed Articles*

The Ancient and Present State of Youghall, Youghall, 1784.

An Answer to the Memoirs of Mrs. Billington. With the Life and Adventures of Richard Daly, Esq., and an Account of the Present State of the Irish Theatre, London, 1792.

APPLETON, WILLIAM W., *Charles Macklin: An Actor's Life*, Cambridge, Massachusetts, 1960.

BAKER, DAVID ERSKINE, *Biographica Dramatica; or, A Companion to the Playhouse*, London, 1812. 2 v.

BARRINGTON, SIR JONAH, *Personal Sketches of His Own Times*, London, 1827. 2 v.

BEAUFORT, DANIEL AUGUSTUS, *Memoir of a Map of Ireland*, London, 1792.

BENN, GEORGE, *The History of the Town of Belfast*, Belfast, 1823.

——*A History of the Town of Belfast*, London, 1877.

BERNARD, JOHN, *Retrospections of the Stage*, Boston, 1832. 2 v.

BIGGER, FRANCIS JOSEPH, 'Mrs. Siddons and the Stage of Belfast', *Belfast News-Letter*, 28 November 1925.

BOWDEN, CHARLES T., *A Tour through Ireland*, Dublin, 1791.

BURKE, REV. WILLIAM P., *History of Clonmel*, Waterford, 1907.

BUSHNELL, GEORGE H., 'The Original Lady Randolph', *Theatre Notebook*, xiii (1959).

CALLWELL, J. M., *Old Irish Life*, Edinburgh, 1912.

CAMPBELL, THOMAS, *Life of Mrs. Siddons*, London, 1834. 2 v.

CARR, SIR JOHN, *A Stranger in Ireland; or, A Tour in the Southern and Western Parts of that Country in the Year 1805*, London, 1806. 2 v.

CHETWOOD, WILLIAM RUFUS, *A General History of the Stage*, London, 1749.

CHURCHILL, CHARLES, *Poems*, ed. James Laver, London, 1933.

CLANCY, JOHN, 'Around the town of Ennis with Father Clancy', *Molua*, Dublin, 1945.

CLARK, WILLIAM SMITH, *The Early Irish Stage: The Beginnings to 1720*, Oxford, 1955.

COOK, DUTTON, *Hours with the Players*, new ed., London, 1883.

COOKE, WILLIAM, *Memoirs of Charles Macklin, Comedian*, 2nd ed., London, 1806.

The Council Book of the Corporation of the City of Cork, ed. Richard Caulfield, Guildford, Surrey, 1876.

CROKER, J. C., *Familiar Epistles to Frederick E. Jones, Esq., on the Present State of the Irish Stage*, Dublin, 1805.

CUSACK, M. F., *A History of the City and County of Cork*, Dublin and Cork, 1875.

DELATOCNAYE, *A Frenchman's Walk through Ireland, 1796–97*, transl. John Stevenson, Dublin and Belfast, [1917].

DERRICK, SAMUEL, *Letters Written from Liverpoole, Chester, Corke, the Lake of Killarney, Tunbridge-Wells, and Bath*, Dublin, 1767. 2 v.

The Diary; or Woodfall's Register, London, 1789–93.

DIBDIN, JAMES C., *The Annals of the Edinburgh Stage*, Edinburgh, 1888.

The Drennan Letters, ed. D. A. Chart, Belfast, 1931.

The Dublin Magazine.

DUNLAP, WILLIAM, *The Life of George Frederick Cooke*, 2nd ed., London, 1815. 2 v.
EDGEWORTH, RICHARD LOVELL, *Memoirs*, London, 1820. 2 v.
EDWARDS, ANTHONY, *The Cork Remembrancer*, Cork, 1792.
EGAN, PATRICK M., *The Illustrated Guide to the City and County of Kilkenny*, Kilkenny, [1885].
—— *Guide and Directory of the County and City of Waterford*, Kilkenny, 1894.
ELLIS, STEWART M., *Life of Michael Kelly*, London, 1930.
ELSTOB, MARK, *A Trip to Kilkenny, from Durham, by Way of Whitehaven and Dublin, in the Year MDCCLXXVI*, Stockton, 1778.
Exshaw's Gentleman's and London Magazine.
FERRAR, JOHN, *An History of the City of Limerick*, Limerick, 1767.
—— *The History of Limerick to the Year 1787*, Limerick, 1787.
FITZGERALD, REV. P., and J. J. M'GREGOR, *The History, Topography, and Antiquities of the County and City of Limerick*, Dublin, 1827. 2 v.
FITZGERALD, PERCY, *The Kembles*, London, 1871. 2 v.
FITZPATRICK, W. J., *Friends, Foes, and Adventures of Lady Morgan*, Dublin, 1859.
FROUDE, J. A., *The English in Ireland in the 18th Century*, London, 1874. 3 v.
GARRICK, DAVID, *The Private Correspondence of David Garrick*, London, 1831–2. 2 v.
GENEST, JOHN, *Some Account of the English Stage, from the Restoration in 1660 to 1830*, Bath, 1832. 10 v.
GILBERT, SIR JOHN T., *A History of the City of Dublin*, Dublin, 1854–9. 3 v.
GILLILAND, T., *The Dramatic Mirror: Containing the History of the Stage from the Earliest Period to the Present Time*, London, 1808. 2 v.
GRATTAN, THOMAS COLLEY, *Beaten Paths; and Those Who Trod Them*, London, 1862, 2 v.
GRIFFITH, AMYAS, 'Wexford', *Dublin Magazine*, August 1764.
—— *Miscellaneous Tracts*, Dublin, 1788.
HARDIMAN, JAMES, *The History of the Town and County of Galway*, Galway, 1820; reprinted Galway, 1926.
HENDERSON, JOHN, *Letters and Poems . . . with Anecdotes of His Life by John Ireland*, London, 1786.
HERBERT, DOROTHEA, *Retrospections, 1770–1798*, London, 1929.
HERBERT, J. D., *Irish Varieties*, London, 1836.
Hibernia Curiosa, Dublin, 1769.
The Hibernian Magazine, Dublin.
HIGHFILL, PHILIP H., 'Actors' Wills', *Theatre Notebook*, xv (1960).
Historical Manuscripts Commission Reports: The MSS. and Correspondence of James, 1st Earl of Charlemont, London, 1894.
HITCHCOCK, ROBERT, *An Historical View of the Irish Stage*, Dublin, 1788–94 2 v.
HODGKINSON, J. L., and REX POGSON, *The Early Manchester Theatre*, London, 1960.
HOGAN, CHARLES BEECHER, 'Eighteenth-Century Actors in the D.N.B. Additions and Corrections', *Theatre Notebook*, vi (1952).

HOGAN, CHARLES BEECHER, 'Eighteenth-Century Actors in the D.N.B. Additions and Corrections (Second Series)', *Theatre Notebook*, xi (1957).
HOGAN, JOHN, *History of Kilkenny*, Dublin, 1884.
HORE, PHILIP H., *History of the Town and County of Wexford*, London, 1906. 5 v.
Journal of a Tour in Ireland Performed in August, 1804, London, 1806.
KEANE, E. T., *A Glimpse of the Days that Are Over*, Kilkenny, 1910.
KEENAN, P., *Old Newry: Some Historical Notes*, Newry, 1945.
KELLY, MICHAEL, *Reminiscences*, London, 1826. 2 v.
KELLY, R. J., 'The Old Galway Theatres', *The Journal of the Royal Society of Antiquities of Ireland*, 6th series, iv (1914).
'Lady Morgan', *Irish Quarterly Review*, ix (1859).
LAWRENCE, W. J., 'The Old Belfast Stage: Its Glories and Romances', *The Irish News*, 21 Nov. 1895.
—— 'The Drama in Belfast', *Sketch*, 25 Dec. 1895.
—— 'The Old Arthur Square Theatre', *The Northern Whig*, 2 Jan. 1909.
—— 'The early Belfast stage: how the drama dawned in the north', *Irish Life*, 11 Apr. 1913.
—— 'Flashlights on the old Belfast stage', *Irish Life*, 25 Apr. 1913.
—— 'The Old Belfast Theatre', *Irish Life*, 3 Oct. 1913.
—— 'Michael Atkins: a noted Belfast actor manager', *Irish Life*, 14 Nov. 1913.
—— 'Flashlights on the old Belfast stage', *Irish Life*, 28 Nov. 1913.
—— 'The oldest Belfast playbill', *Ireland's Saturday Night*, 11 Jan. 1919.
—— 'Bygone Belfast: how they went to the play: when audiences called tunes', *Ireland's Saturday Night*, 2 July 1921.
—— 'First Arthur Square theatre: deadlock over licence: Belfast as "Second Athens" ', *Ireland's Saturday Night*, 17 May 1930.
—— 'First Belfast panto: on stage over wine vaults: strolling group as pioneers', *Ireland's Saturday Night*, 26 Dec. 1931.
—— 'Flashlights on the old Belfast stage', *Ireland's Saturday Night*, 17 Sept. 1938.
—— 'New plays in old Belfast', *Ireland's Saturday Night*, 31 Dec. 1938.
—— 'The old Arthur Square theatre, Belfast', *Ireland's Saturday Night*, 4 Mar. 1939.
—— 'The Early Cork Stage', *Weekly Irish Times*, 16 Dec. 1905.
—— 'The Old Cork Theatre', *Ireland's Saturday Night*, 29 Dec. 1906.
—— 'Old Cork Stage', *Irish Independent*, 26 Mar. 1907.
—— 'The Old Cork Stage', *Saturday Herald*, 18 Apr. 1908.
—— 'Some glimpses of the old Cork Stage', *Irish Life*, 26 July 1912.
—— 'The Cork Stage in the 18th century', *Irish Independent*, 25 Nov. 1913.
—— 'The Old Cork Stage', *The Irish Rosary*, xxiv (Jan. 1920).
—— 'The Dawn of Drama in Derry', *Ireland's Saturday Night*, 21 Oct. 1905.
—— 'The Old Londonderry Theatre', *Irish Life*, 17 Apr. 1914.
—— 'Old Derry Theatres', *Ireland's Saturday Night*, 9 July 1921.
—— 'The bygone drama in Derry', *Ireland's Saturday Night*, 26 Nov. 1938.
—— 'The Bygone Drama in Drogheda', *Saturday Herald*, 4 Mar. 1905.
—— 'Drama in Drogheda', *Weekly Irish Times*, 17 Apr. 1909.

LAWRENCE, W. J., 'The Old Drogheda Theatre', *Saturday Herald*, 24 Jan. 1914.
—— 'Drama in Dundalk', *Irish Independent*, 6 Feb. 1907.
—— 'The Drama in Dundalk', *Irish Life*, 13 Mar. 1914.
—— 'Freemasonry and the Irish stage: ceremonial visits to theatres in eighteenth century', *Irish Times*, 14 Feb. 1936.
—— 'The Old Galway Theatre', *Saturday Herald*, 9 Feb. 1906.
—— 'The Old Galway Theatre', *Irish Life*, 7 Feb. 1914.
—— 'The Old Galway Theatre', *Saturday Herald*, 14 Feb. 1914.
—— 'The Bygone Drama in Kilkenny', *Saturday Herald*, 9 Dec. 1905.
—— 'The Old Limerick Theatre', *Ireland's Saturday Night*, 19 Jan. 1907.
—— 'The Old Limerick Theatre', *Evening Telegraph* (Dublin), 25 Sept. 1909.
—— 'Flashlights on the old Limerick stage', *Irish Life*, 13 Sept. 1912.
—— 'Stories of the old Limerick stage', *Evening Telegraph* (Dublin), 25 Nov. 1922.
—— 'The Bygone Drama in Lisburn', *Belfast Saturday Night*, 20 Jan. 1906.
—— 'The drama in Lisburn: dips into the bygone days of strolling players', *Ireland's Saturday Night*, 24 Sept. 1921.
—— 'Newry's Old Theatres', *Irish Independent*, 20 Oct. 1905.
—— 'The Old Newry Theatre', *Irish Life*, 27 Feb. 1914.
—— 'Newry Theatre: once part of Belfast circuit: the pious old landlady who evicted Richard Rowe', *Belfast Telegraph*, 14 Dec. 1938.
—— 'The Drama in Sligo', *Saturday Herald*, 10 Apr. 1909.
—— 'The Drama in Sligo', *Irish Life*, 20 Mar. 1914.
—— 'The Old Waterford Theatre', *Dublin Evening Herald*, 7 Jan. 1905.
—— 'The Old Waterford Theatre', *Weekly Irish Times*, 16 Jan. 1909.
—— 'The old Waterford stage: some valuable new records', *Evening Telegraph* (Dublin), 27 Apr. 1912.
—— 'The Waterford Stage', *Evening Telegraph* (Dublin), 28 Oct. 1922.
—— 'The Old Wexford Theatre', *Dublin Evening Herald*, 23 Dec. 1905.
—— 'The old Wexford theatre', *Irish Life*, 9 May 1913.
—— 'The Drama in Youghall', *Saturday Herald*, 5 Aug. 1905.
LENIHAN, MAURICE, *Limerick; Its History and Antiquities*, Dublin, 1866.
LEPPER, S. H., and P. CROSSLE, *History of the Grand Lodge of Free and Accepted Masons of Ireland*, Dublin, 1925. 2 v.
Letters which passed between Mr. West Digges, Comedian, and Mrs. Sarah Ward, 1752–1759, Edinburgh, 1833.
LEWES, CHARLES LEE, *Memoirs*, London, 1805. 4 v.
LEWIS, JAMES, *Original Designs in Architecture*, London, 1780–97. 2 v.
LOVE, JAMES, *Poems on Several Occasions*, Edinburgh, 1754.
LUCKOMBE, P., *A Tour through Ireland in 1779*, London, 1780.
MACLYSAGHT, EDWARD, *Irish Life in the Seventeenth Century: After Cromwell*, London, 1939.
MATHEWS, CHARLES, *Memoirs*, London, 1839. 4 v.
MAXWELL, CONSTANTIA, *Country and Town in Ireland under the Georges*, Dundalk, 1949.
Memoirs of Mrs. Billington, London, 1792.
MILLIN, S. SHANNON, 'Arthur Street Theatre', *Belfast Telegraph*, 21 Apr. 1938.

The Monthly Magazine, London.
The Monthly Mirror, London.
MOORE, ALFRED S., *Old Belfast*, Belfast, 1951.
MOORE, THOMAS, *Memoirs*, London, 1853. 6 v.
MORGAN, LADY [Sydney Owenson], *Memoirs: Autobiography, Diaries, and Correspondence*, ed. W. H. Dixon, London, 1862. 2 v.
MUNDEN, JOSEPH, *Memoirs of Joseph Shepherd Munden, Comedian*, London, 1844.
'Newriensis', *A Historical Sketch of Newry*, Newry, 1876.
The Newry Magazine, Newry, 1815–16. 2 v.
NICOLL, ALLARDYCE, *A History of English Drama, 1660–1900*: vol. i, *Restoration Drama, 1660–1700* (4th ed.); vol. ii, *Early Eighteenth Century Drama* (3rd ed.); vol. iii, *Late Eighteenth Century Drama* (2nd ed.), Cambridge, 1955.
Notes and Queries.
O'BRIAIN, LIAM, 'Theobald Wolfe Tone in Galway', *The Irish Sword*, ii (1955).
O'KEEFFE, JOHN, *Recollections of the Life of John O'Keeffe, Written by Himself*, London, 1826. 2 v.
O'NEILL, JAMES J., 'The Early Cork Stage', *The Cork Sportsman*, 4 Dec. 1909.
Ordinance Survey, County of Londonderry, Dublin, 1837.
O'RORKE, T., *History of Sligo*, Dublin, n.d. 2 v.
PAIN, WELLESLEY, *Richard Martin*, London, 1925.
PARKE, WILLIAM THOMAS, *Musical Memoirs*, London, 1830. 2 v.
PASQUIN, ANTHONY (John Williams), *The Eccentricities of John Edwin, Comedian*, Dublin, 1791. 2 v.
[PILKINGTON, J. C.], *The Real Story of John Carteret Pilkington*, London, 1760.
POCOCKE, RICHARD, *A Tour in Ireland in 1752*, ed. Rev. G. T. Stokes, Dublin, 1891.
[ROACH, JOHN], *Authentic Memoirs of the Green Room*, London, 1814.
ROSENFELD, SYBIL, *Strolling Players and Drama in the Provinces, 1660–1765*, Cambridge, 1939.
RYAN, JAMES, 'A Carrickman's Diary, 1787–1809', *Journal of the Waterford and South-East Ireland Archaeological Society*, xiv (1911).
RYLAND, R. H., *The History, Topography and Antiquities of the City and County of Waterford*, Waterford, 1824.
SAMPSON, G. V., *Memoirs Explanatory of the Chart and Survey of the County of Londonderry, Ireland*, London, 1814.
SIDDONS, SARAH, *Reminiscences of Sarah Kemble Siddons, 1773–1785*, Cambridge, Massachusetts, 1942.
SIMPSON, ROBERT, *The Annals of Derry*, Londonderry, 1847.
SMITH, CHARLES, *The Ancient and Present State of the County and City of Cork*, Dublin, 1750. 2nd ed., Dublin, 1774. 2 v.
—— *The Ancient and Present State of the County and City of Waterford*, Dublin, 1746. 2nd ed., Dublin, 1774. 2 v.
SNAGG(E), THOMAS, *Recollections of Occurrences: The Memoirs of Thomas Snagg (or Snagge)*, London, 1951.
SOUTHERN, RICHARD, *The Georgian Playhouse*, London, 1948.

STOCKWELL, LA TOURETTE, *Dublin Theatres and Theatre Customs (1637–1820)*, Kingsport, Tennessee, 1938.

Theatrical Biography; or Memoirs of the Principal Performers of the Three Theatre Royals, London, 1772. 2 v.

The Theatrical Review; or Annals of the Drama, London, 1763.

The Theatrical Review: For the Year 1757 and the Beginning of 1758, London, 1758.

The Thespian Dictionary; or Dramatic Biography of the Eighteenth Century, London, 1802.

TONE, THEOBALD WOLFE, *Autobiography of T. W. Tone*, ed. Sean O'Faolain, London, 1937.

A Tour through Ireland, London, 1780.

A Tour through Ireland in Several Entertaining Letters, Dublin, 1746.

Town Book of the Corporation of Belfast (1613–1816), ed. R. M. Young, Belfast, 1892.

TOWNLEY, CHRISTOPHER, 'Galway's Early Association with the Theatre', *The Galway Reader*, iv (1953).

The Traveller's New Guide through Ireland, Dublin, 1815.

TWISS, RICHARD, *A Tour in Ireland in 1775*, London, 1776.

VICTOR, BENJAMIN, *Original Letters*, Dublin, 1776. 2 v.

WESLEY, JOHN, *Journal*, ed. Nehemiah Curnock, London, 1909–16. 8 v.

WHYTE, SAMUEL, *The Shamrock; or, Hibernian Cresses*, Dublin, 1772.

WILKINSON, TATE, *Memoirs of His Own Life*, Dublin, 1791. 3 v.

WILSON, W., *The Post-Chaise Companion; or, Travellers' Directory through Ireland*, Dublin, 1786.

WOOD-MARTIN, W. G., *History of Sligo*, Dublin, 1892. 3 v.

YOUNG, ARTHUR, *A Tour in Ireland*, London, 1780. 2 v.

YOUNG, M. J., *Memoirs of Mrs. Crouch*, London, 1806. 2 v.

YOUNG, ROBERT M., *Belfast and the Province of Ulster in the Twentieth Century*, Brighton, 1909.

INDEX

This index includes only authors discussed in the text and actors mentioned therein See Appendixes A and B for the complete listing of writers and performers

PRINTED IN GREAT BRITAIN
AT THE UNIVERSITY PRESS, OXFORD
BY VIVIAN RIDLER
PRINTER TO THE UNIVERSITY